THE GOLDEN AGE OF ARAGONESE JEWRY

THE LITTMAN LIBRARY OF
JEWISH CIVILIZATION

Dedicated to the memory of
LOUIS THOMAS SIDNEY LITTMAN
*who founded the Littman Library for the love of God
and as an act of charity in memory of his father*
JOSEPH AARON LITTMAN
and to the memory of
ROBERT JOSEPH LITTMAN
who continued what his father Louis had begun
יהא זכרם ברוך

'*Get wisdom, get understanding:
Forsake her not and she shall preserve thee*'

PROV. 4: 5

The Littman Library of Jewish Civilization is a registered UK charity
Registered charity no. 1000784

THE GOLDEN AGE OF ARAGONESE JEWRY

Community and Society in the Crown of Aragon, 1213–1327

YOM TOV ASSIS

London
The Littman Library of Jewish Civilization
in association with Liverpool University Press

The Littman Library of Jewish Civilization
Registered office: 4th floor, 7–10 Chandos Street, London, WIG 9DQ

in association with Liverpool University Press
4 Cambridge Street, Liverpool L69 7ZU, UK
www.liverpooluniversitypress.co.uk/littman

Managing Editor: Connie Webber

Distributed in North America by
Oxford University Press Inc, 198 Madison Avenue,
New York, NY 10016, USA

First published in hardback 1997
First published in paperback 2008

© *Yom Tov Assis 1997*

All rights reserved.
No part of this publication may be reproduced,
stored in a retrieval system, or transmitted, in any form or by
any means, without the prior permission in writing of
The Littman Library of Jewish Civilization.

This book is sold subject to the condition that it shall not,
by way of trade or otherwise, be lent, re-sold, hired out or
otherwise circulated without the publisher's prior consent in any
form of binding or cover other than that in which it is published
and without a similar condition including this condition
being imposed on the subsequent purchaser

Catalogue records for this book are available from the
British Library and the Library of Congress

ISBN 978-1-904113-76-8

Publishing co-ordinator: Janet Moth
Design: Pete Russell, Faringdon, Oxon.
Typeset by Footnote Graphics, Warminster, Wilts.

Printed and bound in Great Britain by
CPI Group (UK) Ltd., Croydon, CR0 4YY

Preface and Acknowledgements

FOR more than a century the Jews of the Iberian peninsula have been the subject of intensive research. Numerous themes, communities, events, and personalities have been studied in books and articles written in Spanish, Catalan, Portuguese, French, Italian, German, English, Hebrew and other languages. Research on the history of the Jews in the Crown of Aragon has also made great progress. Invaluable collections of sources from the rich Catalan, Aragonese, and Valencian archives published in the past hundred years have enabled historians to describe the life of the Jews in the medieval Crown of Aragon in greater detail and with more precision. Furthermore, historians with easy access to the local archives have uncovered sources which depict the life of the Jews in small towns and villages. Yet despite all this progress, no book has ever been written on the Jews of the Crown of Aragon, a subject treated only in books and monographs dedicated to Spanish Jewry in general. *The Golden Age of Aragonese Jewry* is an attempt to remedy that situation.

The conditions under which Jews lived in the territories of the Crown of Aragon were different from those that prevailed elsewhere in the Iberian peninsula. Here they were subject to a different regime, enjoyed different privileges, and suffered from different restrictions; even the Christian milieu differed in many respects from the Christian surroundings in other areas of the peninsula. Naturally the influence of Christian society on the local Jews varied from region to region. The geocultural position of the Crown of Aragon, and its most important component Catalonia, exposed the Jews to various and contradictory influences. Even within the the Crown of Aragon, there were significant differences in various fields between the Jews living in Catalonia, Aragon, Valencia, Majorca, or Roussillon. The specific subjects and areas of difference are treated separately in this book.

The book covers a period of 114 years from 1213 to 1327, a period of great achievements for the Crown as well as for the Jews. It deals with three major domains in Jewish life: the structure and organization of the community; the nature of Jewish society, its frameworks and characteristics; and religious conduct and institutions, along with cultural and spiritual trends. Economic life has been completely left out to keep the size of the book within a reasonable compass. The subject is fully treated elsewhere.

The book is based on Hebrew and Latin or Romance material, published and unpublished. The use of both internal and external sources is a fundamental principle underlying the research. For the benefit of scholars closely involved in the subject, archival sources are almost invariably cited in the footnotes, followed where appropriate by references to other works where the document has been published or summarized; these references are given in square brackets. The bibliography is not intended to be exhaustive; only books and articles mentioned in the footnotes have been included. Throughout the footnotes, bibliographical titles are given in abbreviated forms; the full titles are found in the bibliography. The glossary contains all important terms used in the book which are not in English. For many readers some of the terms in certain languages will need no explanation; but the glossary has been prepared with a view to catering for the widest possible readership.

The orthography of names of places and persons differs from that used in many standard books and articles on the Crown of Aragon. While I hold regional and linguistic differences in great respect and fully accept the principle that people and places should be given the names by which the local medieval people called them, nevertheless I have deviated from this norm in the interests of the reader. Names of places with a traditional English orthography have been spelt thus: Majorca and not Mallorca, Saragossa and not Zaragoza. In other instances the Castilian (or Aragonese) form was preferred since this is the form with which English readers are familiar: thus Lérida and not Lleida, Gerona and not Girona, and similarly with many other Catalan place names. The forms used in maps and atlases have also determined spellings used.

Names of people proved no less complicated. Names of famous Jews are spelt according to the *Encyclopedia Judaica*; names of other Jews are spelt in accordance with the most prevalent orthography. Names of non-Jews follow the most usual orthography in the sources. Monarchs are called by their Castilian or Aragonese names, and never by their English names. The Catalan names of the monarchs are not used solely for practical purposes; that is the way they are most likely to be identified by English readers. So Jaime and Pedro and not Jaume and Pere or James or Peter. Similarly, the monarchs are designated by their Aragonese rather than their Catalan numbers. First, that is how they are usually presented in English books and articles (with the notable exception of *The Spanish Kingdoms* by Hillgarth, who follows the Catalan orthography and numbers); secondly, there is probably a justification for the use of the Aragonese designations if only because of the variant titles 'king', used in Aragon, and 'count', used in Catalonia. The overriding principle that guided me in these matters of orthography was to give priority to clarity, simplicity, and common sense with the reader's interests in mind. I have also borne in mind the sensitivities of the people who live nowadays in the territories that in the past formed the Crown of Aragon.

I have also consistently used the terms 'Crown of Aragon' and 'Kingdom of Aragon' to designate respectively all the territories ruled by the count–kings of

Catalonia, Aragon, Valencia, Majorca, Roussillon, and Cerdagne, and the kingdom of Aragon proper, the inland kingdom, surrounded by Catalonia, Valencia, Castile, Navarre, and France. Much confusion is caused by the improper and incorrect use of the terms in many works. The only deviation from this distinction is in the title of the book: *The Golden Age of Aragonese Jewry*. The adjective 'Aragonese' in this context applies to the Crown of Aragon as a whole.

*

The origins of this book go back to the academic year 1985/6 when I spent my sabbatical in London. It was at the initiative of the late Dr Vivian Lipman, then a member of the editorial board of the Littman Library, that I was commissioned to write a book on the history of the Jews in the Crown of Aragon. Dr Lipman, who taught me at University College, London in the late 1960s, discussed with me many details about the form and contents of the book. I dearly cherish his memory.

I can never forget the genuine interest that the late Mr L. T. S. Littman, founder of the Library, showed in the book. In a long conversation shortly before his sad death we spoke about Jewish history and historiography, and most especially about Sephardi Jewry and this book, which was then in preparation. This book is dedicated to his blessed memory. I also wish to express my deep satisfaction that through this book I came to know Mrs Colette Littman, whose friendship I greatly appreciate.

I should like to thank Mrs Connie Webber for her care, help, and advice until the first draft of the book was submitted. My grateful thanks are also extended to Ms Janet Moth, who worked with dedication and efficiency until the book was published. I wish to put on record my deep appreciation to Ms Gillian Bromley for her expert work in the preparation of the book. Her suggestions and corrections have greatly improved both style and content. I also thank Professor Jonathan Israel, member of the editorial board of the Littman Library, for his valuable suggestions about the structure of the book. Finally, I wish to put on record my gratitude to my teacher and friend, Professor Haim Beinart, whose guidance and friendship I have enjoyed for the past twenty-five years.

The list of the archives, libraries, and institutions in Spain, Britain, and Israel I wish to thank is too long to mention each individually. Special thanks are offered to the Institute for Advanced Studies at the Hebrew University of Jerusalem, which enabled me to devote the entire academic year of 1991/2 to the preparation of this book. The final stages of the work were completed during my sabbatical at University College, London, and the University of California at Los Angeles in 1993. No words can express my gratitude to the Hebrew University of Jerusalem, where I have had the privilege to work, to teach, and to do research for the past twenty-five years.

I was able to complete this book only because my wife was ready to take over many of the responsibilities that we usually share in raising our family and taking care of our home. Very often she was alone in times of joy, sadness, and crisis while I was engaged in my research. My debt to my wife cannot be measured by the standards of this world. This book is as much hers as mine. No words of love to my beloved children, who suffered from my frequent absences from home, seem appropriate.

YOM TOV ASSIS
The Hebrew University
Jerusalem, 1996

Contents

❧

The Sources	xii
Abbreviations	xiv
Maps	xvii

INTRODUCTION	1
The 'Golden Age'	1
The Crown of Aragon	2
The Jews of Catalonia and Aragon before 1213	4

PART ONE
THE LEGAL AND POLITICAL CONDITIONS

§1.1 The Status of the Jews in the Crown of Aragon	9
§1.2 Royal Privileges	19
§1.3 The Crown, the Church, and the Jews	49

PART TWO
JEWISH SELF-GOVERNMENT

§2.1 The Jewish Community in the Crown of Aragon	67
§2.2 The System of Communal Government	76
§2.3 Elections and Appointments	88
§2.4 Leaders and Leadership	110
§2.5 Communal Functionaries and Synagogue Officials	132
§2.6 The Law and the Judiciary	145

PART THREE
INTER-COMMUNAL RELATIONS

§3.1 Relations between Communities	163
§3.2 Regional Communal Organization	172

CONTENTS

§3.3 The Catalan *Collectas* — 179
§3.4 The *Collecta* in Roussillon — 190
§3.5 Inter-Communal Relations and Organization in Aragon — 192
§3.6 Inter-Communal Organization in Valencia — 195

PART FOUR
THE JEWISH QUARTER

§4.1 The *Call* or *Judería* — 199
§4.2 The Synagogue and House of Study — 210
§4.3 The *Miqve* and Public Baths — 222
§4.4 The Slaughterhouse — 224
§4.5 The Bakery — 230
§4.6 The Cemetery — 232

PART FIVE
JEWISH SOCIETY

§5.1 Social Classes — 237
§5.2 Social Welfare and Mutual Aid — 242
§5.3 Family Life — 255
§5.4 Daily Life and Moral Conduct — 279
§5.5 Crime and Violence in the *Judería* — 288

PART SIX
RELIGIOUS LIFE

§6.1 Jewish Religious Trends in the Crown of Aragon: Between Sepharad and Ashkenaz — 299
§6.2 Scholars and Scholarship — 308
§6.3 Religious Supervision — 315
§6.4 Religious Practice, Divine Worship, and the Crown — 319
§6.5 Pious and Synagogal Fraternities — 325
§6.6 Jewish Education in the Crown of Aragon — 327

CONCLUSION — 333

APPENDIX 1
The Monetary System in the Medieval Crown of Aragon   335

APPENDIX 2
The Sovereigns of the House of Aragon in the Crown of
Aragon, Majorca–Roussillon, and Sicily, 1213–1336   337

Glossary   338

Bibliography   343

Index   363

The Sources

THE use in this book of both Jewish and non-Jewish sources, in Hebrew, Latin, Catalan and Aragonese, is one of the major premises on which the work is founded. These internal and external sources complement each other and present a more comprehensive picture of Jewish life than can be assembled from either category alone: details lacking in one type of source may be found in another, and vice versa; one kind of record emphasizes a particular aspect of its topic and neglects another.[1] The utilization of all available sources to describe the history of the Jews in the Crown of Aragon follows Baer's concept of research. Indeed, it was Baer who laid the foundations of the systematic research of the history of the Jews in the Aragonese Crown, first in his dissertation and later in the first volume of his monumental documentary collection *Die Juden im christlichen Spanien*.[2]

The Hebrew sources are primarily the responsa of the Catalan rabbis of the thirteenth and fourteenth centuries. The responsa of Nahmanides, Asibili, Gerondi, and above all Adret offer a wealth of information about the Jews of the Crown, revealing details of the communal organization, the judiciary, and the religious and social life of the Jews that are hardly to be found in other types of records. Despite certain difficulties that the responsa present to the historian, their use is indispensable for a proper description of Jewish life in the medieval world.[3]

The archival sources in Latin, Catalan, and Aragonese pertaining to the Jews in the Crown of Aragon are the richest at the disposal of the historian of any medieval Jewish community. The Archivo de la Corona de Aragón in Barcelona houses the largest part of these sources, of which the *registros* in the Cancillería Real are by far the most important series. These are the copies of the king's letters, which have been fairly regularly kept since the reign of Jaime I (1213–76). The originals of these letters, the Cartas Reales, have also been extensively utilized. Another valuable series in the same archive is the Archivo del Real Patrimonio, which contains the records of the royal household, including valuable material on the finances of the king.[4]

---

[1] See Assis, 'Crisis'; Romano, 'Responsa'.
[2] Baer, *Aragonien*.   [3] Weinryb, 'Responsa'.
[4] A description of the ACA is found in González, *Guía histórico-descriptiva*. I have gone through all the *Cartas Reales* (more than 20,000) up to the end of Jaime II's reign. The *regesta* of all the *Cartas Reales* concerning the Jews have been published as vols. iv and v in the series Sources for the History

THE SOURCES

Numerous sources from the ACA have been published in full or in summary form by, among others, Bofarull, Fita, Miret, González, Rubió, Carreras, Duran, Jacobs, Régné, Baer, Martínez, Millás, Romano, Riera, and others. The works of Régné and Baer have been used most extensively in this book. Despite its shortcomings, Régné's rich collection on the same period as this book was invaluable.[5]

Rich archival material is found in many ecclesiastical and notarial archives. Some material from the Archivo Capitular de Barcelona, the Archivo Diocesano de Barcelona, Archivo Histórico de Protocolos de Barcelona and the Archivo Histórico de Protocolos de Tarragona has been used in this book. Important works on the Jews of individual communities and entire regions, such as Aragon, Valencia, Majorca, or Roussillon, mostly by local historians, have been based on sources from local archives. The task ahead is still immense and awaits coordination and long-term planning on an international scale.[6]

---

of the Jews in Spain, which I edit in Jerusalem. For a description of the material, see Cinta Mañe's introduction to vol. iv: *The Jews in the Crown of Aragon. Regesta of the Cartas Reales in the Archivo de la Corona de Aragón, Part I: 1066–1327* (Jerusalem, 1993), pp. xvii–lxiii. For vol. v, see under Assis in the Bibliography.

[5] On the shortcomings of Régné's collection, see Romano, 'Análisis'.

[6] The list of all the works is too long to be given here. A detailed discussion on the sources is found in Assis, 'Los judíos de Cataluña'. See also works in the series Sources for the History of the Jews in Spain.

Abbreviations

✣

The following abbreviations are used in the footnotes and bibliography.

Abba Mari	R. Abba Mari, *Minhat Qenaot* (An Offering of Zeal) (Pressburg, 1838)
ACA	Archivo de la Corona de Aragón/Arxiu de la Corona d'Aragó, Barcelona
ACB	Archivo Capitular de Barcelona
ADB	Archivo Diocesano de Barcelona
Adret, i–viii	R. Shelomo ben Adret, *Sheelot u-Teshuvot* (Responsa), vols. i (Bologna, 1539); ii, iii (Leghorn, 1657, 1778); iv (Vilna, 1881); v (Leghorn, 1825); vi, vii (Warsaw, 1868); viii (Adret's responsa attributed to Nahmanides) (Warsaw, 1883)
AHPT	Archivo Histórico de Protocolos de Tarragona
ARP	Archivo del Real Patrimonio, Barcelona
Asher	R. Asher ben Yehiel, *Sheelot u-Teshuvot* (Responsa) (Venice, 1607)
Asibili (Blau)	R. Yom Tov Asibili, *Responsa, The Works of the Ritba (Kitve HaRitba)*, ed. M. Y. Ha-Cohen Blau (New York, 1957)
Asibili (Kapah)	R. Yom Tov Asibili, *Sheelot u-Teshuvot* (Responsa), ed. Y. Kapah (Jerusalem, 1959); numbers indicate the number of the source, followed by specific page numbers where relevant
Assis & Cinta Mañe	M. Cinta Mañe (comp.) and Y. Assis (ed.), *The Jews in Barcelona 1213–1291*, Regesta of Documents from the Archivo Capitular (Jerusalem, 1988)
Baer, *Spanien*	F. Baer, *Die Juden im christlichen Spanien, Urkunden und Regesten*, vol. i: *Aragonien und Navarra* (Berlin, 1929)
BABLB	*Boletín de la Real Academia de Buenas Letras de Barcelona*, Barcelona
Baer, *Aragonien*	F. Baer, *Studien zur Geschichte der Juden im Königreich Aragonien während des 13. und 14. Jahrhunderts* (Berlin, 1913)
BAH	*Boletín de la Real Academia de Historia*, Madrid
Bofarull, Barcelona	F. de Bofarull y Sans, *Los judíos en el territorio de Barcelona (siglos X al XIII), Reinado de Jaime I (1213–1276)* (Barcelona, 1910); numbers refer to document numbers
Bofarull, Montblanch	F. de Bofarull y Sans, 'Judíos en Montblanch', *Memorias RABLB*, vi (1898), 560–73
Bofarull, Montpellier	F. de Bofarull y Sans, 'Jaime el Conquistador y la comunidad judía de Montpellier', *BABLB*, xl (1910), 484–92

ABBREVIATIONS

Cartas Reales	*The Jews in the Crown of Aragon. Regesta of the Cartas Reales in the Archivo de la Corona de Aragón, Part I: 1066–1327*, compiled by M. Cinta Mañe et al. and edited by Y. Assis (Jerusalem, 1993)
CDIA	*Colección de documentos inéditos del Archivo de la Corona de Aragón*, Barcelona
CR	Cartas Reales, Archivo de la Corona de Aragón, Barcelona
Dinur	B. Z. Dinur, *A Documentary History of the Jewish People*, 2nd ser., *Israel in the Diaspora*, 2nd edn., 2 parts, 10 vols. (Jerusalem, 1961–72); references are in the form 'Dinur, ii. 2, p. 9, no. 1', where ii is the volume and 2 the part number
EEMCA	*Estudios de Edad Media de la Corona de Aragón*, Saragossa
EUC	*Estudios Universitaris Catalans*, Barcelona
Ex. s.	Extra serie
fas.	fascicle
fo.	folio
Finke	H. Finke, *Acta Aragonensia*, 3 vols. (Berlin and Leipzig, 1908–22)
Gerondi	R. Nissim ben Reuven Gerondi, *Sheelot u-Teshuvot* (Responsa), ed. L. A. Feldman (Jerusalem, 1984)
González, *Tesorería*	E. Gonzáles Hurtebise, *Libros de tesorería de la casa real de Aragón*, vol. i (Barcelona, 1911)
Guinovart	R. Gallofre Guinovart, *Documentos del reinado de Alfonso III de Aragón, relativos al antiguo Reino de Valencia y contenidos en los registros de la Corona de Aragón* (Barcelona, 1968)
Indice	J. E. Martínez Ferrando, *Indice cronológico de la colleción de documentos inéditos del Archivo de la Corona de Aragón*, part 1 (Barcelona, 1958)
Isaacs	A. L. Isaacs, *The Jews of Majorca* (London, 1936)
Jacobs	J. Jacobs, *An Inquiry into the Sources of the History of the Jews in Spain* (London, 1894)
JQR	*Jewish Quarterly Review*
MF	J. E. Martínez Ferrando, *Catálogo de la documentación relativa al antiguo Reino de Valencia*, 2 vols. (Madrid, 1943)
Morel-Fatio	A. P. V. Morel-Fatio, 'Notes et documents pour servir à l'histoire des Juifs des Baléares sous la domination aragonaise du XIIIe au XVe siècle', *REJ*, iv (1882), 31–56
Nahmanides	R. Moshe ben Nahman, 'Sheelot u-Teshuvot' (Responsa), in S. Assaf (ed.), *Sifran shel Rishonim* (Jerusalem, 1935), 51–119
Perfet	R. Yishaq ben Sheshet Perfet, *Sheelot u-Teshuvot* (Responsa) (Riva di Trenta, 1559)
R	J. Régné, *History of the Jews in Aragon, Regesta and Documents 1213–1327*, ed. Y. Assis (Jerusalem, 1978)
Reg.	registro
RABLB	Real Academia de Buenas Letras de Barcelona

RABM	*Revista de Archivos, Bibliotecas y Museos*, Madrid
REJ	*Revue des Études Juives*, Paris
RP	Real Patrimonio
Rubió, *Documents*, i, ii	A. Rubió y Lluch, *Documents per l'història de la cultura catalana mig-eval*, 2 vols. (Barcelona, 1908–21)
s	sou(s), solidus/i, solido(s), sueldo(s)
sb	sou(s) of Barcelona
sj	solido(s) of Jaca or *jaqueses*
sm	sou(s) melgorien(s)
sr	sou(s) reial(s)
t.	tomo (volume)

MAP 1 *The Expansion of the Crown of Aragon, 1213–1327*

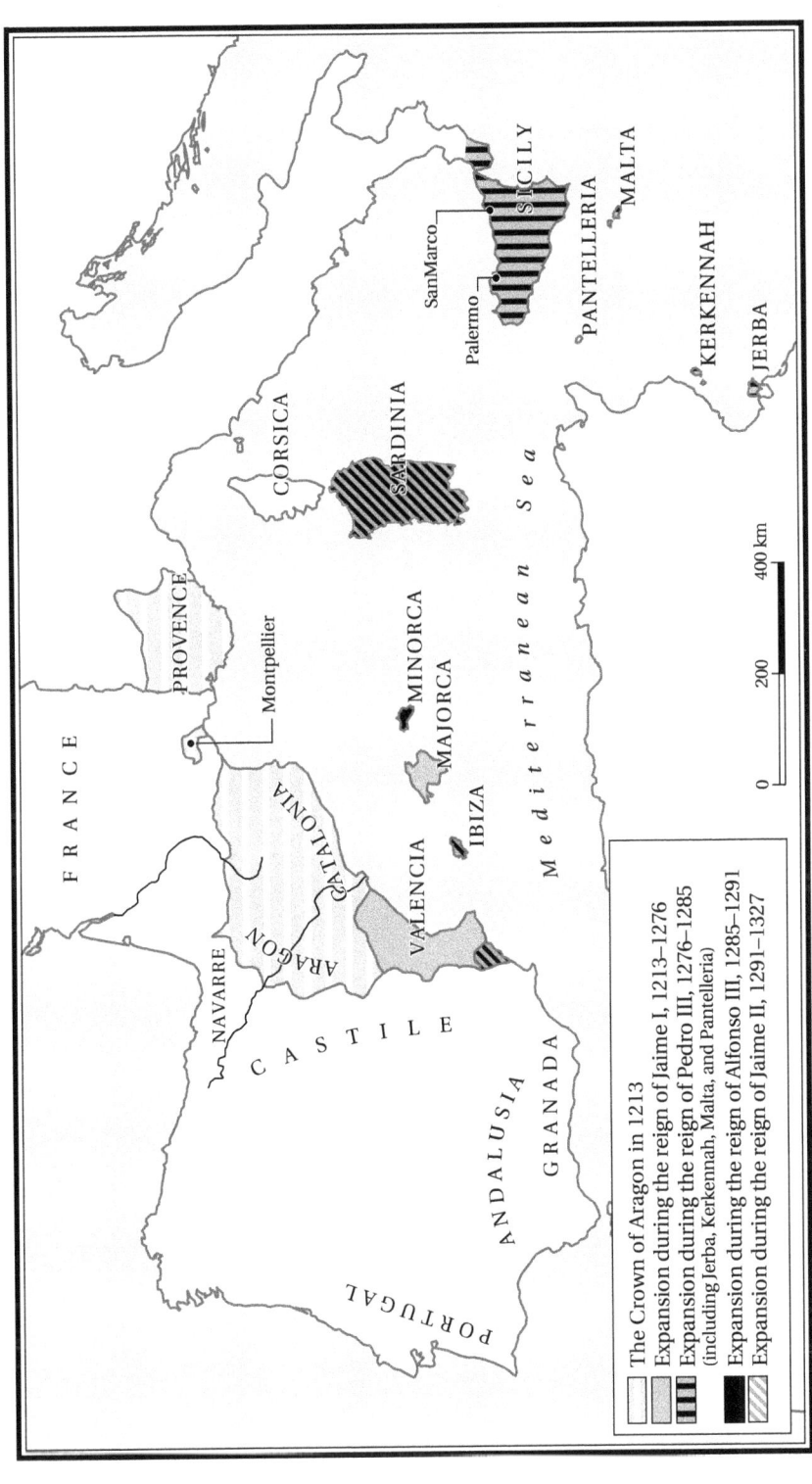

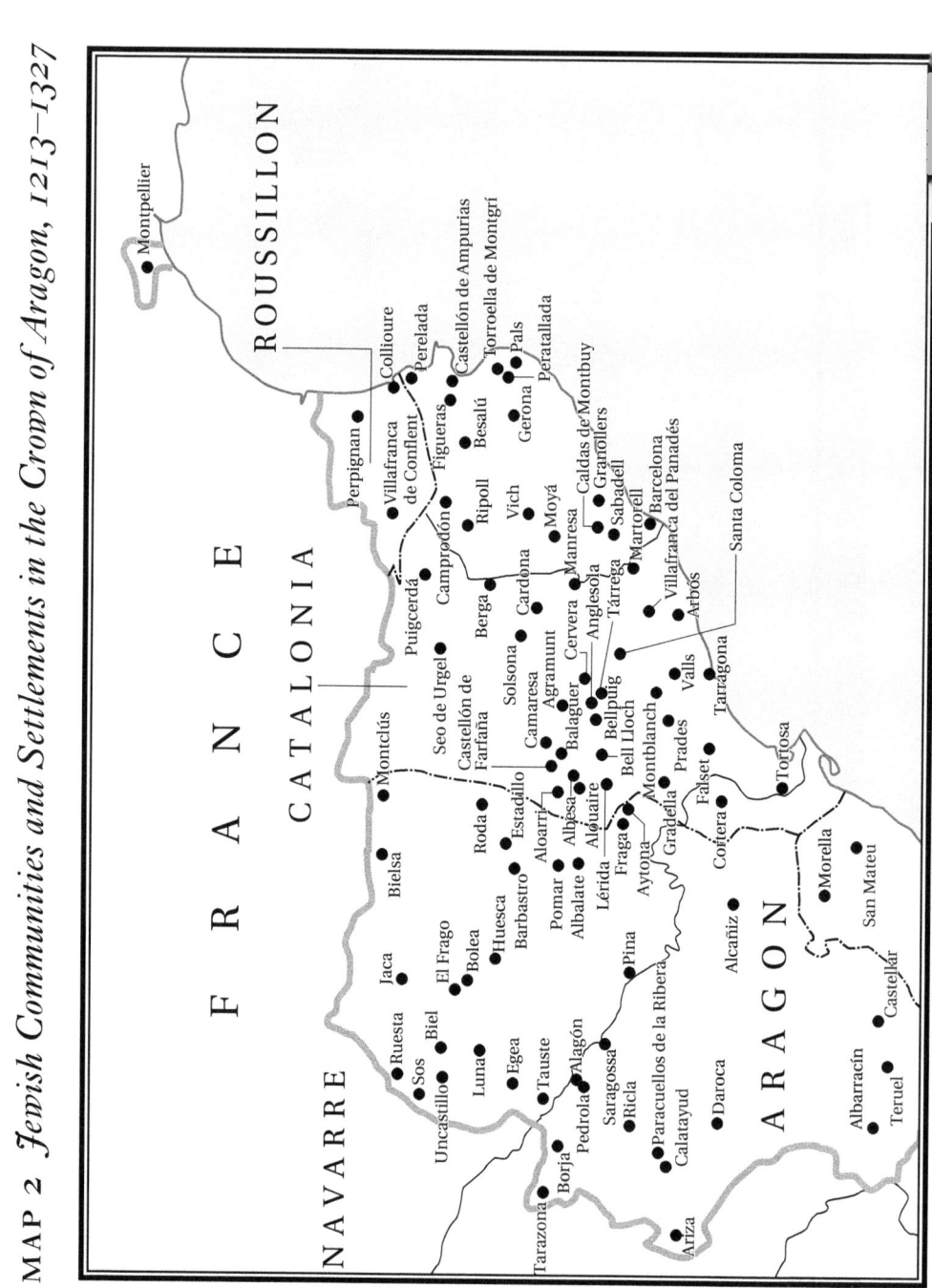

MAP 2 *Jewish Communities and Settlements in the Crown of Aragon, 1213–1327*

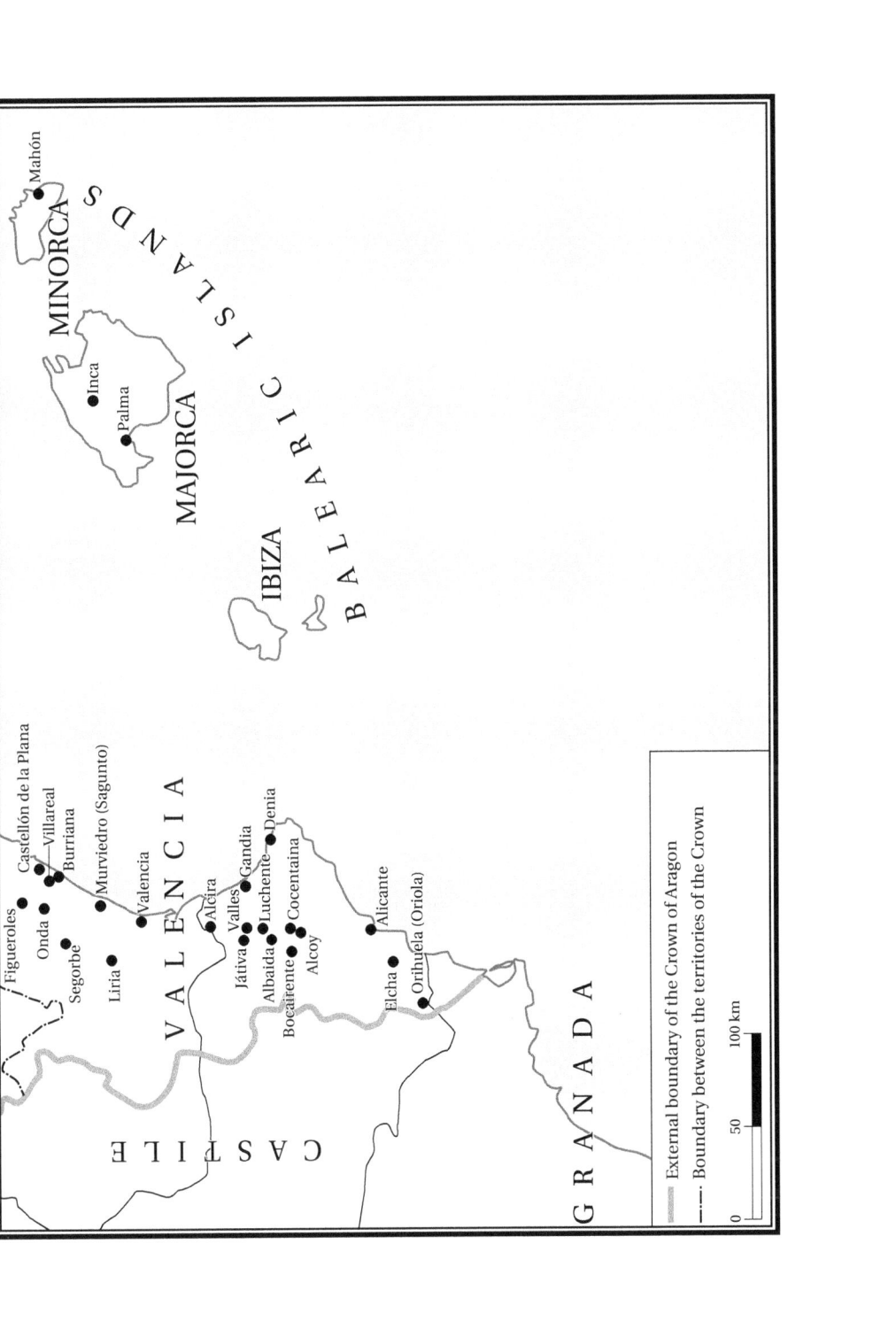

*To my wife, children,
and grandchildren, with love*

INTRODUCTION

THE 'GOLDEN AGE'

THE story of any Jewish community in exilic times is an integral part of two histories. First, it is inseparable from Jewish history, forming one of a long series of interrelated chapters. Each community bears the imprint of all the traditions formed, transformed, and transmitted over many generations, all enriched by the experiences and experiments that are the result of a unique phenomenon in the history of humankind—life in a world-wide and centuries-long diaspora. Not only through correspondence and books but also through intensive travels and migrations, each community received and passed on the experiences of the complex Jewish existence. The story of every community contains elements of the rich, sad, and happy story of a wandering nation that retained its cultural, religious, and national identity throughout its long exile.

Equally, the story of any such community is inseparable from the history of the people among whom it existed. While retaining their Jewish identity, the Jews in every land and region were deeply affected by their surroundings, by the language, culture, music, diet, fashions, and lifestyles of the people among whom they lived. Jewish as well as non-Jewish sources testify to the profound impact that Gentile society made on the Jews. It was not only in superficial and external matters that non-Jewish influence left its lasting mark; in the cultural, religious, and communal fields too, the Jewish community absorbed much from its surroundings.

The Jews of the Crown of Aragon in the thirteenth and fourteenth centuries offer a remarkable illustration of this twofold link. The thirteenth century was undoubtedly the Golden Age of the Crown of Aragon, which reached the peak of its territorial expansion in these years. Crusading spirit and commercial enterprise together produced this most exciting period in the history of that realm. The Jews of the Crown took an active part in various aspects of the process and reached the zenith of their political status and economic power. For the Jews of the Crown of Aragon, this century was to offer the most exciting and fruitful cultural and religious experiences in their history. Significantly but not surprisingly, the Golden Age of the Crown of Aragon and that of its Jews coincided. The conditions outside the Jewish quarter were ripe for the Jews to enter on one of the most productive chapters in medieval Jewish history.

THE CROWN OF ARAGON

Alongside Castile, Navarre, and Portugal, the medieval Crown of Aragon was one of the four Christian Crowns that emerged in the Iberian peninsula as a result of the Reconquista which began in the ninth century. By the thirteenth century the Crown of Aragon included Catalonia, Aragon, Valencia, Majorca, Roussillon, Cerdagne, Sicily, and other territories in the Mediterranean sea and in southern France. Each of these units maintained its own political institutions and legal system and remained independent. They differed in language, culture, currency, and social structure, united only by a common ruler, whose status differed from one territory to another.

From the ninth century the Catalan counties were in the process of colonization by Christians as the Muslims retreated southwards. The counties of Pallars, Urgell, Cerdagne, Roussillon, Besalú, Ampurias, Osuna, Gerona, and Barcelona formed what became subsequently known as Catalonia. At the beginning of the tenth century, Aragon was a tiny county at the foot of the Pyrenees. Eventually the counties of Sobarbe and Ribagorza were to join Aragon, and in 1035, after the death of Sancho the Great, Aragon emerged as a kingdom.

Aragon looked towards Castile, whereas Catalonia was close to Languedoc. The two countries remained different in many respects even after their political union in 1137; yet despite these differences, that political union, which formed the Crown of Aragon, was very durable and continued for as long as the Crown existed as an independent realm. The participation of the Crown of Aragon in the Reconquista was the dominant factor in its change of orientation from Provence to the Iberian peninsula, a change illustrated by the Cazola Treaty of 1179, which divided Muslim Spain between Castile and the Crown of Aragon. The redivision of the realm by Alfonso II between his two sons, with Catalonia, Aragon, and Roussillon going to Pedro II and Provence to Alfonso, was a further factor strengthening the Iberian character of the Crown of Aragon.

In the thirteenth century, its Golden Age, the Crown of Aragon expanded both in the Iberian peninsula and in the Mediterranean basin. The peninsular expansion was due to the leadership of Jaime I (1213–76), whose reign dominated most of the century. His conquest of Majorca in 1229, of the other Balearic islands in the early 1230s, and of Valencia between 1238 and 1244 doubled the area under his control. The acquisition of Majorca and Valencia opened up vast territories for settlement and exploitation, and that of Majorca had some important economic repercussions. The island gave the Catalans a foothold in the western Mediterranean and brought North Africa so much nearer, providing a springboard for subsequent conquests overseas.

Whereas large numbers of Muslims left Majorca after its conquest, the vast majority of the Muslims in Valencia remained. For a long time to come they continued to form the majority of Valencia's population, creating a demographic problem that was not solved until the final expulsion of the Muslims at the beginning of the seventeenth century. By creating a separate Kingdom of Valencia, Jaime I prevented any rivalry or struggle between Aragon and Catalonia for control over the region; he also enhanced his own position as head of the newly established realm, a position he owed to no one but himself, the conqueror and founder of the kingdom.

Like his predecessors, Jaime I did not envisage the Crown of Aragon as a political entity. He divided the realm between his two sons. Majorca, Roussillon, Cerdagne, and Montpellier were given to Jaime, who became Jaime II of Majorca, while Pedro became the King of the Crown of Aragon, which comprised Catalonia, Aragon, and Valencia. The Kingdom of Majorca remained independent until its reincorporation in the Crown of Aragon in the middle of the fourteenth century.

The achievements of Jaime I were acknowledged during his lifetime. His conquests made him the champion of Christendom, while his fifty-three years of rule created a stable government and administration. In his days, the royal chancellery was organized, and at his orders the royal records began to be kept meticulously. Paper registers were introduced and all correspondence was copied before its despatch. His scribes accompanied him even during his campaigns. The chancellery became one of the best organized in Europe, and its registers form one of the richest archives of the continent.[1]

The reign of Pedro III, the Great (1276–85) was crucial in many respects. He continued to develop the administration of the Crown, and attempted—though unsuccessfully—to establish a civil service composed mainly of Jews which could have meant the end of the Crown's dependence on the nobility and higher clergy. He restricted the power of the nobility and put an end to the Crown's feudal relationship with the Pope. Most important of all was his expansionist policy overseas. As no peninsular conquests were possible without fighting Castile, Pedro turned to the sea. His conquest of Sicily in 1283 brought immediate hostile reaction from the papacy and France, but the gain was permanent. The island's economic and strategic importance was immense. However, this aggressive policy created serious problems, inside the realm as well as beyond its borders. As soon as France and the papacy declared war on Pedro, the nobility challenged his authority and succeeded in undoing much of what the king had done to centralize his government and neutralize the aristocracy. Pedro had no choice but to give way to the nobility if he wished to resist his foreign enemies and keep Sicily.[2] Nevertheless, Pedro's campaigns had significant results. Several islands, including Malta and Jerba, were now under Aragonese rule. The Mediterranean expansion meant a considerable development of the Catalan maritime trade and

---

[1] González Hurtebise, *Guía histórico-descriptiva*, esp. pp. 7–8, 89.
[2] Soldevila, *Història*, i, pp. 361–4.

the transformation of the Crown of Aragon into a European Mediterranean power.³

Pedro III was succeeded by Alfonso III, 'the Liberal' (1285–91), whose brief reign was in no way comparable to that of his father. He was followed by his brother Jaime II (1291–1327), whose achievements were impressive in many fields. His foreign policy was a success. He added Murcia and Sardinia to the territories of the Crown; and once the problem of the Murcian border was settled, his relations with Castile became peaceful. His treaty with the Pope in 1295 put an end to the conflict that had isolated the Crown of Aragon in the international arena since the conquest of Sicily. In maritime trade the Catalan, Valencian, and Majorcan merchants continued to prosper.

THE JEWS OF CATALONIA AND ARAGON BEFORE 1213

Very little information is available on the Jews of Catalonia during the Muslim period. In contrast to southern Spain, no cordial relationship characterized the meeting of the Muslim conquerors of Catalonia with the local Jews. Despite its brevity, the Muslim conquest must have affected Jewish life deeply, as it brought the Jews of Catalonia into the orbit of Babylonian Jewry.

Apparently, the Jews of Catalonia welcomed the Christian conquerors led by the Carolingian kings.⁴ Good relations prevailed also between the Jews and the local Catalan princes who had Jews in their service. In the eleventh century, Vidal Salamon was the baile in Barcelona of Ramon Berenguer I.⁵ In the twelfth century, a Jew named Saltell was the baile in Barcelona of Alfonso I of Catalonia, while Jucef was the treasurer of Pedro I of Catalonia.⁶ This early association of Jews with the princes was based on mutual benefit. From their very early stages the Christian principalities, which were to embark on an anti-Muslim crusade that led to their expansion southwards, entered into an unwritten alliance with the Jews that was crucial in determining the status of the Jews in the years to follow.

The political and legal position of the Jews in the Catalan counties is reflected in their economic activities and land ownership. Jews held urban and rural property on a very large scale and held full title to part of the land. In late eleventh-century Barcelona sixty houses were owned by Jews. The amount of real estate in Jewish hands in Catalonia at the end of the twelfth century was estimated at one-third of all owned property. It is not clear to what extent the Jews' ownership of rural land reflected an involvement in agriculture.⁷ On the other hand, the

---

³ Hillgarth, 'The Problem'.
⁴ Baer, *Spanien*, doc. 1.
⁵ Ibid. doc. 7; ADB, Pergaminos de Santa Anna, Carpeta 3–A, doc. 21.
⁶ Baer, *Spanien*, docs. 56, 59.
⁷ ADB, Pergaminos de Santa Anna, Carpeta 2–A, doc. 57; Carpeta 3–B, docs. 215, 342; Carpeta 1, Bolsa 4, doc. 6. The subject is fully treated in Romano, 'Los judíos y el campo'. See also Assis, 'La participación'.

right of the count to Jewish property in some circumstances indicates the subordinate status of the Jew in Catalan counties. The property of childless Jews and of those guilty of crime passed to the count.[8] A number of laws in the Usatges of Barcelona show that the Jews themselves belonged to the prince.

In the cultural field, the Jews of Catalonia attained quite a high level of sophistication, despite their small number. Scholars had a sound knowledge of Hebrew.[9] The eminent scholars of the eleventh century could not have emerged without a fair background of Jewish scholarship. Yishaq ben Reuven Al-Bargeloni was a poet, translator, and Talmudist. Abraham bar Hiyya was a philosopher and a scientist. His work on geometry, *Hibbur ha-Meshikhah ve-ha-Tishboret*, was rather handy for land allotment during the Reconquista. In his *Megillat ha-Megalleh* he attacked Christianity and Islam. Yehudah ben Barzilay al-Bargeloni, author of *Sefer ha-'Ittim* and *Sefer ha-Shetarot*, was the third eminent scholar of this period.[10]

We have no data on the Jews of Aragon until the union of the kingdom with Catalonia in 1137. In the second half of the twelfth century a number of educated Jews from wealthy families were in the service of the king. Together with Jews from rich families of Catalonia, they served the king–count and contributed greatly to the status of the Jews in both lands. Some were exempted from paying taxes with the rest of their community, thus eventually forming the class of *franco* Jews. In fact, most of the privileges these Jews received from the ruler were at the expense of their community, and this caused tension in Jewish society. Those who ate free meat from the community slaughterhouse, for example, were severely criticized.[11]

By the beginning of the thirteenth century Jewish society in Catalonia–Aragon contained both the ingredients of its future greatness and the roots of the social and religious conflicts that were to tear it apart in later generations. Despite the radical differences between the two lands that constituted the Crown of Aragon, the Jews in both lands and in the territories to be annexed later are here treated together. The policy of the king–count towards the Jews contributed to the unity and uniformity that prevailed among the Jews of the Crown. Furthermore, the boundaries between the lands of the Crown neither stopped the free movement of Jews nor created serious barriers between the Jews of the different lands of the Crown. Their common Jewish traditions played an important unifying role. The differences, wherever they exist, are discussed in context as they arise.

[8] Baer, *Spanien*, docs. 2, 4.
[9] Some tombstones discovered in the vicinity of Gerona show a style of Hebrew letters different from that used in Castile. Cantera and Millás, *Las inscripciones*, pp. 190ff.
[10] Schirmann, *Shirim Hadashim*, pp. 196–200; Stitskin, *Judaism as a Philosophy*; Zlotnik, 'Two Passages', pp. 138–97.
[11] For a discussion of food and dietary customs see pp. 286–7 below. On the Jews prior to the thirteenth century, see Baer, *History*, i, pp. 78–96.

PART ONE

THE LEGAL AND POLITICAL CONDITIONS

§1.1 The Status of the Jews in the Crown of Aragon

THE CROWN AND THE JEWS

THE status of the Jews in the Crown of Aragon did not remain constant through the period under consideration since the Jewish policy of the monarchs in the thirteenth and fourteenth centuries was not entirely consistent. Nevertheless, certain principles continued to be valid until the massacres of 1391. One major principle was the concept that 'the Jew belongs to the lord king'.[1] This concept is described in terms related to property and wealth, such as 'the treasure of the lord king', 'our treasure and property', and 'our special royal serfs'.[2] Being the king's property, the Jews enjoyed royal protection.[3] This was a fundamental principle that was retained by all the king–counts going back to Ramon Berenguer IV who united Aragon and Catalonia in 1137. Without it, the existence of Aragonese Jewry would have been in jeopardy. While in the course of time new conditions brought about changes in the Crown's Jewish policy and consequently in the status of the Jews, the Crown never relinquished its claim to proprietorship over the Jews. This contributed to the relative stability enjoyed by the Jews of the realm until 1391.

The Jews' own conception of their status is noteworthy although it had no bearing on their actual legal position. The declaration by a spiritual leader of Catalan Jewry in the mid-fourteenth century that 'the Jews are free men' cannot be ignored.[4] It reflected not only the Jews' view of their own position, but also their respectable standing in society at large.[5] In fact, the Jews' position during this

---

[1] 'Judaei sunt domini regis'; see Mieres, *Apparatus*, i, p. 62b; Bergua Camón, 'Fueros de Aragón', p. 455.

[2] 'Cofres del senyor Rey', 'peculium et thesaurus noster', 'tresor e case nostra propia', 'nostrae camerae servi speciales' are a few examples of such terms. Coroleu, *Documents historichs*, p. 61; Bofarull, *Barcelona*, p. 37; cf. Gorosch, *El Fuero de Teruel*, cap. 568: 'Qual los judios siervos son del sennor Rey et siempre a la real bolsa son cu[u]tados'.

[3] 'Que todos los judios sean . . . en espaecial guarda del senyor rey'; Cabarte, *Fueros y observaciones*, p. 11b; cf. ACA, Reg. 43, fo. 30' [= R 1206], where Pedro III claimed that since the Jews belonged to him, the Church authorities had no jurisdiction over them, even when Jews assisted converts who returned to Judaism.

[4] Baer, *Spanien*, p. 315, para. 2. This declaration was contained in a letter of Crescas Elias, a famous Jewish physician, to the leadership of Catalan Jewry in protest against the attempt by the Jews of Gerona to prevent those who did not pay their taxes from leaving the place. Cf. Baer, *Aragonien*, p. 14, n. 122.

[5] Of similar importance was R. Shem Tov's opinion expressed on the same occasion: 'In the king's

period was far from that of serfs, even royal serfs.[6] Completely free men, however, they were not. The Jews were conscious that 'in the countries in which the entire land belongs to him' the king can 'decree laws as he pleases . . . and the king has power to confiscate property'.[7]

From the Crown's point of view the Jews constituted a major source of income. It follows that in periods when the king's coffers were almost empty the Jews' position generally grew stronger. They were a valuable asset to the king which it was in his interest to keep, and, better still, to increase. Jaime I's famous invitation to the Jews to settle in his realm is clear evidence of the value he attached to his Jewish subjects.[8] The encouragement of Jewish immigration to the lands of the Crown of Aragon remained an important element in the policy of his successors. Pedro III continued his father's policy,[9] and Jaime II both encouraged immigration of Jews and forbade their emigration.[10] The prohibition on Jewish emigration from the realm was meant to prevent financial losses and was thus another aspect of the same policy of the king–counts.[11] Every additional Jew was the treasury's gain. Every attack on Jews or damage to their property produced an immediate reaction by the king, who feared possible losses to his income. Whether it was intended to compensate the king or deter any potential attack, the fine paid to the king for the murder, manslaughter, or accidental killing of a Jew proves the latter's value for the Crown.[12] In short, the attitude of the king was that of an owner towards his property. In reaction to the Archbishop of Tarragona's attempt

---

courts and their castles, it was upheld and confirmed by the kings and their counsellors that all the Jews, in all their places of residence, are free to go where they choose, while no one may protest or coerce them': Baer, *Spanien*, p. 314, para. 1.

[6] Baer, *Aragonien*, p. 14, n. 12.

[7] Adret, viii. 22 (end of responsum); the king's theoretical ownership of Jewish property is clearly presupposed in the law, according to which the king was entitled to receive a third of the price of such property sold to Christians. ACA, Reg. 59, fo. 9ᵛ [= R 921].

[8] Villanueva, *Viage literario*, xxii, pp. 327–8; R 36; Morel-Fatio, 'Notes et documents', p. 32, no. 1. Jaime I remained faithful to this policy throughout his reign. See e.g. ACA, Reg. 16, fo. 199 [= R 443].

[9] On immigration of Jews from North Africa, see ACA, Reg. 40, fo. 80ᵛ [= R 691 = MF ii. 332]; from Castile, see ACA, Reg. 60, fo. 56ᵛ [= R 1032].

[10] On the policy of Jaime II towards Jewish immigration to the Crown of Aragon, see Assis, 'Juifs de France', pp. 294–9; ACA, Reg. 256, fo. 1ᵛ [= R 2674]; Reg. 195, fo. 120 [= R 2675]; and R, index of subjects, 643, s.v. 'Emigration, of Jews to Aragon'. One of the conditions of the peace agreement of 1291 with Castile signed at Monteagudo stipulated that Castile would return to the Crown of Aragon any Jew or Muslim who penetrated its territory: 'Otrossi vos prometemos que si algun judio o moro viniesse del vuestro sennorio al nuestro que nos seamos tenudo de enbiarvoslo con todo los suyo, quando vos lo ffizierdes saber . . .': ACA, Pergaminos no. 59 [= González Antón, *Las Uniones*, ii. 307].

[11] For the prohibition on leaving the lands of the Crown in Jaime I's reign, see ACA, Reg. 10, fo. 37 [= Jacobs 146 = R 94]; in Pedro III's period, see ACA, Reg. 56, fo. 59ᵛ [= R 1337].

[12] There is clear evidence that irrespective of the circumstances a Jew's death was considered a loss to the Crown. A Jew's accidental death was often used as an excuse to demand monetary compensation or a fine to make up for the Crown's loss. In 1307 a fine was imposed on the *aljama* of Montclús

in 1300 to prevent royal officials from collecting taxes from the local Jews in accordance with the decision of the Corts of Barcelona, Jaime II expressed astonishment at this interference and declared that all the Jews of Catalonia were his private property and that he was therefore entitled to tax them as he pleased.[13] It is obvious, therefore, that the Jews were not permitted to submit to any other jurisdiction without the king's prior consent.[14]

During this period, the king's vigilance over the Jews as his property or part of his treasury worked in their favour. In 1290 Alfonso III stopped a judicial procedure initiated by the Count of Ampurias against the Jews of his domain, claiming that only the king had the authority to investigate and judge Jews. He further claimed that the Jews belonged to the Crown and therefore that any harm inflicted on them would be against his interest.[15] Jaime II's answer in 1294 to the Queen of Castile, who had requested him to appoint Salamon Constantin as *jutge* or *rap* (judge or rabbi) over the Jews of Aragon, illustrates well the Jews' advantage in being the king's property. Since the king was aware of their opposition to such an appointment, he refused to the queen's request, arguing that 'she should not wish that for the sake of one Jew he should lose the rest'.[16] Indeed, he spared no effort to avoid forfeiting his jurisdiction over his Jewish subjects, and acted with diligence in their defence and protection in time of distress. He took measures and offered facilities to ensure their welfare, and encouraged Jews to settle in his domain.[17]

This attitude on the part of the king was the result of financial considerations and had nothing to do with his feelings towards the Jews. Jaime II's true feelings

---

for the death of a mother and her son who were buried alive under a wall. The community which buried them without delay, in accordance with the *halakhah*, was in trouble with royal officials. Although the king intervened on its behalf, it is clear from this episode that no burial was permitted until the authorities had examined the possibility or necessity of imposing a fine. See ACA, Reg. 204, fo. 30ᵛ [= R 2868]. In 1296 the community of Majorca obtained a privilege exempting it from responsibility for the accidental death of its members (ACA, Reg. 194, fo. 266 [= R 2623 = Isaacs 74]; the *aljama* of Saragossa relied on such a privilege granted by Jaime I when it requested the king to order his officials not to impose any fine except in case of murder: ACA, Reg. 197, fo. 19ᵛ [= R 2720 = Baer, *Spanien*, doc. 142].

[13] 'Res propie camere nostre': ACA, Reg. 257, fo. 44ᵛ [= R 2725].

[14] The family Avenjahia was heavily fined in 1307 because its head Josef had accepted the jurisdiction of the lord of Montalbán, ignoring the king's authority: ACA, Reg. 204, fo. 73 [= R 2874]. (The reference is to Montalbán in southern Aragon and not to Montblanch, which is in Catalonia, as suggested by Régné.)

[15] Alfonso III based his claim on the decisions taken in the court at Monzón: ACA, Reg. 81, fo. 87 [= R 2107]. See also Reg. 81, fo. 236 [= R 2265], where Alfonso defines the Jews of Gerona who dwelt in the bishop's palace as his Jews.

[16] '... non devedes querer que por un judio perdamos los otros': ACA, Reg. 252, fo. 50 [= R 2551 = Baer, *Spanien*, doc. 136].

[17] On assigning a safe locality to the Jews, see e.g. ACA, Reg. 198, fo. 228ᵛ [= R 2747]; on the king's help to repair their damaged houses, see Reg. 212, fo. 60ᵛ [= R 3029]; for tax reductions, see Reg. 216, fo. 24ᵛ [= R 3089]; on encouragement to settle in the royal domain, see Reg. 213, fos. 258–9 [= R 3057]; Reg. 214, fos. 102ᵛ–103 [= R 3069].

towards his Jewish subjects were expressed in a letter to his daughter Constanza, sent on the occasion of her son's birth in 1321, in which he warned her not to follow the Jews' advice about his education, as she had previously done about other matters.[18] This letter reveals, on one hand, the close relationship that existed between Jews and members of the royal family, and on the other, the king's personal reservations and prejudices towards the Jews as expressed in his private communications. The king–counts were able to suppress their personal feelings and treat the Jews in accordance with the benefits the kingdom could derive from them. By and large, the status of the Jews was determined by the financial benefits, real or imagined, that the kings expected from them.

THE JEWS DURING THE RECONQUISTA

The position of the Jews under Jaime I and Pedro III seemed to be strong and secure while their contribution to the Crown was at its peak. During the reign of Jaime I, the Jews were found suitable to the needs of colonization in newly conquered Majorca and Valencia—a project vital for the king from the points of view of security, demography, and economy. After the conquest there was a substantial emigration (from Majorca in particular) of Muslims, a population whose loyalty to the king was questionable. The Jews were ideal candidates for the task of colonization—from the king's point of view, preferable even to the Christian candidates from the Catalan or Aragonese nobility, who could have been political rivals. Jewish settlement was important not only for raising the proportion of non-Muslims in the conquered territories, but also for colonizing lands abandoned by fugitives or confiscated from the hands of hostile owners. The encouragement of settlers in place of Muslims, who were permitted to emigrate to Granada and North Africa, was a cornerstone of the Crown's policy in the new possessions.[19] The relative tolerance of the Aragonese monarch towards the Muslims was abandoned following rebellions,[20] when royal pressure on the Muslims to emigrate to North Africa increased[21] in equal measure as a welcome was extended to Jews to

---

[18] ACA, Reg. 246, fo. 310 [= Giménez Soler, *D. Juan Manuel*, appendix, no. 374 = Martínez Ferrando, *Jaime II*, ii, doc. 366]. After his greetings and congratulations, he wrote: 'E fiamos en Dios qu'ell vos lo salvara, el vos conservara, mas filla, no fagades como havedes acostumbrado de criarlo a cosello de los judios.' For Juan Manuel's attitude and account in connection with the education and service that members of the Wakar family in Castile could and did offer to the royal household and the Crown Prince, cf. Baer, *History*, i, pp. 182–3.

[19] In the last quarter of the thirteenth century there were apparently approximately 100,000 Muslims living in Valencia and some 25,000 in Majorca, compared to only 30,000 Christians in Valencia. See Vicens Vives, *Historia social*, ii, pp. 39, 50, 61; Martínez Ferrando, 'Repoblación', p. 153. On the Muslims in Valencia, see Dufourcq, *L'Espagne catalane*, p. 154; Alanya, *Aureum*, fo. 36, no. 14; fos. 40, 103ᵛ, no. 10; Burns, *Medieval Colonialism*.

[20] Subsequent to the rebellion of 1254, the king decided to expel the Muslims within one month —a decision which was in many respects impracticable. Zurita, *Anales*, i, fo. 167ᵛ.

[21] ACA, Reg. 9, fo. 28; Reg. 10, fo. 62ᵛ; Dufourcq, *L'Espagne catalane*, p. 187.

come and replace them.²² The Jews' contribution to the economy and colonization of the south was substantial. Furthermore, Jaime I found both in Majorca and Valencia a local Jewish population whose successful integration strengthened the position of the incoming Jews.²³

JEWS IN THE ROYAL SERVICE

During the reign of Pedro III, when foreign policy efforts and resources were directed overseas, towards a Mediterranean expansion including Sicily, Malta, Kerkennah, Pantelleria, and Jerba, the Jews' role in the colonization programme, though not in the financial field, came almost to an end. The Catalano-Aragonese Reconquista was interrupted after the Castilian conquest of the Kingdom of Murcia created a buffer zone between the Crown of Aragon and Muslim Andalusia. As soon as the Catalan interest turned overseas, a certain deterioration in the status of the Jews was to be expected. However, at that time the Jews began to play an alternative role of great importance in the king's policy. In parallel to his vast programme of territorial and economic expansion, Pedro III tried to establish a centralized political system independent of the nobility. He tried to form a civil service based on Jewish officials, and almost succeeded.²⁴ His choice is not surprising. In general, Jews showed a remarkable ability in administration. Their loyalty to the king was total and their dependence on the Crown absolute. The experiment failed when the nobility refused to send forces against the French invasion of 1283 unless Pedro III dismissed his Jewish officials. Their dismissal meant the collapse of the entire project which, had it succeeded, would have deprived the nobility of any political power and position.²⁵

In 1283 Pedro III promised the noblemen of Aragon,²⁶ Valencia,²⁷ and

²² *CDIA*, 'Repartimientos de Mallorca, Valencia', xi, *passim*; R, *passim*.

²³ Vicens Vives, *Historia social*, ii, p. 56. It is obvious that this policy was in total contradiction with the policy concerning the Jews that the Church intended the entire Christian world to adopt in keeping with the decisions of the Fourth Lateran Council. In this case the Crown's security interests in its southern regions overrode all other considerations. This situation was destined, however, to change in the course of time. On Jaime I's attitude, see Baer, *History*, i, pp. 138-50.

²⁴ Klüpfel, 'El règim', xxxv, pp. 34-40, 195-226, 289-327; xxxvi, pp. 18-37, 97-135, 298-331; Romano, 'Estudio histórico'; id., 'Los hermanos Abenmenassé', pp. 243-92; id., 'Los funcionarios judíos', pp. 5-41; id., 'Judíos escribanos', pp. 83-7; id., *Judíos al servicio de Pedro el Grande*; id., 'Cortesanos judios', pp. 25-37; Shneidman, 'Jews as Royal Bailiffs', pp. 55-66; id., 'Jews in the Royal Administration', pp. 37-52; id., 'Protection of Aragonese Jewry', pp. 49-58; Assis, 'Jewish Diplomats', pp. 11-34.

²⁵ See the various articles by Shneidman cited in n. 24 above; also Romano, 'Los funcionarios judíos', p. 31; Klüpfel, 'El règim', xxxv, p. 313.

²⁶ 'Item demandan que los ricos omnes et todos los otros sobreditos que en los regnes d'Aragon et de Valencia ni en Rebagorca ni en Teruel que no aya bayle que judio sea . . .' (Versión romanceada), Biblioteca Universitaria de Zaragoza, MS 207, Noveno Libro, cap. 406, Privilegi General. See Bergua Camón, 'Fueros de Aragón', p. 455; ACA, Reg. 62, fo. 16ᵛ; Reg. 47, fo. 52.

²⁷ On the same day the king accepted the petition of the Valencian aristocracy referring to the illegality of the employment of Jews in the state service: 'Primerament que el sennor Rey mete jodio

Catalonia[28] that no Jew would henceforth be appointed to the post of baile. In December 1283, at the confirmation of the *fueros*, he reiterated his promise to the bourgeois citizens of Valencia, stating that no Jew would exercise the function of baile or 'any other public function which would bestow upon him authority over a Christian'.[29] In January 1284 the Catalan noblemen were informed about the final and definite exclusion of Jews from all public posts.[30] All these promises were in fact an elaboration of a prohibition dating back to 1228 which barred Jews from any position giving them judicial power over Christians.[31]

We must not underestimate the serious consequences for the Jews of the king's submission to the nobility's demands. This was a turning-point in the history of the Jews in the Crown of Aragon, the beginning of a decline in their status and the first stage of a process that was to end in massacres, forcible conversions, and destruction. However, the view that once the king's project had collapsed the Jews were no longer necessary to the Crown and therefore lost the king's favour is totally untenable.[32] Both Pedro III himself and his successor Alfonso III continued to avail themselves of the services of Jewish officials in the same fields as before, without however conferring upon them the title of baile. During this transitional period the Jews continued to be employed by the court until a new Jewish policy was formulated by Jaime II. Furthermore, the Jews, who remained the king's property, continued to be a valuable asset. There remained several fields—for example, medicine and science as well as finance and taxation—in which the Jews so excelled that even the nobility, the Church, and the bourgeoisie could not dispense with them. It is hardly surprising, therefore, that whereas Jews were being expelled by kings of other Christian lands, the Aragonese kings extended a warm welcome to Jewish refugees.[33] The downfall of Pedro's Jewish courtiers and officials was not followed by an economic decline of the Jewish communities;[34] nor did the absence of Jewish officials from the court nullify the importance of the communities, whether real or perceived, and the king expressed his appreciation of them on various occasions.

---

baile en la terra que no lo ydeve meter segunt constumme del Reyno . . .': ACA, Reg. 62, fo. 18; Reg. 47, fo. 53.

[28] On the constitution 'Una vegada l'any', see Soldevila, *Història*, pp. 362ff.

[29] 'Item statuimus et ordinamus quod nullus judeus sit bailus nec teneant baiuliam nec curiam nec sit etiam collector redditum in Valen. nec in alia loco regni, nec officium publicum teneat unde super christianum habeat jurisdictionem': *CDIA*, viii, p. 166 [C= ACA, Reg. 46, fo. 129; Reg. 62, fo. 29'].

[30] We read the following in 'Recognoverunt proceres XCIX': 'Item concedimus capitullum quod aliquis judeus non posset uti jurisdictionem vel districtu super christianos.' Cf. *Constitucions y altres drets de Cathalunya*, ii, p. 49; Carreras i Candi, 'Evolució històrica'; Romano, 'Los funcionarios judíos', p. 31; see also Vives y Cebria, *Usatges de Catalunya*, iv, p. 83, lib. 1, tit. xiii, ley xcix; R 1100.

[31] '. . . ut judei officia iudicandi vel puniendi exercere non presumant.' Cf. Carreras i Candi, 'Evolució històrica'; Archivo Municipal de Barcelona, Llibre vert, i, fo. 79.

[32] See e.g. the end of Shneidman's article, 'Jews as Royal Bailiffs'.

[33] See Assis, 'Juifs de France'.

[34] See Assis, 'The Jews in the Crown of Aragon', pp. 90–5.

JEWISH OFFICIALS AFTER 1283

During the transitional period between 1283 and 1291 several Jews, such as Mosse Ravaya,[35] Muça de Portella[36] his brothers Abraham, Salamon,[37] and Ismael,[38] and Aharon ibn Jahia,[39] fulfilled political and economic duties. In this period the work of Jewish diplomats in the service of the king–count was particularly conspicuous. The missions of these diplomats to Muslim lands were highly appreciated. They were entrusted with the task because of their expertise in Arabic, their understanding of Muslim affairs in general, and their acquaintance with the conditions prevailing in the Muslim states of Spain and North Africa. Among others, Abraham ibn Gallel, the envoy of Pedro III to Granada in 1280 and 1284,[40] also served Alfonso III in diplomatic missions to Morocco, Telmecen, and Granada;[41] Vidal de Porta was sent to Morocco in 1286,[42] and Samuel Alfaquim to both Morocco and Granada on several occasions.[43] These diplomats played an influential role in shaping the Crown's foreign policy towards its Muslim neighbours.[44]

The king and his family continued to use the services of Jewish physicians even after 1283. Samuel ibn Menasse, who was appointed as Pedro III's physician in 1279,[45] remained in this position until October 1285. Bondavid Bonsenyor was the Infante's doctor from the end of 1284 onwards.[46] In 1287 the Infante's doctor was a Jew named Josef.[47] Samuel[48] and Josef de Orta (or Huert)[49] were among the physicians of Alfonso III.

---

[35] He was active in Gerona and Valencia. See Romano, 'Los funcionarios judíos', pp. 32–3.

[36] In several sources he was even called 'baile del Rey y del infante'. His activities took place mostly in Saragossa, Huesca, and Jaca. He joined the infante in 1284 during the Urgel campaign and later was active throughout the lands of the Crown. See Romano, 'Los funcionarios judíos', pp. 33–5; ACA, Reg. 71, fo. 149ᵛ [= R 1129]; Reg. 58, fo. 97ᵛ [= R 1389]; R, index.

[37] Abraham was active in Daroca and Tarazona, while Salamon was employed in Tarazona.

[38] He was active in Tarazona and was in the service of the infante.

[39] He bore the title 'bajulo Aragonum'. See Romano, 'Los funcionarios judíos', pp. 35–6; ACA, Reg. 43, fo. 90ᵛ [= R 1248]; Reg. 57, fos. 144, 188 [= R 1397, 1442]; on his downfall, see Reg. 57, fo. 222ᵛ [= R 1457 = MF ii. 2298].

[40] ACA, Reg. 48, fo. 83ᵛ [= Giménez Soler, 'La Corona de Aragón y Granada', pp. 113–14 = R 810, doc. xii = MF ii 1107]; ACA, Reg. 47, fo. 122.

[41] ACA, Reg. 64, fo. 150 [= R 1701]; Dufourcq, L'Espagne catalane, pp. 211–13, 217.

[42] Dufourcq, L'Espagne catalane, p. 213.

[43] ACA, Reg. 47, fo. 41; Dufourcq, L'Espagne catalane, pp. 225–7.

[44] Assis, 'Jewish Diplomats', pp. 11–34.

[45] ACA, Reg. 43, fo. 129ᵛ [= Romano, 'Los hermanos Abenmenassé', doc. i]; Reg. 46, fo. 178ᵛ [= R 1117].

[46] Romano, 'Los hermanos Abenmenassé', p. 36; ACA, Reg. 62, fo. 109. He was the brother of the famous interpreter and translator Jahuda Bonsenyor.

[47] ACA, Reg. 71, fo. 59 [= R 1747].

[48] ACA, Reg. 70, fo. 190ᵛ [= R 1774].

[49] ACA, Reg. 75, fos. 28ᵛ, 33ᵛ [= R 1780, 1804–5]; Reg. 74, fo. 43 [= R 1843–4]. On Jewish physicians in the Crown of Aragon generally, see Assis, 'Jewish Physicians'.

Jewish scribes, translators, and interpreters worked for the court during this period. Samuel ibn Menasse, Pedro III's physician, was also his secretary for Arabic until the end of 1284,[50] and his brother Jehuda filled the vacancy when Samuel accompanied the king on a campaign to Africa and Sicily. The physician Bondavid Bonsenyor was the Infante's secretary for Arabic in 1285 and continued to serve him as such after his accession to the throne.[51] Abraham ibn Menasse was appointed King Alfonso III's secretary in 1290 and remained in this post under Jaime II.[52]

These examples from the period immediately following 1283 are more than sufficient to show that the king–count did not give up his Jewish officials, counsellors and aids so promptly or completely as his Christian subjects had demanded. This was true despite Alfonso's declaration in 1289 that 'no Jew can occupy the post of veguer or baile',[53] a statement intended to give the impression that the king endorsed the anti-Jewish policy imposed on his father. Whatever the motives behind this declaration were, Alfonso III did not stop appointing Jews to other posts,[54] nor did his successor and brother Jaime II.[55]

ROYAL POLICY AND JEWISH STATUS UNDER JAIME II

A new Jewish policy that was to last until 1391 was elaborated and adopted under Jaime II. This policy was based primarily on old principles that were prevalent in the thirteenth century; while in outlook it was new, in content it was a legacy from his predecessors.

The Jewish courtier, counsellor, or official was no longer the representative of the Jews' status, power, or influence in the eyes of the Jewish public and society at large. Though this figure did not entirely disappear, it was now pushed to the periphery, and while some such individuals retained part of their past glory and prestige, henceforth the *qehilah* and its duly appointed leaders were recognized as responsible for the Jews' destiny. This innovation in the history of the Jews in the Crown of Aragon was reflected especially in the status of the *qehilah*, in the increase of its jurisdiction and power and in the broadening of the basis of its regime, in which more Jews of the lower classes began to take part. Paradoxically,

---

[50] See n. 45 above; also Romano, 'Judios escribanos', pp. 84–5. Under Jaime II he once again acted as secretary for Arabic and as diplomat. See Romano, 'Judíos escribanos', pp. 95–6; Vernet, 'Un embajador', pp. 125–54; Assis, 'Jewish Diplomats', pp. 24–6.

[51] Romano, 'Judíos escribanos', pp. 86, 88–90; id., 'Los hermanos Abenmenassé', p. 30.

[52] Romano, 'Judíos escribanos', pp. 90–5.

[53] '. . . que nengun jueu no puga tenir loc de veguer ne de batle . . .': Carreras i Candi, 'Evolució històrica'.

[54] See e.g. ACA, Reg. 85, fo. 93 [= R 2294]; Reg. 82, fo. 105ᵛ [= R 2337]; see also works cited in nn. 41–3 above; Assis, 'Jewish Diplomats', pp. 22, 27–8, 30 and table on p. 34.

[55] Jewish courtiers were still to be found in Jaime II's reign. In several fields Jews occupied important posts as diplomats, interpreters, physicians, tax-collectors, and suppliers. See Assis, 'The Jews of Aragon under James II', pp. 40–56.

the decline of the court Jews who had to a large extent given the Jewish community its character until 1283 caused an immediate rise in the status of the community. The severe blow suffered by the Jewish officials who were the natural leaders of the community paved the way for a new leadership, caused radical changes in the community's system of government, and turned the community into the protector of the members' rights and property and the chief representative of their religious and cultural uniqueness. There was, so to speak, a silent agreement between the Jews and the Crown which offered the community compensation in the form of constitutional change for the harm inflicted by the dismissal of the influential aristocratic Jewish officials, who, while fully occupied by their work for the Crown, had also functioned as the community's unofficial representatives at court. Alongside the agitation among the lower classes which frequently led to royal intervention and consequent constitutional changes in the Jewish communities, the sudden redundancy imposed on capable and ambitious Jews, whose political careers had been abruptly interrupted in 1283, contributed much in turning the community into the centre of Jewish affairs and politics. Unemployed Jewish administrators, politicians, diplomats, financiers, and other experts formerly in the service of the king now turned their full attention and unfulfilled ambitions to communal politics. Here they found an outlet for abilities and ambitions which could no longer be satisfied outside the boundaries of the Jewish quarter.[56]

Conscious of the paramount importance of the Jewish presence for the welfare of his realm, Jaime II strengthened the status of the *qehilah* as an alternative to the position of individual Jewish statesmen and officials. The decision to dismiss Jews from government service was not an initiative of the king, who took it under duress; the Jews had not suddenly become worthless and dispensable to the Crown. The king needed the Jews not only because of the efficient, capable, and loyal officials they could offer him but also for the resources with which they continued to provide him. The king's failure to use the Jews in the establishment of an efficient civil service cannot therefore be considered as the cause of their downfall and the abrogation of their special position. As they continued to be an important source of income for the treasury the Jews were favourably treated by Jaime II, who consolidated the framework of the *qehilah* and thus gave its members a feeling of security which would have otherwise disappeared after 1283.

We cannot infer from all this that the status of the Jews under Jaime II was based entirely on the Crown's attitude to the community as a whole. The relationship between the Crown and the individual Jewish subject was founded on mutual interest. This is so even when there is no hint as to the nature of the benefit the Crown derived from the Jew. It is indeed doubtful if a complete

[56] Although the beginnings of the lower classes' struggle may be traced to the reign of Jaime I, its most important phase and results occurred under Jaime II. On the beginnings of the agitation, see Baer, *History*, i, pp. 222–31; Assis, 'Crisis'; id., 'Social Unrest'. On the court Jews in Christian Spain, see Beinart, 'The Image of Jewish Courtiers'.

description of this relationship can ever be given. First of all, for various reasons, some of which are obvious, many sources mention no reasons for the king's favour towards a Jew. Secondly, those benefits described in most sources as granted by the king to individual Jewish subjects were such as in one way or another to harm the authority, the prestige, and the economy of their community and of Jewish society in general. Other benefits were not always mentioned in the sources available, since they were not of interest to the public.

The status of the individual Jew is well illustrated in the favours and benefits which the king granted him in many fields, including tax facilities,[57] appointments to communal posts,[58] monopoly rights on certain communal enterprises,[59] freedom from humiliating conditions attached to oath-swearing,[60] and freedom from communal jurisdiction.[61] The advantages which the king derived from Jews as diplomats, interpreters, physicians, tax-collectors, financiers, entrepreneurs, and suppliers were major factors in the formation of his attitude towards the Jews and the shaping of their status. Even though the king's favours to individual Jews frequently caused friction within Jewish society and harm to the authority of the community, on the whole the Jews in the service of the Crown contributed much to its security and privileged status.

[57] On tax exemption, see ACA, Reg. 220, fo. 111ʾ [=R 3204]; Reg. 230, fos. 96ʾ–97. The king's Jewish protégés often had their tax fixed to their advantage; see ACA, Reg. 213, fo. 250ʾ [=R 3055]. For tax deductions, see e.g. ACA, Reg. 227, fo. 191 [=R 3332]. Individual Jews were sometimes exempt from any responsibility *vis-à-vis* other Jews who did not pay their taxes: ACA, Reg. 222, fo. 33ʾ [=R 3225]; Reg, 225, fos. 186ʾ–187 [=R 3292].

[58] See e.g. ACA, Reg. 228, fo. 35ʾ [=R 3369 = Jacobs 853]. The subject is fully treated in Part III below.

[59] See e.g. ACA, Reg. 232, fo. 352ʾ [=R 3081]. [60] See n. 58 above.

[61] ACA, Reg. 215, fo. 243 [=R 3082]; Reg. 213, fo. 250ʾ [=R 3055]; Reg. 225, fos. 186ʾ–187 [=R 3292]; Reg. 228, fo. 134ʾ [=R 3399].

§1.2 Royal Privileges

As in other medieval Jewish communities, communal self-government in the Crown of Aragon was subject to royal consent. For the Jews, however, the *qehilah* drew its power from Jewish sovereignty in antiquity and from its members' readiness to accept its jurisdiction.[1] Although the rabbinic leaders of Catalan and Aragonese Jewry considered the *qehilah* to be the rightful and only heir of ancient Jewish sovereignty,[2] they were nevertheless conscious of the political reality which enabled the Jews to live within the framework of their communities in accordance with Jewish law and lore. With sound political insight and understanding, Adret recognized that in various fields the *qehilah* acted with 'government permission' as dictated by the conditions and necessities of the time, and not so much by the laws of the Torah. Its jurisdiction then came from 'the power of the kingdom'.[3] This 'government permission' was included among the privileges that the king granted to the communities in return for a handsome payment. These privileges were necessary to regulate the life and position of a group that was not integrated in feudal Christian society.

In the confederal Crown of Aragon there was no central inter-communal organization vested with sufficient authority to represent all the Jews of the realm before the monarch. Regional or local inter-communal organizations which developed during this period did not significantly restrict the independence of the individual community.[4] Consequently, most privileges were addressed to the community, which was the basic framework of Jewish self-government.

THE REIGN OF JAIME I

Jaime I pursued his predecessors' policy of encouraging Jewish settlement in the realm and of protecting Jewish communities throughout his territories, which were then in the process of expansion.[5] During his reign the Reconquista was renewed with additional vigour. To Aragon–Catalonia and the royal domains in

---

[1] Baer, 'The Foundations'.   [2] Adret, i. 1206.
[3] Adret, iv. 311 = viii. 279; Assaf, *Punishments*, no. 56; and cf. Adret, iii. 397: '. . . but all the communities have laws and ordinances in this matter which are not based on the Talmud and are allowed to have them . . .'
[4] See Part III below on 'Inter-communal Relations'.
[5] On the attitude of of Jaime I's predecessors towards the Jews, see Baer, *History*, i, pp. 52–9, 81–3, 90–4.

Roussillon and Languedoc were added vast territories in Valencia in the south and in the Balearic islands in the east. In addition to the existing Jewish population in these conquered territories, the king thought it expedient to encourage Jews, both his subjects and foreigners, to settle there. The Jewish policy of Jaime I, who ruled for sixty-three years (1213–76), determined the Jews' status for a long time to come.

This policy, as reflected in the privileges received by many communities, was not the result of a casual attitude but rather a deliberate product of royal initiative and decision. In a letter of protection which Jaime I sent to the Jews of Montpellier in 1258 he declared that although they suffered a life of servitude in the realms of the Christian kings, he was opposed to their humiliation, oppression, and persecution anywhere under his rule.[6] It was his concern for the welfare of his Jewish subjects that made him decide towards the end of his reign that copies of charters of the Jews of Roussillon signed by the local notary should be as valid as originals that had been lost or damaged.[7] The Jews of Roussillon were granted immunity from arrest and confiscation of property during a limited period, as the Christian inhabitants were.[8] This placing of Jews on an equal footing with Christians was not an isolated instance.

In 1261, while Christians and Muslims in the Kingdom of Valencia were required to pay 1,000 sr for the confirmation of their privileges, the Jews were exempt.[9] Such an exemption, however, was exceptional. Confirmation of privileges almost always cost a large amount of money.[10] As no community was ever left without basic privileges, their confirmation was a source of income for the king, who usually instructed his local officials to ensure their observance.[11] Although the circumstances are not always entirely clear, there is reason to believe that a community's application to the king for the confirmation of its privileges was almost invariably the result of pressure exerted by hostile elements or of a danger that the community faced.[12]

Jaime I granted new communities privileges based on those of older ones. Whereas with the beginning of the conquest in 1239 the Jews of Valencia obtained privileges similar to those of the Jews of Saragossa,[13] subsequently, in 1244, the

---

[6] Kahn, 'Documents inédits', p. 261.
[7] ACA, Reg. 20, fo. 267ᵛ [= R 632 = Jacobs 589 = Bofarull, Barcelona, clxi].
[8] ACA, Reg. 16, fo. 159ᵛ [= Bofarull, Barcelona, lxxxviii].
[9] ACA, Reg. 11, fo. 233 [= R 142 = Jacobs 188 = MF i. 353].
[10] ACA, Reg. 13, fo. 183ᵛ = R 264].
[11] The confirmation of the privileges of the Jews of Montpellier was sent, for instance, first to the local consuls and only a day later to the leaders of the community: ACA, Reg. 13, fo. 218 [= R 280 = Bofarull, Montpellier, 487].
[12] On repeated confirmations of privileges to the *aljama* of Majorca, see Villanueva, *Viage literario*, xxii, pp. 328–31; Morel-Fatio, 'Notes et documents', nos. 3, 5; Fita and Llabrés, 'Privilegios', nos 2, 3 [=*España hebrea*, ii, nos. 2, 3]. For the community of Montpellier, see Kahn, 'Documents inédits', pp. 271–2, no. 1.
[13] ACA, Reg. 941, fos. 176–7 [= Baer, *Spanien*, doc. 91].

Valencia Jews received privileges like those of Barcelona.[14] The latter served as models for many communities, including Perpignan,[15] Montpellier,[16] Lérida and its *collecta*,[17] and Gerona–Besalú.[18] At times, the privileges of communities within a *collecta* followed those of the main community.[19] The privileges of the communities were confirmed by successive kings and Infantes and, on the whole, the original wording was retained.[20]

Privileges served first and foremost to attract Jews to settle in a certain locality. It was natural, therefore, that under Jaime I charters were granted to communities found in territories conquered from the Muslims: Valencia,[21] Morella,[22] and Játiva.[23] Even in the privilege given to the community of Valencia in the last year of his reign, the settlement of Jews was mentioned with great favour and sympathy.[24] In places where Jaime I had to share his rule with noblemen or clergymen, he was particularly generous in offering protection and benefits to potential Jewish immigrants who were prepared to settle under his rule.[25]

The main charters refer to the existence of a separate entity in which the Jews could preserve their special identity and live according to their customs. Jaime I knew that without the ability to conduct its own internal affairs, no community would agree or manage to exist. Jewish existence in exile was conceivable only because of the authority given to the Jews to maintain an administrative and judicial system, to observe parts of Jewish law which endowed the scattered Jewish communities in exile with a sense of national unity despite their dispersion, and to uphold all the institutions which were necessary to lead a way of life distinct from the Gentile environment. A common destiny of a nation away from, and deprived of, its own homeland could thus be achieved in exile. From the king's point of view, there was no other possibility in the circumstances of the time but to recognize the separation of the Jews from the rest of society in their self-government in the religious, cultural, and social fields.

Jaime I seems to have understood and accepted these basic principles. The first known privilege established under his rule is that which he granted in 1229 to the Jews of Calatayud, authorizing them to elect their communal management.[26] A

---

[14] See R and bibliography therein.
[15] ACA, Reg. 15, fo. 123ᵛ [=R 394 = Jacobs 431]; Reg. 16, fo. 157 [=R 421 = Jacobs 445 = Bofarull, Barcelona, lxxxv].
[16] ACA, Reg. 15, fo. 123ᵛ [=R 395 = Jacobs 431 = Bofarull, Barcelona, lxxiv].
[17] ACA, Pergaminos de Jaime I, no. 1955 [= *CDIA*, vi, pp. 170–2 = R 400 = Martínez Ferrando, *Indice cronológico*, no. 327].   [18] ACA, Reg. 14, fo. 128 [=R 499].
[19] ACA, Reg. 11, fo. 216ᵛ [=R 150 = Jacobs 182].
[20] ACA, Reg. 37, fo. 34ᵛ [=R 504 = Jacobs 182].
[21] See nn. 13–14 above.
[22] ACA, Reg. 12, fo. 143 [=R 239 = Jacobs 270 = MF i. 512].
[23] ACA, Reg. 19, fo. 108 [=R 582 = Jacobs 536 = MF i. 1665].
[24] ACA, Reg. 20, fo. 242 [=R 620 = Jacobs 573 = MF i. 1813].
[25] R 49.
[26] ACA, Reg. 202, fos. 201ʳᵛ [=R 6]. This is a confirmation from 1305 of the original 1229 privilege.

stable and efficient regime was in the king's interest. From Jaime I's privilege to the Jews of Gerona–Besalú in 1258 it is clear that the collection of taxes, from the Crown's point of view an activity of paramount importance, would be best performed through this privilege. This alone more than justified Jewish self-government.[27] The king's attitude to the authority of the communal leadership is well illustrated in the power he conferred upon the *secretarii* of the *aljama* of Barcelona to put under ban and punish, if necessary, any Jew in the *collecta*. The motive was not concealed: it was to ensure quick and efficient tax collection. More than half a century later, his grandson Jaime II was to confirm this privilege, mainly for the same reason.[28]

Since this confirmation came at the request of the community's representatives we may conclude that the authority vested in them, primarily advantageous to the Crown, was readily accepted and was used also for purposes different from the king's original design. Such a potential weapon can be found in a privilege given in 1269 to the Jews of Valencia, whose *aljama* was empowered to put any Jew under ban and forbid the laying of a tombstone over his grave if he did not pay his part of the tax.[29] The communal leadership did not hesitate to extend its authority over other fields using the power bestowed upon it by the Crown. This use by the community of the king's delegation of power was made with his knowledge and consent. The king sometimes gave his agreement to a *fait accompli* and at times authorized the *aljama* to use in its internal domains the power that was intended to be used on his behalf. The Jews of Gerona and Besalú, who had received, as we may recall, a privilege giving them special powers to collect taxes, obtained fourteen years later, in 1272, a more extensive one which empowered the leaders to extend their authority in matters related to internal community affairs.[30]

The right to establish a judiciary which operated according to Jewish law was undoubtedly the most obvious expression of self-government. In several privileges the king referred to this aspect of Jewish autonomy. In the oldest known privilege, granted by Jaime I to the Jews of Calatayud as mentioned above, the right of the community to set up a judicial system was one of the major clauses.[31] In 1241 the communities of Roussillon and Barcelona,[32] in 1258 those of the *collecta* of Gerona–Besalú,[33] and in 1272 the community of Huesca[34] were each permitted to found a court of law to adjudicate between Jews. It is therefore

---

[27] ACA, Reg. 10, fo. 54ᵛ [= R 97 = Jacobs 151 = Baer, *Spanien*, doc. 97].

[28] ACA, Reg. 219, fo. 208ʳ [= R 355].

[29] ACA, Reg. 16, fo. 159 [= R 418 = Jacobs 453 = MF i. 883]. Martínez Ferrando does not include in his *regestum* the main point of the privilege.

[30] ACA, Reg. 21, fo. 37 [= R 520 = Jacobs 637 = Bofarull, Barcelona, cxiv].

[31] See n. 26 above.

[32] ACA, Reg. 16, fo. 158 [= Bofarull, Barcelona, lxxxxiii = Baer, *Spanien*, doc. 93]. The part published by Baer does not include the communities of Roussillon, while the source in Bofarull is incomplete.   [33] See n. 27 above.   [34] See n. 20 above.

reasonable to assume that such a permission was general and was given to newly founded communities in the territories annexed by the Crown of Aragon in the process of the Reconquista. Thus permission was granted in 1239 to the Jews of Valencia[35] and in 1250 to the Jews of Majorca[36] to bring before the Jewish court all cases involving Jews, except cases of serious crimes such as murder. The king considered the community's judicial autonomy to be as much in the royal interest as in that of the Jews, as stated in the charter of the Saragossa community.[37]

The survival of the Jewish people in the Christian world was justified in Christian thought by theological arguments, according to which, even in his humiliated and oppressed position, the Jew had the right to worship his Creator in his own manner, however mistaken this might be in the Church's opinion. Royal charters which permitted the Jews freedom of worship and observance of their law may therefore seem superfluous. In medieval reality, however, there was a wide gap between theory and practice, working both to the Jews' advantage and to their detriment. The *qehilah* viewed as vital a charter guaranteeing freedom of worship, the observance of the Sabbath and festivals, and the right to consume *kasher* food. It could then rely on this document in its struggle against any attempt to restrict these freedoms. The privileges in this field which were granted by Jaime I were not intended to confirm the community's right to live the Jewish way and persist in its 'heresy', a right which was generally accepted by Crown and Church, but to ensure that discriminatory laws, which often remained no more than a means of applying pressure and a source of anxiety, should not be put into operation.

Since the Jews' right to observe the Sabbath and festivals was never challenged, all privileges on this subject refer to special conditions. In the privileges of the Jews of Valencia[38] and Perpignan,[39] every Jewish prisoner was assured a leave from prison from the eve of the Sabbath and festivals until Sunday or their conclusion respectively. In return, he was expected to give a bail or promise that he would return to gaol at the appointed time. The Jews of Lérida were promised in 1265 that they would not be arrested on Sabbaths and festivals.[40]

The slaughter of animals and the provision of *kasher* food were far more problematic, due to economic considerations connected with animal slaughter and the sale of meat. Various charters, therefore, included the Jews' right to slaughter

[35] See n. 13 above. The relevant passage is found in para. 1.
[36] See n. 12 above.
[37] '... ad utilitatem nostram ...': ACA, Reg. 16, fo. 240ʼ [= R 458 = Bofarull, Barcelona, cii = Jacobs 474].
[38] See n. 13 above, para. 5 of the source. In another privilege from 1262 this immunity was again guaranteed: ACA, Reg. 12, fos. 43ʼ–44 [= R 160 = Bofarull, Barcelona, xxv = Jacobs 210 = MF i. 389].
[39] ACA, Reg. 12, fo. 8ʼ [= R 178 and doc. iv, 418–19 = Jacobs 197].
[40] ACA, Reg. 13, fo. 275ʼ [= R 336]. The three charters refer to Jews who were imprisoned for failure to pay taxes or debts.

according to *halakhah*,[41] and in special conditions there was a need to emphasize their right to eat *kasher* food. Because it was relatively simple to prevent Jewish prisoners from eating *kasher* food, the attempt to do so was prohibited in several charters.[42]

The maintenance, repair, and, above all, construction of synagogues was another area of religious life which caused problems. Despite repeated prohibitions every new Jewish settlement built its new synagogue, while many old ones added new synagogues with the king's knowledge and consent. At every attempt to attack the centre of communal life, the king conceded the Jews' request to build new synagogues[43] or repair old ones.[44]

Another crucial area of the religious field which was provided for in the royal charters was the community's right to bury its dead according to Jewish ritual. Not every community had its own cemetery, but none was prevented from using that of a neighbouring *qehilah*. Numerous difficulties were encountered in connection with the status of the plot on which the cemetery was established or planned, and with projects which were likely to affect the cemetery. Jaime I confirmed in 1268 that the cemeteries of Barcelona and Lérida would not be transferred elsewhere without the communities' consent.[45] In 1274 he allowed the community of Villafranca to acquire a piece of land for burial, and when it chose one which was leased by the Crown, the community was asked to choose a freehold plot.[46]

It is evident that in religious matters royal privileges were given only in those instances in which the observance of the commandment or the implementation of the *halakhah* was in danger. In principle, the right of the Jews to live according to their beliefs and opinions was one of the fundamentals of their very existence as a tolerated minority. Yet, as a minority, the Jews were extremely vulnerable and were not always tolerated. Many factors made them easy prey and the focal point of general hatred. Most of these were not unique to the Crown of Aragon, but prevailed throughout Christendom. In the thirteenth-century Crown of Aragon the Jews enjoyed a particularly strong position which explains the numerous charters given by the king to protect the *aljama* and its members against a multitude of foes. The Jews' strong position in no way removed their vulnerability: quite to the contrary, it contained the very roots of Iberian Jewry's weakness. In the thirteenth

---

[41] See e.g. the privileges granted to Valencian Jewry in 1271 (ACA, Reg. 16, fo. 248ᵛ [= R 468 = Jacobs 476 = MF i. 1175]) and to the Jews of Majorca in 1273 (ACA, Reg. 19, fo. 47ᵛ [= R 562 = Jacobs 516 = Bofarull, Barcelona, cxxii = Pons, *Los judíos*, ii, no. 6] On the right to sell *kasher* meat see n. 174 below.

[42] See n. 39 above.

[43] ACA, Reg. 15, fo. 123ᵛ [= R 394 = Jacobs 431]. The last paragraph in Bofarull, Barcelona, lxxiv, which refers to the privilege granted to the Jews of Perpignan, justifies the permission granted with the word 'cum non habeant', which seems interesting and odd.

[44] ACA, Reg. 15, fo. 114ᵛ [= R 389 = Bofarull, Barcelona, lxx].

[45] For Barcelona, see n. 44 above; for Lérida, see n. 17 above.

[46] ACA, Reg. 19, fo. 123 [= R 588 = Bofarull, Barcelona, cxxxvi = Jacobs 541].

century, however, the royal charters were more than sufficient to enable the Jews to withstand their enemies' attacks.

However paradoxical it may appear, the Jews needed royal protection first and foremost against the discriminatory and aggressive measures of the king's officials and family. It was customary in the territories of the Crown of Aragon for a newly appointed royal official to receive a gift or payment from the local Jewish community, in the interest of maintaining good relations. However, the Jews often found themselves blackmailed and abused by greedy and extortionate office-holders. Naturally, any community which could relieve itself of such oppression did so unhesitatingly. Huesca was among the *aljamas* which obtained a royal charter putting an end to what was in effect the bribe offered to every new royal official.[47]

The Jews' obligation to act as hosts to the king and his retinue in their quarter during any royal stay in their town became at times an unbearable burden. In a confederate realm with no fixed capital, through which the king would travel with his court from one place to another as his political and financial interests required, the *cena*, as this obligation was called, could be exorbitant and very disturbing. The residence of the royal suite in the Jewish quarter was, therefore, occasionally restricted at the community's request.[48] Some communities succeeded in freeing themselves altogether from the obligation to provide such accommodation.[49] The efficacy of such privileges, however, was questionable when the guests were the king and his immediate family.[50]

Far more serious were the degradation and damage suffered by Jews when royal officials conducting an investigation entered their quarter and their homes. Sometimes they were accompanied by a mob who used the opportunity to beat, wound, rob, and abuse. The mere suspicion that the Jews were guilty of a crime or offence gave such attacks on the community a semblance of legality. Aware of this, Jaime I agreed in 1263 to grant the Jews of Perpignan a privilege forbidding the baile or any other office-holder to enter the Jewish quarter in the course of his duties accompanied by more than five people.[51] In most cases entry into the *judería* or *call* was connected with non-payment of taxes and ended with the confiscation of property and house arrest. Jaime I guaranteed in a privilege given in 1264 to the tiny community of Uncastillo that neither the *alcayde* nor any other officer would be allowed to arrest the Jews, confiscate their property, or cut off their provisions in order to force them to pay their taxes. It can be safely assumed that this community was not alone in enjoying such protection.[52] Six months later Jaime I informed the *aljama* of Valencia that none of his officers could arrest its members

---

[47] ACA, Reg. 12, fo. 74ʹ [= R 173 = Jacobs 229].
[48] See Assis, *Money and Power*, ch. vi.   [49] See n. 39 above.
[50] The exemption granted to the Jews of Valencia was wider and included Christian visitors in general. See n. 55 below.
[51] ACA, Reg. 12, fo. 9 [= R 179 = Jacobs 198 = Dinur, ii. 2, p. 88, no. 67].
[52] ACA, Reg. 13, fo. 189ʹ [= R 273]. This privilege was given to the Jews of Uncastillo on condition that those who were accused would report outside the fortress to be arrested.

or confiscate their property for non-payment of taxes.[53] The king's officers often used the synagogue as a place of confinement or arrest. Needless to say, this procedure seriously disrupted communal and religious life and caused bitter feelings in the *judería* or *call*. In 1265 the communities in the *collecta* of Barcelona were granted a charter which put an end to such measures.[54] The community of Valencia, too, obtained in 1273 a privilege which forbade all royal officials to lock the Jews inside the synagogue for the same reason.[55] In other communities where the quarter was closed with gates, the royal officials resorted to the extremely harsh measure of locking the gates, thereby preventing members of the Jewish community from moving into or out of the quarter. Some communities were able to obtain charters which forbade the king's officials thus to blockade them.[56]

The community assumed responsibility for the protection of its individual members not only from cruel and harsh acts by royal officials but also from the irregularities and corruption of the king's judicial system. Some judges and clerks in the royal courts would frequently deviate from the principles of justice when a Jewish litigant stood before them. Furthermore, some elements of the system itself were constructed in a way that automatically operated to the Jews' disadvantage. The community's concern that Jews might not receive fair treatment in the king's courts is reflected in its numerous requests that royal charters include clauses preventing this outcome. Many such charters from the reign of Jaime I were designed primarily to ensure that the Jew should suffer no discrimination in judicial processes. In a privilege granted in 1239 to the *aljama* of Valencia, the Jews were promised that a Christian's charges against a Jew would be pressed according to Jewish law, and vice versa.[57] This striking undertaking raises many questions. Although there is no evidence whatsoever that it was ever put into practice, its very inclusion in a privilege which was given in the middle of a war of conquest illustrates how far Jaime I was prepared to go in his efforts to grant the Jews equal treatment in justice. Such equality was once again assured to the same community in a privilege given in 1262, which stated that judicial procedure against Jews should be conducted according to the custom of Valencia.[58]

The Jews of Perpignan were promised in 1263 that any litigation in which a Jew was involved would be referred to a neutral judge.[59] Some eleven years later the privilege granted to the Jews of Perpignan and all Roussillon was even more extensive: every Jewish defendant was to receive a copy of the charges against him, while the plaintiff was to bear the impending punishment and offer compensation if his accusation proved groundless. The defendant had the right to consult

---

[53] ACA, Reg. 13, fo. 248ᵛ [= R 306 = MF i. 580].
[54] ACA, Reg. 13, fo. 257 [= R 317 = Bofarull, Barcelona, li = Jacobs 324].
[55] ACA, Reg. 19, fos. 56ᵛ–57 [= Danvila, 'Clausura', p. 143, n. 2 = R 566 = MF i. 1536].
[56] In 1265, for example, the *aljama* of Lérida received such a charter: ACA, Reg. 13, fo. 275ᵛ [= R 336]. [57] See n. 13 above.
[58] ACA, Reg. 12, fos. 43ᵛ–44 [= R 160 = Bofarull, Barcelona, xxv = Jacobs 210 = MF i. 389].
[59] See n. 51 above.

a lawyer and enjoyed immunity from having his property confiscated if the plaintiff did not submit to the *lex talionis* principle or law of retaliation. He was further protected from any torture.[60]

The charter of the Jews of Montpellier in 1267 was very comprehensive in respect of its judicial contents. The Jew was permitted to consult lawyers before sentence was pronounced and was promised that no investigation would be initiated without his claims and his lawyer's defence being heard. Moreover, the Jew was assured that any charge would be declared in the presence of the accuser or informer, whose name would appear in the court protocol and who would have to submit the names of two guarantors. The defendant would receive the accusation signed by the plaintiff. The accuser would be punishable according to *lex talionis* if his proofs were found to be invalid. Most importantly, all cases had to be brought in the king's courts (i.e. not in the Church courts).[61] The Jews of Montpellier also enjoyed another privilege, according to which any investigation against them could proceed only following the deposition of an official accusation or information.[62] This privilege was designed to prevent would-be informers from hiding behind anonymity and thereby avoiding counter-interrogation and subsequent punishment in the case of the accusation proving to be false. The impression gained from all these privileges is that the king spared no effort to assure the communal leaders that no discrimination would be exerted from above against Jews appearing in his courts.

In keeping with the concept that the Jews belonged to him, the king objected to any attempt by any party to establish its jurisdiction over them or to interfere in their internal affairs. Jaime I showed great concern over the efforts of the Church authorities to act among the Jews and meddle in their communal life. Although he gave in from time to time to churchmen who engaged in missionary practice and worked for the restriction of Jewish rights,[63] Jaime I took great care that such activities should not seriously damage the status of the Jews. On several occasions he showed foresight by putting a timely end to Church activities directed against the Jews. He was able to recognize the limit beyond which anti-Jewish activities by the Church would endanger the Jews' very existence.

This policy is well illustrated in the charters and letters of protection which

---

[60] ACA, Reg 19, fo. 145 [= R 605 = Bofarull, Barcelona, cxliv = Jacobs 557]. In 1275 the privilege which included the principle of *lex talionis* in cases where the plaintiff's accusation proved to be false was confirmed: ACA, Reg. 20, fo. 267 [= R 628 = Bofarull, Barcelona, clvi = Jacobs 585].

[61] ACA, Reg. 15, fos. 42'–43 [= Kahn, 'Documents inédits', pp. 270–1 = R 356 = Jacobs 409]. This privilege was again confirmed in 1274: ACA, Reg. 19, fo. 134 [= R 601 = Bofarull, Montpellier, pp. 491–2 = J 553].

[62] ACA, Reg. 15, fo. 124 [= Kahn, 'Documents inédits', pp. 271–2 = R 396 = Bofarull, Barcelona, lxxiv = Jacobs 432].

[63] It was in such circumstances that the Disputation of Barcelona was held under the king's auspices. On the examination and eventual burning of Maimonides' books, see ACA, Reg. 12, fo. 106 [= Denifle, 'Quellen zur Disputation', p. 235 = R 212 = Jacobs 243 = Dinur, ii. 2, pp. 539–40, no. 11]; and see n. 64 below.

Jaime I sent to various communities. To begin with, he moderated the Church's missionary activities, which were greatly intensified in the thirteenth-century Crown of Aragon. These activities included the imposed debates which reached their peak in the Disputation of Barcelona in 1263 and the sermons which the Jews were forced to hear from churchmen, especially Dominican friars, many of whom were converts full of zeal in their new faith and hatred towards their old brethren. In 1242 Jaime I forced Jews and Muslims to listen to the sermons of the Dominican and Franciscan friars;[64] however, in the 1260s, after the Barcelona Disputation, while he renewed the obligation of the Jews to attend these sermons, Jaime I issued a series of orders intended to protect Jewish participants from aggression.[65] When the king realized the futility of these orders—unlike the zealous friars and their ardent supporters, who continued to terrorize the Jewish audience—he sent letters of protection to the Jews of Barcelona assuring them that they would not be coerced to listen to the sermons outside their quarter and that preachers in the synagogue would not be accompanied by more than ten people.[66] On the very same day he declared all the Jews of Barcelona and its *collecta* free to answer the allegations that their books contained anti-Christian passages.[67] Some five years earlier, in the midst of the excitement of the Barcelona Disputation, the Jews had been ordered to erase all derogatory references to Christianity, its founders, and its saints.[68] The king's policy *vis-à-vis* the attitude of the Church towards the Jews remained consistent in that he acted according to the circumstances; while yielding to Christian pressure in certain conditions, as soon as that pressure was lifted, alleviated, or increased to the point of danger, he would resume his support of the *qehilah*.

Jaime I objected to the attempts of the Church to impose its jurisdiction over Jews in certain places and under certain conditions, and he guarded with great zeal his exclusive authority over his Jewish subjects.[69] His decision in 1275 henceforth

---

[64] On the decree of Jaime I in 1242 and its confirmation by Innocent IV in 1245, see Grayzel, *The Church and the Jews*, pp. 254–7. About a month after the Barcelona Disputation the order was renewed; see Grayzel, 'Popes', p. 163; ACA, Reg. 12, fo. 107 [= Denifle, 'Quellen zur Disputation', pp. 234–5]. Additional orders issued at the time restricted the preaching friars and moderated the effect of the sermons; see e.g. ACA, Reg. 12, fo. 107ᵛ [= Denifle, 'Quellen zur Disputation', pp. 235–6 = R 215] (29-viii-1263) in which the king demanded that the preachers act with restraint. The following day he ordered that the Jews should not be forced out of their quarter or synagogue in order to hear the sermons: ACA, Reg. 12, fo. 111ᵛ [= Denifle, 'Quellen zur Disputation', p. 237 = Bofarull, Barcelona, xxxiv = Jacobs 247 = R 217 = Dinur, ii. 1, p. 259, no. 42] (30 Aug. 1263). For additional sources and information on compulsory sermons in the lands of the Crown of Aragon, see Assis 'Papal Inquisition', pp. 393–4, n. 8.

[65] ACA, Reg. 12, fos. 107ᵛ, 111ᵛ. For publication details of the source, see n. 64 above.

[66] ACA, Reg. 15, fo. 122ᵛ [= R 386 = Bofarull, Barcelona, lxxiii = Jacobs 424].

[67] ACA, Reg. 15, fo. 122ᵛ [= R 387 = Bofarull, Barcelona, lxxv = Jacobs 425]. This exemption did not include passages against Jesus, Mary, and the saints.

[68] ACA, Reg. 12, fo. 111ᵛ–112 [= Denifle, 'Quellen zur Disputation', p. 237 = R 216 = Jacobs 248 = Dinur, ii. 1, p. 259, no. 42]. On the burning of Maimonides' books that year see n. 63 above.

[69] See e.g. his reaction to bringing Jews in Montpellier to an ecclesiastical court: ACA, Reg. 19, fo. 126ᵛ [= R 596 = Bofarull, Montpellier, 490–1].

to prohibit any legal process against the Jews of Roussillon in ecclesiastical courts as long as they were prepared to appear before the king's courts is noteworthy. A fine of 100 *maravedís* was to be paid by any transgressor of this edict, and severe measures were taken against any clergyman who initiated a lawsuit against Jews in ecclesiastical courts. Provision was made for further measures against witnesses testifying in such lawsuits and against subjects who maintained commercial and economic relations with the plaintiff. At the same time, Jaime I granted the Jews of Roussillon a privilege which denied the Church any authority to ban or expel them.[70]

Some of the privileges intended to protect the Jews against popular attack were the result of agitation and hatred propagated by the Church. The custom of throwing stones at Jews, especially on Good Friday, was widespread in the territories of the Crown of Aragon and was undoubtedly connected with the sermons preached in the churches at that season.[71] A letter of protection in favour of the Jews of Játiva, which Jaime I sent in 1268 to his officers and the local council, contains a detailed description of attacks perpetrated by Christians against Jews, particularly on Good Friday. The king ordered the closure on that day of the tower overlooking the Jewish cemetery and of the area whence, from a ladder placed against a wall, Jewish houses could be bombarded with stones. His instruction that on every Good Friday, during the Mass, a guard should be on duty at the entrance of the Jewish quarter in order to prevent youths from entering the premises clearly shows both the extent of the suffering and damage inflicted on Jews and the king's concern for the protection of Jewish life and property.[72] Quite a number of instances of permission to enclose the Jewish quarter, found in several charters, owed their origin to the wish of the Jews to protect themselves and to the Crown's readiness to defend them.[73] Many a communal charter contained several clauses designed to combat popular aggression against the Jews. One of them forbade the removal of stones from the Jewish cemetery;[74] another separated Jewish and Christian prisoners.[75] In some cases the provisions were more general in character, as was the protection afforded.[76]

[70] ACA, Reg. 20, fo. 267 [= R 630 = Bofarull, Barcelona, clviii = Jacobs 586].

[71] On the prohibition which Jaime I issued against Christians throwing stones at Calatayud Jews, see ACA, Reg. 12, fo. 141ʳ [= R 236 = Jacobs 265].

[72] ACA, Reg. 15, fo. 95ʳ [= R 377 = Jacobs 417 = MF i. 789]. It is interesting to compare in this context the decision of the representatives of Catalan and Valencian Jewry in 1354: 'While Gentile oppressors and imbeciles consider it an act of piety to build during Easter a high structure from which they would throw at us stones . . .' Baer, *Spanien*, doc. 352, para. 3.

[73] On the permission granted to the Jews of Valencia to close the gates of their quarter in order to prevent undesirable Christians from entering, see n. 55 above.

[74] Villanueva, *Viage literario*, xxii, pp. 330–1; R 46; Fita and Llabrés, 'Privilegios', p. 20; Morel-Fatio, 'Notes et documents', p. 34, no. 5.

[75] Villanueva, *Viage literario*, xxii, p. 312; R 560; Fita and Llabrés, 'Privilegios', p. 26; Morel-Fatio, 'Notes et documents', p. 34, no. 7.

[76] On the Jews of Montpellier, see n. 25 above; on the Jews of Gerona–Besalú, see ACA, Reg. 16, fo. 152ʳ [= R 412].

Jaime I's orders concerning the Jews' apparel provide further indication of his protective policy. On the one hand, he demanded that the Jews wear clothes which would distinguish them from their neighbours, in accordance with the Fourth Lateran Council which met during his reign; but on the other hand he took various decisions which alleviated much of the severity of the decree. In 1268 he exempted the Jews of Barcelona and its *collecta*, Gerona, Perpignan, and Montpellier from wearing the badge or any other distinctive sign on the head or body. They were expected to continue wearing the special Jewish gown inside the city, but were permitted to put on an ordinary coat when they left it.[77] The purpose of these provisions was no doubt to ensure as far as possible that the Jews were not exposed to harassment from the Christian population and to eliminate the dangers awaiting the Jewish traveller if his identity were to be conspicuous. The charter given to the Jews of Montpellier sheds light on the king's attitude to the Jews in general. Having granted them the same rights as the Jews of Barcelona, he added that any signs that the Jews of the episcopal part of Montpellier had to bear must also be borne by those of the king's side of the city. However, if the Jews under the jurisdiction of the bishop of Montpellier wore more humiliating clothing than the Jews of the Crown of Aragon, the king's Jews of Montpellier should be treated in the same way as his Aragonese subjects.[78]

Many charters which were granted to the Jews of the Crown in 1268 were primarily intended to protect them from vexations perpetrated by the populace in general and by churchmen in particular. The timing was not accidental; these charters were issued at a significant moment at the request of the *aljamas*, whose position and security were shaken as a result of the agitation following the Barcelona Disputation.[79] Nonetheless, Jaime I was prompted to grant charters to Jewish communities not only by the dangers and attacks to which they were subject but also by his wish to grant the Jews of the realm the maximum security: that their property and homes were protected, that their purchases and ownerships were legal and that their residence was permanent. In this spirit he issued in 1239 a charter to the Jews of Valencia taking their property under his protection and promising them freedom of movement throughout his realm.[80] In 1261 he confirmed again the legality of all the transactions in real estate which were performed by Jews in accordance with the laws of Valencia.[81] Twelve years later the king confirmed their possession of their quarter and their houses, and allowed

---

[77] On the Jews of Barcelona and its *collecta*, see ACA, Reg. 15, fo. 123 [= R 390 = Jacobs 427 = Bofarull, Barcelona, lxxi]. In the same privileges he completely exempted the Jews in his service or in the service of the infante from any special garb. On the Jews of Gerona, see ACA, Reg. 15, fo. 123 [= R 392 = Jacobs 429 = Bofarull, Barcelona, lxxii]. For the Jews of Perpignan, see ACA, Reg. 15, fo. 123ᵛ [= R 394 = Jacobs 431].

[78] ACA, Reg. 15, fo. 123ᵛ [= R 395 = Jacobs 431 = Bofarull, Barcelona, lxxiv].

[79] Against such a background we can understand the need of the Jews of Barcelona and its *collecta* to seek confirmation of a privilege which guaranteed the possession of their religious institutions; see n. 44 above.

[80] See n. 13 above.

[81] ACA, Reg. 11, fo. 202ᵛ [= R 141 = Jacobs 176 = MF i. 357].

them to buy Christian houses in the Jewish quarter, the purchase of which by other Christians was forbidden.[82] In 1269, in a charter granted to the Jews of Majorca, Jaime I ratified their right to buy property inside and outside the city and to dwell in purchased or rented houses without fear of expulsion.[83] Four years later he confirmed this charter and moreover permitted them to buy new houses from Christians.[84] In 1275, just before he died, Jaime I declared that any land acquired by the Jews of Perpignan for the purpose of building a house was exempt from the payment of the lease unless the land were to be transferred to a Christian.[85]

The mutual suspicions that marked Judeo-Christian relations were the result of the character that each side ascribed to the other. In some of the charters reference was made to the Jewish oath, namely, the oath a Jew defending himself against a charge of an illegal act was required to take declaring that the accusation was untrue. The compulsion to take this oath both revealed the weakness of the Jews and reflected the doubts and mistrust felt by Christian society towards them. In Catalonia, according to an eleventh-century source, Jews swore to Christians but Christians never swore to Jews.[86] In twelfth-century Aragon, however, a Christian swore over a cross in a trial with Jews or Muslims, and a Jew swore from a tablet, while holding in his hand a scroll of the Law.[87] The tablet, if it did not contain the Maledictions, bore the Decalogue and a portrait of a man wearing a gown in the customary style of the Jews.[88] When the Jew took the 'oath of the Maledictions'[89] he submitted himself to the curses included in the oath if he swore falsely. In such a case the punishment incurred, which was set by the Crown, was severe.[90]

Which version of the oath was to be used, and the manner in which it was to be

---

[82] See n. 55 above.

[83] Fita and Llabrés, 'Privilegios', p. 235, no. 8; R 433. On the king's assurance that the Jews would not be expelled, see Fita and Llabrés, 'Privilegios', pp. 22–3, no. 7; R 432.

[84] ACA, Reg. 19, fo. 47ʻ [= R 562 = Jacobs 516 = Bofarull, Barcelona, cxxii = Pons, *Los judios*, doc. 6]. The only qualification here was that Jews should not dwell together with Christians in one building with a common entrance. In Montpellier, in the charter of 1259, this right did not include the property of the king; see n. 97 below.

[85] ACA, Reg. 20, fo. 267 [= R 627 = Jacobs 387 = Bofarull, Barcelona, clv]; Alart, *Privilèges*, p. 337.

[86] 'Judeis jurent christianis; christiani vero illis numquam': d'Abadal and Valls, *Ustages*, p. 21, para. 51; Baer, *Spanien*, doc. 5; 'Judeus juren a crestians, mas crestias no juren a jueus': Rovira, *Ustages*, p. 79, para. xliv.

[87] '. . . Et christianus iuret ad iudeo et ad mauro super cruce et iudeus iuret ad christiano in carta, sua atora tenendo . . .': Baer, *Spanien*, doc. 17, para. 37. On an attempt to swear over a scroll of *haftarot* (the weekly Prophetic passages) see Asibili (Kapah), 186.

[88] In Tortosa, Jewish witnesses for or against Christians took an oath over the Law of Moses, whereas Jews brought to justice by a Christian or Muslim over a sum exceeding 5 s took an oath over the tablet of Maledictions. '. . . con testimoni deven fer jueus contra cristian o per cristian juren sobre la Lig de Moysen, quels posa hom devant, . . . Mas si jueu ha afer escondiment a cristia oa serrai . . . de V sous a amunt, juren sobre les Maledictions . . .': Archivo Municipal de Tortosa, Llibre iv, Rub. xi, de testibus, costum xxxviii; Carreras i Candi, 'L'aljama', p. 21. On the tablet of the Decalogue, see Adret, iii. 218. [89] 'Jurament de les malediccions'.

[90] Adret, i. 1148.

taken, were subject to negotiation between the Jewish communities and the Crown. There were, therefore, differences in the administration and contents of the oath. The 'oath of the Maledictions' was meant to arouse anxiety and fear in the Jew. He knelt in front of the judge and held a candle during the recital of the curses from an open book. He repeated in a loud voice the oath as pronounced by the judge. This oath, which was often taken in public, was most humiliating. In Barcelona, for example, the Jew swore in front of the gate of the Jewish quarter in Sant Jaume Square. It is not difficult to imagine the behaviour of the people gathered there. Many communities therefore tried to obtain easier conditions. In the above-mentioned charter granted to Valencian Jewry in 1239, it was explicitly stated that the Jewish oath should be on the Law of Moses.[91] Twenty-three years later Jaime I declared that the oath throughout the Kingdom of Valencia would be taken solely on the Decalogue.[92] In 1259 it was decided with the consent of the consuls of Montpellier that the local Jews should swear on 'the holy Law of Moses'.[93] In 1273 the Jews of Lérida were no longer required to take the oath on the tablet of Maledictions in lawsuits with Christians; instead, they could now swear in the synagogue on the tablet of the Decalogue.[94]

Self-government and protection of their life and property, though essential, were not sufficient conditions to ensure the welfare of the Jews, who constituted a most valuable asset for the king. First and foremost, it was necessary to take certain measures which would enable the Jews to engage fairly freely in economic and commercial activities. Their prosperity was, in a way, the king's; hence on more than one occasion Jaime I ordered the appraisal of the Jews' wealth. This necessitated investigations which naturally disturbed the Jews and aroused their suspicions as to the monarch's intentions. Jaime I was aware of the gravity of such a situation and on occasion agreed to suspend the investigations, as for example in 1254 in a privilege he granted to the Jews of Majorca.[95]

In the course of these investigations, the Jews had to declare all their loans. However, in some exceptional cases the king freed the Jewish moneylenders from

[91] 'Item si judeus voluerit jurare christiano, quod juret suoper legem Moysi'; see n. 3 above.

[92] 'Concedimus etiam volumus et statuimus quod quandocumque vos vel aliquem ex vobis oportebit facere juramentum super facto usure et aliquarum causarum quas habebitis cum christianis vel super facto aliquorum contarctuum juretis et faciatis ipsum juramentum per decem mandata legis Moisen et non aliter nullo modo'; see n. 38 above.

[93] '... sacra lege mosaica': Kahn, 'Documents inédits', pp. 261–2; R 115. It is important to note that this decision was taken in consequence of Christian complaints and as a gesture in favour of the plaintiffs. Nevertheless, the clause on the oath contained no derogatory or humiliating details; see Saige, Les Juifs du Languedoc, p. 24.

[94] 'Item fuit eis concessa alia littera quod non teneatur jurare super aliquibus causis quas cum christianis habeant seu petitionibus prestare sacramentum super librum maledicionem set tantum super X precepta legis quod quidem etiam sacramentum faciant cum illud facere habuerint in posse et presencia baiuli Ilerde vel sui nunciis quem ipse ad illud recipiendum elegerit intus sinagogam eorum': ACA, Reg. 19, fo. 65ᵛ [= R 570 = Jacobs 523 = Bofarull, Barcelona, cxxiv].

[95] Villanueva, Viage literario, xxii, pp. 331–2; Morel-Fatio, 'Notes et documents', p. 34, no. 6; Fita and Llabrés, 'Privilegios', p. 21, no. 5.

the obligation to declare their loans, as in the 1254 privilege to Majorcan Jewry. The same privilege undertook not to hold the Jews responsible for any transgressions their brethren in the community might commit against the laws of credit. Jewish moneylenders were assured again and again that the payment of their loans would not be postponed. In certain cases, the king even promised to force their debtors to pay their debts.[96] Despite the general prohibition on confiscation of goods brought by Christians to the markets of Gerona and Besalú, Jaime I gave permission to Jewish moneylenders from these two communities to confiscate such goods, with the help moreover of his senior local officials.[97]

After the enactment in 1241 of the famous law of Jaime I limiting interest rates to 20 per cent or four *solidi* per *libram*, many Christian debtors used it as the basis for complaints to the court and withheld payment of their debts. Apart from the financial loss suffered, Jewish moneylenders were involved in exhausting legal complications. In 1264, in response to the request of the communities belonging to the *collectas* of Barcelona and Gerona, Christians were no longer permitted to open legal proceedings against Jews on the basis of this law.[98] In 1265 Jaime I offered the Jews of the *collecta* of Barcelona a charter which allowed them to receive both loan and interest in return for a stolen pledge after they swore they did not know the thief.[99] One of a series of privileges addressed to the Catalan communities in 1268 confirmed the loans of the Jews of Barcelona and Lérida on condition that the legal rate of interest was observed.[100] A year later, Majorcan Jews were granted the same right as those of Catalonia to bring to court those of their debtors who had not paid their debts for five and a half years.[101]

To note all these privileges in favour of Jewish moneylenders may give a misleading impression: for, just as the king took such favourable decisions when they seemed appropriate, so he did not hesitate to take harsh measures when he deemed it expedient, or even to cancel promises made to the Jewish communities concerning their lending activities. Like his successors, Jaime I had no scruples in exploiting Jewish moneylenders and often did not feel bound by the undertakings given in the charters.[102]

Jaime I was far more consistent in the undertaking he gave his Jewish subjects that they could trade freely. The right to purchase provisions from Christians

---

[96] ACA, Reg. 10, fo. 48 [= R 114 = Bofarull, Barcelona, xix = Jacobs 149]. In this charter to the Jews of Montpellier the rights and privileges granted exceeded the customary standard in the Crown of Aragon.

[97] For Besalú, see ACA, Reg. 13, fo. 227ᵛ [= R 287 = Bofarull, Barcelona, xlv = Jacobs 303]; for Gerona, see Reg. 13, fo. 229 [= R 289 = Bofarull, Barcelona, xlvi = Jacobs 308].

[98] ACA, Reg. 13, fo. 233ᵛ [= R 293–4 = Bofarull, Barcelona, xlviii = Jacobs 316, 310].

[99] ACA, Reg. 13, fo. 265 [= R 322]. This privilege was included in a charter given fifteen years earlier to Majorcan Jews. See n. 12 above.

[100] For Barcelona, see ACA, Reg. 15, fo. 123 [= R 391 = Bofarull, Barcelona, lxii = Jacobs 428]; for Lérida, see n. 17 above. [101] See n. 83 above.

[102] The sources are numerous and it is sufficient here to cite two examples: ACA, Reg. 14, fo. 127ᵛ [= R 486 = Bofarull, Barcelona, cvii = Jacobs 395]; Reg. 10, fo. 155ʳᵛ [= R 609.

was, of course, vital for the very existence of the Jewish community in medieval conditions. This right, which was incorporated in the charter received in 1268 by the Jews of Barcelona, was by no means a novelty but was most probably reiterated to reassure the Jews, who may have had some cause for concern at this time.[103] A similar interpretation may be put on the confirmation of freedom to trade made to the *aljamas* of Aragon and of Valencia and Murviedro in 1271.[104] The need for such a confirmation was undoubtedly caused by particular problems at the time, for in general the king never challenged this right.[105] The commercial privileges granted were adapted to the local conditions prevalent at the time and recognized the Jews' participation in the slave trade.[106]

Finally, there were charters which offered their beneficiaries tax reductions, exemptions, and other facilities. Some of these cancelled all levies and subsidies except the annual tax.[107] Others were clearly designed to attract new Jewish settlers,[108] and offered exemption for a limited period only.[109]

THE CHARTERS OF PEDRO III

Pedro III pursued his father's Jewish policy of providing protection and support to the Jews and preserving their rights and security.[110] In some fields Jewish rights were comparable to those of Christians.[111] In accordance with the prevalent custom of the time, and at the request of the communities, Pedro III confirmed charters granted by his father. Although we lack even partial documentation, we have clear indications of such confirmation.[112] Only very rarely, however, did Pedro III add new charters to those he confirmed.[113]

The process of confirmation of the communal charters was not a simple one. In this respect, the reign of Pedro III may be divided into two periods. In 1278, two

[103] ACA, Reg. 15, fo. 122ᵛ [= R 388 = Bofarull, Barcelona, lxix = Jacobs 426].

[104] For the communities of Aragon, see ACA, Reg. 16, fo. 252 [= R 490 = Jacobs 478]; for Murviedro, see ACA, Reg. 16, fo. 239ᵛ [= R 494 = Jacobs 473]; for Valencia, see n. 55 above.

[105] For a reconfirmation to the Jews of Barcelona see n. 99 above; for the right of the Jews of Lérida to engage in commerce, see n. 17 above.

[106] The material on the participation of Jews in the slave trade is extensive and scattered in many archives and other sources. Here we are only dealing with their right to engage in such a trade, contained in charters granted to Jewish communities. For a hint at Majorcan Jews' share in this trade, see n. 74 above.

[107] ACA, Reg. 12, fo. 8ᵛ [= R 178 and pp. 418–19, doc. iv = Jacobs 197]; Reg. 16, fo. 152ᵛ [= R 412].

[108] See nn. 23–9 above.

[109] ACA, Reg. 18, fo. 105 [= R 581 = Bofarull, Barcelona, cxxxi = Jacobs 505 = Dinur, ii. 2, p. 45, no. 1.

[110] See e.g. the case of the Jews of El Frago: ACA, Reg. 43, fo. 43 [= R 1217].

[111] ACA, Reg. 42, fo. 243 [= R 771].

[112] ACA, Reg. 40, fo. 80ᵛ [= R 697]. In this document the *justicia* of Teruel was ordered to respect the privileges of the *aljama* since the king had confirmed them at his accession to the throne.

[113] ACA, Reg. 39, fo. 155ʳᵛ [= R 674 and pp. 423–4, doc. x].

years after his coronation, the king ordered investigations into the legality of the charters granted by his predecessors to many Catalan, Aragonese, and Valencian Jewish communities, claiming that many of them harmed his rights, authority, and jurisdiction.[114] This sudden order to examine the charters came after the king had already confirmed most of them.[115] This change of royal policy, which seems surprising, was in fact an attempt to extract money from his Jewish subjects in the easiest possible way. Ten months later, in March 1279, Pedro III renewed his order to collect together all the charters of the communities of Catalonia, Aragon, and Valencia.[116]

This policy was abandoned in 1280 and replaced by a new strategy during the second period of Pedro's reign. From 1280 onwards the king's attitude towards the Jews of his realm came to be largely based on, or reflected in, the charters given by his father Jaime I. Some of these charters clearly indicate their confirmation by Pedro III;[117] in others, an examination preceded confirmation.[118] It is obvious that his father's charters were now acceptable to him[119] and that they became the basis for the protection of Aragonese Jewry under his reign also.[120] Any of his officials who ignored this new policy and the validity of the charters were ordered to respect them.[121] Likewise, in 1282 the king instructed all his officials to consider any copy of a charter drawn up by a notary and signed by a royal official as equally valid as the original.[122] Nevertheless, many problems relating to the authenticity and the text of the privileges continued to trouble various communities right through the reign of Pedro III.[123]

Only in the mid-1280s did Pedro III authorize the Catalan communities to maintain a communal government and other necessary institutions. He further allowed them to initiate and develop inter-communal relations and either reach a consensus or exchange views on their different positions in order to reach a common policy on certain issues. The communities of Aragon were also granted

---

[114] The king's claim was mentioned in a letter that he sent on 29 May 1278 to the local baile: ACA, Reg. 22, fo. 84 [= R 699]. In a letter sent to the communities on 3 June 1278 such claims were not mentioned, but the communities were required to hand over their charters within two or three days for an examination: ACA, Reg. 40, fo. 111ᵛ [= R 700]. A month later, the king renewed his order that all charters be collected and examined and cancelled their validity until the conclusion of this examination: ACA, Reg. 40, fo. 84 [= MF ii. 419].

[115] The abovementioned two letters were also sent to the baile and *aljama* of Teruel. Since we know that this community's charters had already been confirmed with the king's accession to the throne (see n. 112 above), we are led to this conclusion.

[116] ACA, Reg. 41, fo. 50ᵛ [= R 720 = MF ii. 502].

[117] See n. 111 above.

[118] ACA, Reg. 48, fo. 63ᵛ [= R 799].

[119] ACA, Reg. 48, fo. 107 [= R 822]; Reg. 44, fo. 188 [= R 824]; Reg. 49, fo. 27 [= R 859]; Reg. 50, fo. 187 [= R 884].

[120] ACA, Reg. 62, fo. 63ᵛ, 66 [= R 1152, 1154]; Reg. 43, fo. 28ᵛ [= R 199 = MF ii. 2026].

[121] ACA, Reg. 48, fo. 175 [= R 851, = MF ii. 1204].

[122] ACA, Reg. 59, fo. 131ᵛ [= R 975].

[123] ACA, Reg. 60, fo. 71 [= R 1037]; Reg. 56, fos. 21ᵛ, 96ᵛ [= R 1305, 1350 = MF ii. 2211].

a similar charter.[124] The confirmation of past charters enabling the Jews to enjoy self-government was taken for granted. The need for such confirmation generally arose out of internal strife:[125] from time to time, community leaders had to rely on royal charters in order to assert their authority over their members.[126] Some charters authorizing the community to elect its leadership also conferred the right to operate a judicial system of its own.[127] Such a charter was necessarily general in character and was addressed to all the communities. This did not prevent many individual communities from seeking to obtain their own copies, duly written and sealed.[128] The charter that regulated the communal judiciary included three elements: the validity of the *halakhah* and Jewish custom;[129] the appointment of *dayanim*, experts in *halakhah*;[130] and the obligation of Jewish litigants to appear before them.[131]

Side by side with the right to establish self-government and look after their own internal affairs, it was no less important for the Jews to obtain privileges which guaranteed them the basic right to fulfil the commandments of the Torah in their own manner. During the reign of Pedro III there were no records of serious disturbances in this area and there was consequently no need to reissue the relevant charters. From time to time, privileges on religious and ritual matters were mentioned as part of general charters or whenever a community felt that some aspects of its religious life were threatened.[132] The most important rights which came to be endangered and were therefore reconfirmed by the king included those to establish a synagogue, to slaughter according to their rite and sell the meat,[133] and to bury their dead according to Jewish custom.[134]

---

[124] On Catalan communities, see ACA, Reg. 44, fos. 187ʳ-188 [= R 823 = Baer, *Spanien*, doc. 121 = Dinur, ii. 2, p. 418, no. 8 and pp. 446–7, no. 2]. On Aragonese communities, see ACA, Reg. 59, fo. 56 [= R 942].

[125] In 1282, the Infante Alfonso issued an order for the respect of charters dealing with the election of a communal government and *berure tevi'ot* which had been previously granted by his father and other kings. The order was issued as a result of an internal crisis in the community of Gerona. See ACA, Reg. 59, fo. 115ʳ [= R 974 = Baer, *Spanien*, doc. 123].

[126] ACA, Reg. 50, fo. 206 [= R 886].

[127] See e.g. the privilege granted to Catalan and Aragonese Jewry, n. 124 above.

[128] ACA, Reg. 59, fo. 23 [= R 930]; Reg. 46, fos. 221ʳ-222 [= R 1172 and p. 428, no. xiv = MF ii. 1058].

[129] ACA, Reg. 43, fo. 8ʳ [= R 1177].

[130] See n. 128 above; also ACA, Reg. 43, fo. 8ʳ [= R 947].

[131] ACA, Reg. 43, fo. 114 [= R 1270 = MF ii. 2128].

[132] In 1280 the king reminded the Bishop of Saragossa that he had already forbidden him to prevent the Jews of Tauste from erecting a synagogue: ACA, Reg. 48, fo. 57ʳ [= R 797].

[133] In 1277, for example, together with other privileges, there is a reference to the right of the Jews of Calatayud to slaughter in accordance with Jewish law; see n. 113 above. In 1285, however, they were ordered to produce the privilege, which they claimed to possess and which permitted them to sell *kasher* meat: ACA, Reg. 56, fo. 21ʳ [= R 1305]. In 1279 Alfonso ordered the municipal leaders of Tarragona to refrain from harassing the local Jewish community over the slaughtering and sale of meat: ACA, Reg. 41, fo. 59ʳ [= R 722].

[134] ACA, Reg. 48, fo. 108 [= R 822].

THE REIGN OF ALFONSO III

Alfonso III's ascent to the throne did not mark any significant change in the attitude of the Crown towards the Jews as it had crystallized in the last years of his father Pedro III. There is no record of any difficulties arising from the confirmation of charters granted by Jaime I and Pedro III. On the contrary, the king instructed his officials to respect any charter which was challenged or opposed until he had examined the document.[135] The information at our disposal indicates Alfonso's general readiness to confirm the Catalan communities' past privileges. Between June 1290 and February 1291 the king confirmed important charters that his grandfather and father had granted to the Jews of Catalonia in general,[136] while the communities of Barcelona and its *collecta*,[137] the *collecta* of Gerona–Besalú,[138] and Lérida[139] had various of their privileges confirmed before 1286.

Of the Aragonese communities, we know that Calatayud[140] and Tarazona[141] were confirmed in their charters from the two previous reigns. In 1287 a charter granted by Pedro III to the Jews of the Kingdom of Valencia was endorsed by Alfonso.[142] Almost all the charters of the Jews of the city of Valencia which were confirmed by Alfonso III were valid in communities throughout the kingdom, although there might have been some privileges which were specific to isolated communities.[143] As soon as he ascended the throne, Alfonso III confirmed six charters which the community of Majorca had received between 1231 and 1273.[144]

---

[135] For the case of the privileges of the communities of Huesca and Saragossa, see ACA, Reg. 64, fos. 132–3 [= R 1661].

[136] For the privileges confirmed from the days of Jaime I see ACA, Reg. 83, fo. 55ᵛ [= R 2148], reconfirmed eight months later, Reg. 83, fo. 112 [= R 2304]. For those confirmed from the reign of Pedro III see ACA, Reg. 83, fo. 53ʳᵛ [= R 2141–2], reconfirmed eight months later, ACA, Reg. 83, fo. 111ᵛ–112 [= R 2301–2]. Their contents and importance are discussed below. The reconfirmation of old privileges at the request of the communities within such a short period suggests an urgency perhaps arising from emergencies in the communities.

[137] ACA, Reg. 83, fos. 52ᵛ, 112 [= R 2304, 2538]; Reg. 70, fo. 19ʳᵛ [= R 1685]; Reg. 75, fo. 43ᵛ [= R 1832]; Reg. 80, fo. 56ᵛ [= R 1997].

[138] ACA, Reg. 64, fo. 17 [= R 1501]; cf. R 1511–13, 1681. For a confirmation of a general charter, see ACA, Reg. 83, fo. 37ᵛ [= R 2110]. For a confirmation of other privileges, see R 2141–2, 2148, 2304.

[139] For a general confirmation, see ACA, Reg. 80, fo. 32 [= R 1982] and R 2304. For the examination of the claim of the Jews of Lérida concerning a charter they had received from Jaime I see ACA, Reg. 74, fo. 98ᵛ [= R 1908].

[140] ACA, Reg. 66, fos. 235ᵛ–236 [= R 1671–2]; Reg. 74, fo. 21 [= R 1816]; Reg. 83, fo. 87 [= R 2202]. The last two privileges dating back to the reign of Jaime I were also confirmed by Pedro III.

[141] ACA, Reg. 79, fo. 27 [= R 1935].

[142] ACA, Reg. 74, fo. 2 [= R 1789 = Guinovart 883]; Guinovart's regestum does not refer to this matter.

[143] ACA, Reg. 80, fo. 5ᵛ [= R 1961 = Guinovart 1334]. For privileges specific to individual communities, see e.g. ACA, Reg. 85, fo. 127 [= R 2347].

[144] ACA, Reg. 63, fo. 23ʳᵛ [= R 1478 = Isaacs 26]. An additional confirmation was obtained a short while before his death: ACA, Reg. 83, fo. 133 [= R 2364].

To all these Alfonso III added new charters of his own. The Jews of Majorca received at the beginning of 1286 an extensive new privilege on the same day on which their old privileges were confirmed.[145] In 1290 the king issued a very important charter to the *aljama* of Majorca, permitting the Jews to establish a walled and closed *call* or quarter, a synagogue, and a bakery. The charter also granted the Jews the right to refuse lodgings to Christians.[146]

Together these charters reflected a favourable policy towards the Jews based on the conception that their existence was a permanent interest of the state—an interest which was exclusively financial. This did not mean that the Crown refrained from making occasional immediate profits in return for the granting of a charter. In 1286, for example, a sum of money had to be paid for charters given to all the Jews of the Crown.[147] According to a document from 1290, the Jews of the *collecta* of Gerona–Besalú owed money to the king for charters they had received.[148] The charter of 1290 addressed to the *aljama* of Majorca cost the Jews 12,000 *solidi*.[149] These charters were not the only ones which brought financial profit to the monarch: one way or another, behind every charter, we may assume, there was a worthwhile gain for the Crown. Charters were used to attract Jewish settlers to places that the king wished to colonize.[150]

THE REIGN OF JAIME II

Jaime II did not deviate from the Jewish policy formulated by his predecessors. In 1291–4, the first years after he ascended the throne, he confirmed the old charters of the *aljamas* of Saragossa, Calatayud, Daroca, Valencia, and Tortosa.[151] This partial list proves the general rule. The process of royal endorsement sometimes lasted many years and the circumstances behind such delays are not always clear. In 1296, at the request of the community of Lérida, Jaime II declared that all the Jews of the *collecta* would be entitled to the same rights as the Jews of Lérida.[152] In 1298 the king confirmed the privileges given by Jaime I and Alfonso III to the communities of the *collecta* of Gerona–Besalú;[153] in 1303 he confirmed those which Alfonso III had granted to the *aljama* of Villafranca.[154]

---

[145] ACA, Reg. 63, fo. 30 [= R 1479 and pp. 438–9, doc. xx = Isaacs 27].
[146] ACA, Reg. 83, fos. 99ᵛ–100 [= R 2267–8 and pp. 440–1, doc. xxii = Isaacs 63–4].
[147] ACA, Reg. 70, fo. 14 [= R 1684].
[148] ACA, Reg. 81, fo. 87ᵛ [= R 2108].
[149] ACA, Reg. 83, fo. 100 [= R 2269 = Isaacs 65]; cf. R 2270. The establishment of the bakery was expected to cause no loss to the Crown: ACA, Reg. 83, fo. 100ᵛ [= R 2271 = Isaacs 67].
[150] See ACA, Reg. 81, fo. 196ᵛ [= R 2233 = Dinur, ii. 2, p. 47, no. 11] dealing with the colonization of Albarracín.
[151] Saragossa: ACA, Reg. 191, fo. 27ᵛ [= R 2392]; Calatayud: Reg. 191, fo. 40 [= R 2401]; Daroca: Reg. 192, fo. 54ᵛ [= R 2422]; Valencia: Reg. 87, fo. 19ᵛ [= R 2463]; Tortosa: Reg. 194, fo. 95 [= R 2546].
[152] ACA, Reg. 194, fo. 258 [= R 2622].
[153] ACA, Reg. 196, fo. 214 [= R 2705].
[154] ACA, Reg. 200, fo. 191ᵛ [= R 2811].

Some of the charters confirmed by Jaime II were quite old. At the beginning of the fourteenth century he confirmed charters of Alfonso II dating from 1145 and 1161.[155] The royal confirmation of these old charters was however far from a guarantee of their observance in the way the communities expected, as illustrated by the complaint of the Jews of Calatayud in 1301 that endorsed old charters were not fully respected.[156] Nevertheless, the *aljamas* were most anxious to preserve the copies of the charters so that they could produce them in times of emergency. Sometimes the king consented to renew the copy of the charter which was in the hands of the community, by permitting either its transcription anew or the replacement of its worn out seal.[157]

The charters confirmed by Jaime II relate to all fields of communal life. Some of them were designed to protect Jewish life and property,[158] while others were intended to ensure the proper administration of the community. In 1305 Jaime II endorsed the important charter that the community of Calatayud had obtained from his grandfather Jaime I in 1229, which had granted the Jews a very extensive autonomy, including the right to impose the death penalty.[159] In 1321 he renewed the charter that the *aljama* of Barcelona had received from Jaime I in 1266 and in which the basis of its self-government was laid down.[160]

Some of the charters which were confirmed by Jaime II were designed to protect the Jew in the king's judicial system. A most important principle in this domain was the necessity for a double testimony of a Jew and a Christian as a condition of its validity. In this matter Jaime II pursued the policy of his father, Pedro III, and his brother, Alfonso III.[161] In 1302 he confirmed a charter of Pedro III which had freed from arrest any Jew from Gerona, unless accused of murder, for the payment of a bail of 100 *maravedis*. Jaime II, it is true, modified it slightly by excluding also Jews accused of crimes for which the sentence might involve severe corporal punishment, but the charter remained essentially the same.[162] He also confirmed the charter that his grandfather had granted to the same community in which royal officials were denied the right to act as prosecutors or attorneys against any Jew from Gerona–Besalú, that is, to open legal proceedings, unless an official complaint had been laid against him.[163]

Not surprisingly, there was strong opposition to the confirmation of charters which were considered harmful to the Christian community. Subsequent to the

---

[155] ACA, Reg. 202, fo. 156 [= R 2826]; Reg. 203, fos. 103ᵛ–104 [= R 2848].
[156] ACA, CR, Jaime II, C 13, no. 1716.
[157] ACA, Reg. 205, fo. 234 [= R 2889]. This privilege of 1234 granted by Jaime I to the community of Huesca needed a new wax seal instead of the original one, which had disintegrated. For a new copy of the 1266 charter of the Barcelona *aljama* see ACA, Reg. 219, fo. 208 [= R 3167].
[158] See e.g. n. 157 above.
[159] ACA, Reg. 202, fo. 201 [= R 2836]; and see n. 26 above.
[160] ACA, Reg. 219, fo. 208 [= R 3167]; cf. R 355.
[161] ACA, Reg. 194, fo. 272 [= R 2621].
[162] ACA, Reg. 199, fo. 134ᵛ [= R 2797].
[163] ACA, Reg. 199, fo. 134ᵛ [= R 2798].

king's decision that in criminal cases involving Christians and Jews in Lérida the city's court was authorized to adjudicate between the litigants, the Jews brought up a charter from 1277 which had referred all such cases to the baile. Instructions were therefore sent to the baile in 1308 and again in 1309 to assert his authority. The municipal leaders did not give up their struggle. In 1316 they were promised that Jews accused of injuring Christians would be judged by a municipal court. In 1320, however, the community succeeded once again in obtaining the confirmation of its old charter entrusting the Jews to the jurisdiction of the baile. This confirmation was finally endorsed in 1322.[164] Jaime II similarly confirmed old charters designed to facilitate the Jews' autonomous life within the Jewish quarter.[165]

Jaime II inherited numerous charters related to taxation which he ratified as the need arose. Among these was a series of charters which set a limit to a community's annual tax,[166] or cancelled some taxes and duties altogether.[167] Conversely, it sometimes happened that communities were required to return such charters which had granted tax reductions.[168]

In addition to ratifying his predecessors' charters, Jaime II granted many new ones at the request of the communities. Some of these reflect his support for Jewish communal self-government. Two years after the temporary incorporation of Majorca in the Crown of Aragon, Jaime II offered the Jews of the island a charter regulating communal administration and jurisdiction.[169] Nine months later, the same community was authorized to issue ordinances in accordance with its needs.[170] At the request of the Jews of Lérida, Jaime II issued a charter setting out the administration's jurisdiction and functions in all fields of communal life; this charter was based on that which had been given by Pedro III to the Jews of Catalonia.[171] The right to impose a purchase tax on various commodities was also included in some privileges of several communities, although this tax aroused opposition among both the Christian and the Jewish population, often causing the abrogation of the privilege.[172]

The fulfilment of the commandments of the Torah and the observance of

[164] ACA, Reg. 221, fo. 212 [= R 3217 = Jacobs 805].

[165] ACA, CR, Jaime II, C 32, no. 4032 [= *Cartas Reales* no. 143]. Jaime II gave orders in 1311 to abide by the charters dealing with the sale of *kasher* meat in Elche as they were in force in the days of the Infante Manuel.

[166] ACA, Reg. 193, fo. 143 [= R 2424]; Reg. 195, fo. 113^v–114 [= R 2671].

[167] ACA, Reg. 211, fo. 278 [= R 3018]; Reg. 160, fo. 219 [= R 3041 = Bofarull, Montblanch, 84 = Dinur, ii. 2, p. 56, no. 60]; Reg. 203, fos. 103^v–104 [= R 2849]; Reg. 219, fos. 176^v–177 [= R 3157].

[168] ACA, Reg. 200, fo. 143 [= R 2802–3].

[169] ACA, Reg. 194, fo. 266 [= R 2623 = Isaacs 74].

[170] ACA, Reg. 253, fo. 2^v [= R 2648 = Isaacs 77].

[171] ACA, Reg. 195, fo. 44 [= R 2629 = Baer, *Spanien*, doc. 139].

[172] Such a charter granted to the *aljama* of Saragossa was strongly opposed by the city council, which succeeded in including a clause stipulating that the Christians suffer no harm: ACA, Reg. 223, fo. 211^v [= R 3257]. In another case, in Calatayud in 1323, local opposition caused the cancellation of the privilege: ACA, Reg. 223, fo. 258^v [= R 3260].

Jewish rituals were also provided for in privileges granted by Jaime II. The right of the Jews to abide by their laws and the traditions of their forefathers was not normally challenged, and therefore the need for a charter in this field was exclusive to cases which had economic implications and repercussions and those in which outsiders were involved. The arrest of a Jew on the Sabbath or festivals for defaulting in his tax payment was very frequent; numerous privileges were, therefore, granted in order to avoid such a contingency.[173] Very often, too, these privileges contained a promise that Jewish prisoners would be regularly provided with *kasher* food.

Dietary laws in general and ritual slaughter in particular had some economic aspects; in addition, the question of Jewish ritual slaughter raised certain technical problems, such as suitable places for slaughtering animals and selling the meat. Charters were necessary to regulate these matters.[174] These charters imposed restrictions as well as granting rights. Among these restrictions we find prohibitions on slaughtering a greater quantity of meat than the community required; on selling *kasher* meat to Christians; and on displaying *kasher* meat outside the allocated premises. Any attempt to ignore the right of the Jews to slaughter according to *halakhah* or to obstruct the provision of *kasher* meat to the members of the community aroused immediate and strong opposition.[175] The opposition of the *qehilah* was strongest when Christians were given a monopoly on the sale of *kasher* meat to Jews.[176]

The status and rights of the Jews in trials against Christians were defended in various charters which Jaime II agreed to grant to the communities of his kingdom. The principle of the dual testimony in vogue throughout the thirteenth century remained valid in all the communities and applied also to all those who had recently entered into the royal domain.[177] Whenever necessary, the king reiterated the validity of this principle.[178] Occasionally there was need to remind the royal officials of the Jews' rights in mixed trials.[179] The king was similarly

---

[173] ACA, Reg. 197, fos. 126ʳᵛ, 140 [= R 2738–9, 2742 = Miret, 'Le Massacre', p. 257]; Reg. 198, fo. 313ᵛ [= R 2758]; Reg. 201, fo. 25ᵛ [= R 2821]; Reg. 207, fo. 162 [= RR 2917].

[174] For Barcelona, see ACA, Reg. 200, fo. 140 [= R 2800]; for Elche, see ACA, CR, Jaime II, C 39, no. 4876.

[175] ACA, Reg. 203, fo. 172 [= R 2857 = Bofarull, Montblanch, 90]; Reg. 55, fo. 69 [= R 2859]; and esp. CR, Jaime II, C 18, no. 2397].

[176] In addition to the monopoly offered to a convert in Montblanch, see for the *aljama* of Játiva ACA, CR, Jaime II, C 134, no. 232 [= *Cartas Reales*, no. 453].

[177] ACA, Reg. 89, fo. 7 [= R 2538]. On 15 September 1294 the Infante Pedro promised the Jews of Vich who entered his jurisdiction all the customs and privileges enjoyed by the Jews of Catalonia. The principle of the dual testimony was particularly emphasized.

[178] This was how the king acted in 1326 vis-à-vis the community of Calatayud, which underwent great disorder following legal actions taken against it. The religious and economic reasons behind these actions made this principle doubly important. See ACA, Reg. 227, fo. 278ʳᵛ [= R 3358, 3382 = Jacobs 849].

[179] ACA, CR, Jaime II, C 13, no. 1715 [= *Cartas Reales*, no. 78]. This was a reminder from 1301 concerning the Jews of Saragossa.

prepared to sign charters protecting Jews against cruel methods of interrogation and judicial procedure,[180] and especially to treat with sympathy complaints by communities that their members were subjected to torture.[181] In 1318 his undertakings on this subject to the *aljama* of Huesca and its *collecta* were very prominent: no Jewish offender could be tortured without the king's express permission.[182] At the same time instructions were sent that, apart from execution for violence committed against Christians, which was within the *justicia*'s jurisdiction in Huesca, for all other offences the baile should act as a judge. Evidently the Jews preferred to be subject to the baile, who was the king's representative or *albedin* of the community, rather than to the judges.[183] The preference was not unjustified, for the judges continually harassed and pressurized the Jews in connection with the oath. Jaime II usually acquiesced in the *aljama*'s requests in this matter, and in the case of Calatayud, for example, he ordered that the oath be taken before the *zalmedina*, as in Saragossa.[184] In Huesca, when the Jews involved in trials with Christians were required to take the 'oath of the Maledictions' the leaders of the *aljama* produced two charters, the object of which was to prevent harm to their members.[185]

The king, considering the Jews part of his patrimony, took them under his direct protection; he referred to this principle at every opportunity and warned all persons and institutions against any act of interference in the Jews' affairs.[186] Some communities possessed charters which denied any official, except the baile, the exercise of any jurisdiction over them.[187]

Certain privileges issued by Jaime II were designed to protect the Jewish public and its quarter. Sometimes these privileges were granted at the establishment of the *aljama*, or the settlement of the first Jews in the locality. One of the clauses found in these privileges was the prohibition on the sale to Christians of houses in the Jewish quarter. In theory, the Jews' property belonged to the royal treasury, so that such a transaction could affect the status of the house as well as giving rise to the security risk associated with Christians living within the boundaries of the *judería*. Consequently, the reaction of the communal leadership

---

[180] See the charter that the king granted to the *aljama* of Daroca in 1320: ACA, CR, Jaime II, C 53, no. 6500.

[181] Concerning the Jews of Teruel, see ACA, Reg. 222, fo. 117ᵛ [= R 3239].

[182] ACA, Reg. 216, fo. 80ᵛ [= R 3096].

[183] For the community of Daroca, see ACA, CR, Jaime II, C 52, no. 6409 [= *Cartas Reales*, no. 220]. For Teruel, see CR, Jaime II, C 133, no. 99 [= *Cartas Reales*, no. 321].

[184] ACA, CR, Jaime II, C 13, no. 1719 [= *Cartas Reales*, no. 73].

[185] Following the complaint of the Jews, the judge of Huesca Domingo Tamarit sent copies of the two charters to the king, who was expected to send him instructions: ACA, CR, Jaime II, C 116, no. 748. The document bears no date.

[186] See e.g. Jaime II's letter to the local authorities in Vich: ACA, CR, Jaime II, C 134, no. 163 [= *Cartas Reales*, no. 377].

[187] The community of Teruel possessed such a charter: ACA, CR, C 133, no 5 [= *Cartas Reales*, no. 231]. It was mentioned in connection with the property of a Jew who was executed after having been falsely accused of poisoning the water with another Jew.

to this kind of development was immediate and resolute. When certain Jews sold to Christians houses in the Jewish quarter of Játiva, in the Kingdom of Valencia, the king responded to the complaint of the community by issuing prompt instructions for an investigation. If the investigation should confirm the objections of the *aljama*, all transactions in contravention of the charter establishing the quarter would be declared null and void.[188]

From time to time the king reasserted the validity of charters granted for the protection of the community.[189] When the Jewish quarter was attacked, for example in 1322 after Christians invaded the Jewish quarter in Villafranca,[190] he demanded that the perpetrators be punished and measures be taken to prevent similar attacks in the future. A year later he once again ordered that no harm should be done to the life and property of the Jews, especially on Fridays and on Christian festivals when they remained inside the *judería*. In this letter the king made explicit mention of the violence, aggression, and serious attacks which the Jews of Villafranca had suffered.[191] Subsequent to such attacks, Jaime II would seek and obtain information on the events with the aim of bringing the guilty to trial. From a letter to the *veguer* of Barcelona in 1308 we know of the stoning of the Jewish quarter on a Christian festival. After this incident, an investigation and legal proceedings were initiated against the aggressors.[192]

Royal protection was also extended to individual members of the community. Relying on their communities' charters, Jews turned to the monarch to redress grievances and combat oppression. It was the monarch whom the Jews trusted to protect the lives of their families, or, failing that, at least to punish the criminal. On principle, the king demanded the trial of the accused and the punishment of the guilty in any case of a Jew's murder. He took an active part in the procedure and even in the final verdict.[193] Those who were entrusted with the investigation and trial of cases of murder of Jews often received instructions from the palace.[194] These instructions were particularly necessary when attempts were made to obstruct the proper conduct of the investigation or the trial. On 25 March 1326 Galceran Andreu, the baile of Manresa, sent a letter to the king admitting his

---

[188] ACA, CR, Jaime II, C 39, no. 4919 [= *Cartas Reales*, no. 168]. According to this source dated 10 June 1314, the Jewish quarter was called *algema* (a variant of the usual term *aljama*), as was customary in the Kingdom of Aragon.

[189] ACA, CR, Jaime II, C 45, no. 5581 [= *Cartas Reales*, no. 196]. This declaration from 1317 referred to the community of Calatayud.

[190] ACA, CR, Jaime II, C 57, no. 6974 (21 March 1322).

[191] ACA, CR, Jaime II, C 133, no. 10 [= *Cartas Reales*, no. 257] (9 February 1323).

[192] ACA, CR, Jaime II, C 27, no. 3477 [= *Cartas Reales*, no. 128]. The attack took place on Sunday, which was the festival of Domingo de Ramos.

[193] In November 1316 the *justicia* of Oriola sent the file of the trial which was opened at the demand of the king against Miguel Garces, from Castellón, who was accused of the murder of the Jew Mosse Abendino: ACA, CR, Jaime II, C 45, no. 5542.

[194] Investigators of the murder of Jews from Figueras, for example, sought instructions from the king: ACA, CR, Jaime II, C 135, no. 378.

inability to bring to justice the murderer of Yucef Baro's wife, the nobleman en Pere de Puig, unless he were authorized to summon some specific witnesses.[195] Even when the Jew's death was the result of accidental manslaughter or attack by an animal, Jaime II did not remit the fine.[196] Cases of royal pardon accorded to murderers of Jews must be seen as a deviation from the official policy.[197]

Jaime II considered physical attacks against the Jews short of murder equally menacing and dangerous, for they might lead to serious disturbances. He would therefore demand the immediate and severe punishment of such aggressors. In June 1319 the Infante Alfonso ordered the arrest of a Christian who had wounded a Jewess from Agramunt.[198] The authorities did not even give up their pursuit of those who sought sanctuary in churches and monasteries after committing physical violence against Jews.[199]

There is ample evidence of royal protection of Jews facing pressure, threats, and persecution. While it was the interests of the king and the authorities that determined this attitude, its significance and importance in the daily life of the individual Jew cannot be overestimated. This policy of protection was put into practice in various areas and various ways, including the expression of concern over the condition of Jewish women imprisoned in Barcelona;[200] instructions sent to local officials to protect Jews against Christians and Muslims,[201] or against threats and violence by Christians as a result of economic rivalry;[202] and intervention on behalf of Jews attacked by robbers.[203] In many cases the king even insisted that the Jewish victims be compensated.[204]

Jaime II's interest in the welfare of those of his Jewish subjects who were confronted with problems outside the territories of the Crown is particularly striking. In August 1321, for example, at the request of the community of Barcelona, he despatched a letter to the consuls of Narbonne concerning Juceff Sachs (or Jaches), who was there on business and to visit relatives, and who had suffered

---

[195] ACA, CR, Jaime II, C 134, no. 150 [= *Cartas Reales*, no. 366].

[196] In 1300 the king ordered that the price of the mule which caused the death of a Jewish child should be paid to the father. ACA, CR, Jaime II, C 7, no. 1007 [= *Cartas Reales*, no. 65].

[197] ACA, CR, Jaime II, C 35, no. 4381.

[198] Concerning Na Mira, see ACA, CR, Jaime II, C 50, no. 6192. On the trial of a Christian who wounded a Jew from the region of Gerona, see CR, Jaime II, C 68, no. 8298 [= *Cartas Reales*, no. 346]. For the case of the Jewess from Agramunt, see CR, Jaime II, C 135, no. 369 [= *Cartas Reales*, no. 513].

[199] That is what happened to P. Berenguer Tororo, who found shelter in the monastery of San Pedro de Besalú after wounding a Jew from the same locality. ACA, CR, Jaime II, C 135, no. 399 [= *Cartas Reales*, no. 542].

[200] ACA, CR, Jaime II, C 66, no. 8151 [= *Cartas Reales*, no. 333].

[201] ACA, CR, Jaime II, C 133, no. 109 [= *Cartas Reales*, no. 334]; C 134, no. 163 [= *Cartas Reales*, no. 377]. [202] ACA, CR, Jaime II, C 134, no. 172 [= *Cartas Reales*, no. 385].

[203] ACA, CR, Jaime II, C 34, no. 4227.

[204] The request of the King of Majorca addressed to the King of Aragon in April 1320 that certain Jews from Majorca be compensated is an interesting example: ACA, CR, Jaime II, C 57, no. 6992 [= *Cartas Reales*, no. 219].

arrest and the confiscation of his goods. The king also sent without avail a letter to the King of France.[205]

Jaime II had also to protect his Jewish subjects against arbitrary attitudes on the part of his officials. Jews did not hesitate long before turning to the king for support of their charters, rights, and customs if they felt threatened by royal representatives and officials. From time to time the king issued instructions that no investigation into Jewish affairs should be opened without his express order.[206] No doubt such instructions were the result of investigations conducted by his men which the Jews found oppressive and unjust. From letters sent by the king to his local officials, warning them not to breach the Jew's privileges, we may infer that this was not a rare offence.[207] Indeed, Jaime II interfered quite frequently in the work of his functionaries whenever he thought that they were likely to harm the Jewish community or individual Jews.[208] His orders forbidding his officers to confiscate their shops and businesses in cases of non-payment of taxes or debts are especially noteworthy.[209] An interesting case was that of Jews from Castellón de Ampurias who protested when their property in Gerona was confiscated by the local *veguer* and the baile because of a debt of the Count of Ampurias. The king intervened on their behalf.[210]

Although by the reign of Jaime II the territorial expansion of the Reconquista had long been completed, and consequently the role of the Jews in colonization considerably diminished, the Crown still showed interest in using Jews as settlers in certain places. The king had to offer generous charters to actual or potential settlers in specific localities. Jaime II showed particular interest in Jewish settlement in newly conquered territories in the south, and encouraged foreign Jews in particular to settle there.[211] Privileges identical to those of the Kingdom of Valencia were granted to all Jews who would settle in Elche, Oriola, and Alicante, which were conquered by Jaime II.[212] Jews who were invited to live on the lands of princes and noblemen received equally advantageous charters.[213]

The rights of new or small communities were often modelled on those of

---

[205] The letter to the consuls is found in ACA, CR, Jaime II, C 55, no. 6824. For the letter to the French king see CR, Jaime II, C 135, no. 373 [= *Cartas Reales*, no. 517]. Concerning the request of the community of Barcelona see CR, Jaime II, see C 133, no. 3 [= *Cartas Reales*, no. 229].

[206] ACA, Reg. 197, fos. 112, 131 [= R 2734, 2737].

[207] See e.g. ACA, Reg. 201, fo. 71 [= R 2821] for the king's letter to the *merino* of Saragossa, and ACA, CR, Jaime II, C 77, no. 9416 [= *Cartas Reales*, no. 448], for a letter sent on 30 May 1327 by the Infante Alfonso to the *veguer* of Urgell and the baile of Agramunt, warning them against any harm to the Jews.

[208] ACA, CR, Jaime II, C 134, nos. 177, 229 [= *Cartas Reales*, no. 390, 450].

[209] ACA, Reg. 196, fo. 172 [= R 2695].

[210] ACA, CR, Jaime II, C 55, no. 6796 [= *Cartas Reales*, no. 228]. For a safe-conduct sent to one of the Jews involved, see ACA, Reg. 220, fo. 82'.

[211] Under Jaime II the region of Alicante in the north of Murcia was conquered. For privileges offered to Jews who were prepared to settle there, see ACA, Reg. 195, fo. 120 [= R 2675].

[212] ACA, Reg. 212, fo. 145 [= R 3037].

[213] During Jaime II's reign there was a large movement of Jews from the royal domains to those

older or bigger *aljamas*. Communities that passed from one domain to another would receive new charters compatible with their new status.[214] Small communities would frequently have their charters compared to those of the leading community in the *collecta* or district.[215] Thus the privilege that exempted the Jews of Montblanch from wearing the badge and permitted them to wear the same clothes as the Jews of Barcelona, Tarragona, and Villafranca was granted in 1311 to the community as it belonged to the same *collecta*.[216] For the same reason, Jaime II decreed in 1325 that the Jews of Cervera and Tárrega should enjoy the same rights as the Jews of Lérida.[217]

On matters of taxation and finance the Jews often needed new charters. New Jewish settlers were usually promised easy conditions for the payment of their taxes.[218] Some charters were designed to protect the community from measures which were usually taken by royal officials whenever taxes were not paid. These measures included the confiscation of the Jews' property, arrest on Sabbaths and festivals, and the cutting off of food supplies to the entire community while the gates of the Jewish quarter remained shut. The effects of such measures were naturally very serious and some communities obtained charters forbidding them.[219] In 1302 all the communities of the Crown of Aragon received a charter exempting all Jewish prisoners from the *carcelatge* (prison tax) and forbidding any attempt to disrupt food supplies.[220] The *aljama* of Jaca was promised in its 1307 privilege that its members would not be imprisoned outside their quarter so that their wives and daughters would not be harassed on their way to bring them food.[221] Other charters conferring exemption from or reduction of various kinds of taxes were granted to various *aljamas*, and the king's officials were warned not to ignore communal charters in matters of taxation.[222]

---

of the nobility. This emigration is also referred to in Hebrew sources, while the archival material on the subject is abundant. For the request of the infante that the king permit Tomas Çacosta to settle ten Jewish families in Algerri see ACA, CR, Jaime II, C 134, no. 228 [= *Cartas Reales*, no. 449]. For the very favourable charter granted by the Infante Alfonso to the Jews who came to settle in Alcolea de Cinca, see ACA, Reg. 383, fo. 40–2 [= Baer, *Spanien*, doc. 175].

[214] For Jews who passed from the domain of a nobleman to that of the infante see ACA, Reg. 89, fo. 7 [= R 2538]; for the renewal of the charters of the Majorcan *aljama* with the temporary return of the island to Aragonese rule, see ACA, Reg. 194, fo. 266 [= R 2623 = Isaacs 74].

[215] ACA, Reg. 194, fo. 258 [= R 2622]; Reg. 196, fos. 151ᵛ, 172 [= R 2688, 2695 = Dinur, ii. 2, p. 54, no. 48]; Reg. 229, fo. 248 [= R 3401]; Reg. 228, fo. 107ᵛ [= R 3407].

[216] ACA, Reg. 208, fo. 12 [= R 2928 = Bofarull, Montblanch, 83].

[217] ACA, CR, Jaime II, C 133, no. 92. A copy of the king's letter is found in Reg. 226, fo. 137ᵛ [= R 3328].

[218] ACA, Reg. 87, fo. 12 [= R 2459]. This is a charter promising all Jews who settled in Arbós the same conditions of tax payment as the Jews of Sabadell.

[219] For example, Lérida in 1300: ACA, Reg. 197, fo. 140 [= R 2742]; Tortosa in 1314: Reg. 207, fo. 162 [= R 2917].

[220] The charter was sent in seven copies to all the *aljamas* of the Crown: ACA, Reg. 199, fo. 68ᵛ [= R 2772 = Jacobs 748].

[221] ACA, Reg. 204, fo. 73ᵛ [= R 2875 = Jacobs 757].

[222] On tax exemptions or reductions, see ACA, CR, Jaime II, C 39, no. 4876; Reg. 218, fos.

Under Jaime II Jewish communities also received charters dealing with commerce, assuring their members, for example, that their businesses and goods would not be confiscated because of debts,[223] and that strict supervision of weights and measures would be enforced.[224] Some charters regulated the conditions of loans to Christians,[225] while others enabled the Jews to exact unlimited interest from Muslims.[226] Particularly important were the charters which undertook not to allow late payment of debts to Jews.[227]

Finally, the attitude of Jaime II towards repeated attempts to bypass or abrogate the Jewish communities' charters merits attention. As a rule, the king insisted on the validity of these charters. In this respect the letter of the baile of Majorca addressed to the king in 1297 is noteworthy. The baile complained that the local population was strongly opposed to the charter which had invested the *aljama* and its leaders with judicial authority, in contravention of the privileges of the inhabitants, royal jurisdiction, and even the local Jews' wishes.[228] Three years later, the municipal leaders on the island applied once again to Jaime II requesting the abrogation of the charter which authorized the Jews to elect their own leaders/judges, claiming that the extensive jurisdiction of these figures was in conflict with their own rights.[229] Such charters aroused strong opposition among the local population, particularly since they considerably reduced the jurisdiction of the local Christian judiciary. The opposition was even greater when the Jews enjoyed privileges which put them beyond the authority of the local institutions in trials between Jews and Christians. When the Jews of Lérida produced a charter from 1277, according to which these trials had to be conducted by the baile, Jaime II withdrew his consent that such trials should be within the jurisdiction of the municipal court. Against this charter, the city leaders quoted a privilege from 1316 authorizing them to judge cases where Jews and Muslims were accused of damages inflicted on Christians and for which the punishment would be corporal. In 1320, however, the Jews of Lérida obtained the king's promise that their charter would be honoured; and again in 1322, despite all opposition, Jaime II decided to uphold the charter that the Jews of Lérida had held from his father.[230]

156ʼ–157; Reg. 221, fos. 155ʼ–156; Reg. 222, fos 26ʼ, 127 [= R 3223, 3145, 3152]. On the warning to royal officials, see CR, Jaime II, C 48, no. 5974.

[223] ACA, Reg. 196, fo. 172 [= R 2695]; the Jews of Saragossa were guaranteed by a charter that the goods of the Jewish cloth merchants would not be confiscated because of debts, as long as they held other property: ACA, CR, Jaime II, C 38, no. 4809; cf. C 40, no. 5015, concerning the Jews of Tortosa. [224] ACA, Reg. 196, fo. 172ʼ [= R 2696].

[225] ACA, Reg. 228, fo. 107ʼ [= R 3407]. The original letter is found in ACA, CR, Jaime II, C 134, no. 193 [= *Cartas Reales*, no. 406]. The importance of the CR is clear from this instance.

[226] ACA, CR, Jaime II, C 13, no. 1717 [= *Cartas Reales*, no. 81].

[227] For such a charter granted to the Jews of Montblanch, see ACA, CR, Jaime II, C 133, no. 38 [= *Cartas Reales*, no. 272]. For a privilege to the Jews of Montclús, see n. 225 above.

[228] ACA, CR, Jaime II, C 1, no. 325. [229] ACA, CR, Jaime II, C 5, no. 754.

[230] ACA, Reg. 221, fo. 212 [= R 3217 = Jacobs 805].

In general, both the king[231] and the infante[232] were ready to instruct officials and local authorities to abide by the charters of the communities which sought their help. The reaction of the *aljama* of Saragossa to the orders sent to its leaders to produce their registers so that accusations that they had hidden part of their property to avoid tax could be checked is worth noting. The leaders appeared before the king with a charter given by Jaime I which guaranteed the complete secrecy of the community's records and registers. Thereupon Jaime II cancelled his orders.[233] In another case the king ordered that the charter of the Jews of Tortosa, stating that the Jews pay no more than the Christians for *carcelatge*, be upheld.[234] The king even stood by the community in its struggle against violent attempts by some of its own members to disregard its charters. In 1311, for instance, he supported the case of the *aljama* of Huesca against the physician Vidal Abulbaca, who refused to hand over to the communal archive charters which he continued to hold despite the *aljama*'s formal demand for their return. The demand was made in the synagogue under the threat of ban in case of disobedience.[235]

At times, however, Jaime II gave orders in favour of Jews who acted contrary to the charters of the *qehilah*.[236] Not surprisingly, most of these Jews belonged to the upper classes of Jewish society. In quite a number of cases the king's attitude to the charters, which he himself or his predecessors had granted to the community, seemed cynical or ambivalent. In 1327 he instructed the *veguers* of Barcelona and its vicinity to postpone the payment of a Christian's debts as he himself was unable to do, since such a decision would contradict a charter that he had given to the Jews.[237]

The favourable charters granted to the Jews of the Crown of Aragon in the thirteenth and early fourteenth century reflect the high esteem in which they were held by the monarchs, and the kings' recognition that the Jews were a most valuable asset in need of their protection. As in the rest of Christian Europe, however, these charters contained no more than a limited guarantee of royal protection. The charter itself implied a precarious situation and a transient privileged status which revealed the Jew's almost total dependence on the Crown. In retrospect, the charter not only betrayed the Jews' weakness but also contained the hidden roots of future disasters.

---

[231] The king reacted favourably to the request of the *aljama* of Saragossa in 1297: ACA, Reg. 253, fo. 43 [= R 2649]; and to the request of the community of Calatayud in 1301: ACA, CR, Jaime II, C 13, no. 1716. However, Jaime II did not cancel the right he granted to a Christian in 1320 to appoint the *shohatim* in Valencia. When the *aljama* mentioned its charter from the days of Jaime I, which forbade this, the king agreed that the charter would become valid once again after the death of that particular Christian: ACA, Reg. 219, fos. 214ᵛ–215 [= R 3168].

[232] For the community of Valencia, see ACA, CR, Jaime II, C 67, no. 8288 [= *Cartas Reales*, no. 345]; for the community of Huesca, see C 133, no. 87.   [233] ACA, Reg. 197, fo. 106 [= R 2733].

[234] For the king's orders to respect the charter on the *carcelatge* or *carcellagium*, see ACA, CR, Jaime II, C 13, no. 1711 [= *Cartas Reales*, no. 79].   [235] ACA, Reg. 207, fo. 182 [= R 2918].

[236] ACA, Reg. 209, fo. 226 [= R 2959].   [237] ACA, CR, Jaime II, C 134, no. 255.

§1.3 The Crown, the Church, and the Jews

In the thirteenth century the Church reached the peak of its power throughout Western Europe. Its policy towards its opponents became more aggressive; its war against heretics and deviants was total. Its efforts to impose unity and uniformity on its own members were generally successful, thanks to capable popes and enthusiastic friars. The continued survival of Jews in the midst of Christendom was no longer tolerated by zealous friars whose missionary spirit was reinvigorated in the newly formed orders of the Franciscans and Dominicans. The latter particularly developed new methods and adopted novel attitudes in their missionary activities. They studied Arabic and Hebrew and changed their polemical tactics and strategy. The conversion of the Jews to Christianity was a major Christian aim, with which, in theory, the kings and princes of Christian Europe, including those of the Crown of Aragon, were fully identified. Reality, however, was far more complex. Bitter rivalry existed between the secular and the religious authorities. Kings and princes were alarmed by the rise of papal power and suspicious of the pope's political designs.

CHURCH POWER AND JEWISH SPLENDOUR

No Christian king could openly oppose the Church programme to bring the Jews to the baptismal font. Many among them were, however, determined not to lose their control over the Jews, whom they considered part of their patrimony. While Christian influence penetrated deep in all sections of society and was eventually to play a leading role in shaping the Jewish policy of the kings, the Aragonese monarchs, who like many European leaders derived political and financial benefits from the Jews, were unwilling to cooperate with any group or institution whose policy would lead to financial losses for the royal treasury. The Aragonese kings of the thirteenth and fourteenth centuries saw no contradiction between their Christian loyalty and their protection of Jewish life and property.

The renewed Christian missionary activities of the thirteenth century coincided with the Reconquista and the overseas expansion in the Mediterranean of the Crown of Aragon. The great successes of the Reconquista, the holy wars waged by the Christians against the Muslims, raised the crusading spirit, the hopes and enthusiasm of the missionary forces operating in the territories of the

Crown of Aragon. The period was also the greatest in the history of the Jews of the Crown. Jaime I, whose conquests in the name of the Cross earned him the admiration of Christendom, was also the great benefactor of his Jewish subjects whose potential and contribution to his realm he appreciated. With his reign a new era of splendour in Jewish life was ushered in. The status and achievements of the Jews reached their highest point. In the same period, new methods began to be employed by Christian missionaries in their attempts to convert the Jews. Public debates and new polemics were also features typical of the period.

THE DISPUTATION OF BARCELONA

The Disputation of Barcelona in 1263 between the apostate Paulus Cristiani and the famous Talmudist Nahmanides could not have taken place without the king's consent. Jaime I shared neither the aim nor the optimism of Paulus and his Dominican colleagues. While the Disputation was being held, he continued to show favour to the Jews. The freedom of speech he granted Nahmanides was most remarkable.[1] On the one hand, he permitted the missionaries to stage their great show—and by doing so acted in keeping with his reputation as the champion of the Christian faith—while on the other, he had no intention of allowing religious fanaticism to shape his Jewish policy. What seemed an ambivalent attitude was rather a carefully calculated pragmatic policy that placed his own interest and that of the Crown above all others.

Some of the decisions taken by the king at this time illustrate the point well. About a month after the Disputation, on 26 August 1263, Jaime I ordered the Jews to attend the Dominicans' sermons delivered in synagogues;[2] two days earlier he had approved the establishment of a new synagogue in Barcelona.[3] On 28 August the king ordered the confiscation of all copies of the book of Judges of *Mishne Torah*, which he condemned to burning because of the blasphemies it contains against Jesus;[4] two days later, he forbade the Dominicans to force the Jews to attend sermons given outside the Jewish quarter.[5] Following the publication of his account at the request of the Bishop of Gerona, Nahmanides was accused of blasphemy. The king refused to inflict on him any punishment more than two

---

[1] A Latin account of the Disputation is found in ACA, Reg. 12, fos. 110–11. The text published in Villanueva, *Viage literario*, xiii, pp. 332–5 is based on another source found in Gerona. See Riera and Feliu, *Disputa de Barcelona*. A short while after the Disputation Nahmanides published a Hebrew account of his own version of the events; see Chavel, *Works of Nahmanides*. Nahmanides gave a copy of his account to the Bishop of Gerona: ACA, Reg. 13, fo. 265 [= *CDIA*, vi, p. 168 = Villanueva, *Viage literario*, xiii, pp. 336–7 = Bofarull, Barcelona, liii = Dinur, ii. 2, pp. 540–1, no. 14]. For further bibliography see R 323, 726, and Chazan, *Barcelona*, and bibliography therein.

[2] ACA, Reg. 12, fo. 107 [= R 209 = Jacobs 244].

[3] ACA, Reg. 12, fo. 104ᵛ [= R 208 = Bofarull, Barcelona, xxxiii = Jacobs 241].

[4] ACA, Reg. 12, fo. 106 [= R 212 = Jacobs 243 = Dinur, ii. 2, pp. 539–40, no. 11].

[5] ACA, Reg. 12, fo. 111ᵛ [= R 217 = Bofarull, Barcelona, xxxiv = Jacobs 247 = Dinur, ii. 1, p. 259, no. 42].

years' banishment and the burning of his work.[6] As this sentence seemed too light in the Dominicans' eyes, Jaime I did not bother to punish Nahmanides at all; indeed, he had rewarded him a few days earlier with 300 sb.[7] These seemingly contradictory decisions are indicative not of vacillation but rather of pragmatism. Jaime I, himself a devout Christian, was prepared to encourage individual Jews to accept Christianity but was strongly opposed to all measures of coercion and pressure that were designed to destroy Jewish life. Jaime I acted as a Christian king as long as there was no danger to Jewish life and property.

The Disputation of Barcelona was not an isolated public performance of missionary propaganda, but part of a well-planned anti-Jewish campaign that began in the early 1240s and continued throughout the thirteenth and fourteenth centuries. The Judeo-Christian polemics continued on various levels and in different forms throughout the period.[8] Yet despite the innovations in methods and approach, Paulus Cristiani did not succeed in his plan to bring masses of Jews to baptism through argument and persuasion. His use of the Talmud to prove the veracity of Christianity was revolutionary, but his efforts bore no fruit. Nahmanides was a formidable disputant and an expert Talmudist. Paulus himself might not have been sufficiently ready for the task; and in any case the Jews were far from being easy prey to Christian propaganda, even if it were based on Talmudic passages.

Less than a year after the Disputation, Jaime I reduced the sentence pronounced against Astrug de Porta from Villafranca, who had been condemned for blasphemies. The king took into consideration Astrug's family, and particularly the rights of his wife, daughter, and daughters-in-law. The accused was the brother of Benveniste de Porta, who was in the king's service. The stance taken by the king in this affair was not determined exclusively by Christian considerations.[9]

As noted above, following the Disputation of Barcelona Jaime I accepted the Dominicans' demand to confiscate and burn one of the books of *Mishne Torah*. As for the remaining books, the Jews were required in August 1263 to erase within three months all passages containing references to Jesus and Mary and any other passage identified by the heads of the Dominicans, who included Paulus Cristiani and Raymundus de Peñaforte. From later sources we may infer that the 1263 decision was not fully implemented. In 1268 the king defined the passages to be erased as those that contained direct references to Jesus and Mary and the saints; these cases apart, the Jews did not have to show their books to their Christian adversaries.[10]

---

[6] ACA, Reg. 13, fo. 265 [= Villanueva, *Viage literario*, xiii, pp. 336–7 = *CDIA*, vi, pp. 167–9].

[7] ACA, Reg. 14, fo. 70 [=R 319 = Jacobs 373].

[8] See e.g. Adret, iv. 187; Perles, *R. Salamo b. Abraham b. Adreth*; Cohen, 'The Christian Adversary'; Longpre, 'Le B. Raymond Lulle'; Assis, 'Papal Inquisition'.

[9] ACA, Reg. 13, fo. 178ᵛ [=R 262 = Bofarull, Barcelona, xxxix = Jacobs 130–1].

[10] On the burning of Maimonides' books, see n. 4 above. On censorship see ACA, Reg. 12, fos.

THE MISSIONARY SERMONS

The methods and means employed by the Dominicans to convert the Jews became more efficient and sophisticated at a time when the Jews reached the zenith of their power and achievements. This paradox is well illustrated in the king's attitude to the conversionist sermons delivered by the Dominican friars. These sermons intensified after the Barcelona Disputation.[11] In his early instructions after 1263, the king informed the Jews of the Crown that he sent Paulus Cristiani to show them the right path and to teach them the Scriptures, in their synagogues and homes or anywhere else. The Jews were required to listen carefully to his sermons and respond in humility. They also had to produce any of their books for which the missionary asked. These instructions, which were severe and uncompromising, were somewhat softened in a letter sent the following day in which Jaime I prohibited the use of violence in taking the Jews outside their quarter to listen to the sermons. Furthermore, the Jews were granted complete freedom to decide whether to listen to these sermons or not, even when they were given in the synagogue or in the Jewish quarter. In fact, this letter cancelled out much of the king's previous order and left the missionary sermons quite ineffective.[12]

Five years later, in October 1268, Jaime I repeated his orders not to force Jews to listen to conversionist sermons outside their quarter so that they should not be exposed to dangers and harassments. Similarly, he forbade the entry of the preachers into the quarter if they were accompanied by more than ten people. These decisions were taken at the request of Catalan communities that had experienced violence by religious zealots accompanying the preachers.[13]

Under Pedro III the sermons to the Jews were renewed with enthusiasm by the Dominicans, who were inspired and encouraged by the pope. The king supported these missionary activities and took converts under his auspices,[14] in

---

111ˇ–112 [=R 216 = R 248 = Dinur, ii. 2, p. 540, no. 12]. On renewed instructions, see ACA, Reg. 13, fo. 156 [= *CDIA*, vi, pp. 164–6 = R 249 = MF i. 518 = Indice 318]. On the exemption of 1268 to the Jews of Barcelona see ACA, Reg. 15, fo. 122ˇ [= R 387 = Bofarull, Barcelona, lxxv = Jacobs 425]; for Lérida, see *CDIA*, vi, p. 170.

[11] The missionary sermons preceded the Disputation. Jaime I was the first king to order the Jews to listen to sermons in 1242 and was highly praised by Pope Innocent IV. See Grayzel, *The Church and the Jews*, p. 256. In 1247 the Corts of Lérida repeated the Jews' and Muslims' obligation to attend the sermons: *Cortes*, ii, pp. 217–18.

[12] On the king's orders to the Jews to attend the sermons, see n. 2 above. The order was published in Denifle, 'Quellen zur Disputation', pp. 234–5. Three days after the general order the letter about Paulus Cristiani was sent: ACA, Reg. 12, fo. 107ˇ [= R 215 = Dinur, ii. 2, p. 539, no. 9]. For the freedom granted to the Jews to attend the sermons, see ACA, Reg. 12, fo. 111ˇ [= R 217 = Bofarull, Barcelona, xxxiv = Dinur, ii. 1, p. 259, no. 42].

[13] ACA, Reg. 15, fos. 122ˇ–123ʳˇ [= R 386, 392, 394 = Bofarull, Barcelona, lxxiii, lxii = Jacobs 424, 429, 431; *CDIA*, vi, pp. 170–2; Indice 327].

[14] ACA, Reg. 41, fo. 61ˇ [= *CDIA*, vi, p. 194 = R 723]. On the prohibition of Christian participation in forcing Jews to listen to sermons, see ACA, Reg. 41, fos. 93ˇ–94 [= R 731–3, 735, 740].

apparent contravention of his policy of incorporating a large number of Jews in his administration, appointing many of them to senior positions. Despite his approval of the missionary sermons to the Jews, Pedro imposed restrictions on the number of Christians who could accompany the preachers, as Jaime I had also done, as soon as reports showed that acts of violence were frequently committed during and after these sermons.

During the reign of Pedro III violence against the Jews spread fast in Aragonese communities. Excited and incited by extremely anti-Jewish sermons, the mobs attacked both the Jews themselves and their property. Some synagogues suffered severe damage. From the sources it is clear that the attacks were the direct result of very hostile sermons and that Jews were dragged to baptism against their will. Sometimes crowds of Christians participated in anti-Jewish processions during which Jewish ceremonies and customs were ridiculed. Mock Jewish rituals were staged to the great amusement of the Christian public.[15] These anti-Jewish attacks contradicted a fundamental principle of Jewish existence under the protection of the king—the right to live in accordance with their laws and beliefs. Throughout the period, the kings of Aragon had the power and the will to oppose this threat. Pedro III did not ban the missionary sermons, but he imposed very strict conditions not only on the members of Christians who could accompany the preachers but also on the permissible style of preaching.[16]

MISSIONARIES AND APOSTATES

The conversion of the Jews under duress, which was in any case contrary to Christian doctrine, was also explicitly opposed by Pedro III, who reminded the friars that the Jews should be converted by persuasion rather than force.[17] Those who converted of their own accord were afforded the king's protection against retaliation and acts of vengeance by other Jews. Nevertheless, Pedro III was quite tolerant towards Jewish pressure on potential or actual apostates.[18]

While Pedro III encouraged and supported converts to Christianity, he prohibited conversions of Jews to Islam and of Muslims to Judaism. In a land where Christians, Muslims, and Jews lived side by side and where, apart from wars between Muslims and Christians, members of all three groups met and debated the merits of their respective religions, conversion was a matter of social intimacy as much as of doctrine. There were instances of both Muslims and Jews adopting the other faith, and Hebrew sources of the thirteenth century confirm that Judeo-Muslim polemics took place in the Crown of Aragon.[19] As early as the period of

[15] For an anti-Jewish procession in Huesca, see ACA, Reg. 41, fo. 94 [= R 734 = Baer, *Spanien*, doc. 117].
[16] ACA, Reg. 41, fo. 94 [= R 736]; Reg. 42, fos. 148ʹ–149 [= R 746–7 = MF ii. 684–5].
[17] ACA Reg. 42, fos. 148ʹ–149ʹ [= R 747–8 = MF ii. 685–6].
[18] ACA, Reg. 43, fo. 30ʹ [= R 1206]. On Jaime I's tolerant attitude, see ACA, Reg. 20, fo. 225 [= R 618 = Bofarull, Barcelona, cxlviii = Jacobs 566].
[19] Adret, iv. 187. Adret's responsum was written following debates that took place in Lérida

Jaime I, the Corts of Tarragona imposed the death penalty on any Muslim or Jew who converted to the other religion. In 1280 Pedro III decided to press charges against three Jews who converted to Islam, and in 1284, following a precedent from his father's days, he ordered a Jewess who converted to Islam to be put to death. This severe punishment did not, however, deter Jews from converting their Muslim concubines, particularly when they became pregnant, as the law was not always applied.[20]

Missionary activities among the Jews were intensified during the reign of Jaime II, and no doubt contributed to the increase in the number of apostates.[21] The king was himself partly responsible for this. He renewed the permission that had been given to the Dominicans to preach Christianity to Jews and Muslims; and in an order of 1296 Jews and Muslims were instructed not only to listen to the sermons but also to participate in religious debates with the Dominicans and to amend their books in accordance with the friars' ruling. Apostates were also obliged to attend the sermons of the Dominicans so that they could improve their conduct, mend the ways they inherited from Judaism, and strengthen the beliefs they acquired from Christianity.[22]

As under his predecessors, during Jaime II's reign the Dominican sermons caused serious harm to the Jews. During these highly antagonistic, indeed venomous, addresses the Jewish audience was humiliated and harassed. When they were forced to listen to sermons in churches, the Jews were exposed to much greater dangers. Both in the church and on the way back to their quarter, the Jews were an easy target for Christians motivated by religious zeal or simply a taste for trouble. In such circumstances the Jews had no option but to seek the king's help. In 1296 the Jews of Majorca complained about the dangers to which they were exposed each time they had to listen to the friars' sermon in the church. Following in the footsteps of his predecessors, Jaime II decided that the sermons should be delivered inside the Jewish quarter in the presence of no more than ten Christians.[23]

---

between a Muslim scholar and the Jews of Lérida. See also Adret's arguments against the anti-Jewish attack of Abu Muhammad ibn Hazm in his 'Maamar 'al Yishma'el' (A Treatise on Islam): Schreiner, 'Die apologetische Schrift', p. 39.

[20] On the decision of the Tarragona Corts, see *Cortes*, i, p. 126. On the conversion to Islam of three Jews, see ACA, Reg. 48, fo. 159 [= R 847–8]. On the woman who converted to Islam see ACA, Reg. 46, fo. 221ʳ [= R 1171 = MF ii. 1957]. These sources were published in Romano, 'Conversión'. The responsa contain material on the conversion of concubines from Islam. On a concubine who was converted to Judaism in 1286, see ACA, Reg. 67, fo. 1 [= R 1543]. The source refers to the *halakhah* that the ethnic–religious identity of offspring from mixed parents follows the identity of the mother. On the conversion of Muslim concubines, see Assis, 'Sexual Behaviour', pp. 36–40.

[21] On some aspects of these activities, see Coll, 'Escuelas'.

[22] On the renewal of the permission, see Rubió, 'Notes sobre la ciencia oriental', p. 392; ACA, Reg. 104, fo. 62 [= Rubió, *Documents*, vol. ii, no. xii]. The source was also published in Alanya, *Aureum*, fo. xl, where the relevant passage on the apostates' participation in the sermons is included.

[23] ACA, Reg. 194, fo. 267 [= R 2624 = Isaacs 75].

The presence of apostates in the audience added to the agitation. They spared no effort to prove their attachment to their new faith and showed extreme antagonism to their ex-brethren. In some cases the preacher himself was a convert from Judaism, and his sermon would be particularly anti-Jewish. In 1297 the Jews of Saragossa complained about the serious attacks and harassment they suffered whenever the sermons they had to attend were given away from their quarter. The king asked that the sermons should be milder and be delivered only in the synagogues. Moreover, the king allowed debates to follow the sermon. All the signs indicate that pressure on the Jews to convert constantly increased, and that the collaboration between the Crown and the missionaries, which was potentially disastrous, became ever closer. A good illustration of this collaboration was the permission Jaime II granted in 1299 to Ramon Lull to preach on Saturdays and Sundays in synagogues and mosques throughout the land. Yet although Jaime II ordered the Jews to attend Lull's sermons, he limited the number of Christian participants to five or six men; and although he permitted the Jews to answer the Christian arguments, he forbade anyone to force them to respond.[24]

It seems that Jaime II, more than any of his predecessors, supported the efforts of the missionaries to bring Jews into the Church, without however depriving them of his protection. During his reign there was a marked increase in the number of permissions given to preachers, including apostates, to deliver sermons to Jews in their synagogues. Also during this period, these sermons received the sanction of the Cortes. Such strong support of missionary activity by the king had serious repercussions.[25]

The positive attitude of Jaime II towards converts is well illustrated by the favours and protection he granted them. In his various decisions the king offered the convert conditions that made his integration in Christian society easier. His social, cultural, religious, psychological, and material difficulties were more easily overcome with some help from the king or his representatives. The king's most efficient contribution was in resolving some of the convert's financial problems. Contrary to the Church's prevalent usage, Jaime II decided in 1295 that a convert would not lose the property he had held while a Jew. This decision aroused opposition in both Jewish and Christian circles, so that the king apparently needed to reiterate it some time later. The concern of the king for the convert's comfort was genuine, for allowing him to keep his property meant, at least in theory, its loss to the Crown. The king's aim was to disseminate Christianity among Jews, as explicitly stated in the 1295 decision.[26]

---

[24] On converts' sermons, see ACA, Reg. 253, f. 43 [= R 2650]. On Lull, see Reg. 114, fo. 44' [= Llabrés, 'Permiso concedido a Ramón Lull', p. 104 = Rubió, *Documents*, vol. i, no. xiv]. Cf. Kayserling, 'Raymond Lulle', pp. 148–9; R 2719.

[25] On permissions to preach granted to apostates, see Rubió, 'Notes sobre la ciencia oriental', p. 393; Kayserling, 'Raymond Lulle', p. 148; R 2862. On the decision of the Cortes, see *Cortes*, ii, p. 218.

[26] Alanya, *Aureum*, fo. xl, col. 1. In 1311 the Cortes took a similar decision: ACA, Reg. 268, fo. 109 [= *Cortes*, i, pp. 217–18 = Baer, *Aragonien*, p. 33. Apparently, this decision was not taken under the

The king and members of his family took additional steps to improve the material welfare of the converts. Some of them received commercial monopolies; others were employed in the king's service. In other instances the convert benefited from gifts from the king or prince. An entry in the account book of the king's baile in 1303 refers to an expense for the purchase of clothes for the convert Bonanat. In 1305 the queen gave the convert Bertrand de Jorba the monopoly on the sale of *kasher* meat in Montblanch. Two years later, Jaime II took under his protection the ex-Jewish physician Vicente Stefan to reward him for his diligent work on behalf of his new faith. In the same year, 1307, the king appointed the convert Juan Ferrand to the post of baile of the Jews and Muslims in Teruel. These examples are more than sufficient to show the king's warm and encouraging attitude towards converts and his deep concern for their well-being.[27]

An element in this special attitude towards converts was the king's appreciation of their influence on Jewish society. Abandoning the Jewish camp was a drastic act that left its mark behind. Jews with doubts about their Jewish faith found the convert's decision encouraging and inspiring. Some converts turned their attention back on their old community, and their enthusiasm in the struggle against Judaism is noteworthy. Their participation in the anti-Jewish campaign overshadowed in its intensity any similar moves by Christian zealots born and bred in the Church.

Typical of this hostility was the attempt by apostates in Monzón to persuade the ecclesiastical authorities to prohibit the consumption by Christians of meat, wine, and bread prepared by Jews. They did not hesitate to make libellous allegations against the Jewish community. The local Jews had to offer bribes to the judges and priests in order to counteract the apostates' attempts.[28] Apart from the active role they played in missionary sermons and the feelings of shame and anger they aroused upon their appearance in the synagogue, many converts caused serious trouble to the Jewish community. Some were involved in blackmail, sometimes acting as informers and causing the Inquisition to proceed against Jews.[29]

The attitude of the Jews towards converts combined hostility, contempt, and suspicion. In giving expression to these antagonistic feelings the Jews distinguished clearly between apostates whose hatred for their former faith was well

---

pressure of the Council of Vienna which met between 16 October 1311 and 6 May 1312 since the Cortes decision was taken on 16 October 1311 and was in keeping with the king's previous decisions.

[27] On Bonanat, see González Hurtebise, *Libros de tesorería*, para. 719. On the monopoly in Montblanch, see ACA, CR, Jaime II, C 18, no. 2397; Reg. 203, fos. 50ᵛ, 62, 172 [= R 2844–5, 2857 = Bofarull, Montblanch, 88–90]; Reg. 55, fo. 69 [= R 2859 = Baer, *Spanien*, doc. 160].

[28] Adret, i. 1091 [= iii. 401].

[29] In 1324, for instance, a convert by the name of Ramón informed on the scribe of the community, who was imprisoned by the Inquisition, and exacted money from his wife. ACA, Reg. 248, fo. 244ᵛ [= Finke, ii. 542]. On the part played by the converts in the activities of the Inquisition, see Assis, 'Papal Inquisition'.

known and others whose conversion had occurred under duress or out of weakness, adopting a warm and brotherly attitude towards the latter but treating voluntary apostates with utter contempt and abhorrence. On occasion the king had to intervene on behalf of the converts and prohibit the use of derogatory terms and insults against them.[30] The Cortes, too, proclaimed in 1311 a warning against those who insulted converts.[31] A Hebrew source from Lérida confirms the custom among the Jews to give derogatory names to converts. We are told about a Jew who quarrelled with a convert whom he called *meshumad*, that is, 'apostate'. The convert reported him to the authorities, since he was told that the meaning of the word was *renegat* or heretic.[32]

Conflicts between Jews and apostates caused problems for the community whose leaders, if not all its members, were held responsible for the acts of the individual. In 1294 the leaders of the community of Huesca were punished for failing to prevent Abrahim Abingavet from spitting at the convert Martin Pere. It is, therefore, not surprising that the leaders of the community of Montblanch were most severely punished after they had not only assisted two Germans to convert to Judaism but also helped a repentant convert, whose Christian name was Juan Ferrand, to return to Judaism, and killed another apostate. Jaime II reduced the punishment but, understandably, did not cancel it.[33]

The Jews tried various means to bring repentant converts back into the fold, despite the dangers. The convert's return to Judaism was a grave crime severely punished by the Christian authorities, and individuals and communities implicated in a repentant's resumption of his former faith were mercilessly prosecuted.[34]

Naturally, any such return to Judaism was conducted in secret, but in many instances the event was nevertheless discovered. As a result, the very existence of communities was put in jeopardy. The community of Montblanch faced such a danger in 1312 when local Jews persuaded a convert to return to Judaism. It appears that the repentant was one of three Tarragona Jews who had converted some time earlier to escape punishment for having helped two German proselytes. It is not unlikely that the person in question was Benvenist Barzilay. The king's reaction to the episode was surprisingly tolerant: the guilty members were fined, but he did not permit the Inquisition to punish the entire community.[35]

---

[30] In 1297 he prohibited the use of the words *tornadiç* or *renegat*. See Alanya, *Aureum*, fo. xl; Roca Traver, 'Un siglo de vida mudéjar', p. 151, n. 92.   [31] *Cortes*, i, pp. 217–18.

[32] Adret, iii. 352.

[33] On Huesca, see ACA, Reg. 88, fo. 252 [= R 2529]. On Montblanch, see Reg. 210, fos. 30'–31 [= R 2966 = Baer, *Spanien*, doc. 168].

[34] On attempts to bring converts back to Judaism, see ACA, Reg. 251, fo. 79 [= R 2954]; Reg. 207, fo. 245' [= R 2926]. On the fine paid by the family of Benvenist Barzelay, who returned to Judaism after being baptized, see ACA, RP, t. 279, fo. 9' [= Baer, *Spanien*, pp. 205–6]; Reg. 211, fo. 291 [= R 3016].

[35] ACA, Reg. 209, fos. 236'–237 [= R 2952 = Baer, *Spanien*, doc. 166]. On Benvenist Barzelay, see n. 34 above.

The king was quite consistent in his policy, as the Calatayud affair indicates. The Jews of Calatayud were persecuted by the Inquisition in the second decade of the thirteenth century because they offered help to repentant converts. The Inquisition, which conducted the investigation, was correct in its claim that a repentant convert and two converts from Christianity, and those who assisted them, came under its jurisdiction;[36] however, the king converted the punishment pronounced by the Inquisition, namely the destruction of the community, into a heavy monetary fine.

THE PAPAL INQUISITION AND THE JEWS

The Papal Inquisition, established to combat heresy at first in Languedoc, turned its attention to neighbouring Catalonia at the end of the twelfth century, intending to investigate refugees from southern France who hoped to find a haven there. Following the spread of heresy in north-eastern Spain in the thirteenth century, the Inquisition extended its operations and penetrated into Valencia.[37] It first dealt with Jews or Jewish affairs in the Maimonidean Controversy of 1232 and the Paris Disputation of 1240, at which time its activities against heretics were decreasing as the Cathar movement grew weaker. This development was very significant for relations between the Church and the Jews.

In the Crown of Aragon, the Disputation of Barcelona in 1263 was a turning-point in the attitude of the Inquisition to the Jews. That the punitive measures against Nahmanides and others accused of blasphemy proposed by the Dominicans were not taken was due to the king's opposition to the designs of the friars. The very proposals, however, indicated gloomy days in the future.[38] The involvement of the Inquisition in the religious life of the Jews was probably justified by the argument of Paulus Cristiani that Talmudic Judaism is guilty of blasphemies against Christianity. Paulus was a member of the censorship committee whose task it was to expurgate blasphemous passages from Jewish books. It seems that Paulus played an important role in linking the Jews with heresy. In this context the bull issued by Pope Clement IV in 1267, in which he wrote to Jaime I that Christians, under Jewish influence, were abandoning their faith and ordered the Inquisition to take all the necessary steps to eradicate this heresy, is significant. Although we have little information about the structure and organization of the Inquisition in the thirteenth century, there is no doubt about the obvious and close link between it and the activities of the friars.[39]

[36] ACA, Reg. 229, fo. 239ᵛ [= R 3419 = Jacobs 873]; and see below on the king's attitude towards the trials of the Inquisition.

[37] Marqués Casanovas, 'Alfonso II el Casto', pp. 218–19; Fort, *Catalonia i la inquisició*, pp. 31–6; Carreras, 'Evolució histórica', pp. 504ff.

[38] On the proceedings against Nahmanides, see ACA, Reg. 13, fo. 265 [= Villanueva, *Viage literario*, xiii, pp. 336–7 = *CDIA*, vi, pp. 167–9 = R 323 = Bofarull, Barcelona, liii = Jacobs 323 = Indice 321 = Dinur, ii. 2, pp. 540–1, no. 14].

[39] On Paulus Cristiani's arguments against the Talmud, see the sources and bibliography on the

The Dominicans who headed the Inquisition were the driving spirit behind the campaign against any deviation from official Christian doctrine. They were able to obtain the cooperation of the Aragonese kings in launching their attack against heretics, many of whom were fugitives from southern France. This campaign strengthened the Inquisition in the Crown of Aragon. In 1286 Alfonso III issued instructions ordering his officials to offer every help to the inquisitors. The latter were permitted to move throughout the land.[40] The help the inquisitors received from the royal officials was very significant, and the results of this cooperation were very impressive during the reign of Jaime II. In 1292 the king ordered the banishment of all heretics from his realm and asked all officials and judges to help the Dominican inquisitors. The campaign against the Templars, inspired by France, was a source of renewed energy for the Inquisition. Its war against heresy was without mercy or limit.[41]

The Aragonese kings greatly helped the Inquisition, which lacked both structural organization and manpower, by offering it the services of royal officials. Nevertheless, they had no intention of allowing it to operate without restraint as far as the Jews were concerned. Quite to the contrary: knowing very well the grave consequences that the Inquisition might have for the Jews if it were allowed to operate without restraint, the kings acted accordingly. The flight of Jews from the realm was to be avoided as highly detrimental to the Crown. Therefore, all royal officials were ordered to protect the Jews from inquisitorial proceedings.[42] When, at the request of the Inquisition, Jaime II issued in 1292 the order mentioned above expelling all heretics and instructing his officials to extend help to the inquisitors, he did not intend that the Jews should be included among the heretics. When that year the Inquisition took steps against Jews in the *collecta* of Gerona–Besalú, Jaime II immediately informed the Dominican inquisitors that the Jews did not come under their jurisdiction as they were not Christians. If Jews caused harm to Christians, he claimed, he as king, and not the Inquisition, should judge and punish them: he therefore ordered the Inquisition to suspend its investigation of the case.[43]

Jaime II followed in the footsteps of his grandfather and father. Jaime I, who endorsed the Church's attitude towards the Jews, nevertheless retained full control over the Jews, denying the Church any right to exercise jurisdiction over them.[44] Pedro III likewise declared in 1284 that the Jews belonged to him and

---

Disputation of Barcelona (no. 1 above) and Cohen, *The Friars and the Jews*, pp. 122–8. On the censorship committee, see n. 10 above. For the bull of Clement IV, see Grayzel, 'Popes, Jews and Inquisition', pp. 173–4. On Paulus, see also Shatzmiller, 'Paulus Christiani'.

[40] ACA, Reg. 66, fo. 144' [= Carbonel, 'Opuscules inédits', p. 75].

[41] LLorente, *Historia crítica*, i, p. 56, ii, p. 462. Of special interest was the Inquisition's condemnation of Arnaldo de Vilanova's views.

[42] Gonzálo Rubió, 'Zaragoza en la historia', p. 101.

[43] ACA, Reg. 92, fo. 144 [= Baer, *Spanien*, doc. 133].

[44] The charter that Jaime I granted to the Jews of Lérida in 1268 expresses this policy well. See

came under his exclusive jurisdiction, and consequently that those Jews who hid converts in their homes should not be judged by the Inquisition.[45]

The kings' policy did not however deter the Inquisition from repeatedly attempting to claim jurisdiction over the Jews. These attempts became more frequent and more dangerous at the beginning of the fourteenth century. Jews who were accused of blaspheming near the church during their stay in Alexandria were interrogated by the Inquisition under Juan de Llotger, who claimed that the transgression was a religious one. Jaime II absolved the suspects of any punishment in return for the payment of 6,000 sb.[46] During this period inquisitorial accusations against Jews increased considerably; however, Jaime II's policy remained unchanged throughout his reign. When in 1305 a Dominican friar from Huesca accused one of the wealthiest Jews of the region Açach Çalema, a man from Biel, of blasphemies against Jesus and Mary, the king demanded that the Inquisition drop all charges, claiming that the accusation was false.[47]

The stance taken by Jaime II in the inquisitorial trials that deeply affected two communities deserves special attention. The first case involved the community of Tarragona. Despite the intervention of the king, its consequences were disastrous. At this time, around 1311, the Inquisition opened a series of proceedings against converts who returned to Judaism and against Jews who had helped two German proselytes. The inquisitorial court was headed by Juan de Llotger and the Archbishop of Tarragona. At the time of a previous trial, conducted in 1303 by Bernardo de Podio against the Jews of Tarragona, Jaime II had expressed his displeasure and reprimanded the inquisitor. The king was annoyed that these renewed proceedings provoked many Jews into leaving the city, and protected many of the individuals on trial, among them Jucef Maçana from Barcelona, who was interrogated by Juan de Llotger. Others who were found guilty, however, had their property confiscated in 1312 by the Archbishop of Tarragona and were banished. The *aljama* was heavily fined, the amount exceeding its annual tax payment; however, the king reduced the punishment. After three of the ten leaders of the community were baptized the king granted his pardon to all the condemned, including the Jews of nearby Valls who were also involved in the affair. The king put further pressure on the Archbishop of Tarragona, who in March 1313 commuted the expulsion verdict to a banishment from Tarragona. For this protection, the Jews paid the king various sums of money.[48]

Grayzel, 'Popes, Jews and Inquisition', p. 181; Parkes, *The Jew in the Medieval Community*, pp. 403–4; Darwin Swift, *The Life and Times*, pp. 296ff.

[45] ACA, Reg. 43, fo. 30ᵛ [= R 1206].

[46] ACA, CR, Jaime II, C 135, no. 397 [= Finke, iii. 49; in Finke the number of the C is not updated]; Reg. 199, fo. 95 [= R 2781]; González Hurtebise, *Libras de tesorería*, para. 209; Assis, 'The Jews of Barcelona in Maritime Trade'.

[47] ACA, CR, Jaime II, C 135, no. 396 [= Finke, iii, p. liv; in Finke the number of the C is not updated]; Reg. 137, fo. 5ᵛ [= Baer, *Spanien*, p. 188].

[48] Finke, ii. 859; Sánchez Real, 'La judería de Tarragona', p. 342; ACA, Reg. 207, fo. 245ᵛ [= R

Meanwhile the archbishop transferred his attention to Montblanch, where he pressed charges against Jews who were accused of helping a convert to return to Judaism. The community, apprehensive of imminent trouble, sought the king's help in 1312; many Jews had already fled, while others lived in fear. The king asked the archbishop not to harm the Jewish public in general. Undoubtedly, he expected the flight thereupon to end and many who had left to return. Five months later, however, in March 1313, the community of Montblanch had still not recovered from the blow it had suffered and was once again in need of the help of the king. The Jews of the city were accused of extending help to converts to return to Judaism and to Christians to become Jewish. The king reduced the fine demanded of the Jews from 20,000 s to 12,300 s and ordered the return of the promissory notes and declarations of property that had been taken from them. In return, the Jews of Montblanch paid the king a handsome sum.[49]

The Inquisition maintained its pressure on the Jews of Tarragona and Valls and in 1323 Jews were still appearing before it to answer charges. On this occasion the Inquisition confiscated property belonging to Jews from the two communities: the king's intervention on their behalf cost them 15,000 sb. A month later Issach Nisim fled from Valls after being condemned to death for having offered shelter to a convert who returned to Judaism. His property was ordered to be burnt; but the king opposed its burning for fear that the fire might spread, and took half of the house himself. Apparently, the king thought that matters had got out of control, and demanded that no further inquisitorial proceedings should be initiated without his permission. Bernardo de Podio, however, disregarded the royal order and both prosecuted the Jews of Tarragona and opened proceedings against the Jews of Lérida. The king was furious and claimed that the Inquisition would ruin the law of the kingdom. Realizing that the Inquisition was challenging his authority, he called the inquisitors to the palace. Yet despite some success in mitigating their punishments the king was unable to stop the activities of the Inquisition, and the tribunal did not cease to act against the Jews.[50]

The second community over which the Inquisition and the king clashed was Calatayud. Tense relations existed here between Jews and apostates. In 1324 Jews from Calatayud complained to the king about an apostate blackmailer who caused a scribe who refused to pay him to be imprisoned, then extorting the money from the scribe's wife.[51] Meanwhile the Inquisition intensified its investigation against the entire community, which stood accused of helping two proselytes from Germany and of supporting one convert who wished to return to Judaism. Part of

2926]; Reg. 210, fo. 40 [= R 2971]; Baer, *Spanien*, p. 205; Sánchez Real, 'Los judíos en Tarragona', pp. 15ff.

[49] ACA, Reg. 251, fo. 79 [= R 2954]; Reg. 210, fos. 30ʳ–31 [= R 2966, 2968 = Baer, *Spanien*, doc. 168].

[50] ACA, Reg. 223, fos. 227, 251 [= R 3256, 3259 = Baer, *Spanien*, doc. 180]; Reg. 248, fo. 28 [= R 3276 = Finke, ii. 540]; Reg. 224, fo. 135ʳ [= R 3288].

[51] ACA, Reg. 248, fo. 244ʳ [= Finke, ii. 542].

the heavy fine that was imposed on the community went to the king, who assigned it to his daughter María, a nun in the monastery of Sigena.[52] The affair did not end with the fine. Soon afterwards, the Inquisition opened proceedings against Calatayud Jews accused of heresy. In a strong letter sent in February 1325 to the deputy head of the Inquisition in Aragon, Jaime II accused him of using un-Christian and unfair methods and demanded the he should act, judge, and punish only according to ecclesistical law.[53] The Infanta María who had benefited from the fine imposed on the *aljama* in October 1324, in 1326 sought to cancel her agent's part in that fine. She also asked that he be given the right to trade and exact his loans from Christian debtors, and that his property be protected from confiscation. The infanta did not hide her interest; in explaining her request, she informed her father that this Jew provided her every week with the money she needed.[54]

The special treatment received by individual members of the community had no bearing on the fate of the Jewish public in general. The inquisitorial investigation against the Jews of Calatayud led to the confiscation of their books. Some of these books, including the Hebrew Bible, R. David Qimhi's *Sefer ha-Shorashim*, and some Talmudic tractates, were given by the king to the Franciscan Ramon de Miedas in 1326.[55] Still the Inquisition was not satisfied and persisted in its investigations against the badly battered community of Calatayud. The sources leave us in no doubt that the aim of the Inquisition was the total destruction of the *aljama*. Calatayud could have become a test case. After the confiscation of the Hebrew books, the Inquisition intended to confiscate the two *bate midrash* (houses of study) of the community. Realizing the significance of the plan, Jaime II expressed his fear in a letter to the Inquisitor-General at the end of December 1326 that such a step would destroy the community, a view based on reports received from his local officials.[56] In the last year of his reign Jaime II cancelled the enormous fine that the Inquisition imposed on an oppressed and persecuted community by now on the verge of complete ruin.[57]

THE END OF AN ERA

The Calatayud affair illustrates well the rise in the power of the Inquisition and the change in the Jewish policy of the king. The king and his family continued to

---

[52] ACA, Reg. 284, fo. 272 [= Martínez, *Jaime II*, p. 425].
[53] ACA, Reg. 248, fo. 243 [= R 3325 = Finke, ii. 543].
[54] ACA, CR, Jaime II, C 135, no. 376 [= Baer, *Spanien*, doc. 184; in Baer the number of the C is not updated]. It is interesting to note that the tax paid by the agent Açach Abenalafu (Issach Avenhalaut) was fixed by the baile separately from that due from the community. See ACA, Reg. 228, fo. 131` [= R 3399].
[55] ACA, Reg. 285, fo. 172 [= Rubió, *Documents*, vol. ii, no. lii].
[56] ACA, Reg. 249, fo. 277 [= Finke, ii. 548]. The style of the letter is rather delicate.
[57] ACA, Reg. 229, fo. 239` [= R 3419 = Jacobs 873].

derive benefits from Jews and to oppose the destruction of Jewish communities, but the strong, unequivocal statements of all the Aragonese kings on the status of the Jews up to the beginning of the fourteenth century, from Jaime I to Jaime II, were no longer being matched as the clear expressions of royal policy. The principle that the Church, and therefore the Inquisition, had no jurisdiction over Jews, who belonged to the Crown no matter what transgressions they committed, was still valid but was emphasized less than before. The change that occurred in Jaime II's policy concerning the Jews might not have been the result of any institutional weakness *vis-à-vis* the Church but rather the outcome of the anti-Jewish tendencies advocated by the friars and the Inquisition which penetrated the palace. The last decade of Jaime II's reign is characterized by hesitation and doubt. On the one hand, the king cancelled a very heavy fine which would have meant the utter ruin of the Calatayud community; on the other, he gave its confiscated books to a Franciscan friar. On the one hand, he prevented the confiscation of the community's synagogues; on the other, he enjoyed the share he received from the heavy fine imposed by the Inquisition. Whereas previously the Aragonese monarchs had claimed that the Inquisition had no authority whatsoever to judge Jews, Jaime II asked the Inquisition in 1325 only to refrain from using in its investigations methods that were contrary to Christianity, and to judge and punish Jews according to Christian law.

Another factor that strengthened the Inquisition was the expulsion of the Jews from France in 1306. Some of the French refugees settled in the Crown of Aragon. Quite a number of French Jews who were baptized north of the Pyrenees decided to return to Judaism in the Crown of Aragon. The geographical proximity, the presence of French and Provençal Jewish refugees, and hospitable Jewish communities made the territories of the Crown of Aragon attractive to repentant converts. This development led inevitably to an increase in the activities of the Papal Inquisition.[58]

Having lost their political power at the end of the thirteenth century, the Jews of the Crown of Aragon showed the first signs of decline in the 1320s when their religious life was at last seriously and successfully attacked. True, these were only the first signs; but in retrospect they assume great importance and mark the end of a golden age in the history of the Jews in the Crown of Aragon. However, for the Jews who lived in north-eastern Spain at the time, the foundations still seemed intact and unshaken, and the tolerant and moderate Jewish policy of Jaime II still seemed valid. His policy of restricting the activities of some zealous sectors of the Church remained more or less unchanged throughout the fourteenth century until the massacres of 1391.

[58] Assis, 'Juifs de France'; id., 'Papal Inquisition'.

PART TWO

JEWISH SELF-GOVERNMENT

§2.1 The Jewish Community in the Crown of Aragon

JEWISH existence in the Middle Ages presupposed a degree of self-government by Jewish communities, whether under Christian rule or Muslim domination. The absence of communal autonomy meant nothing less than the disintegration and ultimate disappearance of Jewish life in medieval society. The *qehilah* became the Jews' miniature homeland in which they were able to conduct their religious, cultural, social, and national life with an intensity which enabled them to preserve their separate identity. Within the framework of this autonomy, the Jewish communities dispersed among the nations found ways and means, and availed themselves of opportunities offered to them, to achieve uniformity in important spheres which contributed much to the unity of the Jewish people. While this unity could not conceal the diversity and pluralism that characterized medieval Jewish life, it was however a source of spiritual strength and comfort which compensated a little for the absence of institutions and conditions which seemed vital in the life of other nations.[1]

The Jewish *aljama* in the Crown of Aragon was no exception to this overall picture, and displayed features similar to those of other medieval Jewish communities. However, while its foundations followed the general pattern, in many fields the community in the Crown of Aragon differed from others and developed its own distinctive character. First and foremost, it served as a bridge between the communities in Christian Europe and those in Muslim lands. Because of its proximity to both, it absorbed influences from north and south alike. Furthermore, the Muslim and Christian occupations both left their mark on numerous aspects of communal life and organization. The *aljama* in any of the territories of the Crown of Aragon retained some institutions and posts, to which in some cases their names bear witness, typical of Jewish communities under the previous rulers of Muslim Spain.

Naturally, there was no uniformity in this respect across the lands of the Crown, since the process was determined primarily by an ever-fluctuating border. Traces of the Muslim past were much stronger in the newest acquisitions, whereas very clear influences from north of the Pyrenees were to be found in the regions that had been longest under Christian rule. In a realm where Muslims remained for quite a long time the predominant population in some regions, it is not

---

[1] On the Jewish community in the Middle Ages in general, see Finkelstein, *Jewish Self-government*; Baron, *The Jewish Community*; Baer, 'The Foundations'.

surprising that the Jews did not abandon overnight the Arabic language and culture and some features of the communal life and system of government that characterized Jewish life in Muslim Spain. In the course of a gradual process of adaptation, Jewish communal government and institutions suffered no radical upheavals and often underwent little change. Containing different elements from various sources and periods, the *qehilah* in the Crown of Aragon was an organic structure that must be reviewed in its totality.[2]

THE *ALJAMA*: AN INDEPENDENT COMMUNITY

The *aljama* in the Catalan–Aragonese realm was unique in so far as it was profoundly influenced by the structure of the Crown, which was different from most medieval kingdoms of Christian Europe. The lands of the Crown of Aragon in the thirteenth century were united only by a common ruler, count or king as the case may be. The various component states were divided from each other by different languages, legal systems, social structures, currencies, and political administrations. This composite character of the Crown of Aragon prevented the emergence of an inter-communal organization embracing all the communities of the realm. It also assisted any opposition to the creation of a central rabbinic authority for the entire Jewish population. This largely decentralized framework and administration strongly enhanced the natural tendency of the local Jewish community to protect its independence and helped to neutralize some later attempts to include it within a larger inter-communal organization. The *aljama* in the Crown of Aragon remained basically an independent unit, jealously defending its separate autonomous existence.[3]

Consequently, we should be very cautious in making any general statement about the *aljama*, including its system of government. The commonest characteristic of the communities in the Crown of Aragon was the individuality of each. Sources that refer to all the *aljamas* of the realm or of any of its constituent lands are rare. In dealing with the history of the Jews of the Crown of Aragon, we must therefore search the innumerable sources dealing with individual communities for patterns prevalent in all or most of them. There are three principal fields in which research must be concentrated: the common background and traditions of all Jewish communities; the Jewish policy of the Aragonese monarchs; and the influence of the city on the *aljama*.

[2] It is sufficient at this stage to draw attention to the various terms used in communal organization which illustrate clearly the origins of its foundations. The name of the Jewish community throughout the Iberian peninsula, *aljama*, was in fact the name of the Muslim one; and the appellation of certain office-holders, such as *muqademin* in Aragon, in contrast to Catalonia, and the designation of Jewish law and ban by the words ҫ*unna* and *alatma* respectively, further demonstrate the point.

[3] The character of the community is discussed in detail below. All attempts to appoint a chief rabbi or *dayan* for the whole Crown or for any of its lands failed completely. See below and ACA, Reg. 252, fo. 50 [= R 2551 = Baer, *Spanien*, doc. 136] and other sources mentioned in Baer, *Spanien*, docs. 151–2.

Despite the rich diversity that characterized them, the communities of the Crown of Aragon shared traditions of Jewish autonomous life and used sources of Jewish law and customs common to most Jewish communities in the Middle Ages. Judicial, legislative, procedural, and punitive methods and traditions and administrative and institutional customs deriving from Jewish sources served to balance the isolationist or separatist tendencies of the communities. A very significant illustration of the unifying role played by Jewish sources common to most communities is the rapid spread of Maimonides' *Mishne Torah* throughout Spain and its adoption by a growing number of communities in the Crown of Aragon in the course of the thirteenth century as the code of Jewish law. From the order issued in August 1263 to burn parts of *Mishne Torah* because of anti-Christian blasphemies, we may infer its wide circulation in the country. A letter written by Pedro in 1382 proves that a few generations earlier *Mishne Torah* had become the standard code in the realm, not only in Valencia, to which the letter refers.[4]

THE COMMUNITY IN ITS CHRISTIAN CONTEXT

The kings' attitude to their Jewish subjects and their policy towards the Jewish communities also created a balance between diversity and uniformity in communal life. The kings saw all their Jewish subjects as a special class bound to their patrimony and dependent exclusively on them. Uniformity in the system of communal government and organization made perfect sense to them. We have already seen how a privilege granted to one community became the basis for many others. Royal consent for constitutional reform in one community inspired Jews in other communities to follow suit. Although there exists only a very limited number of royal decisions affecting the entire realm or one of its lands, nevertheless the Jewish *aljama*, its system of government, and its institutions did not develop in isolation. They were all influenced by, and in turn exerted influence on, other sister communities.[5]

Hardly any other medieval Jewish community was influenced by its town to so great an extent as the *aljama* in the Crown of Aragon. While maintaining its Jewish characteristics, the community reacted promptly to any changes that affected urban life and municipal administration. Since the structure of Jewish society was almost an exact duplicate of Christian urban society, some similar developments in municipal government and communal administration were only natural. Certain similarities, it can be argued, were the result of analogous circumstances pertaining in both societies. Social classes and class struggle in city and *qehilah*, class representation in the local governing bodies of both societies,

---

[4] See ACA, Reg. 12, fo. 106 [= R 212 = Jacobs 243]; Reg. 939, fo. 221 [= Baer, *Spanien*, doc. 343]; also Perfet 478. On the spread of *Mishne Torah* in Spain, see Septimus, *Hispano-Jewish Culture in Transition*, pp. 40, 47, 55–7, 73–4.

[5] The policy of the kings towards the *aljamas* and its consequent effects on the status of the Jews and the privileges of the communities are treated in Part I above.

and the subsequent constitutional and institutional reforms in both municipal and communal administrations are strikingly similar and contemporaneous. Changes in social structure and the system of government which transformed Jewish society from the end of the thirteenth century onwards cannot be understood without reference to the events and developments that occurred in the cities and towns of Catalonia and Aragon. Of course, inner forces for change and reform were also at work in Jewish society, and social contradictions and reformatory ideals were part of Jewish life for generations. But the centrality of municipal and urban influences, as well as other developments affecting both societies, produced a Jewish community typically Aragonese or Catalan.[6]

THE *ALJAMA* AND THE *QEHILAH*

As elsewhere in the medieval Jewish world, the Jews of the Crown of Aragon saw in the *aljama* a framework in which they were able to live in accordance with their laws and customs and maintain a well-organized communal life. The scholars and leaders of the Jews were well aware of the special conditions prevalent in the country. They recognized that in certain fields they were prevented from leading their communities according to Jewish law and that the *aljama*'s power was restricted by the Christian ruler. Its authority depended on concessions granted by the ruler, while its judicial system in many cases deviated from Jewish law and, 'vested with authority from the state', operated and judged 'with government's permission in accordance with temporal conditions'.[7] It was within these limitations that Jewish life was governed in the Crown of Aragon.

The *aljama* in the Crown of Aragon was a legally recognized corporation which usually included the entire Jewish population in the locality, that is the *qahal*. The *qahal* or *'edah* was the demographic basis of the *aljama*, while its authority was designated as *ma'amad ha-qahal*, *da'at ha-qahal*, or *harshaat ha-qahal*.[8] The terms *aljama* and *qehilah* were not synonymous in all contexts. Whereas the former designated the corporate entity of the Jews, legally recognized by the authorities, the latter meant the legal embodiment of the community in Jewish law. Thus the smallest Jewish settlement enjoyed the status of a *qehilah* without constituting an *aljama*. The only condition for the existence of a *qehilah* was that the members had to pledge their commitment to a common jurisdiction. In the second half of the thirteenth century in several regions of the Crown of Aragon, where there were many tiny Jewish settlements scattered in villages, the question arose as to the minimum number of Jews required to form a *qehilah*. R. Shelomo ben Adret's

---

[6] For the similarities in social structure and agitation in cities and *aljamas*, see Assis, 'Social Unrest'. References to similarities in both societies are found in various parts of this book.

[7] Adret, iv. 311, viii. 279. See also Assis, 'Jewish Attitudes'.

[8] The term *qahal* is found frequently in the sources. For the term *'edah*, see Adret, v. 253. For the various terms denoting communal authority, see Adret, iii. 294, 434 and n. 7 above.

answer that any ten male adults in any locality could establish themselves as a *qehilah* can be accepted as halakhically authoritative, but not necessarily valid from the king's point of view.[9]

The dual origin of the community's authority is easily discernible. The king's bestowal of power and authority was a prerequisite for Jewish self-government, but is not sufficient to explain fully the mechanism of Jewish autonomy. Internally, the legitimacy of communal government was derived from Jewish sovereignty dating from pre-exilic antiquity and the readiness of its members to accept its yoke voluntarily. The leaders of Catalan and Aragonese Jewry, led by R. Shelomo ben Adret, considered the *qehilah* the sole and legitimate heir of Jewish sovereignty of the past.[10] Adret fully supported the autonomy of the *qehilah* and confirmed its right to enact ordinances and cancel the rights of the individual member when necessary.[11] The community's right to enact ordinances and to impose restrictions and fines, he stated, was as legal and binding 'as Biblical law'. Aware of doubts cast on the legal validity of communal *taqanot*, he reiterated his view that the *qahal*'s decision was as binding as a decree of the supreme court of antiquity, irrespective of whether the *qehilah* was small or large.[12] Adret's opinion was all the more significant since he and his disciples were aware of the political conditions prevalent in exile and admitted that certain communal enactments were not in accordance with Talmudic law. Adret admitted that the community's right to punish transgressors was based on royal patents, and with political shrewdness and realism he declared that in various fields the community deviated from the 'laws specifically written in the Torah' and enacted by 'royal permission' because of the dictates of circumstances prevalent throughout the Crown of Aragon.[13]

AUTHORITY AND JURISDICTION WITHIN THE *ALJAMA*

Towards the end of the thirteenth century, the extent of the *aljama*'s authority was a subject of public debate among the Jews of the Crown of Aragon. It was then ruled that with the consent of its members the community was authorized to issue ordinances and even confiscate a member's property for the benefit of the public.

---

[9] Adret, v. 403.   [10] Adret, i. 1206.

[11] In his *responsum* to the community of Huesca, Adret based his decision on the principle *hefqer zibbur hefqer*, that is 'the requisition made by the public is valid': Adret, iv. 142. It was not by sheer accident that he changed the original Talmudic formula *hefqer beth din hefqer*—'the requisition of the *beth din* is valid': *Tosefta, Sheqalim,* i, 1, 1; Babylonian Talmud, *Yebamot,* 89b and *Gittin,* 36b.

[12] For the *qahal*'s right to act not in accordance with Biblical law, see Adret, iv. 185; Assaf, *Punishments,* no. 56. For his comparison of communal *taqanot* to the decrees of the ancient supreme court, the Sanhedrin see Adret, v. 126; on the validity of ordinances irrespective of the size of the *qahal,* see Adret, v. 253.

[13] Adret, iii. 397; also n. 7 above; Assaf, *Punishments,* no. 57.

Although the representatives of the public were empowered to administer communal affairs as they saw fit, the *qahal* or the members of the community did not thereby relinquish their ultimate power. Any decision taken by the majority was binding as far as the leadership and the majority were concerned, 'inasmuch as the majority of the public is like the whole public'.[14] Therefore, no group had any moral or legal right to impose its leadership on the people without the consent of the latter, irrespective of its policy.

The principle that the minority could not act on behalf of the majority was clearly and eloquently expressed by the formula that 'the majority is not subjugated to the minority.'[15] Furthermore, even those who were duly appointed or elected were duty bound to pursue the policy adopted by the public, any deviation from which would be considered null and void. However, 'no man had the power to challenge' the decisions taken legally by the leaders.[16] All this does not imply that a democratic principle was the guideline in a society that was divided into classes of unequal sizes and rights. R. Yom Tov Asibili justified the majority's right to decide on the grounds that 'the majority of the important members is considered as the entire public.' The support of a scholar enhanced further the decisions of the community.[17]

The consideration and tolerance that must be shown to the views of the individual and the position of the minority in no way affected the validity of the majority's stand. No Jew had the right to exclude himself from the congregation or free himself from the *qehilah*'s jurisdiction, its ordinances, and its decisions. The jurisdiction of the *qehilah* over its members was almost absolute.[18] It follows that any attempt by a minority to organize an opposition to communal decisions was totally rejected. Even if such opposition was voiced during the debate, it did not offer sufficient grounds for continued dissent once a majority decision had been taken. When contradictory interests of the various classes in the *aljama* resulted in independent actions and representation on the part of dissenting groups, this infringement of the communal jurisdiction was stopped through

---

[14] On the authority of the communal leadership, see Adret, i. 1206. On the majority's power, see Adret, ii. 279.

[15] The formula is found in Adret, iii. 245. For the rejection of a minority group's claim to impose its leadership, see Adret, iii. 428, where he says that no group is allowed to act 'without the consent of the whole community'. See also Adret, iii. 294; Elfenbein, 'Jewish Communal Government', pp. 105–6. Adret also rejects the validity of a *herem* pronounced by unauthorized people; see Adret, ii. 280, iii. 428.

[16] For the leaders' obligation to pursue the *qahal*'s policy, see Adret, iii. 434; the community's obligation to abide by the leaders' legal decisions is contained in Adret's responsum to the *aljama* of Lérida: Adret, i. 729, iii. 438.

[17] Asibili (Kapah) 114. On the scholar's support, see n. 7 above. In financial matters, decisions in Castile were taken according to wealth: see Asibili (Kapah) 80.

[18] Adret, v. 242, viii. 280: 'Know that every community has jurisdiction over its members since it is authorized to decree and enact in its town as the Supreme Court can for all Israel.' On tolerance and consideration for the minority, Adret says that in many places in the country they took into account 'the early protests of the members': Adret, v. 126.

constitutional reforms in the first quarter of the fourteenth century that ensured representation for all classes in the communal government of many *aljamas*.[19]

The jurisdiction of the *qehilah* extended to the Jewish quarter, the *judería* or *call*, and all its inhabitants as well as those of its members living outside it.[20] Each *aljama* in the Crown of Aragon was an independent unit; however, the development of an inter-communal framework inevitably gave the major *aljamas* greater power, leading to a considerable extension of their jurisdiction to the detriment of the smaller ones.[21]

As long as the Jew did not undergo baptism he remained under his community's control, even in localities where there were so few Jews that there was no *aljama*. No Jew could escape the *aljama*'s control unless he had the king's support. Occasionally, the kings of the Crown of Aragon freed certain Jews from their community's jurisdiction. Unable to oppose the king's decision, the community would nevertheless express its profound discontent at such brutal interference in its internal affairs. The exclusion of any member from communal control contradicted a basic principle of Jewish autonomy and was totally rejected by communal and spiritual leaders alike.[22] Mere condemnation of this widespread practice was insufficient to prevent wealthy and powerful Jews from seeking royal privileges which, by restricting the *aljama*'s jurisdiction, also inflicted irreparable damage on its prestige. During the period of constitutional reforms coinciding with Jaime II's reign, several communities tried to remedy the situation by including in their constitution an injunction on all members to give up their privileges and a prohibition on seeking new ones in the future.[23]

JEWISH AUTONOMY AND ROYAL POWER

The nature of the relations between the Crown and the Jewish community, as described in Part I, renders any further explanation of the kings' constant interventions in communal affairs unnecessary. No aspect of Jewish life remained unaffected by royal interference.

While until the middle of the thirteenth century the sources are scarce, those

---

[19] Adret, iii. 394, viii. 280. The constitutional reforms are discussed later in this part. Examples of separate representations of different classes are found in Assis, 'Social Unrest'. Professional and social confraternities parallel to the guilds in Christian society were permitted, notwithstanding a certain infringement of the *aljama*'s jurisdiction. These organizations had a free hand in matters affecting their own members but having no bearing on the rest of the community: Adret, iv. 185; Assaf, *Punishments*, no. 56; Assis, 'Welfare and Mutual Aid'.

[20] See e.g. Salarullana, 'Estudios históricos', pp. 69–70.

[21] This subject is fully treated in Part III below.   [22] Adret, iii. 434.

[23] Thus the *aljama* of Barcelona included as the first article of its new constitution in 1327 its decision 'que hayen a renunciar tota la aliame e els sengles dequella en general e en especial de tota letra, privilegi o manament obtengut del senyor rey . . .'; ACA, Reg. 230, fo. 106 [= Baer, *Spanien*, doc. 189, para. 1].

from the last twenty-five years of Jaime I's reign, that is from 1250 to 1276, show clearly that he refrained from frequent interference in Jewish internal affairs. His interventions were for the most part restricted to matters of taxation.[24] With Pedro III, however, a clear change in royal policy may be discerned. The new king did refrain from interfering in communal appointments and imposing his own candidates. This may be due to the extensive employment of Jews in the administration of the Crown of Aragon during his reign: the various fields in which Jews served the king were more than sufficient to provide posts for all the ambitious and capable among his Jewish subjects.[25] However, Pedro III frequently intervened in other ways, for example showering privileges on his Jewish officials and making the community bear the cost. Considering his brief reign, the frequency of his interference in the community's affairs on behalf of his Jewish courtiers is striking.[26] Pedro also gave numerous orders concerning the community's activities, amounting to the exercise of strict control over the Jews.[27]

Pedro's successor Alfonso III interfered very little in the internal affairs of the Jewish community and his supervision of it was comparatively loose. His interventions were frequently designed to promote the interests of favourite influential Jews or leaders of the community. Alfonso was no innovator in this field, following the established policy.[28]

Jaime II, by contrast, was far more involved in the inner life of the community and its routine activities than any of his predecessors. Nevertheless, he was careful not to detract too much from Jewish autonomy. He found it convenient to leave in the hands of the Jewish community sufficient power to fulfil its tasks and obligations *vis-à-vis* the Crown. Jewish autonomy remained a natural condition within the structure of medieval society and in the territories of the Crown of Aragon with their different norms, laws, customs, languages, and institutions the Jews were even more than elsewhere in the medieval world naturally separated from the rest of society. Accordingly, the king's claim of exclusive rights over the

[24] ACA, Reg. 9, fo. 1ʳ [= Jacobs 105 = R 74 = Bofarull, Barcelona, ix]; Reg. 13, fo. 164ʳ [= Jacobs 282 = R 257–8].

[25] On the Jews in the service of Pedro III, see Romano, 'Los hermanos Abenmenasse'; id., 'Judíos escribanos'; id., *Judíos al servicio de Pedro el Grande*; Shneidman, 'Jews in the Royal Administration'; Assis, 'Jewish Diplomats'.

[26] ACA, Reg. 41, fo. 62 [= R 725]; Reg. 61, fo. 122 [= R 1056 = Baer, *Spanien*, doc. 125]; Reg. 43, fos. 13ʳ, 15, 114 [= R 1183, 1181, 1270 = MF ii. 2128].

[27] See e.g. ACA, Reg. 39, fo. 197 [= R 681]; Reg. 46, fos. 221ʳ–222 [= R 1172 and pp. 427–8, doc. xiv]; Reg. 57, fo. 223 [= R 1459 = MF, ii. 2300]; Reg. 41, fo. 6 [= R 712–13 = Baer, *Spanien*, doc. 115, paras. 1–2]; Adret, i. 617.

[28] ACA, Reg. 63, fos. 40ᵛ–41 [= R 1486 = Guinovart 42]; Reg. 64, fo. 47 [= R 1527]; Reg. 66, fo. 100ᵛ [= R 1571]; Reg. 74, fo. 78ᵛ [= R 1880–1]. As long as this group controlled communal government, the sources contain no criticism of their conduct, but reveal incriminating evidence which explain the subsequent social unrest. These Jews belonged to the upper class of Jewish society and the king's open support for their cause entrenched further the sense of bitterness and injustice felt by poor Jews, whose opposition to the communal establishment and struggle for social reform grew considerably towards the end of the thirteenth century. See ACA, Reg. 74, fo. 68ᵛ [= R 1871].

The Qehilah

Jews made more sense in the Crown of Aragon than anywhere else in Christian Europe. Jaime II opposed repeated attempts by the Church and the Inquisition to extend their own jurisdiction over the Jews, claiming that 'they are neither Catholics nor subordinate to Catholic law and, therefore, if they act against the law, only I can punish them.'[29] In the circumstances, Jaime II's simultaneous encroachment on Jewish autonomy and his policy of supporting the power of the community were not as contradictory as they seem.

Jaime II played a major role in the changes that took place in the system of government and leadership of the Jewish community. He often interfered in the appointment or dismissal of Jewish leaders and functionaries.[30] Like his predecessors, Jaime II rewarded and compensated some of his Jewish favourites at the expense of the community, disregarding its autonomous rights. His support of individual Jews in conflict with the community had an equally negative effect on Jewish autonomy.[31] The king's involvement in the affairs of the community was frequently connected with taxation. His intervention necessarily restricted the community's autonomy, while his support of individual taxpayers against it greatly damaged its prestige. At times the community was seriously humiliated and the monarch's measures, such as the closure of the *judería*'s gates or the arrest of its leaders, dealt a severe blow to its rights.[32] Tax exemptions and reductions granted to Jews usually of the wealthy class constituted both a financial burden on the community and an infringement of its jurisdiction.[33]

---

[29] ACA, Reg. 92, fo. 144 [= Baer, *Spanien*, doc. 133]; cf. Grayzel, 'Popes, Jews and Inquisition', pp. 181–2.

[30] ACA, CR, Jaime II, C 134, no. 198 [= *Cartas Reales*, no. 408]; C 133, no. 343.

[31] ACA, CR, Jaime II, C 49, no. 6040 [= *Cartas Reales*, no. 204]; C 133, no. 116 [= *Cartas Reales*, no. 337]; C 43, no. 5331 [= *Cartas Reales*, no. 188]; C 14, no. 1828 [= *Cartas Reales*, no. 99]; C 133, no. 23 [= *Cartas Reales*, no. 246]; C 134, nos. 196, 207 [= *Cartas Reales*, nos. 407, 416].

[32] ACA, Reg. 197, fos. 153ᵛ–154 [= R 2745 = Baer, *Spanien*, doc. 146]; Reg. 239, fos. 18ᵛ–19 [= Baer, *Spanien*, doc. 164]; ACA, CR, Jaime II, C 134, no. 249 [= *Cartas Reales*, no. 468]; C 10, no. 249 [= *Cartas Reales*, no. 1328]; C 2, no. 420; ACA, Reg. 229, fos. 260ᵛ–261, 274ᵛ–275 [= R 3432, 3436]; Reg. 211, fo. 337ᵛ [= R 3020].

[33] ACA, CR, Jaime II, C 35, no. 4423 [= *Cartas Reales*, no. 153]; C 67, no. 8272 [= *Cartas Reales*, no. 344]; C 80, no. 9731 [= *Cartas Reales*, no. 472]; C 39, no. 4847; C 99, no. 12364 [= *Cartas Reales*, no. 486]; C 134, no. 207 [= *Cartas Reales*, no. 416]; C 23, no. 2956; C 133, no. 66 [= *Cartas Reales*, no. 297]; C 134, nos. 206, 252 [= *Cartas Reales*, nos. 415, 471].

§2.2 The System of Communal Government

No field of Jewish life in the territories of the Crown of Aragon underwent a more radical change in this period than the system of government in the Jewish community. The traditional regime in the *aljama* was that of aristocratic oligarchy allied with scholars who often belonged to the same class. This coalition ran the affairs of the Jewish communities of Catalonia and Aragon until late in the thirteenth century and also controlled the communities in Majorca and Valencia, newly conquered from the Muslims by Jaime I. Until then, we hear very little of complaints against the system by the lower classes; the only signs of conflict came from rival families and individuals among the aristocracy. Admittedly the sources at our disposal originated in the same aristocratic circles, and therefore we can hardly interpret their silence as definite proof that there was no unrest in the Jewish communities, where a large majority of members had no say in communal affairs. Nor can we expect to find political self-criticism, for that matter. Latin sources until the second half of the century are scarce and, in any case, they too reflect exclusively aspects of Jewish life of the upper classes.

The scarcity of documentation would have rendered impossible a detailed description of the Jewish system of communal government, were it not for the rich sources available from the beginning of the fourteenth century which deal with the changes and reforms of the system. As a full description of these changes appears below, it is sufficient here to note the general characteristics of the communal regime.

THE TRADITION OF OLIGARCHY

The oligarchy of the wealthy and educated in communal government continued almost undisturbed until nearly the end of the thirteenth century. Members of rich and well-established aristocratic families retained power through a system that perpetuated itself. Each family considered it correct and prestigious to be represented in the governing body of the *aljama*. Until the reforms of Jaime II's reign, the number of leaders in a community depended primarily on the number of wealthy families. 'Often', says Adret, 'the large number of *ne'emanim* is purely for honorific purposes, since all the families in town wish to see one of their sons nominated only for the glory of the family.' It was not the candidate's education but his property that made him eligible, and he was nominated 'whether or not he was versatile in books'.¹ The system worked very simply by allowing every leader to nominate his successor or for the outgoing leadership to choose the next leaders *en bloc*.²

Both methods perpetuated the power of the elite in Jewish society. There is hardly any evidence that elections in which a significant number of electors participated were held at all during the reign of Jaime I. In 1229 Jaime I permitted the Jews of Calatayud to select four *adelantados* for any period they chose, with the consent and in the presence of *arrab*, their rabbi. While we have no details about the method of selection, the power of veto given to the rabbi and the unlimited term of office show clearly the oligarchical character of communal leadership in the early thirteenth century. The ruling elites held very extensive powers, including the right to impose the death penalty.³ A leadership of this type needed measures to protect its interests and standing, since its authoritarian and sometimes even dictatorial character was likely to cause discontent and arouse opposition.⁴ The fines imposed on those guilty of contemptuous behaviour towards their leaders were sometimes exorbitant.⁵

The access of the leaders to information on the assets of members of the community, and the secrecy with which such information was guarded, even when transmitted to other office-holders, invested them with real power, confirmed by Hebrew acts or royal privileges, at times by both. The extent of this power had almost no parallel in other medieval communities, except Castile, and the capital punishment they could inflict on those who resisted their jurisdiction was carried out by royal officials.⁶

Significantly, the earliest information on elections or nominations of communal leaders comes from Saragossa after the rebellion of the lower classes against the aristocratic regime in 1263. Side by side with very moderate changes in the system of communal government we find a slight increase in royal intervention in these

---

¹ Adret, iii. 399.

² In one community there was a *taqanah* according to which 'if each one of the *berurim* wishes to nominate his successor, he may do so': Adret, iii. 425. In another, we are told that 'ten people agree among themselves to nominate *berurim*': Adret, v. 125. For *berurim* and *yo'azim* who appointed their successors; see Adret, v. 284–5.

³ ACA, Reg. 202, fo. 201ʳ [= R 6]. This is a confirmation by Jaime II in 1305 of the original privilege granted by Jaime I in 1229.

⁴ Such measures are mentioned in Latin and Hebrew sources. In 1241 and 1269 Jaime I confirmed the right of the Barcelona leaders and those of Perpignan, Cerdagne, and Roussillon respectively to punish severely anyone who insulted them: ACA, Reg. 16, fo. 158 [= R 29 = Baer, *Spanien*, doc. 93]. The privilege of 1241 is quoted in that of 1269 [= Jacobs 450 = R 417 = Bofarull, Barcelona, lxxxiii]. This in itself shows that the 1241 protective measures were known beyond the region of Barcelona and were copied elsewhere years later.

⁵ On fines imposed for contemptuous attitudes towards Crown-appointed rabbis, see Adret, i. 475. For insults pronounced against communal leaders, see ACA, Reg. 13, fo. 274 [= R 335].

⁶ Some of the early thirteenth-century sources on the authority and power of the communal leaders are: ACA, Reg. 10, fo. 54ʳ [= Jacobs 151 = R 97 = Baer, *Spanien*, doc. 97]; Reg. 13, fo. 163 [= Jacobs 279 = R 253]; Reg. 16, fo. 240ʳ [= Jacobs 474 = R 458 = Bofarull, Barcelona, cii]; Reg. 21, fo. 126ʳ [= Jacobs 665 = R 552 = Baer, *Spanien*, doc. 107].

matters. The sweeping changes that put an end to the monopoly of the wealthy families were yet to come.⁷

Towards the end of the thirteenth century, the rich still held power in most communities, occupying all the important offices. In one community it was clearly stated that only a member enrolled in the tax roll for at least three *solidi* was eligible to the office of *baror*. The rich tax-payers protested strongly when the *berurim* were elected without their consent. In some communities, a leader's impoverishment led to his dismissal.⁸ The system designed to control communal expenditure that evolved in the thirteenth century, most probably as a result of public criticism, was also in the hands of the rich. In one of the communities the control committee consisted of 'ten members from among the biggest taxpayers'. In a responsum of R. Yom Tov Asibili from 1308, we learn that no money was spent in the *aljama* of Lérida without consulting the ten people 'from [among] the greatest and most important men without whose consent no decision could be taken'.⁹

The attitude of the spiritual leaders of Catalan and Aragonese Jewry to the communal oligarchy was somewhat ambivalent. Adret declared his preference for a *qehilah* run by scholars. As a second-best alternative he advocated a type of leaders described by the sages as the 'seven notables of the town', who should be acceptable to the public. The 'seven notables' in the Hebrew sources were often identical with the Jewish *probis homines* in the Latin documents. Other types of leaders who acted against the will of the public were considered by Adret to be outlaws. However, he admits that in the circumstances prevailing in the Crown of Aragon 'in most places, now, those who are greater in counsel and authority in the community, attend to all communal affairs' since 'it is impossible that women, minors and the intellectually weak should run their own affairs.' It is not too difficult to identify the 'intellectually weak' members of the community with the masses who were deprived of political rights in the communities. It is equally easy to understand that 'the men of counsel' who, 'acting naturally as their guardians, supervise all the affairs' of the community were none other than the local leaders who controlled the communities by virtue of their wealth and pedigree. In the last quarter of the thirteenth century, however, popular discontent could no longer be ignored. Adret therefore admits that 'if some in the community, even though they were among those who were not great in counsel, protest, their protest is valid,' unless they had explicitly accepted the authority of the *berurim*, *muqademin*, or *ne'emanim*.¹⁰

---

⁷ ACA, Reg. 12, fo. 148 [= Jacobs 277 = R 245 = Baer, *Spanien*, doc. 98]. On the protection of rebellious elements by the king, see Reg. 12, fo. 144 [= Jacobs 272 = R 244]. For more details, see sources quoted in n. 6. above.

⁸ Such was the situation in the *aljama* of Valencia: Adret, iii. 417; ACA, Reg. 87, fo. 19ʿ [= R 2464]; ACA, Reg. 195, fo. 46 [= R 2661]. On eligibility for the office of *baror*, see Adret, iv. 312. On tax-payers' consent to the election, see Adret, v. 125.

⁹ On the status of the controllers, see Adret, iii. 386, 434, 443; Asibili (Kapah) 114.

¹⁰ Adret, iii. 428, iv. 185. His views were well expressed in his responsum to the community of

The first evidence of popular opposition to the oligarchic leadership in the communities of the Crown of Aragon is the revolt of the poorer classes against the aristocratic government in the *aljama* of Saragossa. This revolt was caused by the method of distributing the tax burden and the share borne by the less wealthy in the total sums paid to the king. Any significant change in the system necessitated constitutional and administrative reforms to allow the poorer classes some representation on the various bodies in the *aljama*. That this was temporarily achieved with the blessing of the king is clear evidence that the popular agitation was very serious.[11] Although the achievements of the Kat ha-Havurah, as the rebels of the lower class called themselves, were meagre, the process that they initiated could no longer be stopped indefinitely or reversed. The struggle was renewed with vigour, and spread to other communities of the kingdom.

Meanwhile, the last quarter of the thirteenth century witnessed something of a novelty in Aragonese communal life. During Pedro III's reign we have the first series of sources dealing with changes in the system of communal government and details about elections. During this period we find a new institution emerging: the *'eza* or council. Depending on the size of the community, the *'eza* consisted of ten to thirty *yo'azim* or councillors and fulfilled a function similar to that of the municipal *concell* in Catalonia. The appointment of various officeholders in the *aljama* and important financial decisions fell within the council's jurisdiction. The principle of elections and appointments for a limited term of office, from one to five years, became universal in Catalonia, Aragon, and elsewhere.[12]

Such innovations were not welcome among the traditional governing class of the community. In Saragossa, where the lower classes began their struggle against the ruling class, members duly elected to office refused to occupy their posts and were not ready to come to terms with the new conditions. Some were not prepared to assume the responsibility of leading a community so divided and troublesome.[13] Nor did the reform measures prove enduring in all communities. The old and well-established ruling class was more than a match for the inexperienced representatives of the poorer classes. Jewish aristocrats were not prepared to give up easily the political status they had achieved in the *aljama* and looked for the first opportunity to strike back. In Saragossa and in other *aljamas* such as Lérida and Jaca, by 1285 all these changes were anulled. The leaders were simply allowed

---

Murviedro. On the *probi homines*, see ACA, Reg. 195, fos. 44, 51ˇ [= R 2629, 2663 = Baer, *Spanien*, docs. 139–40].

[11] On the Saragossa episode, see Baer, *History*, i, pp. 222–4; Beinart, 'Hispano-Jewish Society', pp. 220–38. Full details and sources can be found in Assis, 'Crisis'.

[12] On the *'Eza*, see ACA, Reg. 44, fo. 177ˇ [= R 776 = Baer, *Spanien*, doc. 118]; on elections in Catalonia, see Reg. 44, fos. 187ˇ–188 [= R 823 = Baer, *Spanien*, doc. 121 = Dinur, ii. 2, p. 418, no. 8 and pp. 446–7, no. 2]; for Aragon, see Reg. 59, fo. 56 [= R 942].

[13] It was so in 1280 (ACA, Reg. 48, fos. 117, 119ˇ [= R 829, 833]) and again in 1290 (ACA, Reg. 83, fo. 87ˇ [= R 2227]). See also ACA, Reg. 80, fo. 46ˇ [= R 2000].

once again to choose their successors, thus perpetuating their power. Rich families were back in control of communal administration.[14]

One of the factors in this reaction was the dismissal of Jewish officials from the administration of Pedro III in 1283 under pressure from the nobility, which left many ambitious and capable members of aristocratic Jewish families redundant. Communal politics and government offered a convenient alternative to royal political and administrative employment, an outlet through which they could satisfy their ambitions locally after the 1283 setback.

MINORITY VERSUS MAJORITY

The question of minority and majority in the procedure of communal decision-making was already a topic of debate in eleventh-century Spain. Although Alfasi was of the opinion that no communal ordinance could be enacted without the consent of the majority in the community, it appears that his opinion, which did not go unchallenged, was by no means adhered to in all the *aljamas*.

When Adret was asked whether a *qehilah* had the right to prohibit a wedding unless it was conducted in the presence of ten men, he confirmed the *qehilah*'s right on condition that its members agreed to it and that no local halakhic authority expressed opposition.[15] Elsewhere he defines the members' agreement as the agreement of the majority, 'since the majority of the public is like the entire public'.[16] No minority could impose its will on the rest, even with a meritorious case. Hence the majority did not have to abide by the decision of the minority even if the latter included the leaders and dignitaries of the community. The legal basis of the communal regime was the mandate it received from the majority. With such a mandate at its disposal the executive body of the *qehilah* could then administer its affairs and its decisions would be binding on the entire *qahal*.[17] No one could avoid the authority of such a body and its decisions by claiming to have been absent when the mandate was conferred.[18] This mandate remained, however, totally dependent on the majority's will, and at the appointed time and in the established form it could be withdrawn.[19] There were exceptions to this principle: for example, in Castile at the beginning of the fourteenth century, in financial matters involving expenditure the view of those who contributed most and not that of the majority prevailed.[20]

By the 1280s the majority principle was well enough established for the king or infante to quote it as the basis of communal government. When in 1282 some

---

[14] For Lérida, see ACA, Reg. 57, fo. 187 [= R 1429]. For Jaca, see ACA, Reg. 57, fo. 199 [= R 1438]. For Saragossa, see Assis, 'Crisis'.   [15] Adret, i. 1206.

[16] Adret, ii. 279, where he also states that 'whenever the majority of the community decide on any matter or proclaim a ban, it is forbidden to act against their ban or ordinances.'

[17] Adret, iii. 428, v. 125–6, 129, 245.   [18] Adret, v. 125   [19] Asibili (Kapah) 114.

[20] Asher, pt. vii, no. 3. Cf. Asibili (Kapah) 80.

members of the *aljama* of Gerona were obstructing the election of the *berurim de tavioz* (civil magistrates) the Infante Alfonso ordered that they should proceed with the elections in accordance with the majority principle. Even after the temporary return to the old oligarchical order, Alfonso III, now king, demanded in 1287 that the forty electors choose the *adelantados* by majority vote.[21] During the reign of Jaime II, the majority vote was upheld consistently by the Crown. Jaime II was sensitive to the inclinations of the majority and in matters of elections, as in important items affecting the community in general, he generally supported this principle.[22]

Over the whole area of the respective rights and power of the majority and minority in the community, the progress that had been achieved by the end of this period was impressive. By the beginning of the fourteenth century, Adret's description of the situation found in his late thirteenth-century responsum to the community of Saragossa must have seemed extremely obsolete:

The custom of different places in these matters is not uniform, for there are places where their affairs are entirely in the hands of their elders and men of counsel, while in other places even the majority are not permitted to do anything without the agreement of the whole congregation, and in yet others, the people appoint over themselves for a specified period well-known men whose decisions in all fields they abide by and these men are their guardians.[23]

So far we have discussed the principle of majority voting in the election of the executive body and in its application to the power of the general membership of the community. But for decision-making in the various bodies governing the *aljama*, the principle of unanimity was very widespread, especially in decisions involving expenditure. The decisions of the control committee supervising the expenses made by the *berurim* were usually taken by a unanimous vote. In some communities the *berurim* in charge of finance were permitted to spend up to a certain amount beyond which they needed the confirmation of all or the majority of the *berurim* in the town, depending on the sum. According to a *taqanah* of Lérida in 1308, a committee of ten had to authorize unanimously any expense higher than two *solidi*. Such a committee operated in many communities.

The difficulties arising from the need for a unanimous vote were immense. Any member could veto any expenditure and paralyse the work of the community. Adret however rejects the implication that the entire public could be thus enslaved to the fancies and tendencies of one *baror* whom they themselves elected to office.[24] Yet since in several communities during the thirteenth century the *berurim* and *yo'azim* appointed their own successors, each was in a position to

---

[21] ACA, Reg. 59, fo. 115 [=R 974 = Baer, *Spanien*, doc. 123]; Reg. 70, fo. 129ᵛ [=R 1731].
[22] ACA, Reg. 86, fo. 135ᵛ [=R 2444]; Reg. 206, fos. 43ᵛ–44 [=R 2902]; Reg. 222, fo. 120ᵛ [=R 3241].   [23] Adret, iii. 394.
[24] Adret, iii. 386, 434. For the *taqanah* of Lérida, see Asibili (Kapah) 114.

paralyse the communal administration.[25] Even when the principle of majority vote was already the accepted norm in the elections of leaders and in the procedure of executive and legislative activities, the necessity for a unanimous vote remained the practice in several other spheres.[26]

THE LOWER CLASSES' STRUGGLE FOR POWER

Despite the success of the Jewish aristocratic families in recovering part of the power they had lost, the lower classes, whose feelings of grievance had not been appeased, did not give up their struggle to gain a share in communal government. Their campaign was parallel to, and was no doubt inspired by, a similar social unrest and dissatisfaction with exclusion from power that characterized municipal life. The struggle of the lower and middle classes bore fruit from the beginning of the fourteenth century onwards, the popular demand for constitutional and institutional reforms spreading wide and fast. Prior to these reforms, relations between the old, wealthy families in control of the *qehilah* on the one hand, and the newly emerging middle class together with the poorer Jews on the other, were extremely strained and were marked by mutual suspicion and distrust. Jaime II, without whose help the lower classes could never have achieved any of their political aims, gave moderate support to their claims in a policy dictated by a pragmatic evaluation of the discontent and its potential consequences.

Open antagonism existed between the ruling elite and the lower classes in Valencia, where as late as 1297 the leaders were chosen from among the upper class.[27] Three years later, during the apportionment of royal and communal taxes among the members, the representatives of the lower classes complained to the king that the rich oppressed and harmed them in many ways. In response, the king decided to change the tax system and the structure of the body in charge of tax-collection. The committee before which every tax-payer had to take his oath henceforth included a member of each of the three classes. These three would be chosen by a twelve-member *concilium*, composed of four representatives from each class. The same *concilium* or *'eza*, together with the outgoing *berurim*, would choose the new *berurim*.[28] Some time later it was decided that the outgoing *berurim* could not be eligible for re-election for three years.

---

[25] Adret, iii. 425, v. 284–5. In courts of law majority voting was the rule. See Asibili (Kapah) 85; Adret, ii. 104. The same applied to the appointment of communal officials: Adret, v. 129.

[26] In some communities, unless stated otherwise, the interpretation of communal ordinances had to be unanimously agreed by the leaders: Adret, v. 289. The body appointed to protect the community's rights *vis-à-vis* the individual in Lérida took its decisions mostly by unanimous vote: Adret, v. 126. Majority vote prevailed in the decisions of the governing body: ACA, Reg. 195, fo. 44 [= R 2629 = Baer, *Spanien*, doc. 139]. [27] ACA, Reg. 195, fo. 46 [= R 2661].

[28] The lower classes claimed that 'maiores judei et diviciis opulanti mediocres et minores in eis diversimode agravant et molestant': ACA, Reg. 197, fos. 153ʳ–154 [= R 2745 = Baer, *Spanien*, doc. 146].

The old regime, which was primarily based on privileges enabling the oligarchs to perpetuate their power, was now abolished. Equally important was the prohibition on electing relatives of existing *berurim*. The constitution of 1300 did not put an end to the rivalry and agitation between the various groups in the Valencian *aljama*; however, despite the continuing need for royal intervention, the principle that all the three classes should be represented on all the communal institutions remained a permanent feature of communal life.[29]

The Valencian episode was part of a phase of general unrest and set a pattern to be followed by other communities. In neighbouring Murviedro, following long disputes, the king decided in favour of an electoral college of six members, two from each class, who would elect all the leaders every two years.[30] In Aragon, too, various communities witnessed similar developments. In Huesca,[31] Barbastro,[32] Teruel,[33] and Calatayud[34] the opposition of the poorer classes brought down the ruling oligarchies and the right of the leaders to appoint their own successors was abolished. The king's sympathetic attitude, a product of his political realism and pragmatism, made these changes possible: in every case the representatives of the lower classes turned to him for help. Despite various fluctuations, the greatest achievement of the middle and lower classes in this process, their gain of a share in the communal administration through the election of representatives from among their number, was permanent in many communities. Vestiges of the rich families' privileges remained, however, a source of continuous strife in several Aragonese communities.[35]

The Catalan *aljamas* were not immune from the social unrest that characterized the Valencian and Aragonese communities. Here the most radical changes in the system of communal government were introduced in 1308 in Lérida, where in the first stages the upper and middle classes seem to have agreed to share the *qehilah*'s administration, leaving out the lower classes. The latter intensified their struggle and obtained Jaime II's support for the 1315 reforms, which included them in the communal leadership.[36] The principle that outgoing officers should be ineligible for re-election for three years, designed to break the monopoly of the upper class, caused difficulties here as elsewhere. Since each class, irrespective of its numerical strength, was represented by an equal number of people, the upper

---

[29] ACA, Reg. 214, fo. 23 [=R 3064]; Reg. 229, fo. 274 [=R 3434 = Baer, *Spanien*, doc. 188].

[30] ACA, Reg. 230, fo. 59 [=R 3442].

[31] ACA, Reg. 210, fo. 79 [=R 2976]; Reg. 225, fo. 280ʳ [=R 3299]; Arco, 'La aljama judaica de Huesca', pp. 282–3.

[32] ACA, Reg. 210, fos. 86–7 [=R 2977]; Reg. 229, fos. 177ʳ–178 [=R 3404].

[33] Baer, *Spanien*, doc. 163.

[34] A most interesting letter by the representatives of the poor in Calatayud to the king, complaining about the ruling class, is found in ACA, CR, Jaime II, C 135, no. 411, and published in Assis, 'Social Unrest', p. 144, n. 96.

[35] See n. 33 above; ACA, Reg. 227, fo. 191ʳ [=R 3333]; R 218, fos. 92ʳ–3 [=R 3135 = Baer, *Spanien*, doc. 174].

[36] Asibili (Kapah) 114; ACA, Reg. 212, fos. 30ʳ–31 [=R 3026]; Reg. 216, fo. 83 [=R 3095].

class found it difficult to provide so many candidates. Attempts to solve the problem within the framework of the new reformed principle failed, causing the entire system to collapse. Efforts to uphold the principle of equal representation finally proved futile. The exclusion of the lower classes from the governing bodies of the community in Lérida, having once participated in them, should however be seen as an exception to the general trend.[37]

THE EXTENT OF REFORM

The constitutional reforms and the changes in the communal system of government were sufficiently clear and well established in various communities at the beginning of the fourteenth century for Adret to write that 'now it is customary in all the communities to appoint men for all public offices for a limited period and when the time comes the old management leaves and the new one takes over.'[38] We have already seen that additional measures limiting the power of the elected leaders were taken. In addition to the ineligibility of outgoing office-holders for re-election until a certain period had elapsed, and the prohibition on the election of relatives of incumbent officers, these measures included a prohibition on spending more than a certain amount without the consent of the councillors, a supervisory role exercised by the newly founded *'eza, consell*, or *concilium* over the *berurim* or *muqademin*.

The *'eza* was a very significant institutional innovation. In many communities the new body included representatives of all the classes, and its wider membership permitted more debates. In many fields it controlled the smaller executive body of the *berurim, muqademin, ne'emanim*, or *secretarii*.[39] The earliest information about the council comes from the 1260s, but at this period is very vague and limited. We know that in the 1280s the Council of Saragossa had twenty-five members.[40] From the beginning of the fourteenth century the sources show the existence of a council in various communities. The number of its members depended on the size of the community.[41]

Another innovation of the new system was the appointment of judges by the council or the electors in the *qehilah*. The number of the judges and their term of office varied from one community to another. The importance of this development, which dates back to the period of Pedro III, is clear. The official royal confirmation of periodically held appointments of judges ensured that no individual or group could treat the judicial system as their domain by virtue of family

---

[37] ACA, Reg. 216, fos. 84ʳ, 122ʳ–123 [=R 3097, 3106].
[38] Adret, v. 283.
[39] Adret, iii. 386, 434, 443, v. 284–5; ACA, Reg. 223, fo. 196 [=R 3255].
[40] Adret, ii. 33.
[41] Baer, *History*, i, pp. 224–8. In Lérida there were 10 members (Asibili (Kapah) 114); in Barcelona, 30 (ACA, Reg. 230, fos. 106–7ʳ [= Baer, *Spanien*, doc. 189]; in Gerona in 1352, there were 26 *yo'azim* (Loeb, 'Actes', pp. 118–22; id., 'Les Administrations', pp. 263–4).

ties, tradition, or even expertise in Jewish law.⁴² The radical character of the new procedure in several communities where local politics had been dominated by a few powerful families can best be illustrated by the reaction of the latter to the new system.⁴³

Systematic elections or appointments of judges were bound to hurt those members of the aristocratic families who saw themselves as the rightful occupants of these posts. It is reasonable to assume that the reluctance of several appointees to take up their posts was due in no small measure to the vehement opposition of certain members of the upper class who did not hesitate to use force against their rivals.⁴⁴

Additional obstacles made the appointment of judges a recurrent problem in many communities. In some communities there was a need for further reform; in others, the problem brought royal intervention. Again and again, the early reform of Pedro III's times was quoted as the basis of the judicial system, in its various adjusted forms.⁴⁵ Other parties, too, such as the municipal authorities, had an interest in the type of judiciary and its methods of work as they developed in the Jewish community, and made attempts to have a say in the matter.⁴⁶

THE COMMUNAL INSTITUTIONS

The *qehilah* in the Crown of Aragon developed a sophisticated system of government which combined elements from the medieval Jewish world and newly created institutions to suit its special needs and prevalent local conditions. The

---

⁴² In 1280 the king conferred on the *aljamas* of Catalonia the right to appoint their judges annually. The Aragonese were granted a similar right at about the same period. For the sources, see n. 12 above.

⁴³ A noteworthy example is the Alconstantini family in Saragossa, whose members tried repeatedly to occupy the post of chief judge of Aragon. In 1232, 1271, 1294, and 1329 attempts by members of the family to act as such aroused opposition from rabbinic authorities, rival families, and members of the community. See Baer, *History*, i, p. 105; ACA, Reg. 16, fos. 261ᵛ–262 [= R 461 = Jacobs 483 = Bofarull, Barcelona, ciii = Baer, *Spanien*, doc. 104 = MF i. 1096]. Significantly the 1271 attempt came after the *taqanah* that three judges be appointed in the community: ACA, Reg. 16, fo. 240ᵛ [= R 458 = Jacobs 474]; Reg. 252, fo. 50 [= R 2551 = Baer, *Spanien*, doc. 136]; Reg. 481, fo. 249; Baer, *Spanien*, pp. 151–2.

⁴⁴ On the reluctance of Jews to accept their appointment as judges, see ACA, Reg. 48, fos. 117, 119ᵛ [= R 829, 833]. On violence exerted by Mosse Alconstantini and Meir Elazar against a Jew who gave the baile certain information and advice, see ACA, Reg. 48, fo. 134 [= R 841 = Dinur, ii. 1, p. 204, no. 10].

⁴⁵ For Lérida, see ACA, Reg. 195, fo. 44 [= R 2629 = Baer, *Spanien*, doc. 139]; Reg. 256, fo. 28 [= R 2680]. For the complications relating to the appointment of judges in Saragossa, see Reg. 89, fo. 121ᵛ [= R 2587]; Reg. 197, fo. 19ᵛ [= R 2720 = Baer, *Spanien*, doc. 142]. Note the reference to the 1280 privilege of Pedro III in the last-named source.

⁴⁶ For an interesting example in Majorca, see ACA, CR, Jaime II, C 5, no. 754 [= *Cartas Reales*, no. 67]. For arrangements stipulating the appointment of judges in the island's community during the brief period of Aragonese domination in Jaime II's time, see ACA, Reg. 194, fo. 266 [= R 2623 = Isaacs 74].

system of communal government that emerged did not distinguish between the different elements according to that different backgrounds, but fused all into one integral system. Whether of ancient origin and hence considered part of traditional Jewish self-government, or recently imported, adapted, or modified to cater for contemporary Jewish needs, the communal institutions all together formed the *aljama* in the Crown of Aragon.

The supreme body in the community was the general assembly of all the male members and heads of families.[47] It was known by the name *qahal*, which is found in numerous Hebrew sources. Although in theory this body represented the will of the entire community, in reality it enjoyed little power in the running of most communities, although in some it did exercise real influence.[48] For example, after the electoral reform of the early fourteenth century, in some communities the *qahal* was active in the election of the leaders. Some important decisions were also taken by the entire assembly.[49] All important ordinances were read solemnly in the assembly, an act which enhanced their validity. The public *herem* was also proclaimed in its presence;[50] and it was the official forum in which the Jewish public heard the formal announcements of the governing bodies of the *aljama*.[51]

The general assembly met in the main synagogue, the *sinagoga mayor*, at certain fixed times of the year and whenever an important item was put on its agenda by the *berurim* and *yo'azim*.[52] The annual oath, for instance, that was to be taken according to the requirement of the authorities, took place in the assembly on a fixed day.[53]

The term *qahal* was also used in some Hebrew sources as the name of the executive board that administered the *qehilah*.[54] In other sources the term for this board is more specific, such as *rashe ha-qahal*[55] or *berure ha-qahal*;[56] or else it is referred to by the terms for its members, the *berurim* or the *adelantados, muqademin* or *ne'emanim* (also known by the more widespread names of *parnas, gabbay*, etc.)[57] This body was the organ that governed the community on a day-to-day basis and appointed most of the community functionaries.[58]

The *berurim* were originally members of the wealthiest families and the intellectual elite. As constitutional reform was introduced in many communities from the beginning of the fourteenth century, the executive board became the representative body of the three social classes in Jewish society. Henceforth the number of its members was a multiple of three, so that the lower, middle, and upper classes could be equally represented. In the course of time, this executive committee became known as the *ma'amad*, that is the organ in which each

---

[47] Adret, iii. 443.   [48] Adret, iii. 394, v. 278–9.   [49] Adret, ii. 279, iii. 304.
[50] Adret, i. 815, iii. 443.   [51] Adret, i. 551.   [52] Adret, vii. 244.
[53] ACA, Reg. 19, fo. 65ᵛ [= R 570 = Jacobs 523 = Bofarull, Barcelona, cxxiv]; Reg. 42, fo. 136 [= R 743].
[54] Adret, i. 644, 955; Asibili (Kapah) 156, 159.
[55] Adret, i. 967, iv. 315.
[56] Adret, i. 1187.   [57] Adret, i. 617, 644.   [58] Adret, i. 594.

ma'amad or class was represented.⁵⁹ The name was retained by the Sephardi refugees both in the east and in the west.⁶⁰

The *berurim* performed all executive tasks as well as some legislative and judicial functions. Some were in charge of special departments or fields and bore special names, such as *berure 'averot, berure tevi'ot, berurei midot*, and the like. They were assisted by a number of officers and wardens, known by a variety of names; the next section treats these in more detail. Some of the most important officers were the treasurers, charity officers, tax-assessors, and tax-collectors.

A larger consultative body with some degree of control over the executive board was the council or *'eza*, which, as noted above, was established in some communities in the latter part of the thirteenth century. Its members, the councillors or *yo'azim*, numbered between twelve and thirty. It was modelled on the *concilium, concejo*, or *consell* found in the Christian cities. In communities where constitutional reform took place, the three classes were equally represented on the council.

The council was in control of certain activities and could veto some of the decisions of the *berurim*. It had wide legislative power and enacted the *taqanot* or ordinances that regulated life in the community. The councillors elected some of the officers and often the *dayanim* or judges, many of whom were answerable to them. In the course of the fourteenth century the council became a most important organ of Jewish self-government in all the major and middle-sized communities of the Crown of Aragon.⁶¹

---

⁵⁹ The word *ma'amad* is also used to denote the presence and authority of the public; see Adret, v. 125, viii. 288.

⁶⁰ See Hacker, 'The Sephardim', pp. 118–21; Kaplan, 'The Sephardim', pp. 273–6.

⁶¹ Full details of the council's authority and functions can be found in communal constitutions confirmed by the king, as well as other sources. See e.g. ACA, Reg. 44, fo. 177ᵛ [=R 776 = Baer, *Spanien*, doc. 118]; Reg. 939, fos. 99–103ᵛ [= Baer, *Spanien*, doc. 342] (Saragossa); Reg. 230, fos. 106–7ᵛ [= Baer, *Spanien*, doc. 189]; Baer, *Spanien*, doc. 333; Reg. 948, fos. 114ᵛ–122ᵛ [= Baer, *Spanien*, doc. 381]; Reg. 1815, fos. 51ᵛ–52 [= Baer, *Spanien*, doc. 386] (Barcelona); Reg. 653, fos. 15ᵛ–16 [= Baer, *Spanien*, doc. 229]; Reg. 926, fos. 39ᵛ–42; Reg. 1898, fos. 196–199ᵛ [= Baer, *Spanien*, doc. 256] (Huesca); Reg. 1580, fos. 90ᵛ–91 [= Baer, *Spanien*, doc. 308] (Valencia); Reg. 1439, fos. 8–11 [= Baer, *Spanien*, doc. 318, para. 3]; Reg. 1689, fos. 213–16 [= Baer, *Spanien*, docs. 330, 371] (Perpignan); Reg. 941, fos. 176ᵛ–179 [= Baer, *Spanien*, doc. 348] (Jávita); Reg. 2041, fos. 37ᵛ–40 [= Baer, *Spanien*, doc. 396] (Gerona); Adret, v. 284 (Lérida?).

§2.3 Elections and Appointments

ELECTIONS AND THE CROWN

AN important component of the communal regime was the system of elections and appointments to the various positions in the communal administration. There was no single procedure that was applied in all the communities of the Crown of Aragon. Until the end of the thirteenth century in most communities the leaders were appointed; only in a few were elections held.[1] Several communities were ruled by a despotic regime that was severely criticized by R. Shelomo ben Adret.[2] Whatever the system, the king's consent to all appointments was necessary. In principle, however, the king granted every community the right to chose its own leaders freely, as did noblemen to Jews living in their domains.[3]

The need for the king's approval of the administrative system reveals one of the weaknesses of Jewish autonomy and its dependence on an all-powerful external factor. Royal confirmation of a new constitution for a community, and the recognition by the monarch of its elected or appointed leadership, although welcomed by the Jews, were nevertheless obvious examples of royal involvement in the community administration.

The king confirmed the right of the Jewish community to elect its own leaders and, if the Jewish public was not split over the issue, he did not interfere with the system of elections or appointments. Extant charters granted to Jewish communities and confirmed by successive monarchs include this right. In 1229 Jaime I approved the constitution of the *aljama* of Calatayud, which authorized the election of four *adelantados* with the consent of their rabbi for a period of its choice. The rabbi's consent was in accordance with Jewish custom. The unlimited term of office reflected the oligarchical character of the regime in most Jewish communities at the time.[4]

Every *aljama* had its constitution, including its election or appointment system, approved by the monarch. This approval was not only a necessary formality offering a handsome income to the monarch, but was often necessary because of internal strife in the community. Successive monarchs confirmed the election

---

[1] Adret, iii. 428.
[2] Adret, v. 245.
[3] ACA, Reg. 194, fo. 266 [= R 2623 = Isaacs 74]; Salarrullana, *Estudios históricos*, pp. 69–70.
[4] This charter was confirmed by Jaime II in January 1305: ACA, Reg. 202, fo. 201ʳᵛ [= R 6].

systems of various *aljamas*. Jaime II was very much involved in this process.[5] Under his reign many *aljamas* had their system of elections confirmed. In some cases, the king approved proposals put forward by the community, in others, he played a leading role in the formulation of the system. The *aljamas* of Lérida, Barbastro, and Barcelona had their election systems confirmed as part of their constitution.[6] Certain changes in these electoral systems were introduced or approved by Jaime II during his reign. The Jews of Lérida, who had a new constitution approved in 1297, had changes in their electoral system made in 1315, 1318, and 1319. Those of Barbastro had their electoral system of 1313, which was proposed by Jaime II, changed in 1326. The instability of the communal regimes was first and foremost reflected in the changes that were introduced, with royal approval, in the election system.[7]

The king's involvement reached its peak in his direct intervention in the appointment and dismissal of the *adelantados* or secretaries of the *aljama*. Following a serious crisis in relations between the leaders of the *aljama* and the poor of Saragossa in 1263-4, Jaime I nominated the four *adelantados* in April 1264. The community of Saragossa continued to be dogged by problems in choosing its leaders. In 1280 Pedro III ordered the *aljama* to elect three leaders to run its affairs, and those three had to accept the posts.[8] In June 1292 Jaime II ordered the *adelantados* of Valencia to co-opt four or five Jews as secretaries.[9] Such a measure, however, was almost invariably the direct result of disagreements and disputes within the community. It was often the party that was dissatisfied with the results of the elections, or that was opposed to the actual leadership, that turned to the king for help and brought about his direct intervention. What was in principle a negative step from the community's point of view sometimes had favourable results. Such was the case when a group of Jews in Huesca complained to the king about the election results in their community in 1313. The king thereupon proclaimed a new constitution that remedied some of the distortions of the old system.[10] Similarly, agitation and dissent that accompanied the elections in the *aljamas* of Valencia and Murviedro in 1327 led to royal intervention and changes in the election system in both communities.[11]

In some extreme cases the king or the infante simply wished to appoint his favourites to the communal leadership. For example, in 1326 Pedro asked his brother Alfonso, the crown prince, to appoint Astruc Saltell, son of Saltell Gracia

---

[5] ACA, Reg. 195, fo. 144; Reg. 202, fo. 210.

[6] ACA, Reg. 195, fo. 51` [=R 2663 = Baer, *Spanien*, doc. 140]; Reg. 210, fos. 86`-87; Reg. 229, fos. 177`-178 [=R 2977]; Reg. 230, fos. 106-107` [=R 3454 = Jacobs 892 = Baer, *Spanien*, doc. 189.

[7] For Lérida, see ACA, Reg. 212, fos. 30`-31 [=R 3026]; Reg. 216, fos. 84`, 122`-123 [=R 3097, 3106]; for Barbastro, see ACA, Reg. 210, fos. 86`-87 [=R 3404 = Jacobs 866].

[8] [ACA, Reg. 13, fo. 163 [=R 253 = Jacobs 279]; Reg. 48, fos. 117, 119` [=R 829, 833].

[9] ACA, Reg. 86, fo. 136 [=R 2445].

[10] ACA, Reg. 210, fo. 79 [=R 2976].

[11] ACA, Reg. 229, fo. 274 [=R 3434 = Jacobs 878 = Baer, *Spanien*, doc. 188]; Reg. 230, fo. 59 [=R 3442 = Jacobs 884].

of Barcelona, as the seventh *secretarius* in Barcelona, a post vacated on the death of one of the leaders.[12] Similarly, in 1268 Jaime I nominated two Jews to the post of tax-collector in the community of Montpellier.[13]

Sometimes it was at the initiative of the leaders of the community that the king intervened. Naturally, they wished the king to intervene in their favour against their opponents. Leaders sought the king's support for changes they wished to introduce in the election system and which they considered advantageous to them or to the *aljama*. The changes the king was asked to approve varied from determining the qualifying criteria for candidates to various posts to permitting an additional term of office and changing the number of the candidates to be elected.[14]

The king was the highest authority in all matters related to elections in the Jewish community. Any change in the election system which aroused opposition could only be effected with the king's consent. The Jewish community lost some of its autonomy in consequence of such internal conflicts. The harm caused to Jewish self-government by the selfish conduct of the parties involved cannot be overestimated. The king perceived the limits of his involvement in the elections within the *judería* rather differently from the parties in conflict. This process, which began as a Jewish initiative, did not stop at the Jews' behest. It was not under their control, nor did the king's intentions necessarily coincide with those of the Jews. When Valencian Jews complained in 1292 against the leaders of their community, the infante sacked the latter and ordered his officials to appoint new leaders, holding no elections. When the *adelantados* failed to appoint the secretaries as ordered by the infante, once again the royal officials were instructed to appoint the secretaries. The infante dismissed two of the appointed members whom he disliked. Eventually, however, the infante gave in to the opposition of the *adelantados* and, cancelling his orders, agreed that the secretaries should be appointed by the *adelantados*.[15]

This degree of intervention was not exceptional, as can be seen from the sources. In 1289, as the Jews of Barcelona and its *collecta* could not reach an agreement about the election of new secretaries, Alfonso III sent instructions that the Jews meet to elect their leaders without fail. In 1326 the secretaries of the same *aljama* were appointed by a royal officer at Jaime II's command.[16] The king's interference in the elections in the *judería* diminished considerably when there was no conflict in the community, in which case all that occurred was royal confirmation of the election results, generally as an automatic act.[17]

---

[12] ACA, CR, Jaime II, C 134, no. 152 [= *Cartas Reales*, no. 367].

[13] ACA, Reg. 15, fo. 124 [=R 397 = Jacobs 433 = Bofarull, Montpellier, 489].

[14] ACA, Reg. 195, fo. 46 [=R 2661]; Reg. 214, fos. 23, 83 [=R 3064, 3095]; Reg. 225, fo. 280ᵛ [=R 3299 = Jacobs 837]; Arco, 'La aljama judaica', p. 282.

[15] ACA, Reg. 86, fos. 131, 157ᵛ, 158 [=R 2442, 2451]; Reg. 87, fos. 19ᵛ, 34 [=R 2464, 2467].

[16] For 1289, see ACA, Reg. 80, fo. 49ʳᵛ [= R 2002]; for 1326, see Reg. 228, fo. 70 [=R 3381 = Jacobs 858 = Baer, *Spanien*, doc. 182].   [17] ACA, Reg. 228, fo. 70; Reg. 229, fo. 193 [=R 3406].

In view of the importance of the task, the election of tax-assessors and collectors was a matter of dispute in some communities. This led to frequent royal intervention. In the *collecta* of Gerona–Besalú the five tax-collectors who were chosen took an oath promising not to reveal the information provided to them by the secretaries of the community and to fulfil their task properly.[18]

The appointment of judges or *dayanim* was also performed with the approval of the king. In 1241, for instance, Jaime I allowed the Jews of Barcelona to appoint two or three judges,[19] and during this period the right to appoint judges was conferred upon the Jewish communities throughout the land. Under Pedro III all the *aljamas* of the realm were authorized to appoint between two and seven judges to adjudicate in lawsuits between Jews. This privilege was maintained under his successors.[20] Under the brief period of Aragonese rule over Majorca in the last decade of the thirteenth century, it was decided that three to four *adelantados* should serve as judges. The judicial power exercised by the Majorcan *adelantados* raised opposition in municipal circles. Following the return of the island to the Kingdom of Majorca, the municipal authorities raised objections in 1300 to the appointment of four *adelantados* as judges, claiming that they and the baile had judicial authority over Jews.[21] In the Crown of Aragon the principle that the Jews should elect their own judges was generally upheld.

THE CANDIDATES

Only tax-paying members of the *aljama* were eligible to the post of *adelantado* or secretary. In most communities a candidate had to pay a minimum amount of tax, which varied from one place to another.[22] Before the introduction of constitutional reform in some *aljamas* of the Crown of Aragon, the leaders traditionally belonged to the rich families in Jewish society. Until the first protests were heard, it was widely accepted that the leaders of the communities were chosen from a limited number of aristocratic and wealthy families. It was the norm that the administration of the community was in the hands of the biggest tax-payers. Certain families were permanently represented in the community administration: each family appointed its representative, or the outgoing member chose his successor.

In communities where it was established that a minimum sum be paid as tax by the candidate, changes in his fortunes subsequent to his election to office sometimes had serious repercussions on his political future. Leaders who lost their wealth after they had taken office were challenged by their rivals. According to R. Shelomo ben Adret it was the candidate's financial status at the time of taking

---

[18] ACA, Reg. 10, fo. 54ʳ [= R 97 = Jacobs 151 = Baer, *Spanien*, doc. 97].
[19] ACA, Reg. 16, fo. 158 [= R 29 = Baer, *Spanien*, doc. 93].
[20] ACA, Reg. 44, fos. 187ʳ–188 [= R 823 = Baer, *Spanien*, doc. 121]; Reg. 59, fo. 56 [= R 942].
[21] ACA, CR, Jaime II, C 5, no. 754 [= *Cartas Reales*, no. 67].   [22] Adret, iv. 312.

office that counted; political reality, however, was harsher than the halakhist's opinion, and impoverished leaders found themselves ousted from their posts before the end of their term of office. Not only did the king confirm the minimum tax-payment condition, he also supported any step against leaders who no longer fulfilled that criterion.[23] This condition must have been widespread in Aragonese communities as the constitutions of 1313 in Huesca and Barbastro indicate. In both communities, the *adelantados*, the secretaries, and the councillors were elected from among the biggest tax-payers.[24]

In addition to the financial criterion, family relationship also limited eligibility. In some communities, where the outgoing leaders chose their successors, the former were not allowed to appoint their immediate relatives, defined as those relatives who were halakhically disqualified from testifying in their trial. This limitation was quite extensive and indicates the care taken to avoid extreme forms of oligarchy and nepotism.[25] In communities where the electorate was large this principle was more generally adhered to. Councillors, *berurim*, or *ne'emanim* could not sit with close relatives on the same board.[26]

Another qualifying criterion for any candidate for office was residence in the locality. Even when the royal authorities imposed their own non-resident candidate on the community, they made the appointment conditional upon the transfer of his residence to the new place.[27]

It was in 1313 that the prohibition on re-election for consecutive terms was first mentioned, in Barbastro, where the outgoing *adelantados* could not seek re-election for two years. In Barcelona, according to the 1327 constitution, the secretaries could not seek re-election before one term of office had passed.[28] The period varied from one community to another and depended on the size of the Jewish population. The principle spread in many communities but was neither popular with the leaders themselves nor easy to put into practice. In 1317 the *aljama* of Valencia asked the king to cancel the prohibition on re-election within three years, claiming that there were not sufficient candidates for such frequent rotation. The cancellation was temporary; the prohibition reappeared in 1327 in connection with the election of the three *berurim–dayanim*.[29] A similar request, for the same reason, was submitted by the *aljama* of Lérida in 1318. The king suggested that a reduction in the number of candidates would solve the problem.[30]

---

[23] ACA, Reg. 87, fo. 19ʾ [=R 2464]; Reg. 195, fo. 46 [=R 2661].

[24] ACA, Reg. 210, fos. 79, 86ʾ–87 [=R 2976–7]; Reg. 299, fos. 177ʾ–178 [=R 2977].

[25] Adret, v. 284; cf. id., iv. 188. On the *halakhah*, see Maimonides, *Mishne Torah*, Book of Judges, Hilkhot 'Edut, ch. 13.

[26] ACA, Reg. 210, fo. 79 [=R 2976]; Reg. 229, fo. 274 [=R 3434 = Baer, *Spanien*, doc. 188]; Reg. 230, fos. 106–107ʾ [=R 3454 = Baer, *Spanien*, doc. 189].

[27] ACA, Reg. 228, fo. 70 [=R 3381 = Baer, *Spanien*, doc. 182].

[28] ACA, Reg. 210, fos. 86ʾ–87 [=R 2977]; Reg. 230, fos. 106–7ʾ [=R 3454 = Baer, *Spanien*, doc. 189].

[29] ACA, Reg. 214, fo. 23 [=R 3064], Reg. 229, fo. 274 [= R 3434 = Baer, *Spanien*, doc. 188].

[30] ACA, Reg. 216, fo. 83 [=R 3095].

The claim of the *aljamas* of Valencia and Lérida that there were not sufficient candidates for the various posts of community leadership is somewhat surprising. In both communities there were bitter conflicts between ambitious rivals. The explanation for this rivalry may lie in the small number of people eligible for these posts as a result of the above-mentioned restrictions; moreover, the process of democratization which started around the beginning of the fourteenth century and which led in many aljamas to equal representation for three numerically unequal classes restricted further the number of candidates for the upper class, while the traditional leadership found it difficult to abandon its positions of power and prestige.

THE ELECTION SYSTEM

Throughout the thirteenth century the established systems of elections in the Jewish community fitted well with the oligarchical character of the regimes. There was no universally accepted procedure and the method differed in various details in different communities. In almost all the communities the leaders remained in office for many years. Those who took office in 1277 were in most cases still the heads of their communities in 1284.[31] The principle of majority voting was to be found hardly anywhere in the Crown of Aragon. In most communities the system was not too different from that elaborated in an ordinance of the *aljama* of Lérida, where 'the appointment of the *berurim* and the councillors is not to be by majority vote but every *baror* and councillor may appoint his successor even without his colleagues' consent.'[32] This system operated in the *aljama* of Lérida and, as we shall see later, in other communities, such as Jaca, in the latter part of the thirteenth century and probably earlier.[33] It produced serious problems, of which the gravest was the refusal of the outgoing leaders to nominate their candidates, either in an attempt to retain power or as a way of exerting pressure on their colleagues' choices; this could cause a paralysis of the community administration. An effective measure designed to prevent the disruption of communal management by this tactic was the *ostages* system, which placed the electors somewhere outside the *judería*, prohibiting their exit or contact with the outside world until they had all nominated their successors. They had to eat and sleep in quarantine until the new administration was chosen. In some communities, the outgoing leaders appointed the new administration together. Under this system too, the electors were in *ostages* until they reached an agreement on the composition of the new management.[34]

Despite all the precautionary measures, the system did not operate smoothly. The *ostages* method was relatively new in the second half of the thirteenth century and was differently interpreted in some communities which adopted it. In Lérida,

[31] ACA, Reg. 43, fos. 29', 31' [=R 1201, 1204]. [32] Adret, v. 284.
[33] Adret, iii. 423; for archival sources see below. [34] Adret, iii. 425, v. 285.

for instance, it was not clear to the *adelantados* whether they had to be in one particular place or whether they could be anywhere they pleased outside the *judería*. The latter interpretation would have seriously impaired or totally undermined the efficiency of the system. Adret was of the opinion that all the electors had to remain in quarantine, in one particular place not far from the town, until a complete list of the new elected officers was produced.[35] Despite occasional difficulties, the community of Lérida continued to follow the system whereby the leaders appointed their own successors. The king favoured stability and gave his support to the system in Lérida and elsewhere. In 1285 Pedro III ordered the *aljama* of Jaca to adopt it.[36] In 1297 a slight change was introduced into the system, though this did not alter its basically oligarchical character: the outgoing leaders now had to co-opt five other Jews, and together this group had to choose, by majority vote, their successors. The five were certainly members of the most influential families.[37]

Soon after its introduction, however, the system proved inefficient in several communities and the delaying and obstructing tactics employed by some community leaders caused concern at court. In October 1282, for instance, the Infante Alfonso, wishing to put an end to such tactics in Gerona, ordered the *aljama* to elect the *adelantados* or *berure tevi'ot* (*berurim de tauioz*) by majority vote. The system was not altogether novel and had apparently been tried beforehand elsewhere.[38] Reform was most needed where the crisis reached dangerous proportions. In Saragossa political differences tore apart the Jewish public and caused frequent conflicts and violent rivalries. In 1287 Alfonso III decided to propose a new system of election to the community. An electoral college of forty members was to be constituted and charged with electing the *adelantados* by majority vote. This proposed system was by far the most democratic of any among the Jews of the Crown of Aragon at this date, but was not enough to uproot the oligarchical system. It certainly did not satisfy Jews of the lower classes, as the forty electors belonged to the prestigious and wealthy families in the community.[39] As noted above, the changes introduced in Lérida did not produce any radical difference in the character of the regime at the end of the thirteenth century.

The first constitutional changes that broadened the basis of the communal leadership occurred at the beginning of the fourteenth century following growing pressure from the lower classes. The Jews of Lérida, who had taken the lead in reforming the old election system, were also the pioneers in the new reform that permitted representatives of the lower classes to share in the communal administration. By 1315 the pressure of the lower classes was bearing fruit and a new system was introduced. The old system, whereby the five leaders appointed their

[35] Adret, iii. 422.
[36] ACA, Reg. 57, fos. 187, 199 [= R 1429, 1438].
[37] ACA, Reg. 195, fo. 51ᵛ [= R 2663 = Baer, *Spanien*, doc. 140].
[38] ACA, Reg. 59, fo. 115ᵛ [= R 974 = Baer, *Spanien*, doc. 123].
[39] ACA, Reg. 70, fo. 129ᵛ [= R 1731].

successors, was abandoned. The new system provided representation to all three classes. Eighteen tax-payers, six from each class, were to be elected at the beginning of every year. These included six *adelantados*, two from each class, and twelve secretaries, divided equally among the three classes. The baile was to supervise the elections and ensure that they were conducted legally.

The new system did not last long: it collapsed three years later, when in 1318 it was decided that the six *adelantados* and the three secretaries would elect their successors for the following year under the baile's supervision. The equal representation of the classes was maintained, but the suffrage was greatly reduced. Power in the community now lay in the hands of a few families from each social stratum. Even this semblance of social reform in the administration was short-lived. Some six months later, in March 1319, there was hardly anything left of the reform of 1315. Four Jews elected by the *aljama* were empowered to select the *adelantados* and the secretaries for a six-year term of office. No trace was left of any of the electoral reform initiated three and a half years earlier.[40]

The election system in the *aljama* of Barcelona also underwent changes. R. Shelomo ben Adret, who headed the *yeshivah* in Barcelona, favoured a community governed by the leading families and rabbinic scholars. His ideal of community government had a strong impact on the actual regime and the election system.[41] There were occasional conflicts between the *aljama* of Barcelona and those of its *collecta* over the elections of the secretaries.[42] The constitution adopted in 1327 provided for a council of thirty members who chose the *ne'emanim* or secretaries, putting an end to the old system whereby communal posts had been in the hands of privileged individuals supported by the king. The new constitution imposed heavy fines on any person who attempted to obtain office in this way. The members of the 'Council of Thirty' were elected from the most distinguished families for three years by a majority vote of the *ne'emanim* and the judges. Close relatives were not to be elected for the same term of office. This regulation was certainly a significant improvement on the old system. Within three days of their election the councillors had to take an oath that they would fulfil their duty to the best of their abilities. The councillors appointed all the community administrators: *ne'emanim*, judges, charity officers, and accountants. The *ne'emanim* were appointed for one or two years and could not be re-elected for successive terms. This measure was also designed to prevent the perpetuation of power in the hands of a few aristocratic families. Despite the larger number of Jews taking part in the communal government and the restrictive measures against successive terms of office, the new constitution did not offer the lower classes representation on the various bodies of the communal government.[43] The aristocratic character of the leadership remained unchanged until the very end of

[40] ACA, Reg. 212, fos. 30ʻ–31 [= R 3026]; Reg. 216, fos. 84ʻ, 122ʻ–123 [= R 3097, 3106].
[41] Adret, iii. 394, 399, 428.
[42] ACA, CR, Jaime II, C 48, no. 5908 [*Cartas Reales*, no. 197].
[43] ACA, Reg. 230, fos. 106–7ʻ [= R 3454 = Baer, *Spanien*, doc. 189].

the community's existence.⁴⁴ The Barcelona constitution was copied by other *aljamas* in the Crown of Aragon, despite its shortcomings, being adopted in 1364 by Valencia and in 1374 by Huesca.⁴⁵

Following the social and political unrest in the community of Saragossa and the constitutional reform introduced there, other Aragonese communities followed the example of the metropolis. In several communities representatives of the lower classes were included in the administrative body. In 1313, electoral reform was introduced in Huesca, where previously five *adelantados* and twenty councillors ran the affairs of the community. Many Jews complained to the king that the system was prejudicial to their interests and did not permit them to take part in the administration of their own community. Jaime II found their complaints justified and ordered extensive reform in the electoral system. According to the new constitution, the tax-payers would elect each year eighteen councillors, six from each of the classes, of whom six, two of each class, would act as *adelantados*. The baile was ordered to supervise the elections and ensure that no relatives were elected to either post. The eighteen leaders could not seek re-election before three years had passed. A committee of six Jews who had not served as leaders during the previous five years were to assist the baile in conducting investigations into the work of those who had served as leaders during the same period. It is noteworthy that the king did not wait for the results of the investigations to order electoral and constitutional reform.⁴⁶ In 1324, at the request of the *aljama*, Jaime II confirmed some modifications of the system. Six *adelantados* and six councillors, representing equally the three classes, were to be elected. No near relatives, fathers, sons, or brothers, could succeed the outgoing leaders, who could seek re-election after the passage of two years.⁴⁷

In Barbastro, too, radical changes in the electoral system were adopted the same year. Until 1313 the six elders who served as *adelantados* appointed their own successors. Local Jews complained about the system. Jaime II accepted the need for reform and decided that henceforth nine tax-paying Jews, three from each class, were to be elected every year. Three of them would act as *adelantados* and the remaining six as councillors. Two years had to pass before any of the nine could stand for office again. The new system put an end to the monopoly of the Jewish aristocracy and guaranteed rotation in the communal government.⁴⁸

In the kingdom of Valencia, the communal regime was unstable for some time after the conquest of the territory in 1238–45. Various systems were tried without success, while inner conflicts led to frequent royal interventions. In 1292, following the dismissal of the Valencian *adelantados* by the authorities, their successors were ordered to co-opt four or five *secretarii*. As the *adelantados* could not reach

⁴⁴ Perfet 214, 228.
⁴⁵ ACA, Reg. 928, fo. 25; Reg. 926, fos. 39ʻ–42; Reg. 1898, fos. 196–9ʻ; cf. Baer, *Spanien*, doc. 256.
⁴⁶ ACA, Reg. 210, fo. 79 [= R 2976].
⁴⁷ ACA, CR, Jaime II, C 133, no. 63 [*Cartas Reales*, no. 294].
⁴⁸ ACA, Reg. 210, fos. 86ʻ–87 [= R 2977]; Reg. 229, fos. 177ʻ–178 [= R 3404 = Jacobs 866].

Elections and Appointments 97

an agreement, the king's officials appointed four *secretarii*, a move that displeased both the *adelantados* and the general public. Despite the infante's insistence on upholding the appointments, the authorities had to withdraw at the beginning of 1293 in the face of strong Jewish opposition.[49] The situation remained unsettled and there were constant clashes between various groups advocating different systems of election or appointment. It was only in 1300 that a serious attempt was made to solve the problem. A council of twelve members, four from each of the three classes, joined the retiring *adelantados* in the election of new leaders. The council also appointed the three tax-assessors from the lower, middle, and upper classes. If the members of the council failed to elect the three within eight days, they would enter the synagogue where they would stay until an agreement was reached. The new system did not bring peace to the Valencian *aljama*. Serious conflict among factions led to outside interference: in 1327 Jaime II decided to introduce certain changes in the system. Meeting in the synagogue, the members of the community would now choose six instead of twelve councillors, two from each class, who should not be related to one another. The six could not leave the synagogue until they had elected the three *adelantados*. The latter were elected for one year and could not be re-elected for a consecutive term.[50]

In the provincial communities of the Kingdom of Valencia conditions were no better. In Murviedro, crisis preceded and followed the elections. In 1327 Jaime II decided that the Jews of Murviedro should adopt the same constitution as Valencia. Six electors, two from each class, chosen by the members of the community, would in turn appoint the leaders and other office-holders for two years. The unending strife that accompanied all the elections deepened the involvement of the king and his officials. Jewish self-government did not grow in strength.[51]

NUMBERS OF LEADERS

The number of the various office-holders depended on the size and regime of the community and frequently changed in accordance with political life in the community. The number of the *berurim*—the community leaders, known as *muqademin* or *adelantados* in Aragon and Valencia, and as *ne'emanim* or *secretarii* in Catalonia—varied between three and six. When all three classes were represented the number was naturally three or its multiple. The number of other officers, known by various names—*secretarii*, *prohomens*, or *yo'azim*—was anything between three and thirty.

In Barcelona, for instance, there were six *ne'emanim* or *secretarii* until 1326; at the end of that year the number rose to seven, while according to the 1327 con-

---

[49] ACA, Reg. 86, fos. 136, 157ʳ–158 [=R 2445, 2451]; Reg. 87, fo. 34 [=R 2467].
[50] ACA, Reg. 197, fo. 153ʳ [=R 2745 = Baer, *Spanien*, doc. 146]; Reg. 229, fo. 274 [=R 3434 = Baer, *Spanien*, doc. 188].
[51] ACA, Reg. 230, fos. 59–60 [=R 3442; Chabret, *Sagunto*, pp. 343ff. and doc. viii].

stitution three *secretarii* were elected by the thirty councillors.[52] In Lérida there were five *adelantados* during the thirteenth century.[53] One more had to be added in 1315 when it was decided that the three classes should each have an equal number of *adelantados*. Besides these six, there were also twelve *secretarii*. Three years later, the number of the *secretarii* was reduced to three. This was due to the lack of candidates, particularly because of the prohibition on seeking re-election before the passage of three years.[54] At the beginning of the fourteenth century the council in Lérida numbered ten members.[55]

According to an ordinance from approximately 1290, the community of Saragossa was led by twenty-five *muqademin* and *berurim*, apparently five of the former and twenty of the latter, who constituted the twenty-five-member council or *'eza*.[56] In Huesca until 1313, five *adelantados* and twenty *secretarii* headed the communal administration. Following the reform introduced that year, the numbers were changed, to effect the equal representation of the three classes, to six *adelantados* and twelve *secretarii*. In 1324 the number of the latter was further reduced to six, probably due to the inability of the upper classes to provide new candidates every year who were unrelated to the sitting officers.[57] In Barbastro six *adelantados* led the *aljama* until 1313. With the introduction of the new constitution, nine leaders, representing the three classes, were elected annually. Three served as *adelantados* while six acted as councillors.[58]

In the second half of the thirteenth century, the *aljama* of Valencia was led by three *adelantados* and four or five *secretarii*. By the beginning of the following century the number of holders of each post in the community was a multiple of three. During the brief period when Majorca was part of the Crown of Aragon three *adelantados* ran the affairs of the community.[59]

It appears that the changes in the numbers of communal leaders varied in accordance with the class struggle that took place in Jewish society at the end of the thirteenth century. In the first stage the number increased; subsequently it decreased following the collapse of reform or the claim of the rich that they could not put forward every year a list of new candidates who were unrelated to one another. While the numbers of some office-holders depended generally on the size of the community, efficiency of administration was almost never a decisive factor.

---

[52] ACA, Reg. 228, fo. 70 [= R 3381, 3406 = Baer, *Spanien*, doc. 182]; cf. Baer, *Spanien*, doc. 169; Reg. 229, fo. 193; Reg. 230, fos. 106–7` [= R 3454 = Baer, *Spanien*, doc. 189].

[53] Adret, iii. 425.

[54] ACA, Reg. 212, fos. 30`–31 [= R 3026]; Reg. 216, fos. 83, 84` [= R 3095, 3097].

[55] Asibili (Kapah) 114.

[56] The ordinance was enacted in consultation with R. Aharon Ha-Levi de Na Clara from Barcelona. On the ordinance, see Perfet 388. On the council, see Adret, ii. 33.

[57] ACA, Reg. 210, fo. 79 [= R 2976]; Reg. 225, fo. 280` [= R 3299 = Jacobs 837]; cf. del Arco, 'La aljama judaica', p. 282.

[58] ACA, Reg. 210, fos. 86`–87 [= R 2977].

[59] ACA, Reg. 194, fo. 266 [= R 2623 = Isaacs 74].

TERMS OF OFFICE

Until the end of the thirteenth century, in most communities the leaders remained in office for a period in many cases not limited by any legislation. The community government was in the hands of a few wealthy families who appointed their representatives by rotation. The sources indicate that many communities were led by the same people for very long periods. In 1284, for instance, the leaders of almost all communities in Catalonia, Aragon, and Valencia had already served seven years without interruption.[60] During Alfonso III's reign the situation did not change. According to a document from 1289, the leaders of the Barcelona community had been in power for four years.[61] The long term of office was a characteristic feature of the oligarchic regimes that prevailed throughout the communities.

Before the end of the thirteenth century the term of office was reduced in several communities as constitutional reforms arose out of widespread discontent among the poorer Jews who had no share in the communal administration. As already noted, many communities adopted at the beginning of the fourteenth century regular elections at fixed intervals; several communities enacted ordinances instituting annual elections,[62] and the term of office was now generally one to three years. According to the constitutional reform of 1313 the elections in the Aragonese communities of Huesca and Barbastro were held annually;[63] in Majorca, too, under Aragonese rule, the leaders were elected for a year.[64]

In Lérida, even in the 1315 constitution, which cancelled some of the earlier gains achieved by the lower classes, the one-year term of office remained unchanged until 1319. That year, with the abrogation of almost the entire reform, the leaders were henceforth appointed for six years.[65] This instability of regime was not restricted to Lérida: in the Catalan capital, in the 1327 constitution that left the political power in the hands of the upper classes, the *secretarii* were elected for one or two years, on the decision of the *'eza*, while the councillors were elected every three years.[66]

In the Kingdom of Valencia, the principle of a limited term of office was upheld even when, following serious dissent, the king himself appointed the leaders. The duration of office was not altered in the constitution that was adopted in 1327.[67]

---

[60] ACA, Reg. 43, fos. 29ʽ, 31ʽ [=R 1201, 1204 =MF, II. 2032].
[61] ACA, Reg. 89, fo. 66ʽ [=R 2010].
[62] Adret, v. 284.
[63] ACA, Reg. 210, fos. 79, 86ʽ-87 [=R 2976-7].
[64] ACA, Reg. 194, fo. 266 [=R 2623 =Isaacs 74].
[65] ACA, Reg. 195, fo. 51ʽ [=R 2663 =Baer, *Spanien*, doc. 189]; Reg. 212, fos. 30ʽ-31 [=R 3026]; Reg. 216, fos. 84ʽ, 122ʽ-3 [=R 3097, 3106].
[66] ACA, Reg. 230, fos. 106-7ʽ =R 3454 =Baer, *Spanien*, doc. 189].
[67] ACA, Reg. 86, fo. 131 [=R 2442]; Reg. 87, fo. 34 [=R 2467]; Reg. 229, fo. 274 [=R 3434 =Baer, *Spanien*, doc. 188].

TIME AND PLACE OF ELECTIONS

The Hebrew sources, confirmed by Latin and Romance sources, mention Rosh Hashanah as the accepted time for elections and appointments.[68] All the documents refer to a period prior to the Jewish High Holidays. The elections were not, of course, intended to be held on the festival itself, but on a day close to it. Royal orders concerning forthcoming elections around the New Year were usually sent during August.[69] The constitutions of some communities stated clearly that the elections were held at Rosh Hashanah.[70]

When the electors chose the leaders according to the *ostages* system, they had to stay in a locality outside the town.[71] Such was the case in Lérida until it was decided that every leader would appoint his successor.[72] Otherwise, general elections took place in the synagogue, which was the religious, administrative, social, educational, and political centre of the Jewish community.[73]

It was in the synagogue that the results of the elections were announced. The announcement was an impressive ceremony at a time which was in any case very solemn in the Jewish calendar. The proclamation of the elected leaders in the synagogue was a necessary step before they could take office. In the synagogue, during the service, the *hazan* or *capella*, the official in charge of the divine services, announced to the public the names of the newly elected leaders.[74] The list had to be complete; a partial reading would invalidate the entire procedure.[75] The detailed description of the ceremony in Lérida was more or less true of other communities too. In Valencia, the newly elected leaders took an oath that they would fulfil their duty faithfully. A similar oath was taken by the councillors in Barcelona. It seems that this procedure was adopted in many communities throughout the Crown of Aragon.[76]

RESIGNATION, DISMISSAL, AND DEATH

The vacancy caused by the resignation, dismissal, or death of a leader created a problem requiring immediate attention. The question arose whether there was a need to appoint someone else to the vacant post, and the answer depended on the

---

[68] Adret, iv. 312, v. 284.
[69] ACA, Reg. 210, fos. 79, 86ᵛ–87 [= R 2976–7].
[70] For the constitution of Lérida, see ACA, Reg. 212, fos. 30ᵛ–31 [= R 3026].
[71] Adret, v. 284.
[72] Adret, iii, 422–3.
[73] ACA, Reg. 197, fo. 153ᵛ [= R 2745 = Baer, *Spanien*, doc. 146]; Reg. 229, fo. 274 [= R 3434 = Baer, *Spanien*, doc. 188].
[74] Adret iii. 422, 424, v. 284.
[75] Adret, v. 285, iii. 425.
[76] For Valencia, see ACA, Reg. 229, fo. 274 [= R 3434 = Baer, *Spanien*, doc. 188]; Reg. 230, fos. 106–7ᵛ [= R 3454 = Baer, *Spanien*, doc. 189].

regime prevalent in the community. In most cases the new officer served for the remaining part of the term.

In case of a dismissal of the community leadership en bloc, the king either appointed another team or ordered the community to do so.[77] The same applied to the dismissal of one or several leaders.

The absence of leaders from their home community raised problems, especially where certain decisions had to be taken unanimously or by majority vote of a particular magnitude. Some communities took measures to cope with absentee leaders. The Barcelona constitution of 1327 included a provision for a temporary appointment to fill the post of a councillor who was absent from the city. The appointment was made by a majority vote and required the consent of the *secretarii* and the *dayanim*.[78] The principle behind such a clause was the necessity for a full house for decisions of the board and council. When in 1326 one of the *secretarii* of the Barcelona community died, the remaining six could not continue their work without royal approval. In the end a new *secretarius* was appointed of in place of the deceased.[79]

THE APPOINTMENT OF *DAYANIM*

An essential component of medieval Jewish autonomy was a judiciary incorporating essential parts of Jewish law. The *dayan* or judge, who was supposed to be expert in Jewish law, was an integral part of the system. Despite its universal character, the Jewish court or *beth din* was influenced by local internal and external conditions, and the appointment of the *dayan* was not immune from such influences. In the Crown of Aragon the appointment of the Jewish judges was made by 'royal concession'. The interest of the monarch in the appointment is obvious when it is remembered that part of the fines imposed by the *beth din* reached the king's treasury.

All the monarchs, though they confirmed the right of the Jewish community in principle to appoint its own judges, sometimes nominated their own candidates to the post. In some instances the opposition of the community brought about the king's substitution of his own candidate; in others the appointment was forced on the Jewish public. In 1270, Jaime I appointed Naci Azday as rabbi and judge in the *aljama* of Lérida with the right to co-opt two more people to form a *beth din*.[80] The document mentions no opposition. In Saragossa the king's appointment did not go smoothly. In the early years of his reign, Jaime I had appointed Salamon Alfaquim, a member of the Alconstantini family, as a judge for the Jews of Saragossa and of the whole Kingdom of Aragon. Jahuda de la Cavallería, a

---

[77] ACA, Reg. 86, fo. 131 [=R 2442].
[78] ACA, Reg. 230, fos. 106–7' [=R 3454 =Baer, *Spanien*, doc. 189].
[79] ACA, Reg. 228, fo. 70 [=R 3406]; Reg. 229, fo. 193.
[80] ACA, Reg. 16, fo. 202 [=R 446 =Jacobs 462].

member of a rival family, was at the head of a group of Jews who decided that Salamon should be joined by two more Jews, their nominees, as judges. Their intention was clearly to neutralize Salamon, who had since 1258 appointed his nephew Mosse Alconstantini as his assistant and substitute in the Kingdom of Valencia. It was Mosse who turned to the king in 1271 to punish Jahuda and his party. Mosse lost his case and had to flee.[81] His brother Salamon Alconstantini asked the Queen of Castile to intervene on his behalf at the court of Jaime II to appoint him *jutge o rap* over all the Jews of the Kingdom of Aragon, claiming that he occupied the post under Pedro III and Alfonso III. The king refused to accede to the request because of the opposition of the Jews and the harm that might therefore arise.[82] Another Saragossan Jew, Salamon Avenbruch, who was appointed judge by Pedro III, was murdered in 1284. It is noteworthy that Salamon Avenbruch was himself among those who opposed the claims of Mosse Alconstantini to the post of judge.[83]

Most of Jaime I's reign is characterized by a lack of an established method of appointing judges, and hence by frequent royal interference as the king imposed his own favourites on the communities. Jaime I did, however, come to realize the necessity of regulating the appointment of judges. Grave incidents and growing violence in the *aljama* of Barcelona led him to initiate in 1272 a system whereby the community was empowered to choose two or more judges.[84] In most communities two to three people were appointed to adjudicate between Jews.[85] Some communities insisted that three judges were chosen, as required by Jewish law;[86] others did not do so for lack of suitable candidates. The large communities that did not suffer from a shortage of suitable people were authorized by the king to form a *beth din* of three. Saragossa was naturally one of these.[87]

Pedro III continued the process of regulating the appointment of a properly constituted *beth din*. Saragossa was one of the first communities to be ordered to choose *dayanim*.[88] Judicial appointments during this reign were made in accordance with a special privilege such as that granted in 1280 to all the *aljamas* of Catalonia to elect between two and seven elders as judges. From a later source we know that the Aragonese communities received a similar charter.[89]

---

[81] ACA, Reg. 16, fos. 261ᵛ–262 [= R 461 =Jacobs 483 =Bofarull, Barcelona, ciii].
[82] ACA, Reg. 252, fo. 50 [= R 2551 =Baer, *Spanien*, doc. 136].
[83] For details about his appointment and murder, see ACA, Reg. 46, fo. 184 [= R 1119]; for other sources about his murder see R 1118, 1128, 1144, 1176, 1192, 1224, 1235, 1354.
[84] ACA, Reg. 21, fo. 32ᵛ [= R 517 =Baer, *Spanien*, doc. 106 = Jacobs 634 =Bofarull, Barcelona, cxii].
[85] Adret, iii. 385–6, 390; Assaf, *Courts of Law*, p. 42.
[86] Adret, iii. 418.
[87] ACA, Reg. 16, fo. 240 [= R 458 =Jacobs 474 =Bofarull, Barcelona, cii].
[88] ACA, Reg. 44, fo. 177ᵛ [= R 776 =Baer, *Spanien*, doc. 118].
[89] ACA, Reg. 44, fos. 187ᵛ–188 [= R 823 =Baer, *Spanien*, doc. 121]. For the Aragonese communities see Reg. 197, fo. 19ᵛ [= R 2720 =Baer, *Spanien*, doc. 142].

With the inclusion of Majorca in the Crown of Aragon for a brief period from 1296, the Jewish community there was permitted to appoint three or four judges.[90] These charters were confirmed by later kings. In 1282 the Infante Alfonso issued orders to the community of Egea to abide by his father's charter.[91] In 1299, at the request of the Jews of Saragossa, Jaime II confirmed their right to choose their judges as granted by Pedro III.[92] According to these charters, the judges were elected for one year by the *adelantados*. In the case of Saragossa, Pedro III ordered the community in 1280 to choose, with the consent of the twenty-five councillors or the majority of members, three judges for five years.[93] Following serious disagreements in Lérida, Jaime II modified Pedro's charter in 1297 and decreed that, a month after their election, the *adelantados* should co-opt three elders, and that this group together should appoint the judges for that current year. It appears that the king's decision did not put an end to the conflicts in Lérida, for eight months later the king had to repeat his orders.[94]

In most communities the judges were appointed by the leaders of the community.[95] In some communities, however, for example those of Valencia and Majorca, the *adelantados* acted as judges, that is, appointed themselves to the post. This was possibly due to the lack of competent *dayanim*. At the beginning of the fourteenth century the judges of Valencia were appointed by a twelve-member collegium; in 1327 their number was reduced to six, two of each class, who chose three judges. The elections took place eight days after the general elections in the synagogue, where the councillors remained until the judges had been chosen.[96]

The Hebrew sources do not reveal the full extent of royal involvement in the process of appointing the *dayanim*. The king was equally involved in the appointment of expert Jewish jurists to handle specific trials between Jews. In 1322 Jaime II ordered the baile of Montblanch to appoint two experts in Jewish law for the trial between Jucef Azday, of Gerona, and Mosse Aieig, of Montblanch. Naturally, such interventions were the result of an initiative taken by one of the parties.[97] Despite certain appointments of favourites as judges and frequent temporary allocation of trials to halakhists, on the whole the king's intervention in the appointment of judges, or even his request for Jewish judges and halakhic

---

[90] ACA, Reg. 194, fo. 266 [= R 2623 = Isaacs 74].

[91] ACA, Reg. 59, fo. 56 [= R 942].

[92] Jaime II's modification of the charter for Lérida constituted, in fact, its confirmation. For the confirmation of Saragossa's charter, see ACA, Reg. 197, fo. 19ˇ [= R 2720].

[93] ACA, Reg. 44, fo. 177ˇ [= R 776 = Baer, *Spanien*, doc. 118].

[94] ACA, Reg. 195, fo. 44 [= R 2629 = Baer, *Spanien*, doc. 139]. The orders were repeated in February 1298. See Reg. 256, fo. 28 [= R 2680].

[95] See e.g. the charter granted to the Jews of Alcolea de Cinca by the Infante Alfonso in 1320: ACA, Reg. 383, fos. 40–2 [= Baer, *Spanien*, doc. 175].

[96] ACA, Reg. 229, fo. 274 [= R 3434 = Baer, *Spanien*, doc. 188 = Jacobs 878].

[97] ACA, CR, Jaime II, C 133, no. 26 [= *Cartas Reales*, no. 248].

authorities of the calibre of R. Shelomo ben Adret, were not meant to weaken the Jewish judiciary.[98]

THE APPOINTMENT OF SPECIAL *BERURIM* AND *NE'EMANIM*

Certain positions in the community leadership were considered sufficiently important or delicate to necessitate special provisions for the election or appointment of their holders. Such a post was that of the *barurim daveros* in Catalonia in the fourteenth century. This post, which reached its full development under Pedro IV,[99] was established during the reign of Jaime II, when Jews began to appoint *berurim* whose task was to eradicate transgressions against Jewish law. The appointment was made with the consent of the royal authorities.[100] The post spread also in some neighbouring communities in Aragon.[101] We have no information on the method of the appointment of the *berure 'averot*, although it may be reasonably assumed that they were chosen by their fellow *berurim*.

In some communities special *ne'emanim* for tax collection were appointed.[102] Their number varied in accordance with the size of the community, and the method of their appointment differed from one community to another. As the position was considered highly influential, in certain communities the election of the *ne'emanim* for tax collection was different from that of the other *ne'emanim*. In some *aljamas* they were appointed by a specially constituted electoral college;[103] in others they were chosen by lottery from a list of candidates. In Valencia five tax *ne'emanim* were appointed in such a manner from among twenty candidates, from the richest families, who were chosen by the public. In 1300, as part of the process of democratization, four electors from each of the three classes elected the three tax-collectors, one from each of the three classes.[104] Unable to reach agreement on the election of tax-collectors and assessors or collectors of specific taxes, some communities petitioned the king to decide on the matter. Thus in 1322, the *aljama* of Barbastro asked the king to see to the appointment of two to three Jews for the collection of the *cisa*.[105]

In thirteenth-century Saragossa the tax-collectors were elected annually by the community. Before the protest movement of the poorer classes in 1263 they all belonged to the upper class. After an interim period of instability the three

---

[98] For trials or cases referred to judges or famous halakhists, see ACA, Reg. 60, fo. 33 [= R 1017]; Reg. 43, fo. 24` [= R 1192 = Baer, *Spanien*, doc. 127].

[99] Baer, *Spanien*, doc. 205; 2; p. 412; doc. 317; doc. 338, 2; p. 546.

[100] For the institution under Jaime II, see Riera and Udina, 'Els documents en hebreu', pp. 21–36. See also Adret, iv. 311, viii. 279 [= Assaf, *Punishments*, no. 57].

[101] For Jaca, see Adret, iii. 318. [102] Adret, v. 283. [103] Adret, iii. 399.

[104] Adret, iii. 417. For the reformed system of 1300, see ACA, Reg. 197, fos. 153`–154 [= R 2745 = Baer, *Spanien*, doc. 146].

[105] ACA, CR, Jaime II, C 133, no. 18 [=*Cartas Reales*, no. 242].

collectors represented the three classes.[106] In Calatayud, the Jews were authorized to choose four tax-collectors. In Teruel, in the years 1310–13, there were two *collidores*. In 1325, four to five *berurim* were elected to handle the taxes.[107] Even when the poorer classes succeeded in having representatives among the tax-collectors, the rich did not lose their paramount influence at court. Thus in 1320 Jaime II decided that the Avenfalaud family should have its representative join the collectors when they deliberated on its share of the tax.[108]

In 1285 Pedro III introduced an important change in the composition and election of the tax-assessors in the Aragonese communities. Henceforth his official would choose two to three members in every community to supervise the tax tests and fix the tax of every tax-payer.[109]

In Lérida the tax-collectors were chosen by the *adelantados*.[110] In 1285 Pedro III ordered the *aljamas* of Villafranca, Tarragona, Montblanch, and Cervera, all constituent communities of the *collecta* of Barcelona, to choose two or three persons per *aljama* who would be in charge of submitting to the secretaries of the *aljama* of Barcelona the accounts of the taxes of their members.[111] The 1327 constitution of Barcelona stipulated that no Jew should seek any position, including that of *tatxador*, in the community administration. The councillors elected annually three *tatxadors* and two *sobratatxadors*.[112]

In some communities accountants were appointed by the *adelantados* or the councillors. At the beginning of the fourteenth century in Murviedro, the accountants were appointed by a six-member council, representing equally the three classes.[113] At that time, five *recebedores de compte* in Barcelona were appointed by a majority vote of the council of thirty.[114]

THE APPOINTMENT OF COMMUNAL FUNCTIONARIES

In principle the administrative body of the *aljama*, that is the *berurim* and the *ne'emanim*, the *muqademin* or the *adelantados*, appointed and dismissed the various functionaries whose salaries were paid from the communal budget or assets. Some of the functionaries were engaged by contract for a limited period, while others were employed with no legally binding document.

The appointment of the *albedi* or *bedin* in Aragonese communities, where he

---

[106] ACA, Reg. 12, fo. 148 [=R 245 =Jacobs 277 =Baer, *Spanien*, doc. 98].
[107] Baer, *Spanien*, doc. 163; ACA, Reg. 227, fo. 191ᵛ [=R 3333].
[108] On the appointment of the collectors, see ACA, Reg. 13, fos. 184ᵛ–185 [=R 267 =Jacobs 293]. On the privilege granted to the Avenfalaud family, see ACA, Reg. 218, fos. 92ᵛ–93 [=R 3135 =Baer, *Spanien*, doc. 174].
[109] ACA, Reg. 43, fo. 111ʳᵛ [=R 1266 =Baer, *Spanien*, doc. 128, 1].
[110] ACA, Reg. 15, fo. 96ᵛ [=R 378 =Jacobs 418 =Bofarull, Barcelona, lxv].
[111] ACA, Reg. 57, fo. 215 [=R 1452].
[112] ACA, Reg. 230, fos. 106–7ᵛ [=R 3454 =Baer, *Spanien*, doc. 189].
[113] ACA, Reg. 230, fo. 59 [=R 3442].
[114] ACA, Reg. 230, fo. 106–7ᵛ [=R 3454 =Baer, *Spanien*, doc. 189].

fulfilled some sort of a police task, including the collection of fines, was sometimes a controversial issue in the community, leading on occasion to royal intervention. The appointment was made with the baile's knowledge and consent. In 1310–13 the communities of Daroca and Luna dismissed their *albedin* and appointed another one without, however, informing the baile of their move,[115] and were fined as a consequence.

The intervention of the king in the appointment of synagogue functionaries seems at first sight surprising. For example, only in 1320 were the Jews of Saragossa promised that the king would not intervene in the appointment of the rabbis of their synagogues and the *shohatim* of the community.[116] In 1315 there were two candidates for the post of rabbi in Lérida. Çadia Abenaçaya was Jaime II's candidate, while the *aljama* presented another candidate, Mosse Jumiz, who obtained an absolute majority. The baile, who informed the king about the results, also sent him the full lists of the voters for both candidates.[117] In 1321 the *aljama* of Valencia protested at the appointment of its slaughterers by the king's scribe. The latter acted, no doubt, with the king's blessing. When the *aljama* told Jaime II that the scribe's action contradicted his grandfather's explicit privilege, the king refused to cancel the appointment but promised that after the death of the scribe, the *aljama* would once again appoint its own slaughterers.[118] In fact, the ruler constantly interfered in the choice of these appointments and no promise could guarantee the community complete freedom of action. The king's interest was twofold. There were obvious financial considerations in the appointment of slaughterers, while the post of rabbi was a convenient one with which to reward Jews for services rendered.

The *berurim* and the *ne'emanim* usually appointed the *darshan*, the *hazan*, and the *shamash*. There was no accepted form of appointment, and the matter therefore led to internal strife and external interference. In Tárrega, for instance, when the administration did not succeed in choosing a *hazan*, the king accepted the proposal that the appointment should be made by the entire congregation by a majority vote.[119] The dismissal of a synagogue functionary could also result in royal interference. In 1325 some of the leaders of Saragossa intended to dismiss the *rabisse* of the *sinagoga mayor*, Ceti, who had worked there for over twenty years. The *rabisse* sought the help of the Infante Alfonso, who ordered the *adelantados* not to permit her dismissal.[120]

As the work of the *sofer* or the scribe involved receiving payments of fees for documents drawn up according to Jewish law and certain notarial activities for which the parties needed registration from the Jewish authorities, the post was very much in demand. The scribe's activities were also a source of income to both

---

[115] Baer, *Spanien*, doc. 163.   [116] ACA, Reg. 218, fo. 155^v [= R 3144].
[117] ACA, CR, Jaime II, C 43, no. 5313 [=*Cartas Reales*, no. 186].
[118] ACA, Reg. 219, fos. 214^v–215 [= R 3168].   [119] Adret, v. 273.
[120] ACA, CR, Jaime II, C 133, no. 125 [=*Cartas Reales*, no. 343]. On the possible meaning of *rabisse*, see below.

Elections and Appointments

the king and the community. The king's frequent involvement in the appointment of a scribe and the monopoly that the king granted to Jewish scribes are naturally related to the financial benefits that he could derive. Jaime II, for instance, gave Jahuda son of Astrug Bonsenyor the monopoly over all the Hebrew documents drawn up in Barcelona.[121] In 1307 Jaime II appointed the Jewish scribe in Barbastro.[122] Rabi Azariam, the scribe and notary of the *aljama* of Saragossa, was so busy in his medical work that the king permitted him to appoint a replacement or deputy.[123] It is clear, therefore, that the Jewish scribe or notary was appointed by the king. The reason was purely financial. In 1318 Jaime II appointed Jaffuda Acdarra as the scribe of the *aljama* of Valencia for life; the post was to remain in the hands of his descendants. Jaffuda had to pay the king a certain amount per annum for this lifelong position. Nine years later, Jaffuda passed the post to two other Jews whose greed and lack of understanding aroused bitter opposition in the community.[124]

Other functionaries, including charity officers or *almoyners*, were appointed by the leaders of the community, who also chose the representatives or delegates of their *aljama*.[125] It was also the *berurim* who appointed people for special missions. Thus the community of Monzón appointed members whose task was to collect the debts and interest due to members of the community.[126]

EXEMPTION FROM POWER AND SERVICE

An unusual aspect of the political life of the Jewish community was the attempt by some Jews to be freed from any political or administrative duties or positions. In some communities those appointed or elected to a post had to accept the nomination; however, the king could grant an exemption. The ordinance prohibiting duly appointed individuals from refusing office was enacted following the shortage of candidates in some communities, and has a long history in Sephardi communities, as can be seen in the *haskamot* of many of them after the expulsion. There was a variety of reasons for the refusal of some Jews to accept nomination to positions in the community. Its origins go back to the thirteenth century, when many Jews served the ruler in various capacities and had no time for politics in the Jewish community. Moreover, the growing responsibility of communal leadership and the heavy punishments and fines imposed on Jewish leaders whose community failed to satisfy the ruler deterred many potential candidates. In view of the rules that restricted re-election, and the small number of candidates from the

---

[121] ACA, Reg. 194, fo. 108ᵛ [= R 2556].
[122] Kayserling, 'Critical Notes', p. 491.   [123] ACA, Reg. 211, fo. 220 [= R 3001]
[124] For his appointment, see ACA, Reg. 232, fo. 352ᵛ [= R 3081]. For the transfer of the post, see ACA, Reg. 229, fo. 274ᵛ [= R 3435 = Jacobs 879].
[125] Adret, iii. 394, v. 283; ACA, Reg. 230, fos. 106–7ᵛ [= R 3454 = Baer, *Spanien*, doc. 189].
[126] Adret, iii. 300, 416.

upper class available to fill the required posts, the concern of the community to restrict this trend is readily understandable. It is difficult to assess the extent of this trend, as the archival sources primarily contain information about those instances where the king agreed to exempt the applicant from any office. Likewise, royal decisions against those who refused to take office do not provide exact figures.

The communities needed the king's support to ensure that none of its members refused the post to which he was elected. In 1280 the three leaders elected in Saragossa refused to take office; Pedro III ordered his baile to force the three to fill their posts.[127] The community was not, however, always fortunate enough to obtain the king's support. Royal policy was not consistent, changing in accordance with various pragmatic considerations. Alfonso III, for instance, in 1286 asked the community of Saragossa not to appoint the two brothers, Vidal and Ismael Thercullut, to any office against their will. The same king sent instructions in 1289 to the Jews of Saragossa that all those elected to office must fulfil their tasks without fail.[128]

At the end of the thirteenth century one of the rich Jews of Valencia, who had announced his wish not to become a *ne'eman*, was elected to the post. Adret, who was asked about the individual's right not to serve the community, declared that 'no one had the right to free himself from the ordinances and decisions of the public.'[129] Several communities had enacted an ordinance forbidding any member to refuse serving in any post. Nevertheless, many Jews did ask the king to exempt them from communal office. In 1314, taking into consideration the applicant's heavy medical duties, the king exempted Omar Tahuyl, a Jewish physician from Valencia, from any work or position in the community. The exemption was renewed in 1317. Some three months later, in 1318, Tahuyl's son Abraham, also a physician, received a similar exemption.[130] Also in 1318 two brothers of Valencia, Içach and Abraffim Abnayub, were given three years' exemption from serving as leaders in their community. The same day a Valencian Jew, called Juceff son of Jaffudan Abnayo, received an unlimited exemption. The three were most probably brothers, since their father's name was Jaffuda. In 1320 Abraffim had his exemption renewed.[131] Abraffim had good reason to keep away from communal politics: he had served as *baror* in the years 1294–1304 and as a member of the administration that was accused of corruption was subsequently heavily fined.[132]

---

[127] ACA, Reg. 48, fos. 117, 119ᵛ [=R 829, 833].
[128] On the privilege granted to the two brothers, see ACA, Reg. 66, fo. 100ᵛ [=R 1571]. His instructions of 1289 are found in Reg. 80, fo. 46ᵛ [=R 2000].   [129] Adret, iii. 417.
[130] On Omar Tahuyl, see ACA, Reg. 211, fo. 235ᵛ [=R 3005]; Reg. 215, fo. 185ᵛ [=R 3075]; on Abraham, see Reg. 215, fo. 254ᵛ [=R 3083].
[131] ACA, Reg. 215, fos. 215ᵛ, 222 [=R 3079–80]; on the renewal of Abraffim's exemption, see Reg. 219, fos. 191ᵛ–192 [=R 3159]; on their father's name see also n. 132 below.
[132] ACA, Reg. 202, fo. 203 [=R 2833].

The same pattern was found elsewhere in the Crown of Aragon. In Saragossa the Jewish physician and rabbi Salamo Avenjacob received an exemption in 1302 just as his colleague Baron Almelich did in 1303, so that they could more easily devote themselves to their profession.[133] In 1316 Jaime II informed the same *aljama* that Jahuda Golluf was freed for a year from any communal task since he served as the guardian of his nephews.[134] The number of Jews in Saragossa who were permitted not to hold office was so high in the first quarter of the fourteenth century that it was seen as a serious stumbling-block for the efficient running of communal government. The community had no option but to turn for help to the monarch who was, of course, the source of all exemptions from office. The situation must have been very serious, for in 1326 Jaime II cancelled all such exemptions.[135]

Meanwhile, Jews in other Aragonese communities were equally determined to avoid communal politics and responsibility. In 1311, for instance, Jaime II ordered the *aljama* of Huesca to uphold the privilege that Queen Blanca had granted to the two brothers David and Jossuas Abnarrabi, both local silversmiths and jewellers, to exempt them from appointment as tax-collectors. The following day, the king advised the same *aljama* that Çalema Çuri, a silk manufacturer, and Abrahim Cucumbrell were to be similarly free from appointment to the post of tax-collector. In the case of Çalema Çuri the reason is explicit: he provided silk to the royal family. It does not require much imagination to suppose that the brothers Abnarrabi, too, found favour in the queen's eyes thanks to some beautiful jewels they provided to the ladies of the court.[136]

It is clear that in all matters connected with elections and appointments in the Jewish communities, it was ultimately his own interest that determined the extent of the king's involvement and the community's degree of self-rule.

[133] ACA, CR, Jaime II, C 14, no. 1828 [=*Cartas Reales*, no. 99]; Reg. 201, fo. 21 [=R 2820].
[134] ACA, Reg. 213, fo. 253 [=R 3056].   [135] ACA, Reg. 228, fo. 35ʼ [=R 3369 =Jacobs 853].
[136] ACA, Reg. 207, fo. 242ʼ [=R 2921]; Reg. 208, fo. 9 [=R 2922].

§2.4 Leaders and Leadership

LEADERS IN THEIR COMMUNITY

LEADERSHIP in the Jewish communities of the Crown of Aragon did not differ essentially from that in the rest of the medieval Jewish world. All medieval Jewish communities shared common characteristics and traditions of self-rule which exercised a profound impact on patterns of leadership that had to be adjusted to exilic conditions. To be a leader under almost absolute obedience to the ruler of the land was a universal Jewish feature. In such circumstances all leaders had to assert their authority in their communities. In some, traditions of royal or princely descent helped immensely to establish authority and command respect. In others, leaders had to rely heavily on well-developed Jewish concepts of leadership. In all forms, the authority of Jewish leaders was ultimately dependent on the nature and extent of support lent to them by the non-Jewish rulers. This close relationship between the Gentile government and the Jewish leadership was an important factor that distinguished between the leaders of different communities. Leaders and leadership in the Jewish communities in the different parts of the Crown of Aragon were affected by local practices and conditions; and yet at the same time all were subjected to the policies and preferences of a single ruler. These contradictory trends in the external influences on Jewish leadership necessitate careful analysis to identify those features common throughout the Crown and those specific to each of the component territories.

TERMINOLOGY

Various names in different languages are used in the sources to describe the leaders of the Jewish communities in the Crown of Aragon. The Hebrew, Latin, Catalan, and Aragonese names are confusing and are not necessarily synonymous. So far no definitive description has been given, and a discussion of the terms employed is necessary.[1] The Hebrew texts employ the following terms: *berurim, ne'emanim, muqademin,* and *yo'azim.* In Latin sources we find *probi homines, procuratorii, adenantati,* and *secretarii.* Their almost-equivalents in Catalan and Aragonese sources are respectively *sindichs, prohomens, adelantats, secretaris* and *procuradores, adelantados* or *delantados,* and *secretarios.*

[1] The subject has been treated in the following works: Loeb, 'Les Administrations', pp. 263–4; Elfenbein, 'Jewish Communal Government', pp. 102–3; Neuman, *Jews in Spain,* i, pp. 35ff.; Baer, *History,* i, pp. 217–18; Beinart, 'Hispano-Jewish Society', pp. 220–38.

Leaders and Leadership

It is very difficult to establish the equivalence between the Hebrew terms and the terms in the other languages. An examination of the Hebrew sources seems to indicate that the term *baror* (plural *berurim*) had the widest and the most general meaning. It denoted the elected or appointed leaders of the community. All the leaders were called *berurim*, but those with special duties had additional titles, sometimes compound ones including the word *baror*. Some *berurim*, those who had a specialized judicial field, fulfilled the task of a judge or *dayan*.[2] Some dealt with civil complaints between fellow Jews, called in Hebrew *tar'omot*.[3] There were also *berurim* whose duty was to eradicate religious and criminal offences;[4] from the fourteenth century onwards these were known as *berure 'averot*.[5] Other *berurim* were in charge of the finances of the community,[6] the collection of its taxes,[7] and weights and measures.[8]

In time, with the growing number of functions assumed by the larger communities, the division of the functions became more institutionalized. Those who served as judges were known as *berure hadayanim*.[9] The civil magistrates were known as *berure tevi'ot* or, as in one Latin source, *berurim de tauioz*. One of the earliest references to the post goes back to 1282.[10] Mention has already been made of the *berure 'averot* who were appointed to deal with criminal and religious cases. In many instances, the contents of the source indicate the *baror*'s special duty in the Jewish administration.

It is obvious that the term *baror* covers more than one term in non-Hebrew sources. There are several sources which help us to clarify the term. A document from 1282, referring to the *adelantados* of the community of Saragossa acting as judges, says explicitly that in Hebrew they are called '*borurim*'.[11] In another document from the same year the *adelantados* of Gerona are also given by their Hebrew name, *berurim de tauioz*, as mentioned above.[12] In 1286, the *secretarii* of the *aljamas* of Gerona and Besalú are also called by their Hebrew name *berurim*.[13] A comparison between the ordinances of Barcelona from the end of the thirteenth

---

[2] Adret, iii. 385 [= Assaf, *Courts of Law*, p. 42], 393, v, 261, 290 [= Assaf, *Punishments*, no. 53]; ACA, Reg. 43, fo. 58 [=R 1229].

[3] Adret, iii. 386, 388.

[4] Adret, iv. 311 = viii. 279 [= Assaf, *Courts of Law*, no. 57], i. 1187.

[5] ACA, Reg. 599, fo. 127ʳ [= Baer, *Spanien*, doc. 205, 2]; Baer, *Spanien*, doc. 412; Reg. 931, fos. 141–4ʾ [= Baer, *Spanien*, doc. 317]; Reg. 1271, fo. 2ʾ [Baer, *Spanien*, doc. 338, 2]; Reg. 941, fo. 55ʾ [= Baer, *Spanien*, doc. 355]; Baer, *Spanien*, doc. 546; Reg. 1815, fos. 51ʾ–52 [= Baer, *Spanien*, doc. 386]; Reg. 2041, fo. 70ʾ [= Baer, *Spanien*, doc. 447].

[6] Adret, iii. 386–7.

[7] Adret, v. 221–2.

[8] Adret, i. 590.

[9] Asibili (Kapah) 156.

[10] For the 1282 source, see below; for later sources see ACA, Reg. 1271, fo. 2ʾ [= Baer, *Spanien*, doc. 338, 2]; Baer, *Spanien*, p. 546; Reg. 1815, fos. 51ʾ–52 [= Baer, *Spanien*, doc. 386].

[11] ACA, Reg. 59, fo. 67ʾ [=R 947].

[12] ACA, Reg. 59, fo. 115ʾ [=R 974 = Baer, *Spanien*, doc. 123].

[13] ACA, Reg. 64, fo. 17ʾ [=R 1503].

century and the 1327 constitution of the same community shows also that the terms *baror* and *secretarius* denoted the same post.[14] Thus it can be definitely established that the term *berurim*, which applied to leaders in general, was equivalent in many instances to the terms *adelantat* or *adelantado* and *secretarius*.

In Catalan *aljamas*, and particularly in the *collecta* of Barcelona, the members of the executive body were called the *secretarii*, while in Hebrew sources their name was *ne'emanim*.[15] Outside Catalonia, in Aragonese and Valencian communities, both terms, *adelantado* and *secretarius*, are found. While the term *adelantados* was invariably used in Aragon and Valencia as the equivalent of the Hebrew *muqademin*, in more than one community we come across both terms. The reference in the same sources to *adelantados* and *secretarios* serving in the same community suggests that outside some of the Catalan communities, particularly those of the *collecta* of Barcelona, a distinction was made between the two posts.[16]

Following the constitutional reform a new institution, the council, was formed in many communities in Catalonia and Aragon. The council, known in Hebrew as the *'eza* and in the Romance languages as *concejo* or *concell*, was modelled on an institution bearing the same name in Christian cities. The council appears for the first time in the second half of the thirteenth century.[17]

LEADERS AND THEIR DUTIES

All the affairs of the community fell under the jurisdiction of the leaders. Our information on the various functions fulfilled by the leaders is derived from a variety of sources which do not necessarily reflect the reality of communal life in its correct proportions. For instance, the documents emanating from the court naturally provide ample data on the leaders' work in all the stages of the collection of the royal taxes, while the responsa tend to emphasize far more their administrative work within the *judería*.

Documents that give us a full picture of the *berurim*'s duties are rare.[18] One such document was the charter that Pedro III granted the *aljamas* of Catalonia in July 1280. The Catalan *aljamas* were authorized to choose between two and seven *probos homines* who would be in charge of all judicial matters, legislative work, and

[14] Adret, v. 284; ACA, Reg. 230, fos. 106–7ʳ [= R 3454 = Baer, *Spanien*, doc. 189].

[15] On the term and the post see Loeb, 'Les Administrations', 263–4.

[16] See Asibili (Kapah) 157 (the source is from 1296) and ACA, Reg. 59, fo. 78 [= R 961 = MF, ii, 1551]; Reg. 74, fo. 66 [= R 1852] (the sources are from 1282 and 1288 respectively and refer to Valencia); Reg. 46, fo. 154ʳ [= R 1110] (Lérida, 1284). It should be noted that in more than one field the Jews of Lérida, a bone of contention between Catalonia and Aragon for some time before its final inclusion in the former, were subjected to influences from both east and west.

[17] For the earliest references to the *'eza* as an already established institution, see Adret, ii. 33 and ACA, Reg. 44, fo. 177ʳ [= R 776 = Baer, *Spanien*, doc. 118] for Saragossa and Adret, v. 284 for Barcelona.

[18] Unless another term is required by the specific context, *berurim* or 'leaders' is used throughout this section.

administrative affairs in their communities.[19] The legislative work consisted mostly of enacting ordinances in accordance with the needs of the community.[20] Their authority to enact ordinances was backed by their right to proclaim the ban against any transgressor.[21]

The elected leaders were also in charge of all the economic activities in which members of their community were engaged. The *secretarii* of the Catalan *aljamas* obtained from Pedro III and Alfonso III charters permitting their members to engage in economic activities almost without restriction.[22] The *berurim* supervised the various institutions of the *aljama*, including the synagogue, the slaughterhouse, and the like.[23] Various other aspects of the religious life of the community also came under their supervision and responsibility.[24] They represented their community on any occasion and on any subject, at court or before any other authority.[25] There was almost no field affecting the Jewish public that lay outside the jurisdiction of the *berurim*, although in certain matters their authority was limited.

AUTHORITY AND JURISDICTION

The *berurim* and all other leaders, whatever their titles, enjoyed the authority vested in them by the ruler and the community. Specific charters were issued to different communities enabling their elected leaders to rule and take measures against members who failed to abide by their decisions. Communities enacted ordinances to ensure that the public observed the leaders' decisions and respected their authority. A most severe punishment was reserved for Jews who disobeyed the leaders and turned to the non-Jewish authorities for support. Such people were denounced and treated as *malshinim* or informers, and could even be executed under emergency regulations.[26] Another form of punishment was to put disobedient members and law-breakers under ban in all its forms: *niduy* or *herem*.[27]

The authority granted by Jaime I to the four *adelantados* he appointed after the crisis of 1263–4 in Saragossa emanated on the one hand from the royal document itself, demanding that all members abide by the decisions of their leaders, and on

[19] ACA, Reg. 44, fos. 187ᵛ–188 [= R 823 = Baer, *Spanien*, doc. 121].
[20] ACA, Reg. 195, fo. 44 [= R 2629 = Baer, *Spanien*, doc. 139]; Asibili (Kapah) 114; Perfet 388 [= Baer, *Spanien*, doc. 143, 14].
[21] ACA, Reg. 216, fo. 55ᵛ [= R 3091].
[22] ACA, Reg. 83, fo. 53ʳᵛ [= R 2141].
[23] ACA, Reg. 292, fos. 245ᵛ–246ᵛ [= Baer, *Spanien*, doc. 185].
[24] Leaders of some communities, for instance, took care that their Hebrew books should not be confiscated for unpaid debts: ACA, Reg. 83, fos. 55, 113 [= R 2147, 2308].
[25] ACA, Reg. 85, fo. 87ᵛ [= R 85], fo. 87ᵛ [= R 2262].
[26] For the authority bestowed on the *berurim* by the community see Adret, viii. 279; for punishment inflicted on disobedient Jews see Adret, viii. 240.
[27] ACA, Reg. 87, fo. 57 [= R 2473].

the other hand from a Hebrew document on which it was explicitly based, expressing the will of the Jewish community and drawn up jointly by the Jews and Jahuda de la Cavallería, the Jewish baile of the city.[28] The authority of the *adelantados* was greatly enhanced by the king's support, but this added strength could easily turn into weakness should the king use his power in the opposite direction.[29] The authority and prestige of the community leaders were greatly reduced when the king granted privileges to his favourite Jews and their families, putting them in many respects outside the communal leaders' jurisdiction.[30] The king was primarily interested in ensuring that the Jews' leaders had all the necessary power to collect taxes and punish anyone who failed to abide by their decisions, but the Jewish leaders used royal support to the full to establish their authority in every field of communal life. Hence the interest of the Jewish leadership in seeking the confirmation of royal charters.[31]

The king's support for the leaders in their clashes with members of the community was of crucial importance for the maintenance of their authority, just as his decision to exclude certain Jews from their jurisdiction had the gravest consequences for that authority. The king's help was vital in communities where disobedience was widespread, for example in enabling the leaders of the community to assert their authority over Jews who refused to take the oath or accept any communal responsibility or position.[32] Also noteworthy was the king's sympathetic attitude towards the grievances and claims of the poorer classes, as opposed to the policy of the *adelantados*. The king's favourable attitude towards this challenge to the leaders' authority had some serious repercussions in Aragonese communities where the opposition was strongest.[33]

In times of serious crisis affecting the authority of the *berurim* and involving a large number of members, drastic measures were needed. The crisis of 1263–4 in Saragossa, when the poor members of the community challenged the old aristocratic leadership, was followed by some constitutional reform, as has been noted above.[34] Around 1290 a number of Jews in Valencia complained against the leaders of their community over some money matter. The king appointed a commission of eleven people to arbitrate between the plaintiffs and the leaders. The commission declared the claims of Isach Abingalell, Juceff Alorqui and Jonas, Vidal, and Açach Çibili to be legitimate and ordered the leaders of the community

---

[28] ACA, Reg. 13, fo. 163 [= R 253 = Jacobs 279].

[29] For royal support lent to the *berurim*, see ACA, Reg. 20, fo. 312ᵛ [= R 650 = Jacobs 608]; Reg. 70, fo. 129ᵛ [= R 1731]; for the king's support of individuals against the leaders, see Reg. 59, fos. 67ᵛ, 74ᵛ [= R 947, 954–6]; Reg. 43, fo. 24ᵛ [= R 1193]; Reg. 57, fo. 181 [= R 1424].

[30] ACA, Reg. 74, fo. 78ᵛ [= R 1880].

[31] A charter given to the *aljama* of Barcelona by Jaime I in 1266 was confirmed by Jaime II at the request of the Jewish delegates in 1321: ACA, Reg. 219, fo. 208ʳᵛ [= R 355].

[32] For the king's support see ACA, Reg. 13, fo. 274 [= R 335]; Reg. 83, fo. 87ᵛ [= R 2227]; for protection to individuals see Reg. 37, fo. 31ᵛ [= R 495 = Jacobs 725].

[33] ACA, Reg. 81, fo. 9 [= R 2060].

[34] Assis, 'Crisis'; id., 'Social Unrest'.

to pay them various sums of money. The leaders did not pay until complaints reached Alfonso III.[35]

The king used the *adelantados* to give effect to his wishes pertaining to individuals and groups within the Jewish community. The use of the community leaders to carry out the king's personal favours to individuals, often in breach of law and custom, did not contribute to their authority.[36]

The leaders of the community saw themselves as the representatives of the Jewish public and spoke on its behalf whenever the need arose.[37] They turned to the king to seek his help or support on many issues affecting Jewish life in the community, and at times to request his help for Jews of other localities.[38]

The most obvious task of the *berurim* was to administer the affairs of the community. They generally enjoyed broad rights in this respect, including the right to delegate certain duties to members of their community. In most communities members had no right to refuse the duty they were asked to fulfil; therefore, from time to time the *berurim* would be ordered to exempt from such duties Jewish favourites of the kings.[39]

The *berurim* or the *adelantados* and *secretarii* fulfilled certain constitutional and political duties in their community. The *secretarii* in Barcelona fixed the date of the convention of the Council of Thirty and determined the synagogue in which the meeting was to take place. Together with the *dayanim*, the *secretarii* appointed a replacement for any absentee councillor, as thirty members had to be in post at all times. Any differences of opinion among the *secretarii* on the choice of candidate were settled by the *dayanim*. This triple interdependence of *secretarii*, *dayanim*, and councillors was designed to ensure continuity, stability, and mutual control, though not necessarily efficiency, in the Jewish community. The *secretarii* or the *ne'emanim* in Catalonia, the *adelantados* or the *muqademin* in Aragon, acted as the executive body of the community. The community leaders, in consultation with the councillors, appointed the delegates of the *aljama*.[40] Until the end of the thirteenth century, the *berurim* in Valencia elected the *ne'emanim* (or *secretarii*).[41] The *berurim* in most communities appointed the various officials of the community, sometimes together with other members.

The authority of the *berurim* extended beyond the limits of their own *judería* to cover Jews who lived in surrounding settlements. Similarly, the leaders of the chief community in the *collecta* had a certain jurisdiction over the satellite

---

[35] ACA, Reg. 81, fos. 173–5 [= R 2187–9]; Reg. 84, fo. 18ʳ [= R 2297].
[36] ACA, CR, Jaime II, C 133, no. 116 [= *Cartas Reales*, no. 337].
[37] Corbella, *La aljama*, p. 205, doc. 54.
[38] ACA, Reg. 200, fo. 140 [= R 2800]; Reg. 203, fo. 189ʳ [= R 2860 = Jacobs 752].
[39] ACA, Reg. 59, fo. 75ʳ [= R 957].
[40] ACA, Reg. 230, fos. 106–107ʳ [= R 3454 = Baer, *Spanien*, doc. 189 = Jacobs 892]; Adret, iii. 402.
[41] ACA, Reg. 86, fos. 136, 157ʳ–158 [= R 2445, 2451]; Reg. 87, fo. 34 [= R 2467].

communities, just as those of the *aljama* of the capital had authority over the rest of the territory.[42]

The leaders were in charge of all properties that belonged to the community. They administered and took care of buildings used for public purposes and let or leased other properties that were not used by the community.[43] A substantial part of the communal property was bequeathed to the *aljama* by members. The leaders were responsible for the maintenance of the entire Jewish quarter and for the repairs of its walls.[44]

The *berurim* performed several administrative tasks for the king. They were usually required to make the king's announcements in public and proclaim the ban on any member who did not comply with a royal decision. The king made full use of the administrative mechanism headed by the *berurim* for any purpose connected with Jews, for the system was free, time-saving, and efficient.[45]

THE COLLECTION OF TAXES

The most important work the *berurim* performed was the collection of the taxes for the king's treasury. That this was so from the king's point of view can be easily deduced from the abundance of documents on the subject that were dispatched from his chancellery. The use of the *berurim* as a tax-collecting mechanism saved time and money for the royal treasury; and was far more efficient than any alternative. If the *berurim* were to act on the king's behalf, a formal arrangement would have to be established with the Jewish community. Accordingly, in 1286 Alfonso III authorized all the *aljamas* of Aragon, Catalonia, and Valencia to employ their *adelantados* and other officers for the collection of taxes.[46] The next step for the king was to lend the leaders his full support in fulfilling their tasks, and most particularly in the apportionment and collection of the taxes due to him.

The apportionment of taxes among the taxpayers was not an easy job, and the *adelantados* relied heavily upon the support of the king in determining the shares of the total to be borne by all tax-paying members. His support gave them additional authority that was sometimes desperately needed for this task.[47] It was no easier to collect the taxes and hand them over to the king. Here, too, the latter's help proved to be very effective.[48] The *berurim* of the capital or the head

---

[42] The sources on the subject are abundant. See ACA, Reg. 67, fo. 80ᵛ [= R 1641]; Reg. 198, fo. 310 [= R 2757]; Reg. 217, fo. 148ᵛ [= R 3114]; Reg. 222, fo. 63ᵛ [= R 3233].

[43] ACA, Reg. 16, fos. 202ᵛ, 232 [= R 445, 457 = Jacobs 463, 471 = Bofarull, Barcelona, ci].

[44] For the repairs of the *call*'s walls undertaken by the *secretarii* of Barcelona in 1287, see ACA, Reg. 70, fo. 37ʳᵛ [= R 1722].   [45] ACA, Reg. 63, fo. 40 [= R 1490].

[46] ACA, Reg. 66, fo. 28 [= R 1518, 1522].

[47] ACA, Reg. 57, fo. 187 [= R 1432]; Reg. 64, fo. 17ᵛ [= R 1503].

[48] ACA, Reg. 13, fo. 163 [= R 255 = Jacobs 280]; Reg. 46, fo. 152ᵛ [= R 1105]; Reg. 66, fo. 16 [= R 1509].

community of the *collecta* had a say in the distribution of the taxes between the communities.[49]

It was the king who frequently instructed the community leaders what to do with individual tax-payers who did not comply with their decisions.[50] They were responsible to the king for the collection of all his taxes; all his demands for taxes and subsidies were addressed to the *adelantados* or *secretarii*.[51] In general they could rely on his support, as their success in their task was first and foremost in the king's interest; in specific instances, however, his approach varied as the circumstances seemed to him to require. Whether in his own interest or at the request of members of the Jewish public, the ruler sometimes permitted the community members to choose some from among their number who would assist the leaders, and in some instances control them, reporting any mismanagement to the king, and also act as mediators between the leaders and Jewish tax-payers.[52] The king's intervention in the work of the leaders in allocating taxes had greatest repercussions in the case of the poor classes. The case of Saragossa is most illustrative. Following the protest of the poor who formed the Kat ha-Havurah in 1263-4, Jaime I made some concessions to them which were to the detriment of the *berurim*. The poor were now entitled to have representatives on the administrative board.[53] The crisis, however, was not over and the tension between the poor and the rich continued for years to come. In 1290 Alfonso III, considering the complaints of the poor in Saragossa just, ordered the *adelantados* not to impose the tax on the poor, except in the method of *solidum et libram*, the system of 'declaration' according to which the tax-payer declared under oath his income or assets. He also instructed them that they had to keep the agreement to implement this system signed between the upper and the lower classes in the *sinagoga mayor*, in the presence of their rabbi.[54] Several months later, as he was informed that the poor could not pay their tax, the Infante Pedro informed the *adelantados* that two of his officials would decide how the community had to act. Thus the leaders were almost completely stripped of their power.[55] Nonetheless, the *berurim* were normally in charge of all matters of taxation and any Jewish settler automatically came under their jurisdiction.[56]

In many communities the *adelantados* faced problems of jurisdiction over tax-payers. Naturally the aim of the community leaders was to include the maximum number of tax-payers on their list. There was no clear-cut policy and the leaders

---

[49] For the Kingdom of Valencia, see ACA, Reg. 67, fo. 80ʳ [= R 1641]; Reg. 74, fo. 49ʳ [= R 1836]. For the *collecta* of Barcelona, see Reg. 81, fo. 130 [= R 2153]. For the *collecta* of Lérida, see Reg. 70, fo. 23 [= R 1693, doc. xxi; see end of document on p. 440].
[50] ACA, Reg. 57, fo. 222ʳ [= R 1457 = MF, II. 2298]; Reg. 62, fo. 115 [= R 1262].
[51] ACA, Reg. 52, fo, 39ʳ [= R 1096]; Reg. 71, fo. 149ʳ [= R 1129].
[52] ACA, Reg. 10, fo. 54ʳ [= R 97 = Jacobs 151 = Baer, *Spanien*, doc. 97].
[53] Assis, 'Crisis'; id., 'Poor and Rich', pp. 125-6.
[54] ACA, Reg. 81, fo. 9 [= R 2060].
[55] ACA, Reg. 85, fo. 15ʳ [= R 2112].
[56] ACA, Reg. 10, fo. 121ʳ [= R 122 = Jacobs 172a].

had to cope with conflicting interests. The payment of taxes by Jews doing business and holding shops outside their community was one problem facing community leaders. Their policy on this issue reflected the interest of the community, the number of non-resident Jews involved in local trade, and the volume of that trade compared to their own members' operations outside their *aljama*. The *adelantados* of Saragossa, for instance, insisted that non-resident Jews should pay tax with them for all business transacted in the city. The leaders of Saragossan Jewry were ordered on more than one occasion not to exact tax from Jews who came to Saragossa to trade or held shops in the city.[57]

Once the taxes were collected, the *berurim* handed them over to the king or his representative. In return the *berurim* or their delegates were given a receipt. The distance between the community and the locality where the king was staying at the time determined the number of the leaders or delegates who came to court. When the king was in the city or its vicinity the leaders themselves paid the tax.[58] It should be remembered that as the Crown of Aragon lacked a capital city, the court was rather mobile. The payment of the tax was the occasion for one or more of the leaders to submit the accounts for the current tax payment.[59]

As noted above, any communications connected with the payment of taxes were addressed by the king to the *berurim*.[60] When payment was delayed, the king asked the leaders to ensure immediate payment.[61] He occasionally demanded personal guarantees from the leaders. In January 1300 Jaime II ordered the *secretarii* of Barcelona to mortgage their property as security for the sum of 25,000 sb which the *aljama* had to pay on his behalf to the Infanta Lascara.[62] If there was a shortage of money in the community, it was the *berurim* who had to find the funds to pay the tax. In the search for loans, they had to be personally responsible to the creditors for their payment. It was not easy to find other members of the community to join them as guarantors for loans needed to pay taxes or subsidies. The leaders aroused much antagonism by seeking the king's help to force others to add their names as guarantors.[63] This financial responsibility was a serious matter which had far-reaching consequences. Holding them responsible for their

---

[57] ACA, CR, Jaime II, C 67, no. 8272 [= *Cartas Reales*, no. 344].

[58] ACA, Reg. 21, fos. 32, 37 [= R 516, 519 = Jacobs 633, 636 = Bofarull, Barcelona, cxvi]; Reg. 21, fo. 155 [= R 608 = Jacobs 559]; Reg. 43, fo. 18ᵛ [= R 1187]; Reg. 46, fo. 50 [= R 850 = MF ii. 1198]; Reg. 50, fo. 38ᵛ [= R 1208]; Reg. 51, fos. 29ᵛ, 34ᵛ, 39ʳᵛ, 40 = R 916, 1141, 1223, 1236]; Reg. 52, fos. 29ᵛ-30 [= R 917]; Reg. 71, fo. 152ᵛ [= R 1135]; Reg. 82, fos. 60, 70, 179 [= R 2170, 2195, 2320].

[59] ACA, Reg. 51, fo. 29ᵛ [= R 915].

[60] ACA, Reg. 71, fo. 78 [= R 1779]; Reg. 79, fo. 23 [= R 1924–5] Reg. 80, fo. 158 [= R 2049]; Reg. 82, fos. 51ᵛ, 65ᵛ [= R 2159, 2196]; Reg. 81, fo. 190 [= R 2204–5]; CR, Jaime II, C 8, no. 1088 [= *Cartas Reales*, no. 52].

[61] ACA, Reg. 41, fo. 6 [= R 710 = Baer, *Spanien*, doc. 114, 2]; Reg. 46, fo. 59; Reg. 52, fo. 20ᵛ [= R 888].

[62] ACA, CR, Jaime II, C 5, no. 723 [= *Cartas Reales*, no. 45].

[63] ACA, Reg. 19, fo. 128 [= R 595 = Jacobs 551 = Bofarull, Barcelona, cxli]; Reg. 66, fo. 52ᵛ [= R 1538]; Reg. 67, fo. 84ᵛ [= R 1645].

communities' tax payments, the king insisted on having the names of all the community leaders.[64] Even after their term of office was over, their personal responsibility did not cease. The four *secretarii* of the community of Barcelona some time before 1285, who included the famous halakhist R. Shelomo ben Abraham de Adret, were still considered responsible for the money they borrowed for the community after a new board had been elected.[65] In all probability, the money had been borrowed to pay the royal tax. The financial burden of responsibility for the tax payments was probably the most serious reason for the refusal of many Jews to accept leadership positions.[66]

From time to time the *berurim* were ordered to appear before the king to present the accounts of all the tax payments for a period of several years. In 1275 the *secretarii* of the communities of the *collecta* of Barcelona brought Jaime I the tax accounts of the past seven and a half years.[67] In September 1284 Pedro III ordered the leaders of all Catalan, Valencian, and Aragonese communities to bring him, within a few days, the tax accounts for their seven-year period of office.[68] About six months later he conducted an extensive investigation following accusations that the leaders of the Aragonese communities were guilty of fraud in the payment of taxes. He demanded full accounts and examined all the ordinances they enacted.[69] In 1289 Alfonso III asked the leaders of the Jews of Barcelona to present their tax accounts since the beginning of his reign.[70] In accordance with the king's orders, the accounts were sometimes submitted by delegates appointed by the *adelantados*[71] and sometimes by the leaders themselves to the king's representatives.[72] In 1304 twelve Jews from Valencia and one from Murviedro were prosecuted for their negligence and mismanagement of the tax-collection in their *aljama* during their ten years of office as *secretarii*. The accusation was levelled against them by the *aljama* of Valencia.[73] On 31 December 1304 they were pardoned in return for payments of various sums, ranging from 50 to 800 sr. One of the accused was Azmell Abengalell, whose Catalan account-book of six folios for the tax year of 1300 gives us a good idea of the way the accounts were kept and calculated.[74]

The investigations into the accounts of the *aljamas* implicated first and foremost the leaders of the community; it is not surprising, therefore, that the impetus for these investigations sometimes came from their rivals. In April 1327

---

[64] See e.g. the end of the following document: ACA, Reg. 57, fo. 187ʳ [=R 1433].
[65] ACA, Reg. 57, fo. 139ʳ [=R 1391].
[66] ACA, Reg. 80, fo. 49ʳˑ [=R 2002].
[67] ACA, Reg. 20, fo. 294ʳˑ [=R 641–2 = Jacobs 595–6].
[68] ACA, Reg. 43, fos. 29ʳ, 31ʳ [=R 1201, 1204 = MF, ii. 2032].
[69] ACA, Reg. 56, fo. 126 [=R 1344; doc. xvi = Baer, *Spanien*, doc. 129].
[70] ACA, Reg. 89, fo. 66ʳ [=R 2010].
[71] ACA, Reg. 67, fo. 84 [=R 1638].
[72] ACA, Reg. 72, fo. 37ʳˑ [=R 1721]; Reg. 80, fo. 45ʳ [=R 1990]; Reg. 81, fo. 71ʳ [=R 2093].
[73] ACA, Reg. 202, fo. 303 [=R 2833].
[74] ACA, CR, Jaime II, C 132, no. 118 [= *Cartas Reales*, no. 42].

Jaime II ordered that the proceedings against the *secretarii* of Barcelona should continue, and should include anyone else in his administration who might have been involved in the fraud. The investigation was renewed at the instigation of Astruc Saltell and other Jews from Barcelona.[75] The same Astruc Saltell was the subject of a request by the Infante Pedro to the Infante Alfonso a year earlier to order the baile of Barcelona to appoint Astruc Saltell to replace one of the seven *secretarii* who had recently died.[76]

The authority of the *berurim* was severely impaired when the king chose to exclude his favourite Jews from their jurisdiction in matters of taxation.[77] The *berurim* had little choice but to accept the king's orders, which overrode all their decisions and warnings. It was little comfort that these Jews belonged to the same aristocratic families as most of them did. These exemptions, as well as reductions and other benefits, caused real harm to the prestige and authority of the leaders.[78] The same effect resulted when the king acceded to requests from individual Jews in ordering the community leaders not to raise the applicants' taxes or to tax them according to a certain system.[79]

INTERNAL FINANCE

The *berurim* were, in general, responsible for the revenues and expenses of the community and all aspects of the economy affecting Jewish life. In some communities special *berurim* were in charge of routine financial transactions.[80] These transactions were very varied and their extent depended on many factors relating to the particular community. Part of the communal expenses went to the king and local authorities, as regular and extraordinary payments, gifts and bribes.[81] These expenses were often a bone of contention between different parties in the community, sometimes causing friction between the leaders and some members, and even division among the members of the board.

As the community was often short of money, the expenses had to be met by the members, who would in principle be reimbursed as soon as financial conditions permitted it. The reimbursement of members was not always a simple procedure since the money available at any given time was not sufficient to repay all members who had advanced money. In 1280 a crisis broke out in Saragossa after some members who received their money back prevented others from being

---

[75] ACA, CR, Jaime II, C 134, no. 223 [= *Cartas Reales*, no. 367].
[76] ACA, CR, Jaime II, C 134, no. 152 [= *Cartas Reales*, no. 443].
[77] ACA, Reg. 13, fo. 164ᵛ [= R 257 = Jacobs 282].
[78] ACA, Reg. 64, fo. 32 [= R 1526]; Reg. 70, fo. 77 [= R 1709]; Reg. 74, fo. 27ᵛ, 41ᵛ, 66 [= R 1823, 1839, 1852, 1865]; Reg. 76, fo. 28ᵛ [= R 1906].
[79] ACA, CR, Jaime II, C 133, no. 66, 95 [= *Cartas Reales*, nos. 297, 317].
[80] Adret, iii. 386.
[81] Adret, v. 183, vii. 191.

similarly repaid.[82] For certain expenses the community leaders claimed that Jews in neighbouring settlements or *aljamas* had to contribute their share; but the matter was not simple.[83] The *berurim* had also to take into account the expenses of the *aljamas* of an entire region, and had to contribute the share borne by their community.[84]

When the community was in financial distress and could not pay its debts and obligations or raise the necessary funds among its members, the leaders had no other recourse but to borrow money.[85] The leaders borrowed in their own names and were therefore held personally responsible for repayment. Many leaders whose communities borrowed found themselves in serious legal complications.[86] The debts were sometimes so burdensome that the king was prepared to offer the *berurim* easy terms.[87] From the creditors' point of view, the leaders who had taken out the loan remained responsible for it even after they had left office.[88] In some cases, the *berurim* lent money to their community and were not repaid until long after they had left their posts, sometimes only after royal intervention.[89] The community leaders sometimes had difficulty too in recovering the expenses they incurred while on duty and for services they undertook on behalf of their *aljama*. Here, too, the king's help was often necessary.[90]

For the Crown, the leaders of the community were more than the financial administrators and representatives of their community. In some respects they were the king's hostages. If he was in great and urgent need of cash, there were several possibilities open to the king for getting the money from Jewish sources. One convenient way was to make the leaders of the *aljama* assume his debts. The community leaders would then either collect the money from among the members or borrow the money on behalf of the community, although formally they would be held personally responsible for the loan contracted for the ruler. While the king could raise money this way from many communities, promising at best that the loan would be deducted from the future taxes of the community, the Jewish leaders found themselves under great royal pressure and their power abused for royal convenience.[91] The leaders' task was particularly hard when the king asked for a very large loan from the community, exceeding its tax liability.[92] The *berurim*

---

[82] ACA, Reg. 48, fo. 119 [=R 831].
[83] R 2329; I was unable to trace the document recorded by Régné.
[84] ACA, Reg. 56, fo. 107 [=R 1360 = MF ii. 2216].
[85] Adret, iii. 412, vii. 263.
[86] ACA, Reg. 79, fo. 21ᵛ [=R 1923]; see also R 2332.
[87] ACA, Reg. 75, fo. 50ᵛ [=R 1861].
[88] ACA, Reg. 70, fo. 77ᵛ [=R 1714].
[89] ACA, Reg. 57, fo. 217ᵛ [=R 1454].
[90] ACA, CR, Jaime II, C 134, no. 190 [= *Cartas Reales*, no. 402].
[91] ACA, Reg. 14, fos. 59ᵛ, 17ᵛ [=R 274 = Jacobs 363; =R 292]; Reg. 37, fos 61ᵛ [=R 599]; Reg. 46, fo. 13ᵛ [=R 742].
[92] ACA, Reg. 71, fo. 7ᵛ [=R 1699 = Isaacs 46]; Reg. 72, fo. 4ᵛ [=R 1704 = Isaacs 47]; Reg. 80, fo. 3 [=R 1958].

were sometimes given guarantees or pawns, if future taxes were already totally engaged for previous loans or if the borrower was a member of the royal family other than the king.[93] In some communities, hard hit by loans to the king, where there was great anxiety among potential leaders, special measures were taken to alleviate the conditions. A *taqanah* of the community of Valencia is noteworthy. It was decided that any loan by a member to the king would automatically become the common loan of the entire *aljama*.[94] In other communities the principle was established that, though the leaders were formally the borrowers of the loan, the community as a whole was to repay the debt. This commitment of the general Jewish public to repay the loans contracted by the leaders on behalf of the community was upheld by Jewish jurists.[95]

The *berurim* had jurisdiction over all aspects of the economy that in any way affected Jewish life. They enacted ordinances regulating real estate transactions. These ordinances were of no less consequence in the economic life of the Jews than the laws and norms of the king. Their relevance to daily life is attested to in the numerous responsa concerning economic and financial problems within the Jewish community.[96] As already noted, there were special *berurim* in charge of weights, measures, and prices.[97] Jewish autonomy is perhaps best exemplified in the ability of the community and its leaders to create an entire set of economic and financial laws and regulations parallel to those of the kingdom.

RELIGIOUS AND MORAL DUTIES

Religious life in the *judería* or the *call* was also under the control of the *berurim*. Every Jew in the *aljama* was expected to abide by Jewish law and the local *taqanot*. Any deviation from Jewish norm or transgression of the *halakhah* was punishable within the community, which enjoyed a very extensive autonomy in matters of religious and moral conduct. In general, the right of the *berurim* to supervise the moral and religious conduct of the members of their community was widely accepted and the *berurim* acted accordingly.[98] Their jurisdiction included marital life and problems related to marital and sexual life were therefore addressed to them.[99]

As the kings in the Crown of Aragon fully supported the community's right

---

[93] In 1271 the *secretarii* of the Jews of Barcelona received from the Infante Pedro some precious objects as pawns for a loan of 10,000 sb and 200 golden *maravedis alfonsines*: ACA, Reg. 35, fo. 63ʳ [= R 465]. For another instance, see ACA, Reg. 82, fo. 53ʳ [= R 1186].

[94] ACA, Reg. 74, fo. 41ʳ [= R 1840]. The *taqanah*, which was designed to protect fellow-members, especially the leaders, was easily abused by the king, to whom it offered an easy way to obtain Jewish loans.

[95] Adret, v. 251, vii, 353. [96] See e.g. Adret, ii. 95.
[97] Adret, i. 590. [98] Adret, i. 1187, iii. 318.
[99] There is an abundance of material on the subject, suffice it to refer here to Adret, i. 1209.

and duty to supervise Jewish life in the Jewish quarter, the task of the *berurim* as defined by Jewish law became relatively easy. In a charter granted by Jaime I to the *aljama* of Barbastro in 1273, the *adelantados* were authorized to co-opt ten members to assist them in their supervision of religious life. They were empowered to prosecute any Jew suspected of immoral behaviour or accused of being an informer or *malsin*, whom they could summon to the local baile. Once the *adelantados* and the supervisors had submitted their accusation under oath, the baile had to prosecute, judge, and if necessary punish—even to the extent of the death penalty where appropriate. In keeping with the medieval notion that the Jew belonged to the royal treasury, for every execution the *aljama* had to pay 500 sj.[100]

The *berurim* had overall responsibility for the pursuit of religious life, the maintenance of public worship, and the provision of *kasher* food in the community. They had to supervise the slaughtering of animals and the sale of *kasher* meat. In the case of serious problems, severe measures were taken by the community leaders. The *berurim* controlled the work of the slaughterers, tested their performance, and checked their knowledge of *shehitah*. A *shohet* who failed such tests would be dismissed.[101] In 1283 the *adelantados* of Alagón expelled from the Jewish quarter for four years six Jews who were butchers and forbade the six to act as butchers in Alagón during this period.[102] Here too, royal intervention occurred. In 1284 the *adelantados* of Jaca forbade the butcher Genton to work as a butcher. At Genton's request, the infante informed the leaders of the community that it would please him if they were to cancel their decision.[103] In 1315 Jaime II asked the *adelantados* of Huesca to lift the one-year ban on the butcher Gavarell after four months if he behaved well.[104] The community leaders would punish butchers for rivalry and misbehaviour.[105]

In some communities the *berurim* also controlled the prices of *kasher* wine. This was an item that could easily be abused by unscrupulous merchants, *kasher* wine being a necessary commodity that could not be purchased everywhere.[106]

The *berurim* were in charge of the religious services in the synagogue and all the rituals and the decorum related to them. On Succoth, they provided the congregants with *ethrogim*.[107]

It was likewise the duty of the *berurim* to take care of problems in the fields of public morality and ethics. They did so by enacting ordinances and taking other measures.[108] We know that in some communities there were Jewish prostitutes.[109]

---

[100] ACA, Reg. 21, fo. 126ᵛ [=R 552 = Jacobs 665 = Baer, *Spanien*, doc. 107].
[101] Adret, i. 218.
[102] ACA, Reg. 61, fo. 135ᵛ [=R 1066].
[103] ACA, Reg. 62, fo. 55 [=R 1130]. Genton is the Romance form for Yom Tov.
[104] ACA, Reg. 212, fo. 21ᵛ [=R 3022].
[105] Asibili (Kapah) 67.
[106] Adret, i. 590.   [107] Adret, i. 406.   [108] Adret, i. 416.
[109] Assis, 'Sexual Behaviour', pp. 44–5.

It was the duty of the leaders to ensure that the prostitutes operated in a place and in a manner that did not disturb the Jewish public in general. When Muça de Portella, the Jewish baile of Saragossa, complained in 1283 that Jewish prostitutes had begun to operate in a house adjacent to his in the *judería*, whereas previously they were not allowed to use the Jewish quarter for their professional purposes, the infante ordered the *adelantados* to take immediate action and expel the women.[110]

THE *BERURIM* AS JUDGES

In addition to their mainly executive jurisdiction and limited legislative work the *berurim* acted also as judges, often as a *beth din*.[111] Such was the case in Saragossa in the latter part of the thirteenth century.[112] Their judicial power was recognized by the king, as is made explicit in some of the charters. They dealt with monetary, criminal, and religious cases.[113] The status of the *berurim* judges in comparison to the *dayanim*, members of a halakhically constituted *beth din*, deserves careful examination. A full discussion of this topic is found in the section below on 'The Judiciary'. Suffice it to say here that *berurim* in many communities of the Crown acted as judges but were by no means necessarily experts in *halakhah*. Despite their judicial duties, they were not always the only judges: in some communities we find the *baror*, with some judicial duties, working alongside a *dayan*.[114]

In the charter given to the Jews of Calatayud in 1229 the community was authorized to elect, with the consent of their *arrab* (rabbi), four *adelantados* whose jurisdiction included judicial matters, such as the prosecution of suspects and the punishment of those found guilty by imprisonment or even death.[115] A document from 1272 relating to the Jews of Huesca shows that the *adelantados* formed a tribunal that adjudicated between Jews. Such tribunals existed in other communities as well.[116] Under Pedro III and Alfonso III *adelantados* continued to act as judges for their fellow Jews. Although this practice was widely adopted in Aragon, *adelantados* of other communities also performed judicial acts.[117] The number of *adelantados* in these communities varied between two and seven, but not all of them acted in the capacity of judges.[118] We have information from several communities on how these *adelantados* exercised their judicial role. In the Aragonese community of Egea in 1283 the *adelantados* pronounced their sentence

---

[110] ACA, Reg. 61, fo. 134 [= R 1053].
[111] Adret, ii. 300.
[112] ACA, Reg. 59, fo. 67ᵛ [= R 947] (1282); Adret, ii. 229 (1283).
[113] Adret, iii. 388, 393.
[114] Adret, i. 1126.
[115] ACA, Reg. 202, fo. 201ʳᵛ [= R 6].
[116] ACA, Reg. 37, fo. 34ᵛ [= R 504 = Jacobs 726].
[117] For instances from Valencian and Catalan *aljamas* see ACA, Reg. 43, fo. 114 [= R 1270 = MF ii. 2128]; Reg. 74, fo. 2 [= R 1790]; Reg. 80, fo. 91 [= R 2025].
[118] ACA, Reg. 59, fo. 56 [= R 942].

in favour of one Jew against another. The judges heard the appeal of one of the litigants and rejected it, causing the litigant to complain to the infante. The question arose whether, according to the legal tradition of Egea, the litigant had the right to appeal to the judges of Saragossa as a higher authority.[119]

In Valencia, too, the king recognized the *berurim* as judges. Unlike the Catalan communities, in Valencia the *berurim* served as judges according to the 1327 constitution.[120] For the most part they dealt with financial disputes and moral behaviour.[121]

It appears that in Aragon, more than anywhere else in the Crown, the *adelantados* acted as judges. The explanation may partly lie in the shortage of halakhically qualified judges (see section on 'The Judiciary' below). On the other hand, although there were leaders who were ignorant of Hebrew and Jewish law, there were also among the *adelantadi* or the *secretarii*, some who were highly versed in *halakhah*, even renowned halakhists. Hebrew records show that community leaders were not elected for their scholarship, and that among them there were some who were known for their lack of learning.[122] As noted above, the famous halakhist and author of these very records, R. Shelomo ben Adret himself, was for a while a member of the board in Barcelona. The ban of 1305 against secular studies was signed by scholars and the *ne'emanim* of Barcelona, some of whom were known for their learning.[123]

INTERNAL AND EXTERNAL PRESSURE ON JEWISH LEADERS

The leaders of the Jewish communities in the Crown of Aragon worked under pressure, as did their colleagues in other lands. In the thirteenth and fourteenth centuries the very pronounced social tensions in Jewish society rendered their position far more vulnerable. The *berurim*, who belonged to the aristocratic class, were challenged by the lower classes for the first time in the latter part of the thirteenth century, and the king's partial support of the masses' claims was a severe blow to the power of the leaders.

In addition to internal pressure, the community leaders were exposed to pressure from the royal court. On top of the constant demands and instructions they received from the king and his representatives, in certain circumstances they faced investigation, prosecution, arrest, and even dismissal as a result either of Jewish complaints or of the king's displeasure with the leaders' performance. Prosecution of the *berurim* for ordinances they had enacted was not a rare occurrence.

[119] ACA, Reg. 61, fo. 122 [= R 1056 = Baer, *Spanien*, doc. 125].
[120] ACA, Reg. 229, fo. 274 [= R 3434 = Jacobs 878].
[121] ACA, Reg. 89, fo. 60' [= R 2568]; Reg. 202, fo. 204 [= R 2832].
[122] Adret, i. 617, ii. 290, iii. 399.
[123] Adret, i. 415 [= Abba Mari, no. 79]; Adret, i. 417 [= Abba Mari, no. 81].

Jews were often behind these proceedings against their own leaders. In 1277 four Jews accused the *berurim* of Lérida of serious misconduct and of promulgating ordinances against the king's interest. First the informers were arrested, but then Pedro III ordered a full investigation and the leaders' suspension from office until the investigation was over.[124] In 1278 the leaders of the *aljama* in Saragossa were prosecuted by the Jewish baile of Saragossa, Mosse Alfaquim, for ordinances they enacted, one of which affected the *francos*.[125] The leaders of the *aljama* of Gerona were accused of attempted perjury in 1281 when they were ordered to appear before a judge in connection with certain matters. They were supposed to bring along with them a book of the Torah on which to take an oath, and it was claimed that they substituted for it another book, with the obvious intention of lying. Since only a Jew could identify the contents of the book, we must assume that there was an informer. The leaders were heavily fined.[126]

OTHER POSTS AND POSITIONS

Besides the *berurim, muqademin*, or *ne'emanim*, there were additional executive positions in the communal administration. Their number varied from community to community, depending on its size and the degree of sophistication of its administration. Some of the *berurim* or *muqademin* bore titles indicating their special tasks in the executive body. The following posts are found in Hebrew, Latin, and Romance sources: *gabay, gabae ha-mas, gabae zedaqah, gizbar, gizbar ha-heqdesh, gabay ha-heqdesh, parnas, shamay, poseq, gove ha-mas; reebadors de compts* or *receptores compotorum, taxadores, tatxadors, collidores, clavarios, talliadores, elemosinarii.*

In communities in which there were more than three *berurim*, two of them were usually in charge of finance and the assets and property of the community. In most communities their right to spend money without prior permission was limited to a certain amount. In many communities the names *gizbar* and *gabay* were interchangeable. In non-Hebrew sources, they were called *reebadors de compts* or *receptores compotorum*. They were either nominated by the *berurim* or appointed by electors.[127]

Two important economic positions were those of the tax-assessors and collectors. The tax-assessors were known as *shamain, poseqim, taxadores, tatxadors*, or *talliatores*, while the collectors were called *gove ha-mas, ne'emanim 'al ha-mas, collidores*, and *clavaris*, among other titles. By the thirteenth century most of the

---

[124] ACA, Reg. 39, fo. 197 [= R 681].
[125] ACA, Reg. 41, fo. 6 [= R 709 = Baer, *Spanien*, doc. 114, 1].
[126] ACA, Reg. 50, fo. 184ᵛ [= R 882].
[127] Adret, iii. 386–7, v, 249, 268; Asibili (Kapah) 56; Asibili (Blau) 12; ACA, Reg. 230, fos. 59, 106ᵛ–107 [= R 3442, 3454 = Jacobs 884, 892 = Baer, *Spanien*, doc. 189]; ACB, Bernat de Vilarrubia 1295, fos. 3ᵛ–4ʳ, 4ᵛ, 12ʳ, 13ᵛ, 26ᵛ, 73ʳ, 75ʳᵛ, 76ᵛ, 85ᵛ–86ʳ, 103ʳᵛ.

aljamas had their own tax-assessors and collectors. In the smaller communities the two functions were performed by the same person, whereas in the larger ones, like Barcelona, there was a hierarchy in charge of the taxes.[128]

In the larger communities a special treasurer was appointed to administer the property of the *aljama* or the *heqdesh*. He was called the *almoyner* or *gabay ha-heqdesh*. He enjoyed great influence and prestige as he was in charge of distributing some of the revenues from communal assets.[129] Closely related to this post was that of the charity wardens, called *gabae zedaqah, elemosinarii, almoyners*. They were responsible for administering the charity funds of the community, which were part of the *heqdesh*, and for dispensing charity to the poor. The charity wardens were appointed in the same way as the other officers of the community. The office was created either because of the funds for charity donated by Jews or because the community decided to adopt a welfare policy.[130]

The *berurim* and the *yo'azim* sometimes represented their communities in negotiations with outside bodies, whether Jewish or otherwise; in other cases special delegates were appointed by the *berurim* or the council. These delegates, known in the sources as *shelihim, sheluhe ha-qehilot, procuradores, missatgers*, etc., were paid fees and expenses by the community, although very often this caused serious disputes. The most important delegates were those sent to the king, either at his command or on the initiative of the community.[131]

Jewish envoys played an important role in inter-communal relations. Delegates of communities of a territory or region gathered regularly to divide between them the taxes due to the king or whenever they had to deal with an issue that was of common interest. Meetings of the delegates of the communities of the entire Crown of Aragon were very rare as the Jews of the Crown, in accordance with the structure of the realm, were not considered one unit. One such meeting did take place during the reign of Jaime II when delegates of the Jews of Catalonia, Aragon, and Valencia met in Tortosa in 1302 to distribute between them the sum of 100,000 sj they were required to pay for the Sicily campaign.[132]

More frequent were the meetings of delegates of the communities of each of the three constituent territories: Aragon, Catalonia, and Valencia.[133] In Aragon, the delegates of the *aljamas* met annually, originally in Saragossa and later in Alagón,

---

[128] Adret, iii. 428, v. 283; Baer, *Spanien*, doc. 163, pp. 256, 481, 488, 493, 497; ACA, Reg. 227, fo. 191` [= R 3333]; Reg. 230, fos. 106–7` [= Baer, *Spanien*, doc. 189].

[129] Adret, viii. 268, iii. 293, iv. 64, 239; Asibili (Kapah) 34, 167, 206.

[130] Adret, iii. 292, 394, v. 283; ACA, Reg. 230, fos. 106–7` [= Baer, *Spanien*, doc. 189]; Reg. 229, fo. 258 [= R 3427].

[131] ACA, Reg. 207, fos. 245`–246 [= R 2924]; Reg. 230, fos. 106`–107 [= Baer, *Spanien*, doc. 189]; Reg. 56, fo. 132` [= R 1387 = MF, ii. 2227]; Reg. 57, fo. 223 [= R 1459 = MF, ii. 2300]; ACA, CR, Jaime II, C 133, no. 55 [= *Cartas Reales*, no. 354]; Adret, iii. 402.

[132] ACA, CR, Jaime II, C 135, no. 382 [= Baer, *Spanien*, doc. 151 = *Cartas Reales*, no. 525].

[133] ACA, Reg. 59, fos. 151`–152, 156` [= R 984 = MF, ii. 1604; = R 986]; Reg. 62, fo. 50 [= R 1116].

though the place changed at the king's request. The number of the delegates from each community varied, sometimes according to size.[134]

Delegates of the Jews in the Catalan *collectas* also met regularly to deal with the tax load of each community and settlement, as we shall see below.

COUNCILS AND COUNCILLORS

The latter part of the thirteenth century saw the emergence and consolidation of a new institution in the communities of the Crown of Aragon. The council or *'eza* became the supreme supervisory and advisory body in the larger communities and the highest authority in the communal administration, enjoying sometimes the power of veto and usually the right to appoint, together with the *berurim*, several of the officers, or at least to confirm their appointment. While its emergence preceded the class struggle, its development was closely related to the conflict that broke out between the classes in the second half of the thirteenth century and the beginning of the fourteenth. The members of the council were originally recruited from the richest and most powerful families, but following the constitutional reforms of the later thirteenth century its structure changed accordingly[135] to represent in equal numbers the three social classes. The councillors were known as *yo'azim*, *ba'ale 'eza*, *prohomens*, *probi homines*, *viri boni consilium*, or *consellers*. During the fourteenth century the authority of the council increased further.

The council or *'eza* was modelled on the institution bearing the same name in the Christian municipality and offers the most obvious example of the striking similarities in the form of government between the *qehilah* and the Christian municipality. Although they were totally separate and distinct in their jurisdiction, their proximity explains the inevitable influence of the municipality on the *judería*. *'Azat ha-Sheloshim* (the Council of Thirty) of the *aljama* of Barcelona was undoubtedly modelled on the *Consell de Cent* (the Council of One Hundred) of the city of Barcelona.

Both Barcelona and Saragossa had their councils in the latter part of the thirteenth century. According to a *taqanah* from the late thirteenth century, the *yo'azim* in one of the Catalan communities elected their own successors annually.[136] Despite local differences in their duties and jurisdiction, the status of the councillors was similar to that of the *berurim* and the *ne'emanim*. The

---

[134] ACA, Reg. 59, fo. 56 [= R 942]; Reg. 61, fos. 117, 159 [= R 1052, 1072]; Reg. 46, fo. 166 [= R 1240]; Reg. 43, fo. 90ʻ [= R 1248]; Reg. 74, fo. 78 [= R 1878].

[135] Baer's statement that 'the conflict of class interests led, in the late thirteenth and early fourteenth centuries, in Barcelona and elsewhere in Catalonia, to the creation of the 'Etza' seems to be inexact, as the very *taqanah* he quotes immediately shows its oligarchical character. See Baer, *History*, i, p. 236.

[136] Adret, v. 284 [= Baer, *Spanien*, doc. 143, para. 11].

signatories of the 1305 twin ban of Barcelona on the study of secular sciences and on allegorical interpretations of the Bible included the seven *ne'emanim* or *secretarii* and the thirty *yo'azim* of Barcelona, all described by Adret as dignitaries of the community.[137]

According to the 1327 constitution the *yo'azim* of Barcelona appointed all the leaders, judges, and other officers of the community and were themselves elected every three years by the *ne'emanim* and the judges. While members of the council were eligible for re-election, close relatives could not serve concurrently. The members of the Council of Thirty were given more power than their counterparts on the municipal council. In the second half of the fourteenth century their power and prestige were undiminished.[138] Until 1386 the composition of the council of Barcelona remained essentially aristocratic. The regime enabled the same wealthy families of merchants and scholars to perpetuate their power. However, the new constitution promulgated that year gave equal representation to the three classes. Ten councillors had to withdraw every year so that the council was constantly injected with fresh members. In order to make communal administration more efficient, a small council was created, composed of five councillors from each class and the three *ne'emanim*. This reform, which was fully endorsed by Pedro IV and followed social unrest and a long struggle between the classes, was simultaneous with a similar one that was introduced in the *Concell de Cent*. However, the new council was short-lived: the massacres of 1391 destroyed the *aljama* and with it Jewish life in Barcelona.[139]

In other Catalan communities councils were established later in the fourteenth century. In Perpignan a council of twenty to twenty-eight members existed in the 1380s. The councillors were appointed for life, and upon the death of a member a new councillor was co-opted by the council. Unlike Barcelona and Majorca, where physicians were barred from membership in the council, in Perpignan, where science was highly esteemed, there were always several physicians on the council.[140]

In Gerona, in accordance with the 1341 constitution, a dual council was established: one part had twenty-six members and the other had sixteen.[141] In 1391, just before the massacres, a new constitution created a twenty-three-member council: twenty-one councillors represented the Jews of Gerona and two were representatives of Jews from settlements in the *collecta*. Sixteen councillors were appointed for life. They could delegate their seats for limited periods to their sons or brothers. Fifteen other candidates filled the remaining seats on the council, five

---

[137] *Minhat Qenaot*, 81; Adret, i. 416 [= Halper, *Post-Biblical Hebrew Literature*, i, pp. 137–41; Eng. trans. in ii, pp. 176–82]; Baer, *History*, i, pp. 303–4.
[138] Perfet 228.
[139] ACA, Reg. 948, fos. 114ᵛ–122ᵛ [= Baer, *Spanien*, doc. 381].
[140] ACA, Reg. 1689, fos. 213–16 [= Baer, *Spanien*, docs. 330, 371].
[141] ACA, Reg. 1670, fo. 75ᵛ [= Baer, *Spanien*, doc. 366]; Reg 1822, fo. 87, 116 [= Baer, *Spanien*, p. 569; and doc. 385]; Reg. 1815, fos. 51ᵛ–52 [= Baer, *Spanien*, doc. 386].

at a time, by rotation every three years. The two councillors of the Jews from the surrounding villages came from a list of six candidates who each served for three years by rotation.[142]

In Lérida in the latter part of the thirteenth century the *yo'azim* chose their successors annually in secret conclave according to the *ostages* system.[143] In Cervera, according to a document of 1348, there were seventeen councillors.[144]

In Majorca, after its reincorporation in the Crown of Aragon in 1344, the influence of the Jews on the Catalan mainland grew. During the period of independence, besides the *ne'emanim* there was a council of eight elders who served in an advisory capacity. We have no exact data, but it appears that no elections were held for these offices. Following much struggle and dissension, a Council of Thirty was established in Majorca in 1378. Its early existence was not trouble-free. The wealthy were not prepared to relinquish their traditional position easily and in the early years they enjoyed the support of Pedro IV. Despite continuous struggle by the poorer members, no reform was introduced in the composition of the council.[145]

In Valencia, a Council of Thirty existed in the second half of the fourteenth century. The council was considered the representative body of the community and made most of the appointments in the *aljama*.[146]

About the middle of the thirteenth century, Saragossa already had its *'eza*. In the 1280s it had twenty-five members.[147] The struggle of the 'little people' in the *aljama* of Saragossa had its effect on the structure of the council. In Aragon, at least part of the *muqademin* formed part of the *'eza*. In the 1380s the three classes participated in the election of the councillors and all three classes were represented on the council.[148]

In Huesca until 1324 the council had twelve members, three from each class. It appears that the six *adelantados* were also members of the council. In that year the number of the councillors was reduced to six, two from each class.[149] In Barbastro, a council of six members was constituted in 1313 and operated alongside the *adelantados*.[150]

The council that emerged in the second half of the thirteenth century spread throughout the Jewish communities of the realm in the course of the fourteenth

---

[142] ACA, Reg. 2041, fos. 37ᵛ–40 [= Baer, *Spanien*, doc. 395].
[143] Adret, v. 284 [= Baer, *Spanien*, doc. 143, para. 11].
[144] ACA, Reg. 653, fos. 15ᵛ–16 [= Baer, *Spanien*, doc. 229].
[145] Fita and Llabrés, 'Privilegios', nos. 91, 106; ACA, Reg. 1439, fos. 8–11 [= Baer, *Spanien*, doc. 318]; Reg. 1438, fo. 19ʳ [= Baer, *Spanien*, doc. 319]; Reg. 1440, fos. 32ᵛ–33, 168ᵛ [= Baer, *Spanien*, docs. 323, 328].
[146] ACA, Reg. 1580, fos. 99ᵛ–91 [= Baer, *Spanien*, doc. 308]; Baer, *Spanien*, doc. 325.
[147] Adret, ii. 33; ACA, Reg. 44, fo. 177ᵛ [= R 776 = Baer, *Spanien*, doc. 118].
[148] ACA, Reg. 2041, fos. 23ᵛ–26ᵛ [= Baer, *Spanien*, doc. 341]; Reg. 939, fos. 99–103ᵛ [= Baer, *Spanien*, doc. 342].
[149] ACA, Reg. 225, fo. 280ᵛ [= R 3299 = Jacobs 837].
[150] ACA, Reg. 210, fos. 86ᵛ–87 [= R 2977]; Reg. 229, fos. 177ᵛ–178.

century. The institution became so much part of the community administration that the word *solacim*, from the Hebrew *sheloshim* (thirty), was found in archival sources.[151]

[151] ACA, Reg. 1580, fo. 68 [= Baer, *Spanien*, doc. 307].

§2.5 Communal Functionaries and Synagogue Officials

MANY Jewish communities in the Crown of Aragon, like other medieval communities, appointed a number of salaried functionaries to perform certain works inside the Jewish quarter. The number of functionaries in any one field, and the number of fields covered by communal workers, varied from one community to another, depending primarily on the community's size and wealth. In some communities certain functions were performed free by members. The appointment of functionaries became over the course of time part of the tradition of Jewish self-government in the Crown of Aragon.[1] The king, favouring stability in the Jewish community, gave his support to the orderly appointment of the community functionaries.[2]

According to R. Abraham ben Shelomo ibn Tazrat, R. Shelomo ben Adret's disciple, most communities in the Crown of Aragon appointed a scribe, a slaughterer, a teacher, a *hazan*, a *mohel*, and a physician, among others.[3] We may reasonably assume that Tazrat meant the larger communities, and even in these, it is doubtful if all the positions existed in every case. Tazrat must have generalized.

THE COMMUNITY SCRIBE OR *SOFER*

All official Hebrew documents had to be prepared by an expert scribe.[4] The *sofer* or *scrivano dela aljama* was appointed by the leaders of the community[5] or a special board of electors.[6] The non-Jewish authorities considered him a Jewish notary and referred to him thus.[7] The incumbent was usually one of the most learned members of the community, as the post demanded a thorough knowledge of Hebrew, a fair knowledge of Jewish jurisprudence, and a good calligraphy. The evidence shows that in large communities there was more than one scribe at the

---

[1] Adret, v. 283.
[2] Del Arco, 'La judería', 327–8; ACA, Reg. 225, fo. 237.
[3] Tazrat, *Huqat Ha-Dayanim*, no. 156.
[4] The English word 'scribe' is used here to distinguish him from the Christian notary public. The scribe of the community was not necessarily the one who wrote the scrolls of the Torah, the *tefillin* and the *mezuzah* and other liturgical items, and worked as copyist of manuscripts.
[5] Adret, i. 729 = iii. 438.
[6] Adret, v. 129.
[7] See e.g. ACA, Reg. 1202, fo. 183 [= Baer, *Spanien*, doc. 272].

time. As the scribe received his fees from the people who needed the documents, the post was very much in demand. The competition between rival candidates and the prospect of some gain for the royal coffers explain the special interest of the king in the post.

The king was particularly interested in the post of scribe in large communities, where he would often go as far as appointing his own candidate. These scribes had a right of monopoly over the post which they could transfer to others, with the king's permission. In some cases the post passed by inheritance as late as the end of the fourteenth century.[8] In December 1294 Jaime II appointed Jahuda son of Astrug Bonsenyor as notary public for Arabic documents and as scribe for Hebrew in Barcelona and its vicinity. Jahuda enjoyed a monopoly which must have aroused the envy of his rivals.[9] In 1314 the *sofer* of Saragossa, R. Azariah, asked the king's permission to appoint a substitute to enable him to visit the sick.[10] In 1305, the king dismissed the *sofer* of Barbastro and appointed Vidal to the post.[11] For an annual fee, in 1311 Jaime II appointed Jahuda Adarra as the scribe of the community of Valencia for life with full monopoly. In 1327 Jahuda transferred his post to two Jews as sub-contractors. As they charged exorbitant fees, the community complained to the king, who ordered his baile general to negotiate with the *adelantados* so that reasonable and fixed fees could be determined for Hebrew notarial acts.[12]

It appears that in most communities the scribe or *sofer* was not a functionary of the *aljama*. In some Hebrew sources he is called 'the city scribe' or 'the local scribe'.[13] His appointment, often for life, as well as the fees chargeable for every document, contributed to detach the *sofer* from the communal administration. The double appointment of Jahuda Bonsenyor as scribe for all Arabic and Hebrew documents in the region of Barcelona is further proof of the independence of the post from the communal administration in many communities. Moreover, there is evidence that the prospect of a handsome income rendered the post attractive to some leaders of certain communities who coveted the post. R. Joce Avenjacob, who acted as scribe of the Saragossan community in 1311, was at the same time one of its three *adelantados*.[14]

The scribe was expected to draw up all the documents required by Jewish law, such as the marriage contract (*ketubah*), divorce bill (*get*), will, etc., and prepared any other contractual document which the parties were required to sign according to Jewish law. He also wrote and edited the ordinances (*taqanot*) of the

---

[8] Perfet 195.

[9] ACA, Reg. 194, fo. 108ᵛ [=R 2556]. For the appointment in 1291 of Sabahon Jucef de Centurbio as the notary of the community of Palermo in Sicily, which was under the rule of the House of Aragon, see ACA, Reg. 192, fo. 100ʳᵛ [=R 2407–8].

[10] ACA, Reg. 211, fo. 220 [=R 3001].

[11] ACA, Reg. 203, fo. 222.

[12] ACA, Reg. 232, fo. 352ᵛ [=R 3081]; Reg. 229, fo. 274ᵛ [=R 3435 = Jacobs 879].

[13] Adret, ii. 111, viii. 65; Asibili (Kapah) 56.

[14] ACA, Reg. 207, fos. 239ᵛ–240ᵛ [=R 2919].

community and was in charge of the community archives, the secrecy of which he undertook to keep. As the archives contained the list of all the tax-payers and their assets, it was important that anyone who had access to them should not divulge any information.[15] The *sofer* also drew up and signed bills of sale and transfer of property.[16]

The recognition of the validity of documents drawn up by the Jewish scribe in the Crown of Aragon enhanced the status both of Jewish law and of the scribe. In 1264 Jaime I decreed that all deeds in Hebrew concerning dowry and other financial matters between couples were as valid as any document prepared and signed by the notary public, if drawn up by the scribe according to *halakhah* (*azuna* in the source) and countersigned by two witnesses.[17] The recognition by Christian authorities and courts of documents prepared by Jewish scribes was extensive. In the late thirteenth century, Hebrew promissory notes were valid outside the Jewish community and even involved non-Jews. The legality of such a deed prepared by 'Rabi' Mahir, the *sofer* of Huesca, was not questioned in 1290.[18] In some communities a document signed by the *sofer* had the same validity as one signed by two witnesses, as required by Jewish law. Lérida, for instance, adopted such an ordinance at the end of the thirteenth century.[19] This rule was in accordance with the decision of R. Shelomo ben Adret, the leading halakhist in the country.[20] This halakhic decision followed the law of the land, which considered the copy kept by the notary as proof of the authenticity of the promissory note. The ordinance was designed to solve many problems that ensued from the death or absence of witnesses.[21]

Most scribes belonged to the intellectual class in Jewish society. They were Hebraists and knowledgeable in Jewish law. Some were linguists, others scientists or physicians. Jahuda Bonsenyor was a scholar and linguist. He was commissioned to compile in Catalan an anthology of parables from Hebrew, Latin, and Arabic literature. He also translated scientific books into Catalan. His appointment illustrates the intellectual level and the high prestige of a scribe or notary public for Hebrew in a large community like Barcelona.[22] As mentioned above, in 1314 the scribe of Saragossa, R. Azariah, was a physician, and as he bore the title 'Rabbi' we may assume he was learned in the Torah. In fact, in Saragossa the scribes

---

[15] ACA, Reg. 197, fo. 106 [R 2733].
[16] Asibili (Kapah) 56 [= Asibili (Blau) 12].
[17] ACA, Reg. 13, fo. 163 [= R 254 = Jacobs 280]. The validity of Hebrew documents in the country and the legality of notarial acts in Jewish courts, a very important theme in the history of the *halakhah* and of Jewish autonomy, deserve special treatment. Here interest is focused on the status and work of the scribe.
[18] ACA, Reg. 85, fo. 18ᵛ [R 2119].
[19] Adret, i. 729 = iii. 438.
[20] Adret, ii. 111, iv. 199.
[21] Adret, viii. 65.
[22] Jahuda's book *Llibre de paraules e dits de savis e filosofs* has been published. For sources on the author, see Rubió, *Documents*, vols. i, ii, and indexes, and Cardoner, 'Nuevos datos', pp. 287-8.

generally must have been known for their Jewish erudition, for in a document from 1300 the scribes of the community were called *rabis*.[23] In 1311 and 1321 the post was occupied by *Rabi* Joce Avenjacob, *scrivano*, obviously a rabbinic scholar and one of the leaders of the community.[24]

The status of the scribes in the communities of the Crown was not uniform. In some communities the scribe was appointed by the king and had a monopoly on most types of Hebrew documents. In several others, one of the leaders of the community obtained the post. In yet others, the scribe was a functionary appointed by the community or its representatives. In some communities the scribe was attached to the *beth din*.

THE *ALBEDIN*

The *albedin, bedin, bidin*, or *mandadero* was found only in the communities of the Kingdom of Aragon and in neighbouring Castile.[25] The word obviously comes from the Hebrew *beth din*, with the Arabic definite article *al*. The *albedin* was an executive officer who carried out the decisions of the *beth din* and the *adelantados*. He was also in charge of the collection of fines from Jewish litigants in trials with Christians. The Jewish community would want the *albedin*, rather than the Christian judge, to collect such fines.[26] The *albedin* collected both the fines imposed by the court and those fixed by law that he was empowered to impose on Jews guilty of violence. Within the context of the law he could also confiscate and inflict other punishments. It seems that he had some judicial power and acted in some cases as a *dayan*. The number of the *albedin* depended on the community leaders.[27] The authority of the *albedin* was confirmed in a privilege by Jaime I that was reasserted in 1299 by Jaime II.[28] The *albedin* was appointed by the *adelantados* and the *secretarios*.[29] The post existed throughout the fourteenth century in Aragonese communities.[30]

The *albedin*'s task was facilitated by close cooperation with the local baile. However, the authorities were not always constant in their support of the *albedin*.

---

[23] For R. Azaria, see ACA, Reg. 211, fo. 220 [= R 3001]. For the scribes of Saragossa, see Reg. 197, fo. 106 [= R 2733] and Beinart, 'A 15th Century Hebrew Formulary', pp. 77–8.

[24] ACA, Reg. 207, fos. 239ʻ–240 [= R 2919] (this source is in Aragonese, and not in Catalan as suggested by Régné); Reg. 239, fos. 18ʻ–19 [= Baer, *Spanien*, doc. 164].

[25] Beinart, 'Hispano-Jewish Society', p. 235; Tilander, *Los Fueros de Aragón*; Gorosch, *El Fuero de Teruel*.

[26] The Jews of Teruel, for instance, asked Jaime II in May 1325 to ensure that the fines imposed on Jews in mixed trials be paid to the *albedin*: ACA, CR, Jaime II, C 133, no. 99 [= *Cartas Reales*, no. 321].

[27] ACA, Reg. 942, fo. 55 [= Baer, *Spanien*, doc. 357].

[28] ACA, Reg. 197, fo. 19ʻ [= R 2720 = Baer, *Spanien*, doc. 142].

[29] ARP, t. 1688, fo. 73 [= Baer, *Spanien*, doc. 163, para. 5].

[30] ACA, Reg. 1678, fos. 107–12 [= Baer, *Spanien*, doc. 215]; Reg. 1202, fo. 183 [= Baer, *Spanien*, doc. 272].

The fines imposed by the *albedin* were sometimes modified by the king. In 1319, for instance, the fines imposed by the *albedin* of Calatayud on two Jews who attacked another Jew were reduced by Jaime II.[31] The *albedin* was eager to collect the fines as he received 7 per cent of the sum.[32] Although the *albedin* was appointed by the leaders of the community, his status in the communal bureaucracy was somewhat ambivalent. The fact that the *albedin* was also in charge of collecting the fines that his own *aljama* or part of the Jewish public had to pay strained the relations between the *albedin* and his community. As an appointee of the community, he could often find himself in an embarrassing and uncomfortable situation.

Sometimes the dismissal of an *albedin* by the leaders of his own community caused royal intervention. In the second decade of the fourteenth century, the leaders of the Jews in Daroca dismissed the *albedin* Manuel, son of Açach Manuel, who had been appointed by their predecessors. Their decision brought an immediate reaction by the baile.[33] In those days informers were often involved in uncovering the misdeeds of the community and the public, for which fines were imposed. In Luna, the three *adelantados* were denounced to the baile for having dismissed the *albedin* Jento Caracallo and appointed their own candidate to the post.[34]

The *albedin* himself was often seen as an informer. Whether this was because that was the nature of his work, or because he was overenthusiastic in the pursuit of his commission, it is difficult to determine. As the *albedin* was present with the *adelantados* while Jews took their oath, he was well placed to report any breach of oath. In one case, the *albedin* Jento d'Abdella was present when a Jew from Tarazona took an oath that he would not gamble again. The fine was collected and transmitted to the baile. The *albedin* of Sos was witness to the oath taken before the *adelantados* by two Jews who reported that a fellow Jew charged interest higher than the maximum rate. The *albedin* had little option but to give the full information on the case.[35]

THE GATE-KEEPERS

Very few Jewish quarters were completely enclosed in the thirteenth and fourteenth centuries. Where such quarters existed, the community sometimes (though not always) employed a *portero* or gate-keeper in charge of the gates. He was responsible for the opening and closing of the gates at appointed times and guarded the gate.

---

[31] ACA, Reg. 217, fos. 149ʳ-150 [= R 3115].
[32] ARP, t. 1688, fos. 46, 48ᵛ [= Baer, *Spanien*, doc. 163, paras. 2, 4].
[33] ARP, t. 1688, fo. 73 [= Baer, *Spanien*, doc. 163, para. 5].
[34] ARP, t. 1688, fos. 96-7 [= Baer, *Spanien*, doc. 163, para. 9].
[35] ARP, t. 1688, fos. 96-7 [= Baer, *Spanien*, doc. 163, paras. 10, 14].

Astrug Obrador, the gate-keeper of the *call* of Barcelona, was among the ten Jews (forming a *minyan*, or quorum) who were permitted to participate in the funeral of Içach Çaporta, executed for crimes in 1291.[36] Four years later, the gate-keeper of the same *call* was Jucef.[37]

THE COMMUNITY PHYSICIAN

Several communities engaged the services of a physician for the benefit of the sick among the poorer Jews. Clear evidence that some communities had such a physician on their pay-roll is found in Tazrat's *Huqat ha-Dayanim*.[38] It is unlikely that many communities did, however, since the sources referring to physicians are so few. According to a document from 1313, R. Azraiah Abenjacob, the physician and the scribe of the community of Saragossa, was authorized to choose his own substitute.[39] It is not clear whether he wanted to be replaced as physician or as scribe of the community, or as both. In 1314, we may recall, he asked the king to permit him to have a substitute as a scribe, so that he could devote himself to his patients.[40] From these documents, however, we can draw no definite conclusion that he was employed by the community. He could have been a physician who served the sick in a private capacity, as the expression 'the physician of the community' is ambiguous. Even in those *aljamas* where it appears there was a community physician, the payment he received left him free to offer his services also to the Christian population and the royal family.

THE *HAZAN*

The *hazan* or *capella* was the most important functionary of the Jewish community.[41] A *hazan* was in charge of one synagogue, usually the major one in the *judería*, although other smaller synagogues might have had their own *hazanim* as well. He was paid from the community budget or from a special levy imposed on the congregants,[42] as was the case with the *capella del ascola major* in Valencia in 1299.[43] In those communities where a special levy was raised to pay the *hazan*, there were often arguments as to whether the levy should be distributed according to wealth or according to the number of people in the family.[44] The *hazan* was paid to conduct the services and perform a variety of other functions related to communal and synagogal life, including weddings, funerals, and other

---

[36] ACA, Reg. 86, fo. 59ᵛ [=R 2426].
[37] ACB, Notaria Capitular, Bernat de Vilarrubia 1295, fos. 70ᵛ–71.
[38] Tazrat, *Huqat ha-Dayanim*, no. 156.
[39] ACA, Reg. 447, fo. 147; Reg. 860, fo. 213 [=R 2985].
[40] ACA, Reg. 211, fo. 220 [=R 3001]. In 1323 R. Azaria left both his posts to accompany one of the infante's councillors to Sardinia.
[41] See Assis, 'Synagogues', pp. 27–8.   [42] Adret, iii. 381.
[43] ACA, CR, Alfonso III, Ex. s., no. 131 [= *Cartas Reales*, no. 35].   [44] Adret, v. 15.

ceremonies. In several communities it was enacted that only weddings that took place with a *minyan* and a *hazan* were valid.[45] Certain *hazanim* were expected to write Hebrew documents, such as the *ketubot*.[46] They enjoyed several privileges, including tax exemption.[47]

The appointment of a *hazan* was a major occurrence, due to the importance of the post and its usually long occupation by the same person. In many communities the entire adult male population, or, where the appointment was for one of the *aljama*'s synagogues, all the congregants of that synagogue, participated in the election. In a few communities the leaders appointed the *hazan*. As the qualities looked for were so many and varied, and their importance was differently evaluated, dissent and arguments during the process were almost inevitable. Division within the community on this issue was at times so severe that the parties turned to the king for support. In 1309, when the Jews of Tárrega could not elect a *hazan*, Jaime II ordered that the election be made by majority vote.[48]

Even where there were some people suitable to lead the services on a voluntary basis, communal leaders and rabbinic authorities in many *aljamas* preferred to hire a *hazan*. This decision was designed to prevent unsuitable people from acting as *hazanim*, a problem experienced in several communities which had to take measures to prevent members from acting in this capacity without the consent of the leaders.[49] Furthermore, only a salaried *hazan* could be expected to comply with the community's requirements and be meticulous in the fulfilment of his duties.[50]

A contract was usually signed between the community and the candidate. Some communities encountered serious difficulties in their search for a suitable candidate. Often the community had to find its *hazan* from afar, with all the complications that this entailed. Even after a contract was signed, the community was not absolutely sure that the candidate would take the position.[51] The contract was sometimes for life, and in a number of cases one family had a monopoly on the post. Such was the case of the *hazan* of Huesca in the second half of the thirteenth century, whose father and grandfather were also the *hazanim* of the same synagogue. After he had occupied the post of *hazan* for thirty-eight years he decided to bring in his son as his assistant, a move opposed by the community leaders. Although he had many supporters among the the congregants of his synagogue,

---

[45] For the ordinance on weddings, see Adret, i. 550, v. 314; Asibili (Kapah), 68. R. Meir Abulafia's description of the *hazan*'s duties applied equally to the Crown of Aragon as to Castile. See Abulafia, *Responsa*, 241. [46] Adret, i. 300.

[47] ACA, Reg. 383, fos. 40–2 [= Baer, *Spanien*, doc. 175].

[48] ACA, Reg. 206, fos. 43ᵛ–44 [=R 2902].

[49] See e.g. the case of Montpellier, where the community leaders asked Jaime I to forbid any Jew from serving as *hazan* without their consent: ACA, Reg. 16, fo. 148ᵛ [=R 438 = Jacobs 440 = Bofarull, Montpellier, 490]. [50] Adret, i. 450, 691, iii. 439, vii. 265.

[51] For the problems that the community of Majorca had in engaging a *hazan* from Perpignan in the fourteenth century see Gerondi 65.

the *sinoga mayor*, the leaders objected to the appointment of his son, whose voice was not pleasant, and insisted that he should either continue to serve in accordance with his contract or vacate his post.[52] In the course of time, more and more communities opted for a limited contract. Irrespective of the type of contract signed, a *hazan* would not normally be dismissed unless he was guilty of serious misconduct.[53]

In addition to the services he conducted, the *hazan* fulfilled various other tasks. Not only was he present at weddings, as mentioned above, he also performed the wedding ceremony.[54] He made all the important announcements in the synagogue.[55] He proclaimed the *herem* and the *niduy* during the service, and their abrogation.[56] He read the *taqanot* or ordinances of the community in the synagogue, after which they became valid.[57] He also announced the election results in the synagogue.[58]

COMMUNAL RABBI AND COURT RABBI

The communities of the Crown of Aragon in the thirteenth and fourteenth centuries had spiritual and rabbinic leaders of world fame whose works had great influence on world Jewry both in their own time and for generations to come. Among these leaders were R. Mose ben Nahman, R. Jonah Gerondi, R. Shelomo ben Adret, R. Aharon Ha-Levi de Na Clara, R. Bahye ben Asher, R. Yom Tov Asibili, R. Nissim Gerondi, and R. Yishaq ben Shehet Perfet. None of these scholars, as far as we know, was a salaried rabbi, employed by the community: they were leaders of the community, merchants, moneylenders, physicians, teachers in the *yeshivot*. Their great halakhic and Talmudic erudition was further promoted by their financial independence and freedom from any communal patronage. Most of these great authorities belonged to the aristocratic stratum in Jewish society.[59]

The rabbis who were paid a salary by the community formed a different category altogether. Their duties were related to synagogal life. Some were engaged as *darshanim* or preachers to preach in synagogues on the Sabbath and at festivals. The leaders of the community hired the preacher by contract. From an extant contract we have a good idea of the conditions of his work.[60] It seems that during this period many communities employed preachers. Some rich Jews

---

[52] Adret, i. 300 contains the text of the contract.   [53] Adret, v. 283.
[54] Asibili (Kapah) 69 [= Adret i. 1180].   [55] Asibili (Blau) 5; (Kapah) 156, 165.
[56] Adret, i. 815, iii. 304, 306; ACA, Reg. 219, fo. 208ʳᵛ [= R 355].
[57] Adret, iii. 395. For Barcelona see ACA, Reg. 230, fos. 106–107ᵛ [= R 3454 = Jacobs 892 = Baer, *Spanien*, doc. 189].
[58] Adret, v. 284 [= Baer, *Spanien*, doc. 143, para. 11].
[59] The scholars of the Crown of Aragon are not included in this chapter as they were not part of the communal administration in so far as they were rabbinic scholars (see Part VI on religious life and scholars and scholarship).   [60] Adret, v. 273.

bequeathed money towards their salaries.[61] Although most of the preachers were unknown figures of modest calibre, there were a few famous individuals, such as R. Bahye ben Asher, who were outstanding scholars. R. Bahye preached at the beginning of the fourteenth century in a synagogue at Saragossa, where his sermons probably formed the basis of his book *Kad ha-Qemah*.[62] Not all preachers, however, were of the same standard, and the teachings of the less proficient were severely criticized by R. Shelomo ben Adret, who said of one such: 'Heavens forbid! He is neither a wise man nor a scholar but a wicked and foolish man . . . who has failed and caused others to fail and deserves to be under ban.'[63]

The professionalization of the rabbinate in the Crown of Aragon was a gradual process. Before the end of the thirteenth century few communities employed rabbis. The functions of the communal rabbi were not clearly defined and there were regional variations. There was no uniformity even within one region, as the needs and wishes of the individual community determined the rabbi's duties. The communal rabbi would act as a preacher, a teacher, a *hazan*, a *shohet*, a *sofer*, or a judge on top of his work as a religious guide, as the needs of the community required. In Lérida the rabbi's salary was paid from a fund established by Ismael Avinabez de Ablitas, a Jew from Tudela, to teach the children of the poor.[64] In the second decade of the fourteenth century, Davi, *rabi del aliama de los judios de Darocha*, served as a slaughterer, while the rabbi of the small community of Tauste was Hacen, son of the physician Salamon, from Egea. In Daroca, rabbis served as judges and scribes as well.[65] At that time, the community of Saragossa also employed a salaried rabbi and in 1320 obtained a confirmation to choose its own rabbis.[66] Some of the immigrant rabbis from Franco-Germany and Provence who settled in the Crown of Aragon in the course of the fourteenth century became salaried rabbis. Famous among them was R. Perez Ha-Cohen, a protégé of R. Nissim Gerondi. In fourteenth-century neighbouring Castile as well, the appointment of salaried rabbis became a widespread practice. Some small communities debated whether they should engage a *hazan* or a rabbi, if their resources could only maintain one of them.[67]

In most communities the rabbis served in several capacities, in fields connected with ritual, liturgy, education, and justice. In most cases the salaried rabbi of the community performed technical duties, in contrast to the rabbinic leaders who were financially independent of the community and who fulfilled a vital role in Jewish jurisprudence, Torah studies, and Talmudic scholarship. In communities where the public was not satisfied with the programme of teaching, if any, that

---

[61] Asibili (Kapah) 161.
[62] The structure of his book shows that it may have been compiled from series of sermons delivered over the years. See *Kad ha-Qemah*, Kippurim, ii. 227.   [63] Adret, i. 180.
[64] ACA, Reg. 392, fos. 245ᵛ–246ᵛ [= Baer, *Spanien*, doc. 185 = Assaf, *Sources*, ii, pp. 45, 47].
[65] ARP, t. 1688, fos. 96–7 [= Baer, *Spanien*, doc. 163, paras. 1, 4, 13].
[66] ACA, Reg. 218, fo. 155ᵛ [=R 3144].
[67] On R. Perez ha-Cohen see Shatzmiller, 'Rabbi Isaac Ha-Cohen'; on Castile, see Asher, vi. 1.

their leaders offered, there were attempts by groups to find alternatives. In one community, ten Jews hired a rabbi to teach them as the community had failed to provide a satisfactory programme of adult education.[68]

Some of the communal or regional rabbis were appointed by the king. The Jewish communities throughout the kingdom resisted attempts by the king or his entourage to impose on them rabbis whom they had not chosen themselves. These rabbis could hardly be considered genuine communal rabbis, but as they intended to occupy the post, although via royal favouritism rather than the community's consent, they are treated here. The court rabbis did not owe their position to their rabbinic expertise but rather to their influence at court. R. Shelomo ben Adret writes that 'in our country there are rabbis of the kingdom who do not even know how to read properly. What should be done to a Jew who insulted them?' In his answer, Adret states that such rabbis do not fall under the category of scholars, if insulted, but are to be treated like any ordinary Jew.[69]

Adret's low opinion of the court rabbis was shared by the Jewish public, who opposed vehemently any move to appoint king's favourites to rabbinic posts. Such moves were made exclusively in Aragon. The candidates were all members of the aristocratic elite that aroused so much antagonism among the lower classes, among them Ismael de Portella and Salamon and Bahye Alconstantini.[70]

In 1294 Jaime II rejected the request of his mother-in-law, the Queen of Castile, to appoint Salamon Alconstantini as *jutge o rap sobre todos los judios d'Aragon*, a post he had held during the reign of his predecessors Pedro III and Alfonso III. Explaining that such an appointment would cause great harm to all the Jews of the land, the Aragonese monarch argued that it would be unreasonable to ask him 'that for one Jew he should lose the others'.[71] The same king, however, disregarded this sound argument nine years later when he appointed Ismael de Portella as judge of appeal for the Jews of Aragon.[72] In 1312 Bahye Alconstantini obtained the post.[73] Needless to say, Jaime II had good reason to favour these Jews and to allow them to occupy a post for which the rabbinic scholars of the period found them totally unfit. However, these repeated efforts to impose rabbis never had lasting results as the Jewish community on the whole refused to accept the halakhic pre-eminence of people who were unqualified to fill the position.

THE COMMUNITY TEACHER

Until quite late in the history of Iberian Jewry no systematic education was provided by the community. (The development of an educational system in the

---

[68] Adret, viii. 1.
[69] Adret, i. 475, viii. 245.
[70] See Beinart, 'The Image of Jewish Courtiers', pp. 55–71.
[71] ACA, Reg. 252, fo. 50 [= R 2551 = Baer, *Spanien*, doc. 136].
[72] ACA, Reg. 231, fo. 13 [= R 2837 = Baer, *Spanien*, doc. 153, para. 5].
[73] ACA, Reg. 481, fo. 249 [= Baer, *Spanien*, pp. 151–2].

Jewish community is discussed in Parts V and VI below.) Children of the rich and the middle classes were taught by tutors who were paid by the parents and guardians.[74] Education was largely a private matter in which the community was not involved.[75] Nevertheless most poor boys received some education thanks to the generosity of rich individuals who left assets to fund their tuition. The teachers who were paid from these funds were not employees of the community.

Although the change occurred rather late, even in the thirteenth century we find pioneering work initiated by some communities which set up schools for children, mostly from poor families. Teachers were engaged and paid from the funds of the community. From several documents related to the appointment of a teacher, it is clear that the pupils were poor and that the teacher's salary came mostly from funds specifically donated for this purpose.[76] Eventually, the establishment of funds specifically allocated for education led the community to hire teachers. Even then, the matter remained part of the charity policy of the community. Thus we find in some communities that it was the *gizbar heqdesh*, that is, the officer in charge of charity funds, who engaged a teacher for the pupils of the poor.[77] In other cases, the entire enterprise seemed to remain completely in private hands: a member would hire a teacher to teach the children of the poor and pay him from his own pocket.[78]

It was in the course of the fourteenth century that more and more communities began to appoint a teacher to educate the children of the poor, although the operation tended to remain part of the community's charity policy. In the first quarter of the fourteenth century in Huesca, a regular fee was collected from the members to pay the teacher of the poor children. When some Jews complained that the collectors were not doing their job properly, the Infante Alfonso ordered that the accounts be submitted to him.[79] Although Tazrat listed the teacher among the communal functionaries whose salary was paid from public funds, such teachers were not found in every community.[80]

THE *SHAMASH*

In some communities, the leaders hired a *shamash* to attend to the needs of the synagogue. The *shamash* or sacristan was responsible for the order, cleanliness, and maintenance of the synagogue. Apart from these traditional duties, the *shamash* of the communities in the Crown of Aragon also performed some special duties: for example, he invited the members to the meetings of the community.[81]

The *shamash* was appointed by the members or the leaders (though not all

---

[74] Adret, i. 643, 645, v. 229.
[75] Adret, i. 1042, viii. 1.
[76] ACA, Reg, 392, fos. 245ʳ–246ʳ [= Baer, *Spanien*, doc. 185 = Assaf, *Sources*, ii, pp. 46, 47].
[77] Adret, i. 1157.
[78] Adret, i. 1157.
[79] ACA, CR, Jaime II, C 134, no. 144 [= *Cartas Reales*, no. 431].
[80] Tazrat, *Huqat ha-Dayanim*, no. 156.
[81] Adret, v. 15.

synagogues had a *shamash* officially appointed). As with the *hazan*, the hiring of the *shamash* did not always go smoothly. The community of Tárrega, which had trouble in appointing a *hazan*, had a similar problem in hiring a *shamash*. The king, we may recall, ordered that the choice be made by majority vote.[82]

The *shamash* received a regular fee, paid in the same way as the *hazan*'s.[83] Payments to the *shamash* of the synagogue were recorded in the community's registers, and expenses reports were sent to the king to be set against tax. In a list of expenses submitted by the *aljama* of Valencia in 1299, one of the items was a payment of 49 s to the *sagrista dela escola major*.[84]

Was there a woman functionary who did equivalent or similar work to that of the *shamash*? Was there a woman who worked in the synagogue? Was there a woman employed by the community whose duty was to look after the synagogal needs of the female worshippers? As noted earlier, a document from October 1325 relates the case of a Jewess from Saragossa called Ceti, *rabisse* of the Jewish women of the great synagogue, whom some wanted to dismiss after more than twenty years of work. The Infante Alfonso ordered the *adelantados* not to permit her dismissal. The title *rabisse*, used normally for the wife of the rabbi, suggests that Ceti performed some sort of religious work connected with synagogue services, probably leading the service in the women's section of the synagogue or assisting the women worshippers in their prayers.[85]

THE *SHOHET* OR SLAUGHTERER

Most communities, if not all, had their own *shohet*, appointed by the leaders of the community or a specially formed committee.[86] Even where there was no Jewish slaughterhouse, there was a duly appointed *shohet* who slaughtered in the Christian or even the Muslim abattoir.[87] The appointment involved both religious and economic considerations. On the one hand, the candidate had to be an expert in ritual slaughter, on whose religious and honest conduct the Jewish public could rely. On the other hand, as the sale of *kasher* meat was one of the major sources of revenue for the community, the leaders had to consider the best possible candidate whose cooperation could be secured in raising the levy on meat.

The appointment of the *shohet* was not without problems, since the prospects for financial gain led many outsiders to interfere in the process. To safeguard their rights, Jewish communities turned to the king for support. Some obtained an explicit privilege empowering them to appoint their *shohet* without outside

---

[82] ACA, Reg. 206, fos. 43'–44 [= R 2902]. [83] Adret, v. 15.
[84] ACA, CR, Alfonso III, Ex. s., no. 131 [= *Cartas Reales*, no. 35].
[85] ACA, CR, Jaime II, C 133, no. 125 [= *Cartas Reales*, no. 343].
[86] Nahmanides 77; Adret, v. 129.
[87] ACA, CR, Jaime II, C 8, no. 1684; Reg. 383, fos. 40–2 [= Baer, *Spanien*, doc. 175, para. 3]; Adret, i. 345, 786.

interference. Many communities, however, found themselves deprived of their right to choose their own slaughterers. When in 1321 Jaime II gave his secretary the right to appoint the slaughterers in the *aljama* of Valencia, the latter protested and referred the king to the privilege of Jaime I permitting the Jews to appoint their own slaughterers. Jaime II did not cancel his appointment; he only conceded that after the death of the beneficiary, the *aljama* would regain its right to appoint its own slaughterers.[88]

For financial and religious reasons there was a very strict supervision of ritual slaughter, both by the community and by the king. The *shohatim* in Barcelona, and presumably elsewhere, had to take an oath before the baile every year that they would not slaughter more than was needed for Jewish consumption.[89] The communal supervision was twofold; financial and ritual. The *shohet* and the tax-collectors kept a record of all the animals slaughtered, and the registers served as a basis for the computation of the meat tax and for control by the royal authorities. The method might have been rather similar to that of Navarrese Jewish communities whose registers are extant.[90]

The community's leaders and its rabbinic authorities supervised the competence and the ritual aptitude of the *shohet*.[91] If the latter was not careful with his knife and slaughtering, he would probably be immediately put under ban or dismissed; at the least, strict supervision would be established on his slaughtering.[92] This measure was far from satisfactory, but it might have been taken in cases where there was no other candidate for the job. In the early fourteenth century, Davi, *Rabi de la aliama*, was put under ban in accordance with the ordinance of the community as his slaughtering was found to be inadequate. Some Jews turned to the baile general, requesting him to reinstate the *shohet* in office and put an end to his poverty.[93]

In some communities the *shohet* was also the butcher, and in this case his interest in the sale of *kasher* meat was even greater. In those communities where there was more than one butcher the competition sometimes led to physical violence, involving even their wives, and to their eventual dismissal or the issue of a ban against them.[94]

---

[88] ACA, Reg. 219, fos. 214ˇ–215 [=R 3168]. The community of Saragossa was more successful in its attempts to have the slaughterers of its choice. Two months earlier, Jaime II agreed that the *aljama*, not his officials, should appoint its own slaughterers: ACA, Reg. 218, fo. 155ˇ [=R 3144].

[89] ACA, Reg. 200, fo. 140 [=R 2800]. The problem of selling Jewish meat to Christians is discussed in Part IV on 'The Jewish Quarter'.

[90] See Assis and Magdalena, *The Jews of Navarre*, doc. 17, pp. 159–66, doc. 18, pp. 166–74; Assis et al., *Aljamía romance*, docs. 33–5, 38.

[91] Adret, viii. 161.   [92] Asibili (Kapah) 121.

[93] ARP, t. 1688, fo. 39 [= Baer, *Spanien*, doc. 163, para. 1].   [94] Asibili (Kapah) 67.

§2.6 The Law and the Judiciary

THE LEGAL FOUNDATIONS

FOR the Jewish communities of the Crown of Aragon, the almost exclusive predominance of Jewish law or *halakhah* as the basis of their judicial system was a matter of principle shared with Jews all over the world. The king's recognition of Jewish law as the foundation of the system enhanced its validity significantly. The privileges granted to Jewish communities authorizing them to adjudicate between Jews according to their laws were followed by the equally important royal support of the verdicts rendered *secundum legem iudeorum*.[1]

Records from the second half of the thirteenth century state clearly that disputes between Jews should be settled according to Jewish law. The fact that Jewish law or *halakhah* is referred to as *açuna*, the word in Arabic for law, in documents from 1264 and 1270 concerning the Jews of Saragossa and Lérida respectively leaves no doubt that this was merely a confirmation of a situation dating back to periods preceding the early Reconquista.[2] The use of an Arabic term for Torah or *halakhah* in *aljamas* that had been under Christian rule for almost a century and a half since their conquest from the Muslims indicates that there was no interruption in the tradition.[3] The term was used throughout the period to denote Jewish law, and in most sources it appears in connection with the king's policy advocating its use in litigation among Jews. This policy was clear and explicit. All trials between Jews in all Jewish communities had to be conducted according to Jewish law.[4] The charter of Pedro III granting the Jews of Catalonia the right to adjudicate between their members according to Jewish law even in civil and criminal lawsuits, as long as the baile was informed, was confirmed by Jaime II.[5]

In matrimonial cases, the principle was that the settlement should be in accordance with the *halakhah*, and the Aragonese monarchs were consistent in their support of Jewish matrimonial law. The divorce procedure and women's rights as prescribed by their *ketubah*, and many other details connected with marriage and

---

[1] See the charter of the Valencian Jews from 1239: ACA, Reg 941, fos. 176ᵛ–177 [= Baer, *Spanien*, doc. 91]. For the king's support of halakhic verdicts, see Reg. 16, fos. 261ᵛ–262 [= R 461 = Jacobs 483 = Bofarull, Barcelona, ciii = Baer, *Spanien*, doc. 104 = MF i. 1096].
[2] ACA, Reg. 13, fo. 163 [= R 254 = Jacobs 280]; Reg. 16, fo. 202 [= R 446 = Jacobs 462].
[3] Saragossa and Lérida were captured in 1118 and 1149 respectively.
[4] ACA, Reg. 59, fo. 21 [= R 924]; Reg. 43, fos. 8ᵛ, 50ᵛ [= R 1177, 1220]; Reg. 75, fo. 52 [= R 1831].
[5] ACA, Reg. 195, fo. 44 [= R 2629 = Baer, *Spanien*, doc. 139].

divorce, came within the strict boundaries of the *halakhah*.[6] Refusal by a husband to give a *get* (divorce bill) to his wife could create an impasse which was difficult to overcome in certain cases unless the king ensured that the obstinate husband appeared before a properly constituted *beth din*.[7] The financial rights of women according to their marriage contracts and their alimony in accordance with Hebrew acts were protected by orders of the king, as were halakhic verdicts in their favour.[8] Particularly noteworthy is the order issued by Pedro III in 1285 to all his officials in the Kingdom of Valencia guaranteeing women's rights to their husbands' assets and property according to Jewish law, if their husbands were involved in legal proceedings.[9] In the exchange of correspondence between the royal court on the one hand and the king's officials and the Jews on the other, there was no question but that all matrimonial matters were resolved according to Jewish law.[10]

Complicated matrimonial cases were referred by the king to the leading halakhic authorities of the land. In 1289 Alfonso III asked R. Shelomo ben Adret and R. Aharon de Na Clara to settle a certain case in Barcelona.[11] In the case of a beaten wife who abandoned her conjugal home in 1293, the infante asked the *dayan* of Calatayud not to force the fugitive wife to return home, if that were not in contradiction with the Jewish *açuna*.[12] Even in lawsuits on matters of dowry brought before a Christian magistrate, the latter was ordered to consult Jewish jurists, since the verdict had to be in accordance with Jewish law.[13]

In matrimonial law as in religious precepts, at the very least, from a Jewish point of view the *halakhah* supersedes the laws of the land in almost all circumstances. It was, therefore, a great achievement that the king accepted this principle. In the case of polygamy, prohibited in the Crown of Aragon, the Aragonese monarchs gave precedence to Jewish law that permitted such marriages. Permissions for bigamous marriages became particularly frequent in the fourteenth century, when rabbinic opposition to bigamy increased, following growing influence from Franco-German Jewish circles.[14] Whenever there was a clash between Jewish

---

[6] See e.g. ACA, Reg. 50, fo. 168 [= R 875]; Reg. 59, fo. 23 [= R 929]; Reg. 60, fo. 33 [= R 1017]; Reg. 43, fo. 58 [= R 1229].   [7] See e.g. ACA, Reg. 63, fo. 83ᵛ [= R 1498].

[8] ACA, Reg. 46, fo. 107ᵛ [= R 1090]; Reg. 61, fo. 124 [= R 1057]; Reg. 62, fo. 130 [= R 1297]; Reg. 56, fo. 59 [= R 1333]; CR, Jaime II, C 133, no. 107 [= *Cartas Reales*, no. 331].

[9] ACA, Reg. 57, fo. 223 [= R 1461 = MF ii. 2302].

[10] ACA, Reg. 66, fo. 247ᵛ [= R 1678]; Reg. 70, fo. 84ᵛ [= R 1714]; Reg. 80, fo. 95ᵛ [= R 2030]. Noteworthy was the extensive use of Hebrew matrimonial legal terminology in notarial acts written in Latin or Romance. For numerous instances see Secall, *Els jueus de Valls*, 120–33.

[11] ACA, Reg. 80, fo. 77ᵛ [= R 2022]. In Régné the names of the two rabbis are totally distorted.

[12] ACA, Reg. 87, fo. 118ᵛ [= R 2488].   [13] ACA, Reg. 85, fo. 217 [= R 2377].

[14] ACA, Reg. 15, fos. 64ᵛ–65 [= R 359 = Bofarull, Barcelona, lxii]; Reg. 216, fo. 114 [= R 3102]; Reg. 218, fo. 29 [= R 3129]; Reg. 222, fo. 142ᵛ [= R 3243 = *CDIA*, vi, pp. 240–1 = Indice 475]; Reg. 223, fo. 169ᵛ [= R 3249]; Reg. 226, fo. 43ᵛ [= R 3306, 3308]. On polygamous marriages see Assis, 'The "Ordinance of Rabbenu Gershom" '.

matrimonial and civil law and the law of the land, the latter was superseded, and the Jew was explicitly allowed to act in accordance with his law.[15]

Marriages performed contrary to Jewish law could be met with automatic cancellation or some punishment, depending on the severity of the prohibition flouted. In general, the royal authorities confirmed the halakhic position, despite a certain ambivalence.[16] In some cases where the *halakhah* was more stringent than the law of the kingdom, the king ordered that the *halakhah* should apply.[17]

In cases of inheritance, closely related to matrimonial law, the *halakhah* was upheld by the king whenever his interest was not at stake.[18] The validity of a Hebrew will, drawn up according to Jewish law, was not challenged.[19] It was a principle from which there was almost no deviation throughout the period. It was stressed in royal documents that problems of inheritance among Jews involving children and particularly widows had to be resolved according to the Jewish *açuna*.[20]

Even in civil and financial litigations between Jews, when no interest or law of the kingdom was in breach the kings supported the application of Jewish law or the *açuna* and referred suits to the *beth din* or renowned halakhists such as R. Shelomo ben Adret, R. Aharon Ha-Levi de Na Clara, or R. Shelomo Gratiani.[21] From extant Hebrew contracts we know that, on the whole, property transactions between Jews were subject to Jewish law and the *beth din*.[22] The verdicts of the *beth din* were fully endorsed by the Crown.[23] Even in monetary litigation between Jews in Gentile courts, and in some instances in criminal proceedings against Jews, the application of Jewish law was a principle followed by Aragonese monarchs throughout the thirteenth century. Royal officials were often instructed to apply the *halakhah* in litigations between Jews and in any case not to decide lawsuits in contradiction of the *açuna*.[24]

The king's general support of the Jews' right to have their courts adhere to

---

[15] ACA, Reg. 74, fos. 81, 86ᵛ [=R 1892, 1898].

[16] ACA, Reg. 225, fo. 287ᵛ [=R 3301].

[17] ACA, Reg. 49, fo. 95 [=R 866].

[18] ACA, Reg. 50, fo. 156ᵛ [=R 885]; Reg. 44, fo. 226 [=R 906]; Reg. 57, fo. 204 [=R 1450]; Reg. 70, fo. 172ᵛ [=R 1769]; Reg. 74, fo. 50 [=R 1846].

[19] ACA, Reg. 15, fo. 117ʳᵛ [=R 384]; Reg. 21, fos. 54, 56 [=R 526, 531, and doc. vi, pp. 420–1 = Jacobs 641, 646 = Bofarull, Barcelona, cxvii]; Reg. 63, fo. 39ᵛ [=R 1489].

[20] ACA, Pergaminos de Alfonso III, no. 93 [=R 1542].

[21] ACA, Reg. 21, fo. 37 [=R 520 = Jacobs 637 = Bofarull, Barcelona, cxiv]; Reg. 42, fo. 243ᵛ [=R 772]; Reg. 57, fo. 191ᵛ [=R 1435]; Reg. 66, fo. 162ᵛ [=R 1615]; Reg. 74, fo. 78 [=R 1877]; Reg. 81, fo. 9 [=R 2055]; Reg. 85, fo. 96ᵛ [=R 2310].

[22] ACA, Reg. 80, fo. 91 [=R 2025]. For Hebrew documents of transactions and *beth din* verdicts see Miret and Schwab, *Documents*; Millás, 'Documents'; Riera and Udina, 'Els documents en hebreu'.

[23] ACA, Reg. 66, fo. 9ᵛ [=R 1507].

[24] ACA, Reg. 42, fo. 217ᵛ [=R 766]; Reg. 59, fos. 52ᵛ, 74, 180ᵛ [=R 934, 953, 993]; Reg. 43, fo. 54ᵛ [=R 1224]; Reg. 57, fo. 155 [=R 1412]; Reg. 63, fo. 39 [=R 1488]; Reg. 70, fo. 103ᵛ [=R 103]. For criminal proceedings see ACA, Reg. 66, fos. 44, 54, 236ᵛ [=R 1533, 1537, 1674].

halakhah and his concern for the minutest details of its application are remarkable. In the thirteenth century the king gave preference to Jewish courts, rather than Christian ones, to deal with cases involving Jews.[25] It is particularly remarkable that even in trials conducted in royal courts, Jews' arguments based on Jewish law in their appeal to the king seem to have been taken seriously.[26]

In addition to the *halakhah*, the total repository of Jewish jurisprudence, the medieval community enacted its own by-laws or *taqanot* to deal with its local problems. Each community had the right to promulgate its own ordinances, which were as binding on its members as Jewish law was on all Jews.[27] This right was based on Jewish law and royal charter. From the Jewish point of view, the *taqanah*, from the Hebrew root that means to mend or to improve, is for the benefit of the public and is needed where there is no explicit *halakhah* to cope with a particular problem. The absence of an explicit halakhic solution, the nature of the problem, or circumstances rendering it inappropriate to follow the *halakhah* were primary causes for the enactment of *taqanot*.[28]

The *taqanah* was issued by the assembly or council of the community or by its representative leaders, the *berurim* or *adelantados*.[29] Its confirmation by a leading halakhic authority added to its prestige and moral validity, while the king's approval of the community's right to enact statutes ensured its application.[30] By the same token, the king and his advisers examined carefully the contents of the communal ordinances, which would be revoked if found to be detrimental to the king's interests.[31]

The ordinance was read in the main synagogue, at least, and was duly signed by appropriate witnesses.[32] Hebrew copies were kept in the archives of the community and in the hands of some leading members. The confirmation of the ordinance by the king implies that there was a translated copy in a Romance language.

Any infringement of the communal ordinances would entail the punishments prescribed, often with the king's full consent. The culprits could have very well been the leaders of the community and the transgressions included forging the text of the *taqanot*.[33] The king also knew that this legislative power of the Jewish communities could very well be placed at his disposal.[34] In other cases, however,

---

[25] ACA, Reg. 80, fo. 3ᵛ [=R 1959].

[26] ACA, Reg. 61, fo. 122 [=R 1056 = Baer, *Spanien*, doc. 125]; Reg. 43, fo. 54ᵛ [=R 1224].

[27] Adret, i. 769, iii. 417, iv. 185, vii. 490, viii. 280.

[28] Adret, ii. 107, iii. 395.

[29] ACA, Reg. 44, fos. 187ᵛ–188 [=R 823 = Baer, *Spanien*, doc. 121 = Dinur, ii. 2, p. 418, no. 8, and pp. 446–7, no. 2]; Reg. 195, fo. 44 [=R 2629 = Baer, *Spanien*, doc. 139]; Reg. 253, fo. 24 [=R 2648 = Isaacs 77]; Reg. 256, fo. 28]; Reg. 219, fo. 198ᵛ [=R 3163].

[30] ACA, Reg. 16, fo. 240ᵛ [=R 458 = Jacobs 474 = Bofarull, Barcelona, cii]; the community also sought the support of the king to annul a statute: Reg. 230, fo. 52 [R 3440].

[31] ACA, Reg. 213, fo. 265 [=R 3058].

[32] Adret, iii. 395.

[33] ACA, Reg. 51, fo. 43ʳᵛ [=R 1200]; Reg. 199, fo. 78 [=R 2776]; Reg. 206, fo. 22 [=R 2894].

[34] ACA, Reg. 58, fo. 106ᵛ [=R 1441].

he would relieve favourite Jews of their obligation to comply with the *taqanot*,[35] or cancel their fines for transgressing the ordinances of their community.[36]

The communal ordinances reflected the legal solutions to the communal, social, religious, and economic problems that Jewish society confronted. Most decisions concerning the communal regime were in the form of *taqanot*, which were usually confirmed by the king in their Romance translations. Hence we may expect to find both the Hebrew or Judeo-Romance ordinances on communal administration and their parallel Romance versions that were confirmed by the king. Any changes in the original version required royal approval; if attempts were made to alter *taqanot* without seeking such approval, there were bound to be some Jews who, dissatisfied with the change, reported it to the king. This happened, for instance, in 1295 when the *taqanah* on the election of *dayanim* in Saragossa was changed.[37]

A substantial number of ordinances dealt with various aspects of tax. They were usually proclaimed in the synagogue.[38] There were also ordinances issued by several communities.[39] Among the ordinances that regulated economic life in the community, those that related to the prices of *kasher* food were particularly important; ordinances also served as an efficient weapon in the hands of communities that competed for the sale of their wine product. Some were designed to introduce order in financial transactions within the Jewish community; others to control the spending power of the leaders. Many ordinances referred to money-lending.[40]

Many communities tried to establish control over their members by means of ordinances. Communities enacted ordinances against potential emigrants, informers, and other members whose behaviour was not compatible with the norm. Extravagant clothes were also forbidden by communal ordinances.[41] Many communities issued ordinances regulating the religious and moral life of their members. With the active support and involvement of a recognized halakhic figure, a leading community would sometimes issue an ordinance for all the communities. The best example is the ban of 1305 against the study of philosophy and sciences before the age of twenty-five, issued in Barcelona and signed by R. Shelomo ben Adret and the leaders of the *aljama*.[42]

---

[35] ACA, Reg. 213, fo. 250ᵛ [=R 3055]; Reg. 215, fo. 243 [=R 3082].

[36] ACA, Reg. 224, fo. 92ᵛ [=R 3286].

[37] ACA, Reg. 89, fo. 124ᵛ [=R 2587].

[38] Adret, v. 279; ACA, Reg. 13, fo. 211 [=R 276 = Jacobs 299]; Reg. 48, fo. 183ᵛ [=R 854]; Reg. 56, fo. 126 [=R 1344 and doc. xvi, pp. 430–2 = Baer, *Spanien*, doc. 129].

[39] Such was the *taqanah* of Barbastro: ACA, Reg. 43, fo. 111ʳᵛ [=R 1266–7 = Baer, *Spanien*, doc. 128, paras. 1–2].

[40] Adret, i. 590, ii. 335, iii. 443; ACA, Reg. 74, fo. 41ᵛ [=R 1840]; Reg. 86, fos. 99ᵛ–100, 144 [=R 2439, 2448 = Baer, *Spanien*, doc. 131.

[41] ACA, Reg. 228, fo. 26ᵛ [=R 3367]; Adret, iii. 384; ACA, Reg. 60, fo. 25 [=R 1021 = MF ii. 1666]; Reg. 56, fo. 92 [=R 1342].

[42] Adret, i. 415.

THE COURTS AND JUDGES

In one of the earliest documents of Jaime I's reign, the Jews of Calatayud were permitted to choose, with the consent of their *arrab* (rabbi), four *adelantados* who were authorized to exercise wide-ranging judicial power.[43] It seems clear that no distinction was made between the executive–administrative and the judicial functions of the *adelantados*, who prosecuted, judged, and punished transgressors while governing the community. Calatayud was not an isolated case: in Huesca in Pedro III's time or in Valencia under Jaime II the *adelantados* served also as judges.[44] Similarly, the charter granted to the *aljama* of Majorca during the brief Aragonese occupation in the last decade of the thirteenth century authorized the three elected *adelantados* to adjudicate between Jews.[45] Nevertheless, there is extensive evidence that in many *aljamas* there were specially appointed Jewish judges who sat in judgement between Jews.[46]

The judges were elected by the leaders of the community and a number of electors.[47] The judges sitting in one *beth din* could not be relatives and were forbidden to judge their relatives.[48] They were advised to behave in a manner befitting their eminent position and never to insult or deprecate the litigants.[49] The *dayanim* enjoyed no immunity; charges were brought against them like any other community member.[50]

The judges were sometimes subjected to pressure and even violence. Even so eminent an authority as R. Shelomo ben Adret was stoned in Villafranca in 1281 while he was commissioned to act as a judge there.[51] Salamon Avenbruch, who had been appointed as judge of the *aljama* of Saragossa by Pedro III, was assassinated in 1284,[52] most probably a victim of the class struggle in the community. He was a prominent member of the community and was very active during the reigns of Jaime I and Pedro III. Many were imprisoned but no one was convicted of the murder.[53]

The right of the Jews to have all their lawsuits tried by Jewish judges according to Jewish law does not necessarily imply that in every community there was a

---

[43] ACA, Reg. 202, fo. 201ʳ [= R 6].

[44] ACA, Reg. 37, fo. 34ˤ [= R 504 = Jacobs 726]; Reg. 89, fo. 60ˤ [= R 2568].

[45] ACA, Reg. 194, fo. 266 [= R 2623 = Isaacs 74].

[46] For Gerona see ACA, Reg. 10, fo. 15ˤ [= R 92 = Jacobs 128 = Bofarull, Barcelona, xiii]; Reg. 56, fo. 96 [= R 1347 = MF ii. 2210].

[47] ACA, Reg. 195, fo. 44 [= R 2629 = Baer, *Spanien*, doc. 139]; Reg. 256, fo. 28 [= R 2680].

[48] Adret, i. 750, vii. 392, vi. 6–7.

[49] Adret, vii. 496.

[50] ACA, Reg. 60, fo. 76 [= R 1039]; Reg. 207, fo. 244 [= R 2923].

[51] ACA, Reg. 50, fo. 169 [= R 873 = Dinur, ii. 3, p. 272, no. 26].

[52] ACA, Reg. 46, fo. 184 [= R 1119].

[53] See R 461, 1118, 1128, 1144, 1176, 1192, 1224, 1235, 1354; R. Shelomo ben Adret, who was consulted on the case, hesitated to get involved: ACA, Reg. 43, fo. 24ˤ [= R 1192 = Baer, *Spanien*, doc. 127].

permanent *beth din*. In places where no permanent court existed, an ad hoc court was constituted as the need arose. The alternative was sometimes to turn to non-Jewish courts, a move condemned by rabbinic authorities except in some financial disputes.[54] In some communities a permanent *beth din* was established later in the period as the need for one increased.[55]

Until the second half of the thirteenth century, the post of *dayan* was filled in many communities by powerful Jews who owed their appointment to the king and who acted alone. Many were lay leaders, not necessarily legal experts, although in some localities, where the right candidates were available, rabbis or halakhists filled the post. In 1270, for instance, Neci Azday, a rabbi *in mandatis Legis veteris*, was the judge in Lérida. He was to co-opt two Jews and thus they constituted a three-member *beth din*.[56] According to a *taqanah* of 1271, the Jews of Saragossa were to appoint three Jews as judges of the community. The appointment of the three, which was made with the full support of Jahuda de la Cavallería, the baile of Saragossa, contradicted an earlier appointment by the king of Salamon Alfaquim as the sole judge in all lawsuits in the city and in the Kingdom of Aragon. Cavallería, a rival of the Alconstantini family, of which Salamon was a member, led the move for the establishment of a three-member *beth din*, which included, apart from Salamon Alfaquim, Samuel Almeridi and Açach Abenbruch, members of leading Saragossan families. The move angered the Alconstantini family, who claimed that Salamon had acted as the judge of Aragonese and Valencian Jewry under Jaime I for many years before. Despite the protest, led by Salamon's nephew who had filled the post in his uncle's absence, Jaime I confirmed the newly constituted *beth din*.[57] The process of reform could not be reversed and the establishment of a properly constituted *beth din* could no longer be challenged even by the most powerful families. In 1280 Pedro III ordered the *aljama* of Saragossa to appoint in consultation with the twenty-five councillors or the majority of the community three judges who would serve for five years. A three-member *beth din* operated in the community in the following years.[58] The same year all the Catalan communities were authorized to elect between two and seven people who would act as judges.[59] From later sources we know that a similar charter was given to the Aragonese communities.[60] The charter was confirmed on several occasions, both to individual communities and to the Jews of an entire region.[61] In Valencia, too, a three-member *beth din* operated

[54] ACA, Reg. 59, fo. 23 [= R 930]; Adret, vii. 137; Assis, 'The Jews of Spain in Gentile Courts'.
[55] Adret, ii. 222.
[56] ACA, Reg. 16, fo. 202 [= R 446 = Jacobs 462].
[57] ACA, Reg. 16, fos. 240', 261'-262 [= R 458, 461 = Jacobs 474, 483 = Bofarull, Barcelona, cii–ciii = Baer, *Spanien*, doc. 104 = MF i. 1096].
[58] ACA, Reg. 44, fo. 177' [= R 776 = Baer, *Spanien*, doc. 118]; Reg. 60, fo. 76 [= R 1039].
[59] ACA, Reg. 44, fos. 187'-188 [= R 823 = Baer, *Spanien*, doc. 121 = Dinur, ii. 2, p. 418, no. 8, and pp. 446–7, no. 2].
[60] ACA, Reg. 59, fo. 56 [= R 942].
[61] ACA, Reg. 195, fo. 44 [R 2629 = Baer, *Spanien*, doc. 139]; Reg. 197, fo. 19' [= R 2720].

in the thirteenth century, and the king referred lawsuits to a court of three judges.[62]

In many civil and financial matters the Jewish court consisted of one person.[63] Although sometimes the king asked one or two judges to look into cases involving Jews, he was quite aware that in certain trials the participation of three judges in the panel of the court was imperative. When this law was ignored and one of the parties complained that the composition of the court was illegal, the king ordered a retrial.[64]

Lawsuits between communities and individuals or appeals from the local *beth din* were referred by the king to the famous halakhists of the period. A lawsuit between the *aljama* of Saragossa and a Jew from the community concerning buildings that belonged to the community's *heqdesh* or *elmosine* was referred in 1278 to the two famous jurists of Barcelona, R. Shelomo ben Adret and R. Aharon de Na Clara.[65] Litigation involving Jews from different *aljamas* was also occasionally brought to the attention of eminent halakhists. R. Aharon de Na Clara was asked in 1280 to handle a lawsuit between Jews of Lérida and Valencia.[66] Some matrimonial lawsuits were also referred by the king to the same halakhists. The king's interference in divorce cases is particularly noteworthy since that matter came under the exclusive jurisdiction of the Jewish court.[67]

In two particular types of litigation the king appointed judges: when his favourites were involved, or when the accusation was considered very grave.[68] Because of its gravity the case of Vidal de Porta, accused of being an informer, was left in 1279 to the care of the *magistris in lege ebrayca*, R. Shelomo ben Adret from Barcelona and Benedict Jona from Gerona.[69] Meanwhile all the communities of the Crown of Aragon were ordered to entrust the examination of the case to tribunals of three members who would collect all the relevant testimony. It is reasonable to assume that the communities decided that the matter should be dealt with by the *beth din*.[70] Some serious offences were tried in double trials, both in the king's court and in the *beth din*. David Mascaran, a very controversial figure accused of serious crimes, was tried in 1286 in the court of the *veguer* of Lérida and in the court of R. Shelomo ben Adret, the latter assisted by Zarch Malet and Saltel Astruch.[71] It seems that R. Shelomo ben Adret presided over his own

---

[62] ACA, Reg. 57, fo. 181 [= R 1424].

[63] ACA, Reg. 12, fo. 100 [= R 191 = Jacobs 204]; Reg. 91, fo. 148ᵛ [= R 2409].

[64] ACA, Reg. 74, fo. 86ᵛ [= R 1898].

[65] ACA, Reg. 41, fo. 6 [= R 712–3 = Baer, *Spanien*, doc. 115, paras. 1–2]. A matrimonial case was referred by Alfonso III to the same two rabbis in 1289: ACA, Reg. 80, fo. 77ᵛ [= R 2022].

[66] ACA, Reg, 42, fo. 243ᵛ [= R 772].

[67] ACA, Reg. 50, fo. 193ᵛ [= R 881 = Dinur, ii. 3, p. 272, no. 25]; Reg, 60, fo. 33 [= R 1017].

[68] For appointments of judges in cases involving influential Jews, see ACA, Reg, 63, fo. 83ᵛ [= R 1498]; Reg, 85, fo. 96ᵛ [= R 2310]; Reg, 66, fo. 162ᵛ [= R 1615]; Reg. 80, fo. 95ᵛ [= R 2030].

[69] ACA, Reg. 41, fo. 62 [= R 725 = Baer, *Spanien*, doc. 116, para. 1]; Reg. 42, fo. 169ᵛ [= R 751 = Baer, *Spanien*, doc. 116, para. 2]. [70] ACA, Reg. 41, fo. 76 [= R 728 = MF ii. 540].

[71] ACA, Reg. 66, fo. 9ᵛ [= R 1507–8].

beth din which operated as a high court and was probably independent of any communal control.

Expert jurists were sometimes asked to examine the decisions and the verdicts of a local *beth din* and serve as a court of appeal. A sentence handed out in 1285 by three judges in Barcelona would have been examined by R. Shelomo ben Adret, had one of the litigants objected to the verdict. The well-known halakhist examined cases that had already been sent for appeal.[72]

In the thirteenth and fourteenth centuries, the *beth din* in the communities of the Crown of Aragon had a very extensive jurisdiction. It had the power to imprison and even to impose capital punishment.[73] In practically all communities the *beth din* had the power to fine, expel, and ban.[74] The *beth din* had the power to impose its decisions as it was accepted throughout the medieval Jewish world.[75] It also had the right to force people to appear before it and use all means at its disposal to achieve this.[76] The court's right to dispose of a Jew's property was far from absolute, however, and eminent halakhists expressed their reservations or opposition on this matter.[77]

The *beth din* dealt with matrimonial, civil, financial, and religious cases; in criminal law it had limited jurisdiction, varying according to the community and the period.[78] In some communities the *beth din* was expected to consult the royal authorities or the elders of the community in criminal cases before pronouncing its verdict.[79] Its remit was not always strictly judicial. It had a wide but ill-defined jurisdiction in several fields related to religious life and public morality. Certain religious standards had to be maintained by force, if persuasion failed.[80]

The jurisdiction of the Jewish court in cases involving litigants from different communities was frequently contested. The problem was often resolved according to the principle of seniority of the court, a criterion which was often disputed, or by referring the case to a neutral body.[81] The *beth din* of larger communities, some of which were headed by eminent rabbis, served as courts of appeal for decisions by courts in provincial communities.[82] Litigation between communities was usually referred to a neutral court of a third community.[83]

---

[72] ACA, Reg. 57, fo. 224 [=R 1464]; Reg. 66, fo. 138 [=R 1597].

[73] ACA, Reg. 202, fo. 201ʳᵛ [=R 6].

[74] ACA, Reg. 21, fos. 32ᵛ, 37 [=R 517, 520 = Jacobs 634, 637 = Bofarull, Barcelona, cxii, cxiv = Baer, *Spanien*, doc. 106].

[75] Adret, i. 692–3, iii. 411.

[76] Adret, i. 940.

[77] Adret, iv. 247.

[78] ACA, Reg. 16, fo. 240ʳ [=R 458 = Jacobs 474 = Bofarull, Barcelona, cii]; Reg. 43, fo, 58 [=R 1229]. For instances of jurisdiction in specific fields, see Reg. 87, fo. 118ʳ [=R 2488]; Reg. 89, fo. 116ʳ [=R 2585].

[79] Adret, ii. 290.

[80] Adret, i. 472.

[81] Adret, i. 1149, viii. 47.

[82] ACA, Reg. 61, fo. 122 [=R 1056 = Baer, *Spanien*, doc. 125]; Reg. 66, fo. 138 [=R 1597].

[83] ACA, Reg. 86, fo. 187 [=R 2455 = Baer, *Spanien*, doc. 134, para. 2].

The principle that all cases between Jews should be tried by a Jewish court was upheld by the king. Alfonso III indicated his preference for a Jewish court over a Christian one in trials of Jews.[84] This favourable attitude of the king towards the Jewish court was maintained throughout the period. Even his instructions to the judges did not damage their status.[85]

In civil cases, Jewish law permits the litigants to choose their own arbitrators. Once the two sides had agreed on the names of the arbitrators and the ceremony of *qinyan* had been performed, neither side was allowed to retract.[86] A duly signed document contained the names of the chosen arbitrators whose judgment the parties undertook to accept.[87] The arbitrator was sometimes an eminent halakhist, as can be seen, for instance, in the case of two Jewish litigants from Saragossa who agreed in 1282 to have as arbitrator Jenton Assibili, who was the great Talmudist R. Yom Tov Asibili.[88] The occasional need for the king to ratify the arbitrators' decision seems to indicate that it was not always readily accepted.[89] Naturally, the arbitrators' methods of work and terms of reference were far less rigid than those of the ordinary courts.[90]

Some cases were resolved by arbitration at the king's orders. The king's interest in arbitration and in the implementation of the verdict is readily understood when we realize that he received a large part, sometimes half, of any financial settlement.[91]

PUNISHMENTS AND FINES

The community had various ways of exercising its authority over its members. The punishments and fines that the *berurim* and the *beth din* imposed on wrongdoers constituted its most efficient methods. Some of the punishments were as prescribed by Jewish law and were the same as those found in most medieval communities; others were typical of the communities in the Iberian peninsula in general, and of those in the Crown of Aragon in particular. In principle the community imposed its punishments with the king's permission, which was incorporated in its charters.[92] In 1280 Pedro III issued a general charter to all the Catalan communities empowering them to punish and fine all Jews found guilty

---

[84] ACA, Reg. 80, fo. 3` [= R 1959].
[85] ACA, CR, Jaime II, C 4, no. 563 [= *Cartas Reales*, no. 37].
[86] Adret, i. 1126, vii. 432.
[87] Nahmanides 78.
[88] ACA, Reg. 59, fo. 23 [= R 927].
[89] ACA, Reg. 19, fo. 141`ᵛ [= R 604 = Jacobs 556]; Reg. 256, fo. 25 [= R 2678].
[90] ACA, Reg. 42, fo. 217` [= R 766]; Adret, ii. 104.
[91] ACA, Reg. 50, fo. 156` [= R 885]; Reg. 81, fo. 166` [= R 2183].
[92] For Barcelona, see ACA, Reg. 16, fo. 158 [= R 29 = Baer, *Spanien*, doc. 93]; for Perpignan and the whole of Roussillon and Cerdagne, see Reg. 16, fo. 158 [= R 417 = Jacobs 450 = Bofarull, Barcelona, lxxxiii].

by their courts and leaders.[93] Jaime II confirmed his predecessors' charters[94] and, whenever it was felt necessary, reiterated the power of the individual community to punish and fine its culprit members.[95] The halakhic experts in the realm made no effort to conceal this dependence of the Jewish judiciary on the Crown, including its right to deviate from Jewish law.[96]

Capital punishment in Jewish law ceased even before the end of the Second Jewish Commonwealth in 70 CE, and in any case no Jewish court had criminal jurisdiction outside the Land of Israel—except for Spain, where, contrary to *halakhah*, the Jews exercised criminal jurisdiction and imposed the death penalty and corporal punishment, including mutilation. This extraordinary jurisdiction originated in the Muslim period and continued in the Hispanic kingdoms under Christian rule. The special political circumstances that prevailed in Spain, particularly the incessant wars between the Muslims and the Christians, had a deep impact on society in general and on the Jewish judicial system in particular. In Castile, Jewish criminal jurisdiction was more extensive and lasted longer than in the Crown of Aragon. Jewish jurists explained this deviation from the *halakhah* as 'an emergency measure'.[97]

In the Crown of Aragon, the right to impose capital punishment was included in early charters granted to some communities. In the 1229 charter of the Jews of Calatayud, the death penalty was listed as one of the punishments that the *aljama* could impose on Jewish criminals. Although the charter was confirmed by Jaime II in 1305, we have no information on the penalty being imposed in the fourteenth century by a Jewish court.[98] In 1273 the Jews of Barbastro received a charter that promised to pronounce the death penalty for informers, called *malsins* in the source. It appears that the *adelantados* declared the person as *malsin*, while the baile was the authority to judge and execute the sentence.[99] Some Hebrew sources suggest that the Jews also carried out the death penalty,[100] but this seems very unlikely. As far as we can tell, no death penalty was executed by the Jews in the Crown of Aragon throughout the thirteenth century. In neighbouring Castile the secret execution of Joseph Picho, an official of Enrique II, in 1379 caused criminal jurisdiction to be withdrawn from the Jews.[101] The case of Vidalon de Porta, executed as an informer at the end of the 1270s and the last Jew condemned

---

[93] ACA, Reg. 44, fos. 187ᵛ–188 [= R 823 = Baer, *Spanien*, doc. 121 = Dinur, ii. 2, p. 418, no. 8, and pp. 446–7, no. 2].

[94] ACA, Reg. 195, fo. 44 [= R 2629 = Baer, *Spanien*, doc. 139]; Reg. 197, fo. 19ᵛ [= R 2720 = Baer, *Spanien*, doc. 142]; Reg. 100, fo. 187 [= Baer, *Spanien*, doc. 137].

[95] ACA, Reg. 222, fo. 103ᵛ [= R 3237 = Jacobs 816].

[96] Adret, ii. 279, iv. 411 = vii. 279 [= Assaf, *Punishments*, no. 57]; Adret, iv. 185 [= Assaf, *Punishments*, no. 56].

[97] Literally 'the need of the hour': Adret, v. 238.

[98] ACA, Reg. 202, fo. 201ʳ [= R 6].

[99] ACA, Reg. 21, fo. 126ᵛ [= R 552 = Jacobs 665 = Baer, *Spanien*, doc. 107]; Adret, v. 290. [= Assaf, *Punishments*, no. 53].   [100] Asibili (Kapah) 179.

[101] Baer, *History*, i, pp. 375–6.

to death in the Crown of Aragon, shows the immense complications of imposing the death penalty.[102] Halakhic experts such as Adret and Benedictus Biona, known as R. Jonah Gerondi, the cousin of R. Jonah Gerondi the elder, had serious doubts about capital punishment.[103] Charters granted or confirmed subsequent to this episode made no reference to capital punishment.[104]

Corporal punishment was found among Jews as late as the first half of the fourteenth century.[105] The Hebrew records show that the Jewish community inflicted a variety of corporal punishments, some of which were prescribed by Jewish law and practice.[106] In Castile, and to a lesser degree in the Crown of Aragon, corporal punishment included flagellation and even mutilation. These were considered emergency measures that were not covered by *halakhah*.[107] Flagellation, called in Latin sources *malcuç*, from the Hebrew, was therefore not the punishment prescribed by the Torah, which was limited to thirty-nine strokes, and could lead to the death of the convict.[108]

From an appeal against a verdict directed to R. Yom Tov Asibili it is obvious that corporal punishments in Castile and in the Crown of Aragon were inflicted with the full knowledge and consent of the authorities.[109] In several charters, corporal punishment is included among those that the community was permitted to inflict on Jewish convicts, although the punishment was often carried out by the local baile.[110] Corporal punishment was inflicted for two kinds of transgressions: sexual and marital misdemeanours, and acts by informers.[111]

All medieval Jewish communities had the power to pronounce the *herem* or ban against any member who violated the law and its ordinances. The *herem* ostracized the condemned person, cut him off socially from the rest of the community, and prevented his participation in various religious events. It also had serious financial implications, as it forbade any transaction with him. Sometimes the *herem* carried with it expulsion from the Jewish quarter.[112] In the communities of the Crown of

---

[102] ACA, Reg. 41, fos. 62, 76 [= R 725, 728 = Baer, *Spanien*, doc. 116, para. 1 = MF ii. 540]; Reg. 42, fo. 169ʻ [= R 751 = Baer, *Spanien*, doc. 116, para. 2]. The epistle of Adret (Oxford Codex Pococke no. 2218 [old no. 280b]) was published in Kaufman, 'Jewish Informers', pp. 221ff.; and see Assaf, *Punishments*, no. 52.

[103] For the execution of murderers see Urbach, 'Responsa of the RaShBA'; Adret, v. 290, viii. 240.

[104] ACA, Reg. 195, fo. 44 [= R 2629 = Baer, *Spanien*, doc. 139]; Reg. 256, fo. 28 [= R 2680]; Reg. 202, fo. 210 [= R 2826]. The charter of 1320 to the Jewish settlers in Alcolea de Cinca was an exception. See ACA, Reg. 383, fos. 40–2 [= Baer, *Spanien*, doc. 175].

[105] Asibili, *Novellae on Makot*, fo. 22 [= Assaf, *Punishments*, no. 80].

[106] Adret, ii. 280, and cf. 279; iii. 393, iv. 264, 311.

[107] Adret iv. 314, v. 66, 238; Asibili (Kapah) 131; Adret, viii. 240; Urbach, 'Responsa of the RaShBA'.

[108] Asibili, *Novellae on Makot*, fo. 22 [= Assaf, *Punishments*, no. 80]; Asibili (Kapah) 179.

[109] Asibili (Kapah) 131.

[110] ACA, Reg. 195, fo. 44 [= R 2629 = Baer, *Spanien*, doc. 139]; Reg. 383, fos. 40–2 [= Baer, *Spanien*, doc. 175].

[111] Asibili (Kapah) 131, 179; Adret, v. 288; and see above on Alcolea de Cinca.

[112] ACA, Reg. 81, fo. 193ʻ [= R 2230].

Aragon the intensity, severity, and duration of the ban, called *herem*, *niduy*, or *alatma* in the sources, varied a little depending on the circumstances and conditions. The *herem* or *alatma* was the severer form. The *niduy* was generally for a shorter, limited period, usually a month.[113]

The *herem* was included in many ordinances of the community, in which cases it would operate automatically in case of an infringement. The Christian sources use the Hebrew names *herem* and *niduy* (or *nitduy*) as well as *alatma*, an Arabic term. As a punishment it was considered one of the harshest and was included in the charters of many communities.[114] In 1280 Pedro III authorized all the Catalan communities to put under ban members who violated the law.[115] It was pronounced in the synagogue by the *hazan* or *capellano*.[116]

The ban was also an efficient method of putting pressure on witnesses who hesitated to come forward with their testimony.[117] Some bans were proclaimed on specific occasions and for set times against Jews whose acts were considered harmful to the king. On 1 October the Jews throughout the Crown of Aragon were expected to take an oath under *alatma et nitduy* that they would act honestly and lawfully in tax and credit matters.[118] In general, it appears that the *herem* was used no less by the king for his own interest than by the community to penalize its members.

Simultaneously, the ban usually involved social and economic measures. Some of the sanctions associated with the *herem* were applied in religious life. One of the severest bans stipulated that the person under ban would be deprived of a tombstone. In Valencia the king permitted the *aljama* to apply this severe sanction against Jews who did not pay their tax.[119] Some Jews under *herem* were prevented from entering the synagogue. Alternatively, those present would stop the service and leave the synagogue premises if the banned person entered. In short, the person under ban would not be permitted to participate in any public service. Our information about the suspension of the prayers comes mostly from archival sources since they all deal with the king's interference on behalf of the person under ban. Significantly, the Hebrew sources are silent on the subject.[120] Jews who refused to pay their debts to fellow Jews were barred from entering the

---

[113] ACA, Reg. 71, fo. 55ʳ [= R 1738].

[114] For Barcelona, see ACA, Reg. 21, fo. 32ʳ [= R 517 = Jacobs 634 = Bofarull, *Barcelona*, cxii = Baer, *Spanien*, doc. 106]; for Gerona, see Reg. 21, fo. 37 [= R 520 = Jacobs 637 = Bofarull, *Barcelona*, cxiv].

[115] See n. 2 above.

[116] ACA, Reg. 219, fo. 208ʳˇ [= R 355].

[117] ACA, Reg. 15, fo. 124 [= R 398 = Jacobs 434 = Bofarull, *Montpellier*, 489]; Reg. 66, fo. 149 [= R 1605]; Reg. 81, fo. 9 [= R 2055].

[118] In 1308 the date coincided with Sukkot, and the Jews of Lérida asked for the date to be changed: ACA, CR, Jaime II, C 26, no. 3319 [= *Cartas Reales*, no. 130].

[119] ACA, Reg. 16, fo. 159 [= R 418 = Jacobs 453 = MF i. 883].

[120] ACA, Reg. 14, fo. 63 [= R 275 = Jacobs 364 = Baer, *Spanien*, doc. 100]; Reg. 37, fo. 31ʳ [= R 495 = Jacobs 725].

synagogue, and if this injunction failed the prayers were suspended as soon as the culprit who was under *herem* entered the synagogue. Jaime II fully supported the right of the community of Tortosa to prevent borrowers who defaulted from participating in public prayers.[121]

There is a basic difference between the institution of interrupting the prayers in Franco-Germany and the suspension of prayers in the Crown of Aragon. Whereas in Franco-German communities the interruption was a measure taken by an individual to exert pressure on a fellow Jew who refused to give satisfaction to him, in the Crown of Aragon it was a move by the community against the individual member who did not perform his duty. The few sources that are known show clearly that communities in the Crown of Aragon used their power to prevent a rebellious Jew gaining access to the synagogue or participating in prayers. In 1264 Jaime I cancelled the ban imposed on Jucef Abinhalim and his two sons Azach and Jacob from Calatayud for having ignored the property tax decided upon by the tax assessors. The king also ordered the community to allow them to enter the synagogue and not to permit those present to go elsewhere to pray when any of the three entered.[122] Another document refers to a safe-conduct granted by the Infante Pedro to the three brothers Junis, Jahuda and Jucef Avinceit, in which he forbade the Jewish community of Lérida to put the three under ban or to suspend prayers when they arrived in the synagogue or joined the service, wherever it was held.[123] This document is particularly noteworthy since the only Hebrew source which mentions the suspension of prayers as a punitive measure is connected with Lérida. It was there that a father sued his son for refusing to support him, pronouncing a ban against him and declaring him unfit to pray with a *minyan*.[124] There is likewise only a single source which speaks of the interruption of prayers according to Ashkenazi custom. In 1261 the widow of Rabbi Shemuel HaSardi obtained the large sum of money to which she was entitled according to her *ketubah* after interrupting prayers for a long time.[125] It seems that her act was exceptional in the Iberian peninsula and was probably inspired by Ashkenazi sources. Considering the growing influence of Franco-German Jewry in Spain, this single record is hardly indicative of adoption of the practice by the Jews of Iberia. In Franco-Germany the interruption of prayer indicates the weakness of the community which did not have sufficient powers of coercion; the suspension of prayer in the communities in north-eastern Spain illustrates the strength of the community *vis-à-vis* the Jew under ban.[126] The community of Montpellier, which was exposed to divergent and contradictory influences from the north and the

---

[121] ACA, CR, Jaime II, C 40, no. 5015 [= *Cartas Reales*, no. 171].
[122] ACA, Reg. 14, fo. 63 [= Jacobs 364 = R 275 = Baer, *Spanien*, 100].
[123] ACA, Reg. 37, fo. 31ᵛ [= Jacobs 725 = R 495].
[124] Adret, iv. 56.
[125] Millás, *Documents hebraics*, 75.
[126] On the interruption of prayers in Franco-Germany see Finkelstein, *Jewish Self-government*, pp. 15–18, 119, 128–9; Grossman, ' "Stopping the Service" '.

south, offers an interesting case of the clash of the two traditions. In 1270, at the request of the leaders of the community, Jaime I forbade the interruption of prayers in the synagogue by any Jew, as was customary in Franco-German communities, while allowing only the leaders of the *aljama* to do so, as was the practice south of the Pyrenees.[127]

In several communal ordinances provisions for imprisonment were included, while some charters mentioned prison sentences for convicted Jews.[128] Some communities had a prison in the precincts of the *judería*; in others, prisoners were held in the city prisons and were provided with *kasher* food by their families.[129] The length of the prison sentences varied with the offence and the prisoner was required to pay for his stay in prison a fixed sum, the *carcellagium* or the *carcelatge*.[130] The prisoners maintained some contact with their families and with the outside world through brief visits of relatives and correspondence.[131]

Most prison sentences were given in cases of theft and financial transgressions.[132] Jews who transgressed rabbinic injunctions in marital matters, such as divorce and concubinage, and refused to mend their ways, were also subject to imprisonment.[133]

The community also had the power to prohibit Jews from leaving the *judería* or the *call*. This confinement was often taken as a measure against debtors and taxpayers who did not pay their dues.[134]

Expulsion from the Jewish community, which often meant banishment from the Jewish quarter as well, was a severe punishment. It was not easy for the expelled to find a place of refuge. The right to expel from the community and the city was sometimes explicitly mentioned in the charters. It was designed to remove from the community Jews whose religious and moral behaviour was unacceptable in Jewish society or whose continued presence in the *judería* was considered harmful.[135] Expulsion was a severe punishment that was thought appropriate for sexual offences and serious religious transgressions, but it was often cancelled by the king or the infante.[136] This measure was also used against unwanted elements in Jewish society The king's occasional cancellation of the *aljama*'s expulsion sentences must have greatly reduced the efficacy of the system,

---

[127] ACA, Reg. 16, fo. 148ᵛ [= R 438 = Jacobs 440 = Bofarull, Montpellier, 490].
[128] Adret, v. 242 [= Assaf, *Punishments*, no. 51]; ACA, Reg. 202, fo. 201ʳ [= R 6]. See n. 2 above.
[129] Asibili (Kapah) 179.
[130] See e.g. ACA, CR, Jaime II, C 13, no. 1711 [= *Cartas Reales*, no. 79].
[131] ACA, CR, Jaime II, C 135, no. 389 [= *Cartas Reales*, no. 533].
[132] Asibili (Kapah) 159; ACA, Reg. 210, fo. 102 [= R 2982].
[133] Adret, ii. 276; Asibili (Kapah) 179; Adret, v. 242 [= Assaf, *Punishments*, no. 51].
[134] ACA, Reg. 62, fo. 119ᵛ [= R 1274]; Reg. 207, fo. 166ᵛ [= R 2916].
[135] ACA, Reg. 16, fo. 158 [= R 29 = Baer, *Spanien*, doc. 93]; ACA, Reg. 21, fo. 32ᵛ [= R 517 = Jacobs 634 = Bofarull, Barcelona, cxii = Baer, *Spanien*, doc. 106]; Reg. 100, fo. 187 [= Baer, *Spanien*, doc. 137]; Reg. 194, fo. 266 [= R 2623 = Isaacs 74]; ACA, Reg. 202, fo. 201ʳ [= R 6]; Reg. 61, fo. 135ᵛ [= R 1066]; Asibili (Kapah) 159.
[136] ACA, Reg. 89, fos. 49, 55ᵛ [= R 2555, 2559]; Reg. 202, fo. 204 [= R 2832].

but it should be remembered that it is mostly those cases in which the king interfered that were recorded in the archival sources.

Practically every charter establishing judicial autonomy included the right of the Jewish community to fine Jews who were found guilty of misdemeanours.[137] As the fines were usually paid to the king, his support for the community's right to impose fines is understandable.[138] Part of some fines in Aragon was paid to the *albedin*, the judges, and the scribe of the community; another part was paid to the community or the *berurim*.[139] Halakhists admitted that the fines paid by Jewish transgressors as decided by the *beth din* were not within the framework of the Torah but by permit of the king.[140] Fines were imposed for lesser crimes, such as insults against communal officers,[141] and also for religious and moral transgressions.[142]

According to Jewish law the community had the right to confiscate the property of the individual. Practically all communities employed this means of punishment and enforcement. It was one of the modes of punishment that the community exercised to penalize members for non-payment of taxes and debts.[143] The responsum of R. Shelomo ben Adret about the nature and extent of confiscation which was sent to the *aljama* of Saragossa was confirmed by numerous Latin and Romance sources.[144] The king frequently intervened on behalf of Jewish tax-payers whose property was confiscated by the community, thus rendering ineffective the most efficient weapon in the hands of the community against defaulting tax-payers.[145]

---

[137] See e.g. the charter of Barcelona from 1272 referred to above: ACA, Reg. 21, fo. 32` [= R 517 = Jacobs 634 = Bofarull, Barcelona, cxii = Baer, *Spanien*, doc. 106].

[138] ACA, Reg. 82, fo. 73 [= R 2208]; Reg. 383, fos. 40–2 [= Baer, *Spanien*, doc. 175]; Reg. 82, fo. 90` [= R 2261].

[139] Baer, *Spanien*, doc., 163; Adret, iii. 318.

[140] Adret, iv. 311 = viii. 279 [= Assaf, *Punishments*, no. 57], iv. 185 [= Assaf, *Punishments*, no. 56].

[141] Adret, v. 290 [= Assaf, *Punishments*, no. 53], v. 288, 272, vii. 496, viii. 245; ACA, Reg. 224, fo. 92` [= R 3286].

[142] Adret, iii. 318, iv. 315; Baer, *Spanien*, doc. 163, para. 10.

[143] Adret, i. 1206.

[144] Adret, iii. 400; ACA, Reg. 89, fo. 97` [= R 2581]; Reg. 88, fo. 259` [= R 2530]; Reg. 89, fos. 98, 125, 148 [= 2582, 2589, 2599]; Reg. 216, fo. 55` [= R 3091].

[145] ACA, Reg. 230, fos. 67`–68 [= R 3443 = Jacobs 886]; Reg. 205, fo. 243` [= R 2892]; Reg. 211, fo. 235` [= R 3005]; Reg. 208, fos. 16`–17 [= R 2929].

PART THREE

INTER-COMMUNAL RELATIONS

§3.1 Relations between Communities

RELATIONS between the Jewish communities of the Crown of Aragon were affected by various external and internal factors. A major internal factor was the attempt by the larger communities to influence, control, or dominate the affairs of the smaller. The dependence of the latter on main Jewish centres for some of their needs both facilitated such attempts and was used to justify them. An important external factor was the need to create a united front in conducting negotiations, and to establish appropriate channels for the Jews' contacts, with the outside world, particularly the Crown.

JEWISH CENTRAL INSTITUTIONS

In the Crown of Aragon there was no permanent inter-communal institution representing all the Jewish communities. Representatives of the Jews of Catalonia, Aragon, and Valencia, the main constituent territories of the Crown, met when the necessity arose to discuss topics of common interest—usually relating to royal demands for new taxes and subsidies. Under Jaime I only one meeting of Jewish delegates from different territories took place, in September 1271 in Saragossa, and in this case the initiative was taken by the king. Delegates of all Aragonese and Valencian *aljamas* and those of Tortosa were convened to discuss the king's financial demands.[1] There was no permanent arrangement for such meetings and, significantly, no delegates of the major Catalan *aljamas* attended the meeting. In fact, under Jaime I the Jews of each of the territories of his expanding realm were treated separately.

It was under Pedro III that a Jewish policy affecting all the Jews of the Crown was adopted.[2] This was a significant development. The uniform treatment of the Jews by Pedro III was consonant with his general policy of centralization and his privileging of the interests of the Crown as a whole over those of the individual territories. It was equally compatible with his policy of using the Jews extensively in his central administration. In July 1280, in an important charter granted to the Jews of Catalonia, Pedro III authorized the *aljamas* to appoint delegates who could meet and take decisions for all the Jews of his dominions.[3] Nevertheless, there

[1] ACA, Reg. 18, fo. 63ᵛ [= R 482 = Jacobs 500 and doc. v, p. 131].

[2] For instances of a uniform Jewish policy throughout the Crown, see ACA, Reg. 41, fos. 50ᵛ, 76, 108 [= R 720, 728, 741 = MF ii. 502, 540, 601]; Reg. 44, fos. 183ᵛ–184, 187ᵛ [= R 791, 819 = MF ii. 1086, 1118]; Reg, 71, fo. 129ᵛ [= R 1000 = MF ii. 1640]; Reg. 46, fo. 155 [= R 1111].

[3] ACA, Reg. 44, fos. 187ᵛ–188 [= R 823 = Baer, *Spanien*, doc. 121 = Dinur, ii. 2, p. 418, no. 8, and pp. 446–7, no, 2].

is no evidence that such a general meeting of the Jewish representatives of the *aljamas* of the Crown ever took place during his reign.

Under Alfonso III the same policy was pursued.[4] During his reign it seems that the delegates of the Catalan, Aragonese, and Valencian *aljamas* appeared together to arrange the payments due to the royal treasury, but we have no information on any Jewish efforts to meet and formulate a common programme.[5]

During the reign of Jaime II, Jewish delegates from all the regions of the Crown met in order to divide among themselves the subsidies demanded by the king. Such a meeting took place in 1302 in Tortosa to deal with the Jews' pending payment for the Sicilian campaign.[6] Nine months later the delegates met again in Tortosa to discuss with the king his recent demands of the Jews of the Crown.[7] Another meeting of the delegates from Catalonia, Aragon, and Valencia took place in Barcelona in 1326.[8]

Throughout the period, all the meetings that united the Jews of the Crown took place either at the king's initiative or in reaction to his demands. There was no concerted attempt to regularize the meetings of the delegates or to initiate such meetings to deal with problems of general Jewish concern. It took a major crisis in the middle of the fourteenth century to bring the delegates of the Catalan and Valencian communities to Barcelona. Among the measures agreed by that conference was the establishment of a permanent executive committee composed of two delegates each of the Catalan and Aragonese Jews and one each of the Valencian and Majorcan *aljamas*. The conference decided that the committee would be in charge of negotiations on behalf of all the Jews of the Crown with the ruler and the Cortes, and be empowered to take any necessary decisions or steps in the name of all Jews in the realm.[9] The framework of the executive body was not new, as representatives of the Jews of the different territories did meet in the thirteenth century, as we have just seen; but the duties it was intended to assume were new. The change was not in the policy of the ruler towards a central Jewish institution, but in the Jews' conception of such an institution.

The absence of an adequate and efficient central institution to cater for the Jews of the entire Crown of Aragon during the period under consideration here was due to differences in traditions of self-rule and in the structure of the communal organization of the Jews in each of the territories of the Crown. The absence of inter-communal structures, however, did not prevent cooperation in various fields, as can be seen from the sources cited above.

---

[4] ACA, Reg. 63, fo. 31ᵛ [=R 1481 = Isaacs 29]; Reg. 65, fo. 39 [=R 1487]; Reg. 71, fo. 6ᵛ [=R 1696 = Isaacs 43].

[5] ACA, Reg. 70, fos. 14, 19 [=R 1684, 1689].

[6] ACA, CR, Jaime II, C 135, no. 182 [= Baer, *Spanien*, doc. 151 = *Cartas Reales*, no. 526]. The numbers of the *caja* and the document in Baer are obsolete.

[7] ACA, Reg. 200, fo. 174 [=R 2807].

[8] ACA, Reg 228, fos. 105–7 [=R 3392]

[9] Baer, *Spanien*, doc. 253; Baer, *History*, ii, pp. 25–8; Feliu and Riera, 'Els acords'.

INTER-COMMUNAL COOPERATION

Though remaining, in principle, independent units, the *aljamas* did need one another in a variety of fields. Those Jewish settlements that were not sufficiently large to constitute legally recognized communities or *aljamas* were even more in need of the cooperation and collaboration of their neighbouring *aljamas*. Small Jewish communities and settlements were not able to provide their residents with all the services needed to lead a Jewish life, lacking some or all of the necessary facilities, such as a cemetery, a *beth din*, or a slaughterhouse. For some time the Jews of Burriana and Cervera did not have a cemetery of their own, and therefore had to bury their dead in the nearest Jewish cemeteries.[10]

The Hebrew and archival sources do not provide us with adequate information on the extent of cooperation and collaboration that existed between various *aljamas* in many fields, as they are mostly silent when the relations between the communities were harmonious and friendly, usually reporting only the problems and conflicts. Here and there, however we do catch a glimpse of the support that Jewish communities lent to one another. A very important instance of such support can be seen in the attempt of the Jews of the Kingdom of Valencia to seek the cancellation of a clause in the *fur* of Valencia that was adopted at the suggestion of the heads of the capital city. This clause, which was approved by Pedro III, cancelled the old rule that required at least one Jewish witness in any Christian testimony against Jews. In January 1284 a delegation of Valencian Jewry came to Barcelona to beseech the king to withdraw his support for the clause. The leaders of the *aljama* of Barcelona joined the Valencian delegates and appeared with them before Pedro III. Their joint effort failed, but it did offer a fine example of the kind of inter-communal cooperation that was not usually recorded in the sources.[11]

CONFLICT AND CRISIS BETWEEN COMMUNITIES

Unlike harmonious and cooperative relations, conflicts between the communities are fully described in the sources. As the conflicts between communities within each particular region are treated in sections 3–6 below, attention will be focused here on problems that affected relations between communities of different regions and territories of the Crown.

The jurisdiction of the community within the limits of its geographical boundaries was a fundamental issue over which communities clashed. The authority of the *qehilah* over its members as a matter of principle was not questioned. Jews who lived in the locality, whether inside the *judería* or outside it, were accountable to the legally constituted institutions of the community. The problems arose when the jurisdiction of other communities was involved.

---

[10] For Burriana, see ACA, Reg. 229, fo. 211ᵛ [= R 3409]. For Cervera, see Adret, iii. 291.

[11] ACA, Reg. 46, fos. 152ᵛ–153 [= R 1106].

The jurisdiction of the *beth din* when one of the litigants was a member of another community was one of the causes of friction between communities. Property of Jews within the boundaries of communities other than their own was another major bone of contention. The conflict over the status of such property for tax purposes divided the Jews of Monzón and Barbastro in the thirteenth century. Their conflict was referred to Jaime I in 1271. The Jews of Monzón, who were subjects of the Templars, had asked the Master of the Templars in the town to intercede on their behalf in Jaime's court. The latter decided that property tax should be paid with the community where that property was situated.[12] (It is noteworthy that, faced with the same question, R. Shelomo ben Adret gave a halakhic decision that coincided with Jaime I's order.[13]) When, nine years later, the Jews of Alagón decided to apply the same principle *vis-à-vis* the Jews of Saragossa, Pedro III confirmed the opposite decision taken by Jucef Ravaya, one of the highest officials in the royal chancellery.[14] The Jews of Egea and Tauste were divided over the same problem during the reign of Alfonso III, who upheld the decision of Pedro III.[15] Jaime II also adopted a similar policy. Not only did he decide in 1315 that the *aljama* of Saragossa had no right to tax Jewish merchants from Lérida who came to trade in the city, but he also ordered in 1325 that the same *aljama* refrain from demanding tax from a Jew of Barcelona who owned shops in the Aragonese capital.[16] This policy, which remained consistent, did not prevent further clashes on the matter. Relations between the communities of Monzón and Barbastro remained very tense after the 1271 decision. The Jews of Monzón pronounced a ban on the import of wine from Barbastro. Some time around the beginning of 1288, Alfonso III ordered the Jews of Monzón to abrogate the ordinance they had enacted and lift the ban. No doubt the intervention of the king came after the *aljama* of Barbastro complained about the boycott. Subsequently, in March 1288, the king explained that the cancellation of the boycott was not meant to restrict the Jews of Monzón in their choice of wine.[17]

At times, emigration of Jews from one community to another caused conflict between the two. Communities were as opposed to losing taxpayers as they were eager to gain new ones.[18] In the last decade of the thirteenth century, some Jews of Montclús moved to Barbastro, where they undertook to pay taxes with their new community for four years. At the end of the period, these Jews decided to return to Montclús. The Jews of Barbastro were not pleased with their loss and demanded that the departing group continue to pay taxes with their hosts. The

---

[12] ACA, Reg. 16, fo. 252ᵛ [=R 491 = Jacobs 479].

[13] Adret, i. 788. The problem must have been quite serious for the *aljama* of Saragossa to enact an ordinance forcing those who had left to pay all their debts up to the time of their departure: Adret, iii. 405–6.

[14] ACA, Reg. 48, fo. 126 [=R 840].   [15] ACA, Reg. 80, fo. 9 [=R 1964].

[16] ACA, CR, Jaime II, C 67, no. 8272 [= *Cartas Reales*, no. 344].

[17] ACA, Reg. 74, fo. 88ᵛ [=R 1903].

[18] A full discussion is found in Assis, *Jewish Economy*, ch. ix.

crisis between the communities was resolved only with the intervention of Jaime II in 1297 in favour of Montclús.[19]

Communities were in constant conflict over the distribution of taxes and subsidies, and these disagreements were often solved by royal intervention.[20] These conflicts sometimes ended in lawsuits, such as that in which the *aljama* of Fraga was involved with the Catalan communities in the early 1280s over the allotment of taxes.[21] At that time, the Jews of Saragossa and Ruesta were at odds because the latter claimed to be unjustly overtaxed by the former.[22] Some years later Granollers, another small Jewish settlement, had the same complaint against the *aljama* of Barcelona.[23] In all known cases the dispute led one party to complain to the lay authorities, and in most instances the conflict was between a small and a large community or between an *aljama* in the capital and one in the provinces.[24] Sometimes, members of provincial communities turned to the institutions of the *aljama* in the capital for arbitration between them and their community, or in appeal against a decision of their community.[25]

THE KING'S JEWS VERSUS THE NOBLES' JEWS

The settlement of Jews on the lands of the nobility caused harm to the Jewish communities they left, which lost tax-payers who were financially very successful—indeed, it was precisely their financial contribution that made them attractive settlers in baronial domains. The king, who gave his permission for the transfer, lost nothing, since the financially weakened community continued to pay the same tax as before. The damage was particularly serious when Jews living on baronial land possessed property in the royal domain but did not contribute to the king's taxes.

The result was tense relations between the communities of the Crown and those of the nobility. Baronial Jews felt persecuted and maltreated by the king's communities, of which in many cases they were former members and which demanded their participation in royal taxes. One of the baronial communities decided to compensate any of its members who suffered as a result of its decision not to pay taxes with the royal community.[26] The baronial Jews felt constantly harassed by the royal communities, and naturally they turned to their lords for help. In February 1326, at the request of the nobleman Oto de Montcada, Jaime II ordered the leaders of the *aljama* of Lérida not to molest the Jews who lived in

---

[19] ACA, Reg. 253, fo. 55` [=R 2659].
[20] See ACA, Reg. 48, fo. 87 [=R 812]; Reg. 59, fo. 192 [=R 996].
[21] ACA, Reg. 60, fos. 1, 2` [=R 1003–4].
[22] ACA, Reg. 60, fo. 19 [=R 1015].
[23] ACA, Reg. 74, fo. 86 [=R 1896].
[24] ACA, Reg. 46, fo. 152` [=R 1105].
[25] ACA, Reg. 61, fo. 122 [=R 1056 = Baer, *Spanien*, doc. 125].
[26] Adret, v. 286.

Aytona and not to require them to pay past taxes and levies. Despite these warnings, the Jews who had settled in Aytona with the king's permission continued to suffer pressure from Lérida.[27]

The emigration of Jews to baronial lands assumed dangerous proportions in some periods and areas from the point of view of some of the communities they left. Towards the end of the thirteenth century the *aljama* of Saragossa issued an ordinance designed to reduce the damage caused by emigrants, stipulating in particular that any Jew wanting to emigrate from Saragossa to Pedrola must first pay all his debts to the community. The effect of the ordinance depended entirely on the king's attitude, as emigration depended on royal permission. Following the emigration of Saragossan Jews to Pedrola, which belonged to Lope Ferrench de Luna, the two communities entered into a serious conflict. Adret, who was asked to arbitrate between the communities, decided that emigrants who paid all their debts before leaving Saragossa would not be required to pay any taxes for any period after their departure.[28] At the beginning of the fourteenth century the emigration changed direction as Jews left Pedrola to settle in Saragossa and Alagón, both communities of the king. This emigration caused a renewed deterioration in their relations, and both communities were infuriated when Jaime II, in an effort to appease the nobleman, decided that the emigrants should return to the baronial community.[29]

Jews who settled in 1315 in the upper part of Vich, which belonged to the bishop and the House of Montcada, refused to be considered part of the *collecta* of Barcelona. The community of Barcelona decided to retaliate by denying the Jews of Vich any of the rights that were included in the privileges granted to the Jews of Catalonia, claiming that these privileges were granted only to the king's Jews. The Jews of Vich retorted that they were Catalan Jews and deserved to enjoy all the rights given to the Jews of Catalonia, irrespective of their royal or baronial allegiance. Barcelona's answer was of fundamental importance. Those who want to enjoy the benefits of the privileges, it asserted, must be prepared to share the obligations, above all to pay taxes. It was hinted that all the privileges were paid for by the Jews. A community that was prepared only to benefit from the privileges paid for by others, without participating in the expenses, deserves to be under ban, the leaders of Barcelona threatened indignantly. The Jews of Vich claimed that they paid taxes to their lord. A ban was finally pronounced on the Jews who lived in the part of the city belonging to the House of Moncada,[30] while in the lower part of the city, which belonged to the king, life followed its normal course. Gerona, too, tried to include the Jews of Vich under its jurisdiction. When, finally, Vich passed into the king's dominion, all the Jews of Vich became part of the *collecta* of Barcelona.[31]

[27] ACA, CR, Jaime II, C 133, no. 79 [= *Cartas Reales*, no. 360]; Reg. 228, fo. 26ᵛ; Reg, 230, fo. 110 [= R 3366].

[28] Adret, iii. 421.

[29] ACA, Reg. 199, fo. 85 [= R 2780].

[30] Corbella, *La aljama*, pp. 126–30.

[31] Ibid., docs. 52, 54.

In 1326 there was a wave of emigration of Jews from the royal to the baronial domain. Some settled, as mentioned above, in Aytona, others in the domain of the Infante Ramón Berenguer. The leaders of the communities from which the emigrants came resorted to various tactics in order to make their former residents continue to pay tax with them, while the king decided in favour of the Jewish settlements in the infante's domain, as long as the number of settlers from any given community did not exceed six households.[32]

Relations between the royal and baronial communities remained unfriendly and tense. The established *aljamas* tried constantly to prevent their members emigrating, but these moves were resisted by some rabbinic authorities who claimed that the Jew's freedom of movement should not be removed. The emigrants were expected, however, to pay all their debts in respect of past taxes and subsidies before their departure.[33]

ROYAL MEDIATION BETWEEN COMMUNITIES

In the absence of a centralized institution for all the Jews of the Crown of Aragon, and given the weakness of the regional communal organizations, as described below, the role of the king as mediator between communities in conflict assumed special importance. The king himself arbitrated in many conflicts between communities or delegated a third party, either one of his high officials or a leading rabbinic scholar, to do so.

The king's mediation was most frequently needed to resolve disputes between communities over taxation. In some cases he was asked to determine whether Jews of certain settlements or communities were to be included in a certain tax zone, as was usually claimed by the main community of the zone; in other cases, he was called upon to decide if certain Jewish communities under baronial or princely jurisdiction should pay any royal taxes with other communities of the realm, as we have seen above.[34] In most cases the king or his baile settled a dispute between two communities, related for tax purposes, which failed to agree on their respective proportions of the tax liability. The two communities in such cases were usually of unequal size and status, often involving the main community in the tax zone and one of the smaller communities. The king's interest in seeing that small communities repaid their share of the sums that had already been advanced by the major *aljamas* is clear in his decisions. Equally firm was the king's insistence that no large community should exploit smaller communities and settlements. The king's protection of the small communities is noteworthy.[35] In some extreme cases

---

[32] ACA, Reg. 229, fo. 159; Reg, 230, fo. 73 [= R 3400].

[33] See the strong words of R. Cresques Elias from the middle of the fourteenth century, referring to this emigration and the attempts to prevent it: Baer, *Spanien*, doc. 224a, para. 1.

[34] ACA, Reg. 16, fo. 252ᵛ [= R 491 = Jacobs 479]; Reg. 61, fo. 188 [= R 1070].

[35] ACA, Reg. 48, fo. 87 [= R 812]; Reg. 57, fo. 222ᵛ [= R 1458 = MF, ii. 2297]; Reg. 66, fo. 47ʳᵛ

the king decided to put an end to the official connection between the fighting communities.[36] Many of the disputes settled by the king were between one community that claimed to be overtaxed and the other communities of the region.[37]

Reference has already been made to the king's role in determining the tax liabilities of Jews who resided in one community and held property in another.[38] In major disagreements that led to an impasse between the communities of the territory or tax zone, the king's interest in a swift and efficient solution for the distribution of the tax can be easily recognized in his instructions to the communities involved. If he offered no solution, he at least sent procedural instructions,[39] or referred the case for arbitration to Jewish legal experts. In 1292 Jaime II referred to Adret the dispute over taxation between Lérida on the one hand and Agramunt and Pons on the other.[40]

The king was also involved in inter-communal disputes over expenses incurred by one *aljama* on behalf of others. The king invariably lent his support to any community that had spent money in the common interest, and with the consent of other communities, but was not promptly reimbursed. The *aljama* of Barcelona had great difficulty in reclaiming the money it had advanced to the treasury on account of the episode of David Mascaran, who was murdered by fellow Jews following the 1285 tax ordinances, in which he was involved. It took a long time for the three major Aragonese communities to pay their parts, and even the king's repeated orders had little influence.[41] In 1292 the conflict between Barcelona and the Aragonese *aljamas* was still unresolved when Jaime II asked two rabbis of Huesca to arbitrate between the *aljamas* of Barcelona and Saragossa. The two were then ordered to delay their verdict until the arrival of the king in Huesca.[42]

Since most of these expenses were incurred by delegates sent to the palace or court, the king's interest in settling these disputes was obvious. Similarly, the failure of smaller communities to reimburse the main community promptly for payments advanced to the king led to royal intervention.[43] The king suggested a procedure to resolve a deadlock when the Jewish communities in the same tax area could not reach agreement on the payment of their debts.[44] Some Jewish settlements objected to the demands of major communities that they contribute to

---

[= R 1531, 1535]; Reg. 74, fo. 86 [= R 1896]; Reg. 80, fos. 31–2, 49 [= R 1976, 1981, 1983, 2005]; Reg. 81, fo. 130 [= R 2153]; Reg. 171, fo. 197ʳᵛ [= R 3178–9 = Bofarull, Montblanch, 86–7].

[36] ACA, Reg. 227, fo. 197ʳᵛ [= R 3339].

[37] ACA, Reg. 60, fo. 45ᵛ [= R 1026]; Reg. 61, fo. 125 [= R 1058–60].

[38] ACA, Reg. 48, fo. 146 [= R 840].

[39] ACA, Reg. 62, fo. 50 [= R 1116]; Reg. 57, fo. 215 [= R 1452]; Reg. 81, fo. 109 [= R 2127].

[40] ACA, Reg. 98, fo. 82 [= Baer, *Spanien*, doc. 132].

[41] ACA, Reg. 74, fo. 49ᵛ [= R 1838]; Reg. 81, fo. 213ᵛ [= R 2248]; Reg. 84, fo. 23 [= R 2315].

[42] ACA, Reg. 92, fo. 160ᵛ [= Baer, *Spanien*, doc. 134, paras. 1–2 = R 2455]; del Arco, 'La aljama judaica', p. 279.

[43] ACA, Reg. 46, fo. 152ᵛ [= R 1105]. [44] ACA, Reg. 70, fo. 90 [= R 1711].

expenses other than taxes and subsidies. The king's attitude was on the whole fair. He ordered an investigation of the case, sometimes referring the problem to the care of a rabbinic expert, such as R. Shelomo ben Adret.[45]

The kings opposed antagonistic measures taken by one community against another. Bans and boycotts between the communities were unmistakable signs of unrest and struggle which the kings were very eager to discourage. We may recall the boycott by Monzón of wine produced by Barbastro in the 1280s. The king disapproved of the measure and ordered its cancellation, but refused to force the Jews of Monzón to buy wine they did not want.[46]

[45] R 2329, 2336.   [46] ACA, Reg. 74, fos. 74ʳ, 88ʳ [=R 1891, 1903].

§3.2 Regional Communal Organization

THE structure of the medieval Crown of Aragon profoundly affected the inter-communal institutions of the Jews. The various components of the realm remained independent units, although governed by one ruler, and that ruler's status and title were different in each of the component regions. In practically every field—language, culture, society, economy, coinage, judiciary, administration, and demography—Catalonia, Aragon, Valencia, Majorca, and Roussillon remained distinct throughout the period. Although the boundaries between these territories did not constitute an obstacle to the development of various general trends in Jewish life across the territories of the Crown, local characteristics impressed their mark on the structure of Jewish autonomy, and necessarily on inter-communal organizations. Instead of a permanent structure for the Jews of the entire Crown, there emerged a different organizational framework for the communities in each state of the Crown; the three major states, Catalonia, Aragon and Valencia, will be examined here in turn.

THE CATALAN *ALJAMAS*

The communities of Catalonia constituted the most important unit of Jewry within the Crown of Aragon. Despite the scarcity of the sources, there is evidence that already during the reign of Jaime I the Catalan communities formed a unit distinct from the rest.[1] Under Pedro III the Jews of Catalonia were treated as one body in various fields. The constitution issued at the end of July 1280 offered a uniform system of communal government to all the Jews of Catalonia.[2] With certain limitations, this constitution was confirmed by Jaime II in 1297.[3] In a series of charters issued by Pedro III on the very same day as the constitution, Catalan Jews obtained privileges and guarantees in judicial and financial matters.[4] Both Pedro III and Alfonso III granted all the Catalan communities charters that regulated their financial and commercial life.[5] During the reign of Pedro III Catalan Jews appear as a distinct group enjoying their own privileges and represented by their

[1] ACA, Reg. 83, fos. 55ᵛ, 112 [= R 2148, 2304].
[2] ACA, Reg. 44, fos. 187ᵛ-188 [= R 823 = Baer, *Spanien*, doc. 121 = Dinur, ii. 2, p. 418, no. 8, and pp. 446-7, no. 2].
[3] ACA, Reg. 195, fo. 44 [= R 2629 = Baer, *Spanien*, doc. 121].
[4] ACA, Reg. 44, fo. 188ʳᵛ [= R 824, 826-7].
[5] ACA, Reg. 83, fo. 53ʳᵛ, 111ᵛ-112 [= R 2141-2, 2301-3].

own delegates at meetings of all the Jews of the Crown. Jaime II confirmed the judicial rights of Catalan Jews that had been granted by Jaime I and Pedro III.[6]

All the *aljamas* and Jewish settlements in the *collectas* of Barcelona, Gerona, Lérida, and Tortosa formed part of Catalan Jewry, although the exact list of constituent communities was not definitive throughout the period. In 1283, when their part of the subsidy was fixed by the Jews of Barcelona, the Jews of Tortosa claimed that they were never included with Catalan Jewry for the purpose of subsidies.[7] The border between Catalonia and Aragon was not finally determined until late in the thirteenth century, so that some Jewish settlements in the border area wavered between the two regions. One such community was Monzón, which was included with the Catalan communities before finally being incorporated into Aragonese Jewry.[8]

For purposes of tax and subsidy the Jews of Catalonia were considered by the monarch as one unit. Delegates appeared in the palace representing all the Catalan *aljamas*.[9] As the tax that each Catalan *collecta* had to pay was known, there was no need for the Catalan *aljamas* to meet, except when problems arose. In 1283 each Catalan *aljama* had to send three delegates to Barcelona to deal with the claims and objections of the Jews of Lérida.[10] As for the subsidies imposed on Catalan Jewry, the representatives of the *collectas* usually met in Barcelona to divide the sum among them.[11] The final sum of the subsidy was determined following negotiations conducted between the representatives of Catalan Jewry and the ruler.[12] The subsidies strained the relations of the *aljamas* in Catalonia, and each demand for a subsidy was followed by disagreements that led to royal intervention.[13] The *aljama* of Barcelona enjoyed a special status. Its leaders received the payments of all the Catalan communities which they in turn transmitted to the king.[14]

The Catalan *aljamas* were the subject of special legislation by the Catalan Corts, which devoted some of their debates to the Jewish communities of the county. Their decisions affected all these communities.[15] In language, names, clothes, and customs the Jews of Catalonia differed from the Aragonese. The structure of their *qehilah* and institutions, as already noted, their specific inter-communal organization, the titles of their leaders, and the name of their quarter were all influenced by local conditions. Letters sent from the chancellery to Catalan Jews were

---

[6] ACA, Reg. 89, fo. 7 [=R 2538].   [7] ACA, Reg. 61, fo. 125 [=R 1058–9].

[8] See e.g. ACA, Reg. 61, fo. 187 [=R 1069]; Reg. 62, fo. 14ˇ [=R 1092]; Reg. 58, fo. 101 [=R 1404].

[9] The sources are numerous. A few of them are: ACA, Reg. 51, fo. 33 [=R 1107]; Reg. 86, fo. 87 [=R 1292–3]; Reg. 56, fo. 122ˇ [=R 1384].

[10] ACA, Reg. 60, fo. 45ˇ [=R 1026].

[11] ACA, Reg. 59, fo. 147ˇ [=R 981–2].   [12] ACA, Reg. 71, fo. 130ˇ [=R 1005].

[13] As an example see the disagreement between the *aljamas* of Barcelona and Lérida following the subsidy of 200,000 sb that Pedro III imposed on Catalan Jewry: ACA, Reg. 57, fos. 183ˇ, 185 [=R 1426, 1428].   [14] ACA, Reg. 57, fo. 214ˇ [=R 1453].

[15] ACA, Reg. 257, fo. 44ˇ [=R 2725]; Reg. 208, fo. 199ˇ [= *Cortes*, ii, pp. 217–18 = R 2934].

written in Catalan, as were letters by the Catalan Jews addressed to the court or the authorities.[16]

Compared to the assembly of delegates of the Aragonese *aljamas*, the framework of the Catalan communities was rather loose. This was due to the strong local inter-communal organization that developed in Catalonia, the *collecta*, which is discussed in more detail in section 3.

THE ASSEMBLY OF THE ARAGONESE DELEGATES

The union of the Kingdom of Aragon and the County of Barcelona under one ruler in 1137 proved to be a most successful and enduring act. Their common political destiny and shared head did not however obliterate the fundamental differences and separate identities of Aragon and Catalonia. The Jews of the Kingdom of Aragon were a separate entity. They differed from their Catalan brethren culturally, socially, and economically. The Aragonese *aljamas* formed their own separate union, which, like its Catalan counterpart, was treated by the authorities as a distinct organization. In economic and judicial matters the Aragonese communities received general charters.[17] The regime of the Aragonese communities was also treated in general charters affecting the entire kingdom.[18]

For tax purposes, the Aragonese communities formed a separate unit in the Crown of Aragon. Under Jaime I and Pedro III the total annual tax paid by the Jews of the kingdom was 50,000 sj, a sum divided among all the Aragonese *aljamas*.[19] The entire collected sum had to be paid by the representatives of the communities to the high-ranking official appointed by the king, either in Saragossa or in any other place that was convenient for the king. Detailed instructions about the collection were sent to all the *aljamas*.[20] Under Alfonso III the power that had been given to the communal leadership for the distribution and collection of taxes, as well as the arrangements for the transfer of the taxes collected, remained essentially the same.[21] During his reign extra power and responsibility were given to the delegates of the three major Aragonese *aljamas*: Saragossa, Huesca, and Calatayud. These six delegates acted on behalf of all the other *aljamas*.[22] The major Aragonese communities continued to play a central role under Jaime II.[23]

---

[16] See Baer, *Spanien*, 148–9, 151, 156, 189.

[17] ACA, Reg. 16, fo. 252 [= R 490 = Jacobs 478]; CR, Jaime II, C 13, nos. 1715, 1717 [= *Cartas Reales*, nos. 78, 81].   [18] See e.g. ACA, Reg. 59, fo. 56 [= R 942].

[19] ACA, Reg. 19, fo. 168ᵛ [= R 611 = Jacobs 560]; Reg. 59, fo. 156ᵛ [= R 985].

[20] ACA, Reg. 38, fo. 24ᵛ [= R 663]; Reg. 43, fo. 18ᵛ [= R 1187]; Reg. 58, fo. 89ᵛ [= R 1314]; Reg. 57, fo. 187ᵛ [= R 1433]; Reg. 56, fos. 127–9ᵛ [= R 1362 and pp. 433–4, doc. xvii, 1363–78]. The letters sent to the *aljamas* are in Aragonese, not in Catalan as suggested by Régné.

[21] ACA, Reg. 66, fo. 28 [= R 1518]; Reg. 65, fos. 2ᵛ, 50ᵛ, 98ᵛ [= R 1471, 1493, 1506].

[22] ACA, Reg. 66, fo. 28ᵛ [= R 1519]; Reg. 74, fo. 49ᵛ [= R 1838].

[23] ACA, Reg. 91, fo. 222 [= R 2425]; Reg. 230, fos. 97–8 [= R 3448 = Jacobs 889].

The subsidies that the king demanded from the Jews of his realm were usually imposed on the Jews of Aragon en bloc;[24] the total sum was then divided among the communities in accordance with the same criterion used for the regular taxes.[25] In some cases, however, the king decided the sum each community had to contribute to the subsidy, thus relieving the assembly of its task.[26]

The Aragonese *aljamas* were Saragossa, Calatayud, Huesca, Teruel, Daroca, Barbastro, Borja, Tarazona, Alagón, Egea, Jaca, Uncastillo, Tauste, Ruesta, Luna, Monzón, and Montclús. Some of the small communities do not appear in all the lists, either because they did not always exist as legally constituted *aljamas* or because, for one reason or another, they were included for tax purposes with the larger neighbouring communities. Saragossa, where the representatives of Aragonese Jewry originally met,[27] was obviously the most important *aljama*. The meeting-place was switched in the course of time as a result of dissent between the communities and claims that the *aljama* of the capital exerted extreme pressure on the others. However, in 1283 it was the community of Calatayud that objected to the meeting taking place in Alagón instead of Saragossa.[28]

From the king's correspondence we know that the meeting-place often changed. In December 1284 Pedro III ordered that the assembly of the Aragonese Jews meet in Huesca on 31 January 1285. He further ordered the delegates to remain in Huesca until agreement was reached about each community's quota. The *aljamas* of Saragossa and Huesca had five delegates each, while the rest were represented by two each. A document of two weeks later refers to Calatayud as the meeting-place, whereas one of 23 January 1285 had mentioned Alagón as the site of the meeting.[29] In the end the delegates did assemble in Alagón for their deliberations and were ordered to appear before the king in Rueda on the Monday following 27 January.[30] The reason for these changes of location seems to have been the extremely tense relations that prevailed among the Aragonese communities. Under Alfonso III and Jaime II, the assembly of the Aragonese delegates continued to meet in Alagón.[31]

The decisions of the assembly and the distribution of the tax fixed by it did not always please the king: in some cases his protégés would feel dissatisfied and complain to him, exacerbating internal strife and dissension among the tax-payers

---

[24] ACA, Reg. 71, fo. 129ʳ [=R 1001]; Reg. 67, fo. 25 [=R 1573]; González Hurtebise, *Libros de tesorería*, paras. 18, 208, 1393–4, 1396–8 and *passim*.

[25] ACA, Reg. 67, fo. 18ᵛ [=R 1565]; Reg. 71, fo. 62ʳ [=R 1753].

[26] ACA, Reg. 68, fo. 51ᵛ [=R 1740]; Reg. 82, fo. 39ᵛ [=R 2116].

[27] ACA, Reg. 23, fo. 3ᵛ [=R 615]; Reg. 48, fo. 57ᵛ [=R 790]; Reg. 59, fo. 156ᵛ [=R 986].

[28] ACA, Reg. 61, fo. 117 [=R 1052 = Baer, *Spanien*, doc. 124].

[29] ACA, Reg. 46, fo. 166 [=R 1240]; Reg. 43, fos. 90ᵛ, 11ʳ [=R 1248, 1266–7 = Baer, *Spanien*, doc. 128, paras. 1–2 = Cubells, 'Documentos', p. 214]. Contrary to what Régné says, the last documents addressed to the Aragonese *aljamas* were naturally in Aragonese and not in Catalan.

[30] ACA, Reg. 45, fo. 113 [=R 1271].

[31] ACA, Reg. 70, fo. 27ʳ [=R 1700]; Reg. 74, fo. 78 [=R 1878]; *CDIA*, Rentas, xxxix, p. 223.

which was itself a matter of concern to the king. The consequent royal interference both damaged the authority of the community and led to further strife, with the complainants called traitors. There is reason to believe that information was leaked to the king from the deliberations of the assembly by some elements who were dissatisfied with its decisions.[32]

In the assembly of the community representatives decisions affecting all the Jews were taken and ordinances for all the Aragonese communities were enacted. Bans were also issued against individuals who acted against the interest or the decisions of the Aragonese *aljamas*.[33]

The framework within which the Aragonese communities operated was far more highly developed than that of Catalonia. This may be due to the different general systems that existed in the County of Catalonia and the Kingdom of Aragon. A more centralized and autocratic regime in Aragon facilitated or encouraged the emergence of a more efficient and powerful general assembly of the communities of the territory.

THE COMMUNITIES OF THE KINGDOM OF VALENCIA

The third major component of the Crown of Aragon was the last to join the union. After its conquest in 1238–45, Jaime I created on the ruins of the Muslim sultanate a Christian kingdom in which the Jewish population, as well as Jewish participation in its administration, were most welcome.[34] The framework of the Valencian communities was strongly influenced by political developments in the area. Parts of Valencia, north of the river Xúcar, had been incorporated in the Crown of Aragon as early as 1151.[35] The renewed Reconquista under Jaime I added the rest of the kingdom, including the capital, the city of Valencia; and with the inclusion of Valencia within its boundaries, the Reconquista for the Crown of Aragon was over. With the exception of a small part of the Kingdom of Murcia that was annexed later, which included Alicante, Elche, and Oriola, the peninsular boundaries of the Crown of Aragon had now reached their permanent shape.[36] The history of the Jews in the Kingdom of Valencia in general, and inter-communal organization in particular, were deeply influenced by these developments.

The communities of the Kingdom of Valencia were grouped separately from the Catalan and Aragonese communities. The Valencian *aljamas* developed under special political and cultural circumstances. A recent Muslim and Arabic

---

[32] ACA, Reg. 56, fo. 126 [=R 1344 & pp. 430-2, doc. xvi = Baer, *Spanien*, doc. 129].

[33] For the ordinances of Barbastro see ACA, Reg. 43, fo. 111ʳ [=R 1267 = Baer, *Spanien*, doc. 128, para. 2]. For bans, see Reg. 43, fo. 113 [=R 1272].

[34] On the Kingdom of Valencia see Burns, *The Crusader Kingdom*.

[35] Rovira, *Història*, iv, p. 113.

[36] On the conquest of Murcia and the final boundary in the south, see Martinez, *Jaime II de Aragón*, i, pp. 106-7; Soldevila, *Història*, i, pp. 409-10; Giménez, Soler, *Juan Manuel*, doc. cxix.

background, as well as a Christian colonization policy that favoured Jewish settlement in a Christian kingdom with a Muslim majority, left their mark on Jewish life in Valencia. Alongside the Valencian dialect of Catalan, Arabic remained an important language in the Jewish communities.[37]

The Valencian communities appeared as the third group among the Jews of the realm from the reign of Pedro III onwards. The first references to the Valencian communities as a distinct group date from 1279, the reign of Pedro III.[38] In 1280, among the communities of Valencia that were ordered to pay a subsidy towards Pedro's war expenses, we find the *aljamas* and Jewish settlements of Valencia, Játiva, Murviedro, Morella, Segorbe, Onda, Alcira, Burriana, Castellón de la Plana, and Gandia.[39] From then on the Jews of Valencia appear frequently as the third major group of Jews in the Crown. The authority of the capital's *aljama* reached beyond the borders of its *judería*, and all Jews who did not belong to the provincial *aljamas* came under its direct jurisdiction.[40] After the *aljama* of the capital, those of Murviedro and Játiva were the most important; the representatives of the three sometimes acted together on behalf of all Valencian Jewry.[41]

The status of the community of Valencia in the kingdom was unlike the position of Barcelona and Saragossa in their respective territories. Unlike them, it had no rivals, being by far the largest community in the kingdom: at the beginning of the fourteenth century it had 400 heads of households,[42] while the largest communities other than Valencia had no more than fifty families each.[43] Relations between Valencia and the provincial communities were however frequently tense.[44] The crisis in the first decade of the fourteenth century over the proportion of the royal tax that each community had to pay led to the creation of a committee consisting of two representatives each from Valencia, Játiva, and Murviedro, and one from Burriana.[45]

In many fields, but particularly in tax matters, the king addressed Valencian Jewry as one. Many orders and regulations were issued for all the *aljamas* of the kingdom.[46] As the Valencian Jews were the most recent addition to the communities under the Crown, there exist many decisions of principle that related to all of them. For example, the Jews of the kingdom were treated as one unit as far as testimony in lawsuits involving Jews and Christians was concerned, where the

---

[37] See e.g. Millás, 'Un manuscript', p. 341. On the linguistic problem in Valencia, see Burns, *Jaume I i els Valencians*, pp. 303–30.

[38] ACA, Reg. 41, 50ᵛ, 76, 108 [= R 720, 728, 741 = MF ii. 502, 540, 601].

[39] ACA, Reg. 48, fo. 7ᵛ [= R 781 = MF ii. 1003]. [40] ACA, Reg. 74, fo. 49ᵛ [= R 1836].

[41] ACA, Reg. 65, fo. 107 [= R 1360 = MF ii. 2216] is one of many sources for the leading role played by the three communities.

[42] The computation is based on several sources, lists of residents of the community. See Millás, 'Un manuscrit', 341–51; ACA, CR, Jaime II, C 14, no. 1854 [= *Cartas Reales*, no. 97].

[43] Baer, *History*, i, pp. 140–1.

[44] ACA, Reg. 197, fos. 153ᵛ–154 [= R 2745 = Baer, *Spanien*, doc. 146].

[45] ACA, CR, Jaime II, C 21, no. 2678 [= Baer, *Spanien*, doc. 159 = *Cartas Reales*, no. 119]. The *caja* in Baer is no longer up to date. [46] ACA, Reg. 48, fo. 119 [= R 834 = MF ii. 1127].

Jews had to take the 'oath of the Maledictions'. In 1284 delegates of Valencian Jewry cooperated with Catalan delegates in an attempt to have cancelled the clause in the *fur* of Valencia that abolished the requirement to have the testimony of at least one Jew in any suit brought by Christians against Jews.[47] Also in 1284, Pedro III decided that the Valencian Jews should wear the same special apparel as the Jews of Barcelona.[48] The rights of Valencian Jewish women whose husbands were involved in litigation were guaranteed by Pedro III in 1285; these rights were protected by Jewish law, but it was significant that they were upheld by the king.[49] The right of Valencian Jews to trade with Christians was confirmed by Alfonso III in 1286.[50] In 1321 all the *aljamas* of Valencia obtained the right to enact ordinances and adopt a communal constitution.[51]

In February 1285 Pedro III ordered that the leaders and delegates of all the communities submit their financial accounts.[52] The delegates would be ordered to appear before the king to pay the sums promised, as were the Aragonese and Catalan delegates.[53] Subsidies parallel to those of Catalonia and Aragon were imposed on all the *aljamas* of Valencia.[54] As in the other territories, the *aljama* of the capital sometimes advanced money to the king and then had to seek the king's help to recover the contributions of the other communities, which in some cases took quite a long time.[55] The importance of the *aljama* of the capital in relation to the rest of the kingdom is reflected in the payment of 20,000 s to the king in the first decade of the fourteenth century, of which the community of the capital was to pay 6,000 s while the rest was to be paid by the provinces.[56]

The information at our disposal on the taxes paid by the Jews of the Kingdom of Valencia is rather limited and incoherent. It may be stated, however, that the payment of taxes and subsidies was made by two groups of Valencian *aljamas*: the northern and the southern. The border was the river Xúcar. The two groups emerged as a result of historical conditions, mentioned above and described further in section 6 below.[57]

[47] ACA, Reg. 46, fos. 152ʳ, 152ᵛ-153 [=R 1102, 1106].
[48] ACA, Reg. 46, fo. 152ᵛ [=R 1103].   [49] ACA, Reg. 57, fo. 223 [=R 1461 = MF ii. 2302].
[50] ACA, Reg. 66, fo. 47 [=R 1530].   [51] ACA, Reg. 219, fo. 198ᵛ [=R 3163]
[52] ACA, Reg. 56, fo. 7ᵛ [=R 1290 = MF ii. 2158].   [53] ACA, Reg. 71, fo. 83ʳ [=R 1787].
[54] ACA, Reg. 59, fos. 151ᵛ-152 [=R 984 = MF ii. 1604]; Reg. 58, fo. 87 [=R 1294 = MF ii. 2160].
[55] See e.g. ACA, Reg. 57, fo. 222ᵛ [=R 1458 = MF ii. 2297]; Reg. 66, fo. 47ᵛ [=R 1531, 1535].
[56] ACA, CR, Jaime II, C 21, no. 2678 [= Baer, *Spanien*, doc. 159 = *Cartas Reales*, no. 119]. The *caja* in Baer is no longer updated.   [57] ACA, Reg. 219, fos. 167-8 [=R 3146].

§3.3 The Catalan *Collectas*

THE *COLLECTA*

THE *collecta* was a group of communities centred on a major *aljama* that formed one area for tax collection, as its name indicates. It was originally a Catalan creation designed to facilitate and improve the collection of the taxes from the ruler's point of view. In the rare references to it in the Hebrew sources it is called *tevah*, literally 'case' or 'box'.[1] In most places, writes R. Shelomo ben Adret, each city had its own tax borders as set by the authorities.[2] Adret gave halakhic legitimacy to the authority exercised by the main community over all the smaller ones within the boundaries of the *collecta*, including Jewish settlements under baronial jurisdiction.[3]

In the thirteenth and fourteenth centuries many payments of taxes and subsidies were made by the Jews of Barcelona, Gerona, Lérida, and Tortosa in the name of Catalan Jewry. In 1311, for instance, representatives of the four communities gathered in Montblanch and voulantarily put themselves under 'house arrest' for fifteen days to decide on the apportionment of the tax. If they failed to reach an agreement within those fifteen days, the king would decide.[4] Two years earlier, the Catalan communities that contributed to the expenses of the war against Granada were Barcelona, Gerona, Lérida, and Tortosa.[5] In both cases the question arises whether these were the only Catalan communities which paid taxes and subsidies. The answer lies in the *collecta* system: the four above-mentioned communities were, in fact, the four *collectas* that included all the Jews of Catalonia.

We have sufficient evidence to indicate that there were no *collectas* other than these four and that the sums of tax and subsidy paid by these *collectas* amounted to the total sum that was imposed on Catalan Jewry. In 1314, for instance, the Catalan communities were required to pay 90,000 sb for the purchase and annexation of Urgell. The *collectas* of Barcelona and Gerona paid 36,000 sb each, Lérida paid 10,000 sb and apparently the remaining 8,000 sb were paid by Tortosa.[6] Repeatedly in the sources the four *collectas* appear as the only Catalan communities to pay taxes and subsidies.[7]

[1] Adret, iii. 411.   [2] Adret, i. 664 = iii. 440.   [3] Adret, v. 286.
[4] ACA, Reg. 254, fos. 153ʻ–154 [= R 2931].   [5] ACA, Reg. 206, fos. 29ʻ–30 [= R 2900].
[6] ACA, Reg. 219, fos. 184ʻ–185 [= R 3147–50 = Jacobs 775]. Most accounts of the payment are misleading since they speak of four communities.
[7] González Hurtebise, *Libros de tesorería*, paras. 8, 10–11, 19; *CDIA*, Rentas, xxxix, pp. 20, 33, 49, 59, 72.

The early records under Jaime I refer frequently to the *collectas* of Barcelona and Gerona. Later, we have very few sources on the *collecta* of Lérida. Under Pedro III, the three *collectas* appeared for the first time on all the occasions where reference is made to Catalan Jewry. The payments made by each indicate their relative economic and, probably, demographic strength. For example, the amounts that the three were asked to pay to subsidise the war against the Moors were as follows: Barcelona 30,000 sb, Gerona 15,000 sb, and Lérida 6,000 sj.[8] It is noteworthy that the Jews of Lérida had to pay in Aragonese currency. The communities of this *collecta* were in a borderline area between Catalonia and Aragon. The status of Lérida itself was uncertain until late in the thirteenth century, as we shall see below. Nevertheless, during the reign of Alfonso III, Lérida appears as one of the Catalan *collectas*.[9]

The advantages of the *collecta* system from the king's point of view were enormous. It was a sophisticated and indeed an ingenious system that made the collection of taxes very efficient. It operated in the king's favour but cost him nothing. It was based entirely on the Jewish communal administration and infrastructure, allowing the ruler to do away with an expensive bureaucracy. The Jews had little choice in the matter, but were very satisfied with the creation of an inter-communal structure that proved to be advantageous in many respects.

THE STRUCTURE OF THE *COLLECTA* SYSTEM

The importance of the *collecta*'s major function explains the king's grant to the *collecta* of jurisdiction over all Jews within its territory. For this purpose the Jews were authorized to elect special officers and set up the necessary mechanisms.[10] The main *aljama* was naturally the dominant force in the *collecta*, playing a leading role in all its affairs, but the status of the others was by no means negligible. Adret insisted that, despite its demographic and economic predominance, Barcelona could not impose its will on the other communities in the *collecta*. All the decisions were taken in consultation with the representatives of the other *aljamas*. Only when a decision could not be reached through negotiations would the main *aljama* turn to the king for help against dissenting communities.[11] Members of the main *aljama* represented all the Jews of the *collecta* at meetings with the king or his officials. These meetings took place wherever the king was at the time, whether in Catalonia or elsewhere in the territories of the Crown.[12]

Representatives of the *aljamas* within the *collecta* met regularly in the main community. Extraordinary sessions were also held when the need arose. Each of the constituent *aljamas* had its own jurisdiction over smaller communities and

---

[8] ACA, Reg. 39, fo. 209` [= R 682].   [9] ACA, Reg. 83, fo. 112 [= R 2304].
[10] ACA, Reg. 10, fo. 54` [= R 97 = Baer, *Spanien*, doc. 97 = Jacobs 151].   [11] Adret, iii. 411.
[12] ACA, Reg. 12, fos. 39`–40, 59`–60 [= R 156, 164 = Jacobs 208, 224 = Bofarull, Barcelona, xxvi]; Reg. 15, fos. 124`–125 [= R 399 = Bofarull, Barcelona, lxxvi = Jacobs 434a].

settlements within its orbit. The existence of 'sub-*collectas*' in Catalonia has not hitherto been noted. The structure of the *collecta* was far more complex and sophisticated than has hitherto been suggested. We now know that representatives of the smaller Jewish communities or settlements held meetings in the synagogue of the main *aljama* in the sub-*collecta*. Most of these meetings were naturally connected with the distribution of the tax among all components of the *collecta*. Apart from the Jews living in baronial lands or in the domain of the infantes, there was no community or settlement in Catalonia that was not included in one of the *collectas*.

THE PAYMENT OF TAXES AND SUBSIDIES

As the original purpose of the *collecta* was the collection of the king's taxes, most sources relate to this aspect of its operation. The annual tax imposed on all the Jews of Catalonia was divided among the *collectas* according to a scale that was determined in accordance with the demographic and economic strength of each *collecta*. The same proportional system applied to the subsidies that Catalan Jewry had to pay, and the same principle was used within each *collecta*. Every constituent *aljama* paid an agreed part of the tax, and proportionately of the subsidy, in turn dividing its share among the communities and Jews within its sub-*collecta* where that variant existed. As a rule, the king dealt with the whole *collecta*.[13]

In November 1282 Pedro III demanded the sum of 100,000 sb from Catalan Jewry to meet the growing expenses of his foreign policy. The *collectas* of Barcelona, Gerona, Lérida, and Tortosa, and exceptionally the Aragonese *aljamas* of Monzón and Fraga were ordered to send delegates to Barcelona during December to decide how to distribute the subsidy.[14] For the subsidy of 1291 the *collecta* of Barcelona had to pay 60,000 sb, those of Gerona and Lérida 30,000 sb each.[15]

The system did not always function as smoothly as might appear, however. The sources contain abundant information about conflicts between the communities of the *collecta*, and particularly between the main *aljama* and its satellites. The king often had to intervene at the request of one party or the other. Sometimes the main community had to pay money in advance and had difficulty in getting the smaller communities to pay back their parts of the tax or subsidy.[16] There were also problems between the *collectas* on their respective parts in the tax or subsidy liability. In the meeting of December 1282 the *aljama* of Barcelona played a major role in determining the part that each *collecta* or community had to contribute. It

---

[13] ACA, Reg. 12, fo. 68 [=R 168 = Jacobs 226]; Reg. 13, fo. 230' [=R 291 = Jacobs 309].

[14] ACA, Reg. 59, fo. 147' [=R 981–2]. The two Aragonese communities were eventually part of Aragonese Jewry.

[15] ACA, Reg. 82, fos. 117'–119' [=R 2353].

[16] Cf. e.g. the problems between Barcelona and Monzón over the latter's share of the 1282 subsidy; ACA, Reg. 59, fo. 192 [=R 996]; Reg. 61, fo. 187 [=R 1069].

ended up, however, paying the part of Tortosa.[17] Lérida, too, seems to have had its share of trouble with the other *collectas*.[18]

THE OTHER FUNCTIONS AND JURISDICTION OF THE *COLLECTA*

Although the primary and original function of the *collecta* was the collection of the royal taxes, over the course of time it assumed additional functions and became a convenient vehicle for various purposes. The communities of the *collecta* drew great advantages from this development, and the king encouraged it as it permitted an efficient and simple way of dealing with all matters pertaining to the Jews.

For the Jews, it was advantageous to be able to conduct negotiations on behalf of a number of communities; the communities of the *collecta* were more likely to obtain satisfaction when they acted in unison than separately, and their joint requests carried greater weight in the king's court. The smaller communities, in particular, benefited from this collaboration: the experience and prestige of the main *aljama* were a great asset to them. For the king, the system saved a lot of time and bureaucracy. Adret informs us that the *collecta* fulfilled a variety of functions as required by the king.[19]

It was convenient for both the king and the Jews that the *collecta* should perform a variety of tasks and serve purposes other than the collection of tax. Charters were sometimes given to all the communities of the *collecta*; royal instructions and regulations on legal and economic matters were conveniently sent to the head community of the *collecta*, whose task it was to forward them to the other Jews in its district.

A few examples are sufficient to illustrate the point. On 19 December 1257 the king sent two letters addressed to the *collecta* of Barcelona. One contained an important ruling declaring valid documents drawn up for Jews by ecclesiastics acting as notaries; the other promised the Jews of the *collecta* that no moratorium would be granted to their debtors for five years.[20] In a series of letters all sent to the same *collecta* on 13 September 1261, Jaime I dealt with various matters affecting trade and credit.[21] In 1263 the right to give testimony inside the *call* or to appeal in any legal process was given to all the Jews of the *collecta* of Barcelona.[22] In another series of decisions in February 1265, Jaime I ordered that the Jews of the Barcelona *collecta* should neither be detained in their synagogues

---

[17] ACA, Reg. 61, fo. 162ʳ [= R 1075].
[18] ACA, Reg. 46, fo. 154ʳᵛ [= R 1110]; Reg. 57, fo. 185 [= R 1428].   [19] Adret, iii. 411.
[20] ACA, Reg. 9, fo. 2ʳ [= R 76–7 = Bofarull, Barcelona, xi = Jacobs 106–7].
[21] ACA, Reg. 11, fos. 215ʳ–216 [= R 145–7, 149 = Jacobs 179, 181]. These and similar charters were confirmed by Pedro III and Alfonso III. See e.g. Reg. 83, fo. 53ʳᵛ [= R 2141–2].
[22] ACA, Reg. 12, fo. 120 [= R 224, 226 = Jacobs 254–5].

nor forced to engage in polemics with Dominican friars.²³ Some important achievements of the Catalan *collectas* were in the field of Jewish law, the rights of Jewish women, and the validity of their *ketubah* and free access to their books, which were protected from confiscation.²⁴ The privileges of the main *aljama* would generally constitute a precedent or a model for other communities in the *collecta*; in some instances it was understood that these privileges applied equally to the provincial communities in the *collecta*.²⁵

THE *COLLECTA* OF BARCELONA

The *aljamas* and Jewish settlements on the Mediterranean coast from the north of Barcelona to the southern parts of Tarragona were included in the *collecta* of Barcelona. Explaining the mechanism of the *collecta*, R. Shelomo ben Adret writes that 'the city [Barcelona] is the head of all' and that 'we [the *aljama* of Barcelona] and the communities of Villafranca, Tarragona, and Montblanch have one account and a joint budget . . . for the payment of taxes and subsidies.'²⁶ The *collecta* included many other communities which were organized in a framework that is described below. This is clear from the earliest sources referring to the *collecta*.²⁷

In the earliest references to the *collecta*, from 1257–60, Barcelona, Villafranca, and Tarragona are mentioned as the principal communities.²⁸ From 1261 onwards Montblanch was added to the list, and occasionally other *aljamas* or settlements, such as Cervera and Caldas de Montbuy, were named as part of the *collecta*.²⁹ The taxes collected by the *aljamas* of the *collecta* were brought to Barcelona, whose leaders' duty it was to transmit the total sum to the king or his representative. For Barcelona, its status as principal *aljama* gave it not only prestige but also responsibility.³⁰ Tensions between the *aljama* of Barcelona and the provincial communities sometimes ran very high, requiring the king to intervene in order to pacify the two sides. When the crisis between the *aljamas* paralysed the *collecta*, causing financial repercussions, the king gave specific instructions to the *aljamas* to settle their differences.³¹

The Barcelona *collecta*'s importance is evident from the amount of tax and

---

²³ ACA, Reg. 13, fo. 257 [= R 317–18 = Bofarull, Barcelona, l, li = Jacobs 324–5].
²⁴ ACA, Reg. 75, fo. 52 [= R 1831]; Reg. 37, fo. 26ᵛ [= R 487]; Reg. 74, fo. 46ᵛ [= R 1835]; Reg. 83, fo. 55 [= R 2147].
²⁵ ACA, Reg. 11, fo. 216ᵛ [= R 150 = Jacobs 182].
²⁶ Adret, iii. 411. Cf. Sarret, *Jueus*, p. 33.
²⁷ ACA, Reg. 10, fo. 28ʳ [= R 75 = Bofarull, Barcelona, x = Jacobs 135].
²⁸ ACA, Reg. 10, fo. 28ʳ [= R 75 = Bofarull, Barcelona, x = Jacobs 135]; Reg. 9, fos. 2ᵛ–3 [= R 76–7 = Bofarull, Barcelona, xi = Jacobs 106–7]; Reg. 11, fo. 229 [= R 130 = Bofarull, Barcelona, xx].
²⁹ ACA, Reg. 11, fo. 215ᵛ [= R 145–6 = Jacobs 179]; Reg. 14, fo. 127ᵛ [= R 496 = Bofarull, Barcelona, cvii = Jacobs 396].
³⁰ ACA, Reg. 67, fo. 49 [= R 1606]; Reg. 80, 49 [= R 2005].
³¹ ACA, Reg. 57, fo. 215 [= R 1452]; Reg. 70, fo. 90 [= R 1711]; Reg. 81, fo. 109 [= R 2127].

subsidy it paid. Under Alfonso III, in 1290, the *collecta* paid a tax of 95,000 sb.[32] Its usual annual tax, however, was around 21,000–24,000 sb. During the reign of Jaime II, the *collecta* paid 24,000 sb in tax.[33] In 1269, it contributed 40,000 sb for Jaime's overseas campaign in addition to its annual tax of 21,250 sb or sm.[34] The *collecta* enjoyed a special status among the Catalan *collectas*.[35] According to sources from 1320, it paid 36,000 sb out of 90,000 sb that all Catalan Jewry was asked to contribute for the purchase of Urgell.[36]

The *collecta* of Barcelona scored several achievements in the economic and judicial fields,[37] and served as a model for the other *collectas* in Catalonia and those of Roussillon.[38]

As noted above, the *collecta* was divided into sub-*collectas*. Each of the major *aljamas* had several Jewish settlements within its orbit. The *aljama* of Barcelona constituted a sub-*collecta* of its own. From the period of Pedro III, the Jews of Solsona, Cardona, Vich, Manresa, Berga, and Granollers were all part of the sub-*collecta* of Barcelona.[39] All these Jews remained under the direct control of Barcelona throughout the period.[40] The *aljama* of Cervera was the most important group connected directly with Barcelona. In some of the sources it is enumerated along with the four or five *aljamas* of which the *collecta* consisted.[41] From several sources we can deduce that the Jews of Cervera were directly linked with Barcelona.[42] The ten Jewish families who lived in Vich and belonged to the Crown came under the jurisdiction of Barcelona. The other Jews of Vich, who belonged to the lords of Montcada, were excluded from the *collecta*. The proximity of Vich to Gerona explains the latter's attempts to include it in its *collecta*—attempts which nevertheless failed due to the strong opposition of the *aljama* of Barcelona.[43]

The sub-*collecta* of Villafranca had a special relationship with Barcelona because of their geographical proximity.[44] It kept, however, its separate frame-

---

[32] ACA, Reg. 81, fo. 130 [= R 2153].

[33] *CDIA*, Rentas, xxxix, pp. 33, 72.

[34] ACA, Reg. 15, fos. 124ʳ–125ʳ [= R 399 = Bofarull, Barcelona, lxxvi = Jacobs 434a]; Reg. 16, fo. 144ʳ [= R 406 = Bofarull, Barcelona, lxxviii = Jacobs 438]; Reg. 20, fo. 294ʳᵛ [= R 641–2 = Jacobs 595–6].

[35] ACA, Reg. 57, fo. 214ʳ [= R 1453].

[36] ACA, Reg. 219, fo. 185 [= R 3149].

[37] ACA, Reg. 14, fo. 128 [= R 501 = Bofarull, Barcelona, cix = Jacobs 397]; Reg. 19, fo. 50 [= R 564 = Bofarull, Barcelona, cxxiii]; Reg. 83, fo. 52ʳ [= R 2138].

[38] ACA, Reg. 13, fos. 265, 273ʳ [= R 322, 334]. For Roussillon, see R 329.

[39] ACA, Reg. 48, fo. 67ʳ [= R 803]; Reg. 74, fo. 86 [= R 1896].

[40] Sarret, *Jueus*, pp. 33, 60; Baer, *Aragonien*, p. 120.

[41] See e.g. ACA, Reg. 196, fo. 148ʳ [= R 2683].

[42] ACA, Reg. 229, fos. 260ʳ–261 [= R 3432].

[43] ACA, Reg. 216, fo. 24ʳ [= Corbella, *La aljama*, doc. 17 = R 3089]; Reg. 216, fo. 86 [= R 3098]; cf. Corbella, *La aljama*, doc. 54.

[44] See e.g. ACA, CR, C 3, no. 448 [= *Cartas Reales*, no. 32]; Reg. 88, fo. 266 [= R 2536]; Reg. 253, fo. 3ʳ [= R 2638].

work within the larger *collecta*.⁴⁵ The sub-*collecta* included the Jews of Sabadell, Martorell, and Arbós. The relations between these communities and Villafranca were sometimes very problematic.⁴⁶ The *aljama* of Villafranca exercised jurisdiction over Jews of these settlements, who enjoyed similar rights to those of the *aljama*.⁴⁷

The sub-*collecta* of Tarragona enjoyed a status similar to that of Barcelona. Despite being the see of the archbishop, it was emphasized that the Jews here were under royal jurisdiction and were therefore no different from the rest of the Catalan Jews.⁴⁸ Among the Jewish communities and settlements in this sub-*collecta* were Valls, Alforja, Vallmoll, and Alcover. The Jews of Valls were fined in 1312 by the Archbishop of Tarragona in connection with two Germans who wanted to convert to Judaism, because they formed part of the *aljama* of Tarragona that gave shelter and protection to the pair. Ten years later, Jews of Tarragona and Valls were still suffering the effects of this episode. We may recall that under incessant pressure some of the leaders of the Tarragona sub-*collecta* embraced Christianity.⁴⁹ Representatives of the Jewish settlements of the sub-*collecta* brought to Tarragona their parts of the tax that was fixed by the main *aljama*. The meetings between the delegates took place in the synagogue in Tarragona.⁵⁰

There were constant conflicts between Tarragona and the Jews in the area of its jurisdiction. In 1321 a serious dispute erupted, related to the apportionment of taxes. The delegate from Valls registered his complaint and protest against the *aljama* of Tarragona with the notary. The agreement that preceded the conflict had received the blessing of the *aljama* of Barcelona, the principal community in the *collecta*. That same year the three delegates of Alforja claimed that the agreement about their part of the tax reached between the communities of Barcelona and Tarragona was made without their consent. The Jews of Alforja claimed that they were not the only ones who were wronged, and that the Jews of Alcover and Vallmoll, in the same sub-*collecta*, also suffered injustice.⁵¹

Jews in the vicinity of Montblanch paid their taxes with the local *aljama*. This was the smallest sub-*collecta* concerning which the sources are rather scarce.⁵²

---

⁴⁵ ACA, Reg. 217, fo. 144ᵛ [=R 3111]; Reg. 220, fo. 14ᵛ [=R 3184].
⁴⁶ ACA, Reg. 87, fo. 12 [=R 2458].
⁴⁷ ACA, Reg. 85, fo. 221ᵛ [=R 2378]; Reg. 87, fos. 10, 12, 57, 65 [=R 2457, 2473, 2476, 2459]; Reg. 88, fo. 259ʳᵛ [=R 2530–1].
⁴⁸ ACA, Reg. 196, fo. 151ᵛ [=R 2688]; Reg. 211, fo. 278 [=R 3018]; Reg. 217, fo. 144 [=R 3111]; Reg. 257, fo. 44ᵛ [=R 2725].
⁴⁹ ACA, Reg. 209, fos. 236ᵛ–237 [=R 2952 = Baer, *Spanien*, doc. 166]; Reg. 223, fo. 227 [=R 3256 = Baer, *Spanien*, doc. 180].
⁵⁰ Sánchez Real, 'La judería', pp. 343–4.
⁵¹ Ibid.
⁵² ACA, Reg. 55, fo. 69 [= Baer, *Spanien*, doc. 160]; Reg. 196, fo. 168ᵛ [=R 2697].

THE *COLLECTA* OF GERONA–BESALÚ

The *collecta* of Gerona–Besalú consisted of the two northern *aljamas*, which jointly ran the affairs of the *collecta*. Four secretaries of Gerona and two of Besalú formed an executive body for the *collecta*.[53] The predominance of Gerona is obvious from its share of the tax liability and even more in its power to impose its will on its partner Besalú, sometimes with the support of the king.[54] Among the settlements included in the *collecta* was Figueras, where the Infante Pedro encouraged Jews to settle,[55] and Torroella de Montgrí.[56] Jewish inhabitants of Camprodón were part of the *collecta* and were directly linked to Besalú. However, when the village was given to a nobleman, Alfonso III denied Gerona the right to include the Jews in its *collecta*.[57] Jewish settlers in villages and also in Perelada and Ripoll on the whole paid their taxes with the *collecta*.[58] Sources from the 1320s suggest that the Jews of Castellón de Ampurias and La Bisbal might also have belonged to this *collecta*. According to a document from 1342, the Jews of Bañolas, Figueras, Camprodón, Olot, and San Lorenzo de Lamuga were part of the *collecta* of Gerona. In that year Besalú, long the junior partner of Gerona in the *collecta*, was finally allowed to break away from the union.[59]

The annual tax of the *collecta* was around 15,000 sb, although under Jaime II it was reduced to 13,300 sb.[60] In 1269 the *collecta* paid 10,000 sb as a subsidy for Jaime I's overseas campaign. This was a quarter of the sum paid by the *collecta* of Barcelona.[61] Of the 90,000 sb paid by all Catalan Jews for Urgell, the *collecta* of Gerona paid 36,000 sb a sum equal to that paid by Barcelona.[62]

The heads of the *collecta* were in constant touch with Jaime I and conducted a very active policy, as can be seen from the frequent decisions of the king in favour of the *collecta* and, for example, from the series of letters sent by the king on 13 August 1271 in connection with the *collecta*.[63] Soon after Alfonso III came to the throne the *collecta* obtained a series of guarantees and confirmations. These were particularly appreciated as the Jews of the *collecta* had suffered severely as a result of the French invasion during the reign of Pedro III.[64] Under Alfonso III the Jews

---

[53] ACA, Reg. 37, fo. 61ᵛ [= R 599].
[54] ACA, Reg. 62, fo. 114 [= R 1261]; Reg. 71, fo. 160 [= R 1263]; Reg. 70, fo. 19ᵛ [= R 1690]; Reg. 84, fo. 22 [= R 2313].
[55] ACA, Reg. 17, fo. 103 [= R 405 = Bofarull, Barcelona, lxxii = Jacobs 495].
[56] ACA, Reg. 81, fo. 87ᵛ [= R 2108].
[57] ACA, Reg. 19, fo. 89 [= R 575 = Bofarull, Barcelona, cxxix = Jacobs 530]; Reg. 81, fo. 129 [= R 2150].
[58] R 2329, citing a fragmentary Reg. of Alfonso III.
[59] ACA, Reg. 1676, fos. 8–10 [= Baer, *Spanien*, doc. 214]. For Castellón de Ampurias and La Bisbal, see ACA, Reg. 220, fo. 82ᵛ [= R 3192]; R 3356; Torroella, *La jueria de Banyoles*, p. 32.
[60] *CDIA*, Rentas, xxxix, pp. 20, 58–9; Baer, *Aragonien*, p. 130.
[61] ACA, Reg. 16, fo. 153 [= R 413 = Bofarull, Barcelona, lxxx = Jacobs 442].
[62] ACA, Reg. 219, fo. 185 [= R 3150].
[63] See e.g. ACA, Reg. 37, fos. 22ᵛ–23 [= R 472–5].
[64] ACA, Reg. 64, fos. 17–18, 147 [= R 1501–5, 1511–13, 1681]; Reg. 83, fo. 37ʳᵛ [= R 2109, 2111].

of the *collecta* continued to benefit from royal favour.⁶⁵ In 1298 Jaime II confirmed the privileges granted to the Jews of the *collecta* by his predecessors.⁶⁶

THE *COLLECTA* OF LÉRIDA

The first reference to the *collecta* of Lérida is from 1268, when the Jews of the *collecta* were promised the same privileges as the Jews of Barcelona.⁶⁷ Compared to the *collectas* of Barcelona and Gerona, that of Lérida was rather passive. The ambiguity relating to Lérida's identity, namely whether it should be considered Catalan or Aragonese, delayed the emergence of certain institutions typical of the Catalan communities and, to a certain extent, left it different from the rest of the Catalan *aljamas* even after its final inclusion within Catalonia. Even as late as 1284, the inclusion of Lérida with the Aragonese or Catalan communities was still a matter of debate. It appears that Jaime I had changed his own decision about the Jews of Lérida. First he included them in Aragon; later he decided they would be part of Catalonia.⁶⁸ By 1285, under Pedro III, the *collecta* of Lérida was finally considered Catalan.⁶⁹ Under Alfonso III the *collecta* began to enjoy a status similar to the other Catalan *collectas* and received similar treatment.⁷⁰

The information about the *collecta* until the reign of Alfonso III is meagre. The Jews who settled in Agramunt were included in Lérida according to a decision of Jaime I in 1273.⁷¹ During the reign of Pedro III the *collecta* was definitely part of the Catalan structure, and included within its boundaries the Jews of Tárrega, Villagrassa, and other localities.⁷² The *aljama* of Lérida had jurisdiction over Jews who lived in localities that were in Aragonese territory, namely those of Fraga and Monzón. The Jews who lived in Albalate, Alcoletge, Pomar, Estadilla, and Gradella were dependent on Monzón, and all belonged to the Templars. The *aljama* of Lérida claimed that its authority over the Jews of this Aragonese zone was well established in tradition.⁷³ This claim was supported by Alfonso III against the demands of the Templars.⁷⁴ Similarly, Alfonso III supported Lérida in its claim that the *aljama* of Fraga had to pay its taxes with its *collecta*.⁷⁵ Both

---

⁶⁵ ACA, Reg. 81, fo. 87ʳ [=R 2108]; Reg. 83, fos 36ʳ–37 [=R 2104, 2110].
⁶⁶ ACA, Reg. 196, fo. 214 [=R 2705]; Reg. 199, fo. 134ʳ [=R 2798]; Reg. 211, fos. 187ʳ–188].
⁶⁷ *CDIA*, Procesos, vi, pp. 170–2; R 400.
⁶⁸ ACA, Reg. 46, fo. 173ʳ [=R 1115].
⁶⁹ ACA, Reg. 57, fos. 185, 214ʳ [=R 1428, 1453].
⁷⁰ ACA, Reg. 75, fo. 52 [=R 1831]; Reg. 74, fo. 79 [=R 1868]; Reg. 83, fos. 112–13 [=R 2305, 2307–8]; Reg. 84, fo. 33 [=R 2325].
⁷¹ ACA, Reg. 21, fo. 122 [=R 550].
⁷² ACA, Reg. 70, fo. 23 [=R 1693 and doc. xxi, pp. 439–40]; Reg. 74, fo. 79 [=R 1827]. For the period of Alfonso III, see R 2336.
⁷³ ACA, Reg. 80, fos. 31–2, 75 [=R 1976, 1981, 1983, 2019].
⁷⁴ See e.g. ACA, Reg. 81, fos. 92ʳ–93 [=R 2114]; Reg. 84, fo. 2 [=R 2275].
⁷⁵ ACA, Reg. 85, fos. 43ʳ–4 [=R 2176].

the Jews of Fraga and those of Monzón were included in the *collecta* for the subsidy of 1291.⁷⁶

The *collecta* of Lérida included, apart from the principal *aljama* and the Aragonese communities of Fraga and Monzón, the communities of Tárrega, Balaguer, and Agramunt, and Jewish settlers living in the area. Some sort of a sub-*collecta* system developed in the *collecta* of Lérida, with Tárrega, Villagrassa, and Jews in nearby villages forming one unit. From a document from 1286 it is clear that in the sub-*collecta* there were Jews who lived outside the two localities.⁷⁷ In the north of Tárrega there was another sub-*collecta* around Agramunt, to which the Jews of Pons belonged.⁷⁸ Balaguer and some villages in its vicinity formed another unit. There were Jews in baronial domains in the area, where the infante too held some settlements. However, the permission given to the Infante Alfonso to let Jews settle in Balaguer, Agramunt, Pons, and Castellón de Farfaña did not exempt them from paying their taxes with the *collecta* of Lérida.⁷⁹ About six months later, however, in June 1317, Jaime II changed his decision and freed these Jews from the *collecta* of Lérida.⁸⁰ The status of these Jews in the *collecta* of Lérida was not clear and certainly not stable.

As noted above, the two Aragonese towns Monzón and Fraga and the villages within their orbit, were part of the Lérida *collecta* until the last decade of the thirteenth century. The Jews of Albalate, Alcoletge, Pomar, and Estadilla paid their taxes with Monzón. This group formed an additional sub-*collecta* within the *collecta* of Lérida.⁸¹ Under Jaime II, Monzón was finally deemed part of Aragon. In the year Jaime II became king the Jews of Fraga and the neighbouring localities Aytona, Zaidin, and others paid their taxes with the *collecta* of Lérida.⁸²

The *collecta* of Lérida paid 3,000 sj annually in the early years of Jaime II's reign.⁸³ For the purchase of Urgell, the *collecta* paid 10,000 s in 1320.⁸⁴

TORTOSA AND ITS SURROUNDINGS

The *aljama* of Tortosa and Jews who lived in the vicinity were not part of any of the above *collectas*. Tortosa eventually emerged as a fourth Catalan *collecta* after Jaime II received the city from Guillem II of Montcada in 1294.⁸⁵ Even under the House of Montcada the Jews of Tortosa belonged to the king, to whom they paid their taxes separately from the northern Catalan communities. The prosperity of the city increased with the change of jurisdiction and its Jewish community

---

⁷⁶ ACA, Reg. 82, fos. 117ᵛ–119ᵛ [= R 2353].
⁷⁷ ACA, Reg. 70, fo. 23 [= R 1693 and doc. xxi, pp. 439–40]; R 2336.
⁷⁸ ACA, Reg. 98, fo. 82 [= Baer, *Spanien*, doc. 132].
⁷⁹ ACA, Reg. 213, fos. 258–9 [= R 3057].   ⁸⁰ ACA, Reg. 214, fo. 103ᵛ [= R 3070].
⁸¹ ACA, Reg. 80, fo. 31ʳᵛ [= R 1976, 1981].   ⁸² ACA, Reg. 86, fo. 9ᵛ [= R 2384].
⁸³ *CDIA*, Rentas, xxxix, p. 49.   ⁸⁴ ACA, Reg 219, fo. 185 [= R 3148].
⁸⁵ Salarrullana, 'Estudios históricos'.

became an important economic factor.⁸⁶ Under Pedro III the Jews of Alcañizo were taxed with the community of Tortosa, forming together one tax zone.⁸⁷ In the last decade of the thirteenth century, Tortosa was mentioned as a *collecta*.⁸⁸

In 1302 Tortosa was listed as the fourth contributor to the Sicilian campaign subsidy.⁸⁹ In 1309, in the subsidy for the war with Granada, the Jews of Tortosa also contributed as the fourth group of Catalan Jewry, after Barcelona, Gerona, and Lérida.⁹⁰ In 1310, as conflict over the method of taxation flared up, the Jews of Tortosa were mentioned separately from the other three *collectas*.⁹¹ Throughout the reign of Jaime II the Jews of Tortosa and its immediate surroundings were treated as a separate unit of Catalan Jewry.⁹² For the acquisition of Urgell, the Jews of Tortosa paid apparently 8,000 s of the 90,000 s imposed on Catalan Jewry.⁹³ It is clear that the Jews of Tortosa remained a unit outside the three Catalan *collectas*.⁹⁴

The *collecta* reached its full development in the fourteenth century. Originally founded as a tax zone to facilitate the collection of the royal taxes, it assumed additional functions. As an inter-communal organization it served the king and the Jews. In the history of Jewish self-government it is a good illustration of external factors exerting a strong impact on Jewish life.

---

[86] Carreras, 'L'aljama'.
[87] ACA, Reg. 48, fo. 143ʻ [= R 845].
[88] ACA, Reg. 194, fos. 300ʻ–301 [= R 2627].
[89] González, *Libros de tesorería*, para. 19
[90] ACA, Reg. 206, fos. 29ʻ–30.
[91] ACA, Reg. 206, fos. 124ʻ–125 [= R 2909].
[92] ACA, Reg. 211, fos. 186ʻ–187, 303 [= R 2996, 3027].
[93] ACA, Reg. 219, fos. 184ʻ–185 [= R 3147].
[94] In 1323 Tortosan Jews were not even included with the rest of the Catalan Jews: ACA, Reg. 224, fo. 117 [= R 3291].

§3.4 The *Collecta* in Roussillon

THE JEWS OF ROUSSILLON

ROUSSILLON, today in southern France at the eastern slopes of the Pyrenees, was part of the Crown of Aragon until its final annexation by France in 1659. From 1275 until 1348 it was part of the Kingdom of Majorca that was established by Jaime I's will and ruled by a branch of the House of Aragon. From a Jewish point of view, the Jews of Roussillon remained part of Catalan Jewry. In religious and cultural terms, neither the Pyrenees nor the political boundary that lasted for about seventy-five years constituted a barrier. In taxation and communal organization the Jews of Roussillon were a distinct entity apart from Catalan Jewry and yet, until the establishment of the Kingdom of Majorca, they were not considered totally separated from their Catalan brethren.[1]

Despite their affinity with Catalan Jewry, the Jews of Roussillon developed their own independent communal structure, the character of which became far more pronounced when they were part of the Kingdom of Majorca. Perpignan was a centre of learning in the thirteenth and fourteenth centuries and attracted many Jewish scholars and students. R. Menahem Ha-Meiri, the most famous scholar of fourteenth-century Perpignan, represents well the character and standard of Jewish scholarship in the area. The important role played by the Jews in finance and trade cannot be divorced from their cultural and religious achievements.[2]

THE *COLLECTA* OF PERPIGNAN

For the period until 1276, when Roussillon was part of the Crown of Aragon under Jaime I, there is abundant information on the Jews of Roussillon in the Archive of the Crown of Aragon.[3] Perpignan was the principal *aljama* in Roussillon. The Jews scattered in many towns and villages of the area, of which Villafranca de Conflent and Puigcerdá were the most important,[4] were all part of

---

[1] In 1274 they appeared as part of the tax-paying Jews of Catalonia. See below.
[2] The most extensive history of the Jews of Roussillon remains to this day Vidal, *Les Juifs de Roussillon*. On the role of the Jews in moneylending and the economy, see Emery, *The Jews of Perpignan*, and several of his articles included in the bibliography.
[3] The richest documentary collections are found in R and Bofarull, Barcelona.
[4] ACA, Reg. 12, fo. 84 [= R 192 = Jacobs 231]; Reg. 19, fo. 145 [= R 605 = Bofarull, Barcelona, cxliv = Jacobs 557].

its *collecta* and under its jurisdiction. The *collecta* was referred to in many sources as 'the Jews of Perpignan, Roussillon, Cerdagne, and Conflent',[5] or simply *aliama judeorum Perpiniani*.[6]

The Jews of the *collecta* shared a single judicial system and enjoyed royal protection in the various non-Jewish tribunals, where their rights were guaranteed by the king.[7] Jaime I opposed attempts to have the Jews of the *collecta* tried before ecclesiastical courts.[8]

Jews living anywhere in the locality of Roussillon had to contribute to the taxes paid by the *aljama* of Perpignan. Only the king could exempt Jews from paying taxes to and with the community of Perpignan.[9] In 1274 the Jews of the *collecta* paid 5,000 sm.[10] In 1275 the *collecta* lent the king 30,000 sb, a sum which indicates the importance of the Perpignan Jews and the readiness of Jaime to offer them a number of favourable charters.[11]

All the king's charters and decisions related to the financial activities, particularly moneylending, of the Jews of Perpignan applied also to the Jews of Roussillon who were part of the same *collecta*. In this respect the policy of Jaime I was most favourable towards the Jews of Perpignan and its *collecta*. Their prosperity was identified with his. This is evident in the series of concessions and decisions issued in 1274.[12] On the whole their status and privileges were similar to those of the Jews of Catalonia.[13]

---

[5] ACA, Reg. 16, fo. 157v [= R 410 = Bofarull, Barcelona, lxxix = Jacobs 444].

[6] ACA, Reg. 18, fos. 64ʳ, 81ʳ–82 [= R 483–4 = Baer, *Spanien*, doc. 103 = Jacobs, docs. vi–vii, pp. 132–3, 501].

[7] ACA, Reg. 16, fos. 157–8 [= R 417, 419, 422 = Bofarull, Barcelona, lxxxiii, lxxxvi = Jacobs 450].

[8] ACA, Reg. 20, fo. 266ʳ [= R 625 = Bofarull, Barcelona, cliii].

[9] ACA, Reg. 12, fo. 84 [= R 192 = Jacobs 231].

[10] For a comparison with the other communities, see ACA, Reg. 23, fos. 3ʳff. [= R 615 = Dinur, ii. 2, p. 52, no. 41].

[11] For the loan, see ACA, Reg. 20, fo. 267 [= R 629, 636 = Bofarull, Barcelona, clvii, clxiv]. For the charters, see ACA, Reg. 20, fos. 266ʳ–268 [= R 625–8, 630–5 = Bofarull, Barcelona, cliii–clvi, clviii–clxi, clxiii = Jacobs 584–7, 589–91].

[12] ACA, Reg. 9, fo. 11 [= R 89 = Jacobs 111]; Reg. 16, fos. 158ʳ–159 [= R 423, 425 = Bofarull, Barcelona, lxxxvii, lxxxix = Jacobs 451, 454]. For the decisions of 1274 see Reg. 19, fos. 127ʳ–128 [= R 589, 591–3, 595, 598 = Bofarull, Barcelona, cxxxvii–cxli, cxliii = Jacobs 544, 546–9, 551].

[13] ACA, Reg. 16, fo. 157ʳ [= R 420–1 = Bofarull, Barcelona, lxxxv = Jacobs 444–5].

§3.5 Inter-Communal Relations and Organization in Aragon

THE communities of Aragon together developed a strong regional organization which left no room for a local inter-communal structure comparable to the Catalan *collecta*. A loose framework did, however, develop in Aragon, as the sources show. The large *aljamas* in Aragon had under their jurisdiction small communities and settlements in their vicinity. This jurisdiction was exercised mostly in the field of taxation.

THE *COLLECTA* OF SARAGOSSA

The earliest references to the *collecta* of Saragossa belong to the period of Pedro III.[1] The sources contain very little information until the beginning of the fourteenth century. Until then, the Jews of Alcañizo were the only Jews mentioned as part of the tax district of the Aragonese capital, the most important *aljama* of the kingdom.[2] In 1300 the *collecta* is mentioned without details of its dependent localities.[3] According to the tax distribution of 1304, the *aljama* of Saragossa included the Jews of Ruesta, Pina, Zuera, Gorrea, and Pedrola. The Jews of the last-named locality had belonged to the nobleman Lope Ferrench de Luna until 1302 and were therefore excluded from the tax district of Saragossa.[4] Hence the opposition of the *aljama* of Saragossa to the emigration of its members to Pedrola.[5] Emigration in the opposite direction was stopped by the Crown, to the disappointment of the capital's *aljama*.[6] In the 1280s Jews of Ruesta complained that the *aljama* of Saragossa dealt with them unjustly in the apportionment of the taxes.[7]

THE *COLLECTA* OF CALATAYUD

Earlier and more detailed information is available on the *collecta* of Calatayud, the second largest *aljama* in Aragon. In records pertaining to the reign of Pedro III,

---

[1] ACA, Reg. 59, fo. 156ᵛ [= R 985]. [2] ACA, Reg. 67, fo. 20ᵛ [= R 1560].
[3] ACA, Reg. 197, fo. 120ᵛ [= R 2727].
[4] ACA, Reg. 235, fo. 241 [= Baer, *Spanien*, doc. 155].
[5] Adret, iii. 406, 421. [6] ACA, Reg. 199, fo. 85 [= R 2780].
[7] ACA, Reg. 60, fo. 19 [= R 1015].

the Jews of Fariza and Ricla were included in this *collecta*.⁸ Some of the Jews of Fariza paid tax with the Christians. Others, objecting to being included in the *collecta* of Calatayud, eventually persuaded Jaime II to separate them from Calatayud.⁹ The Jews of Daroca apparently paid their taxes with the Jews of Calatayud.¹⁰ References to the *collecta* are not frequent but are quite explicit, even when the names of the localities are not mentioned.¹¹

THE *COLLECTA* OF HUESCA

In addition to Jews living around Huesca, several settlements that had been attached to Lérida in the thirteenth century became part of its tax district by the period of Jaime II. After the defeat of the Templars in 1312, the status of the community of Monzón and its dependent Jewish settlements totally changed. These settlements included Albalate de Cinca, Pomar, and Estadilla.¹² Fraga and Jews living in its surroundings, who had also been attached to Lérida, were now included in the district of the *aljama* of Huesca, whose privileges served as a model for all the local communities.¹³

In 1318 the Jews of the *collecta* of Huesca obtained a series of guarantees related to their judicial rights.¹⁴ The annual tax of the collecta was around 6,000 sj.¹⁵ The *collecta* paid various subsidies. Its part in this funding reflected its economic and demographic strength in the Kingdom of Aragon.¹⁶

THE *COLLECTA* OF TERUEL

In the southernmost part of Aragon was the *collecta* of Teruel, to which belonged the Jews of Santa María de Albarracín and Sarrión.¹⁷ The Jews of the district enjoyed the same privileges as those of Teruel.¹⁸ The *collecta* of Teruel was far behind the three major Aragonese tax districts in prominence, and accordingly its

---

⁸ Baer, *Aragonien*, p. 121; ACA, Reg. 48, fo. 66ᵛ [=R 802]; Reg. 235, fo. 241 [= Baer, *Spanien*, doc. 155].

⁹ *CDIA*, Rentas, xxxix, p. 222. On the decision of Jaime II in 1325, see ACA, Reg. 227, fos. 190ᵛ, 197ᵛ [=R 3335, 3339].

¹⁰ ACA, Reg. 48, fo. 87 [=R 812].

¹¹ ACA, Reg. 48, fo. 116 [=R 828]; Reg. 196, fo. 169 [=R 2698]; Reg. 229, fo. 203 [=R 3411]; *CDIA*, Rentas, xxxix, pp. 219, 246.   ¹² ACA, Reg. 80, fo. 31ʳᵛ [=R 1976, 1981].

¹³ ACA, Reg. 80, fo. 32 [=R 1983].

¹⁴ ACA, Reg. 216, fo. 80ᵛ [=R 3096].

¹⁵ *CDIA*, Rentas, xxxix, pp. 186, 287, xii. p. 350; Baer, *Aragonien*, p. 132; ACA, Reg. 235, fo. 241ʳᵛ [= Baer, *Spanien*, doc. 155].

¹⁶ González Hurtebise, *Libros de tesorería*, paras. 1329, 1413; ACA, Reg. 253, fo. 2 [=R 2632]; Reg. 218, fos. 111ᵛ–112 [=R 3139].   ¹⁷ ACA, Reg. 218, fo. 79ᵛ [=R 3383].

¹⁸ ACA, CR, Jaime II, C 133, no. 5 [= Baer, *Spanien*, doc. 177 = *Cartas Reales*, no. 231] (the number of the *caja* quoted in Baer is no longer valid); Reg. 198, fo. 270 [=RR 2748].

annual tax was usually no more than 1,000 sj.[19] While the Jews of Huesca paid 16,166 sj for the purchase of Urgell, those of Teruel paid just 3,539 sj.[20]

OTHER ARAGONESE *COLLECTAS*

The communities of Daroca,[21] Jaca,[22] Barbastro, Egea, Tarazona, and Alcañiz included in their tax-rolls all the Jews who lived in villages surrounding them and exercised jurisdiction over them. The Jews of Barbastro belonged for quite a while to Catalan Jewry and were dependent on Barcelona. In 1298 they were part of Aragonese Jewry, but in 1303 they were once again connected with the Jews of Catalonia. This unstable status continued throughout the period.[23] In the thirteenth century the Jews of Monzón paid their taxes with the *aljama* of Barbastro. The Jews of Monzón, whose special status has already been discussed, included in their tax-roll Jews in their vicinity.[24]

Egea and Tauste were often joined together in one tax district.[25] Tarazona, too, had in its tax district Jews who lived in neighbouring districts.[26] The same relationship existed between Tarazona and Borja.[27]

---

[19] ACA, Reg. 193, fo. 143 [= R 2424]; Reg. 199, fo. 118 [= R 2791]; Reg. 235, fo. 241ʳ [= R 155]; *CDIA*, Rentas, xxxix, p. 208; González Hurtebise, *Libros de tesorería*, para. 871.

[20] ACA, Reg. 218, fos. 11ᵛ–12.

[21] *CDIA*, Rentas, xxxix. 217; González Hurtebise, *Libros de tesorería*, para. 1360.

[22] ACA, Reg. 196, fo. 168ᵛ [= R 2697].

[23] ACA, Reg. 253, fo. 12 [= R 2639]; Reg. 196, fo. 168ᵛ [= R 2697]; Reg. 222, fo. 143; CR, Jaime II, C 17, no. 2164 [= *Cartas Reales*, no. 105].

[24] ACA, Reg. 59, fos. 52, 192 [= R 938, 997].   [25] ACA, Reg. 89, fo. 116ᵛ [= R 2585].

[26] ACA, Reg. 214, fo. 103ᵛ [= R 3068].   [27] ACA, Reg. 67, fo. 103 [= R 1668].

§3.6 Inter-Communal Organization in Valencia

THE territories of the Kingdom of Valencia were conquered by Catalonia–Aragon in stages. A small part of the Muslim Kingdom of Valencia north of the river Xúcar or Júcar was conquered as early as 1151.[1] In 1238–44 the rest of Valencia was conquered and the Crusading Kingdom of Valencia was established as the third major component of the Crown of Aragon.[2] Part of the Kingdom of Murcia was annexed to the Crown of Aragon after final agreement was reached in 1305.[3] Alicante, Elche, and Oriola remained permanently in the Crown of Aragon.[4] Jewish inter-communal organization in Valencia was influenced by these political developments.

THE NORTHERN AND SOUTHERN COMMUNITIES

The way in which political development occurred in Valencia led to the emergence of two regional inter-communal frameworks. Following the annexation of the northern part of the Kingdom of Murcia in 1296 the Valencian communities were grouped in two separate structures. The dividing line was the river Xúcar, but this was only a border in very general terms, as some Jewish communities and settlements south of the river belonged to the northern group. These communities, which included Játiva, Gandia, and Denia, were in the region that was conquered by 1244, fifty years prior to the renewed expansion in 1296. This division between the Valencian communities was parallel to the administrative division of the kingdom.[5]

The regional inter-communal organizations of the north and south appeared for the first time in 1302.[6] The division became a permanent feature after the treaty between Castile and the Crown of Aragon was signed in 1305.[7] The two groups paid their taxes and subsidies separately.[8] The earliest list of the communities in the two regions dates to 1274.[9] The northern communities were headed by the *aljama* of Valencia. Alcira, south of the river, and Morella, San

---

[1] Rovira, *Història*, IV, p. 113.   [2] D'Arabal, *El domini Carolini*, p. 43.
[3] This was the result of a long process that began with the conquest of Murcia by Jaime I in 1266; see Soldevila, *Història*, i, doc. 384; Giménez, *D. Juan Manuel*, doc. cxix.
[4] Martínez, *Jaime II, su vida*, i, pp. 106–7; id., *Jaume II*, pp. 158–9; Soldevila, *Història*, i, pp. 409–10.   [5] See e.g. ACA, Reg. 228, fo. 56ʳ [= R 3386].
[6] ACA, Reg. 199, fo. 85 [= R 2779].   [7] ACA, Reg. 203, fo. 242ʳ [= R 2864].
[8] ACA, Reg. 219, fos. 167–8, 198 [= R 3146, 3162].   [9] R 615.

Mateo, Castellón de la Plana, Onda, Villareal, Burriana, Segorbe, Liria, Gandia, and Denia, all north of the river, belonged to the northern group. The southern communities included those of northern Murcia, annexed to the Crown of Aragon in 1296, Elche, Oriola, Ella, and Alicante, as well as Játiva, Gandia, and other Jewish settlements in southern Valencia. (During a certain part of the period, Játiva and Gandia were part of the northern communities.)

The king favoured Jewish settlement in this frontier land and encouraged it by offering the Jews privileges and tax facilities.[10] By the end of Jaime II's reign, the southern communities had achieved complete independence from the north as far as taxation was concerned.[11]

LOCAL INTER-COMMUNAL ORGANIZATIONS

In the Kingdom of Valencia no inter-communal organization similar to the Catalan *collecta* developed. There were, however, special relations between several communities. Smaller communities tended to be under the auspices of larger communities in their area, which provided religious, social, and judicial services to the smaller settlements. In the northern part of Valencia, the smaller communities were under the auspices of Valencia, Murviedro, and Játiva. Jews who lived in Burriana, Gatova, Marines, Benavides, and Canet had special relations with the *aljama* of Murviedro.[12] Until 1326 the Jews of Burriana buried their dead in the cemetery of Murviedro.[13] The communities of Onda and Segorbe paid their taxes with Murviedro.[14] The Jews of Gandia and Denia were related in their tax payments.[15] The two communities were under the auspices of Játiva. In the southern district the most important community was Elche.

[10] ACA, Reg. 195, fo. 120 [=R 2675]; Reg. 256, fo. 1ˇ [=R 2674]; Reg. 203, fo. 242ˇ [=R 2864].
[11] ACA, Reg. 228, fo. 56ˇ [=R 3374]; Reg. 219, fos. 167–8 [=R 3146].
[12] ACA, Reg. 44, fo. 186; Piles, 'La judería de Sagunto', pp. 353–4.
[13] ACA, Reg. 229, fo. 211ˇ [=R 3409 = Jacobs 870]; Reg. 219, fo. 221. [=R 3169].
[14] R 515; Baer, *Spanien*, doc. 108; Baer, *Aragonien*, p. 135.
[15] Millás, 'Un manuscrit', p. 354.

PART FOUR

THE JEWISH QUARTER

§4.1 The *Call* or *Judería*

THE NAMES GIVEN TO THE QUARTER

THE Jewish quarter in the Crown of Aragon was called by various names. In Aragon it was called *judería*, as in Castile and Navarre. The names *judaismo* and *ebreismo* denoting the Jewish quarter were peculiar to Aragon alone.[1] In Catalonia, Roussillon, and Majorca its name was *call*.[2] In Valencia both *judería* and *call* were used. Only in Lérida was the Jewish quarter known by a unique name as *cuyraça*, *curacia*, or *coiraza*.[3] Opinions among scholars differ as to the etymology of the word *call*. Some claim that the word comes from the Hebrew *qahal*; others suggest a Latin origin, the word *callum*.[4]

In the Hebrew sources the Jewish quarter was referred to as *shekhunat Yisrael*, *shekhunat ha-Yehudim*, or simply *shekhunah*, that is 'quarter', and *migrash ha-Yehudim* or *shekhunat ha-qahal*.[5]

ESTABLISHMENT AND LOCATION

Practically every Jewish settlement had its own quarter where the majority of the Jews lived. In some parts of the Crown of Aragon Jews lived in little villages in very small numbers, perhaps just three or four families living together with some Jews in their service. The question here was whether, if the number of the male Jews there amounted to ten, they could be considered as an organized community or not. In such places, there could have been no Jewish quarter.[6]

The location of the Jewish quarter depended on many factors. In many cities of the Crown of Aragon, the Jewish quarter was in the proximity of the palace, fortress, or cathedral. Here the Jews would be under close supervision and their activities could be carefully watched; on the other hand, as they were considered

---

[1] ACA, Reg. 83, fo. 7ᵛ [= R 2054]; Reg. 654, fo. 29 [= Baer, *Spanien*, doc. 238]; Blasco, 'Ebreismo', pp. 111–13.

[2] ACA, Reg. 9, fo. 48 [= R doc. iii, pp. 417–18 = Bofarull, Barcelona, v]; Reg. 20, fo. 266 [= Bofarull, Barcelona, clii (the archival source is not indicated)]; Gerondi 50; Pons, *Los judíos*, ii, pp. 218–19.

[3] ACA, Reg. 16, fo. 202ᵛ [= R 445 = Jacobs 463]; Reg. 197, fo. 140 [= R 2742].

[4] On the word *call*, see Magdalena, 'Etimología'. On the subject in general, see Romano, 'Aljama frente a judería'. It is interesting to note that Judeo-Spanish speakers to this day refer to the synagogue as *kal*.

[5] Adret, i. 73, v. 150; Asibili (Kapah) 156–7.

[6] Adret, v. 253.

the ruler's property, their protection from hostile neighbours and mob would be better achieved if they were concentrated near public buildings. The very concentration of Jews in a neighbourhood was of course a Jewish concern too. For religious, social, and security reasons the Jews preferred to live together. The Jewish quarter developed into a Jewish miniature city within a Christian city or next to it.[7] It was in many respects similar to the Christian city or town but had parallel institutions. In principle, it was under the direct rule of the king–count. Its total independence from the city created antagonism, which the municipal authorities and citizens expressed in many forms and on many occasions. The legal and institutional, and often physical, separation of the *judería* and the Christian city or town did not mean that there were no Jews outside the official limits of the *judería* and no Christians inside it. In any case, Jews and Christians lived side by side as neighbours even where there was a wall surrounding the Jewish neighbourhood.[8] There were, however, several places where Jews and Christians lived completely apart and no one was allowed to live in the other group's district.[9] Jews sold or let to Christians houses in the *judería* although it was often forbidden.[10] Jews certainly owned property outside their quarter,[11] and Christians continued to own property inside the *judería*.[12]

The locality of many *juderías* suggests that the security of the Jews was a primary motive in the choice of the exact site. The very name *rehov ha-mivtsar shel ha-Yehudim*, that is 'Jewish street or quarter in the fortress', indicates its location in a fortified part of the city.[13] In 1264 Jaime I decided to allocate to the Jews the Tower of Calatayud as their quarter. This was a fortified part of the city, situated by the city wall, where the road to Soria began. The Jews were allowed to build houses in the area between the castle and the tower and to erect a wall between their quarter and the Christian area. The Jews had to guard their part of the wall and the tower.[14] The *judería* was near the castle of Doña Martina, known even today as *castillo de la Judería*.[15]

In Uncastillo the *judería* was inside the castle. The Jews were given permission to sell the houses that they had found outside the castle to Christians.[16] In Egea in 1271 a new quarter was assigned to the Jews in the fortified part of the city. Its limits were defined precisely.[17] The Jews of Ruesta lived in the royal castle, which

---

[7] Adret, i. 761. vii. 314.
[8] Adret, vii. 63, viii. 16, 207. On Christian tenants in the Jewish quarter, see also Adret, iv. 298.
[9] Asibili (Kapah) 50.
[10] Adret, iv. 298. See below on the investigation of Játiva Jews accused of such sale.
[11] See e.g. R 1166 (Teruel); ACA, CR, Jaime II, C 41, no. 5052 [= *Cartas Reales*, no. 172] (Tortosa).
[12] ACA, CR, Jaime II, C 134, no. 218 [= *Cartas Reales*, no. 439].
[13] Asibili (Kapah) 159.
[14] ACA, Reg. 13, fo. 185 [= R 259 = Jacobs 294]. The allocation of the tower was confirmed by Pedro III in 1277: see ACA, Reg. 39, fo. 155^{iv} [= R 674 and doc. x, pp. 423–4].
[15] See Cantera, *Sinagogas*, p. 188; Lacave, *Juderías y sinagogas*, p. 112.
[16] ACA, Reg. 13, fo. 189^v [= R 273].   [17] ACA, Reg. 21, fo. 6^v [= R 476 = Jacobs 627].

they were expected to guard.[18] In Lérida the *cuyraça* was situated in the fortified part of the city,[19] and in Játiva too the *judería* was near the great castle.[20]

In newly conquered territories the Jews were either given the same quarter where Jews had previously lived or allocated a part of the city that the ruler wished to populate. Its extent was meant to attract more Jewish settlers from outside. The limits of the Jewish quarter of Valencia were clearly defined in a charter signed on 20 October 1244 and confirmed in 1273 by Jaime I, who promised never to change its site.[21]

Jaime I gave the Jews of Játiva a place called the *algofna* or *algema* as the site for their quarter, where they were expected to live apart from the Christians. They were forbidden to sell, lease, or mortgage their houses to Christians or Muslims. In June 1314 the *baile general* of Valencia was instructed to open an investigation following the sale of Jewish houses to Christians in Játiva. The same prohibition applied to the Jews of Valencia and other communities in the conquered territories.[22] The houses and property given to the Jews as part of the *repartiment*, the distribution of the properties taken away from Muslims, remained theoretically the king's as long as they were retained by Jews. If acquired by Christians, the status of such houses changed from the king's point of view. The king could naturally confiscate the property of Jews found guilty of crime[23] and order the expropriation of property for a variety of purposes.[24]

The site of the *judería* could change or expand, following substantial changes in the size of the Jewish population and in their conditions or circumstances. The additional area was not necessarily joined to the old *judería*. In Barcelona a second *call* was created in 1257 outside the wall. It was called the *Call Menor*, to distinguish it from the old one, called the *Call Mayor*. The former disappeared following urban changes in the nineteenth century. Only the site of the synagogue has been preserved in the church of Sant Jaume.[25]

In 1250 Jaime I allocated a new site for the Jewish quarter in Majorca.[26] The Jews of Majorca, however, continued to own property both in and outside the Jewish quarter throughout the reigns of Jaime I and Pedro III.[27] Under Alfonso III a new policy was adopted as a result of pressure from the municipal authorities and the Christian population. In January 1286 the king ordered that all the Jews had to live within the same area, and gave them five years to move to their

---

[18] ACA, Reg. 198, fos. 228ʳ, 316ʳ [= R 2747, 2760 = Dinur, ii. 2, p. 50, no. 29].
[19] ACA, Reg. 16, fo. 202ʳ [= R 445 = Jacobs 463].
[20] ACA, Reg. 21, fo. 46ʳ [= R 524 = MF i. 1305].
[21] *CDIA*, xi, p. 290; Danvila, 'El robo de la judería', p. 380; R 31.
[22] ACA, Reg. 211, fos. 193ʳ, 275 [= R 2997, 3017]; CR, Jaime II, C 39, no. 4919 [= *Cartas Reales*, no. 168]. [23] ACA, Reg. 228, fo. 89 [= R 3386].
[24] In 1327 the king authorized one of his Christian officials to expropriate houses needed to establish a slaughterhouse in the *judería* of Valencia: ACA, Reg. 229, fo. 235 [= R 3416].
[25] Fita, 'El Montjui', p. 236. [26] Fita and Labrés, 'Privilegios', p. 20, no. 2; R 43.
[27] Fita and Labrés, 'Privilegios', pp. 23–5, no. 8; R 433.

newly assigned quarter. In December 1290, just a few weeks before the expiration of the five years, the negotiations and preparations for the inauguration of the new quarter were still unfinished. On 21 December 1290 Alfonso III confirmed the site assigned to the Jews of Majorca. It was one street in the Temple and Calatrava area, and no Christians were allowed to reside in this street. For the privilege of having this new quarter the Jews of Majorca were ordered to pay 12,000 s.[28] In October 1294 the new *call* was still under construction.[29]

Elsewhere in the Crown of Aragon, we find similar pressure from the local Christian population leading to the moving of the Jewish quarter. In 1251 Queen Yolanda accepted the request of the inhabitants of Perpignan to move the Jews of the city to a new area that the king had assigned to them. The Jews were required to move there before Christmas.[30] In 1288 Alfonso III established the limits of the *judería mayor* of Saragossa and set the site where the Jewish cloth merchants could open their shops. The exact circumstances of the fixing of the new limits are not clear.[31]

The allocation of a new area to the Jews instead of, or in addition to, their existing quarter necessitated the purchase or rental of the houses there. The process of evacuating the area from its inhabitants was not simple, one problem being the prices sought by the owners. As the latter could have demanded speculative and exorbitant prices, the king's order for fair prices is understandable. It was not always possible to ensure that all Christian inhabitants had been evacuated, and it was therefore necessary for the king to prohibit the erection of gates,[32] to avoid the possibility of Christians becoming confined within the Jewish quarter.

STRUCTURE AND ARCHITECTURE

There was no general rule that applied to the structure of all the Jewish quarters of the Crown of Aragon. Some were not enclosed; some were surrounded by a wall with gates. Even very small quarters could have gates which the Jews erected with the ruler's permission.[33] Certain Jewish quarters which consisted of one street and a few alleys had gates at each end which would be closed at night. At times, one gate served for entrance, the other for exit.[34] In the middle of the thirteenth century the *call* of Barcelona had gates that could be closed and opened at the Jews' discretion. The two gates, one in the east and the other in the west, had direct access to the main streets of the city.[35] There were other communities in the *collecta* of Barcelona that had gates which the Jews were allowed to close for

---

[28] ACA, Reg. 63, fo. 33 [= R 1483 = Isaacs 31]; Reg. 81, fo. 219 [= R 2254 = Isaacs 62]; Reg. 83, fos. 99ᵛ–100ᵛ [= R 2267 and doc. xxii, pp. 440–1, 2269–70 = Isaacs 63, 65–6].
[29] ACA, Reg. 194, fo. 93ᵛ [= R 2543 = Isaacs 72].   [30] Alart, *Privilèges*, p. 200; R 44.
[31] Kayserling, 'Les Juifs à Saragosse', p. 115; R 1936.
[32] ACA, CR, Jaime II, C 133, no. 16 [= *Cartas Reales*, no. 239].
[33] Adret, ii. 134.   [34] Asibili (Kapah) 50, p. 43, col. 1.
[35] ACA, Reg. 9, fo. 48 [= R 71 and doc. iii, pp. 417–18 = Jacobs 123 = Bofarull, Barcelona, vʲ].

their defence.³⁶ In Villafranca the *call* was closed with a gate at one end, called the Gate of Caynamars; the other side was open, and as a result the Jews suffered much serious damage. For their safety, the Jews asked for permission to close their quarter and to build walls and gates wherever necessary. On 5 January 1291 Alfonso III granted the Jews permission to do so, on condition that two keys, one for the Jews and the other for the Christians, were provided. The keys were needed because Christians continued to live inside the *call*. In March 1303 Jaime II confirmed the right of the Jews of Villafranca to have the *call* completely closed. One important clause, however, was added: the gates were not to be closed, either by day or by night, except in Easter week, without prior permission from the municipal authorities.³⁷ Until 1298 the *call* of Montblanch was not closed and had no gates. The Jews complained that they suffered constantly in consequence of their quarter's lack of defences. After consultation with the local baile, Jaime II agreed that, provided no harm was caused to the city, the Jews could build three gates.³⁸ From all these cases it is clear that it was generally the Jews who wanted their quarter closed off and separated from the Christian city by a wall.

In 1315 Jaime II, who promised the Jews of Lérida that they would not have to host members of the royal family in the *cuyraça*, also authorized them, as he did the Jews of Barcelona, Tarragona, and Villafranca, to have the gates of their quarter closed whenever they wanted.³⁹

The maintenance and repair of the walls surrounding the Jewish quarter were the responsibility of the Jews. In 1287, for instance, the wall in the *call* of Barcelona was in danger of collapse in one point of the street called *call juich*. The secretaries of the community were ordered to repair the wall immediately to avoid any danger to passers-by.⁴⁰ In 1325 serious floods swept through the city of Tortosa as a result of the Ebro river overflowing its banks. There were fears that the flooding would soon isolate the *call*. The Jews wished to join Christian and Muslim teams to work to contain the river. The king gave the appropriate instructions on 11 October 1325.⁴¹ The floods, however, continued to devastate Tortosa and many houses in the *call*, the wall, and the towers of the quarter were severely damaged as a result, some so seriously that it was necessary to demolish them completely. The only help the Jews could hope for was the king's promise not to freeze their loans.⁴²

---

³⁶ ACA, Reg. 11, fo. 229 [=R 130 = Bofarull, Barcelona, xx].
³⁷ ACA, Reg. 83, fo. 103 [=R 2281 and doc. xxiii, p. 441]; Reg. 200, fo. 191ᵛ [=R 2282, 2811].
³⁸ ACA, Reg. 196, fo. 202 [=R 2703 = Bofarull, Montblanch, 82].
³⁹ ACA, Reg. 211, fo. 278 [=R 3018]. In 1316 the Jews of Montblanch were also promised that in accordance with previous charters they would not have to host members of the royal family in their quarter: ACA, Reg. 160, fo. 219 [=R 3041 = Bofarull, Montblanch, 84 = Dinur, ii. 2, p. 56, no. 60]. ⁴⁰ ACA, Reg. 70, fo. 92 [=R 1722].
⁴¹ ACA, CR, Jaime II, C 133, no. 124 [= *Cartas Reales*, no. 342].
⁴² ACA, CR, Jaime II, C 135, no, 386 [= *Cartas Reales*, no. 530].

Access to the Jewish quarter of Lérida was also through gates. The gates, which were meant to protect the Jews, were closed by the authorities when the community did not pay its taxes in time, so that the gates erected for the protection of the community turned into a means of coercion and pressure at the king's disposal. Their closure greatly jeopardized life within the walls. The prevention of any passage through the gates amounted sometimes to putting the entire community under blockade and caused food shortages within a very short time. Jaime I in 1265 and Jaime II in 1300 prohibited such measures,[43] yet they continued to be used from time to time, threatening the food supply of many communities which turned to the king for support.[44] On such occasions exceptions were made to suit the king's or the Christians' convenience: Jewish physicians, for example, would be permitted to pass freely through the gates of a blockaded *judería*, while Christian patients also had a free passage.[45]

The *judería* of Saragossa was surrounded by a wall and had many gates. It was apparently for the Jews' safety that in 1327 the infante and later the king decided to close all the gates of the *judería*, except the three main ones, despite the opposition of the municipal authorities.[46]

As noted above, in 1264 the Jews of Calatayud were permitted to erect a wall separating their quarter from the Christians and built gates to control the movement into the *judería*. They were given a free hand to build houses in the area allocated to them between the castle and the city wall and could sell, lend, or let their houses freely. Jews held property in the quarter as well as outside it and in the vicinity of Calatayud.[47] In June 1301 the request of the Jews of Sos was granted and they were permitted to close their *judería*.[48]

In Barbastro the Jewish quarter was by the wall. In 1271 the *aljama* received permission to erect a gate for the passage of loaded animals, on condition that they would be in charge of its maintenance.[49] Many Jewish quarters were adjacent to the city walls, and some of the Jews' houses were actually on the wall. Such was the case in Gerona.[50] This created some architectural problems. Jews who owned houses next to the wall made some changes that apparently affected the wall. In 1287 Alfonso III ordered his baile in Gerona to see that the wall was restored to its previous state.[51]

Following pressure from the Christian population, a new site for a Jewish quarter of Majorca was finally chosen in December 1290. The new *call* consisted of one street where the Jews were permitted to build a synagogue and an oven. The Jews were permitted to build their houses in the *call* as they pleased. The

---

[43] ACA, Reg. 13, fo. 275ʹ [=R 336]; Reg. 197, fo. 140 [=R 2742].
[44] ACA, Reg. 207, fo. 162 [2917]; Reg. 209, fos. 203ʹ–204, 208, 215, 232ʹ [=R 2951].
[45] ACA, Reg. 211, fo. 337ʹ [=R 3020].   [46] ACA, Reg. 230, fo. 45 [=R 3439 = Jacobs 882].
[47] ACA, Reg. 13, fo. 183ʹ [=R 264].
[48] ACA, CR, Jaime II, C 12, no. 1606 [= *Cartas Reales*, no. 76].
[49] ACA, Reg. 16, fo. 260ʹ [=R 460 = Jacobs 482].
[50] ACA, Reg. 61, fo. 114 [=R 1050].   [51] ACA, Reg. 70, fo. 74 [=R 1704].

municipal authorities were instructed to ensure that the *call* was completely enclosed and that gates were erected for access.[52] A Jew, Jucef Coffe, was given the right to build the only oven in the *call*.[53]

The Christian municipality had no jurisdiction inside the Jewish quarter, which came under the authority of the *aljama* leadership and hence under the direct control of the king–count. The *adelantados* normally exercised control over buildings inside the Jewish quarter and had a say in many matters related to property. While the new *call* of Majorca was still being built in 1294, it attracted Jews from elsewhere. In 1295 a widow from Barcelona enlisted the help of the leaders of the Catalan *aljama* and the infante to receive permission from the *adelantados* of Majorca to acquire a house in the *call*.[54] It seems obvious that the secretaries of the community issued sale permits for property inside the *call*. Building problems were usually dealt with by the *berurim*, but the king gave frequent instructions to solve those which were brought to his attention. Building permits which were not straightforward were issued by the king,[55] and plans that were opposed by neighbours eventually reached the king, if the community was unable to settle the dispute.[56] Some of the houses were claimed by more than one owner and there were innumerable conflicts over ownership.[57]

Some of the quarters were overpopulated, and as their limits could not be easily altered there were immense problems connected with extensions, refurbishing, and conversions in the existing buildings. Some of the streets and alleys in the Jewish quarter were very narrow and dark, with high buildings which shut out sunlight. In Calatayud, for instance, one of the streets was so narrow that animals could not pass through. At the request of some of the tenants in that street, Jaime II suggested in 1322 that the street should be widened if the majority of the community agreed. To all whose houses might be affected an indemnity should be paid.[58] Most of the houses were too small and the possibilities for expansion were limited. One way to extend the space of a house was to build a connecting room between two opposite buildings over the narrow street. Such ingenious extensions were frequent and caused many quarrels and legal proceedings that led to royal intervention.[59] Even the rich could not always purchase suitable property to enable them to expand their existing homes. Necessity, however, led some to look for original solutions. In 1323 Vidal Abulbach from Huesca bought new houses in the *barrio nuevo* which faced each other across the street. He received permission to connect the two houses with a wooden bridge, high enough

---

[52] For the site of the *call*, see above. On the erection of the wall and gates, and the construction permit, see ACA, Reg. 83, fo. 100ʳˢ [=R 2268, 2271 = Isaacs 64, 67].

[53] ACA, Reg. 194, fo. 93ᵛ [=R 2543 = Isaacs 72].

[54] ACA, Reg. 89, fo. 60ᵛ [=R 2567 = Isaacs 73].

[55] ACA, Reg. 20, fo. 266 [=R 624 = Bofarull, Barcelona, clii]; Reg. 204, fo. 28ᵛ [=R 2867].

[56] ACA, Reg. 62, fo. 130ᵛ [=R 1300].   [57] ACA, Reg. 57, fo. 174 [=R 1415].

[58] ACA, Reg. 222, fo. 120ᵛ [=R 3241]; CR, Jaime II, C 133, no. 29 [= *Cartas Reales*, no. 252].

[59] ACA, Reg. 20, fos. 303, 325 [=R 647, 652 = Jacobs 604 = MF i. 1938].

not to obstruct anybody.[60] People who had property next to the city wall had more possibilities to expand their houses. In 1325 Jaime II gave permission to Jews who had their houses on the wall of Egea to enlarge their homes and add shops and wine cellars, provided they did so without weakening the fortified wall.[61] The arrival of a large number of Jewish immigrants in the Jewish quarter created serious housing problems. The settlement of sixty Jewish refugees from France in Barcelona in 1306 must have caused grave difficulties.[62]

The buildings in some Jewish quarters, such as Barcelona, were several floors high.[63] Apart from their height, the Jewish buildings differed from the Christians' by the *mezuzah* that appeared on the right doorpost. Only in Gerona, where the buildings were made of stone, can we still find the holes of the *mezuzah*.[64] Some of the houses overlooked the main street, while others had their entrances in side streets or yards.[65] The courtyard was an important feature of many Jewish quarters in the Crown of Aragon. Some of the yards were private.[66] Despite being overcrowded, some of the *juderías* had green spots, and some Jews created gardens in their yards in which they rested and ate in the summer months.[67]

Certain buildings in the *judería* belonged to the community: some of these were communal buildings, such as the synagogue, hospital, and *miqve*, while others belonged to the *heqdesh*, having been donated to the charity funds of the community.[68]

In many *juderías* there were houses that belonged to Christians. Some houses or parts of them passed into Christian hands as mortgaged property if Jews' debts were not paid.[69] In 1273 Jaime I permitted the Jews of Valencia to purchase houses owned by Christians. The latter were not allowed to sell these houses except to Jews. A wall separated the city from the *judería*, and the Jews controlled the gates with the right to refuse entry to any person.[70]

The Jewish quarter was not a self-contained economic unit and the economic interdependence between the city and the *aljama* is obvious. Although practically no Jewish merchant or craftsman could depend for his livelihood exclusively on a Jewish clientele, there were nevertheless shops and workshops inside the *judería* and on its outskirts.[71] We may recall that in Saragossa the Jewish cloth merchants had their shops in the *judería*. Some had several shops. In Huesca, too, Jews had shops for French cloth in the *judaismo*, that is the Jewish quarter.[72] The Jews of Valencia had their own market, called by its Arabic name *açoch*.[73]

---

[60] ACA, Reg. 224, fo. 27 [= R 3266].   [61] ACA, Reg. 227, fo. 203ᵛ [= R 3341].
[62] ACA, Reg. 203, fo. 189ᵛ [= R 2860]; Assis, 'Juifs de France'.   [63] Adret, v. 150.
[64] One *mezuzah* was found in building no. 15 in carrer de la Força and is now in the Biblical Museum of the seminary in the city.   [65] R 1542.   [66] Adret, iii. 153.
[67] Adret, iii. 180.   [68] ACA, Reg. 41, fo. 6 [= R 712 = Baer, *Spanien*, doc. 115, para. 1].
[69] ACA, Reg. 74, fo. 88ᵛ [= R 1899].   [70] ACA, Reg. 19, fos. 56ᵛ–57 [= R 566 = Jacobs 518].
[71] ACA, Reg. 19, fo. 13 [= R 654 = MF i. 1991].
[72] ACA, Reg. 80, fo. 7 [= R 1955]; Reg. 83, fo. 7ᵛ [= R 2054].
[73] ACA, Reg. 230, fo. 77 [= R 3446]. On the *açoch* or *azoch* of Valencia, see Magdalena, 'Un zoco'.

Jews maintained shops outside the Jewish quarter due to shortage of space inside it as well as to economic considerations. The prospects for trade with the non-Jewish population were far better if the shops were outside the *judería*. In Barcelona the *aljama* claimed to have had the right to maintain the *kasher* meat stands outside the *call* ever since the reign of Jaime I. Jaime II permitted the stands to be placed outside the *call* walls, in front of the house of Maymo de Forn. They had to be of a certain size and be folded against the wall after the sale hour, so that they would not obstruct the traffic.[74] However, the municipal authorities forbade the slaughtering of animals outside the *call*. This could be done only inside the Jewish quarter or at the entrance.[75] In more than one community the *kasher* abattoir was at one of the entrances of the *judería*, near the gate. In 1326 two Jewish courtiers of the Infante Alfonso were permitted to establish an abattoir at the gate of the *judería* of Saragossa.[76]

The Jews' interest in having their shops outside their quarter was paralleled by the Christians' wishes to sell their goods inside the *judería*. In Lérida, for instance, where Christian women daily sold cloth, fruits, fowls, and other stuff inside the *cuyraça*, objections were voiced by the municipal authorities, who considered the situation scandalous. Jaime II decided that saleswomen would no longer be permitted to enter the *cuyraça* but instead should display their goods in La Cadena del Romeu place.[77]

THE *JUDERÍA* AND THE CHRISTIAN CITY

The gates of the *judería* originally served as a means of defence for the Jews against Christian assaults and intruders. The Jewish quarter attracted many visitors who were not welcome. As the king moved constantly around the realm, the Jews were required to provide his people with accommodation. This often disrupted life within the *judería*, sometimes causing serious damage. Communities tried to obtain the right to refuse entry to Christians, including the king's people. In 1260 Barcelona and the other communities in its *collecta* acquired the right to close the gates of their *calls* so that no unwanted visitors, including the king's retinue, could enter the quarter.[78] Nine years later, Jaime I allowed the Jews of Gerona and Besalú to decline to host any Christian in their quarter.[79]

The visits of the king's officials to the *judería* became dangerous when disturbances were caused by people who accompanied them. In 1263 Jaime I promised the Jews of Perpignan that his baile would no longer enter the *call* with more than five people.[80] In fact, as far as the king was concerned the Jewish quarter was

---

[74] ACA, Reg. 200, fo. 140 [= R 2800].
[75] Kayserling, 'Les Juifs à Barcelone', p. 110; R 3101.
[76] ACA, Reg. 228, fo. 45ᵛ [= R 3373].   [77] ACA, Reg. 203, fos. 19ᵛ–21 [= R 2839].
[78] ACA, Reg. 11, fo. 229 [= R 130 = Bofarull, Barcelona, xx].
[79] ACA, Reg. 16, fo. 152ᵛ [= R 412].
[80] ACA, Reg. 12, fo. 9 [= R 179 = Jacobs 198 = Dinur, ii. 2, p. 88, no. 67].

never an area that could ever be closed to him or to his representatives, if he wished to enter.[81]

Outside his quarter, the Jew felt insecure. Especially in periods of tension, he was subjected to harassment and abuse, and sometimes to physical violence. For this reason Jaime I agreed to free the Jews of Barcelona from the obligation to testify outside their *call*.[82] Similarly, Jaime II decided in 1307 that the Jews of Jaca could not be detained outside the limits of the *judería*, as their wives and daughters who brought them food were constantly maltreated by Christians.[83] The same decision was taken in 1312 in favour of the Jews of Saragossa.[84] As any Jews of Lérida who were to be detained or imprisoned for non-payment of debts were harassed by Christians on their way to prison, Jaime II ordered their detention within the limits of the *cuyraça*.[85]

Yet more dangerous were the disturbances that occurred during and following the missionary sermons delivered in the Jewish quarter. The Jews who had been forced to attend sermons outside the *judería* complained about the dangers that awaited their wives and children on their way there and back. They soon found out that compulsory sermons within the Jewish quarter would be no less dangerous. The inflamed Christian audience that accompanied the preachers allowed themselves a free hand in the Jewish quarter, insulting and attacking the Jews and causing chaos in the narrow streets of the *judería*. In 1263, a month after the Barcelona Disputation, Jaime I decided that the Jews could not be compelled to go out of their quarter to listen to sermons, and should be allowed to decide whether to attend the sermons delivered in their quarter.[86] The missionary sermons in Majorca usually ended with grave disturbances and serious attacks. In October 1296 Jaime II ordered that the sermons should always take place in the *call* and that the preachers could have no more than ten Christians with them.[87] In 1268 Jaime I restricted the number of Christians accompanying the preachers in Barcelona to ten.[88] However, in June 1279, while the Jews of Calatayud were gathered in the synagogue to hear a missionary sermon, local Christians crossed the wall of the *judería* and broke through the gates. The king's decision not to allow more than fifteen to twenty people to accompany the Dominican friars into the Jewish quarter proved totally ineffective.[89]

For the Jews, the most dangerous period of the year was around Easter when anti-Jewish sermons increased Christian antagonism towards the Jews. Mobs of

---

[81] ACA, Reg. 43, fo. 118 [= R 1278].   [82] ACA, Reg. 12, fo. 120 [= R 224 = Jacobs 255].
[83] ACA, Reg. 204, fo. 73 [= R 2875 = Jacobs 757].
[84] ACA, Reg. 208, fo. 106ᵛ [= R 2942].   [85] ACA, Reg. 213, fo. 173 [= R 3042].
[86] ACA, Reg. 12, fo. 11ᵛ [= R 217 = Denifle, 'Quellen zur Disputation', p. 237 = Jacobs 247 = Bofarull, Barcelona, xxxiv = Dinur, ii. 1, p. 259, no. 42].
[87] ACA, Reg. 194, fo. 267 [= R 2624 = Isaacs 75].
[88] ACA, Reg. 15, fo. 122ᵛ [= R 386 = Jacobs 424 = Bofarull, Barcelona, lxxiii].
[89] ACA, Reg. 41, fo. 94 [= R 736]. On Pedro's prohibition, see R 735.

zealots often left church inflamed by the preaching and attacked the Jewish quarter. In Játiva in 1268 Jaime I ordered measures to be taken to prevent Christians from penetrating the Jewish quarter. The tower leading to the Jewish cemetery was to be closed on Good Friday so that access to the *judería* through the Algesna gate would be blocked.[90]

The attacks against the *call* of Gerona were led by the clerics and their families. The cathedral and the clerics' houses dominated the *call*, so that it was easily bombarded with stones. The attacks were perpetrated every year. Even when Jaime I was in the city, the bells of the cathedral gave the sign for the attack on Good Friday. The Jews' houses and gardens were damaged. The king's interventions bore no fruit. In 1278 Pedro III's messenger was completely ignored and the attack continued. The king had to ask for the bishop's help.[91] In 1293 Christians attacked the *call* of Gerona and pursued Jews inside the cathedral.[92]

In the second half of the thirteenth century the religious hostilities increased and the attacks against the Jewish quarters became more and more frequent. In 1287 the friars of the Hospital of St John broke through the wall in the *judería* of Valencia, at a spot where a gate had been sealed, and staged a procession with crosses through its streets.[93] In some cities, such as Barcelona and Valencia, the municipal authorities ordered the Jews not to leave the Jewish quarter during certain Christian festivals.[94] The proximity of the Jewish quarter to churches and religious houses added further complications as relations between them were mostly far from neighbourly. In Barcelona a convent was adjacent to the *call*. For the Jews this was a cause of much trouble.[95]

Despite all these attacks, the Jewish quarter remained the stronghold of Jewish life. In its main street, sometimes its only one, and narrow alleys, in its houses and synagogues, its inhabitants lived their Jewish lives and carried on their ancient traditions. It was within the walls of the *judería* that the Jew continued to maintain his separate religious, ethnic, and social identity. It is in this context that the restrictions and prohibitions imposed on Christians' visits to the *judería* must be viewed. Particularly strict were the prohibitions on converts and Christian women entering the Jewish quarter.[96] By the king's order, Jewish children baptized during the massacre of 1320 in Montclús were not to be raised in the Jewish quarter, lest they be exposed to Jewish influence.[97]

[90] ACA, Reg. 15, fo. 95ʳ [= R 377 = Jacobs 417 = MF i. 789].
[91] ACA, Reg. 40, fo. 79ʳ [= R 696].   [92] ACA, Reg. 87, fos. 65ʳ–66 [= R 2478].
[93] ACA, Reg. 70, fo. 84ʳ [= R 1715].
[94] For Barcelona, see Kayserling, 'Les Juifs à Barcelone', p. 110; R 3212 (1321). For Valencia, see Danvila, 'Clausura', p. 148, n. 1; R 3405.   [95] See e.g. ACA, Reg. 74, fo. 46ʳ [= R 1825].
[96] For Perpignan, see Vidal, *Les Juifs de Roussillon*, p. 31. For Barcelona, see Kayserling, 'Les Juifs à Barcelone', p. 110; R 3120; and see above for the prohibition on Christian saleswomen entering the *cuyracia*.
[97] ACA, Reg. 220, fo. 55ʳ [= R 3189 = Miret, 'Le Massacre', p. 261 = Jacobs 793].

§4.2 The Synagogue and House of Study

THERE was nothing more characteristic of a medieval Jewish settlement than its synagogue, where its members congregated to pray and study. No other medieval Jewish institution could be so strongly identified with Jewish identity and survival. The synagogue in the Middle Ages was an essential ingredient in Jewish life, without which no form of Jewish existence could be contemplated. Its establishment was the most fundamental condition for the settlement of Jews in any land throughout the ages.

THE CROWN AND THE SYNAGOGUE

Under both Islam and Christianity restrictions were set by law on the building of synagogues. Although these legal restrictions were often the formal causes for the harassment of Jews in periods of persecution, in general no Jewish community was ever left without a house for worship and study. Like other rulers, the Aragonese kings were well aware of the essential role the synagogue played in Jewish life. The closure of the synagogue meant the end of Jewish life in the area. The pro-Jewish policy pursued by the kings of the Crown of Aragon was reflected in their attitudes towards the synagogue. All general charters granted to Jewish communities contained implicit or explicit permission to have at least one synagogue in any Jewish settlement or *aljama*. All Jewish communities in the territories conquered in the course of the Reconquista in its thirteenth-century phase were allowed to retain their synagogues.[1]

The decisions of the king–counts concerning synagogues were generally in accord with their favourable policy towards the Jews and should be interpreted in the wider context of their attitudes towards the Jewish community. The permission granted in August 1263 by Jaime I to Bonanat Salamo to establish a synagogue in one of his houses or anywhere else in the *call* of Barcelona cannot be isolated from the events that deeply affected the life of the community.[2] The permission to install a scroll of the Law in a newly established ark could not have passed unnoticed when the Barcelona Disputation was still very fresh news. The king's permission could only have meant support and encouragement to a

---

[1] On the synagogues of medieval Spain in general, see Assis, 'Synagogues'; Lacave, *Juderías y sinagogas*.

[2] ACA, Reg. 12, fo. 104ᵛ [= R 208 = Jacobs 24 = Bofarull, Barcelona, xxxiii].

community that felt threatened by the religious pressure of the Dominican missionaries.

Although Christian doctrine forbade the construction of new synagogues, it is common knowledge that there was a wide gap between theory and reality, and numerous new synagogues were established throughout the Christian world, wherever and whenever a ruler favoured the settlement of Jews in his territory. The Crown of Aragon was no exception. In the thirteenth century, together with Castile, the Crown of Aragon was the safest land in Christian Europe for the Jews, and permission to build new synagogues was part of the general pro-Jewish policy. In October 1264 Jaime I permitted the Jews of Besalú to build a new synagogue of which they could hold the freehold.[3] In newly assigned quarters it was natural that the Jews were allowed to establish a synagogue. In such circumstances, even churchmen gave their consent to the construction of a new synagogue. In 1290 Alfonso III permitted the Jews of Majorca to build a new synagogue in their newly assigned quarter.[4] In 1319 Jaime II confirmed the permission granted by the Bishop of Vich in 1307 to the Jews of Tárrega to erect a new synagogue on a new site.[5] The king could not object to the opening of new synagogues that were needed due to an increase of the Jewish population in accordance with his policy. Thus in 1326 the Jews of Burriana opened a new synagogue with the king's consent.[6]

The erection of new synagogues, even with the king's permission, nevertheless aroused opposition and criticism. The most obvious opponents were the churchmen, whose protests were nevertheless bound to fail in view of the ruler's stand. In 1280 Pedro III ordered the Bishop of Saragossa to abstain from any further hindrance to the work on the site of the new synagogue in Tauste.[7] The king's attitude was totally different if a synagogue was established without his permission. Such synagogues were not necessarily destroyed, but heavy fines were imposed on those found guilty. In 1300 Jaime II granted his pardon to Samuel Nageri, who had opened a synagogue in one of his houses in Teruel without permission. Abraham Fierro was fined 500 sj for having held services in his home on a festival using a scroll of the Law.[8] Communities guilty of building synagogues without prior royal permission were severely punished, as was the community of Monzón in 1286 which had rebuilt the synagogue that had collapsed. In 1287 Alfonso III ordered the opening of an inquiry to find out whether the Jews of Barbastro had built a synagogue larger than that for which permission had been given.[9] In extreme cases the king ordered the destruction of the illegally built

---

[3] ACA, Reg. 13, fo. 231ʳ [=R 290 = Jacobs 315].
[4] ACA, Reg. 83, fos. 99ʳ–100 [=R 2267 and doc. xxii, pp. 440–1].
[5] ACA, Reg. 217, fos. 147ʳ–148 [=R 3113].
[6] ACA, Reg. 229, fo. 211ʳ [=R 3409 = Jacobs 870].
[7] ACA, Reg. 48, fo. 57ʳ [=R 797].
[8] ACA, Reg. 198, fo. 211 [=R 2736]; Reg. 212, fo. 73ʳ [=R 3033].
[9] ACA, Reg. 71, fos. 4ʳ, 82 [=R 1694, 1784].

synagogue. The synagogue in Montblanch was destroyed and its stones were offered in 1311 to the monastery of Santa María de la Serra.[10]

The Jews' right to repair their synagogues was never questioned. In 1268, Jaime I confirmed the right of the Jews of Catalonia, Roussillon, and Montpellier to take care of the general maintenance of their synagogues and undertake repairs whenever necessary.[11] That such a confirmation was needed is significant; for, although Church doctrine allowed the Jews to repair their synagogues, the Jews seemed concerned that zealots would prevent them from doing so. The pressure of the Dominicans increased considerably in the second half of the thirteenth century. They watched the Jews' every step and the synagogue did not escape their attention. Individual communities felt the need to obtain the king's permission before undertaking any repairs in their synagogues. They were warned not to enlarge their synagogues, as this was forbidden by ecclesiastical law.[12] In 1321 the Jews of Játiva were allowed to repair their synagogue, which was in terrible condition, and even rebuild parts of it, without however altering its size.[13] Deviation from the prescribed measurements of the synagogue led to grave consequences. The Jews of Valencia were heavily fined for the alteration in the size of their synagogue and the *almidraz* following their repairs.[14]

In the thirteenth century the synagogue became a centre of missionary activity. From the 1240s onwards the Dominicans were permitted to preach in synagogues throughout the Crown of Aragon.[15] These missionary sermons disrupted the services and caused frustration and anger in the community. When the preacher was an apostate, the Jewish audience felt very humiliated. A few weeks after the Barcelona Disputation, on 29 August 1263, Paulus Christiani was given permission to preach in synagogues.[16] A similar permission was given to the apostate Jaime Perez.[17] Pedro III followed his father's policy in ordering the Jews to attend the sermons that the Dominican friars delivered in the synagogues. In 1299 Ramón Lull was allowed to preach in all the synagogues of the realm.[18] We have already seen that grave disturbances were caused by Christians who accompanied the preachers. Many Jews felt terrorized by the uninvited Christian guests who could sometimes cause havoc in the synagogue. The king was usually

---

[10] ACA, Reg. 208, fo. 36' [=R 2933 = Bofarull, Montblanch, 476–7].

[11] ACA, Reg. 15, fo. 123'' [=R 389, 392, 394–5 = Jacobs 429, 431 = Bofarull, Barcelona, lxx, lxxii]; CDIA, vi, pp. 170–2.

[12] The warning to Barcelona was given in 1267, in a period of intense anti-Jewish campaigning following the Disputation of Barcelona: ACA, Reg. 15, fo. 50 [=R 357 = Jacobs 410 = Bofarull, Barcelona, lxi].

[13] ACA, Reg. 219, fo. 198' [=R 3164 = Jacobs 788].

[14] ACA, Reg. 202, fos. 202–3 [=R 2828, 2830].

[15] Grayzel, *The Church and the Jews*, pp. 254–7.

[16] ACA, Reg. 12, fo. 107' [=R 215 = Jacobs 245].

[17] ACA, Reg. 204–5, fo. 174 [=R 2862].

[18] For Pedro's permission, see ACA, Reg. 41, fo. 61' [=R 723 = CDIA, vi, p. 194]. For Ramón Lull, see Kayserling, 'Raymond Lulle', pp. 148–9.

sympathetic to the Jews' complaints, restricting the number of the Christians entering the synagogue with the preacher. In a series of decisions Jaime I made the life of the Jews easier.[19] Pedro III was quite aware that many Christians entered the synagogue accompanying the preacher with the object of ridiculing, irritating, and molesting the Jews listening to the sermon. In 1279 he ordered that no more than three or four people could enter the synagogues during the missionary sermons. He also prohibited fanatic and inflammatory anti-Jewish sermons.[20] Such sermons could not have been prevented altogether. Some continued to lead to violence and attacks in the synagogue, as in Pina in 1285 when Christians, joined by Muslims, broke into the synagogue, smashed the ark, and took away various objects.[21]

Synagogues were abused in other ways by the authorities. The king's officials found it convenient to use the synagogue building as a house of arrest for defaulting tax-payers. The synagogue would turn into a prison and prayers would be prevented. Some communities succeeded in obtaining the king's agreement to put an end to this abuse.[22]

SYNAGOGUES IN THE *JUDERÍA*

The number of synagogues in the community depended on a variety of factors. Wherever there was a *sinagoga mayor*, we may assume that there was at least one more synagogue. Besides the synagogues that were established and run by the community, there were others opened by individuals or special groups. Many synagogues were established in communities by benefactors who wanted to fulfil a religious act of some sort, while Jews from the same background who felt the need to pray together established their own synagogue whenever possible.

The *sinagoga mayor* was the main and probably, but not necessarily, the largest synagogue in the *judería*. In Barcelona, Saragossa, Huesca, Calatayud, and other communities there was a *sinoga* or *sinagoga mayor*;[23] in Valencia it was called the *ascola major*.[24] In Saragossa, Huesca, Jaca, and other communities there was a *sinoga menor*, *chica*, or *pequenya*. In Saragossa there existed the synagogue *de los Cazillos*, the *sinoga viella*, and others.[25] Jews from the same origin or who followed the same ritual founded their own synagogue when they settled in sufficient numbers. In Barcelona there was a *sinagoga dels francesos* or *scola Gallarum*

---

[19] See nn. 23, 84, 87 to Part IV, section 1 above, 'The *Call* or Judería'.
[20] ACA, Reg. 42, fos. 148ʾ–149 [= R 746–7 = MF ii. 684–5]; Reg. 253, fo. 43 [= R 2650].
[21] ACA, Reg. 56, fo. 62ʾ [= R 1335].
[22] Assis, 'Synagogues', p. 12.
[23] Adret, i. 300 (Huesca), ii. 272, v. 152; ACA, Reg. 81, fo. 9 [= R 2055]; CR, Jaime II, C 133, no. 125 [= *Cartas Reales*, no. 343] (Saragossa); Perfet 331 (Calatayud).
[24] ACA, CR, Alfonso III, Ex. s., no. 131, fo. 2ʾ [= *Cartas Reales*, no. 35].
[25] Adret, viii. 268; Blasco, *La judería de Zaragoza*, pp. 147–50, 158–61; del Arco, 'Nuevas noticias', pp. 370–1; id., 'Las juderías de Jaca y Zaragoza', pp. 82–3.

founded by Jewish exiles from France in 1306.[26] The *scola de les dones* in Barcelona was most probably a synagogue with suitable accommodation for women. It was also known as the *sinagoga menor*.[27]

The private synagogues were numerous. Many were in one of the founders' houses, as was the case of Bonanat Salamo of Barcelona.[28] In Saragossa there was a synagogue called 'de don Juce Bienbiniest' established by him or in his memory.[29] The establishment of private synagogues did not always meet with the approval of the *aljama*. They seemed to undermine its authority and sometimes reduced attendance in the public synagogues. Calatayud had seven officially recognized synagogues and many private ones that attracted many worshippers from the former. Many Jews who lived far away from the main synagogues preferred to attend services held in private homes. As a result, some of the synagogues were left without a *minyan* or quorum for public prayers. The community therefore decided to issue a ban on all private synagogues and *minyanim*, except the following: the Great Synagogue, the Great Beth HaMidrash, the Beth HaMidrash donated by R. Ya'aqov ben Khalina, the Weavers' Midrash, the Hevrat Heqdesh Synagogue, the Beth HaMidrash established by R. Yom Tov Farhi, and the synagogue in Bahye Alcostantini's home. A minority wished to include under the ban any synagogue that was not enumerated in the list, but the majority objected, claiming that the aim of the ban was to prevent the establishment of private *minyanim* and not to obstruct the opening of new ones. One of the synagogues, named after Don Aharon ben Yahya, was in total ruin. When Don Yosef ben Yahya rebuilt on its site a large and beautiful synagogue, some wanted to prevent its inauguration, claiming that the ban applied to it as well.[30] Calatayud was not unusual in this proliferation: private synagogues were found in many communities.

Some confraternities and charitable societies had their own synagogues. These were mostly found in Aragon, where the number of confraternities was the highest.[31] The establishment of synagogues by confraternities, whose members belonged to the lower classes, had significant social repercussions. In their special synagogue members of the confraternity felt at home and detached themselves from the establishment in one more, and very important, field. In their own synagogue they could participate in the services without being subject to the limits and the formalities of the main synagogues controlled by the rich and the leaders of the community.

In Saragossa the silversmiths had their own synagogue, the *sinoga de los*

---

[26] Assis, 'Juifs de France', p. 304 and n. 120.
[27] Cantera, *Sinagogas*, p. 171.
[28] ACA, Reg. 12, fo. 104ᵛ [= R 208 = Jacobs 241 = Bofarull, Barcelona, xxxiii].
[29] Blasco, *La judería de Zaragoza*, pp. 151–3.
[30] Perfet 331; see also Magdalena, 'Sinagogas, madrazas y oratorios', pp. 117–23.
[31] On confraternities in Spain, see Assis, 'Mutual Aid and Welfare'; on Saragossa, see Blasco, 'Instituciones sociorreligiosas'.

argenteros.³² About 1300 the Hevra Qadisha, that is the Burial Society, known as the Campanya de los enterradores de la Merce, used the *sinoga menor* as their centre.³³ The Society for the Sick, Biqur Holim or Bicurolim, founded its own synagogue in 1382. For this purpose they obtained a special permit to rebuild a house that the society owned in the Jewish quarter of Saragossa.³⁴

According to R. Nissim Gerondi, who lived in the fourteenth century, there were three synagogues in Saragossa, while archival sources from the end of the fourteenth and the beginning of the fifteenth century contain information on more than seven synagogues. The discrepancy may be due either to an increase of synagogues after 1391, as a result of Jewish immigrants who settled in Saragossa and founded their own synagogues, or to a different method of reckoning: R. Nissim Gerondi might not have counted the private and special synagogues, but only the official ones in the community.³⁵

ARCHITECTURE

The synagogues in the Crown of Aragon were generally small. Their modest size was due to several factors, the most important of which was the limitations imposed by the Church. There was also the shortage of space in the Jewish quarter, which was usually overcrowded. Many communities were too small to warrant a large synagogue. Many synagogues were in fact established in private houses converted to their new function. A few, however, were built especially to serve as synagogues. The rebuilt Don Aharon ben Yahya Synagogue in Calatayud is one instance.³⁶ In these specially built synagogues, there was usually a courtyard or *'azara* leading to the prayer hall. The courtyard was often very busy and during services it was full of people. There were sometimes complaints that there were more people outside the synagogue than in it.³⁷ Many worshippers remained outside because they had no seats. The synagogues were often built in *mudéjar* style, that is, the Muslim style that survived in the Christian Kingdoms of Spain. The entrance to the synagogue was usually through the northern or southern wall, and the *'azara* and the side entrance have been explained in terms of Jewish needs: direct entry to the synagogue, facing the ark, would be improper. In reality, both architectural features were related to a prohibition of the authorities. In a document from 1319 concerning the synagogue of Tárrega in Catalonia it was stated that the door should not open directly on to the street, out of respect for Christians' feelings.³⁸

---

³² Blasco, *La judería de Zaragoza*, p. 162.
³³ Ibid., p. 150.
³⁴ ACA, Reg. 1687, fo. 55ᵛ [= Baer, *Spanien*, doc. 351].
³⁵ Gerondi 50. For the archival sources, see Blasco, *La judería de Zaragoza*, pp. 139–62.
³⁶ Perfet 331.   ³⁷ Adret, i. 63, 584, v. 222.
³⁸ ACA, Reg. 217, fos. 147ᵛ–148 [= R 3113].

Restrictions set by the authorities also constrained the size of the synagogue. There were no standard measurements, but each community knew the limits it could not exceed. These limits were decided upon after consultations between the local churchmen and the royal authorities.[39] The abovementioned Tárrega synagogue was built according to measurements fixed by the Bishop of Vich in 1307 and confirmed by Jaime II in 1319. The synagogue was not to exceed 16 metres in length, 8 metres in width and 12 metres in height.[40] The synagogue in Játiva that the community was permitted to rebuild in 1321 was to be no more than 11 metres high and 12 metres down each side.[41] The size of the synagogue also depended, among other things, on Christian building in the vicinity. Changes in the status the Jews enjoyed led to reduction or increase in its size when such flexibility was physically possible.

Many synagogues became too small for a growing population. We know of efforts to enlarge existing synagogues, including cases where individuals offered their own properties adjacent to the synagogue for the purpose. In one such case, when a member of one community, eager to enlarge the synagogue, was prepared to donate his small house which adjoined the *hekhal*, people who had seats by the eastern wall objected to the plan, claiming that the value of their seats would depreciate.[42] The plan therefore had to be modified. Some communities invested considerable money and time in embellishing and decorating their synagogues. It was a matter of prestige to have the synagogue well maintained.[43] The community was greatly assisted by donors who contributed a substantial share of the expense.

Men and women prayed in separate parts of the synagogue.[44] However, some synagogues had no part allocated for women. As suggested above, the *scola de les dones* in Barcelona was most probably one that did have an *'ezrat nashim*, a ladies' prayer quarters. Most women's galleries were on one side and not around the three walls of the synagogue. In some synagogues the women prayed in an adjoining room or in a separated part of the main prayer hall.

As no remains of synagogues exist in any part of what used to be the medieval Crown of Aragon, our knowledge depends on illustrations and descriptions that are extant. The illustrations come from the *Sarajevo Haggadah* at the National Museum in Sarajevo and the *Barcelona Haggadah* in the British Museum. The literary descriptions are found in responsa. The *hekhal* (the ark) and the *tevah* or *bimah* (the platform) were the two principal elements in the synagogue.[45] The ark had doors which were usually kept locked. Sometimes it was a relatively large room. As in other parts of the world, it was customary to inscribe scriptural quotations near the ark. A plaque containing the founder's or donor's name would

---

[39] Asibili (Kapah) 161.
[40] ACA, Reg. 217, fos. 147ʳ–148 [=R 3113].
[41] ACA, Reg. 219, fo. 198ʳ [=R 3164 = Jacobs 788].
[42] Adret, i. 581.
[43] Adret, iii. 443.
[44] Asibili (Kapah) 183.
[45] See Narkiss, 'Heikhal, Bimah, and Teivah'.

usually be placed beside the ark for the public to see. Engraving the names of donors was not however universally approved.[46]

The *hazan* conducted the services from the *tevah*, the word for *bimah* in Spain.[47] This was an elevated platform in the centre of the synagogue, usually surrounded by a high rail or bar. Sometimes a high structure, supported by four or more poles, covered the entire area of the *tevah*. The *Sarajevo Haggadah* and the *Barcelona Haggadah* offer us a good picture of a *bimah* in a Catalan synagogue, and it is clear from the latter source that the *bimah* could be quite elaborate.[48]

SYNAGOGUE FURNITURE AND RITUAL OBJECTS

In most synagogues worshippers sat on benches placed along all the walls in as many rows as space would allow, apart from the area occupied by the *tevah*. All benches faced the *tevah*. The benches were sometimes but not always divided into individual seats. The seats were the property of individual members and were treated like any other commodity. Sometimes the seats were distributed among the families when the synagogue was inaugurated, while in other cases they were allocated to members. According to the method employed in Borja for the distribution of seats of a newly built synagogue, also used elsewhere, a committee of three people had to allocate all the seats, bearing in mind the status of the members.[49] Whichever system was used, the seating arrangement caused innumerable problems.[50]

In the circumstances, it was inevitable that while some Jews owned more than one seat, many others had none. The owner of the seat might not necessarily attend that particular synagogue. Seats could be acquired like any other piece of property, inherited, or given as a gift. One might own part of a seat or a seat in the wrong part of the synagogue, the men's or women's part.[51] Synagogue seats were donated to charity funds, and were also bought and sold for comfort and convenience,[52] and traded for speculative purposes. The high prices of seats caused many Jews to stop attending services. Sometimes drastic measures had to be taken by the community, such as referring seating problems to the *beth din* or to leading halakhic authorities.[53]

Seating problems could even lead to royal intervention. The king would naturally intervene on behalf of protégés of his whose seating plans did not please the community, or would support the claims of one Jew against another.[54] In fact,

---

[46] Adret, i. 581.   [47] Adret, i. 96.
[48] British Library, Add. MS 14761, fo. 65ʳ. See Feller, 'Purim of Saragossa', p. 82.
[49] Perfet 249; and see Assis, 'Synagogues', pp. 18–21.
[50] For problems in Valencia see Adret, iv. 319.
[51] Adret, i. 937, 943, 956, ii. 141, 158, 182, 191, 220, 226, 272, viii. 12; Asibili (Kapah) 101, p. 119, 192, p. 219, 193, p. 221.   [52] Adret, i. 1022, 1156, viii. 26.   [53] Perfet 253.
[54] ACA, Reg. 885, fo. 8 [= Baer, *Spanien*, doc. 226]; CR, Jaime II, C 134, no. 183 [= *Cartas Reales*, no. 394].

through confiscation or other means, the king also came into possession of synagogue seats which he distributed among his favourite Jews. Some of these Jews who were given prominent seats in the synagogue were disliked, even hated, by many in their communities.[55]

Benches and chairs were virtually the only furniture found in the synagogue. Illustrations in the *haggadot* show the oil lamps used in the fourteenth century. Apart from the *ner tamid* (the perpetual light) near the *hekhal*, there were other lamps to illuminate the synagogue. The lighting of the synagogue was expensive and the cost had to be shared. Many refused to pay, either because they had no seat in the synagogue or because their seat was not well lit. There were, however, many who brought oil as a religious act.[56] The *shamash* was usually in charge of lighting the lamps or candles.[57]

The scrolls of the Torah were adorned with '*atarot* (crowns) which were invariably made of silver. They were usually ornamented and were an imitation of a royal crown. Most of them were donated by members whose names were inscribed on them.[58] Sometimes, the Torah scroll was donated as well as the crowns, as was the case with the scroll donated to the synagogue in Huesca.[59] Silver plaques bearing the name of the donor were attached to donated scrolls.[60] In Barcelona, children used to wear the crowns when the scrolls were moved between the synagogue and private houses, where they were kept for safety reasons.[61] The ark with its silver crowns and *rimonim* could attract thieves: two Jews were caught at night in Daroca while breaking the doors of the ark.[62]

The scrolls of the Law were put in mantles or cases, called *tiq*, and were wrapped with a strap, called *mapah*.[63] Was the *tiq* made of cloth or wood? The sources suggest that both styles existed in synagogues in the medieval Crown of Aragon. As the Sephardi Jews in Morocco, Italy, the Ottoman Empire, and western Europe used cloth mantles, it is reasonable to assume that this fashion was predominant in medieval Spain.[64] Donors were emphatic that all ornaments on objects donated by them should be of high quality and beauty. If they were not satisfied with their order, they would instruct the ornaments to be remade or repaired.[65] Some small Jewish settlements could not afford to have a scroll of the Torah, and instead read from ordinary books.[66]

---

[55] For confiscation of seats, see ACA, CR, Pedro IV, C 27, no. 3714. On seats given to the king's protégés, see ACA, Reg. 16, fo. 257ʻ [= R 459 = Jacobs 480 = MF i. 1094].

[56] Adret, iv. 239. [57] Adret, iii. 277.

[58] Asibili (Kapah) 123, p. 144, 161, p. 191. [59] Adret, iv. 243.

[60] Such a plaque from the second half of the fourteenth century, recording the donation of a Torah scroll by R. Nissim Gerondi to the synagogue *Qehilat Ya'aqov* in Barcelona, is in the Israel Museum together with the scroll. [61] Adret, vii. 73, viii. 260.

[62] Asibili (Kapah) 159, p. 187. [63] Asibili (Kapah) 161, p. 191.

[64] For cloth mantles, see the *Sarajevo Haggadah*, fo. 34, and its reproduction in Assis, 'Synagogues', p. 6. For wooden cases, see the *Barcelona Haggadah*, fo. 65ʻ, and its reproduction in Feller, 'Purim of Saragossa', p. 82, and possibly Asibili (Kapah) 161, p. 191.

[65] Asibili (Kapah) 188. [66] Adret, viii. 199.

THE SYNAGOGUE IN JEWISH LIFE

The functions that the synagogue fulfilled in medieval Jewish life were many and varied. It was not only a house of worship, but served also as the political, social, communal, educational, and cultural centre of the Jewish community in the Crown of Aragon, as in any other land. The meetings of the community leaders and the council took place in the synagogue, as did also the general assembly of all the members. The leaders would meet regularly in the synagogue, at least once a week.[67]

It was in the synagogue that ordinances were enacted and bans were pronounced.[68] The ordinances were read out usually by the *hazan*, in the main synagogue, wherever there was more than one.[69] The payment of taxes was effected in the precincts of the synagogue. In this respect, the courtyard was a particularly busy part of the synagogue as the *berurim* used to sit here to receive the taxes.

Elections took place in the synagogue, and the results and new appointments were announced there. In some communities the electors could not leave the premises until the elections were over.[70] The elected leaders had to take an oath in the synagogue. In Valencia a scroll of the Torah was taken out on this occasion.[71] General oaths by the general public were taken in the synagogue after the Jews obtained charters from the king stating that they would not have to do so outside the Jewish quarter.[72]

Various announcements were made in the synagogue when the Jewish public had to be informed of matters of general concern. Certain transactions were announced in the synagogue on several consecutive occasions: only then did they become valid, if no objections were raised.[73] General bans were issued in the synagogue, where they would have the widest possible publicity.[74] Bans against actual transgressors were also proclaimed in the synagogue and were often accompanied by ceremonies intended to instil awe and fear in the hearts of the worshippers, whose cooperation was essential. The ceremony sometimes included the blowing of the *shofar*, while the person who announced the ban would be wrapped with a *talit*.[75] Members of the community who were put under

---

[67] Adret, v. 222.
[68] Adret, iii. 395, vii. 244.
[69] ACA, Reg. 81, fo. 9 [= R 2060]; Reg. 207, fos. 239ʻ–240 [= R 2919].
[70] Adret, iii. 422, v. 284–5.
[71] ACA, Reg. 229, fo. 274 [= R 3434 = Jacobs 878 = Baer, *Spanien*, doc. 188]; Reg. 229, fos. 274ʻ–275 [= R 3436].
[72] Adret, viii. 506; *Cortes*, pp. 133–7; ACA, Reg. 19, fo. 65ʻ [= R 570 = Jacobs 523 = Bofarull, Barcelona, cxxiv]; Reg. 197, fos. 153ʻ–154 [= R 2745 = Baer, *Spanien*, doc. 146]; Reg. 42, fo. 136 [= R 743].
[73] Perfet 388–90; Asibili (Kapah) 50, 156, 165; Adret, i. 393, ii. 95, 339, 399, iii. 159, 161, 403, 414, 431, iv. 142; Gerondi 80.   [74] Adret, i. 657, ii. 3, iii. 93, iv. 104; Asibili (Kapah) 56, 114.
[75] Asibili (Kapah) 159, p. 189; Adret, i, 1235.

ban could find themselves ostracized in the synagogue. They would be deprived from participating in the prayers and find the synagogue's doors shut before them. If need be, prayers would be suspended upon their arrival. Royal intervention in the cases of some prominent Jews placed under ban caused anger and frustration, in the community.[76]

The kings of the Crown of Aragon, aware of the central role the synagogue played in Jewish life, had their important decisions concerning the Jews made public there.[77] The king often ordered the community to proclaim in the synagogue bans against members who failed to fulfil their obligations to him. The general annual pronouncement of the ban concerning taxation also took place in the synagogue.[78] Moreover, the king used the synagogue premises to have bans proclaimed in specific cases to obtain quick results and resolve pressing problems.[79] For the king as well as for the community, the synagogue was an ideal place to communicate with the Jewish public.

Various religious and social events took place in the synagogue. It was in the synagogue that most circumcisions were organized.[80] Betrothals, too, were often conducted in the synagogue. In some communities, the *hazan* performed the *qinyan* ceremony before the guests while the bride-to-be sat on a special chair. It was then that the future bridegroom gave his presents to his bride.[81]

WORSHIP AND DECORUM

The behaviour of the Jew in the synagogue could not be entirely divorced from his conduct outside. Furthermore, the synagogue has always been a familiar and intimate place where the Jew did much more than praying to his Maker. This naturally permitted certain liberties which, in certain circumstances, could lead to misconduct. Yet here again the sources may be misleading, as they report only problems and misbehaviour, rather than normal and proper actions and events.

The *hazan* played the most important role in the synagogue. Great importance was attached to his vocal and musical performance. There were sometimes complaints that the *hazan* prolonged services excessively. In the opinion of R. Shelomo ben Adret, if it is to render the prayers beautiful so that the public's fervour is aroused, the *hazan* should be praised for his efforts. A beautiful voice, he suggests, is one of the qualities that a *hazan* must possess.[82]

---

[76] Adret, iv. 56; ACA, Reg. 16, fo. 148ʳ [= R 438 = Jacobs 440 = Bofarull, Montpellier, 490]; Reg. 37, fo. 31ʳ [= R 495 = Jacobs 725]. On the suspension of prayers in the Crown of Aragon see Part II, section 6 above on 'The Law and the Judiciary'.

[77] ACA, CR, Jaime II, C 135, no. 410 [= *Cartas Reales*, no. 552].

[78] Vidal, *Les Juifs de Roussillon*, p. 31; ACA, Reg. 43, fos. 111ʳ, 118 [= R 1266, 1278]; Reg. 56, fo. 129ʳ [= RR 1378]; Reg. 211, fos. 301ʳ–302 [= R 3019].

[79] ACA, Reg. 66, fo. 149 [= R 1605]; Reg. 81, fo. 9 [= R 2055]; Reg. 207, fo. 182 [= R 2918]; Reg. 211, fo. 275 [= R 3017].   [80] Adret, vii. 536; Gerondi 52.   [81] Adret, i. 1180.

[82] Adret, i. 215.

The Synagogue

Complaints about lack of decorum during the service came from various communities. In Monzón people did not stand while the scroll of the Torah was being displayed. R. Shelomo ben Adret insisted that the public must remain standing from the moment the doors of the ark are open until the *sefer* is placed on the *tevah*. Complaints about people talking during the reading of the Torah were widespread.[83]

Far more serious were the complaints about violence in the synagogue services. Violence outside the synagogue attracted congregants, while violent Jews were even prepared to bring non-Jews to the synagogue to act against fellow Jews.[84] Violence in the synagogue was quite widespread. Jews hit other Jews, broke furniture, and disrupted the prayers. In all cases reported, heavy fines were paid to the king.[85]

---

[83] For Monzón, see Adret, iii. 281. On talking during the service, see Adret, i. 380.

[84] Adret, i. 244, ii. 83.

[85] ACA, Reg. 62, fos. 145, 136ʻ–137 [= R 1304, 1316, and doc. xv, pp. 428–30]; Reg. 82, fo. 90ʻ [= R 2261]; Reg. 84, fo. 23 [= R 2314]; Reg. 202, fos. 203ʻ, 204 [= R 2831–2]. For a general survey of violence in Jewish society, see Assis, 'Crime and Violence', and Part V, section 5 below on 'Crime and Violence in the *Judería*'.

§4.3 The *Miqve* and Public Baths

THE *MIQVE* IN THE MEDIEVAL CROWN OF ARAGON

THE *miqve* or ritual bath was an essential institution of medieval Jewish life. Though the archeological remains are minimal and the documentary evidence is limited, it seems from a consideration of the halakhic discussions by local rabbis that ritual baths must have existed in many Jewish communities in the Crown of Aragon. For some communities, the information on their *miqve* is no earlier than the year of their liquidation following the expulsion of 1492.[1]

If a community as small as Besalú had its *miqve*, it can be safely assumed that it was found in most communities. In December 1964 the first *miqve* in the Iberian peninsula was discovered in Besalú. In 1977 it was finally opened to the public after being restored. This *miqve*, which is near the Fluvia river, is a thirteenth-century romanesque building. In the absence of a nearby river or underground water, in some places the *miqve* was built on the roof of a building so that rainwater could be used more efficiently.[2]

It is difficult to ascertain whether Jewish baths referred to in some sources were ritual or ordinary baths, or both. Such were the Jewish baths of Saragossa, which provided a substantial revenue to the city. In 1266 Jaime I assigned the revenues of the following two years for the construction of a great bridge over the Ebro.[3] It is possible that these Jewish baths were a *miqve*, since from other sources we understand that various communities had their *miqve* in the compound of the public bath. The Jews of Saragossa used the city's baths for their regular needs. In the late 1280s there was an attempt to prevent the Jews from using the Christian baths.[4]

JEWS AND PUBLIC BATHS

In several cities the Jews operated or owned public baths. In 1160 Ramón Berenguer IV, the Count of Barcelona, authorized the *alfachin* Abram to establish

---

[1] In 1992 two baths were discovered in Toledo. One is in the courtyard of the so-called El Tránsito Synagogue built by Don Shemuel HaLevi Abulafia, and the other in the garden of the House of El Greco where Don Shemuel lived. The discoveries are very recent and we are still awaiting publication of the full report on the two sites. On the structure of the *miqve*, see Adret, i. 828.

[2] On the discovery of the *miqve* in Besalú, see Oliva, *Revista de Gerona*, xxix; Millás, 'Descubrimiento de una miqwah'; Múnera, 'Una miqwah judía', pp. 69–79. On ritual baths on roofs, see Adret, i. 800.   [3] Kayserling, 'Les Juifs à Saragosse', p. 116.

[4] For Saragossa see ACA, Reg. 81, fo. 9 [= R 2056]. For a *miqve* in the non-Jewish public bath, see Adret, iii. 224, v. 64.

a public bath in a garden in Barcelona. The count was to receive two-thirds of the income, while Abram was to keep the other third.[5] In 1199 Pedro II gave his two-thirds share to Guillem Durfort, who had bought the third part from the children of Bonastruch Alfaquim, apparently Abram's son.[6] The bath, which was near the Castell Nou, was not far from the *call* and had many Jews among its customers. The Jews of Barcelona also went to the bath of Caldas de Montbuy.[7]

Jucef Avinxaprut, a Jew from Murviedro, obtained a concession from Jaime I in 1273 to operate the public bath in the town, with all its accessories and adjoining parts, for 200 s per annum.[8] Two years later, Astrug Jacob Xixó bought a public bath in Valencia as part of a huge real estate transaction worth 30,000 sr.[9]

---

[5] ACA, CR, Anteriores a Jaime I, Ex. s., no. 1, fos. 1–2ᵛ [= *Cartas Reales*, no. 2 = Baer, *Spanien*, doc. 33]. Baer quotes as his source Villanueva's *Viage literario*.

[6] ACA, Anteriores a Jaime I, Ex. s., no. 1, fos. 2ᵛ–5 [= *Cartas Reales*, no. 3].

[7] In the 1280s the municipal authorities tried to forbid the use of the bath by Jews: ACA, Reg. 70, fo. 91ᵛ [= R 1718].

[8] ACA, Reg. 19, fo. 19 [= R 556 and doc. vii, p. 421 = Jacobs 511 = MF i. 1475].

[9] ACA, Reg. 20, fo. 252ʳ [= R 623 = Jacobs 582 = MF i. 1824.

§4.4 The Slaughterhouse

THE ESTABLISHMENT OF AN ABATTOIR

ONE of the most fundamental ingredients of religious autonomy enjoyed by the Jews throughout the medieval world was their right to slaughter animals for their consumption in accordance with the prescribed Jewish ritual. A special place had to be allocated for this purpose in every Jewish community. The abattoir in the Crown of Aragon was not necessarily for exclusive Jewish use at all times. Depending on the amount of meat consumption, the place was reserved for the Jews' *shehitah* at certain times. In this and similar cases the Jews shared the slaughterhouse with Christians or Muslims. Sometimes the meat was also sold there, but often there were butchers who provided the meat to the consumers.

There was no community in the Crown of Aragon that was prevented from providing *kasher* meat to its members. With the establishment of a new Jewish community, the right to slaughter and therefore the provision of a suitable place to do so were invariably included among its basic rights. When in 1320 the Infante Alfonso decided to set up a Jewish *aljama* in the town of Alcolea de Cinca and invited Jews to settle there, he permitted the Jews to slaughter their animals in the Christian abattoir.[1] In 1267 Jaime I permitted the Jews of the royal part of Montpellier to buy buildings where they could establish their own slaughterhouse. For this privilege, the Jews had to pay 60 s every Christmas.[2]

The occasional confirmations of the Jews' right to continue their slaughter and sale of *kasher* meat in the places they were accustomed to use seems to indicate that there were some who challenged this right and created problems for Jewish meat consumption. Such difficulties were frequent where the Jews used the Christians' abattoir and meat market. In Barcelona, Valencia, and Majorca, Jaime I had to confirm the Jews' right to slaughter and sell their animals in the city's Christian abattoirs.[3] Pedro III ordered his officials in Montblanch and Tarragona to ensure that the municipal authorities of Tarragona did not fine the Jews for slaughtering animals in the town's meat market.[4] In Cervera, the town's administration and the baile prohibited the use of the local slaughterhouse by Jews in

---

[1] ACA, Reg. 383, fos. 40–2 [= Baer, *Spanien*, doc. 175, para. 3].

[2] ACA, Reg. 15, fo. 55ᵛ [= R 361 = Kahn, 'Documents inédits', p. 265].

[3] ACA, Reg. 15, fo. 122ᵛ [= R 388 = Jacobs 426 = Bofarull, Barcelona, lxix]; Reg. 16, fo. 248ᵛ [= R 468 = Jacobs 476 = MF i. 1175]; Reg. 19, fo. 47ᵛ [= R 562 = Jacobs 516 = Bofarull, Barcelona, cxxii = Pons, *Los judios*, ii, doc. 6]; Fita and Llabrés, 'Privilegios', pp. 26–7.

[4] ACA, Reg. 41, fo. 59ᵛ [= R 722]; Régné's reading 'Tarazona' is mistaken.

1285. The Jews complained to Pedro III that they had never been forbidden the use of the town's abattoir, and the king gave instructions that the Jews be allowed to slaughter their animals freely.[5]

As relations between Christians and Jews deteriorated and the pressure of the city on the *aljama* increased, more and more communities found the Christian abattoirs closed to them. Many communities therefore needed to establish their own slaughterhouses for their exclusive use. This trend coincided with the creation of separate quarters for the Jews as a result of growing insecurity. For example, a new Jewish quarter was established in Majorca in 1286 under pressure from the municipal authorities, and in the new *call* the Jews had their own slaughterhouse.[6] The establishment of Jewish abattoirs for the exclusive use of the Jews towards the end of the thirteenth century was, therefore, the outcome of increasing antagonism towards the Jews, and not of a pro-Jewish policy that allowed a greater autonomy.

Until 1312 the *shohatim* of Elche slaughtered all the animals in the town's slaughterhouse, so that the meat sold by the butchers to the entire population was *kasher*. That was scandalous in the eyes of some, who complained to the king. He ordered that the Jews should slaughter two sheep every day for their consumption only.[7] This arrangement, also followed in Valencia, did not satisfy either side. In 1314 the Jewish communities of Elche and Oriola, which were in a region annexed by Jaime II, asked the king to allow them to have their own slaughterhouse. At the beginning of the fourteenth century the Christian butchers of the big abattoir in Valencia questioned the Jews' right to use the premises. The two sides went to court, and the Jews must have won the case since they continued to use the premises for some time thereafter.[8] Until 1322 the Jews and Muslims of Tortosa shared one slaughterhouse. Following constant arguments the Jews asked to have an abattoir of their own. The king acceded to their request, on condition that the Christian lessee should have complete possession of the property and monopoly of the slaughterhouse.[9]

In Montblanch the Jews slaughtered their animals in the Christian abattoir, but this arrangement caused interminable trouble. Originally they had slaughtered animals for the entire population. In order to put an end to this situation, the Jews were permitted in 1321 to have their own slaughterhouse, and Jaime II forbade the Jews to buy meat from Christians.[10] In Barbastro, too, the Jews slaughtered for all the inhabitants. The municipal authorities forbade the purchase of *kasher* meat,

[5] ACA, Reg. 62, fo. 148 [= R 1345].
[6] ACA, Reg. 63, fo. 33 [= R 1483 = Isaacs 31]; Reg. 66, fo. 176 [=R 1630 = Isaacs 40].
[7] ACA, Reg. 209, fo. 147 [=R 2948].
[8] ACA, CR, Jaime II, C 13, no. 1684; Reg. 210, fo. 160` [= R 2990].
[9] ACA, Reg. 221, fos. 226`–227 [= R 3218 = Jacobs 806]. References to problems between Jews and Muslims over joint slaughterhouses are also found in the Hebrew sources. See Adret, i. 345–6.
[10] ACA, Reg. 220, fo. 74` [= R 3196 = Bofarull, Montblanch, 91]; Reg. 221, fo. 230` [=R 3220 = Bofarull, Montblanch, 571–2].

but the king cancelled their ordinance.[11] The consumption of *kasher* meat was very widespread in the Crown of Aragon. The municipal authorities led a campaign against it. In 1290, for instance, the municipal council of Huesca forbade the purchase of Jewish meat by Christians.[12]

JEWS, CHRISTIANS, AND *KASHER* MEAT

In the latter part of the thirteenth century and the beginning of the fourteenth, relations between Jews and Christians in the Crown of Aragon deteriorated as a result of growing religious antagonism and economic competition. Religious and economic causes alike rendered unfit and forbidden the *kasher* meat that had previously been considered perfectly edible for Christians. The change of attitude came from municipal circles rather than the royal court. The municipal ordinances illustrate well the change and reflect the motives behind the anti-Jewish move. Urban Christian society took various steps to restrict the Jews' economic ventures and religious freedom.

The opposition to *shehitah* and the consumption of *kasher* meat by Christians was expressed in religious terms but was primarily economically motivated. Reference has already been made to the ordinances of Huesca in 1290 and of Barbastro in 1297 forbidding the sale of *kasher* meat to Christians.[13] The Huesca ordinance speaks of the indignation that the Christians felt because, while they consumed *kasher* meat and wine, the Jews never touched the Christians' products. The municipal council was also very indignant that Christians participated in Jewish meals while Jews never partook of Christian ones.[14] In 1301 the council of Barcelona decided that a fine of 10 s would be imposed on anyone who sold *kasher* meat outside the *call*.[15] The Jews challenged the decision of the council and were involved in a long legal process with the baile. They claimed that, according to a privilege granted to them by Jaime I, they were entitled to hold meat stands outside the *call*. In November 1302 Jaime II decided to put an end to the conflict by allowing the Jews to set up a meat stand outside the wall of the *call*, in front of Maymo de Forn's house. The stand should display only ritually slaughtered meat, which was presumably for Jewish consumption. The stand had to be of a certain size and had to be put aside once the sale was over. The slaughtering had to take place elsewhere. Most important of all, the slaughterers had to take an oath that they would not slaughter more than the Jews consumed and would sell the Christian butchers only non-*kasher* meat.[16] The arrangement did not work smoothly, for in 1310 the municipal council in Barcelona issued anew the

[11] ACA, Reg. 253, fo. 12 [= R 2640].
[12] del Arco, 'Ordenanzas inéditas', p. 428.
[13] ACA, Reg. 253, fo. 12 [= R 2640]; and see n. 12 above.
[14] del Arco, 'Ordenanzas inéditas', p. 428; id., 'La judería de Huesca', pp. 321–2.
[15] Carreras, 'Ordinacions urbanes . . . de Barcelona'.
[16] ACA, Reg. 200, fo. 140 [= R 2800].

prohibition on the sale of *kasher* meat outside the *call*.[17] In 1319 the council of Valls ordered that the meat sold by Jews should be clearly identified as such.[18]

There can be no doubt that there were economic considerations behind the initiative of the municipal council. First and foremost, they intended to prevent the sale of *kasher* meat to Christians. The price of this meat must have been competitive for Christians to be ready to buy it. The meat in question was not the meat that was subsequently found unfit, that is, *trefa*. It was customary in many communities to sell such meat at a cheap price. In some communities this meat was known as *trufanes*.[19]

THE CROWN AND THE JEWISH ABATTOIR

The Jewish abattoir was a source of income for the king, who received an annual payment for each slaughterhouse. In his confirmation of its charters in January 1277, Pedro III reiterated the right of the *aljama* of Calatayud to slaughter all the animals needed in its slaughterhouse free of any charge except for the annual payment, the *lezda*.[20] This amount had to be paid to the king or to anyone the king appointed. In the early 1280s the Jews of Calatayud were instructed to pay Domingo de la Figera. When they failed to do so, Pedro III ordered on more than one occasion in 1285 that the matter be settled.[21] The income from the Jewish slaughterhouse was often used by the court to pay its debts to Jews.[22] It was sometimes farmed out, to Jews or Christians.[23]

The meat was sold either at the slaughterhouse or from butchers' shops or stands, for which again the king charged a fee. These stands were sometimes provided by the king, who used them as a source of income.[24] At times, the monopoly on the sale of *kasher* meat was given to Christians, who also paid an annual fee. Very often the beneficiaries were the king's officials, who needed to acquire a suitable building in the Jewish quarter where the meat could be sold. In 1292 Jaime II granted a monopoly in the sale of *kasher* meat in Játiva to Miquel de Cariñena, with two stands. This aroused the opposition of the Jewish community.[25]

The case of the *kasher* meat monopoly in Montblanch is worth particular attention. We may recall that in Montblanch the Jews used the Christian abattoir, and that during a certain period *kasher* meat was provided for the entire population.

---

[17] Fiter, 'Bandos', p. 340; Kayserling, 'Les Juifs à Barcelone', p. 110.
[18] Carreras, 'Ordinacions urbanes . . . Valls'.   [19] Carreras, 'L'aljama de juheus', p. 34.
[20] ACA, Reg. 39, fo. 155ʳ [= R 674 and doc. x, pp. 423–4].
[21] ACA, Reg. 43, fo. 118 [= R 1476]; Reg. 56, fo. 21ᵛ [= R 1305].
[22] ACA, Reg. 87, fo. 26 [= R 2465].
[23] ACA, Reg. 221, fos. 226ᵛ–227 [= R 3218 = Jacobs 806] (Christians); Reg. 192, fo. 41 [= R 2406]; Reg. 197, fos. 105ᵛ–106 [= R 2732]; Asibili (Kapah) 44.
[24] ACA, Reg. 44, fo. 166ᵛ [= R 719].
[25] ACA, Reg. 229, fos. 226, 235 [= R 3415–61]. For Játiva, see ACA, CR, Jaime II, C 134, no. 232.

Even the sale to the Jews alone must have been a fairly profitable monopoly. Following some enquiries and correspondence between the king and the baile, Queen Blanca granted this monopoly in 1305 to Bertrand de Jorba, an apostate. For the Jews the appointment of an ex-Jew as the sole supplier of *kasher* meat was preposterous. Christian butchers who supplied meat to the Jews were also understandably opposed to the new monopoly. Christians and Jews alike complained to the king, whose instructions in early 1306 satisfied no one. In June 1306 the queen cancelled the privilege she had granted to Bertrand. At the beginning of August 1306 the king informed R. Shelomo ben Adret that the affair would be closed as soon as the Jews paid 1,000 sb. The Jews continued to buy their *kasher* meat from Christians who were supplied from the slaughterhouse.[26] The situation remained unchanged until August 1321 when, we may recall, Jaime II at last permitted the Jews to have their own abattoir and sale stands. The success of the new arrangement exceeded all expectations. Christians were among the clients of the new stands. In November 1321 the monopoly on *kasher* meat was once again given to a Christian. In April 1322 stricter instructions were issued. The Jews were not allowed to buy meat anywhere except from this privileged Christian.[27] The case of Montblanch shows the financial aspects of the supply of *kasher* meat in the community and their repercussions in daily life. It is clear that the king was sometimes directly involved in fixing the price of the *kasher* meat, as its sale provided him with some income.[28]

The king also used the Jewish slaughterhouses indiscriminately to recompense his favourite Jews at the expense of their community. In 1273 the Infante Pedro granted the Jew Maalux Alcoqui a *libra* of mutton every day, for life, from the Jewish abattoir of Huesca.[29] Ever since the reign of Pedro II some Jews in the service of the king had enjoyed a regular daily provision of free meat from the Jewish slaughterhouse. The privilege was sometimes granted for life, or even made hereditary. R. Salamon Abendavid, the king's *alfaquim* or interpreter for Arabic, received daily two *libras* of mutton, or the money equivalent, from the Jewish abattoir of Saragossa. Salamon and his family continued to eat meat at the expense of the community under the reign of Jaime I. It was only in 1276 that Pedro III cancelled the right of Abraham, Salamon's son, to this daily treat.[30] These rights did not disappear easily. After the death of Abraham, Pedro III confirmed once again the right of Mosse, Abraham's son, to receive the daily portion of meat from the Jewish slaughterhouse.[31] Other members of the family

---

[26] ACA, Reg. 203, fos. 50ᵛ, 62, 172 [= R 2844–5, 2857 = Bofarull, Montblanch, 88–90]; CR, Jaime II, C 11, nos. 2392, 2397. The letter to Adret is found in ACA, Reg. 55, fo. 69 [= R 2859 = Baer, *Spanien*, doc. 160].

[27] ACA, Reg. 220, fo. 74ᵛ = R 3196 = Jacobs 794 = Bofarull, Montblanch, 91]; Reg. 221, fo. 230 = R 3220 = Bofarull, Montblanch, 571–2].

[28] ACA, Reg. 42, fo. 159 [= R 749]. [29] ACA, Reg. 37, fo. 67 [= R 565].

[30] ACA, Reg. 38, fo. 105ᵛ [= R 667–8]. Régné's reading 'Abindeunich' is incorrect.

[31] ACA, Reg. 44, fo. 196 [= R 864].

benefited from the privilege as well. One of them was Mosse Abendavid, Salamon's nephew, who had the privilege confirmed in 1286.[32]

Rich Jews consistently defended their right to receive meat from the Jewish abattoir. They were often at odds with the community and its members, who challenged that right. In 1280 Pedro III referred to Garcia Garces the case of members of the family of Alazar Alfaquim and the sons of Jahuda de la Cavallería concerning the meat that Alazar and Salamon Alfaquim claimed they were entitled to receive from the Jewish abattoir of Saragossa.[33]

[32] ACA, Reg. 64, fo. 47 [= R 1527].   [33] ACA, Reg. 48, fo. 57 [= R 796].

§4.5 The Bakery

BREAD AND *MATZAH*

SOME Jewish communities in the Crown of Aragon maintained their own bakeries. Some privileges that were granted to the communities contained a clause permitting the Jews to open a bakery, although the Jews did not consider it essential to have a bakery run by them. In 1290, in the newly established *call* of Mallorca, the Jews were permitted to build a Jewish bakery. The king as owner retained his rights on the bakery.[1] In some communities the bakery in the Jewish quarter belonged to the king but was operated by Jews.[2] In other communities the Jews did not have their own bakery and used that of the Christians. In most localities the bakery either belonged to the king or was operated by a concessionary who held a monopoly, so that the Jews had little choice but to bake their bread there. In 1282 Pedro III confirmed the concession granted by Jaime I and ordered the baile of Barcelona to ensure that the Jews of the city had their bread baked in the bakery of a noblewoman of Valencia, the wife of G. Grunn. She had the right to establish a second bakery if one should be found not sufficient for the Jews.[3]

While ordinary bread could be baked in Christian bakeries, it was crucial that Jews be allowed to bake their own *matzah* or unleavened bread. Jaime I permitted the Jews to bake *matzah* in their homes.[4] According to the charter given in 1320 to the Jews of Alcolea de Cinca, the latter were given the right to use the Christian bakery throughout the year and to bake their *matzah* for Passover inside their quarter.[5] In 1326 the community of Lérida had difficulties in baking its *matzah*, whereupon Jaime II intervened on their behalf to help them to bake their unleavened bread in time.[6] As in many cities and villages the Jews used the Christians' bakeries, it displeased the Christian bakers to lose their income for the eight days during which the Jews ate no ordinary bread. In some localities they were compensated by the Jews, who had to pay them a suitable sum.[7] In many localities the bakery belonged to the Crown, and its use by the Jews meant an increased income for the king.

---

[1] ACA, Reg. 83, fos. 99ʳ–100ʳ [= R 2267 and doc. xxii, pp. 440–1, 2271 = Isaacs 63, 67].
[2] ACA, Reg. 19, fos. 56ʳ–57 [= R 566 = Danvila, 'Clausura y delimitación', p. 143, n. 2 = Jacobs 518 = MF i. 1536]. [3] ACA, Reg. 46, fo. 86ʳ [= R 911].
[4] ACA, Reg. 16, fo. 159 [= Bofarull, Barcelona, xci].
[5] ACA, Reg. 383, fos. 40–2 [= Baer, *Spanien*, doc. 175, para. 2].
[6] ACA, Reg. 228, fo. 37 [= R 3371]. [7] ACA, Reg. 228, fo. 45 [= R 3372].

CHRISTIANS, JEWS, AND BAKERIES

Using the Christians' bakery was sometimes dangerous for the Jews. This was particularly so around the period of Easter, when attacks on Jews were a frequent occurrence. In 1269 Jaime I authorized the Jews of Besalú to use small ovens in their homes during the period of Good Friday and Easter without having to pay anything to the royal bakery which held the monopoly in the field.[8]

In communities where there was a Jewish bakery, its use by Christians aroused the anger of the city's bakers. Among those who used the Jewish bakery were churchmen and friars. A fourteenth-century by-law in Tortosa forbade churchmen to have their bread baked in the Jews' bakery.[9]

Some privileged Jews were allowed to use the bakery without paying any dues to the local lord.[10]

[8] ACA, Reg. 16, fo. 159 [= R 426 = Jacobs 452 = Bofarull, Barcelona, xci].
[9] Villanueva, *Viage literario*, v, p. 296; Carreras, 'L'aljama', pp. 35–6.
[10] ACA, Reg. 478, fo. 24ʳ [= R 478 = Jacobs 721].

§4.6 The Cemetery

ESTABLISHMENT

ALTHOUGH the cemetery was not in the immediate vicinity of the Jewish quarter, it was however an extension of the *judería*. The community established a cemetery with the king's permission, which was generally granted upon request. In 1274, for instance, Jaime I authorized the community of Villafranca del Panades to have its own burial-place,[1] and in 1298 the *aljama* of Montblanch obtained the right to set up a cemetery.[2] The Jews who settled in Alcolea de Cinca were allowed by the Infante Alfonso to possess their burial place according to a charter of 1320.[3] In 1321 the Jews of Castellón de la Plana were permitted to acquire some land for a cemetery.[4] Not every community or Jewish settlement possessed a cemetery. The Jews of Cervera, for example, had to bury their dead elsewhere.[5] Many such a community subsequently applied for permission to have a burial place. One of the communities that needed a cemetery of its own after a period of growth was Burriana. Until 1326 the Jews of Burriana buried their dead either in Valencia or in Murviedro.[6] The plot chosen proved to be too small, since in 1328 the same community asked Alfonso IV to confirm the use of another burial-ground to replace the old one, which was now completely full.[7] The cemetery of Lérida became too small in the middle of the fourteenth century following the high mortality of the Black Death. Thereupon Pedro IV decided in 1353 that a suitable plot of land should be allocated to the Jews for this purpose.[8] The cemeteries of some communities were filled following massacres: the Jews of Montclús, who suffered heavily at the hands of the *Pastoureaux*, the 'Shepherds' Crusade' of 1320–1, buried their dead in their small cemetery which suddenly became too crowded.[9]

---

[1] ACA, Reg. 19, fo. 123 [= R 588 = Jacobs 541 = Bofarull, Barcelona, cxxxvi].
[2] ACA, Reg. 196, fo. 202 [= R 2703 = Bofarull, Montblanch, 82].
[3] ACA, Reg. 383, fos. 40–2 [= Baer, *Spanien*, doc. 175, para. 25].
[4] ACA, Reg. 219, fo. 221 [= R 3169 = Jacobs 791].
[5] Adret, iii. 291; ACA, Reg. 91, fo. 163 [= R 2441].
[6] ACA, Reg. 229, fo. 211ᵛ [= R 3409 = Jacobs 870].
[7] ACA, Reg. 478, fo. 181 [= Chabret, *Sagunto*, pp. 332–3].
[8] Romano, 'Restos judíos', p. 365.
[9] ACA, Reg. 220, fo. 56 [= R 3190 = Miret, 'Le Massacre', p. 260].

LOCATION

The location of the cemetery depended on several factors, one of which was the availability of suitable land at a reasonable distance from the quarter. In several localities the cemetery was on a hill not far from the town. In Barcelona, the cemetery of the Jews was on the mountain known as Montjuich. This cemetery is very old: sources from as early as the end of the eleventh century speak of old tombstones. The name is commonly translated as 'the Jews' Mountain', although the etymology of the word is obscure. The cemetery is on the side overlooking the sea and was excavated in 1945.[10]

The cemeteries of Gerona and Villafranca were also called Montjuich. In Gerona a very rich collection of tombstones is exhibited in the Archeological Museum, housed in the monastery of San Pedro de Galligans.[11] The exact location of the cemetery in Lérida has been established by Romano. In what used to be the graveyard human bones and tombstones have been found.[12] The second cemetery, established after the Black Death, was the Corda de Gardeny by the Segre river.

Much information about cemeteries in the Crown of Aragon dates back to the period of the expulsion and its aftermath. That is how the exact location of many cemeteries, including that of Saragossa, is known. Some cemeteries, for example that of Calatayud, have never been excavated, although their location is known. The cemetery of Teruel was excavated in 1925 by Floriano.[13]

DESECRATION OF CEMETERIES

Old, unused cemeteries could easily be desecrated, and often their stones were used in buildings all around the town. The Bishop of Vich agreed in 1307 that the Jews of Tárrega should continue to possess their old cemetery and build a fence around it to prevent any desecration. After the bishop's death in 1319, Jaime II confirmed the privilege and prohibited the desecration of the old tombstones.[14] Some charters offered protection to the cemetery and prohibited the removal of tombstones. The charter of Majorca from the mid-thirteenth century contained such a clause.[15] The removal of tombstones from the Jewish cemetery was not a rare occurrence; tombstones from the Jewish cemetery of Barcelona can be found to this very day in the walls of buildings of the city. Particularly interesting is the collection of Jewish tombstones in Palau del Vicrey, the building that, until recently, housed the Archive of the Crown of Aragon in the *barrio gótico*, and the

---

[10] On the excavation and its findings, see Duran and Millás, 'Una necropolis'; on the cemetery and Montjuich, see Fita, 'El cementerio'; Carreras, 'Lo Montjuich'. For an actual burial on Montjuich, see ACA, Reg. 86, fo. 59' [= R 2426].

[11] Fita, 'El Montjui'. [12] Romano, 'Restos judíos'. [13] Floriano, *La aljama*.

[14] ACA, Reg. 217, fos. 147'–148 [= R 3113]. [15] Villanueva, *Viage literario*, xxii, pp. 330–1.

stones found in buildings situated in the streets Moncada and Condes de Barcelona.

The Crown itself was sometimes involved in the desecration of Jewish cemeteries and the confiscation of graveyards. In 1263 Jaime I gave the site of the old cemetery of the Jews to a monastery in Montpellier. The Jews received from the monastery a sum of money to use for the transfer of the bones to a new graveyard.[16] This kind of desecration was a very heavy blow to the Jews. It blatantly destroyed the sanctity of the graves. Some communities tried to avoid their desecration by having precautionary clauses included in their privileges and charters. The Jews of Barcelona had several of their privileges confirmed in 1268, one of which guaranteed that the location of their cemetery would not change without their consent.[17] Cemeteries were at times attacked by Christians, and Jews felt the need to obtain royal protection. The Jews of Villafranca succeeded in obtaining from Pedro III the confirmation of a privilege of Jaime I forbidding any desecration of their cemetery.[18] In 1321 the Jews of Játiva obtained the king's permission to build a wall all around their cemetery. The king stipulated that a gate should be erected through which people could seek refuge during time of war.[19]

---

[16] Kahn, 'Juifs de Montpellier', p. 264.
[17] ACA, Reg. 15, fo. 123 [= R 389 = Bofarull, Barcelona, lxx].
[18] ACA, Reg. 48, fo. 107 [= R 822].
[19] ACA, Reg. 219, fo. 222ᵛ [= R 3174 = Dinur, ii. 2, p. 51, no. 36].

PART FIVE

JEWISH SOCIETY

§5.1 Social Classes

SOCIAL STRUCTURE

JEWISH society in the Crown of Aragon developed characteristics that distinguished it from the rest of Iberian Jewry. Despite the differences that existed between the various components of the Crown, the structure of Jewish society developed more or less along similar lines throughout the realm. It was profoundly influenced by extraneous factors, of which the Reconquista was undoubtedly the most important. Due to the political and social circumstances that prevailed in the twelfth and thirteenth centuries when the Reconquista reached its most significant phase, the gap between the rich and the poor in the *juderías* of the Crown of Aragon was far more sharply accentuated than was the case elsewhere in the Jewish world. The wars of the Reconquista deeply influenced the structure of Jewish society in the Hispanic kingdoms.[1] The extensive need of the king–counts for Jews in the administration of the Crown added great impetus to the growth of the social, financial, and intellectual élite in Jewish society. Lacking a centralized form of government and constantly in desperate need of money, the king–counts found the Jews ideal candidates for certain bureaucratic and financial posts in their administration.[2]

Most Jewish interpreters, translators, diplomats, purveyors, physicians, administrators, and agents in the royal service came from the aristocratic families. Their employment by the king–counts added to their power and prestige within Jewish society. Their access to the court was also appreciated by the *aljama*, as it enabled them to act on behalf of the Jewish community. The large number of courtiers in the thirteenth century contributed much to the growth of the upper class, while the privileges that the king granted to his Jewish courtiers widened the gap and increased the hostility between the rich and the poor.[3] Some of the advantages given by the king were at the expense of other members of the community, whose anger and envy became very marked.

The greatest differences between the upper and the lower classes were in their lifestyle, daily behaviour, and forms of entertainment. Members of the upper class could afford to live in luxury and extravagance. Those who served at court emulated their Christian counterparts in many matters and the Jewish courtiers

---

[1] On Jewish society in Spain, see Beinart, 'Hispano-Jewish Society'.
[2] Romano, *Judíos al servicio de Pedro el Grande*; id., 'Los hermanos Abenmenassé'; Shneidman, 'Jews in the Royal Administration'; Assis, 'Jewish Diplomats'.
[3] Assis, 'Poor and Rich'.

behaved in very much the same way as Christian courtiers.⁴ The poor, on the other hand, had serious difficulties in making ends meet. Those who were destitute and could not even pay taxes often relied on charity. Some worked as domestic servants for the rich. There were Jews so poor that they could not even afford to buy the long robe they were required to wear. The sources hardly mention these destitutes, who were not involved in the economic and political life in the community.⁵ The poor who appear as one of the three classes in Jewish society were those Jews who paid taxes but whose income was low. They were burdened with expenses and high taxes which they could pay only with great difficulty. The king often had to offer them easy terms of payment of their taxes and at times supported the punishment of defaulting poor tax-payers.⁶ As conditions deteriorated, the division in Jewish society became more rigid and entrenched. Luxury and poverty, extravagance and beggary, formed part of the same general social scene. The gap between the rich and the poor led to the eventual crystallization of social strata in Jewish society.

In 1263 the poor in Saragossa appear as an organized group whose interests were totally opposed to those of the rich ruling families.⁷ Two distinct classes with separate fiscal records appear in sources from 1286 referring to communities in the Kingdom of Aragon. From the beginning of the fourteenth century there are records that refer to three classes in Jewish society: the rich, the middle, and the poor classes. The first such reference comes from Valencia in 1300.⁸ From the source it is clear that this division was not completely new. The three-class division was almost an exact replica of the structure of the urban Christian population in Catalonia and elsewhere in the Crown of Aragon. It is significant that the structure of Jewish society was modelled on the Christian system that existed in the cities.⁹

The rich, called in the sources also *má major*, *mano mayor*, or *manus maiori*, were mostly the wealthy merchants who were the largest tax-payers. They formed a thin top layer of Jewish society who owned the bulk of Jewish property and whose financial transactions were of great import in the country. Most intellectuals and some scholars belonged to this class, as did all courtiers. Until the end of the thirteenth century, and in some cases well beyond that time, they ruled the communities unchallenged. The middle class, or the *manus mediocri*, *mano media*, or *má mitjana*, comprised the small merchants, well-to-do craftsmen, physicians,

---

⁴ On Jewish courtiers in Spain, see Beinart, 'The Image of Jewish Courtiers'; on Jewish society in Spain in general, see id., 'Hispano-Jewish Society'. On the lifestyle of the Jews in the Castilian court, see Baer, 'Todros Halevi'.

⁵ Adret, i. 103; ACA, Reg. 46, fo. 152ᵛ [= R 1103]; Reg. 62, fos. 91ᵛ, 70ᵛ [= R 1138, 1157].

⁶ ACA, Reg. 57, fos. 187, 199ʳᵛ [= R 1434, 1437, 1440]; Reg. 65, fo. 136 [= R 1523]; Reg. 75, fo. 12ᵛ [= R 1748]; Reg. 82, fo. 22 [= R 2071]; Reg. 85, fos. 8, 15ᵛ [= R 2101; 2112].

⁷ Assis, 'Crisis'; ACA, Reg. 65, fo. 138 [= R 1524]; Reg. 81, fo. 18ᵛ [= R 2062]; Reg. 82, fo. 22 [= R 2071]; Reg. 85, fos. 8, 15ᵛ [= R 2101, 2112].

⁸ ACA, Reg. 197, fos. 153ᵛ–154 [= Baer, *Spanien*, doc. 146 = R 2745].

⁹ Assis, 'Social Unrest'.

and other professionals.[10] The largest group constituted the small tax-payers—the poor, *manus minor, mano menor*, or *má manor*. These were men who had to work hard to earn their livelihood and 'sweated blood and brought to the fisc their milk and blood', as reported by R. Bahye ben Asher.[11] They included the tradesmen and craftsmen and most community clerks.

THE STRUGGLE BETWEEN RICH AND POOR

The second half of the thirteenth century witnessed the beginning of the struggle that the poor waged against the community leaders who represented the rich Jews. The two issues over which the poor challenged the rich were taxation and representation in the communal administration. The rich and the poor favoured different systems of taxation. The rich, who controlled all communal bodies, including the tax-assessors' committee, advocated the method of assessment, whereas the poor, who had no share in the administration, favoured the declaration under oath. The poor claimed that they were overtaxed while the rich paid less than their share.

The first records dealing with the struggle between rich and poor are from Saragossa and date from 1263–4. The poor established an organization called Kat ha-Havurah (the People's Faction) and sent a delegation to Jaime I to seek his support for reform in taxation and community administration. They brought the king gifts and bribes and returned to their community with charters, including one which introduced the declaration under oath instead of the assessment system. The poor were also promised that their representatives would be among the tax-assessors of the *aljama*.

The joy of the poor in Saragossa was short-lived. The rich sent their own delegates and more valuable bribes to the court, and returned to Saragossa with letters from the king cancelling practically all the achievements of the poor. The leaders of the community, who were members of the rich families, met and decided that all the expenses of the rich delegates, including the gifts given to the king, were to be shared by all the members of the community, irrespective of their social or economic status. This insensitive decision illustrates well the futility of any action to remedy the grievances of the poor so long as the administration of the community remained in the hands of the wealthy.[12]

The unrest that broke out in Saragossa in 1263–4 spread to other Jewish communities in the Kingdom of Aragon. It was no accident that Saragossa was the centre of the social agitation and that the Aragonese communities were so involved in the struggle for reform, for the Aragonese communities were the scene

---

[10] The middle class is first mentioned in Hebrew sources from the beginning of the fourteenth century in connection with Lérida. See Asibili (Kapah) 114.

[11] Bahye ben Asher, *Kad ha-Qemah*, s.v. Gezel (spoliation), tax infringements.

[12] See Assis, 'Crisis'; ACA, Reg. 12, fo. 151ʳᵛ [= R 248 = Baer, *Spanien*, doc. 99].

of the gravest injustices to the poor and the most generous concessions to the rich. Apart from the numerous instances of easy financial terms offered to the rich, a large group of wealthy Jews enjoyed complete exemption from taxes. These *francos* were, in fact, outside any communal jurisdiction. As the amount of tax remained generally constant, tax exemptions and reductions were at the expense of the remaining tax-payers. The burden was particularly felt by the middling and poor tax-payers.

Some communities enacted ordinances prohibiting Jews from seeking tax exemption or reduction from the king. Such ordinances had their limitations, as the community was almost paralysed when one of its members dared to turn to the king despite the ordinance. Usually, such a member would be a powerful and rich person who had reason to believe that he could rely on the king's protection. The community's frustration and the poor Jews' despair sometimes led to violence. The events in Saragossa, where such an ordinance was promulgated, shed light on the social unrest in Jewish society at the time. The ordinance was indeed ignored by a rich family and the protests were strong but futile. One member of the family was subsequently killed by Jews. The murderer or murderers were never found and the investigations, which lasted for years, led nowhere.[13]

Unable to remedy the situation through the internal channels of the Jewish community, the poor class turned to the king for help against the wealthy who controlled the communal government. This step, which could have been considered an act of betrayal or *malshinut*, was taken by the poor of many a community. The letter sent by the poor Jews of Calatayud to Jaime II is most revealing. The *poble menudo* begged the king to help them and save them from the oppressive regime of the rich.[14] The king's attitude is noteworthy. While his policy seemed at times ambivalent, he did lend a sympathetic ear to the complaints of the poor. It was not so much his sense of justice, but rather his realistic appreciation of the true nature of the social unrest that was sweeping through the Aragonese communities, and spreading to Catalonia and Valencia, that made the king look favourably on some of the poor Jews' demands. The tax and constitutional reforms that were introduced with royal blessing were designed to achieve peace and quiet in the *judería* and preserve the Jewish community as a reliable and efficient mechanism in the service of the king.

Right from the beginning of the crisis, it was clear to all concerned that tax reform could not be achieved without constitutional reform. The gradual, and at times short-lived, reform in many communities permitted the middle and poor classes to have representatives on all the communal bodies. Understandably, the rich gave up their monopoly in the communal leadership with reservations, if not under outright protest. In many communities the reform did not last long, and the

---

[13] Adret, v. 279.
[14] See Assis, 'Social Unrest', p. 144, n. 96.

achievements of the poorer classes proved to be temporary. As we shall see in the next chapter, the poor Jews turned to other solutions for their financial and social problems.

§5.2 Social Welfare and Mutual Aid

JEWISH society in the Crown of Aragon created and maintained many of its institutions on the model of traditional Jewish norms and practices, adapting them to local conditions. Other institutions were typical of the communities in the north-east of the Iberian peninsula. Notwithstanding the traditional Hebrew names given to these institutions, their establishment was due entirely to the needs and conditions prevalent in the Crown of Aragon at the time. The sources reveal that most mutual aid confraternities that operated in these communities were set up to solve problems that the *qehilah* was unable or unwilling to solve. Their establishment was, therefore, directly linked to the social unrest and the communal regime that prevailed in these communities.

THE COMMUNITY AND THE POOR

Most communities of the Crown of Aragon did not pursue a welfare policy designed to assist the needy. No institution was created by the community to look after the poor. Contrary to the widespread Jewish norm by which provision for charity funds was made by the *qehilah*,[1] charity remained a private initiative in most communities in the Aragonese realm. It seems that the absence of any clear public charity programme was due mainly to the character of the communal regime and the status of the leaders. The wealthy leadership proved very insensitive to the needs of the poor members of the community. At the end of the thirteenth century most communities had neither a charity fund nor a welfare policy. The dispute that broke out in one community between the rich and the middle class on the question of welfare provides a good illustration of the situation. Members of the middle class proposed that the members of the community pay a tax for the support of their needy. The tax, they claimed, would spare the poor in their community the shame and the embarrassment of begging from fellow Jews. The institutionalization of charity, in their opinion, was the solution to the problem of poverty among their 'flesh and blood'. The opposition of the rich is most significant. They did not want more taxes. They wanted the poor to continue their habitual visits and receive the usual pittance. They promised to continue their 'generous support'.[2]

Even in the fourteenth century many communities still did not have a charitable fund and the poor depended on the generosity of individual members.

---

[1] Maimonides, *Mishne Torah*, Laws of Charity, ix. 3.   [2] Adret, iii. 380.

In Perpignan there was neither a charitable fund nor a benevolent society until the days of R. Nissim Gerondi.[3] In communities where there was a charitable fund or *heqdesh*, it was often established by individual Jews who bequeathed property and money for charitable purposes. The charity fund was usually under the control of the community: the institution became part of the community organization through individual initiative. Thus in some communities charitable funds from *heqdesh* were available for the needs of the poor. These funds were used for such purposes as the education and burial of poor Jews.[4] The community had to appoint treasurers to administer the funds of the *heqdesh* and dispense charity in accordance with the terms of the bequests.[5] The 1327 constitution of the *aljama* of Barcelona refers to the appointment of *almoyners* by the Council of Thirty for one or a maximum of two years.[6] In the 1386 constitution the *almoyners* of Barcelona were to be elected every year.[7] By then the post was well established and very important because of the community's considerable *heqdesh* property, as is evident from sources following the 1391 massacres.[8]

Officers of the *heqdesh* were found in both small and large communities.[9] These treasurers or officers had both urban and rural property to administer and put to profitable use. Buildings in the Jewish quarter were sometimes assigned to public use by the donor or the community, often serving as synagogues, schools, academies, or hospices.[10] Attempts by communal leaders to change the destination of the *heqdesh* money and property were resisted by the halakhic authorities. When no aim was specified by the donor, the halakhists assumed that the money would be used for charity. *Heqdesh* and charity became identical in many communities.[11]

The sources show that the *heqdesh* in most communities was the main institution for charitable provision. In almost all cases it was a function that the community assumed following donations and bequests by donors who specified the poor as their beneficiaries. The economic deterioration that occurred in many communities in the course of the fourteenth century brought about the creation of special organizations or confraternities. Such organizations existed in Barcelona and Perpignan prior to 1391.[12] In Saragossa, the *heqdesh* was first known as

---

[3] Gerondi 75.
[4] Adret, i. 1103, 1157, v. 77. [5] Adret, i. 604, 617.
[6] ACA, Reg. 230, fos. 106–7ˇ [= Baer, *Spanien*, doc. 189, para. 14].
[7] ACA, Reg. 948, fos. 114ˇ–22ˇ [= Baer, *Spanien*, doc. 381, para. 10].
[8] ACA, Reg. 1949, fo. 16ˇ [= Baer, *Spanien*, doc. 434].
[9] Girbal 'Beneficencia', p. 2 [= Romano, *Per a una història*, ii, p. 544]; Secall, *La comunitat*, pp. 155–8, 245.
[10] A dedication stone by R. Shemuel ha-Sardi was found in a building on the site of the *call* of Barcelona. The stone is now in the Museu d'Història and a replica has been placed on the building at the corner of Marlet and S. Ramon del Call where the original was discovered. For buildings donated which served as synagogues, see Asibili (Kapah) 13, 161.
[11] Adret i. 617; Asibili (Kapah) 167; Gerondi 1.
[12] Baer, *Spanien*, doc. 399; ACA, Reg. 1687, fo. 181ˇ [= Baer, *Spanien*, doc. 362].

almosna de la aljama and after 1391 as *confraria de la almosna*.[13] The names *confraria del cahal* or *almosna de la aljama* indicate that the institution was an integral part of the community administration and were meant to distinguish them from the confraternities that were created by groups or individuals on a voluntary basis. After 1391 and during the fifteenth century the charitable fund based on the *heqdesh* spread to most communities,[14] forced upon the community leaders by the new reality that emerged after the massacres of 1391.

The establishment of a charitable fund based on the *heqdesh* did not solve all social problems and did not serve as an alternative to a planned welfare policy. The changes in the organization reflect the spread of poverty and the growing pressure and criticism from below. The main impetus for change, however, came in the form of initiatives by groups of Jews who united in their efforts to solve social problems in frameworks that were not under the control of the community. The *havurot* or confraternities in the Crown of Aragon present an aspect of social history that has not hitherto been recognized.[15]

BENEVOLENT SOCIETIES

The absence of a well-defined social welfare policy in the community led members of the lower classes and some philanthropists to take the initiative in alleviating the lot of the destitute. This was done through the creation of an institution that was known in the Jewish world but assumed in the Crown of Aragon a role that was of great significance in relations between rich and poor. Members of the lower class in Saragossa, who began their struggle against the rich in 1263–4, organized themselves into a group called Kat ha-Havurah. Other communities, particularly in Aragon, followed suit. This was the beginning of a social struggle that often proved futile. Some of the immediate achievements proved to be of very short duration; in some communities the rich regained power; and the participation of representatives of the lower and middle classes in the governing bodies of the community did not produce radical change in the social and economic policy of the community.

Nevertheless, however meagre the structural achievements of the lower classes were, in one field their success was permanent. This was in the establishment of *havurot*, confraternities or societies which were independent of the communal government and institutions. Their aim was to solve problems that the community was unwilling or unable to resolve. It is significant that the rebellious poor of Saragossa called their organization *havurah*, a word used in Jewish history to denote a fraternity. From several sources it is obvious that the confraternities, like

---

[13] Blasco, 'Instituciones sociorreligiosas', pp. 8, 12–18.
[14] Assis, 'Welfare and Mutual Aid', pp. 322–3.
[15] For a full treatment of this subject, see Assis, 'Welfare and Mutual Aid'.

the *heqdesh*, were private or partisan attempts to solve social and financial problems that the community failed to address.[16]

The foundation of a variety of societies in the first part of the fourteenth century in Saragossa, where the gap between the rich and the poor was so wide and the struggle between the classes was so bitter, indicates the background against which the *havurot* emerged. The Rodfe Zedeq or Conpannya de la Merce was one of the earliest to be formed in Saragossa. One of its aims was to arrange the burial of the poor. It did not replace the community's burial society. It also supported the needy and the sick who were too poor to afford proper medical care. The society expanded its activities in the course of time. In the fifteenth century it received permission to collect funds to build a hospice for the sick and poor. The hospice became an important institution in the life of the entire community. The society held its meetings in the *sinoga menor*, the small synagogue, where its members, who came from the lower and middle classes, attended services. The confraternity was run by a council of thirty and headed by two treasurers.[17] In the Aragonese community of Huesca there was also a society called Rodfe Zedeq that looked after the poor and the sick. It held its meetings in the *beth midrash*.[18]

The 'Ose Hesed society in Saragossa was established to assist the poor, and particularly needy brides. The fraternity also provided food for poor families on the eve of festivals. At one stage the community gave the fraternity meat for distribution among the poor.[19] A similar confraternity operated among the Christian population of Saragossa.[20] Later, in the fifteenth century, the dowries the society provided for poor brides were insufficient as the number of needy and orphaned brides in Saragossa kept growing.[21] The problem of marrying off poor girls was widespread throughout the territories of the Aragonese Crown, as is evident from the existence of such societies in even small communities as Santa Coloma de Queralt.[22]

Another charitable fraternity in Saragossa, the Malbishe 'Arumim, provided clothing to poor Jews. However, the earliest information on it belongs to the second decade of the fifteenth century. Despite the late date, its activities, which are recorded in detail, are very important to the present study, for they constitute eloquent proof of the independent nature of the *havurot* vis-à-vis the *qehilah*. It was indeed a *qehilah* within a *qehilah*.[23] The existence of a society called 'Ose

[16] See e.g. Adret, v. 269.
[17] Blasco, 'Instituciones sociorreligiosas', pp. 32–4 and docs. 1–2; Serrano, *Orígenes*, i, p. xliii; Cantera, 'Cofradía', p. 370.
[18] Lacave, 'Las juderías aragonesas', pp. 221–2.
[19] Serrano, *Orígenes*, i, pp. ccclxxv, ccclxxxix; ACA, Reg. 2593, fos. 127ᵛ–128 [= Baer, *Spanien*, doc. 532]. The distribution of the meat is related in the Judeo-Aragonese ordinances published by Lacave, 'La carnicería', pp. 10, 23, 34.
[20] Blasco, 'Instituciones sociorreligiosas', p. 30, n. 176.
[21] See letters from the period in Beinart, 'A 15th Century Hebrew Formulary'.
[22] Secall, *La comunitat*, p. 157, n. 90.
[23] On the society and relevant bibliography, see Assis, 'Welfare and Mutual Aid', pp. 326–7.

Zedaqot in fifteenth-century Epila, where just twenty-one Jewish families lived, shows the importance of these charitable institutions in Jewish society.[24]

CARE OF THE SICK

In general, the Jews in the Crown of Aragon did not lack physicians. There was a sufficient number of Jewish physicians to take care of the Jewish population. Jewish physicians were indeed in great demand in Christian cities and at court, as well as in aristocratic circles. In small communities and villages such as Santa Coloma de Queralt or Besalú, Jewish physicians served both Jews and Christians. The problem for many poor Jews was not the absence of a physician but want of money. Doctor's fees and medical costs were a heavy burden for the sick poor. They could hardly afford to be ill.

The Biqur Holim (Visiting of the Sick) societies which were established in the first half of the fourteenth century aimed to help the sick among the destitute. Members of the Biqur Holim fraternities undertook to visit the sick poor and ensure they did not suffer from isolation, hunger, and lack of medical care and medicines. In the larger communities there were fraternities which specialized in arranging constant supervision of the dangerously ill. Prayers and psalms were recited at their bedside.

In Santa Coloma de Queralt there was a Biqur Holim fraternity at the beginning of the fourteenth century. It was supported by individuals and benefited from bequests left by members of the community. The fraternity both looked after the sick and offered them financial help.[25]

In fourteenth-century Perpignan one of the fraternities operating in the community was a Biqur Holim or Heqdesh Holim. Its assets came from contributions and charity funds. The fraternity was founded by 'good people in the city . . . to assist and visit the sick poor Jews of the community'. The members of the fraternity promised to donate half of any sum they contributed to any charity, except the fraternity dedicated to providing oil for synagogue lamps. The fraternity was administered by treasurers.[26]

The Biqur Holim of Saragossa developed late in the fourteenth century. The society opened its own synagogue, which became a central institution in the *aljama*.[27] The Biqur Holim synagogue was the scene of the struggle that the lower classes conducted in the fourteenth century against the leaders of the community. It was there that the grievances of the poor were voiced. No wonder that announcements of social and constitutional reform were made in the Biqur Holim

---

[24] Cabezudo, 'La judería de Epila', p. 104.
[25] Segura, 'Aplech de documents', p. 268; Secall, *La comunitat*, pp. 245–6, doc. xlvii.
[26] Gerondi 75.
[27] ACA, Reg. 1687, fo. 55` [= Baer, *Spanien*, doc. 351]; Serrano, *Orígenes*, i, p. xliv; Blasco, 'Instituciones sociorreligiosas', 28, nn. 216–17.

synagogue.²⁸ The society and its synagogue existed right up to the expulsion.²⁹ The society was administered by *muqademin*, who took care of its assets and property.³⁰ Other Aragonese communities that had Biqur Holim societies were Huesca and Teruel. The society in Huesca had its own *beth midrash*.³¹

The Shomre Holim (Guardians of the Sick) was another fraternity that took care of the ill. The fraternity undertook to have one of its members beside the sick at all times. Such a society was found in the first half of the fourteenth century in Santa Coloma de Queralt. In 1335 its representatives paid for a *sefer torah* they had ordered. It is probable that the fraternity held its own *minyan*. The revenues of the Shomre Holim came usually from fees paid by its members and from legacies. From records of its administration we may surmise that the fraternity was quite an important institution.³² It is not surprising to find in fourteenth-century Saragossa a Shomre Holim society which provided continuous vigilance at the bedside of the sick. The society included in its programme Hebrew and Torah teaching to sick Jews who were unable to attend any form of educational activity.³³ The society that existed in Murviedro under this name took general care of the sick.³⁴

HOSPICES IN THE JUDERÍA

The institution called 'hospital' in Latin sources was found in both Christian and Jewish societies from the beginning of the fourteenth century onwards. In both societies it fulfilled similar functions. The information on Jewish hospices prior to this period is not clear. Some later sources may suggest that *heqdesh* buildings in some communities were used as hospices in earlier times, but so far no proof of this can be offered. A Latin source from 1414 speaks of a house for the Jewish poor in Perpignan that was called *heqdesh*.³⁵ As in the rest of the Iberian peninsula, the hospices in the Crown of Aragon were founded to give shelter to the destitute and offered accommodation to poor travellers and visitors who fell ill.³⁶

The hospital or hospice was established by a special society or generous member of the community. It emerged against the background of the social unrest that spread in the thirteenth century in many communities of the Aragonese

---

²⁸ ACA, Reg. 2042, fos. 116ʳ-22ʳ [= Baer, *Spanien*, doc. 467].

²⁹ Cabezudo, 'Testamentos', p. 137.

³⁰ Blasco, 'Instituciones sociorreligiosas', p. 138, n. 9.

³¹ For Huesca see Lacave, 'Las juderías aragonesas', pp. 221-2. For Teruel see ACA, Reg. 1687, fo. 55ʳ [= Baer, *Spanien*, doc. 351].

³² Secall, *La comunitat*, p. 153, n. 56, p. 155-6, nn. 69-71, 79. On the readings of *sembraholim* and *sombrefalim* in the Latin sources, see Assis, 'Welfare and Mutual Aid', p. 329, n. 65.

³³ Blasco, 'Instituciones sociorreligiosas', doc. 6.

³⁴ Chabret, *Sagunto*, p. 344.

³⁵ 'Domum hospi (talis) pauperum judeorum que ebrayce vocatur hekdes . . .': Vidal, *Les Juifs de Roussillon*, p. 173, n. 1 (in Vidal's transcription 'heddes', not 'hekdes').

³⁶ On Jewish hospices in Spain, see Gutwirth, 'Jewish Hospices'.

realm, another manifestation of the efforts of Jews who were dissatisfied with the absence of a clear social policy in the community. In a few places the leaders of the community did establish a hospice, either because the donor specified this as the purpose of his contribution or when the leaders, realizing that the establishment of a hospice by private members was inevitable, preferred to take the initiative. Thus we find hospices established by the community, philanthropists, and charitable fraternities.

In some large communities there was more than one hospice. In Saragossa the three types existed side by side. A private hospice was founded by Isaac Vitalis,[37] while the Rodfe Zedeq society in the same city maintained a hospice of its own, and from a source on the eve of the expulsion, we know that the *aljama* also operated its own hospice, *spital de la judería*. This hospice, designed to help the poor, became an important centre in the life of the *judería*. Meetings were held on its premises.[38] Any Jew who was admitted had to abide by rules set by the *hospitaleros*. His belongings were deposited in the hospice while his relatives signed a document renouncing any right to them.[39]

Later sources prior to the expulsion contain references to hospices elsewhere. The date of their foundation is often unknown. Such was the hospice of Huesca, which served as a shelter for Samuel Pariente who returned to Judaism after his conversion in Portugal. In Epila, too, there was a hospice in the Jewish quarter.[40]

In Catalonia, major *aljamas* had hospices. In Barcelona there was a poor-house in the fourteenth century, supported by generous Jews with donations of money and furniture.[41] The hospice was run by the *hospitaleros* and the representatives of the fraternity which maintained it. We do not know its location, but it may have been either in the *heqdesh* building near the synagogue *scola dels parvols* in Jafiel street, or in the building in Marlet street where the dedication stone of R. Samuel ha-Sardi was discovered.

In some small communities a hospice was usually established when money or property were bequeathed for this purpose. In Santa Coloma de Queralt, Mosse Cabrit left in his will in 1410 assets to set up a hospice. In the will he referred to the possible obstacles that could be encountered in establishing the hospice and expressed the hope that the community would help to remove these obstacles. In June 1411 Mosse Cabrit was already dead. His wife Dulcia donated twenty Barcelona libras for the establishment of the institution. The hospice operated until the expulsion. In Hebrew the hospice was called *heqdesh*.[42] The tailors'

[37] Blasco, 'Instituciones sociorreligiosas', p. 45, n. 339; id., 'Los judíos de Zaragoza', p. 183.

[38] Blasco, 'Instituciones sociorreligiosas', p. 45, n. 340, and doc. 12. On the use of the building, see Serrano, *Orígenes*, i, pp. xliii–xliv; Cantera, 'Cofradía', p. 370.

[39] Blasco, 'Instituciones sociorreligiosas', 45, n. 341; Cabezudo, 'Nuevos documentos', pp. 415–16.

[40] On Huesca, see Baer, *Die Juden*, ii, p. 489, no. 410. On Epila, see Cabezudo, 'La judería de Epila', p. 108.

[41] Cardoner, 'El hospital', pp. 373–5.

[42] Secall, *La comunitat*, pp. 224–5, docs. xxiv, xxv; p. 96, nn. 124–5; pp. 98–100, doc. xxvi.

fraternity in Perpignan opened a hospice for the poor, again known in Hebrew as *heqdesh*. The hospice was open to any Jew, who could stay there for as long as the managers of the hospice considered possible or necessary.[43]

Many details about the hospices were not determined by either local needs or practical considerations. In most cases the building was not chosen for its convenient location or its suitable size: rather, it was donated by a member of the community or was the only available building in the *judería* that could be acquired with the money allocated for the purpose. The furniture in the hospices was very basic and the number of beds was limited.[44]

During the same period, Christian hospitals were established by religious orders, guilds, or individuals. Christian society developed a much wider variety of hospices, which were also usually larger than those established by the Jews.[45]

BURIAL SOCIETIES

The oldest of all the charitable confraternities was the burial society. The establishment of burial societies in the Crown of Aragon was connected with the coincidence of the deeply rooted religious precept among the Jews that the dead should in all circumstances be buried and the financial difficulties involved in fulfilling this requirement. If a community had no cemetery of its own, it had to transport the dead to a cemetery in a neighbouring community. In principle every community had the right to bury its dead according to Jewish ritual and was therefore allowed to possess its own cemetery, but some communities did not acquire a plot of land for burial until some time after their establishment. The Jews of Cervera and Burriana lacked a cemetery for a while, and the families of the deceased and others suffered considerably as a result.[46] Such conditions added to the expenses of a funeral, which the poor found it particularly hard to meet.

As the community did not or could not provide the resources that were needed to cover the high expenses of a funeral, a fund was established to assist bereaved poor families. The burial society emerged to administer this fund and make all the arrangements and meet part of the expenses of poor families. In Cervera, where, we may recall, there was no cemetery, the project was quite successful. The money collected was more than sufficient so that the question arose whether part of the money could be used for other purposes.[47]

The burial society was known in Hebrew sources as *havurat ha-qabarim, kat ha-qabarim*, or *hevrat ha-qabarim*, while in archival sources the name appears as

---

[43] Vidal, *Les Juifs de Roussillon*, p. 173, n. 1.

[44] See Gutwirth, 'Jewish Hospices', pp. 147–8.

[45] Sánchez, 'Cofradías'.

[46] At the end of the thirteenth century Cervera did not have its own cemetery: ACA, Reg. 91, fo. 163 [=R 2411]. The small community of Burriana also had no cemetery until 1326 and had to use the cemeteries of Valencia or Murviedro: ACA, Reg. 229, fo. 211ᵛ [=R 3409 = Jacobs 870].

[47] Adret, iii. 291.

Cabarim, Caparins, or *Albahurim del capbarim*. In Latin and the Romance languages the society was called *Cofradia de los cavafuesas, Cofraria de fodientis sepulturis, Cavadores*, and *Cofraria cohoperiendi Corpora mortua*.⁴⁸

The main task of the burial society was to bury the dead of the poor. It functioned as a charitable institution by assisting the family of the deceased to bury him without incurring too much expense. This is confirmed in practically all the Hebrew, Latin and Romance sources. The ordinances of the society in Huesca from 1323 offer clear proof of these arrangements. The poor need no longer worry about any payment; a rotation system operated so that by day and by night, every day of the week, there were members on duty. The members were expected to keep the Sabbath and attend services where the mourners were. They were also duty bound to perform religious acts and observe high moral standards. They were expected to participate in both the happy and the sad occasions of any member of the community. The same ordinances show how the members of the confraternity acted as a mutual aid society; members undertook to help one another and in the case of the death of one of their fellow members they would join the prayers and do whatever was necessary to comfort the family.⁴⁹ Members of the Perpignan society carried their deceased fellow member to his resting-place. They had a series of clauses designed to assist the mourners in their days of sorrow.⁵⁰

One element of the activities of the burial societies had nothing to do with their main task. Mention has already been made of social and religious activities that were included in their constitution. It appears that some of these were intended to fill a perceived gap. The constitution of the burial society of Huesca which was confirmed by Pedro IV in 1348 included new clauses. One of them established a programme of education for the members, whereby the society undertook to engage a rabbi to teach them the Torah in their *beth midrash*. Not only did the society have its own *beth midrash*, but it also felt the necessity to provide its members with Jewish education. It was stipulated that if at least two members of each of the eight watches joined the *muqademin*, the leaders of the fraternity, a rabbi could be hired.⁵¹

The burial society was usually run along similar lines as the *aljama*. It was headed by *muqademin* or *berurim, adelantados* or *procuratores* elected or appointed by one of the prevalent systems.⁵² They were primarily responsible for the finance of the fraternity, the collection of the contributions and the investment of its assets. They also represented the fraternity in its relations with Jewish and

---

⁴⁸ Adret, iii. 309; Asibili (Kapah) 118; ACA, Reg. 387, fos. 225–9 [= Baer, *Spanien*, doc. 179]; Reg. 917, fo. 236ᵛ [= Baer, *Spanien*, doc. 296]; Serrano, *Orígenes*, i, p. xliv, n. 1; Secall, *La comunitat*, p. 156, n. 76; Blasco, 'Instituciones sociorreligiosas', p. 31, nn. 233–4.

⁴⁹ ACA, Reg. 387, fos. 225–9 [= Baer, *Spanien*, doc. 179].

⁵⁰ Gerondi 75.

⁵¹ Baer, *Spanien*, doc. 238.

⁵² For the *ostage* system in Lérida, see Adret, iii. 330.

non-Jewish bodies. In large fraternities a council supervised the work of the *berurim*.⁵³ There exist some extant constitutions of burial societies which suggest a highly sophisticated administration and stringent membership rules. Many fraternities were closed corporations, similar to parallel Christian institutions.⁵⁴ We have no information on any joint activity or representation of the community and the fraternity. The latter invariably petitioned the king directly on any issue, evading any communal control or influence.

The fraternity had access to various sources of revenue. It received a considerable part of its income from bequests. It was well placed to convince Jews to leave it money in their will, for its members also took care of the sick.⁵⁵ The society also benefited from donations. In some communities it was customary to divide unspecified donations between the charitable institutions, apart from the burial society which usually enjoyed a better financial situation than the rest.⁵⁶ As mentioned above, the society invested the money at its disposal to provide a profit. Its treasurers could lend money on interest, sometimes causing halakhic arguments.⁵⁷ A simpler way to invest the money was to transfer it to members of the fraternity and let them use it for a fixed sum. The method did not always work smoothly.⁵⁸ Some societies owned property and received the rent as additional income.

In the larger communities there were additional fraternities that dealt with the dead or the mourners. One such was the Nos'e ha-Mitah, established in Saragossa in 1387. Its task was the laying-out for burial of the bodies of people from poor families. The fraternity also engaged a teacher to teach the orphans of the poor.⁵⁹ The wealthy did not need the society's services.

THE CRAFT ASSOCIATIONS

The Jewish trade guilds that developed in the Crown of Aragon in the thirteenth century were very similar to their Christian counterparts. The Jewish guilds were even more religious in character. Their constitutions contain practically nothing related to their trade but many religious and, particularly, social clauses. They belonged to the social rather than the economic life of the Jews; hence their inclusion in this part of the book. The professional *havurot* in the second half of the thirteenth century were established at the same time as social unrest was besetting communities in Aragon. Two aspects of the Jewish trade associations are noteworthy. First, all of them were organizations formed by craftsmen who belonged to the lower classes. Secondly, the largest number of these professional associa-

---

⁵³ Adret, iii. 330, v. 267; Serrano, *Origenes*, i, p. xlix, n. 1; ACA, Reg. 917, fo. 236ᵛ [= Baer, *Spanien*, doc. 296].
⁵⁴ For the Huesca constitution, see above. For another case, see Adret, iii. 309.
⁵⁵ Adret, v. 267; Secall, *La comunitat*, p. 156, nn. 74, 76; 246, doc. xlvii.
⁵⁶ For Perpignan see Gerondi 75.   ⁵⁷ Asibili (Kapah) 118.   ⁵⁸ Adret, iii. 308, 310.
⁵⁹ Blasco, 'Instituciones sociorreligiosas', doc. 7.

tions were concentrated in the Kingdom of Aragon, the scene of much of the social unrest that troubled the Jewish communities.

The Christian guilds in the Crown of Aragon were under royal control, and therefore the Jewish *havurot* were able to withstand pressure and antagonism from them. The Jewish guilds regulated norms of conduct among their members, and most particularly prevented uncontrolled competition. The guilds enabled their members to reduce the prices of raw materials through wholesale purchase. Most important of all, the Jewish craft associations were very successful in leading the struggle of the poorer classes in communities controlled by the rich. The Jewish guilds offered an additional semi-autonomous framework within the *aljama* for craftsmen of modest social status to conduct their social and religious life in considerably improved conditions. The guilds and their auxiliary institutions offered their members alternative frameworks to those dominated or controlled by members of the Jewish aristocracy.

The communal leaders had no reason to feel pleased by the foundation of these guilds, which seemed to threaten their monopoly and their grip on Jewish society. A clear echo of the concern and opposition that the community leaders felt as they watched the craftsmen in their community becoming organized may be found in a question addressed to R. Shelomo ben Adret. He was asked whether members of the community had the right to form an association and adopt regulations and restrictions among themselves. According to Adret such activities are lawful as long as they are agreed upon voluntarily by the members. It is the same as if 'all the tradesmen in the same town, such as the butchers, the dyers, the sailors and the like, agree on matters relating to their trade'. In his view, 'any guild whose members are of the same craft is like an autonomous city.'[60] It is clear that the communal leadership was opposed to the formation of Jewish societies and guilds within the *aljama*. It is equally obvious that the leaders could not prevent this development. Neither the king nor the *halakhah* was on their side. The treatment of the subject by Adret shows that mutual aid societies were part of Jewish life in the Crown of Aragon.

It is not surprising that the greater part of our information on this subject comes from Aragonese communities, for it was in Aragonese Jewish society that the gap between the rich and the poor became the widest. It was in Aragon that the largest group of wealthy Jews lived outside the jurisdiction of the Jewish community. The *francos* who did not pay taxes with the community, relying on the protection afforded to them by the king, did not hesitate to exploit the community for their own advantage. Many of the leaders of the communities were members of the same families. It was the realization that they could not remedy their lot through the official channels and institutions of the *qehilah* that led craftsmen to found their *havurot*. The charitable societies and Jewish guilds were part of the same process. It was once again in Saragossa that the Jewish trade guilds

---

[60] Adret, iv. 185.

paved the way for other groups to follow. Naturally, a sufficient number of Jews in the same craft were required to set up a guild, and demographic and economic conditions did not permit the establishment of guilds in every community. Only in relatively large communities can we expect one or two guilds to have emerged.

The most famous guild in Saragossa was that of the shoemakers, *confratrie helemosine judeorum sapateriorum* or *hasquafim*. Its constitution was confirmed in 1336 by Pedro IV, but its existence goes back many years. The constitution contains no clause referring to economic and professional matters; all the clauses deal with the social welfare and religious well-being of the guild's members, their periods of joy and grief, and their health and social status.[61]

The Jewish tanners of Saragossa were also organized in a guild. From a document of 1440 we learn that the guild took it upon itself to protect its members from the competition and antagonism of the Christian guilds. Christian supervisors could not enter a Jewish workshop without being accompanied by a Jewish supervisor. Fines were imposed for infringements of the rules of trade, a third of any such fine going to the Christian supervisor.[62] Another guild, whose members were tanners who cut leather, was the *cofradia de los baldreseros*. These worked fine leather and produced gloves and bags. This guild had its own synagogue and premises for social activities.[63] The Biqur Holim synagogue was known in the fifteenth century as the Sinoga de los Torneros (that is, of the turners) which seems to suggest that a turners' guild may have existed in the city.[64]

In Huesca there was a shoemakers' guild, the *confraria de los judios çapateros*, which in the fifteenth century owned two shops.[65] In Perpignan the Jewish tailors created their own guild, which maintained a hospice. There must have been enough tailors to form a guild and sufficient trade to earn a livelihood.[66] In 1381 a sum of money was left to the *confraria dels çabbaterim* in Santa Coloma de Queralt. If this is a shoemakers' guild, it is interesting that in such a small community there should have been enough shoemakers to establish a guild.[67]

THE *HAVURAH* WITHIN THE *QEHILAH*

The sources show that, despite their varied aims, the societies that were created in the Crown of Aragon were primarily part of a process that owed its origin to the

---

[61] Bofarull, 'Gremios', pp. 131–3; Blasco, 'Instituciones sociorreligiosas', doc. 2; Kayserling, 'Les Juifs à Saragosse', p. 116. For an English translation of the guild's constitution, see Wischnitzer, *A History*, pp. 278–9. [62] Serrano, *Orígenes*, i, p. lxii.

[63] Blasco, 'Instituciones sociorreligiosas', pp. 43–4, n. 333; id., *La judería de Zaragoza*, p. 165.

[64] Serrano, *Orígenes*, i, p. xliv, n. 1.

[65] Vendrell, *Rentas reales*, pp. 155–60; Lacave, 'Las juderías aragonesas', pp. 221–2.

[66] Vidal, *Les Juifs de Roussillon*, p. 173, n. 1.

[67] Secall, *La comunitat*, p. 156, n. 78. If the word *çabbaterim* means shoemakers, as indeed I think it does, then the Hebrew plural suffix to the Romance word is most interesting.

social unrest and the struggle between the different classes in Jewish society.[68] They dealt with charitable, social, economic, and medical problems as well as educational and religious matters, even though these functions may not have been mentioned in their original aims.[69] The societies were not part of communal initiatives to solve problems facing Jewish society, but the most efficient measure that individuals and groups could take to solve the problems the communal establishment did not or could not solve. The result was the emergence of a *havurah* operating autonomously on behalf of its members, for them or for any other group, within the *qehilah*.

The growth and success of the fraternities in the Jewish communities of the Aragonese realm were due to the consent of the king to allow their existence in the *judería*. Their spread and development is very proof of the needs they catered for. The key to a proper appreciation of the social programme the *havurot* intended to implement should be searched in the factors that led to the emergence of the Kat ha-Havurah of Saragossa in 1263.[70] Their impact on Jewish society was deep and lasting. The tradition of the *havurot* was brought to the eastern shores of the Mediterranean by the Sephardi refugees who settled in the Ottoman Empire.[71]

---

[68] The educational and religious or synagogal societies are covered in Part VI below.

[69] For instances, see Adret, ii. 260, iii. 435, iv. 124, 192; ACA, Reg. 387, fos. 225–9 [= Baer, *Spanien*, doc. 179].

[70] In addition to all the material scattered in this section, see Adret, iii. 294, iv. 185.

[71] Hacker, 'The Sephardim', p. 124; Barnai, 'Jewish Guilds', pp. 133–48.

§5.3 Family Life

THE Jewish family in the Crown of Aragon had much in common with the Jewish family elsewhere in the medieval world. Its foundations lay in Jewish jurisprudence and tradition, and its formal institution or dissolution was based on the laws and customs prevalent throughout the Jewish world. At the same time it was deeply influenced by local conditions and trends in Christian society. Furthermore, the geographical position of the Crown of Aragon set the Jewish family there at a junction between Franco-German Jewry and the Jews of Islam, where divergent concepts of and approaches to family life clashed and merged.

COURTSHIP

Conflicting attitudes to courtship and relations between men and women can be easily discerned. These relations were neither as austere as is implied in the idealized descriptions of the moral standards which can be found in some Hebrew sources, nor as lax as is implied in some wedding songs sung in Catalonia. R. Shelomo ben Adret's statement that in his communities 'Jewish girls are modest and do not break the fence by choosing their husbands without their fathers' consent' is certainly a sweeping generalization, as we shall see later.[1] Despite the moral and religious restrictions, young men and women were not entirely separated and individual contact led to courtship, and courtship often to marriage.

The fraudulent means frequently employed by men to force young women into marriage indicate that there were no insurmountable barriers between young men and women. Rabbis reacted strongly against men who did not hesitate to abuse the *halakhah* and adopt various improper tactics to marry the woman they desired.[2] It was sufficient for an unscrupulous and deceitful man to ask the woman to try a ring on her finger and say the wedding formula before two witnesses to trap her into a marriage she did not contemplate.[3] Many girls who did not respond to flirtations were victims of tricks that complicated their lives and delayed their marriage to the man of their choice until the issue was settled. Violent men used force and terror to gain the woman they wanted if their attempts to seduce failed.[4]

Although the norm was for a young woman to marry the man that her parents

---

[1] Adret, i. 1219. [2] Adret, i. 706, 774, 1209–10, vii. 221.
[3] Adret, vii. 58. [4] See e.g. Gerondi 62.

chose for her, not every woman agreed to marry blindfold. R. Shelomo ben Adret admitted that some young women insisted on their right to choose their own husband and, in fact, supported the woman's right to do so if she had reached an appropriate age.⁵ In the case of a childless widow who disliked her brother-in-law, Adret was of the opinion that the levirate marriage should take place, if the man refused to perform *halizah*.⁶

Once the two individuals had agreed to get married, the relations between the couple were often relaxed. This permissive attitude was criticized by rabbis, who were displeased that young couples were left alone. They were not mistaken that such intimacy led to pre-marital intercourse.⁷

BETROTHAL

The formal agreement on the marriage took place in public before an invited audience. First, the final terms of the marriage were negotiated and agreed upon. Then the ceremony took place in the presence of the *hazan* in the synagogue: the bride-to-be was seated in a special chair and the *qinyan* ceremony was performed, which consisted of a symbolic act of holding and raising an article; this was a semi-binding engagement.⁸ When the two components, the *irusin* or betrothal and *nisu'in* or marriage, were separated, the betrothal benedictions were followed by a party.⁹ This party was a festive meal attended by many guests, relatives, and friends.¹⁰ The wedding ceremony was sometimes performed in two stages. It was customary for the bridegroom to offer a ring to his bride, after which the bride would sit next to him at the party.¹¹

MARRIAGE

The marriage of their children was the goal of Jewish parents, who were usually fully involved in the choice of a spouse for their child. Numerous Hebrew sources indicate that the father was most active in arranging his daughter's marriage.¹² If the father was unavailable or dead, the grandfather or the mother negotiated the marriage.¹³ At times even the king or the infante was asked to support the efforts of a mother to bestow her daughter's hand.¹⁴ The girls, particularly, were expected to respect the choice of their parents, although the *halakhah* permits a girl who has attained her majority to refuse a husband chosen for her by her

---

⁵ Adret, iii. 211.   ⁶ Adret, vii. 421.
⁷ Adret, viii. 135.   ⁸ Adret, i. 1180.
⁹ Adret, i. 808.   ¹⁰ Adret, iv. 205.   ¹¹ Adret, iii. 283, i. 1189.
¹² A few sources will suffice: Adret, i. 550, 789, iii. 96, iv. 157, v. 237, vi. 1 and *passim*.
¹³ For matchmaking grandfathers, see Adret, i. 771, vii. 121, 502. For a widow see Adret, vi. 279.
¹⁴ ACA, Reg. 89, fo. 60ᵛ [= R 2567 = Isaacs 73].

father. Many girls did exercise their right upon attaining their legal majority and refused to be married to men they did not like.[15]

At the community's request, the king sometimes interfered in matters concerning marriage. Influential Jews, for instance, tried to overcome opposition to a marriage by seeking his support. Opponents of such royal intervention were often threatened and punished.[16] For the king, his intervention on behalf of an influential Jew often meant some sort of profit. A forbidden marriage, which was valid *post factum* according to *halakhah*, was nevertheless an occasion for the Crown to extort an exorbitant fine.[17]

The institution of marriage was considered the only framework in which man and woman could live together. Despite occasional deviations from the norm, the family remained the only legitimate form of relationship sanctioned by Jewish law and the halakhic authorities. The relatively tolerant attitude towards concubinage by some must be considered a concession in a situation which they thought to be almost uncontrollable. Concubinage was the lesser of two evils. Extra-marital intercourse, which was forbidden by *halakhah*, was widespread, and rabbinic and communal leaders resorted to various punitive devices in their attempt to extirpate this behaviour. They were assisted by the king, who was prepared to punish transgressors.[18]

In Hebrew sources great emphasis was put on the need for the respectful treatment of wives. In case of a bigamous marriage, the husband was reminded of his marital duties and sexual obligations towards the less favoured wife: even though the husband chose to have his permanent residence with one of the wives, he had to visit the other regularly. Even if no second wife was involved, husbands who, for one reason or another, had to stay away from home frequently, were obliged to eat and spend the night with their wives on the Sabbath.[19] The rabbis insisted that considerate behaviour increased understanding and love between the spouses. Adret was of the opinion that the husband should never force his wife to do housework which she had not been used to doing while single. But a wife, he said, must do those types of work which would increase marital love, even if the financial situation permitted the wife to engage in no chores whatsoever.[20]

Most women married at a young age and it seems that this was the cause for the inability of some to cope with certain types of housework.[21] Since many sources, among them those quoted above, refer to the refusal of the girl to marry the fiancé selected by her parents, the age of betrothal was obviously below twelve. Girls were betrothed at the age of nine and less, and in one instance, even a baby was promised to a man.[22] As the marriage age of young women tended to decrease rabbis voiced their criticism of the practice. Sometimes the age difference was very wide, and as the young wife grew older relations between the couple

[15] Adret, iv. 324, vii. 502.
[16] ACA, Reg. 15, fo. 33ʳ [= R 352].
[17] ACA, Reg. 225, fo. 287ʳ [= R 3302].
[18] ACA, Reg. 216, fo. 55ʳ [= R 3091].
[19] Adret, viii. 104.
[20] Adret, iv. 169.
[21] Ibid.
[22] Adret, i. 1109, iv. 246.

deteriorated. As it was her parents who had decided to marry her to a much older man, the young wife expressed her disapproval or disgust as soon as she could—sometimes very soon after the wedding.²³

In view of this practice, it is not surprising to find that there were relatively many young widows in Jewish society. Some were burdened with raising the children alone and faced the difficulty of remarrying with small children to take care of. The young widow of a man who made his wife promise not to remarry until their son and daughter grew up was the subject of legal correspondence between scholars. It was feared that preventing the beautiful young widow to marry could lead her to engage in extra-marital relations.²⁴

As in other fields, the sources relating to marital relations tend to be misleading, since in most cases they report only problems. There are no historical records that treat love, harmony, and companionship between spouses, while some of the difficulties in Jewish families were very likely to come up in courts and provide matter for correspondence between legal experts, judges, communal leaders, and the royal court. Rabbis had to deal with problems of the most intimate nature and with spouses who refused to fulfil their conjugal duties.²⁵ They had to offer solutions to delicate problems revolving around the sexual life of the couple. In one case, the halakhic expert had to give his opinion about a woman who refrained from going to the *miqve* in order to prolong sexual abstinence beyond the ritual limits, and her husband who threatened to abstain from intercourse for ever and even divorce her if she did not immerse the first day she was halakhically allowed to do so.²⁶ There were also cases of coercive sexual relations which were brought to the attention of the halakhic experts.²⁷

The sexual tastes and practices of Jewish couples were also among the subjects discussed in the responsa. The husband who objected to his wife's efforts to become pregnant, claiming that it would deform her beautiful body, or the wife who claimed that her husband's sexual practices were the result of his impotence, and other similar matters came to be known only because they eventually led the couples concerned to the law courts. At this distance of time it is difficult to determine their historical significance.²⁸

No incidents of wife-beating have been recorded in the Crown of Aragon. We do, however, know of cases of husbands deserting their wives and children and abandoning their family because the wife did not want to leave.²⁹ The local *beth din* or the leading rabbinic authority in the district were usually the most efficient protectors of maltreated wives.³⁰ When the problem between husband and wife came to the *beth din*, it meant that their relationship had become almost irretrievable. These marriages most probably failed. In a lawsuit, the litigant wife

²³ Adret, i. 572.   ²⁴ Asibili (Kapah) 43.
²⁵ Adret, ii. 244, viii. 270; Gerondi 13.   ²⁶ Adret, i. 854.
²⁷ Gerondi 62. On the subject in general, see Rakover. 'Coercive Marital Relations'.
²⁸ Adret, iv. 122, i. 628.   ²⁹ Adret, v. 204, viii. 146, 267.
³⁰ See e.g. Gerondi 43.

was usually supported by her father. Some suits unresolved in the *beth din* were finally referred to the king's court.[31]

Jews who were dissatisfied with the marriage of a relative turned to the *beth din* with their complaints and claims. In some instances, the king was asked to intervene. Even though the king's decision in marital matters was much influenced by financial considerations, he insisted on the observance of the halakhah or *açuna*.[32] On the whole, the king's approach was favourable to *halakhah* and to the authority of the community and the parents. His officials were instructed to open legal proceedings against those who were implicated in the marriage of a woman against the will of her parents. In the case of an orphan bride, the king insisted that the consent of the majority of her relatives was necessary for her marriage.[33] The king often protected those who fell in the way of violent Jews who behaved as if they could have any woman they desired. There were Jews who raped and took women by force. The king's attitude, however, would be immensely softened when he received money. In some cases, the silence of Jews was achieved through bribes or threats.[34]

THE WEDDING CEREMONY AND PARTY

In many Jewish communities a wedding had to take place in the synagogue in front of at least ten people and had to be conducted by the *hazan*. In many communities, too, the parents of the bride had to be present at the wedding ceremony.[35] This ordinance was meant to put an end to irregularities in weddings and claims of marriage in private that could prevent a young woman from marrying. As well as conducting the wedding ceremony and reading the benedictions, the *hazan* also read the *ketubah*. This was read in Aramaic, which was not understood by everyone.[36] Weddings took place on any day permitted by Jewish law, except for widows, who were usually married at the end of the week.[37]

The wedding ceremony and the party that followed interested the king for a variety of reasons. In the first place, the party reflected the wealth of the family and could help the king's officials to check whether there was any disparity between the amount of tax the family paid and its standard of living. Secondly, as practically all the members of a small community were usually invited to the party, participation at wedding parties was one of the ways used to determine whether a Jew had really emigrated or settled.[38]

---

[31] ACA, CR, Jaime II, C 134, no. 198.
[32] ACA, Reg. 75, fo. 12 [= R 1743]; Reg. 80, fo. 77ʻ [= R 2022].
[33] ACA, CR, Jaime II, C 133, no. 82.
[34] ACA, Reg. 89, fo. 48 [= R 2558]; Reg. 199, fo. 34ʻ [= R 2770].
[35] Adret, i. 550, 1167, iv. 314.   [36] Adret, i. 629.   [37] Adret, iii. 210.
[38] ACA, Reg. 203, fos. 31ʻ–32 [= R 2841 = Jacobs 751]. Fictive emigration was frequently resorted to in order to avoid tax payment.

At the party songs were sung, poems were read, and even gambling took place. In most communities there were *piyutim* that were sung to traditional tunes. The verses, with some variations, were known by most participants, who joined in the singing.[39] Sometimes special songs and poems were composed for the occasion and were meant to cheer the bride and groom. Some contained sexual allusions and were almost pornographic.[40] Gambling during the party was strictly forbidden in some cities. In 1295 in Perpignan gambling in wedding parties was forbidden unless a special permit was issued. Such permits cost a lot of money.[41]

It was customary to hold special dinner parties in honour of the bride and bridegroom during the week following the wedding.[42] Some couples, who were relatives or friends, shared the same party.[43]

THE DOWRY AND THE *KETUBAH*

The *ketubah* in the Aragonese realm contained all the elements prescribed by Jewish law. Very often the financial conditions of the *ketubah* were also included in a notarial protocol. Despite all the legal arrangements, however, disputes over finance between spouses were frequent. Promises of a dowry or gifts that were not fulfilled by one side or the other, for example, would bring the couple to court.

The amount of the dowry or *nedunia* that the wife's family gave the husband depended on the economic position of the bride's family. Whether small or large, in almost every marriage there was a dowry. The dowries among the richer class in Jewish society were often very substantial, and even middle-class Jews supported their daughters very handsomely. One father gave as a dowry to his daughter one of the two houses he owned,[44] while a dowry of 1,000 s was quite frequent.[45] From the sources we know that some brides brought valuable property with them to their newly established family. As a rule, all assets brought with the wife remained hers in case of divorce or widowhood.[46] The fate of the dowry if the wife died depended on the terms agreed upon in the *ketubah*.[47]

Differences between the two sides or families in cases of divorce or death were frequent. Some were solved by the *beth din* or through Jewish arbitration, but many such lawsuits were tried in Christian courts.[48] Some of the lawsuits that were brought to the attention of the king were between father and son-in-law. The father-in-law most frequently complained that the son-in-law did not provide his daughter with the the food and clothes that were prescribed in the *ketubah* and that he neglected her rights. The husband usually demanded that money promised to him before the marriage be paid. The involvement of the king or the Gentile courts created many problems, but marital disputes continued to be raised

---

[39] Adret, i. 469, vii. 386.
[40] See e.g. Lazar, 'Catalan-Provençal Wedding Songs'.
[41] Vidal, *Les Juifs de Roussillon*, p. 47.
[42] Adret, i. 216.
[43] Adret, i. 451.
[44] Adret, iii. 168.
[45] Adret, ii. 149, iii. 410, v. 83.
[46] Adret, ii. 62.
[47] Adret, v. 76. For Castile, see Asher, ll. 6–10.
[48] Adret, vi. 4, 254.

outside the *aljama* after one of the parties had failed to find a satisfactory solution at the *beth din* or in the community in general.[49] Disputes between husband and wife had various implications. The husband was generally suspected of planning to leave his wife without making provision for her rights, above all her *ketubah* and other monetary rights. Jews turned to the king for help to force their sons-in-law to settle the matter before the *beth din*. Usually the king gave instructions to prevent the husband from leaving town without appearing in court.[50]

There were disputes between the two sides even before the wedding which often led to royal intervention and application to Gentile courts. In 1290 Juceff Avenaçfora wrote to Alfonso III to inform him that, on the occasion of his forthcoming marriage to the daughter of Assach Abnelfalir, his brother Jahuda had handed promissory notes to Mosse Alcotanti, the rabbi of Calatayud. The rabbi did not hold the wedding. The king ordered the rabbi to return the promissory notes and the girl's family to return all the gifts that Jahuda had given to his fiancée.[51] Most couples in whose matrimonial financial disputes the king was asked to intervene belonged to the upper class. These were the Jews who could be in touch with the king and the infantes, who needed them in various financial roles. Nor was the king an entirely disinterested party in the financial arrangements of a Jewish couple. The king also had an interest in dowries and gifts promised by Jews who lived outside the Crown of Aragon, especially since the dowries among the rich were quite substantial. A dowry of 6,000 s of Narbonne or Barcelona did not escape the attention of the king. That alone was enough for the king to encourage marriages between Jews from his realm and Provençal Jews which, in any case, became rather frequent.[52]

BIGAMOUS MARRIAGES

In medieval Spain, where bigamy was not forbidden to the Jews, there are records of bigamous marriages in various regions and periods. In the Crown of Aragon, and particularly in Catalonia, the region nearest to Franco-Germany and most open to northern influences, while bigamy was never completely prohibited, there were attempts to introduce a ban by R. Gershom. As bigamy in general was

---

[49] ACA, CR, Jaime II, C 133, no. 104 [= *Cartas Reales*, no. 328]. The Infante Alfonso's letter of 1325, which was sent at the request of Salomo Mercadell of Villafranca, was an order to the baile of the town to execute the sentence in a lawsuit between the abovementioned Salomo and his son-in-law Astruc Salomo concerning his wife Blanca's alimony. In connection with a similar trial in 1285, Don Alfonso required the judge to take the case of a father and daughter against the latter's husband: ACA, Reg. 62, fo. 136 [= R 1317]. On unfulfilled financial promises see ACA, Reg. 44, fo. 226 [= R 906]; Reg. 88, fo. 259ᵛ [= R 2533]. On disputes between a father of a deceased childless daughter and her husband, see ACA, CR, Jaime II, C 133. no. 80.

[50] ACA, Reg. 91, fo. 113 [= R 2400].
[51] ACA, Reg. 81, fo. 67ᵛ [= R 2084].
[52] ACA, CR, Jaime II, C 133, no. 80; Reg. 196, fo. 151 [= R 2687].

prohibited in the Aragonese realm, the Jew who wanted to marry a second wife while keeping his first needed the king's permission. It was repeatedly stated that such permission was based on *halakhah*.[53]

Until the last decade of the thirteenth century bigamy was hardly mentioned in documents emanating from the royal chancellery. Until then, there were only three applications to the king to allow bigamous marriages. In all three instances, both Jaime I and Alfonso III emphasized that their permission was based on the legality of bigamy in Jewish law. In 1259 Jaime I permitted Jucef de Grasse from Montpellier to marry a second woman, even if he did not divorce the first, although the local Jews claimed that such a marriage was forbidden according to Jewish tradition. The king demanded that the rights of the first wife be guaranteed in accordance with the conditions of her *ketubah*, but also warned the Jews of Montpellier against pronouncing a ban on the bigamist.[54]

This case is important in so far as it sheds light on the king's attitude. Otherwise, the Jews of Montpellier who objected to the bigamous marriage were in no way representative of Iberian Jewry. It is very likely that the king's decision was influenced by the attitude of the Catalan rabbis, who differed from their Provençal colleagues who had been exposed earlier to Franco-German influence. In his answer to a scholar of Castellón de Ampurias about the 'Ban of Rabbenu Gershom', R. Shelomo ben Adret admitted that he had no information about the validity and the extent of the ban which, in any case, did not apply to Spain.[55]

In this case, Jaime I chose to treat the Jews of Montpellier in the same way as the Jews of his central territories, where bigamy was permitted. In another instance, eight years later, the king permitted Belshom son of Bonanash from Besalú, the son of a second wife, to inherit his father's property. The permission was granted because, it was claimed, 'according to the Law of the Jews, it is permitted for a Jew to marry simultaneously many wives' and 'the children born to these women and this man are legitimate.'[56] It is clear that in the Crown of Aragon in the thirteenth century Jewish men were allowed to marry more than one wife, as confirmed by Hebrew sources, and that, according to *halakhah*, the children of such marriages were legitimate. It follows that permission was needed because of the law of the realm which forbade bigamy and considered the offspring of these marriages illegitimate. A 'certificate of legitimacy' for an heir who was the son of a second wife was apparently needed to counteract any challenge to his rights in Gentile or Jewish courts. In the Crown of Aragon the Jews were allowed to marry more than one wife in accordance with Jewish law but despite the law of the realm prohibiting the practice for the general population.

The concern of the Crown to uphold the *halakhah* is evident also in the decision of Alfonso III to confirm in 1278 the permission granted by one of his

---

[53] On bigamy in general, see Assis, 'The "Ordinance of Rabbenu Gershom"'.
[54] ACA, Reg. 10, fo. 47ᵛ [= Jacobs 148 = R 113 = Bofarull, Barcelona, xviii].
[55] Adret, iii. 446.   [56] ACA, Reg. 15, fo. 64ᵛ [= R 359 = Bofarull, Barcelona, lxxii].

senior officials to Isach Vives from Barcelona to cancel his marriage to his first wife, who bore him no children, and marry another. The king's confirmation was given, the letter says, to enable Isach to have a child, after the consent of the first wife was obtained and on condition that Jewish law permitted it.[57]

The increase in the number of applicants for permission to undertake second marriages at the beginning of the fourteenth century was due to changes in Jewish society rather than to a change in royal policy. The influence of Franco-German Jewry on the Jews of Spain in general and on those of the Crown of Aragon in particular reached its peak at the turn of the century. Elements of religious and cultural tradition passed from north to south via Provence. The relations of the Jews of Catalonia and Provence became very close and the interchange of views between the two communities became very intense. Students crossed the Pyrenees in both directions. Another channel for the penetration of Ashkenazi influence into Spain was more direct. Scholars from Catalonia studied in French academies, while French and German scholars came to the Iberian peninsula both as visitors and as settlers. Finally, after the 1306 expulsion, Jewish refugees from France settled in the Crown of Aragon.[58]

The French influence on Catalan scholars brought about a change in the attitude of the latter towards bigamy. R. Shelomo ben Adret was the foremost halakhist in Catalonia who came under the sway of Ashkenazi influence. There is evidence that the different positions adopted by Adret on the validity of the ban of R. Gershom reflect the various stages of his acquaintance with Franco-German traditions.[59] Although the attempts to impose an anti-bigamy ban failed, the very campaign for monogamy created a serious obstacle for those who wished to marry a second wife. We can easily understand that the need for royal permission became more urgent as it was the most efficient way to overcome the opposition of scholars and communities to bigamy. Parents who wanted to ensure that their daughter should remain the sole wife of her husband, and some adult women on their own account, insisted on inserting a clause in the *ketubah* forbidding the husband to marry a second wife in her lifetime.[60]

Throughout the fourteenth century, the reasons that led Jews who wanted to contract a bigamous marriage to seek royal permission remained valid. Bigamy never became automatically possible. Even after the king's permission was granted, pressure was exerted on the bigamist. The king's officials were

[57] ACA, Reg. 74, fo. 81 [= R 1892]. Jewish law in any case permits divorce, and certainly the divorce of a wife who has borne no children after ten years. We have to admit that the need for royal permission was due to the law of the realm that prohibited this process and to the wish of the applicant to prevent any future pressure or claims. On the prohibition of divorce in the realm see Adret, viii. 133.

[58] A detailed discussion is found in Part VI, Religious Life. On the relations between the Jews of Spain and Provence, see Twersky, 'Aspects'; Romano, 'La Transmission'; Assis, 'Les Juifs de Montpellier'. On the French refugees, see Assis, 'Juifs de France'.

[59] Assis, 'The "Ordinance of Rabbenu Gershom"', pp. 259–61.

[60] See e.g. Adret, i. 812, iv. 267.

sometimes warned not to prevent permit-holders from marrying a second wife. Permits were granted throughout the fourteenth century but under no circumstances were Jews from the Crown of Aragon allowed to marry a second wife in Muslim lands. The practice of marrying a second wife in another city or country was strongly opposed, as its grave halakhic consequences are obvious. Whatever his motives, the king's opposition to this practice greatly facilitated the community's struggle against it.[61]

As applications for permission to remarry became more frequent under Jaime II, the king became fully aware of the halakhic authorization of bigamy and, although the permits were always issued explicitly on the basis of the *halakhah*, consultation with a Jewish jurist was no longer considered necessary. Sometimes it was sufficient that the applicant declared the legality of bigamy.[62] Among the bigamists were some of French or Provençal origin who settled in the Crown of Aragon.[63] The king's permission did not always prove to have permanent effect, and the influence of those opposed to bigamy can be seen in those cases where the king cancelled the permission.[64]

Despite attempts to eradicate it, bigamy continued in the Crown of Aragon as evidenced by the permission granted to R. Hasdai Cresques (Crescas) in May 1393 to marry a second wife in accordance with Jewish law.[65]

ILLEGAL MARRIAGES AND INCESTUOUS RELATIONS

Marriages forbidden by Jewish law are divided into two categories which differ in both gravity and legal status. There are those that are forbidden *a principio* but are valid once consummated, and others that are forbidden under any circumstances and are null in any case. The marriage of a *cohen* to a divorced or converted woman falls into the first category. In such cases the rabbis expressed their anger and put pressure on the couple to divorce. Their success was limited. There were several measures that were taken against the husband, but the marriage could not be annulled. The husband was not called up to the *sefer* as a *cohen*, but that was merely a protest with little effect. The children of such a marriage were not accepted as *cohanim*.[66]

---

[61] ACA, Reg. 222, fo. 142ᵛ [=R 3243 = *CDIA*, vi, pp. 240–1]; Reg. 223, fo. 182ᵛ [=R 3253]; Reg. 226, fo. 43ᵛ [=R 3308]; Reg. 227, fo. 274 [=R 3355]; Martínez, *Indice cronológico*, 475. On taking a second wife in a Muslim land, see ACA, Reg. 223, fo. 260ᵛ [=R 3262].

[62] ACA, Reg. 216, fo. 114 [=R 3102]; Reg. 218, fo. 29 [=R 3129]; Reg. 223, fo. 169ᵛ [=R 3249]; Reg. 226, fo. 43ᵛ [=R 3306].

[63] See e.g. ACA, Reg. 218, fo. 29 [=R 3129]. See also the case of Jucef de Grasse from Montpellier, noted above.

[64] See e.g. the letter of Don Pedro to his father the king in 1327: ACA, CR, Jaime II, C 134, no. 211. In the letter the infante asked the king not to cancel the permission he had already granted to Astrug Isach from Besalú to marry a second wife.

[65] ACA, Reg. 1906, fo. 125 [= Baer, *Spanien*, doc. 452].

[66] Adret, vii. 21. In Castile, on the other hand, some communities found ways to abrogate legally

The second category includes incestuous relations as defined by Jewish law. These relations were absolutely forbidden and were not recognized by Jewish law in any shape or form. Jews suspected of incest were prosecuted by the Jewish judiciary.[67] The king was sometimes involved in such cases, from which he made a financial profit. In 1310 Jaime II granted an amnesty from a very heavy fine to a Jew from Tortosa who was accused of many crimes, including sexual relations with his daughter-in-law.[68]

CONCUBINES

For a Jewish man in Spain there was an alternative to bigamy: he could have a concubine. Concubinage among the Jews was introduced under the influence of Islam. From Muslim Spain concubinage passed to, or was taken over by, Jews in the Hispanic kingdoms, including the Crown of Aragon.[69] In Spain the custom spread and aroused bitter rabbinic criticism. Had the Jews kept only Jewish concubines, we could have assumed that it was seen as a more convenient alternative to bigamy, but Jews in Christian Spain kept Muslim concubines while in the Muslim south they had Christian ones. The concubine was a woman known to belong to one person with whom she had a fairly permanent relationship.[70]

In the Crown of Aragon, where all Gentile concubines of Jews were Muslim, the number of Jews indulging in this sexual liberty was small compared to Castile. The status of the Muslim concubine varied. Many of the concubines were servants with whom their Jewish masters had sexual relations which developed into a permanent relationship. The concubine would remain both Muslim and servant. The status of the offspring presented a problem. In most cases the Jew was already married with children.[71] A widower sometimes lived openly with a Muslim concubine and, generally, made no attempt to convert her.[72]

From the correspondence of Nahmanides with R. Jonah Gerondi we may assume that concubinage was not uncommon among the Jews in the Crown of Aragon.[73] Since the Jews in the Aragonese realm were engaged in the slave trade in Muslims it was not difficult for Jews to own Muslim servants as concubines.[74]

---

contracted marriages to allow abandoned wives (*'agunot*) to remarry. See Toledano, 'Conditional Marriage', pp. 211–14.

[67] Adret, v. 239.
[68] ACA, Reg. 207, fo. 154 [= R 2915].
[69] On concubinage among Jews in Islamic lands, see Goitein, 'Slaves and Slavegirls'; Stober, 'On Two Questions'.
[70] A concise description of the institution is found in Assis, 'Sexual Behaviour', pp. 36–40.
[71] Adret, i. 1205; Havlin, 'The Taqqanot of Rabbenu Gershon', pp. 237–8, no. v. On the children of concubines see Adret, i. 1183.
[72] Adret, i. 26.
[73] Adret, viii. 284.
[74] Assis, *The Jews of Santa Coloma*, docs. xi, xix; R, index, s.v. 'slave ownership'; Assaf, 'Slavery and the Slave-trade'.

In 1285 Abraham de Torre from Figueras was accused of having killed two babies born to him by a Muslim. He had at home a Muslim concubine who bore him several children.[75] Rabbis were preoccupied with the children of the concubines, who were not halakhically Jewish, and the humiliation suffered by the wives. The insult inflicted on the wife, whose dignity was undermined, angered rabbis and other members of the community.[76]

Some Jews who wanted to define and protect the status of their concubines' children converted their mother, sometimes as soon as she became pregnant. Even after the conversion the status of the children was not entirely unchallenged. Thus a Jew from Huesca who converted his concubine did not succeed in clarifying the status of his children to the local *beth din*.[77] Other Jews in Castile and the Crown of Aragon married their converted concubines but did not give them a *ketubah*.[78]

The surprisingly tolerant attitude of Nahmanides towards concubinage must be understood in the context of the norms and mores prevalent in Spain at the time. Nahmanides thought that a prohibition might have driven men to find sexual satisfaction with many women outside the community. He considered a relationship with one woman who would be exclusively his more tolerable. This view was strongly opposed by his cousin R. Jonah Gerondi.[79]

In fourteenth-century Catalonia, as elsewhere in the Aragonese realm, there were still Jews who had Jewish concubines. These men were publicly and legally recognized as the fathers of the children born to the women known to be theirs. R. Nissim Gerondi followed Nahmanides' view on the subject. R. Isaac ben Sheshet Perfet also considered a woman who lived with a man on a permanent basis to be like his wife in many respects.[80] This rabbinic sanction does not mean that all opposition to concubinage was eliminated. In 1318 a Jew from Lérida who had lasting relations with a woman who bore him a daughter was criticized for living with a woman contrary to the *çuna*.[81] Jewish concubines, however, caused fewer halakhic problems than Muslim concubines, and a bond between a Jew and a Jewess that was not a casual connection was sanctioned by rabbinic authorities.

There were several possible reasons for concubinage in Jewish communities in the Crown of Aragon. For some men, particularly men who were already married, it was convenient to enjoy a lasting relationship and raise a family, very probably a second and younger one, without the formal and financial commitment of a marriage. This form of union produced less tension with the existing wife and reduced the opposition of grown-up children, whose inheritance was less threatened.

[75] ACA, Reg. 62, fos. 136ʳ–137 [=R 1316 and doc. xv, pp. 428–30].
[76] Adret, i. 1205.
[77] ACA, Reg. 67, fo. 1 [=R 1543]. See also n. 58 above.
[78] See e.g. Adret, v. 242.
[79] Adret, viii. 284; Gerondi, *Sha'are Teshuvah*, ch. 43, pp. 94, 131–3.
[80] Gerondi 68; Perfet 217, cf. 351.
[81] ACA, Reg. 216, fo. 55ᵛ [=R 3091].

There were also social factors which promoted concubinage. Many concubines were former maids in the man's household, and marriage with them would not normally be contemplated. The woman belonged to a lower class and was not considered a good candidate for a bride. Coming from a poor family, she was less likely to object to her status of concubine. In a way, she and her family viewed her new status as a concubine of her rich former master as a social promotion. In some cases, however, the man married the maid as soon as she became pregnant. Even in these cases the behaviour was severely condemned by the rabbis; Adret described such conduct as immoral and considered the treatment of a young woman as a harlot intolerable.[82] In another case the maid was left pregnant by her married employer who supported her after delivery but would not pay for the circumcision of the child.[83] In some cases, it was the adult son in the family who seduced the attractive maid, often a Muslim. When the seduced maid was Jewish problems arose if she became pregnant: some parents refused to accept their maid as a daughter-in-law. In one such case the son did not marry the maid, but established and furnished a home for her, and continued to support her as his concubine.[84]

Concubinage among Jews in the Aragonese realm was the outcome of a strong non-Jewish social influence and a wide social polarization in Jewish society. What started as an imitation of standards in non-Jewish society developed as the norm of a rich and spoilt upper class whose members could not permit themselves to marry poor Jewish girls but were unwilling to abstain from enjoying the beauty and attraction they found among the young women of the poorer class.

THE CROWN AND JEWISH DOCUMENTS

Jewish family life and the laws and norms that governed it have been considered the cornerstone of Jewish existence throughout the ages. Their immunity from extraneous influence was a prerequisite of Jewish autonomy. Hence the interference of the king in the affairs of the Jewish family and in matters pertaining to marital status and disputes deserves our attention.

The validity of matrimonial laws and customs seemed to be enhanced in the eyes of the Jewish public when they were approved by the king, although the very need for such approval indicates a basic weakness in the Jewish system. The kings of Aragon accepted the validity of all Jewish documents of marriage and divorce. A notarial validation was sometimes considered advantageous. The decision of the Infante Pedro in 1271 to permit the Jews of Gerona and Besalú to continue to adhere to the traditional form of the *ketubah* with its Latin or Romance validation by the notary reflects the status of Jewish matrimonial law. The financial arrangements of the marriage as stipulated in the *ketubah*, the *donatio propter nupcias* (that is, the wedding gift by the groom), and the amount that was due to the

[82] Adret, iv. 314. [83] Adret, i. 610. [84] Gerondi 68.

relatives of a bride who died childless were all included in both the Jewish and the notarial document.[85]

The dependence of Jewish law on royal support is noteworthy. The view that it was sufficient for the parties to agree in principle that their marriage or divorce be governed by the *halakhah* does not seem to hold. The financial implications may be the primary reason for the need of notarial validation. In these circumstances Jewish law and the Jewish court alone were obviously not enough. The application of all the clauses of the Jewish document was far more efficient if the royal authorities stood behind it, which they usually did. The king's policy was important, as it insured that the stipulations of the Jewish document were respected in Christian courts. That Pedro III adhered to this policy is well illustrated in his instructions of 1285 to his officials in the Kingdom of Valencia to respect the rights of women to their *ketubah* and other financial benefits guaranteed under Jewish law when legal proceedings were opened against their husbands.[86] This attitude did not, however, prevent the king from interfering in disputes between husband and wife, or between father-in-law and groom.

THE CROWN AND JEWISH MATRIMONIAL LAW

Naturally, in matters of marital status differences between husband and wife were settled according to Jewish law. Even in financial disputes that were brought to his attention, the king asked that they be settled according to *açuna* or *halakhah*.[87] The king referred some cases to halakhic experts, while in other instances he ordered the Christian judge to consult rabbis and settle the case according to *halakhah*.[88] At times, the king ordered the case to be tried before a *beth din* or ordered the nomination of Jewish jurists to settle monetary disputes between members of the family. In 1322, at the request of Jucef Hasdai from Gerona, Jaime II ordered the baile of Montblanch to appoint two experts in Jewish law to settle the case of the petitioner and his son-in-law concerning the dowry and clothing of the young woman.[89]

The woman's alimony was very often a bone of contention between the couple. The woman was invariably supported by her father. The local *beth din* was not always successful in applying the verdict or even in bringing the two sides to trial, especially when the couple came from different communities. The result

---

[85] ACA, Reg. 37, fo. 26ᵛ [= R 487].

[86] ACA, Reg. 57, fo. 223 [= R 1461 = MF ii. 2302]. See also Alfonso III's decision in 1289 to leave intact the rights of a Jewess to her *ketubah*: ACA, Reg. 78, fo. 43ᵛ [= R 1940].

[87] ACA, Reg. 44, fo. 226 [= R 906].

[88] In 1291 the infante ordered the baile of Lérida, acting as a judge in a matrimonial lawsuit, to consult halakhic experts concerning the dowry of Goig, wife of Juceff Açanna: ACA, Reg. 85, fo. 217 [= R 2377].   [89] ACA, CR, Jaime II, C 133, no. 26.

was that one side turned to the king or to a Gentile court.⁹⁰ The party that was not interested in a halakhic verdict would naturally turn to the Christian judiciary. The case of Abraham de Tolosa illustrates the problem. Contrary to a Hebrew document which he signed with his mother, Abraham refused to pay alimony to Bonafilia. In 1285 Pedro III ordered the baile of Barcelona to investigate the case and settle it in consultation with R. Aharon Ha-Levi de Na Clara.⁹¹ Similarly, Jaime II instructed the baile to appoint *dayanim* to hear the lawsuit filed by Abamari Adret and his daughter Blanca against the husband Abraham Sento de Forn and his father concerning Blanca's dowry and alimony.⁹²

The frequent consultations with rabbis prove the concern of the king that his intervention in marital disputes of Jews should not harm the law and tradition on which the existence of the Jewish community depended. Nevertheless, there were inconsistencies and deviations. There were decisions of the king or the infante that did not support the application of Jewish law in matrimonial lawsuits.⁹³ These deviations, however, confirm the rule. The kings of Aragon showed a remarkable consistency in their support of Jewish law as expounded by the scholars of their realm. In 1289 Alfonso III wrote to the two prominent halakhic leaders in Catalonia at the time, R. Shelomo ben Adret and R. Aharon Ha-Levi de Na Clara from Barcelona, informing them about the trial between a husband and wife (and the latter's father). The two rabbis were asked to pronounce their verdict in accordance with the *çuna* and the custom of the Jews.⁹⁴ Ten days later, the king informed the baile of Lérida about a lawsuit between two families whose children planned to marry and about some relevant Hebrew documents. The most important element of Alfonso's letter was his demand that the case be tried according to Jewish law and by Jewish judges. The baile was therefore to appoint a suitable judge or arbitrator, acceptable to the two sides.⁹⁵

The king's support of the *halakhah* in matrimonial cases does not mean that he always refrained from interfering in the judicial process. This intervention, which exposed the weakness of the Jewish community, was also responsible for the application of Jewish law and the verdict of the Jewish court. There are abundant sources that confirm this. In one instance the king would require the *dayanim* to adjudicate in one matrimonial case according to the Torah, while in another he would order the baile to appoint a *beth din* that would pronounce judgement in the case of a husband who refused to grant a *get* to his wife.⁹⁶

⁹⁰ On this problem see Assis, 'The Jews of Spain in Gentile Courts'.
⁹¹ ACA, Reg. 56, fo. 59 [= R 1333].
⁹² ACA, CR, Jaime II, C 134, no. 198 [= *Cartas Reales*, no. 408].
⁹³ ACA, CR, Jaime II, C 133, no. 104 [= *Cartas Reales*, no. 328].
⁹⁴ ACA, Reg. 80, fo. 77ᵛ [= R 2022]. Régné's reading does not even allow us to identify the two rabbis.
⁹⁵ ACA, Reg. 80, fo. 95ᵛ [= R 2030].
⁹⁶ ACA, Reg. 43, fo. 58 [= R 1229]; Reg. 63, fo. 83ᵛ [= R 1498].

EXTRA-MARITAL RELATIONS

Although sexual relations between consenting adults, provided the woman was unmarried, were not punishable in Jewish law, the rabbis left no doubt about their disapproval and condemnation of these relations as immoral. R. Jonah Gerondi was the most outspoken critic of extra-marital sex. He believed that such sexual relations were the symptoms of a degenerate society and he fought for the eradication of this behaviour.[97]

Despite this opposition, sexual relations outside marriage were prevalent among Jews in the Crown of Aragon. The problem became far more serious when the men involved were married. The *beth din* had to deal with several scandals in which married men and single women, who subsequently became single mothers, were involved.[98] When the woman was very young, the man was also accused of seduction and the matter was referred to a Christian court. One such instance was the trial in 1318 of Astrug Avincendut for seducing the daughter of a friend who entrusted her to him.[99]

Sometimes the female partners were Christians. Both the Jewish and Christian authorities were equally opposed to sexual relations between mixed couples.[100] The charter that the community of Calatayud obtained from the king in 1227 set a fine of 300 maravedís on any Christian found in bed with a Jewess. The community was moreover empowered to arrest him and hand him over to the authorities.[101] In the south, where the Muslims were numerous, relations between Jews (or Christians) and Muslim women were prohibited. A decree against these relations was proclaimed in Játiva in 1283.[102]

The sources at our disposal show that sexual relations between Jews and Christians were prevalent despite the prohibition. In many cases the evidence against Jews accused of relations with Christian women was not conclusive. Roven, son of Vidal of Gerona, and Vidal Malet of Barcelona were acquitted in 1285 and 1309 respectively. They were accused of having affairs with Christian women, as was Escapat Açach, another leader of the community of Barcelona and a colleague of Vidal.[103] There were many cases where charges against Jews accused of relations with Christians were dropped for lack of evidence. The absence of evidence was sometimes given as a reason for the king's pardon, which was nevertheless expensive to acquire. It is difficult to determine whether such

[97] Gerondi, *Sha'are Teshuvah*, pt. III, ch. 94.
[98] Adret, i. 1610, vii. 55; Perfet, 41, 425.
[99] ACA, Reg. 216, fo. 55ᵛ [= R 3091]
[100] Chavel, *Works of Nahmanides*, i, p. 370. For Christian opposition, see Girbal, *Los judíos en Gerona*, p. 65; Sanpere, *Las costumbres catalanas*, p. 279.
[101] ACA, Reg. 39, fo. 155ʳᵛ [= R 674 and doc. x, pp. 423–4].
[102] ACA, Reg. 61, fo. 101ᵛ [= R 1045 = MF ii. 1726].
[103] ACA, Reg. 62, fo. 128ᵛ [= R 1289]; Reg. 206, fo. 32 [= R 2898–9].

accusations were simply used to extort money or reflected prevalent behaviour.[104] The two possibilities are not necessarily mutually exclusive.

Surprisingly, those who were found guilty had to pay very heavy fines instead of receiving the death penalty dictated by the law of the Crown of Aragon. Technically they were pardoned, for which they paid the king a large sum. Çulema Abinçulana of Valencia had to pay 5,000 sr after he was caught with a Christian woman in his brother's shop and confessed.[105] Jucef Avenhalahu of Jaca was fined 6,000 s for his relations with a Christian woman and similar crimes.[106] Açach Avenecara from Tortosa was another Jew found guilty of sexual intercourse with Christian, Muslim, and Jewish women.[107]

Even those who were not found guilty did not escape the payment of a fine. Belshom Momet of Besalú, against whom no evidence was found that he had had sexual relations with a Christian woman, paid 3,000 sb.[108] Abraham son of Salamo Adret, Astruc Caravida, and others from various communities, falsely accused of illicit relations with Christian women, had to pay various sums of money to the king, whose income from all these acquittals and false accusations was increasing constantly.[109] Some legal proceedings were initiated by the king. The wholesale accusations in 1283 that Jews from Barcelona, Gerona, and Villafranca had carnal relations with Christians raises some suspicion as to the truth behind these charges.[110] Other individuals were also tried on the initiative of the king for similar offences.[111]

In nearly all cases, whether or not the Jew was found guilty of carnal relations with Christian women, he paid money to the king. In the Crown of Aragon we know of only one case in which capital punishment was inflicted on the Jew and his Christian partner. The Christian partner was a nun, and both were executed in 1381.[112] The kings of Aragon clearly preferred fines and monetary compensation to the death penalty. This discrepancy between law and reality may be explained by the king's continuous need for cash. Despite doubts as to the veracity of many of the accusations, the number of Jews who indulged in sexual relations with Christian women was not negligible.

---

[104] ACA, Reg. 12, fo. 96` [= R 206 = Bofarull, Barcelona, xxxii = Jacobs 239]; Reg. 20, fos. 226, 302 [= R 619, 646 = Jacobs 603].
[105] ACA, Reg. 12, fo. 24 [= R 189 = MF i. 453].
[106] ACA, Reg. 203, fos. 150`–151 [= R 2855].
[107] ACA, Reg. 207, fo. 154 [= R 2915].
[108] ACA, Reg. 37, fo. 38` [= R 510].
[109] ACA, Reg. 21, fo. 31`” [= R 515 = Jacobs 632]; Reg. 199, fos. 102, 126 [= R 2788, 2795]; Reg. 203, fo. 201 [= R 2861].
[110] ACA, Reg. 60, fo. 42` [= R 1029].
[111] ACA, Reg. 61, fo. 162 [= R 1074]; Reg. 81, fo. 39` [= R 2065].
[112] Villanueva, *Viage literario*, xxi, p. 219; Morel-Fatio, 'Notes et documents', p. 37.

ADULTERY

Sexual laxity among Iberian Jews led to adultery which, according to Jewish law, was defined as sexual relations between a Jewish man and a married woman. Adultery in Jewish society in the Hispanic kingdoms was more widespread than in other Jewish communities. In the Crown of Aragon the sources, so much richer than elsewhere in the peninsula, allow us to gain a fairly good picture of adulterous relations among the Jews. According to Hebrew sources the relaxation of restrictions on relations between men and women was the first step leading to the ultimate transgression of adultery.[113]

Several accounts of adulterous relations found in the responsa of Catalan rabbis give a good illustration of the permissive conduct that prevailed in certain circles. For an example, we may refer to a case in the late fourteenth century, when Aljohar, wife of R. Ya'aqov ben Yosef, appeared before the *beth din* of Alcira in the Kingdom of Valencia and reported that Yishaq Cohen had been pestering her with his declarations of love. He put pressure on her to participate in kisses and caresses, and invited her to his house under false pretences. She informed the *beth din* that he had had affairs with married women and had been warned a few years earlier by the *berurim* about his amorous advances towards the wife of R. Samuel Peniel. Aljohar had not reported those events to the *beth din* earlier for fear of embarrassing her husband.[114]

Men suspected of adultery were brought to court. If they were found guilty, the legal implications were extremely grave.[115] The responsa literature contains ample information about husbands who accused their wives of adulterous relations and details about the misbehaviour of married women with men other than their husbands.[116] Some women were suspected of committing adultery with Christians. Some sources contain a vivid picture of the misconduct of the people involved. A man who suspected his wife of adultery, even if he withdrew his allegations, could not live with his wife. Husbands who wanted to continue to live with their wives after their initial anger had died down found out that the *halakhah* did not allow them to do so.[117]

Complaints of women's immoral behaviour were frequent. Some of those found in the sources offer details of the men's and women's behaviour.[118] Some men lived openly with married women and were pardoned by the king for large sums. This kind of open defiance of the norms of society and the laws governing the life of the community is indicative of the low moral standards that characterized some Jews.[119] One man was found in bed with a married

---

[113] Adret, v. 241.   [114] Perfet 265.   [115] Adret, i. 596, 1177, vii. 222.
[116] Adret, i. 557, 832.   [117] Adret, i. 1187.
[118] Adret, i. 557, 1250. For full details of Adret, i. 557 see Havlin, 'The Takkanot of Rabbenu Gershon', pp. 219–33.
[119] ACA, Reg. 199, fo. 34ʹ [= R 2770]; Reg. 215, fos. 268ʹ–269 [= R 3084]; Perfet 351.

woman.¹²⁰ The saddest outcome of these adulterous relations was the lot of any child born to an adulteress; the fate of such children was tragic.¹²¹ They were barred from marrying anyone except a person of the same status.

DIVORCE AND THE PROTECTION OF WOMEN

Divorce is occasionally mentioned in the correspondence of the king; indeed, it is striking how frequently the king was involved in the details of divorce cases. He received complaints on behalf of women whose husbands divorced them for no apparent reason, or at the instigation of a third party, or by using false witnesses.¹²² There were also complaints about women who abandoned their husbands. Generally, the king ordered legal proceedings or an investigation to be opened. In cases where the women were found guilty, the king allowed the husband to pay no alimony until the wife returned home. When the wife was proved to have good reason for her conduct, the king demanded that the husband divorce her and pay her *ketubah*.¹²³

Women left their homes and asked for a divorce because they were beaten by violent husbands or neglected by indifferent husbands. That such cases were brought to the attention of the king shows the standing of the people involved. In practically every request by a Jewess for a divorce, the king asked his officials to examine the case and prevent the husband from leaving the town until the investigation was completed. The king played a vital role in protecting women who might have otherwise been seriously maltreated. In all recorded cases Jewish law was strictly adhered to.¹²⁴

The case of Reina, wife of Samuel de Forn, is noteworthy because it illustrates very well the king's attitude to women's rights according to Jewish law, and to the laws and customs that prevailed among his Jewish subjects. In 1281 Reina asked Pedro III to make her husband preserve the value of her *ketubah* and dowry. She claimed that her husband planned to divorce her and deprive her of her property. Reina did not sit idle but took certain measures designed to control her husband's property. Pedro ordered the baile to force the husband to give his wife her dowry and the value of her *ketubah* and provide her with food as prescribed by Jewish law. The king's measure did not satisfy Reina. Two months later, in October 1281, Reina expressed her fear that if Samuel were to divorce her against her will and for no good reason, as he threatened to do, she would suffer seriously. Pedro forbade Samuel de Forn to divorce his wife without consulting R. Shelomo ben Adret and R. Bonjudas Salomo. From a document of July 1282 it appears that all the above precautionary measures were of little help. The prospects of a divorce

---

¹²⁰ Adret, i. 1249.
¹²¹ Adret, ii. 219.   ¹²² See e.g. ACA, Reg. 74, fo. 27ᵛ [=R1824].
¹²³ ACA, CR, Jaime II, C 2, no. 515; Reg. 66, fo. 247 [=R 1678].
¹²⁴ ACA, Reg. 80, fo. 127 [=R 2042]; Reg. 91, fo. 113 [=R 2400]; Reg. 87, fo. 118ᵛ [=R 2488].

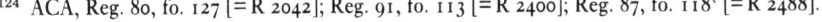

and of the loss of her assets continued to haunt Reina. The king repeated his orders of the previous year and insisted that Jewish law be applied. In February 1283 the couple were in the process of getting divorced, and the Infante Alfonso asked the baile of Barcelona to appoint a suitable and capable legal expert to complete the divorce case between Samuel de Forn and Reina according to Jewish law. The couple and Reina's father Vidal de España were influential members of the Jewish community.[125]

FAMILY DISPUTES

The king and members of his family were from time to time involved in family disagreements and even violent conflicts among relatives. The disputes which were referred to members of the royal family were very varied. Sons and fathers, husbands and wives did not hesitate to seek the support of the king and princes against each other. In one case a father begged the queen not to let his son, accused of gambling and extravagance, leave town. In another, Don Pedro was asked to deal with the kidnapping of a baby by her brother, at his father's request but against the mother's wishes.[126]

WILLS AND HEIRS

The responsa of the Catalan rabbis contain abundant material on wills and inheritance. They reflect the extent of the litigation that was brought to the Jewish courts of law and courts of arbitration, litigation which did not always put an end to the conflicts that could tear families apart. The examination of the file by the great halakhic experts was no guarantee that the dispute would be resolved: hence the frequent involvement of the king in litigations between heirs. These complaints often reached the king after the court of law had reached a verdict or while it was in the process of deliberations; in other instances they were deliberately meant to circumvent the Jewish judiciary.

A testament left by the deceased reduced the risk of conflict between the heirs. The testament was a binding legal document for both the Jewish community and the Christian authorities. It is noteworthy that the need for dual recognition often led to the preparation of two versions, one in Hebrew and the other in Latin, prepared by the authorized agencies according to the specifications of the two systems.[127]

Despite this procedure many wills were challenged, as the numerous Hebrew sources indicate. It was in order to prevent such legal complications that a grow-

---

[125] ACA, Reg. 50, fos. 168, 193ᵛ [=R 875, 881 = Dinur, ii. 3, p. 272, no. 25]; Reg. 59, fo. 23 [=R 929]; Reg. 60, fo. 33 [=R 1017].
[126] ACA, Reg. 56, fo. 63 [=R 1338]; Reg. 85, fo. 57ᵛ [=R 2199].
[127] ACA, Reg. 12, fo. 88 [=R 194 = Jacobs 233].

ing a number of Jews in the thirteenth and fourteenth centuries had their wills confirmed by the king. The need for royal confirmation was felt particularly where the heirs were still minors and guardians were appointed to administer their inheritance, when the king's intervention was sought either to counteract opposition to the appointment of the guardians or to put an end to disputes between the heirs and the guardians.[128] The king was usually ready to confirm the will and order the fulfilment of all its clauses in accordance with the *halakhah*. He also considered the will valid even if there was only a Hebrew version. The legality of a will prepared according to the *halakhah* was never questioned by the king, as the following cases show.[129]

In 1268, while in Villafranca, Jaime I confirmed the validity of the will drawn up in Hebrew by Benvenist de Porta according to which six executors, including the widow and Jahuda de la Cavallería, were appointed. On the same day, meeting the parties in the house of the Dominicans, the king rejected the objections raised by Salamo d'en Adret, acting as the guardian of Belshom son of Bonanasch, who claimed that Bonanasch died leaving no will and that his heirs were his daughter Sara and son Belshom. It is unclear how part of the inheritance fell into the hands of Benvenist, whose heir was his son Vidal. Be that as it may, the executors produced the will of Bonanasch who left all his property to Sara, and Salamo d'en Adret's claims were rejected.[130]

The will of Jahuda de Limos from Lérida is fascinating, for several reasons. In February 1285 Pedro III ordered the baile of Lérida to protect Bonadona, the widow of Jahuda de Limos, who inherited from her husband according to his will as long as she was prepared to appear in court. Ten days later the king was informed that Bonadona, with the help of some conspirators, had in fact dictated the will while her husband was dangerously ill. The will left out other members of the family. Pedro ordered an investigation and, if necessary, the punishment of the culprits. According to a document dated September 1285, legal proceedings were opened against Bonadona and her collaborators accused of forging the will. It appears that in the course of the trial there were attempts to influence witnesses. The king once more insisted that a fair investigation and trial be conducted. Meanwhile Bonadona also raised a formal complaint against the plaintiffs, including her husband's son, and with the help of the baile she ensured that the trial should be conducted according to Jewish law. The king, however, was opposed to any pressure being exerted by his officials on the litigants, and a year after the episode started there was still no verdict. In June 1286 Bonadona again asked for an early end to the trial. In July 1286 Alfonso III issued orders that Bonadona and her associates be compelled to answer the allegations of her stepson Vives. The affair dragged on; in November 1287 the king dealt with

---

[128] ACA, Reg. 21, fos. 54, 81` [= R 526, 544 = Jacobs 641, 657 = Bofarull, Barcelona, cxvii].
[129] ACA, Reg. 63, fo. 39` [= R 1489].
[130] ACA, Reg. 15, fos. 116`, 117` [= R 383-4]. It is probable that Salamo d'en Adret was the famous halakhist R. Shelomo ben Adret.

Bonadona's complaint against the baile who refused, so she claimed, to return her deposit of 500 sj which she had paid at the opening of the trial. The king ordered the return of the deposit. We do not know the fate of Jahuda de Limos' inheritance, or the verdict; but the episode shows how deep the king's involvement in matters of inheritance could be, and the complications that arose in legal proceedings in which rich and influential Jewish heirs appeared as litigants. An important detail is revealed in one of the sources: the handsome deposit that had to be paid by Jewish litigants more than explains the involvement of the Crown in lawsuits between Jews.[131]

Apart from forgeries and other illegalities in the preparation of wills, there were attempts to conceal the document. This serious crime became far graver in the case of a widow named Sol who tried to hide a will that had left 4,000 golden *maravedís* to Pedro III. Alfonso III was nevertheless ready to pardon Sol for the sum of 2,500 sj. This clause in the will reveals an interesting aspect of the intimate relations that existed between some upper-class Jews and the king.[132]

JEWISH HEIRS IN LAWSUITS

The problems that arose following the death of a rich Jew were often extremely complicated. The absence of a testament was naturally an opportune pretext for the heirs to open their struggle for a sizeable share in the inheritance. The situation was further complicated by the king, who lost no opportunity to obtain part or whole of the property of a deceased Jew: when no will was drawn up and the legitimate heirs were not known or available, the king took possession of the deceased's property. Even when heirs were found, the king was able to claim part of the inheritance, particularly in the case of Jews who had been in his service. The king was also the foremost claimant to the inheritance of an apostate, who might have had Jewish heirs. The community, too, sometimes claimed part of the inheritance of Jews who had not paid their debts, had promised property or money to the *qehilah*, or had died without heirs.[133]

When the heirs were known and no one challenged their inheritance, the position of the king *vis-à-vis* their rights and responsibilities was clear. Their rights to their father's or relative's inheritance and their responsibility towards the

---

[131] ACA, Reg. 56, fos. 5, 9 [= R 1286, 1291]; Reg. 57, fos. 198, 204 [= R 1448, 1450]; Reg. 63, fo. 68ᵛ [= R 1495]; Reg. 66, fos. 119ᵛ, 148ᵛ [= R 1587, 1601]; Reg. 74, fo. 16 [= R 1808].

[132] ACA, Reg. 64, fo. 106ᵛ [= R 1625]. See also R 1626.

[133] ACA, Reg. 12, fo. 93ᵛ [= R 204 = MF i. 476]; Reg. 14, fo. 43 [= R 228]; Reg. 41, fo. 59 [= R 721]; Reg. 194, fo. 209 [= R 2610]; Reg. 257, fos. 11ᵛ–12 [= R 2752]; Reg. 206, fo. 22ᵛ [= R 2895]; Reg. 211, fo. 281 [= R 3016]; Reg. 216, fo. 119ᵛ [= R 3104–5]. See also R 1357; MF i. 475. On the king's policy in transferring to the survivors the property of massacred or fugitive Jews, see ACA, Reg. 220, fo. 55ᵛ [= Miret, 'Le Massacre', pp. 261–2 = Jacobs 799 = R 3188].

creditors of the deceased were inseparable. The king also supported the right claims of heirs to anything that was owed to the deceased.[134]

In principle, all inheritance cases were meant to be tried in the *beth din*. However, the financial aspects of the problems that arose, and the difficulties the community encountered in imposing the decisions and verdicts of its court, made the Gentile court the obvious destination of many inheritance cases. Undoubtedly many litigations were brought to the king by Jews whose status and work in the king's service led them to expect his support. Guardians who were among the king's favourites were promised immunity from possible legal proceedings. Naturally all this protection by the king cost heirs and guardians alike no small sums.[135] There were some positive results of the king's involvement in disputes over inheritance, since his intervention usually put an end to the legal complications that split families.

Children of the second marriage of a Jewish bigamist had to make sure that their rights to their inheritance were not denied or challenged. These conflicts could be serious: fathers and sons, mothers and daughters, brothers and sisters pressed charges against one another on account of money and property left by their relatives. The complaints that were addressed to the king show how strained and hostile the relations between family members could be.[136]

The king's involvement in disputes between heirs did not necessarily mean that the case was passed to a Christian court. Sometimes Jewish arbitrators were appointed to deal with the case, while in other instances the litigation was referred to a *beth din* or a halakhic expert. In keeping with their traditional policy, all the Aragonese kings repeatedly emphasized that the *halakhah* or, in their words, the *assuna* or *açuna*, should be the basis of the verdict.[137] Among the scholars to whom the king referred cases of inheritance were R. Shelomo ben Adret, R. Aharon Ha-Levi de Na Clara, and R. Shelomo Graciani.[138]

The right of the widow to receive the part of her late husband's assets due to her by Jewish law was upheld in any Jewish court and consistently supported by the king. The protection of the widow's rights by the king was explicitly based on *halakhah*. Apart from the amount registered in her *ketubah*, which the widow was entitled to receive first from the inheritance, she had the right to take all the gifts she had received from her late husband and all objects she brought from her

---

[134] ACA, Reg. 12, fo. 93ᵛ [=R 204 = MF i. 476 = Jacobs 238]; Reg. 81, fo. 212 [=R 2244]; Reg. 91, fo. 210ᵛ [=R 2420]; Reg. 89, fo. 151 [=R 2601]; Reg. 204, fo. 88ᵛ [=R 2878]; Reg. 219, fo. 241 [=R 3176]; Reg. 171, fo. 197 [= 3177 = Bofarull, Montblanch, 85]. See R 1542.

[135] ACA, Reg. 21, fo. 55ʳᵛ [=R 528–9 = Bofarull, Barcelona, cxxxii = Jacobs 644]; Reg. 19, fo. 115ᵛ [=R 583 = Bofarull, Barcelona, cxxxii = Jacobs 537].

[136] ACA, Reg. 50, fo. 156ᵛ [=R 885]; Reg. 59, fo. 190 [=R 994]. On children of a second wife see ACA, Reg. 15, fos. 64ᵛ–65 [=R 359 = Bofarull, Barcelona, lxii].

[137] The following are sources referring to different kings: ACA, Reg. 19, fo. 141ʳᵛ [=R 604 = Jacobs 556]; Reg. 50, fo. 156ᵛ [=R 885]; Reg. 70, fo. 172ᵛ [=R 1769 = Isaacs 51]; Reg. 74, fo. 50 [=R 1846].

[138] ACA, Reg. 85, fo. 96ᵛ [=R 2310].

parents' home. Even when the inheritance or part of it was in his possession, the king respected the widow's rights.[139]

YOUNG HEIRS AND THEIR GUARDIANS

Where the heir was a minor, the *halakhah* instituted the post of guardian to look after his interests and inheritance. As the position could be abused, various measures were taken to ensure that no losses were caused until the heir reached his legal majority. It was forbidden to use the heir's assets to purchase property outside the area of his residence, and the guardians were not allowed to marry him off or take him out of his home town.[140]

These measures were designed to restrict the guardian's power and prevent abuse of the heir's property. The issue of guardianship, which was treated extensively in the responsa of the period, also occupied the authorities quite a lot. Some relatives raised objections to the appointment of certain guardians in the will. In the face of such opposition the guardians often needed to obtain royal confirmation of their position. Even a widow who was appointed the guardian of her children was not always left in peace to exercise her discretion in administering her husband's assets. The prospect of her remarriage caused concern and suspicion among the relatives, and her appointment as guardian was sometimes made conditional on her remaining unmarried. Some felt the need to strengthen any condition by royal confirmation. In some delicate instances, where the heir was very rich, the king added his own appointees to the guardians named in the will.[141]

All these measures and precautions did not prevent many cases of inheritance appearing before Christian judges. Charges were pressed against many guardians accused of misuse or abuse of their wards' assets, or of fraud. The plaintiffs included relatives of the heirs and sometimes the heirs themselves. The king acted in each case on its own merits. Sometimes he protected the guardian; sometimes he opposed him and ordered legal proceedings against him.[142]

---

[139] ACA, Reg. 10, a single folio between fos. 66 and 67 [= R 104 = MF, i. 128]; Reg. 14, fo. 43 [= R 228]; Reg. 59, fo. 140ᵛ [= R 980]; Reg. 46, fo. 107ᵛ [= R 1090]; Reg. 62, fo. 130 [= R 1297].

[140] ACA, Reg. 21, fo. 74ʳᵛ [= R 539, 541–3 = Jacobs 652, 654–5]; Reg. 201, fo. 15 [= R 2818 = Jacobs 749].

[141] On the confirmation of the guardians, see ACA, Reg. 12, fo. 88 [= R 194 = Jacobs 233]; Reg. 19, fo. 122 [= R 587 = Jacobs 540]. On protection from legal action, see Reg. 15, fo. 116ᵛ [= R 383]. On the obligations imposed on the widow/guardian, see Reg. 13, fo. 159 [= R 252]; Reg. 21, fo. 74ᵛ [= R 540 = Jacobs 653]. On women as guardians, see Reg. 74, fo. 65ᵛ [= R 1854]. On confirmation of guardians' activities see Reg. 21, fo. 74 [= R 539 = Jacobs 652]; Reg. 217, fo. 240ᵛ [= R 3124]. On the appointment of guardians by the king, see Reg. 21, fos. 54, 56 [= R 527, 531 and doc. vi, pp. 420–1 = Jacobs 642, 646 = Bofarull, Barcelona, cxviii]; Reg. 74, fo. 78 [= R 1979].

[142] ACA, Reg. 21, fos. 54, 55ᵛ, 81ᵛ [= R 527, 529, 544 = Jacobs 642, 644, 657 = Bofarull, Barcelona, cxviii]; Reg. 81, fo. 166ᵛ [= R 2184]; Reg. 85, fo. 91 [= R 2287]; Reg. 205, fo. 230 [= R 2885]; Reg. 206, fo. 124 [= R 2908]; Reg. 219, fos. 202–3 [= R 3165–6]; Reg. 63, fo. 67 [= R 1494].

§5.4 Daily Life and Moral Conduct

LITTLE attention has been paid to daily life in the *juderías* of the Crown of Aragon. The lifestyle of the ordinary man in the street and at home did not attract the interest of historians, who looked instead for the personalities and events that, to their mind, shaped the political, intellectual, or religious life of the Jews. The literary product and economic contribution of the Jews occupied a substantial part of historical research and so, inevitably, the history of the Jews in the Aragonese realm depicts the life and achievements of an intellectual and financial elite that controlled Jewish self-government and produced almost all the Jewish sources utilized by historians.

Apart from the fact that many historians tend to see in the political and intellectual leaders of the Jewish community the main, if not the only, matter for historical research, the sources that are at the disposal of the historian belong mostly to the upper circles of Jewish society. The 'silent majority' left few records behind. Most Jews were engaged in hard work to earn their livelihood and raise their families and had neither the time nor the literary talent to describe their thoughts, feelings, and activities. References to the life of the Jewish masses therefore come from sources that are necessarily prejudicial and unbalanced and consequently misleading. They do not reflect the lifestyle of the majority of the common Jews, whose daily conduct did not require any record, but focus on the problems and deviations of some members, whose demographic size and representative character remain a mystery. We hear more of thieves, rapists, prostitutes, men of violence, and the like than of ordinary and well-behaved Jews, simple and hard-working craftsmen, loving husbands and wives, fathers and mothers, friends and neighbours. We read more about violence than love, more about robbery than good deeds, more about how people cursed and fought than how they dressed and ate. We hear the voice of the noisy more than the songs of the quiet, the insults of the quarrelsome more than the compliments of the good-hearted. Despite all these limitations, the story deserves to be told, as long as we bear in mind its shortcomings and one-sidedness.

THE JEWISH HOME

Jews either owned their houses or rented them from Jewish or Christian landlords. The decoration or refurbishing of the house depended on whether the occupying family was the owner or the tenant. The size of the house varied in accordance with both wealth and architectural possibilities. As the boundaries of the *judería* were usually fixed, enlarging a house was no easy matter. In some cases, additional floors could be added, but frequently additional accommodation for the family was achieved by building a bridge across the narrow street of the *judería* between two houses. This bridge construction served as additional quarters. This method of expanding a house was most convenient when one family owned the two buildings facing each other. The connecting room had to be high enough to allow passers-by and horses to pass underneath.[1] As some *aljamas* or Jewish settlements were in small villages, conditions for expanding houses varied from place to place. Security was taken into account in several details of the building, particularly as far as windows and doors were concerned. Houses that were on the border of the *judería* had, whenever possible, their main or only entrance to the street within the quarter.[2] As families expanded, the original buildings underwent changes. Houses were divided and sub-divided. Some neighbours had to use a joint access to their house.[3] Different floors often belonged to different tenants.[4]

In some Jewish quarters several houses had their doors open on to a courtyard where children played and their parents passed their free time. In good weather the family enjoyed sitting in the courtyard and entertained its guests there. In the Catalan *calls* this feature was called the *cort*.[5] The size of the courtyard was varied. Some were rather small, approximately four to six square yards. Some courtyards belonged to the same family, with the surrounding quarters divided between the smaller units within the extended family. In any case, Jews sometimes owned more than one house in the courtyard. Some units were let, although they did not all have their own toilets, as when they were originally constructed for the use of the larger family, a toilet was not considered necessary.[6] Other courtyards belonged to several families. There were courtyards that opened on one side to the street, thus forming a cul-de-sac.[7] When the number of neighbours was small the yard could be used as part of the house.[8] Some were covered with a vault and were even used for eating.[9] Neighbours whose houses were around the courtyard usually sat outside their front door where they worked or chatted and ate their meals.[10]

In some courtyards an upper chamber was built which, while serving as a shade, also offered additional accommodation for the family. In such cases access to the chamber was through the upper floor of the house, sometimes in addition to the stairs reaching the courtyard. Chambers that were built in stages to solve immediate needs eventually proved to be weak and dangerous structures and needed to be reinforced.[11] Some upper chambers were occupied by other families

---

[1] Asibili (Kapah) 125.   [2] Adret, i. 661.   [3] Adret, i. 912; Asibili (Kapah) 87.
[4] Adret, ii. 216.   [5] Adret, ii. 24, iii. 168; Gerondi 35.
[6] Adret, i. 63, 601, ii. 51, 110. For the size, see Adret, ii. 218, iii. 165, 173; Asibili (Kapah) 88.
[7] Nahmanides 87; Adret, ii. 41, v. 148.   [8] Adret, vi. 92.
[9] Adret, iii. 271, iv. 168, vii. 22.   [10] Adret, v. 111, 203.
[11] Adret, i. 880, 892, ii. 47, 301, 306.

who were exposed to the smells of the cooking from below. It was therefore necessary to build chimneys or some sort of outlets to prevent the smoke and the smells from reaching the upper floors.[12] Many houses had fixtures that served as shades.[13] In some yards there was a well which served for the storage of either water or food. The well that provided the water belonged either to all the occupants of the yard or to one family. Some yards also had facilities for cooking.[14] The odour from toilets that were installed in the courtyard caused serious arguments between the proprietor and the neighbours whose windows overlooked the yard.[15] Several houses had a small garden at the back where women did some of their work. In the summer, many families enjoyed eating in the garden.[16]

Since the streets of the *judería* were very narrow, changes to one's house often affected the neighbours. Many disputes between neighbours ended up in the *beth din*. One of the causes of neighbours' protests was the opening of windows overlooking a neighbour's house.[17] In other cases, additional construction could block the view, the light, or the space of the neighbours, who would naturally object. Various types of construction caused innumerable quarrels between neighbours.[18] Sometimes repairs and building in one house actually caused serious damage to the house next door.[19] Even when the owner built an additional floor on his own building, neighbours were sometimes affected.[20]

In some communities there was a *miqve* on the roof which used rainwater. That probably explains our failure to find the ritual baths which we expected to find on ground floors or even underground.[21] Some roofs were occasionally used by the tenant when the weather permitted. A covering would be installed to make this possible.[22] Flat roofs were used to dry fruits and clothes. Most roofs, however, were not usable as they were covered with tiles. The tenants would go up once every two to three years to carry out repairs.[23] The rain from one roof sometimes disturbed the tenants next door, causing damage to property and consequent lawsuits between neighbours. Sometimes the sewage system created by the neighbours did not operate satisfactorily.[24]

Interior decoration was not neglected. Various designs were found on walls and ceilings and beams in the ceilings were decorated.[25] Pillars were sometimes ornamental even when they were also architecturally necessary.[26]

Some arrangements were made to heat the house during the winter months. Chimneys were constructed, but due to the differences in heights between buildings the smoke often caused pollution for neighbours.[27]

---

[12] Adret, i. 907.
[13] Adret, i. 136.
[14] Adret, i. 70, ii. 218, 380.
[15] Adret, iv. 325.
[16] Adret, iii. 161, 180.
[17] Adret, i. 903, 1085, ii. 375, iii. 161, 165.
[18] Nahmanides 81; Adret, i. 1127, 1132–5, ii. 1, 4.
[19] Adret, iii. 164.
[20] Adret, ii. 178, 386, 401.
[21] Adret, i. 800.
[22] Adret, v. 149, vi. 97.
[23] Nahmanides 82; Adret, ii. 43, iii. 156.
[24] Adret, ii. 181, 199, 238, 246, 292, iii. 156.
[25] Adret, i. 55.
[26] Adret, i. 90.
[27] Adret, i. 856, ii. 45.

THE JEWISH DIET

The diet of the Jew differed radically from that of the Christian because of the dietary laws and special Jewish needs, such as the preparation of food prior to the Sabbath and heating it without the desecration of the day. Nevertheless, if we leave aside the forbidden animals and the prohibitions on the mixing of certain foodstuffs, the content of the diet was basically similar, dominated by the availability in the region of the animals, vegetables, fruits, and other ingredients.

Bread has always been a very important item on the table of Jews of all backgrounds. It was usually prepared at home and sent to the bakery or *furn*, which was often operated by Christians under royal licence. That is exactly what they did in Nahmanides' home.[28] In the responsa, we have several recipes of Jews in various communities in the Crown of Aragon. One chicken dish was made by stuffing the chicken with hard-boiled eggs which were mashed and mixed with a variety of spices and then cooked. Eggs were also used in meat soup.[29] In another dish, a chicken was stuffed with spicy minced meat and sewn up.[30] A very popular dish consisted of very thin sliced meat fried with eggs in a pan.[31] Meat soup too was popular.[32] Salt meat was a convenient commodity at a time when refrigeration was not available. Both lamb and veal were sold to the Jewish public. Goat's meat was less often eaten.[33] In communities on the Mediterranean coast, fish was a familiar item on the menu. Even in inland communities, however, salted small fish with eggs was a usual dish. Salted fish was prepared at home.[34]

Meat and fish were fried in a little oil.[35] Salt was widely used as dishes without sufficient salt were not considered tasty.[36] Paprika was dried and ground to be used in dishes. Pepper was used extensively.[37] Some type of pasta was eaten by the Jews.[38] For sweet dishes in some communities honey was used, made from wine.[39]

Of dairy products, cheese was the most popular, and was an important ingredient in a variety of dishes. Cheese in baked pastry was a speciality served on Saturdays as well as on festive occasions.[40] Cheese pies were popular dishes.[41] Among the vegetables available we find that onions,[42] lentils, beans, and olives were eaten in the average house.[43] Almonds and hazelnuts were very popular. Sweet fruits were liked for their sour peels, but the bitter ones were also used.[44] Grapes were the most popular fruit;[45] pears, apples, cherries, and dates were also eaten.[46]

Wine was produced for consumption throughout the year and special wine was

[28] Adret, i. 124.
[29] Adret, i. 449, 710.
[30] Adret, i. 576, vii. 234.
[31] Adret, ii. 251.
[32] Adret, i. 101, 449, 495.
[33] Adret, ii. 256; Gerondi 45.
[34] Adret, i. 129, 522.
[35] Adret, i. 502.
[36] Adret, i. 684.
[37] Adret, i. 400, 497, 924.
[38] Adret, vii. 533.
[39] Gerondi 5.
[40] Adret, i. 681.
[41] Adret, i. 849.
[42] Adret, i. 849.
[43] Adret, i. 274.
[44] Adret, i. 428, 682, 756.
[45] Adret, iv. 93, vii. 253, 362.
[46] Adret, viii. 201, 210; Gerondi 5.

prepared for Passover. It was made of grapes or raisins. Jews produced sparkling wine as well.⁴⁷ Jewish wine was even appreciated by non-Jews.⁴⁸

Oil and honey were bought from Christians without religious scruples.⁴⁹ Cheese and butter produced by Christians were eaten by some Jews and were the subject of some halakhic debate.⁵⁰

JEWISH CLOTHING

As in most medieval communities, there was little that distinguished the Jews from non-Jews in their clothes except the distinguishing garb or restrictions imposed by the authorities. The very need to force Jews to wear a distinctive garment proves the point. Nonetheless, in their style the Jews formed a group that was different from other sectors in Christian society. They were especially easily identifiable on the Sabbath and at festivals.

Men wore a kind of overall made of leather and wool, sewn with flax thread. The leather was of either sheep or squirrels.⁵¹ It was generally permitted to use the skins of rabbits, hares, bears, and foxes to make garments.⁵² In Catalonia, and probably elsewhere in the Crown of Aragon, Jews used to wear a four-cornered mantle or *gonela*.⁵³ This mantle became the Jews' distinctive garb and the text of the Jewish oath that was kept in the courts bore a figure of a Jew wearing this mantle.⁵⁴ During the reign of Jaime I the Jews of Catalonia were exempt from wearing the Jewish sign, but had to wear the mantle in the town.⁵⁵ From 1284 onwards the Jews of the Kingdom of Valencia were required to wear the same mantle as the Jews of Catalonia, except in Jewish settlements where there were fewer than ten Jewish families.⁵⁶ The mantle, called the *capa rotunda* or *capa juhega*, covered the man's clothes and was of a 'simple' colour, not red, nor green, nor purple. Jewish women also wore a mantle, called *aldifara*, similar to that of Muslim women. The mantle covered all their clothes.⁵⁷

It seems that the wearing of the mantle was not consistently enforced during the thirteenth century. In 1286, when the Jews of Barcelona complained that the *veguer* fined every Jew without the mantle, Alfonso III ordered him not to molest the Jews.⁵⁸ However, the Jews of Catalonia and Valencia continued to wear their special mantle in the years that followed.⁵⁹ In 1295 in Perpignan, which was under the rule of Jaime II of Majorca, the baile forbade the Jews to go out without the mantle.⁶⁰

---

⁴⁷ Adret, i. 53, 165.
⁴⁸ Adret, v. 120.
⁴⁹ Adret, i. 497.
⁵⁰ See e.g. Adret, i. 67, 76, 110, 143, iv. 106.
⁵¹ Adret, i. 288.
⁵² Adret, i. 489.
⁵³ Adret, i. 434, vii. 206.
⁵⁴ Adret, ii. 218.
⁵⁵ ACA, Reg. 15, fo. 123ʳᵛ [=R 390, 392, 394 = Bofarull, Barcelona lxxi, lxii = Jacobs 427, 429, 431].
⁵⁶ ACA, Reg. 46, fo. 152ᵛ [=R 1103].
⁵⁷ Carreras, 'L'aljama', p. 29.
⁵⁸ ACA, Reg. 70, fo. 4 [=R 1680].
⁵⁹ ACA, Reg. 81, fo. 10 [=R 2058].
⁶⁰ Vidal, *Les Juifs de Roussillon*, p. 30.

In fact the mantle was worn as an alternative to a distinctive sign as prescribed in the Fourth Lateran Council of 1215. The decision by Jaime I in 1228 to introduce the Jewish badge was neither definite nor final. The Jews, we are told, paid large amounts of bribes to gain permission to reduce the size of the sign by half and leave it out completely if the mantle was worn.[61] The absence of the sign did not mean, therefore, that the Jews wore nothing special, as suggested by some, since the mantle was never abolished.[62] According to the Corts of Lérida in 1300, the Jews had to put a circular sign on their mantle. The sign was half yellow and half red. In fourteenth-century paintings in the cathedral of Tarragona, Jews appear with the round sign in a light colour.[63] Jaime II confirmed the law of Jaime I.[64] In 1302 the municipal council of Barcelona decided that in the city all Jews had to wear the mantle by day and night, except the poor, who had to put on a yellow *capero*.[65] In 1311, at their request, the Jews of Montblanch were allowed to dress like those of Barcelona, Tarragona, and Villafranca, that is, wearing a mantle without a sign.[66] That the sign was not forced on the Jews was confirmed by the Barcelona council that made it compulsory on any Jew who did not wear a mantle.[67] The size and the colour of the Jewish sign changed from time to time and from place to place.[68] In Aragon around 1323 the situation was similar: either the Jewish mantle or the sign had to be worn.[69]

On the Sabbath many Jews put on shoes called *patinas* of leather that tightly wrapped the feet.[70] For general purposes many wore wooden sandals reinforced in the sole with iron pieces.[71] Hats were made of leather and cloth sewn with flax thread.[72]

A woman brought her own trousseau when she got married, including not only her clothes, but also her jewellery.[73] The richer the woman, the larger her wardrobe. Naturally, rich women had expensive clothes made of silk and other luxurious materials.[74] A fashionable style in the latter part of the thirteenth century was a tight dress, open at one side where it was laced with a silk ribbon or lace through loopholes.[75]

Finally mention should be made of ordinances that the community enacted in connection with clothing and fashion. In 1285 the *aljama* of Tarazona prohibited its members from wearing white and light-coloured clothes.[76] The community of

---

[61] Adret, v. 183.
[62] See e.g. Shneidman, 'Jews in the Royal Administration', p. 37.
[63] They are found in the Capilla de Santa Lucia. See Sánchez Real, 'Los judíos en Tarragona', pp. 15ff; id., 'La judería', p. 342.
[64] Robert, 'Etude historique', 92; id., *Les signes d'infamie*, p. 61.
[65] Bofarull, 'Ordinaciones', pp. 97–8.
[66] ACA, Reg. 208, fo. 12 [= R 2928 = Bofarull, Montblanch, pp. 563–4].
[67] Bofarull, 'Ordinaciones', pp. 97–8; Carreras, 'L'aljama', p. 29.
[68] For Barcelona in 1321, see Robert, *Les signes d'infamie*, p. 63.
[69] ACA, Reg. 224, fo. 49 [= R 3272].
[70] Adret, i. 607, vii. 219. [71] Adret, iii. 266. [72] Adret, i. 762, vii. 306.
[73] Adret, ii. 390. [74] Adret, iv. 154. [75] Adret, iv. 266, vii. 360.
[76] ACA, Reg. 56, fo. 92 [= R 1342].

Jàtiva prohibited clothes of various colours.⁷⁷ These ordinances, which were suspended by the king for the benefit of some of his favourite Jews, were designed to combat luxury and extravagance among the Jews. Their aim was the exact opposite of what Jewish clothes imposed by the authorities were meant to achieve.

THE JEWS AND GAMBLING

By the second half of the thirteenth century gambling among Jews had become a matter of serious concern to some religious and communal leaders. Those most affected, however, were members of the gamblers' families, particularly their wives, who complained to scholars, communal leaders, or the local *beth din*. Several communities issued ordinances forbidding gambling and threatening gamblers with severe punishments.⁷⁸ Even when the fine was waived, for whatever reason, the prohibition remained valid.⁷⁹ In fact, gambling was considered forbidden by Jewish law and so, formally, there was no need for any ban or ordinance to prosecute gamblers. They could be prosecuted even after the time limit of their oath was over. Nor was there any necessity to annul the vow taken by a gambler, since gambling was considered illegal.⁸⁰

The king also showed an interest in Jewish gamblers, who were fined by his officials when caught. In view of the spread of gambling among Jews, it is difficult to understand the motives of the *aljama* of Perpignan in its request in 1275 that Jewish gamblers should not pay the fines set by the Infante Jaime.⁸¹ In Perpignan, as in other communities, gambling spread widely. It became fashionable to gamble on minor festivals and at wedding parties. It seems that Jews and Christians also played with dice. The royal authorities issued a general prohibition against all games among the Jews of Roussillon in 1295.⁸²

Often under the pressure of their families, many gamblers who could not resist the temptation swore not to gamble, either ever again or for a limited time. Again and again gamblers failed to keep their oath.⁸³ Indeed, in some cases gambling seemed almost an addiction. Some ex-gamblers found it difficult to adjust themselves and found psychological relief in watching games, if not in actual participation.⁸⁴ Some gamblers who occupied positions of public responsibility lost status in the eyes of the community, as with one butcher whose weakness for gambling made him break his oath.⁸⁵

Some gamblers ruined their own lives and the lives of their families. In some cases they proved to be incapable of maintaining any steady work or of finding

---

⁷⁷ See e.g. ACA, Reg. 15, fo. 95ᵛ [= R 376]; Reg. 60, fo. 25 [= R 1021 = MF ii. 1666].
⁷⁸ See e.g. Adret, vii. 244, 270.   ⁷⁹ Adret, vii. 271.
⁸⁰ Adret, vii. 4, 537, viii. 252.
⁸¹ ACA, Reg. 20, fo. 268 [= R 634 = Bofarull, Barcelona, clxiii = Jacobs 591].
⁸² Vidal, *Les Juifs de Roussillon*, p. 29.
⁸³ Adret, i. 180, 755.   ⁸⁴ Adret, viii. 281.   ⁸⁵ Adret, i. 782.

women ready to bear the consequences of their spendthrift habits.[86] Not every woman was fortunate enough to detect her fiancé's addiction or weakness in time; and sometimes the gambler developed his gambling tendency after marriage. Husbands who borrowed money by pawning their wives' clothes did not have to lose in the game to ruin their family life. Often they eventually left their wife without clothes and without support.[87]

Women whose husbands gambled and lost money became the concern of the judiciary and the halakhists.[88] The gambler was also a natural candidate for both minor and serious crimes which he committed in his despair. We are told of gamblers who joined non-Jews in disreputable gambling houses who would again and again remain there naked, after losing their clothes.[89] Their behaviour was sometimes despicable, sometimes equally ridiculous. No *beth din* could show sympathy to the gambler who, having lost 30 s, filed a complaint against his winning fellow gambler. Gamblers, whether losers or winners, were considered worthy of chastisement for having pursued transient and dangerous worldly pleasure and abandoned honesty and good deeds.[90] Their relatives withdrew their support and tried to withhold the gambler's part of any inheritance, fearing its loss in gaming.[91] In 1285 Izach Daray from Barcelona begged Pedro III not to let his son Jucef administer his property as he was a gambler who lost any money he had.[92]

PROSTITUTION

As noted above in relation to many areas of Jewish life, the sexual behaviour of the Jews as reflected in the sources represents deviance from the general norm in Jewish society rather than the common practices of the multitudes. Nevertheless, even the tastes and deeds of the few assume historical significance when they are compared to the conditions prevalent in other medieval Jewish communities. Spanish Jews who were not completely satisfied with their sexual life at home and had no religious or moral inhibitions availed themselves of the services of Christian and Muslim prostitutes.[93] The existence of Jewish prostitutes is attested in the sources. Its extent was much wider than these sources seem to suggest.

Jewish prostitutes in the communities of the Crown of Aragon did not attract much attention in the records. The few references to them suggest that they were present in many of the major communities. In 1283 the well-known courtier Muça de Portella complained to the infante that Jewish prostitutes offered their services in a building adjacent to his house in the *judería* of Saragossa. From his complaint we understand that the prostitutes had previously conducted their activities out-

[86] Adret, ii. 35. [87] Adret, ii. 286, vii. 47, 501. [88] Asibili (Kapah) 122.
[89] Asibili (Kapah) 149. [90] Adret, vii. 445. [91] Asibili (Kapah) 146.
[92] ACA, Reg. 56, fo. 63 [= R 1338].
[93] For sources in general see Assis, 'Sexual Behaviour', pp. 44–5.

side the Jewish quarter. The infante ordered the *adelantados* of the community to remove the Jewish prostitutes from the *judería*.[94] According to a fourteenth-century source, Jewish prostitutes in Barcelona had a brothel in Castell Nou, very near the *call*.[95]

The idea of young Jewish women turning to prostitution shocked halakhist and moralists.[96] We have to assume that the existence of Jewish prostitutes implies the involvement of other Jews in the business. There must have been intermediaries between the prostitutes and their customers. A similar task was fulfilled by Jews for Christian prostitutes. In 1304 Jahuda Aladef was thrown out of the Jewish quarter of Valencia for a long series of immoral and violent crimes, including adultery, rape, and pimping for Christians.[97]

Jewish prostitution in the Crown of Aragon was not an isolated and unique phenomenon in the Iberian peninsula. Even the limited debate on the topic to which we have access leaves no doubt as to its existence in Castilian and other Jewish communities.[98]

HOMOSEXUALITY

Homosexuality in Jewish society in the Crown of Aragon was closely related to the conditions that prevailed in the region previously under Islam, and in Christian lands in general.[99] In the Aragonese realm, Jewish homosexuals were tried by Christian courts and often pardoned for a large sum of money. It is noteworthy that even when the accused was declared innocent he had to pay the king. Alaçar, grandson of Vives de Limoux of Lérida, was accused of sodomy but pardoned by Jaime I in 1263 as a subject of false accusations, despite the insistence of witnesses against him.[100] In 1274 Vives, son of Jucef Abenvives, baile of the king, was accused of sodomy by some Jews.[101] In 1328 three Jews of Alagón were accused of homosexual relations but were freed at the order of Alfonso IV.[102] In 1374 a Jew was burned to death for having had homosexual relations.[103] We also have some data about homosexual relations among youths.[104]

---

[94] ACA, Reg. 61, fo. 134 [= R 1053].   [95] ACA, Reg. 953, fo. 64ʳ.
[96] See e.g. Adret, i. 1210.   [97] ACA, Reg. 202, fo. 204 [= R 2832].
[98] See the interesting debate between two parties in a Castilian community found in R. Yehuda ben Asher, *Zikhron Yehudah*, p. 17, and the general and bitter attack on Jewish prostitution in Arama, *'Aqedat Yizhaq*, p. 145 on Genesis 20.
[99] For Jewish homosexuals in Muslim Spain, see Roth, 'Deal Gently'. For homosexuality in Christian Europe, see Boswell, *Christianity*.
[100] ACA, Reg. 12, fos. 91, 93ʳ [= R 201, 203 = Jacobs 234, 237].
[101] ACA, Reg. 19, fo. 156 [= R 610 = Jacobs 558 = MF i. 1721].
[102] ACA, CR, Alfonso IV, C 2, no. 155.   [103] ACA, RP, R 1682, fo. 83ʳ.   [104] Adret, v. 176.

§5.5 Crime and Violence in the *Judería*

THE Jews in the Crown of Aragon did not live completely isolated from their non-Jewish neighbours. Quite the contrary: Jewish society in north-eastern Spain was far more open to external influence than many other Jewish communities. The behaviour of some Jews was influenced in varying degrees by the conduct of Christians in the streets of Catalonia, Aragon, and Valencia. In the streets of Barcelona, Majorca, or Perpignan at the end of the thirteenth century and the beginning of the fourteenth violence was widespread. The quick development of the Catalan cities brought with it social instability and unrest.[1]

Gambling and blasphemy were quite frequent in Christian society. Sexual crime and secret marriages spread among all classes, and the number of illegitimate children grew considerably. In 1251 Innocent IV had to cancel the punishments imposed by his representative on churchmen who had mistresses due to the great number of transgressors involved. In 1359, the Bishop of Tortosa forbade the appointment of young men to ecclesiastical posts held by their natural fathers. Quarrels, blasphemies, crime, and violence, however, existed side by side with charitable deeds, religious fervour, and social reform.[2] Contrary to R. Yosef Qimhi's assertions in his polemical work, the Jews were not all innocent angels surrounded by Christian iniquity.[3]

THEFT

In the latter part of the thirteenth century, the punishment for theft imposed by the authorities in the Crown of Aragon ceased to deter potential thieves in some localities. Drastic measures were adopted by several communities to combat the growing number of Jewish thieves.[4] Jewish thieves did not discriminate between Jewish, Muslim, and Christian victims.[5] A Jew from Alcira was caught and fined in 1376/7 for attempting to steal from a Christian's garden.[6] Exorbitant fines were not always sufficient to deter Jewish thieves. In 1314 Yucef Moreno of Huesca was

---

[1] For a description of urban behaviour in Catalan cities, see Hillgarth, *The Spanish Kingdoms*, i, pp. 45-7, 75-7.
[2] On moral behaviour in Christian society, see O'Callaghan, *A History of Medieval Spain*, pp. 630-1.   [3] Qimhi, *Sefer ha-Berit*, p. 26.   [4] Adret, v. 243.
[5] ACA, Reg. 88, fo. 174ᵛ [=R 2511]; Reg. 204, fo. 119 [=R 2884].
[6] ACA, RP, Maestre Racional, t. 1670/1, fo. 2ʳᵛ.

fined 1,000 sj after he was tortured for stealing from a Muslim dyer.[7] It is worth noting that there was occasional cooperation between Jewish and Christian thieves.[8]

On the whole, suspects were arrested as soon as legal proceedings were opened. Intervention on behalf of an accused man by members of the royal family indicates his social status.[9] The conflict between various authorities concerning the arrest of the suspect was no doubt due to the fines they expected to collect. The municipal authorities occasionally clashed with the king's officials on account of these fines.[10] The *beth din* also dealt with cases of theft involving Jews, but because of the fines involved, the execution of the sentence was in the hands of the king's officials. The involvement of various interested parties was used by the litigants to support their case.[11]

The list of items stolen may sometimes seem no less incredible than the plans of the thieves. To steal a cat with the intention of selling its meat as *kasher* is one such example![12] The traffic in stolen goods reached alarming proportions in some places. In Saragossa, Jews were apparently involved in large-scale transactions in stolen textile goods.[13] Some Aragonese Jews controlled a large network marketing stolen goods.[14] Stolen jewellery was sold to foreign Jews by thieves who fled.[15] Jewish thieves from Daroca were involved in stealing the silver ornaments of the Torah from the local synagogue. Two of the thieves who escaped from prison converted to Christianity; the others were expelled from the town.[16] Cases of stealing from relatives were tried in both royal and communal courts. Wives were accused of stealing from their husbands, children from their parents.[17]

QUARRELS AND CURSES

Verbal violence was widespread in the Jewish communities. Curses and insults were uttered against fellow Jews and even rabbis, to the extent that special *taqanot* were necessary.[18] The question whether rabbis appointed by the Crown were included in the ordinance that imposed a special fine on those who insulted scholars was answered in the negative by Adret, who decreed that the case should be treated as an ordinary quarrel.[19] The king's Jewish protégés, however, did not need any communal ordinance to have their insulting opponents punished.[20]

---

[7] ACA, Reg. 211, fo. 200 [=R 2999]. [8] ACA, Reg. 87, fo. 47 [=R 2470].
[9] ACA, Reg. 227, fo. 189ʼ [=R 3331].
[10] ACA, CR, C 56, no. 6862; C 23, no. 2911; Reg. 221, fo. 132ʼ [=R 3210].
[11] Perfet 343–8. [12] Magdalena, 'Delitos', pp. 211–13.
[13] ACA, Reg. 91, fos. 174, 180ʼ [=R 2413].
[14] ACA, Reg. 298, fos. 89ʼ, 96ʳ [=R 2937, 2940–1].
[15] ACA, Reg. 226, fo. 152 [=R 3330]. [16] Asibili (Kapah) 159.
[17] ACA, Reg. 46, fo. 212 [=R 1159–61]; Adret, v. 75.
[18] Adret, i. 179, v. 272; Perfet 220.
[19] Adret, viii. 245. [20] ACA, Reg. 62, fo. 114 [=R 1260]; Reg. 74, fo. 62 [=R 1859].

Wives were verbally abused by their husbands. Some violent husbands wanted their wives to give up their rights to the *ketubah*, or to achieve similar concessions or their agreement to divorce.[21] The latter was particularly important in the Crown of Aragon, where divorce without the wife's consent was forbidden.[22]

In the course of arguments and quarrels a rich variety of curses, insults, and threats was heard.[23] Even these turned out to be a source of income for the Crown, for even when the *beth din* imposed the fines, they were paid to the king's treasury.[24] Synagogues, too, were the scene of quarrels and insults that interrupted the service.[25]

PHYSICAL VIOLENCE

Verbal clashes often led to physical violence. The case of battered wives was discussed in the *beth din* and by halakhists. Adret was asked if a *beth din* could force a husband to take an oath that he would not hit his wife any more. In one case, it was decided to place the couple under supervision; in another, to put the violent husband under ban.[26]

Violence sometimes erupted in large crowds. In 1270 many Jews were involved in a street fight in Besalú. Since one of the participants, Cresques Zarch, who was fined 500 sb, was aided by his servant, we may deduce that some of the fighters belonged to the upper class.[27] Indeed, one of the Jews involved in another street fight that took place in the same community fifteen years later was Belshom Levi, who had previously been the baile of Besalú. Belshom paid a fine of 600 sb while Cresques Zarch, by now an experienced fighter, paid 1,000 sb! Besalú, the beautiful spot in northern Catalonia which was the scene of these violent outbursts, was not exceptional.[28] Astrug Lunel, who had hit Bonjuda, *scapolario scole judee*, paid 100 sb.[29] The Crown did not do badly from all these attacks among Jews. In fourteenth-century Valencia a slap on the face cost the Jews between 11 and 110 sr.[30] In the course of fighting stones and sticks were used; sometimes women were actively involved in these fights.[31]

Synagogues were not spared, and violence violated the sanctity of the house of prayer. The synagogue of Montclús was often the scene of fighting.[32] In 1281, while he walked in the street in Villafranca, the eminent jurist, R. Shelomo ben Adret was attacked with stones by Jews who were not happy with the rabbi's role

---

[21] Adret, i. 692–3, 883. [22] Adret, viii. 133. [23] Adret, i. 855; Perfet 216.
[24] Magdalena, 'Delitos', pp. 200–1, 205–8. [25] Adret, i. 244.
[26] Adret, viii. 102–3, v. 264.
[27] ACA, Reg. 37, fo. 10 [= R 451–3 = Jacobs 714–16].
[28] ACA, Reg. 62, fos. 134ᵛ–135 [= R 1308, 1311–13]. [29] ACA, Reg. 62, fo. 145.
[30] Magdalena, 'Delitos', pp. 189–90. [31] Adret, i. 948; Magdalena, 'Delitos', pp. 191–2.
[32] ACA, Reg. 82, fo. 90ᵛ [= R 2261]; Reg. 84, fo. 23 [= R 2314]. See also Assis, 'Synagogues', pp. 26–7.

in their lawsuit.³³ Jews were also involved in attacks against Christians. Some of their victims were the king's officials or municipal leaders.³⁴

Physical violence spread so much that, in a privilege granted in 1280 to the Jews of Catalonia, Pedro III empowered the *beth din* to try cases of violence according to *halakhah*.³⁵ Indeed, the situation was so alarming that it was deemed necessary to impose punishments far more severe than those provided by Jewish law.³⁶ In some communities, part of the fine imposed on Jews guilty of violence against fellow Jews was paid to the *aljama*.³⁷

Some fights ended with wounded on both sides. Knives, daggers, swords, and other dangerous implements were used by violent Jews with the purpose of injuring fellow Jews.³⁸ The following affair, in which two prominent families from Calatayud were implicated, illustrates well the trend of violence at the time. In 1284, with the cooperation of two other Jews, Jucef Abenalahut of Calatayud wounded Açach el Calvo, who was in the king's service. The king demanded Jucef's extradition after his arrest. From various sources it is clear that several of his relatives helped him. Alfonso III ordered that the accused be judged according to *halakhah*, as was customary in Calatayud. His trial was conducted in a mixed court, where both Jewish and Christian witnesses were heard. Ten years later, in 1297, the Avenalahut family accused Açach el Calvo of wounding and killing the head of the family. Açach el Calvo, indeed, had a previous record of violence: in 1264 he had wounded a fellow Jew with a knife.³⁹

Violence among Jews in the thirteenth and fourteenth centuries was not restricted to any one social stratum but was found in all classes, in all communities, and in all regions. Apart from those already mentioned, Jews from the following communities were implicated in violent incidents according to the sources at our disposal: Calatayud, Lérida, Burriana, Saragossa, Figueras, Valencia, Tárrega, Teruel, and Gerona; and the list is not complete.⁴⁰ Members of aristocratic families, such as the Alconstantini, were involved in violent clashes.⁴¹ Sometimes entire families participated in the fights, leaving behind wounded people.⁴² Among the victims were physicians, rabbis, and women.

---

³³ ACA, Reg. 50, fo. 169 [= R 873 = Dinur, ii. 3, p. 272, no. 26].

³⁴ ACA, Reg. 16, fo. 148ᵛ [= R 409 = Bofarull, Montpellier, 489–90]; Reg. 85, fo. 87ᵛ [= R 2262]; Reg. 91, fo. 91 [= R 2394]; Reg. 203, fo. 171ᵛ [= R 2856].

³⁵ ACA, Reg. 44, fos. 187ᵛ–188 [= R 823 = Baer, *Spanien*, doc. 121 = Dinur, ii. 2, p. 418, no. 8, and pp. 446–7, no. 2].

³⁶ Asibili (Kapah) 131.

³⁷ ACA, Reg. 37, fo. 34ᵛ [= R 504 = Jacobs 726].

³⁸ ACA, Reg. 13, fo. 185 [= R 268 = Jacobs 292]; Reg. 81, fo. 161 [= R 2182]; Reg. 195, fo. 111 [= R 2673]; Magdalena, 'Delitos', pp. 205–6.

³⁹ ACA, Reg. 46, fos. 149, 206 [= R 1099, 1149–50]; Reg. 66, fos. 44, 54, 68, 222 [= R 1533, 1537, 1546, 1655]; Reg. 64, fo. 77ᵛ [= R 1556]. On the murder of the head of the Avenalahut, see Reg. 253, fo. 60 [= R 2660]. On Açach el Calvo's earlier involvement in a knife attack, see ACA, Reg. 46, fos. 149, 206 [= R 1099, 1149–50].

⁴⁰ For sources see Assis, 'Crime and Violence', p. 229, n. 69.

⁴¹ ACA, Reg. 48, fo. 134 [= R 841].   ⁴² ACA, Reg. 48, fo. 134 [= R 841].

There were also women who acted violently and caused serious injuries to men.[43] The king was usually determined to prevent violence and punish those guilty of committing it,[44] but the numerous cases recorded show how little success he had.

Some of the outbursts were not only violent but cruel. In 1319, to cite one example, two Jews from Calatayud attacked a third Jew whom they wounded and dragged quite a distance by his hair.[45] In another case, two butchers and their wives quarrelled almost every day. One day, one butcher attacked the other with a knife, and the wounded man attacked the wife.[46] The results of some attacks were very serious; in one case the victim was blinded in one eye.[47] Violence was so widespread that people tried to secure some extra protection through the king. A Jewish physician from Valencia, Ismael Ibn Crisp, obtained a privilege that threatened with a heavy fine anyone who wounded or insulted him. Two local Jews, not impressed by this royal protection, attacked and wounded him and ended their assault with a bonfire on which they burned the charter, which they had torn into pieces.[48]

RAPE

Rape was an inevitable manifestation of the violence prevalent in Hispano-Jewish society. All our information about Jewish rapists comes from Latin archival records, whereas the Hebrew sources are totally silent on the subject. This may be due to the lack of jurisdiction of the *beth din* over the crime committed by rapists; the prosecution was entirely in the hands of the Crown. Yet it seems odd that they contain no echo whatsoever of this crime. In neighbouring Castile, where the archival material for the period is so meagre compared to the archives of the Crown of Aragon, we have no information at all about Jewish rapists. One possible explanation may be a conspiracy of silence on the part of the people involved not to let the crime be known. This is particularly understandable where the rapists were influential, wealthy men and the victims of low social status. Some of the rapists were violent on occasions other than that of the rape they committed.

Jucef Contatxich of Calatayud was brought to trial in 1279 for allegedly raping a Jewish woman whom he had taken from her home by force. He claimed, however, that he was not present when the witnesses took the oath and that he was not shown the copy of the investigation and file against him.[49] Astruc Caravida, who was accused of other crimes on other occasions, was prosecuted in 1293 for

---

[43] See e.g. ACA, Reg. 199, fo. 31 [= R 2769]; Reg. 222, fo. 27ᵛ [= R 3224]; Reg. 87, fo. 118ᵛ [= R 2488]. On aggressive women, see Adret, i. 948.

[44] ACA, Reg. 81, fos. 76ᵛ, 161 [= R 2098, 2182]; Reg. 224, fo. 31 [= R 3273]; RP, Maestre Racional, t. 1670/1, fos. 3ᵛ, 20ᵛ–21.   [45] ACA, Reg. 217, fos. 149ᵛ–50 [= R 3115].

[46] Asibili (Kapah) 67.   [47] ACA, Reg. 83, fo. 35; Reg. 203, fo. 243 [= R 2865].

[48] ACA, Reg. 199, fo. 31 [= R 2769].   [49] ACA, Reg. 42, fo. 144 [= R 744].

raping Bonafilia, daughter of Druda.⁵⁰ In 1302 Jucef Xaprut from Valencia was accused of raping a married woman. He was pardoned after paying the king a handsome sum.⁵¹ He was also accused of many other transgressions, including attacking a young Jewish woman; again, for a payment of 2,000 sr the king pardoned him. Another Jew from Valencia, Abraham Camis, was prosecuted for attempting to rape a Jewish woman in the public bath. There was widespread discontent with the motives and methods of the king in this field; it was claimed that financial profit was behind some of the royal prosecutions. Jews who reported rape cases to Christian courts were criticized even when the suspicions seemed justified.⁵²

The absence of Hebrew sources on rape should not mislead us into thinking that the Jewish judiciary had no clear stand on the matter. Rape was considered a very serious crime in Jewish law. In 1281 Pedro III wanted to find out whether his officials in Huesca had consulted the *adelantados* in the case of Assach Alcutavi, who had raped Gemila. The king asked them to adopt the penalty prescribed by Jewish law if it was harsher than the *fuero*.⁵³

MURDER

The ultimate and most horrifying evidence of the extent of crime and violence in Jewish society in the Crown of Aragon is the number of murder cases that are recorded. During seventy years, from 1257 to 1327, there were at least sixty murders of Jews by Jews. Almost 60 per cent of all these murders occurred in Aragon. In Calatayud alone nine murders were committed during a period of fifty-five years. In Teruel six Jews were murdered by fellow Jews in fifteen years. All the victims were men except for one woman, one child, and two babies.⁵⁴

Murders were committed in all Aragonese communities. We know of more than one murder committed in each of Saragossa, Daroca, and Barbastro, and at least one murder by Jews took place in each of Huesca, Monzón, Fariza, Uncastillo, and Sos. Considering the small Jewish population in all these communities the figures present an extremely grave picture of morality and social stability. This situation cannot be divorced from the bitter social struggles and extreme social unrest that characterized life in the Aragonese communities and loaded it with tension.

Jewish murderers did not belong to a specific class or group. Some were the favourites of kings and noblemen. They were able to use their contacts to prevent or stop proceedings against them, or, failing that, to reduce or cancel the punishment.⁵⁵ One of them, Salamon Scapa from Barbastro, accompanied the Infante

---

⁵⁰ ACA, Procesos de Audiencia 501/2.   ⁵¹ ACA, Reg. 199, fo. 34ᵛ [=R 2770]
⁵² ACA, Reg. 215, fos. 268–9 [=R 3084]. On reporting of rape, see Reg. 89, fo. 48 [=R 2558].
⁵³ ACA, Reg. 49, fo. 95 [=R 866].   ⁵⁴ ACA, Reg. 66, fo. 100ᵛ [=R 1572].
⁵⁵ ACA, Reg. 46, fo. 200ᵛ [=R 1139]; Reg. 223, fo. 299 [=R 3267].

Alfonso on his campaign to Sardinia in 1324.[56] The king's intervention on behalf of Jewish murderers was not always motivated by legal considerations. That is how we have to interpret certain orders of Jaime II. Thus the king demanded that the judge in Valencia should not limit the movement of Alazar, son of Isaac Allatemi, who was accused of killing Naçan Lobell and was arrested after he had left the city without permission.[57] Another royal order was sent to Calatayud for the protection of Çalema and Azmel Sahadia, who had murdered two Jewish brothers, residents of the same town.[58] Although the king condemned all acts of violence and demanded the punishment of murderers,[59] he frequently departed from his own principles when his interest justified it. In fifteen cases of murder the king granted amnesty or protection to Jewish murderers who paid him handsomely.[60] Normally, however, the king was very strict with murderers and expected their arrest and imprisonment to be efficient. When Astruc Xaprut, murderer of Mosse Bonavia, fled from prison in Valencia the gaoler, fearing the consequences, immediately informed the king and assured him that he was not responsible for the flight.[61] Other Jews were involved in the same murder, and Jucef Morcat, another suspect, the younger brother of Jahia Morcat, also fled. The fugitives were assisted by their relatives, families with whom the king seems to have been on quite friendly terms.[62]

In almost a third of all the murder cases known, more than one person was involved on the side of the guilty party. These murders were committed for political reasons, for vengeance, rivalry, and competition. Family feuds lasted for years. In 1281, eight years after members of the Avenrodrich family were acquitted of the murder of which they had been accused by Jucef de Faro's son, Jucef and his two sons were accused of the murder of a member of the Avenrodrich family.[63] Groups and families hostile to one another did not give up their animosity easily. The result was murder, and dead bodies were found in the streets of the Jewish quarter.[64]

In 1284 Salamon ibn Baruch, a Jew involved in the struggle between the upper and lower classes, was murdered. His murderer was never found. Suspects fled across the border. This was most probably a political killing.[65] Many of the

---

[56] ACA, Reg. 225, fo. 248ᵛ [=R 3296]; Reg. 226, fo. 110ᵛ [=R 3316].
[57] ACA, CR, Jaime II, C 38, no. 4752 [= *Cartas Reales*, no. 155].
[58] ACA, CR, Jaime II, C 35, no. 4411 [= *Cartas Reales*, no. 152].
[59] See e.g. ACA, Reg. 57, fo. 169ᵛ [=R 1414].
[60] This is corroborated in the sources cited here. For other sources see Assis, 'Crime and Violence', p. 231, n. 88.
[61] ACA, CR, Jaime II, C 135, no. 414 [= *Cartas Reales*, no. 556].
[62] ACA, CR, Jaime II, C 100, no. 12501 [= *Cartas Reales*, no. 488]; Reg. 229, fos. 157ᵛ, 258 [=R 3423–4, 3428].
[63] ACA, Reg. 19, fo. 47, [=R 563 = Jacobs 515]; Reg. 50, fo. 176ᵛ [=R 877].
[64] ACA, Reg. 20, fo. 333ᵛ [=R 653 and pp. 422–3, doc. ix = Jacobs 616]; CR, Jaime II, C 35, no. 4411 [= *Cartas Reales*, no. 152]; C 12, no. 1632.
[65] For the sources on this affair, see Assis, 'Crime and Violence', p. 232, n. 96.

murders perpetrated in various communities show Jewish society in its most vulnerable condition.[66] Some Jews hired people to murder their adversaries; others had a Jewish prisoner murdered to ensure he remained silent for ever.[67]

In Aragon, murder among Jews became part of daily life,[68] and the Jews of Valencia were not far behind them.[69] The moral decadence reached its lowest level with the murder of relatives. Brother killed brother, a son-in-law murdered his father-in-law, a husband was poisoned by his wife and in-laws, brothers killed their sister who had slept with a Christian, a husband killed his wife, and a nephew murdered his uncle.[70] In three exceptional cases, Jews killed Christians or Muslims.[71]

MEN OF VIOLENCE

Throughout the period under discussion powerful Jews abused their position to establish control over various aspects of Jewish life. The border between the use of one's influence to govern and the abuse of one's power to coerce was sometimes very vague. Some Jews who occupied important positions in the economy and in the royal or communal administration took advantage of the special relationship they had with the king to force the Jewish community to accept their leadership and their wishes. They hesitated little in using their political power to benefit themselves at the expense of the Jewish community. In many communities Jews exercised power without the consent of the public,[72] and in many cases Jews used the king's support to achieve very specific personal benefits. For example, through royal pressure David Almscaran of Valencia obtained a comfortable seat in front of the ark in the local synagogue.[73]

Some powerful Jews used Christians to impose their will on fellow Jews. One engaged the services of two violent Christian agents to coerce a Jew to divorce his beautiful wife so that she should be free to marry him. The husband was gravely injured with a sword. We know of more cases where Jews employed Christians to get the women whom they were unable to win through conventional methods.[74]

---

[66] ACA, Reg. 43, fo. 79 [=R 1238]; Reg. 66, fos. 149, 157, 221 [=R 1605, 1613, 1648]; Reg. 70, fo. 129 [=R 1737].

[67] ACA, Reg. 253, fo. 60 [=R 2660]; Reg. 199, fos. 11, 77ᵛ, 79 [=R 2766, 2775, 2777].

[68] AC, Reg. 203, fo. 122ᵛ [=R 2851]; Reg. 209, fos. 159ᵛ–60 [=R 2949]; Reg. 217, fo. 207ᵛ [=R 3119]; RP, Maestre Racional, t. 1688, fos. 96–7 [= Baer, *Spanien*, doc. 163, para. 15].

[69] ACA, Reg. 214, fo. 45 [=R 3065]; Reg. 225, fo. 202 [=R 3294]. See the case of Mosse Bonavia above.

[70] ACA, Reg. 13, fo. 248ᵛ [=R 307 = Jacobs 318]; Reg. 19, fo. 117ᵛ [=R 585 = Bofarull, Barcelona, cxxxv]; Reg. 74, fo. 88ᵛ [=R 1902]; Reg. 239, fo. 19 [=R 2919 = Baer, *Spanien*, doc. 164, para. 6]; Reg. 218, fo. 92 [=R 3136]; Magdalena, 'Delitos', p. 200.

[71] ACA, Reg. 9, fo. 12ᵛ [=R 64 = Jacobs 112]; Reg. 21, fo. 43 [=R 522 = Jacobs 639]; Reg. 16, fo. 196ᵛ [=R 441].   [72] Adret, v. 245.

[73] ACA, Reg. 16, fo. 257ᵛ [= MF i. 1084].

[74] Adret, i. 572–3; Gerondi 62.

One powerful Jew prepared an ambush in which a fellow Jew was attacked by Christian gangs.[75] Jewish courtiers used all the means at their disposal to achieve their desires.[76]

The moral decline and corruption perhaps reached their nadir when unscrupulous Jews no longer felt the need to hide their immoral and illegal acts. Rape in public, relations with non-Jewish women that were public knowledge, outrageous behaviour in the synagogue and unrestrained disturbance of public life, open threats to kill, and the use of weapons on Saturdays in synagogues are just some of the immoral and criminal acts that were perpetrated, carried out by Jews who thought they would not be punished. They considered themselves above the law, or indeed outside it. They felt no solidarity with the Jewish community and no compassion towards their victims. Abraham de Torre from Figueras was typical of the worst characters that the Jewish community produced.[77] Salamo Abençaprut of Teruel was accused of killing the wife and sister of Salamon Alfayat; he raped the other sister and then married her.[78] Some of these corrupt and immoral Jews were leaders in the community. Such were Jahuda Alazar of Valencia and Yizhaq ibn Asfura of Saragossa.[79]

The accusations levelled against some of these violent men in Jewish society included adultery, rape, robbery, murder, bribery, incest, and physical attacks. The concise description of their alleged deeds is a reflection of a corrupt generation of spoilt Jews who were totally estranged from their people and from the norms that governed Jewish life.[80] They were often the children or grandchildren of Jews who served their community with love and dedication and who acted in court on behalf of their Jewish brethren. The younger generation born into affluence acquired little of the moral code that served as a guide to many other Jewish leaders of previous and subsequent generations.

---

[75] Adret, v. 245.   [76] Adret, v. 240, vii. 267; Perfet 132.
[77] The following sources represent a fair variety of examples: ACA, Reg. 42, fo. 144 [=R 744]; Reg. 49, fo. 95 [=R 866]; Reg. 62, fos 103ᵛ, 136ᵛ–137 [=R 1242–3, 1316 and pp. 428–30, doc. xv]; Reg. 119, fo. 34ᵛ [=R 2770].   [78] ACA, Reg. 89, fo. 48 [=R 2558].
[79] ACA, Reg. 202, fo. 203ᵛ [=R 2831]; Perfet 395.
[80] AC, Reg. 202, fo. 204 [=R 2832]; Reg. 207, fo. 154 [=R 2915]; Reg. 215, fos. 268ᵛ–269 [=R 3092].

PART SIX

RELIGIOUS LIFE

§6.1 Jewish Religious Trends in the Crown of Aragon: Between Sepharad and Ashkenaz

THE JUDEO-ARABIC TRADITION OF SEPHARAD

THE Judeo-Arabic tradition that transformed the cultural and religious life of Iberian Jewry originated in the east but reached its full fruition in the west, in Sepharad, the medieval Hebrew term for the Iberian peninsula. During the so-called 'golden age' in Al-Andalus, between 950 and 1150, a new trend in medieval Judaism took shape and produced some of the finest works in Hebrew and Judeo-Arabic literature. No field of scholarship was neglected. Talmud and Bible, ethics and philosophy, Hebrew language and poetry, science and medicine developed during the two centuries following the career of Hasdai ibn Shaprut. This flourishing religious and cultural age, which was the outcome of the Judeo-Arabic encounter, came to an abrupt end with the Almohadic invasion of Al-Andalus in 1148. The Almohads, who came to help the Muslims of Spain to halt the advance of the Christian Hispanic kingdoms, destroyed Andalusian culture and outlawed what they considered Muslim, Christian, and Jewish heresy.[1]

The Jewish survivors of the Almohadic persecutions took refuge in both distant and neighbouring lands. Those who settled in Muslim territories made little impact on local Jewish life, since they belonged to the same general Jewish cultural ambience. The exceptional case of Maimonides should not mislead us. Those who emigrated to Provence caused a cultural and religious upheaval, after acquainting the local Jews with the Judeo-Arabic scholarship which they translated into Hebrew. Jewish historiography has however neglected the largest group of Andalusian Jewish emigrants, who crossed the border and joined their brethren in Christian Spain.

Contacts between Jews in Muslim and Christian Spain preceded the decline of Al-Andalus. Jews moved in both directions, across borders that were constantly changing with the fluctuations of the Reconquista wars. It is a fascinating but often forgotten fact that some of the masterpieces of the 'golden age' of Sepharad were produced in Christian Spain, in a different cultural and linguistic environment

---

[1] On the 'golden age' of the Jews in Muslim Spain see Ashtor, *The Jews of Moslem Spain*, i, pp. 228–63. On the Almohadic invasion, see Halkin, 'History of the Almohadic Persecutions'; Corcos, 'The Attitude of the Almohadic Leaders'.

from the much-studied Andalusian surroundings. Moses ibn Ezra felt the necessity to formulate the essence of the Andalusian tradition as a result of his contact with Jews of Christian Spain. This attempt was the product of the cultural crossroads at which the Jews of the Iberian peninsula found themselves.[2]

The religious and cultural symbiosis that took place in Christian Spain was a unique experience and experiment in Jewish history. Jewish culture developed through its contact with two cultures. In his attempt to justify to the Jews of northern Spain the debt of Andalusian Jewish culture to Arabic culture, and to show that the result was far from harmful, Moses ibn Ezra was in fact laying the foundations of the unique Sephardi culture that was to develop in Spain, through contact with both the world of Islam and Christian Europe. Yehudah Alharizi, Israel Israeli, and many others were born under Christian rule. Their absorption of the Judeo-Arabic culture of Andalusia in a Christian milieu is a fascinating phenomenon. The special religious and cultural trend that emerged in the Hispanic kingdoms was not lacking in contradictions, pressures, and competing rival elements, but it was typical of Jews who have gradually passed from an Arabic sphere of influence to a Latin and Romance milieu that was itself in close contact with Arabic cultural and scientific tradition and Muslim religious thought. This religious trend in medieval Jewry differed both from Jewish life in Levantine Muslim lands and from that of Franco-German Jewry. Arabic remained an essential ingredient of this culture, while its broad thematic interest in Jewish studies and general sciences was one of its fundamental characteristics.

From the end of the eleventh century to the end of the thirteenth, Jewish scholars in the Hispanic kingdoms participated in the translation of numerous works of science and philosophy from Arabic into Latin and later into Romance languages. Arabic remained the language of Jewish intellectuals and scholars in Toledo and elsewhere long after their conquest by the Christians. Works in Judeo-Arabic were still produced in the fourteenth century, and in Toledo, Tudela, Saragossa, and Barcelona there were still Jews whose knowledge of Arabic served them both inside and outside the Jewish community. The religious trend that developed in Sepharad was characterized above all by its diversity, its exceptional receptivity, and its attitude to philosophy and science.[3]

Despite their political, social, and economic differences, and even some religious variations, the Jews of the Hispanic kingdoms of Castile and Leon, Navarre and Portugal, Aragon and Catalonia were united by their common broad cultural and religious Judeo-Arabic heritage, which we may conveniently call Sephardi. Their method of study of the Talmud differed from the method that prevailed in the Franco-German *yeshivot*. Their conception of the Hebrew language was also different and their attitude to philosophy and science certainly set them apart from Jews north of the Pyrenees. In their intellectual interests,

---

[2] See Drori, 'The Hidden Context'; Assis, 'The Judeo-Arabic Tradition'.
[3] Romano, 'The Jews' Contribution'.

religious concepts, and mentality the scholars of Sepharad were far from their *tossafist* and pietist colleagues of France and Germany.

ASHKENAZI INFLUENCE IN SEPHARAD

The advance of the Christian conquests opened up new channels of religious and cultural interchange for Spanish Jewry. The Jews in the Crown of Aragon were particularly open to new influences emanating from the north. During the Muslim period, Talmudic scholars from Spain were influential in French *yeshivot*. Similarly, Spanish exegesis and *piyut* left their impact on the traditions of French Jewry.[4] This influence ended with the collapse of Andalusian Jewry during the Almohadic persecutions. Meanwhile, the influence of the French academies was constantly growing in the Jewish communities of northern Spain. One of the first scholars to bring the teachings of the northern *yeshivot* to the attention of Spanish masters and disciples was the Provençal R. Abraham ben Natan Ha-Yarhi, author of *Sefer ha-Manhiq* which reflects his close acquaintance with the customs and rituals of the communities in western Europe which he visited. His arrival in Spain at the beginning of the thirteenth century marks the first stage of a growing penetration of Franco-German influence in the Iberian region.[5] Undoubtedly his stay in Toledo left its mark on local scholars. R. Meir Abulafia must have become more acquainted with the northern traditions through him. It is noteworthy that R. Meir Abulafia was the first scholar to wage war against Maimonides, while the latter was still alive. The alliance of Sephardi scholars with colleagues from France against the Jewish heritage of the Judeo-Arabic age dates back to these early contacts. These led to the growing attraction of students from Spain to the northern *yeshivot* that paved the way for the cultural and religious transformation that was about to occur on Spanish soil.

The number of scholars from Catalonia who studied in France grew. Among those who studied in French *yeshivot* we find the teachers of R. Moshe ben Nahman, R. Yehudah ben Yaqar, and R. Meir of Triquetaille. Nahmanides' relative R. Jonah Gerondi studied in the *yeshivah* in Evreux. During his stay in France R. Jonah absorbed much of the ideals and traditions of the French *tossafists* and established lasting relationships with teachers and colleagues there. There was also some influence of the German pietists, the *hasidim*. After their return from France, these rabbis, deeply influenced by Rashi and the *tossafists*, disseminated their teachings and methods among their colleagues and disciples in Spain.[6] The visit of R. Moshe of Coucy in 1236 was certainly carefully prepared and almost certainly initiated by pro-French Spanish scholars like R. Jonah Gerondi

[4] Grossman, 'Between Spain and France'; id., 'Relations between Spanish and Ashkenazi Jewry', pp. 220–7.

[5] Ta-Shema, 'Ashkenazi Hasidism', pp. 171–3.

[6] Ta-Shema, 'Ashkenazi Hasidism'; Septimus, 'Piety and Power'; Grossman, 'Relations between Spanish and Ashkenazi Jewry', pp. 227–8.

who were more than ready to rally all the forces available for their attack against the representatives of the so-called Maimonidean and rationalist trend.

Nahmanides readily accepted the *tossafists*' method which focused the student's attention on understanding the issue *per se*—a radical change from the Sephardi method that aimed at reaching the halakhic decision through the study of the Talmudic text. Along with the Talmudic method of the *tossafists* and the pietism of the *hasidei Ashkenaz*, there was also a marked kabbalistic trend that emanated from the north and made its way to north-eastern Spain. Gerona's status as a centre of kabbalah owed its origin to Provençal mystics. Nahmanides was also influenced by Ashkenaz in his concept of magic, and was consequently critical of the rationalists' attitude to it.[7]

This immense influence from the north was greatly enhanced by the immigration of Ashkenazi rabbis to Spain. R. Dan Ashkenazi came from France and settled in Toledo.[8] R. Shelomo Zarfati, who also came from France and settled in Majorca at the invitation of Jucef Faquim, brought with him the Talmudic tradition of the north.[9] The most important immigrant, however, was R. Asher ben Yehiel, who settled in Toledo around the beginning of the fourteenth century. He and his family continued to adhere to their Ashkenazi traditions, which they regarded as superior to those of Sepharad, and he clashed with the representatives of the Sephardi Judeo-Arabic tradition. The ground had been prepared for the successful integration of R. Asher and his children; to understand how deep the religious changes of this period were, it is sufficient to note that R. Asher was able to assert his leadership in Toledo, hitherto the centre of Sephardi culture.[10] The expulsion of the Jews from France acted as a catalyst of the northern influence. In the fourteenth century, more rabbis from the north settled in the Crown of Aragon. Apart from R. Shelomo Zarfati, mentioned above, we have to add R. Perez ha-Cohen, who was to be engaged as a professional rabbi at the recommendation of R. Nissim Gerondi. He contributed to deepen further the influence of French scholarship in Catalonia.[11]

The protagonists of the Sephardi trend are generally called rationalists and philosophers, and described as opponents of tradition. It would be wrong however to attribute entirely to the so-called rationalist trend the religious laxity that existed in Jewish Spain. The opponents of the Franco-German trend and the mystics were not necessarily anti-halakhic and they were not opposed to tradition, certainly not to the tradition of Sepharad. They were however opposed to a 'new' tradition that originated north of the Alps. Some of its representatives visited

---

[7] On the northern influence in kabbalah see Idel, 'Jewish Thought', pp. 272–5. On magic, see Adret, viii. 283; *Torat HaShem Temimah*, p. 147, in Chavel, *The Works of Nahmanides*, i, p. 378.

[8] Ta-Shema, 'Rabbeinu Dan'.

[9] On R. Shelomo Zarfati, see Perfet 374–8. His rival on the island, R. Vidal Ephraim Gerondi, acted as the infante's astrologer and had a scientific education, besides Talmudic studies.

[10] Freimann, *Ha-Rosh*.

[11] Assaf, *Texts and Studies*, pp. 173–81; Gerondi 417–20; Shatzmiller, 'Rabbi Isaac Ha-Cohen'.

Spain and preached and taught their doctrines. R. Moshe of Coucy describes his visit, his sermons, and achievements with great enthusiasm.[12] In reality many Jews in Toledo were witnesses to the emergence of a tradition that was different from theirs in numerous details, and many Jews in early fourteenth-century Toledo would have been quite right to be alarmed at seeing their tradition losing ground as R. Asher ben Yehiel and his sons gathered more and more supporters for their imported tradition.

The situation was no different in the communities of the Crown of Aragon, except that here the influence from Franco-Germany was even greater. Not only was the kabbalah centre in Gerona deeply indebted to teachers from Provence and perhaps even from Germany, but Talmudic studies in thirteenth-century Catalonia and Aragon were conducted along the lines of the *tossafists*' approach. The greatest rabbinic masters of Catalonia adopted to a greater or lesser degree the French method of Talmudic study. Even their halakhic writings were saturated with kabbalistic teachings. These masters included R. Moshe ben Nahman, R. Jonah Gerondi, R. Shelomo ben Adret, R. Aharon Ha-Levi de Na Clara, R. Yom Tov Asibili, and R. Bahye ben Asher. Despite this impressive list of prominent rabbinic scholars, the Jews in the Hispanic kingdoms were not all followers of the Ashkenazi trend; had this been so, the conflict and struggle that tore apart Iberian Jewry in the thirteenth and fourteenth centuries would not have occurred.

The northern influence that so deeply affected Jewish life in Spain cannot be understood without reference to the religious and cultural transformation that was taking place during the long period of the Reconquista. Vast territories and masses of people passed from one cultural, religious, and linguistic domain to another. The Christian forces that by the thirteenth century definitely had the upper hand had been for many decades inspired, supported, and influenced by Christians north of the Pyrenees. The Christianization and Latinization of the Iberian peninsula was a long and complex process which left its impact on the Jews as well.

The influence of Cluny brought a fresh and crusading spirit to the Hispanic Church. The French monastery, which was founded in 909, had succeeded in establishing a Cluniac empire in Provence-Languedoc and many houses throughout Spain. Cluny played an important role in recruiting French knights to assist the Hispanic kingdoms in their fight against the Muslims in Spain. Besides the warriors, there were the Cluniac monks who preached their Christian message not only to the defeated Muslims but also to the Mozarabs, the Arabic-speaking Christians who lived under Muslim rule and preserved some Visigothic ecclesiastical traditions besides some customs which developed in the Islamic environment of Al-Andalus.[13]

---

[12] R. Moshe of Coucy, *Sefer Mizvot Gadol*, Positive Commandments, 3.
[13] Morris, *The Papal Monarchy*, pp. 64–8; Hunt, *Cluny under S. Hugh*; Cowdrey, *The Cluniacs and the Gregorian Reform*.

In the south the Christian conquerors found well-established Mozarabic communities. There were many churches in Cordova, Toledo, and Mérida, and fifteen monasteries in the vicinity of Cordova alone. The influence of the Mozarabs in the years immediately following the Reconquista was immense in the field of science and culture. The emigration of Mozarabs to the Christian north from the tenth century brought Arabic influence into the Hispanic kingdoms. The Almoravid and Almohadic invasions in the eleventh and twelfth centuries intensified the Arabic penetration into the north. While the first-generation Mozarabs contributed much to the transmission of the scientific and cultural legacy of the south to the north, their religious influence was seriously contained from the very first stages of their life under Christian rule. The Cluniac trend from the north eventually triumphed. By the thirteenth century a very large majority of the Mozarabs lived in Christian Spain. Their religious traditions and cultural heritage were rejected by their northern coreligionists. In 1080 the Mozarabic liturgy was already replaced by the Roman liturgy by Pope Gregory VII at the Council of Burgos. Apart from a few churches in Toledo which were permitted to use the Mozarabic liturgy, the spirit of Cluny prevailed. The northern trend was presented as the authentic and true religion. Northern preachers, including French ones, came to Spain just as Jewish scholars from Franco-Germany and Provence did in the thirteenth and fourteenth centuries.[14]

Despite the basic differences in content, the processes in Jewish and Christian societies were quite similar. In both cases the southern versions of Judaism and Christianity came under serious attack by representatives of northern French trends, supported by local admirers, in a campaign led by preachers from the north and others who studied there.

The controversies that tore Spanish Jewry apart in the thirteenth and early fourteenth centuries had also their parallel in Christian society. By the twelfth century theology had become an academic discipline of which Paris was the undisputed centre. Neoplatonism and Aristotelianism occupied a major role in Christian theology. Rationalism became a major trait of Christian doctrine. Secular knowledge was employed to understand the Bible. In northern France scholarship was dominated by dialectic and logic. Rationalists and anti-rationalists struggled with no less intensity in Christian society than in Jewish society. The official Church launched a vehemently violent struggle against what it considered 'heresy' in southern France while new orders began their zealous mission in Spain. Jewish society in these areas was equally in turmoil and agitation, and its 'heretics' were banned with great zeal.[15]

---

[14] Simonet, *Historia de los mozárabes*; Cagigas, *Minorías etnico-religiosas*; González Palencia, *Los mozárabes de Toledo*; Aldea Vaquero, Marin Martinez, and Vives Gatell, *Diccionario*, iii (1747).
[15] Vicaire, *S. Dominic*.

THE RELIGIOUS CONTROVERSIES

In its first stages, the conflict between the two trends centred on Maimonides' books, particularly the *Guide of the Perplexed* and the 'Book of Knowledge' in his *Mishne Torah*. Simultaneously with the absorption of Ashkenazi and Provençal influences, Maimonides' masterpiece the *Mishne Torah* was received in Spain with great enthusiasm. Many communities decided to accept it as their code of law. For Maimonides' supporters *Mishne Torah* was the most comprehensive and authoritative codex, which left no question unanswered. His systematic treatment of all the ritual, civil, criminal, and ethical laws without exception was greatly appreciated and valued.

Already during Maimonides' lifetime, however, there was fierce opposition to his *Mishne Torah*. His opponents expressed grave concern that Maimonides' code would lead to the neglect of Talmudic studies. The 'Book of Knowledge' in particular aroused strong criticism for the principles of faith and religious fundamentals that it contained. The rationalist approach evident in his interpretations of these principles was considered heretical by many of his critics.[16] Maimonides' *Guide of the Perplexed* provoked very strong criticism from the opponents of the rationalist trend. As early as 1200 we hear of criticism of Maimonides in Spain. Significantly, R. Meir ha-Levi Abulafia turned to his colleagues in France and Provence to rally their support against some of Maimonides' rationalist articles of faith. We have already noted the presence of R. Abraham ben Natan ha-Yarhi in Toledo when R. Meir headed the *beth din*. There can be no doubt that R. Meir's anti-Maimonidean strategy was carefully prepared in consultation with French rabbis.

Provence, which had become to some extent part of the cultural and religious milieu of Sepharad ever since the arrival of the Andalusian Jewish refugees, took the initiative in the next two rounds of the conflict. This fact, however, should not distract us from the focus of our attention. The conflict was between two religious and cultural trends in Judaism, between Sepharad and Ashkenaz. In 1232 R. Shelomo of Montpellier acted in conjunction with disciples and colleagues from Spain, among whom R. Jonah Gerondi was very active. We should bear in mind that R. Shelomo of Montpellier was in fact originally a Catalan from Barcelona! R. Jonah was sent to France by R. Shelomo of Montpellier to conduct and coordinate the anti-Maimonidean campaign there. In the Catalan and Aragonese communities we find the staunchest supporters and opponents of Maimonides—or rather, defenders of the two trends. Despite the efforts of Nahmanides to calm the situation, the Aragonese communities, followed by the Catalan, issued the counter-ban against R. Shelomo and his supporters. Clearly,

---

[16] On the spread of *Mishne Torah* in Spain, see Asher ben Yehiel, Responsa, xxxi, no. 9; ACA, Reg. 939, fo. 221 [= Baer, *Spanien*, doc. 343]; Baer, *Spanien*, doc. 586, paras. 1, 12. On opposition to the *Mishne Torah*, see Twersky, *Rabad*, pp. 128–97; Septimus, *Hispano-Jewish Culture*, pp. 72–4.

there was still very wide support for the Judeo-Arabic tradition among the Jews of the Crown of Aragon. Among those who signed the ban were Jews who were educated in this tradition and who absorbed philosophy and sciences alongside their Jewish studies.[17]

The conflict entered a new phase around the beginning of the fourteenth century in the communities of the Crown of Aragon before renewed criticism was heard from Montpellier, which was under Aragonese rule, whether within Barcelona or Majorca. In view of the strong opposition to the anti-Maimonidean camp following the 1232 ban on Maimonides' writings and the religious and social unrest at the end of the thirteenth century, it is most surprising that R. Shelomo ben Adret's initial reaction to R. Abba Mari's plea for action against the rationalists in 1303 was rather cool and evasive. His claim that the communities in his land were not faced with the same sort of problem as were the Provençal Jews seems perplexing. The sources indicate otherwise. Even supposing that Adret believed the case to be as he said, why then did he proclaim the ban in Barcelona in 1305? Nothing had radically changed during the short intervening period. It seems most unlikely that Adret, a leader of the highest calibre and a halakhist deeply involved in the communal, social, and religious life of the Jews in the Crown of Aragon, should have failed to detect what any student of history can observe. It was, on the contrary, probably because he feared that a ban on the rationalists might have generated great opposition and a strong reaction in his own community, and wanted to prevent further deterioration in the relations between the two camps, that he was so hesitant to act and even tried to shake off R. Abba Mari's pressure by claiming that the problem did not exist south of the Pyrenees.

It is also possible that Adret did not believe in the efficacy of a ban in context of the *Kulturkampf* between the two major trends which differed on matters of principles, faith, curriculum, and mentality. The ban that was published on 9 Av 1305 in Barcelona had two elements. The first forbade the study of philosophy and sciences, except medicine and geometry, before the age of twenty-five. The other pronounced the ban against Jews who treated the *agadot* lightly and attributed allegorical interpretations to the Torah. In his own community Adret seems to have achieved a great success, since the bans were signed by the six *ne'emanim* and all the members of the Council of Thirty. Yet the bans achieved almost nothing. Each camp continued to adhere to its basic position and uphold its tenets. There is no indication that as a result of the ban the number of science and philosophy students diminished.[18] The bans pleased neither camp. For the anti-rationalists they were too mild and inefficient, while for the rationalists they imposed unbearable restrictions on education.

The clash was between two versions of Judaism which denied each other's

---

[17] On the controversy, see Silver, *Maimonidean Criticism*; Sarachek, *Faith and Reason*; Septimus, *Hispano-Jewish Culture*, pp. 61–74.

[18] On the controversy see Baer, *History*, i, pp. 281–305; Touati, 'La Controverse'.

validity. If we discard some extremists on the fringes, neither camp advocated the abandonment of Jewish values as found in the classical biblical and Talmudic literature and an antinomian attitude. The teachings of the kabbalists in Spain did not represent a tradition older than the various trends of Jewish philosophy in the Iberian peninsula. There is no evidence that the apostates in the thirteenth and fourteenth centuries came from one camp rather than the other: it is sufficient to examine the spiritual and religious background of these apostates to realize this fact.

§6.2 Scholars and Scholarship

THE SCHOLARS AND THEIR WORKS

IN the thirteenth and fourteenth centuries the Crown of Aragon was the leading centre of learning in the Jewish world. It was the meeting-point of various religious and cultural currents from both north and south. In Catalonia, in particular, Judeo-Arabic culture met and clashed with Talmudic traditions from France and kabbalistic teachings from Germany and Provence.[1] The territories of the Crown of Aragon were fertile ground for religious and cultural interaction. To the various conceptions of Judaism that came from other centres the scholars of the Crown of Aragon added their own contribution, and their learning went forth to other communities.

Nahmanides (1194–1270), the greatest of the thirteenth-century scholars, illustrates very well the characteristics of the Jewish centre that emerged in the northwest of the Iberian peninsula. Nahmanides combined in his teaching the *tossafists'* method of Talmudic study, an esoteric kabbalah for a restricted circle, and elements of Judeo-Arabic philosophy. He was a halakhist, an exegete, and a mystic.[2] His halakhic works include commentaries on the Talmud, responsa, and monographs. In his commentaries he opened up new avenues in Talmudic scholarship in Spain by introducing the *tossafists'* approach. It is not surprising that his novellae were to be extensively studied and accepted in the Ashkenazi world. His works of criticism on Maimonides and his refutation of the Provençal critique of Alfasi earned him worldwide fame as a halakhist. His great respect and reverence for other rabbis and for tradition in general did not blunt his sharp criticism and utter rejection of what he considered mistaken views.[3] Nahmanides represented the Jewish side in the Disputation of Barcelona in 1263 (discussed in Part I of this book). His role in the defence of Judaism against the attempts of the apostate Dominican Paulus Cristiani to prove the veracity of Christianity from Talmudic and Midrashic sources is generally known. He spared no effort and no argument, even when this meant going against his own convictions, to destroy Paulus' arguments and credibility. Needless to say, Paulus could have had no greater Talmudic expert for a contestant. The king's attitude towards

---

[1] On the development of the kabbalah in Catalonia see Scholem, *Origins of the Kabbalah*, pp. 365–400; Idel, 'La història de la Cábala'.

[2] On Nahmanides as a mystic and exegete, see respectively Idel, 'We Have No Kabbalistic Tradition on This'; Grossman, 'Biblical Exegesis', pp. 137–42. For a general overview, see Assis, 'El concepto del judaismo' and Idel, 'R. Moses ben Nahman'.

[3] See e.g. *Responsa of Nahmanides*, 46, 49.

Nahmanides during and after the Disputation indicates the high esteem in which the Catalan scholar was held at court. He was a physician and treated Christians, including members of the royal family.[4]

Nahmanides' contemporary and relative R. Jonah Gerondi studied in *yeshivot* in France and Provence and brought back with him to his native land the scholarly traditions and religious approach from north of the Pyrenees. In the Maimonidean Controversy of 1232 he fully supported his teacher from Montpellier in condemning Maimonides' *Guide* and 'Book of Knowledge'. He headed a *yeshivah* in Barcelona, where he taught local and foreign students, before moving to Toledo. He preached his ideas of Jewish ethics and religious behaviour. He wrote commentaries on the Bible and the Talmud as well as ethical works. In ethics, he was a pioneer in Spain. His role in introducing Ashkenazi influence in Spain cannot be overestimated.[5]

R. Shelomo ben Adret (1235–1310) was undoubtedly the greatest and most prolific halakhist of his generation. His thousands of responsa testify to his vast erudition and to the prestige he enjoyed both in the Crown of Aragon and in other lands. Besides his invaluable responsa, his novellae on the Talmud and halakhic works left their impact on Jewish learning for generations to come. He attached great importance to the Aggadic part of the Talmud, on part of which he wrote a commentary. His halakhic works *Torat ha-Bayit* and *'Avodat ha-Qodesh*, as well as his novellae and his responsa, became the cornerstone of Jewish jurisprudence. His *yeshivah*, which housed reliable ancient manuscripts of the Talmud, attracted scholars from various lands, including Germany.[6]

Adret's spiritual leadership in the Crown of Aragon was undisputed. The king's constant consultations with him on matters of Jewish law and public order are eloquent testimony to his high status. Although accomplished in philosophy and the sciences, he followed in the footsteps of his two teachers Nahmanides and R. Jonah Gerondi in adopting the *tossafist* method and in his respect for Ashkenazi scholarship.[7] He was deeply influenced by the kabbalist current in Catalonia of the second half of the thirteenth century. He was in close contact with Christian dignitaries and churchmen, with some of whom he conducted religious polemics. He was well acquainted with Christian polemics against Judaism and issued instructions offering Jewish counter-arguments to Christian ones.[8]

In the early period of his life Adret lent money to Christians. Some fifty promissory notes endorsed by his Hebrew signature are found in the Archivo Capitular de Barcelona.[9] As late as 1283 Adret was involved in the family business

---

[4] Adret, i. 120.

[5] Ta-Shema, 'Ashkenazi Hasidism'; Septimus, 'Piety and Power'. [6] Adret, i. 395.

[7] In many of his responsa he refers to them as his teachers. See e.g. Adret, i. 189, 427, 497, 1011, 1206, ii. 2, 100, 108, 112, 230, 259 and *passim*.

[8] On his discussions with Christians, see Cohen, 'The Christian Adversary'. His polemical instructions are found in Adret, iv. 187 and reference to the treatise he published in Adret, iv. 31.

[9] See *Cartas Reales*, index of persons, s.v. 'Salamon Adret'.

and moneylending transactions.[10] From various sources we know that Adret was actually involved in the administration and politics of his community, Barcelona: in the late 1270s and early 1280s he served as one of the *ne'emanim* or *secretarii* of the community.[11]

Adret's colleague and critic R. Aharon Ha-Levi de Na Clara also taught in Barcelona. The two men shared some of the same students and had frequent discussions on Jewish law. They appeared on many occasions as a team or on the same *beth din*, sometimes at the request of the king. In his *Bedeq ha-Bayit*, Na Clara criticized Adret's *Torat ha-Bayit*. He wrote novellae on the Talmud and a commentary on Alfasi's *Sefer ha-Halakhot*.

R. Yom Tov Asibili was a disciple of both R. Shelomo ben Adret and R. Aharon Ha-Levi. He was active in the first half of the fourteenth century. Like his teachers, he was very much influenced by the *tossafists*, as his novellae on the Talmud seem to indicate. His responsa show how active he was in settling lawsuits and clarifying halakhic problems.[12] A contemporary rabbi and student of the same teachers was R. Abraham ben Shelomo Tazarte, author of *Huqat ha-Dayanim*. R. Bahye ben Asher was *dayan* and preacher in Saragossa at the end of the thirteenth century and the beginning of the fourteenth. His commentary contains four different modes of exegesis: literal, homiletical, rationalist, and kabbalistic. The last method was his favourite as he was himself a kabbalist. He used the Zohar extensively. His commentary became very popular. His *Kad ha-Qemah* is a collection of homilies, apparently based on sermons he preached in the synagogue in Saragossa. They contain much information about the social problems that Aragonese Jewry encountered in his day.[13]

In the middle of the fourteenth century R. Nissim Gerondi was the spiritual head of the Jews in the realm of Aragon. While he sent his responsa near and far, wrote a commentary on the Torah, and prepared novellae on the Talmud and a commentary on Alfasi's *Halakhot*, he also served as a physician and treated the sick, including members of the royal household.[14] He was the teacher of R. Yishaq ben Shehet Perfet, the last great rabbinic figure before the massacres of 1391. Many of his responsa belong to the period prior to his flight to North Africa after 1391.[15]

---

[10] ACA, Reg. 59, fo. 193 [= R 998 = Dinur, ii. 3, p. 272, no. 24].

[11] ACA, Reg. 51, fo. 29ᵛ [= R 915]; Reg. 52, fos. 29ᵛ–30 [R 917]; Reg. 43, fo. 28 [= R 1196]. In a document of June 1285 he was referred to as a past secretary of the *aljama*: Reg. 57, fo. 139ᵛ [= R 1391 = Dinur, ii. 3, pp. 272–3, no. 27].

[12] On R. Yom Tov Asibili, see Asibili (Kapah), introduction.

[13] Rabbenu Bahye's *Commentary on the Pentateuch*, introduction.

[14] Gerondi, introduction.

[15] Hirschman, *Rabbi Isaac ben Sheshet Perfet*.

THE CROWN AND THE RABBI

Most of the rabbis mentioned above maintained a special relationship with the king–counts. Their reputation in the Jewish world in general and in the communities of the Crown of Aragon in particular was well noted in the court. The esteem in which many of the scholars were held by the royal administration reflected the king's realistic evaluation of the status of the rabbis in the Jewish community. In all royal communications addressed or referring to the halakhic experts and rabbinic leaders, the king's appreciation and respect are evident.

The king addressed some lawsuits that remained unsettled by local *dayanim*, and disputes that were not resolved by the community judiciary, to the famous halakhists of his realm. The relatively brief reign of Pedro III (1276–85) offers rich documentation on this subject, and the status of the great Catalan halakhists did not change under his successors. Among the rabbinic authorities consulted on legal issues or required to adjudicate between litigants were R. Shelomo ben Adret, R. Aharon Ha-Levi de Na Clara, R. Yom Tov Asibili and R. Jonah Gerondi.

As noted above, R. Shelomo ben Adret and R. Aharon Ha-Levi de Na Clara acted as a team on several occasions. In October 1278 they were asked by Pedro III to take charge of the lawsuit between the *aljama* of Saragossa and an individual member concerning houses that belonged to the *heqdesh*.[16] Under Alfonso III, a dispute over taxation between the *aljama* of Gerona and Jews settled in localities in the vicinity was submitted to Adret in March 1291 for arbitration.[17] In April 1279 Pedro III asked Adret and R. Jonah Gerondi, the younger cousin of his namesake the famous pietist, to sit as judges in the trial of Vidalon de Porta, who was eventually condemned as an informer.[18] Adret and Gerondi hesitated for about a year before they were forced by the king to take a decision.[19] In another difficult case, in which the courtier David Mascaran was the plaintiff, Pedro III decided that if the compromise reached by a Barcelona Jewish court were challenged by one of the litigants, R. Shelomo ben Adret should act as the judge of appeal.[20] Eventually, Adret and his *beth din* did take charge of the case, as can be seen from the order by Alfonso III in March 1286 that Adret and his two colleagues Zarch Malet and Saltell Astruch pronounce their verdict. Clearly, the judges had difficulty in completing their inquiry on the crimes allegedly perpetrated by David Mascaran.[21]

David Mascaran, who was hated by many Jews for his role in the oppressive

---

[16] ACA, Reg. 41, fo. 6 [= R 712–13 = Baer, *Spanien*, doc. 115, paras. 1–2].

[17] The source is from a fragmentary register of Alfonso III. See R 2329.

[18] ACA, Reg. 41, fo. 62 [= R 725 = Baer, *Spanien*, doc. 116, para. 1]; Reg. 42, fo. 169ʻ [= R 751 = Baer, *Spanien*, doc. 116, para. 2].

[19] On the case, see Kaufman, 'Jewish Informers'.

[20] ACA, Reg. 57, fo. 224 [= R 1464].

[21] ACA, Reg. 66, fo. 9ʻ [= R 1507–8].

tax impositions of 1285, was murdered in 1290 by one of his many enemies in the Jewish community. Adret's reservations about getting involved in the case were well founded.[22] Following the assassination, the *aljamas* of Barcelona and Saragossa disagreed on the way to apportion the sum that the Jews of the Crown were ordered to pay. Two rabbis from Huesca, Salomon Avenlatemi and Juceph Alphavel, the translator of Maimonides' commentary on the Mishnah, were asked in 1292 to arbitrate between the chief communities of Catalonia and Aragon.[23]

At the king's request, Adret sometimes served as an appeal judge for cases tried by a local *beth din*. One such was the case between two Jews over claims on a vineyard, tried in Egea in 1283. One of the litigants appealed to the *beth din* in Saragossa, whose verdict did not satisfy him; when he complained to Pedro III, Adret was asked to examine the case. At the end of June 1286 the matter was still unresolved. Alfonso III ordered that the other litigant appear before Adret.[24] In 1300, after fourteen months in prison, Jucef Alatronay from Valencia wrote to Jaime II requesting that his case against the leaders of the community of Valencia be reviewed by Adret according to *halakhah*. Somehow, certain elements in the Jewish community succeeded in preventing Adret's involvement in the case. No communication was received by Adret on the matter.[25]

In matrimonial cases, Adret's legal opinion was sought at the king's order. In October 1281, for instance, Pedro III suggested that Samuel de Forn consult both Adret and his colleague Bonjudas Salamo before deciding to divorce his wife.[26] A matrimonial case was referred to Adret and R. Aharon Ha-Levi de Na Clara by Alfonso III in October 1289.[27] In 1304 Jaime II ordered the rabbis of Lérida, who were trying a Jewess accused of adultery, to consult Adret.[28] In 1306 the king asked Adret to examine the case of a father and a daughter from Tarragona against the latter's husband from Gerona.[29] Adret's involvement in such cases was due to difficulties related to problems of jurisdiction of the courts when the litigants resided in different communities.

Adret's arbitration and verdict were also called for in disputes between *aljamas*. When a conflict over taxation between the community of Lérida on the one hand, and those of Agramunt and Pons on the other, reached an impasse in 1292, Jaime

---

[22] On the case of David Mascaran, see R, index.

[23] ACA, Reg. 92, fo. 160ʳ [= Baer, *Spanien*, doc. 134, para. 1]; del Arco, 'La aljama judaica', p. 279. A month later the order was cancelled: ACA, Reg. 86, fo. 187 [= R 2455 = Baer, *Spanien*, doc. 134, para. 2].

[24] For the case, see ACA, Reg. 61, fo. 122 [= R 1026 = Baer, *Spanien*, doc. 125]. For the appeal to Adret, see Reg. 66, fo. 138 [= R 1597].

[25] ACA, CR, Jaime II, C 135, no. 389 [= Baer, *Spanien*, doc. 144 = *Cartas Reales*, no. 533]. The number of *caja* quoted by Baer was changed subsequent to the rearrangement of the CR.

[26] ACA, Reg. 50, fo. 193ʳ [= R 881 = Dinur, ii. 3, p. 272, no. 25].

[27] ACA, Reg. 80, fo. 77ʳ [= R 2022].

[28] ACA, Reg. 133, fo. 66ʳ [= Baer, *Spanien*, doc. 154].

[29] ACA, Reg. 139, fo. 58 [= Baer, *Spanien*, doc. 162]; fo. 158, as reported in Baer, is erroneous.

II asked him to arbitrate between the sides.³⁰ Adret's prestige reached its peak when he was asked to adjudicate in cases of dispute between Jewish and Christian institutions.³¹

R. Aharon Ha-Levi de Na Clara was sometimes asked to act alone, as was his colleague Adret on so many occasions. In April 1280 Pedro III entrusted him with the trial between a Jewess and her daughter from Lérida and Benito de Limos, a Jew from Valencia, over a financial dispute.³² At the king's request, R. Aharon performed similar missions in and outside Barcelona. In November 1284 Pedro III granted the rabbi a guarantee of safe conduct and ordered all his officials not to charge him any of the duties and customs imposed on travellers. As R. Aharon had to be in Saragossa, presumably on duty, the local community was required not to exact from him any payment during his stay there.³³ Alfonso III also took R. Aharon under his protection. In January 1291 the Infante Pedro issued a similar guarantee of safe conduct, extending it to other members of his family.³⁴ R. Aharon de Na Clara was also consulted on matters of matrimonial law. In April 1285, for instance, the baile of Barcelona had to consult him, by the king's order, before taking the final steps against Abraham de Tolosa, who refused to support his wife as stipulated by the *ketubah*.³⁵

In June 1282 Pedro III confirmed the choice made by two Saragossan Jews for their arbitrator: Genton Assibili, that is, R. Yom Tov Asibili, the well-known halakhist.³⁶ The king valued Asibili's status as a jurist highly and asked for his opinion in cases of litigants' complaints against the verdicts of the courts.³⁷

It is obvious that lawsuits committed to the care of the Crown's greatest jurists were difficult cases. These were lawsuits between a community and an individual, or between litigants from different *aljamas*, or very difficult trials involving very serious crimes. The involvement of the rabbis in some of these trials did not always please all parties, as is evident from the serious incident that occurred while R. Shelomo ben Adret was on such a mission in Villafranca in 1281, when he was attacked and stoned in the street by night. Pedro III demanded an immediate inquiry.³⁸ In some criminal trials involving Jews Adret was asked to advise the Christian judge. Adret, who had been harassed by the family of the condemned before, as in the case of Vidalon de Porta, expressed his fear of a similar reaction when he was asked in August 1284 to advise the Christian judge who was investigating the murder of Salomon Avenbruch (Ibn Baruch). Pedro III assured him that no harm would come to him.³⁹

[30] ACA, Reg. 98, fo. 82 [= Baer, *Spanien*, doc. 132].

[31] In 1306 Adret was asked to resolve the dispute between the Jews of Montblanch and the apostate who was given the monopoly over the sale of meat in the same community; ACA, Reg. 55, fo. 69 [= R 2859 = Baer, *Spanien*, doc. 160].

[32] ACA, Reg. 42, fo. 243ʽ [= R 772].
[33] ACA, Reg. 43, fo. 69ʽ [= R 1237].
[34] ACA, Reg. 85, fo. 91 [= R 2290].
[35] ACA, Reg. 56, fo. 59 [= R 1333].
[36] ACA, Reg. 59, fo. 22 [= R 927].
[37] Asibili (Kapah) 131.
[38] ACA, Reg. 50, fo. 169 [= R 874].
[39] ACA, Reg. 43, fo. 24ʽ [= R 1192 = Baer, *Spanien*, doc. 127].

The spiritual leaders of the communities in the Catalano-Aragonese realm were not paid officials of the community. Their financial independence strengthened their authority, while their judgements and opinions were generally immune from pressure and manipulation. Some were physicians, others had their own businesses. The physician–rabbi enjoyed an excellent reputation, as is evident in their treatment of members of the royal family.

Sources from the royal archives contain records of payments to the famous rabbis of Catalonia. These payments were either for services rendered or part of unrelated financial transactions. In January 1258 Jaime I ordered the *aljama* of Gerona to advance him 40 golden *maravedís* from the tax due the following Christmas, the amount to be paid to the rabbi of Gerona, Bonastrug de Porta, the Catalan name of Nahmanides.[40] In October 1260 the king gave him for life the royal mill and all the royal revenues from the market of Gerona.[41] In his account of the Barcelona Disputation, Nahmanides claims that he received from the king 300 sb as a gift. There is a record from early 1265 that such a sum had indeed been paid to him on behalf of the king.[42]

We may recall that, early in his life, R. Shelomo ben Adret was engaged in moneylending. His financial transactions apparently included some with the king himself. A document from 1262 refers to the king's debt of 1,616 sb to Salomon Adret, from Barcelona, and Benedict of Gerona. Jaime I ordered the *aljama* of Gerona to pay them 1,000 sb on account of their forthcoming tax payable on the feast of St John. It is very likely that the Jewish lenders were R. Shelomo ben Adret and R. Jonah Gerondi.[43]

---

[40] ACA, Reg. 10, fo. 30 [= R 84 = Jacobs 138].
[41] ACA, Reg. 11, fo. 182 [= R 137 = Jacobs 173].
[42] ACA, Reg. 14, fo. 70 [= R 319 = Jacobs 373].
[43] ACA, Reg. 12, fo. 50ʹ [= R 157 = Jacobs 215 and p. 130, doc. iii]. There is a record of the payment in February 1263: ACA, Reg. 14, fo. 11 [= R 182 = Dinur, ii. 3, p. 271, no. 22].

§6.3 Religious Supervision

COMMUNAL CONTROL IN RELIGIOUS LIFE

IN the medieval Jewish world, the supervision of religious practice and moral behaviour lay within the community's jurisdiction. The community in the Crown of Aragon enjoyed extensive power, so that its control of religious behaviour was tight. This control in the religious and ethical domain should not mislead us into thinking that the community was able in any way to impose uniformity of beliefs and opinions in any area that did not come within the strict definition of the *halakhah*. Not only would such an attempt have been futile, as the bans proclaimed during the Maimonidean controversies show, but no claim was ever made that the community had the right to punish members for their religious views and ideological tendencies. The above-mentioned bans constituted a deviation from communal authority. There was no provision in the framework of Jewish autonomy that could have sanctioned coercive and punitive measures in the field of opinions and beliefs.

In religious practice and moral conduct, the Jewish community in the Aragonese realm developed ways and means of supervision and punishment. Special officers, known as *berure 'averot*, were appointed to eradicate transgressions. Communities therefore enacted ordinances that empowered them to seek permission from the king to punish and fine transgressors as they saw fit.[1] Such an ordinance existed in Jaca.[2] In small communities where there were no *berure 'averot*, some of the *berurim* would be put in charge of prosecuting any transgressor as the necessity arose.[3] In some communities the *beth din* was given ample powers, similar to those found in Castile, to punish moral decadence and irreligious behaviour.[4] In addition to the general charter given by the king enabling the community to punish members who broke the precepts of the Torah,[5] in some communities the king permitted some of his favourites to combat transgressions and punish transgressors without the community's authority. This was usually opposed by the public and by most leaders of the communities.[6]

---

[1] Adret, iv. 311 = viii. 279; Assaf, *Punishments*, no. 57.
[2] Adret, iii. 318.
[3] Adret, iii. 304.
[4] Asibili (Kapah) 131.
[5] ACA, Reg. 100, fo. 187 [= Baer, *Spanien*, doc. 137].
[6] Adret, ii. 279. The community's regulations relating to weddings and family life and behaviour in the synagogue are discussed respectively in Part V, section 3, on family life, and Part IV, section 2, on the synagogue and the house of study.

THE SABBATH AND FESTIVALS

The observance of the Sabbath and festivals by all members inside and outside the *judería* was a major concern of the *berurim*. On the one hand, they had to ensure that no disturbance was caused by external factors on these days, and on the other hand, it was considered their duty to prevent their desecration and punish any desecrators inside the community. In both matters they needed the king's cooperation. Many communities obtained a privilege that guaranteed that they would not be disturbed by the royal officers. These privileges forbade the arrest of Jews and the confiscation of their property, usually for defaulting tax payments, as well as the demand of any payments, on Sabbaths and festivals.[7] The king's favourable policy in this field did not prevent occasional abuses of Jewish holidays by his officials. At the beginning of the fourteenth century the *muqademin* of Saragossa complained to the king about their arrest on the Sabbath because of the community's debt.[8] The leaders of the community took care that the atmosphere of the festivals should not be spoilt as a result of duties imposed by the king. The communities in the Crown of Aragon had to proclaim a ban every year on 1 October against all who broke the interest law. In 1308 the *adelantados* of Lérida asked that the date be changed since the scheduled day fell on Sukkot.[9] In 1315 the heads of the *collecta* of Barcelona asked to move by one day the proclamation of the *herem* as 1 October fell on a Saturday. Other communities obtained the same concession.[10] Kings and princes realized that respecting the Jews' Sabbath and festivals was one of the necessary conditions of attracting them to settle in localities where they were needed.[11]

There was no need for any communal legislation for the *berurim* to take action against Jews whe profaned the Sabbath in public. It was only in circumstances in which the *halakhah* might not be sufficiently clear that communities felt the need to enact an ordinance. It was on the basis of such a *taqanah* promulgated by the *aljama* of Jaca that the *berurim* fined a Jew whose son's wet-nurse bathed on the last day of Passover.[12] In another community a ban was pronounced by the twelve leaders against a member whose workers, engaged on a contractual basis, continued work on his building on Sabbaths and festivals.[13] The observance of the Sabbath by the public remained a primary concern in any halakhic debate.[14]

---

[7] ACA, Reg. 13, fo. 275ᵛ [= R 336] (Lérida); Reg. 197, fos. 126ᵛ, 140 [= R 2738–9, 2742]; Miret, 'Le massacre', p. 237 (Barbastro, Montclús, Lérida); Reg. 207, fo. 162 [= R 2917] (Tortosa).

[8] ACA, CR, Jaime II, C 135, no. 392 [= Baer, *Spanien*, doc. 147 = *Cartas Reales*, no. 536]. In the latter *regestum* the detail of the arrest is not mentioned. In Baer the number of the *caja* is no longer correct.

[9] ACA, CR, Jaime II, C 26, no. 3319 [= *Cartas Reales*, no. 130].

[10] ACA, Reg. 211, fos. 301ᵛ–302ᵛ [= R 3019].

[11] See e.g. ACA, Reg. 383, fos. 40–2 [= Baer, *Spanien*, doc. 175, para. 10].

[12] Adret, iii. 318.   [13] Adret, iv. 315.   [14] Adret, i. 875, 878.

SUPERVISION OF MEAT AND WINE

The supply of *kasher* meat and wine was under the control of the community's governing body. Most communities succeeded in establishing their own abattoir or using the facilities of the Christian slaughterhouse on mutually agreed days. Many communities encountered obstacles in running their abattoir since economic interests were involved in the slaughter and sale of *kasher* meat.[15]

The ritual fitness of the meat sold to Jews was the responsibility of the community leaders, who supervised all stages of the process. Once an abattoir was established, the leaders' next concern was the appointment of the *shohet*, who was chosen for both his expertise and his piety. Failure in providing the community with strict *kasher* food or religious and moral misconduct on his part were rigorously punished.[16] Punitive measures were taken against any *shohet* who was not meticulous in his duty and such discrediting jeopardized his livelihood.[17] Any rumours or information that a *shohet* was allowing non-*kasher* meat to be sold to Jews led to an immediate investigation and, whenever necessary, the punishment and dismissal of the culprit. If the leaders could not obtain reliable information on the *shohet*'s performance, they would take certain measures, including placing a supervisor on the premises.[18] The leaders dismissed any *shohet* who knowingly sold non-*kasher* meat to Jews. While they sought the king's support for their action, it was often the king who intervened on behalf of the dismissed *shohet*.

In Aragonese communities this problem seemed somewhat widespread and frequent. In 1283 six butchers or slaughterers were expelled from Alagón for four years for transgressing the community's ordinance on *kasher* food. The Infante Alfonso asked the community to cancel its decision and reinstate them. Three years later the same butchers were put under ban and their meat forbidden, for having acted against the community's *taqanah*. This time King Alfonso III demanded that the community lift the ban and allow them to practise their trade.[19] In the Aragonese communities of Daroca and Huesca, we know of three slaughterers who were dismissed and put under *herem* for failing in their duty to provide *kasher* meat. Once the fine was paid, the king would order their return to their post. Needless to say, that fine was paid to the royal authorities.[20] The community faced a grave problem in its commitment to provide *kasher* food when it lacked the support of the king. Admittedly, only the cases in which the king or the infante intervened are recorded in the archival sources.

---

[15] See e.g. ACA, CR, Jaime II, C 134, no. 232 [= *Cartas Reales*, no. 453] for Játiva; and, for a general survey, see Part IV, section 4 above, on the slaughterhouse in the *judería*.

[16] Adret, i. 20.

[17] Adret, i. 619–20, 632, ii. 245, viii. 161.

[18] Asibili (Kapah) 121.

[19] ACA, Reg. 61, fo. 135ʳ [= R 1066]; Reg. 66, fo. 93ʳ [= R 1561].

[20] ACA, Reg. 208, fo. 14 [= R 2927]; Reg. 212, fo. 21ʳ [= R 3022]; Baer, *Spanien*, doc. 161, para.

Individuals who ate ritually unfit food were considered unreliable witnesses and were denounced in harsh terms.[21]

The production of *kasher* wine was also the community's responsibility. The communal authorities took care that the vessels for its production and the wine itself remained in Jewish hands.[22] Communities enacted ordinances to cope with conditions in which a Christian was involved in any way in the production, handling, and sale of *kasher* wine.[23] The prospects for profit through the sale of *vinum judayicum* necessarily caused the involvement in its sale of Christians who enjoyed the support of the king.[24] The consumption of non-Jewish wine was prohibited. It is noteworthy that the prohibition was repeated by successive rabbis, a fact that suggests that some Jews did not themselves abstain from drinking Christian wine. It seems that certain Jews advocated a lenient policy on drinking Christian wine.[25] Some communities, like Jaca, issued a *taqanah* prohibiting the sale of non-Jewish wine by Jews.[26] From an ordinance of the city of Huesca from 1290 we may deduce that Jews sold *kasher* wine to Christians and drank with them.[27] This behaviour was condemned by the Christian as well as the rabbinic or communal authorities.

[21] Adret, ii. 32, vii. 248.
[22] The amount of material on the topic shows that the problem was very real: ACA, Reg. 211, fos. 187ᵛ–188 [= R 2993, 2995–6]; Reg. 229, fo. 203 [= Jacobs 869 = R 3411].
[23] For Lérida see Adret, iii. 236.
[24] ACA, Reg. 80, fo. 90 [= R 2028].
[25] See e.g. Adret, i. 633, iv. 107, 178.
[26] '. . . techana com alatma sobre venda de lures vinos . . .'; ACA, RP, Maestre Racional, Reg. 1688, fos. 20ᵛ–31.
[27] del Arco, 'Ordenanzas inéditas', p. 428; id., 'La judería de Huesca', pp. 321–2.

§6.4 Religious Practice, Divine Worship, and the Crown

ALL the Aragonese kings recognized the Jews' right to live their religious life in accordance with their own understanding and beliefs. This recognition was a cornerstone in the relationship between the Jews and the monarch. In principle, the latter refrained from interfering in religious and ritual matters pertaining to the Jews, but even in this field he asserted his authority whenever he thought his interest was at stake.

THE SYNAGOGUE AND PRAYERS

The synagogue, the very centre of Jewish life, could not be built, refurbished, or repaired without the ruler's permission. As in the rest of Christian Europe, it was officially prohibited in the Crown of Aragon to erect new synagogues, but the Jews were allowed to repair their old ones.[1] Despite this prohibition, the Jews were permitted to establish many new synagogues, both in new settlements and in old communities. The king kept control over many details of the synagogue building and imposed many limitations with which the Jews learned to live. In addition to the king's consent, the community would often seek the local bishop's permission as well. Both permissions were generally paid for by the Jews. In the first part of the fourteenth century a Jewess from Oriola bequeathed in her will buildings 'which should serve as a synagogue with the king's and the bishop's permission for daily prayers of men and women'. She donated a large sum of money to be used first and foremost to pay the king and the bishop and, of course, for the building of the synagogue. The donor assumed as a matter of course that the authorities had to be bribed.[2] The local church authorities were often involved in authorizing the Jews to repair their synagogues and even to build new ones.[3] In many instances, similar considerations guided the ruler and the bishop.

Not only were the building and dimensions of the synagogue under the strict control of the king, he also showed an interest in the order of service and activities that occurred inside it. Jaime I interfered in every aspect of synagogal

---

[1] ACA, Reg. 219, fo. 198ᵛ [= R 3164 = Jacobs 788]. The subject is treated fully in Part IV, section 2 above on the synagogue and house of study, and in Assis, 'Synagogues'.

[2] Asibili (Kapah) 161. Kapah's correction of the shortened Hebrew form for *jaqueses* is mistaken. The passage in question means 'thousands of *solidos jaqueses*' or of Jaca.

[3] For permission granted by the bishop of Vich to build a synagogue on a new site, see ACA, Reg. 217, fos. 147ᵛ–148 [= R 3113].

life. When his protégés were involved, he cancelled the community's decision to prevent those under ban from participating in the services and even prohibited Jews from walking out in protest at their entry into the synagogue.[4] The king's involvement in the allocation of seats in the synagogue was a cause of much frustration.[5] On the other hand, we may reasonably assume that Jaime I's intervention in synagogal matters was often at the community's request.[6]

The king's interference in the appointment of the rabbi or *hazan* of the synagogue caused serious damage to religious life. By supporting his favourite candidate for the post the king aroused the anger of the community and, worse still, contributed to lack of respect and ill-feeling towards the rabbi or *hazan*. Moreover, his choice was not necessarily the best. In 1315 Jaime II favoured Çadia (Sa'adiah) Abenaçaya to the post of rabbi in Lérida against the community's candidate, Mosse Jumiz. In 1323 Çadia was already dead when the same king permitted his son Abraham to marry a second wife while his first was still alive. It is obvious that special relations existed between the king and the family.[7]

THE SABBATH AND FESTIVALS

There are no records that there was any serious royal interference in the celebration of the Sabbath and festivals. Arrests on such days by the king's officials for non-payment of taxes or debts were eventually forbidden by charters granted to many communities. The attempts by many communities to obtain such charters indicate the widespread and frequent use of this practice, which disrupted the Jewish festivals, but the king was generally prepared to guarantee their quiet celebration. Some charters also promised that no legal proceedings would be opened against Jews on their festival days.[8]

Purim was the most problematic of all the festivals. The Jews' excessive joy and noisy celebrations on this occasion were viewed as scandalous and immoral. Purim was the only festival on which Jews might have drunk alcohol to excess, inevitably leading to unusual and atypical conduct for Jews. It is not improbable that, along with the names of Haman and Vashti, those of Christian saints might have been pronounced for ridicule by high-spirited Jews. Even when such was not the case, the Christian masses interpreted the festivities as suited them, and the games and plays performed on this festival added further ammunition for Christian accusations. In 1291, following the celebration of Purim in Villafranca, an investigation was opened against the Jews. In July 1291 Jews from this community were

[4] ACA, Reg. 14, fo. 63 [= R 275 = Jacobs 364 = Baer, *Spanien*, doc. 100]; Reg. 37, fo. 31ʳ [= R 495 = Jacobs 725].

[5] See Part IV, section 2, no. 54–5 above.

[6] See e.g. ACA, Reg. 16, fo. 148ʳ [= R 438 = Jacobs 440 = Bofarull, Montpellier, 490].

[7] ACA, CR, Jaime II, C 43, no. 5313 [= *Cartas Reales*, no. 186]. For the king's permission to Abraham, see ACA, Reg. 223, fo. 169ʳ [= R 3249].

[8] Adler, 'Provençal and Catalonian Responsa', p. 144; ACA, Reg. 201, fo. 25ʳ [= R 2821].

ordered to appear in Barcelona before the infante in connection with a lawsuit brought against them in the local court. They were accused of misconduct and the game of 'Purim' they played. At the end of August, the infante ordered that the charges relating to the play and games they had organized half a year earlier on Purim be dropped: the leaders of the community had succeeded in pursuading the infante that their celebration was innocent and in keeping with Jewish tradition.[9]

The Villafranca incident was not an isolated case, and Purim continued to create problems for the Jewish community. In 1294 Jews from Villafranca were condemned because of a game they played on Purim, as was customary. Once more, the king's intervention on behalf of the condemned and the cancellation of their punishment illustrate the Aragonese kings' favourable attitude to the Jews' right to celebrate their festivals and fulfil their commandments.[10] Many sources show that Christians frequently attacked the Jews and spoilt their festivals, to say the least. The attacks were most serious in the Passover period. Some communities tried to protect themselves by seeking charters that forbade Christian attacks on Jewish festivals. Throwing stones at Jews was a frequent occurrence.[11]

KASHER FOOD

As elsewhere in the medieval Jewish world, the Jews in the Crown of Aragon were allowed to eat and drink according to their religious precepts. This tolerance in principle was however frequently brushed aside when it was in the interest of the Crown to do so. The king's involvement in the production and sale of *kasher* food was motivated primarily by economic considerations. The sale of *kasher* meat and wine could be quite a profitable enterprise. The monopoly over these two products was sometimes given to the king's favourites, who might be Christians, even apostates. Alfonso III's order in 1289 that the Jews of Tarazona should buy 'Jewish wine' (*vinum judaycum*) solely from Arnaldo de Bastida and that the *aljama* should refrain from creating any obstacle to the marketing of *kasher* wine through Arnaldo illustrates the point. It was the abuse of Jewish religious life for economic profit.[12]

Although such was not his intention, the king's manipulation of the *kasher* food supply caused serious disruption of Jewish religious life. The contradiction between the Crown's readiness to permit the Jews to practise their traditions and laws and its eagerness to make profit from the sale of *kasher* food remained a permanent feature of royal policy.

[9] ACA, Reg. 86, fo. 6 [=R 2380]; Reg. 90, fo. 12ˇ [=R 2385].
[10] ACA, Reg. 99, fo. 216 [= Baer, *Spanien*, doc. 135].
[11] See e.g. ACA, Reg. 217, fos. 147ˇ–148 [=R 3113].
[12] ACA, Reg. 80, fo. 90 [=R 2028].

The Jews had to bake their bread either in ovens owned by the king or in those of one of his agents. Passover was the only occasion when the Jews were allowed to bake their own unleavened bread in their homes.[13] Moreover, when certain communities had difficulties in baking their *matzah*, the king helped them to overcome these problems. When the community of Lérida was unable to obtain the wheat needed for the *matzah* due to confiscation and debts, Jaime II intervened on its behalf and made sure that *matzah* was available.[14] In those settlements where the Jews had to bake their bread in Christians' bakeries, the privilege of the Jews to bake their own bread for more than a week at Passover displeased them. In some communities, the Jews had to pay bribes or compensation.[15]

The difficulties the *kasher* wine-makers and merchants encountered were also due to economic competition. As it was impossible for every *qehilah* to produce its own wine, it was important that it should be marketed freely.[16] The Jews' concern that at no stage of its production should the wine be handled by Christians caused complications and led to royal intervention. In 1298, for instance, the community of Lérida had to send an emissary to explain to the king the religious reasons behind the ordinance that forbade the letting of the Jews' wine-press and wine-cellars to Christians.[17] Jews, however, did not always refrain from selling their wine to Christians, or even drinking with them, as can be gathered from an ordinance of the city of Huesca in 1290.[18]

The king, who understood the importance of *kasher* wine for the Jews, used the confiscation of the wine and its vessels of production as a means of pressure if taxes were not paid. As this measure caused serious disruption in religious life, communities tried to obtain the king's promise that their wine and its vessels would not be confiscated.[19] In places where the general import of wine was banned, the prohibition did not generally include *kasher* wine, as long as it was

---

[13] For permission granted by Jaime I in 1269 to the Jews of Besalú to bake their *matzah* in their homes two days before Easter (!) and the day after, see ACA, Reg. 16, fo. 159 [= Bofarull, Barcelona, xci]. The Infante Alfonso gave a similar permission in 1320 to the Jews of Alcolea de Cinca: ACA, Reg. 383, fo. 40 [= Baer, *Spanien*, doc. 175, para. 2.].

[14] ACA, Reg. 228, fo. 37 [=R 3371].

[15] In Murcia the Jews paid the Christian bakers a sum of money for the right to bake their *matzah*: ACA, Reg. 228, fo. 45 [=R 3372].

[16] The order of Pedro III to his officials that they should not refrain from issuing permits to send wine from Murviedro and its surroundings by Jucef Abenshaprut may be related to this problem: ACA, Reg. 48, fo. 166 [= MF ii. 1185].

[17] ACA, CR, Jaime II, C 1, no. 368.

[18] 'Et muytos de los cristianos o cristianas . . . compran publicament de las carnes et vino de los dictos judios et encara coman et bevian con ellos . . .': del Arco, 'Ordenanzas inéditas', p. 428; id., 'La judería de Huesca', pp. 321–2.

[19] In 1314 the communities of Gerona, Besalú, Barcelona and its *collecta*, Tortosa, and Lérida obtained such a promise, providing they owned movables that covered the amount of their debts: ACA, Reg. 211, fos. 185, 186'–187 [=R 2993, 2995–6]. A similar promise was given in 1326 to the *collecta* of Calatayud: ACA, Reg. 229, fo. 203 [=R 3411 = Jacobs 869].

sold to Jews in the *judería*.²⁰ Sometimes the Jews were included in the import ban, in which case they had to produce their own wine.²¹

The right of the Jews to eat *kasher* food was never challenged. Even Jewish prisoners were permitted to receive *kasher* food provided by their families. Many communities obtained the king's promise that Jewish prisoners would not be deprived of their food.²²

The most important item ritually was meat. The attitude of the ruler in every phase of its preparation was crucial. We may recall how involved the king was in various aspects connected with slaughterhouses and the appointment of *shohatim*.²³ Just as the leaders of the community appointed the *shohatim*, so they could dismiss them for failing to fulfil their duties. The leaders dismissed permanently or suspended temporarily any *shohet* who failed halakhically in his work, whether knowingly or unknowingly, through negligence or ignorance.²⁴ The king, however, did not always support the decision of the community leaders. The king's interference on behalf of a *shohet* dismissed for religious reasons was a serious blow to the efforts of the leaders, who were in charge of maintaining the religious standards in their community. In 1311 Bonafos Adit, *shohet* in Huesca, was dismissed by the community and fined by the baile for having slaughtered and sold ritually unfit meat. Jaime II ordered the return of Bonafos to his post, once he had paid the requisite fine, and the Jews were to be forced to buy meat from him.²⁵ The same year, the *shohet* of Daroca lost his job and was put under ban for acting against the ordinance of the *aljama* in his slaughter. A fine of 105 sj was paid to the baile.²⁶

The king's interference in a religious matter of grave consequence in Jewish life was due to financial considerations. It created a dangerous precedent and enabled *shohatim* who benefited from the king's support to ignore the community's supervision and deviate from the *halakhah* with impunity.²⁷ The community could not accept that an appointment that had religious repercussions should be taken out of its jurisdiction. Communities that were affected worked hard to persuade the king not to free the *shohatim* from their control. Some succeeded in reasserting their authority in a field that was considered vital in

---

²⁰ In Fraga, which belonged to the lord of Moncada, the ban on the import of wine between the feast of San Miguel and Pentecost did not affect the Jews. See Salarrullana, 'Estudios', pp. 69ff. This permission to the Jews was originally given in 1309 and was confirmed by Jaime II in 1322: ACA, Reg. 222, fos. 87ᵛ–89ᵛ. A source from 1324 repeated the ban on importing wine into Fraga, and once again the Jews were excluded from the prohibition.
²¹ Carreras, 'Ordinacions urbanes . . .': Valls', p. 199.
²² ACA, Reg. 209, fos. 203ᵛ, 204, 208, 215 [= R 2951]; Reg. 210, fo. 97ᵛ [= R 2981].
²³ See Part IV, section 4 above on the slaughterhouse in the judería. To avoid repetition, only those details that bear on religious life are mentioned here.
²⁴ Asibili (Kapah) 121.
²⁵ ACA, Reg. 208, fo. 14 [= R 2927].
²⁶ ACA, RP, Maestre Racional, Reg. 1688, fo. 39 [= Baer, *Spanien*, doc. 163, para. 1].
²⁷ Asibili (Kapah) 67.

their religious life.[28] Charters that granted the community religious autonomy, including control of all posts related to ritual and religious life, were no guarantee that attempts would not be made by the king to appoint his own favourite candidate to the position of *shohet*.[29]

---

[28] In 1320 the Jews of Saragossa were authorized to appoint their own *shohatim*: ACA, Reg. 218, fo. 155ʼ [=R 3144].

[29] ACA, Reg. 219, fos. 214ʼ–215 [=R 3168].

§6.5 Pious and Synagogal Fraternities

PRAYER AND PIETY

IN the days of religious conflict and intensifying polemics in matters of faith and practice, some individual Jews found religious and spiritual comfort in joining fellow Jews in acts of piety and dedication. Groups were formed in and around the synagogue for the purpose of meticulous observance of certain precepts or performance of certain prayers. Jews who decided to be extra careful in prayer joined together to form a brotherhood in which they expected to be stronger than in isolation. This type of fraternity was consonant with the spirit of repentance prevalent in some circles.

Many groups left no records behind, as their activity in the synagogue was informal and necessitated no special act. This was not so, however, with those fraternities that were involved in financial and organizational transactions. Such was the society called Ashmoret ha-Boqer (*confradria de la Maytinal*, or *d'Azmuro*) which was established in Saragossa in 1378. The members of the fraternity undertook to rise before dawn and pray at sunrise. Their purpose was also to distribute charity and perform good deeds among their fellow Jews. The existence of the fraternity is known because of the property and funds it possessed.[1] Other such fraternities with no assets remain unknown to posterity.

SYNAGOGAL FRATERNITIES

Groups were also formed to take care of the synagogue or of particular aspects of synagogal life. They were known in various parts of the Iberian peninsula as the *cofadria de la sinoga* or *confraria de la teba*.[2] The *ma'or* society took care of the supply of oil and the lighting of the synagogue. A *ma'or* society existed in Perpignan in the first half of the fourteenth century.[3] In Santa Coloma de Queralt, too, a special society was responsible for the synagogue lights.[4]

Scrolls of the Torah, prayer books and other books required for study and prayer were expensive. The rich could afford their own books, which they kept at home for private use and the tuition of their children but brought to synagogue

---

[1] ACA, Reg. 1682, fo. 160ᵛ [= Baer, *Spanien*, doc. 320]; Beinart, 'Hispano-Jewish Society', p. 238; Blasco, 'Instituciones sociorreligiosas', docs. 3, 10.
[2] Assis, 'Welfare and Mutual Aid', p. 339.
[3] Gerondi 75.
[4] Secall, *La comunitat*, p. 246, doc. xvii.

for the services. Some wealthy Jews, indeed, possessed impressive libraries.[5] The establishment of public libraries and the provision of liturgical books in synagogues proved to be a very difficult task. The community did not always come up with the necessary funds to purchase books for public use.

Members of the lower and middle classes were generally involved in the establishment of book societies. Such a society functioned in Saragossa;[6] called *hevrah de sefarim* or *conffraria de Ceffarim alias de las Atoras*, it was apparently responsible for the Torah scrolls and books used in the synagogue. The poor were the main beneficiaries of the activity of such societies. Members of the book society of Saragossa cooperated with other fraternities in the community.[7] The book society was headed by two or three *muqademin* and had a council of eleven members. Their meetings were held in the *sinoga menor*.[8] According to its Judeo-Aragonese constitution, the income of the society came partly from the indirect tax on meat and wine.[9] Another source of income was the property the fraternity owned. Its buildings were identified by the inscription at the entrance, which read *de la conffraria de las Atoras*.[10]

---

[5] Secall, *La comunitat*, pp. 173–87; Millás and Batlle, 'Inventaris', p. 545; Soberanas, 'La biblioteca', pp. 200–1; Hillgarth and Narkiss, 'A List of Books', pp. 297–320.

[6] Blasco, *La judería de Zaragoza*, pp. 247–8, doc. 36.

[7] Serrano, 'Notas', p. 335.

[8] Blasco, 'Instituciones sociorreligiosas', p. 236, n. 36.

[9] Lacave, 'La carnicería', p. 15.

[10] Serrano, *Orígenes*, i, p. xliv, n. 1, cccclxxv–vi; Blasco, 'Instituciones sociorreligiosas', p. 25, nn. 201–2.

§6.6 Jewish Education in the Crown of Aragon

As in other medieval Jewish communities, the education of the young and of adults alike in the communities of the Crown of Aragon was the exclusive concern of Jewish society. Formally, the education was Jewish; in reality, the curriculum was affected by currents that were the product of external influences, as described in section 1 above on 'Jewish Religious Trends in the Crown of Aragon'. Despite the ancient tradition of Jewish education and the establishment of educational institutions for the young and adults that go back to antiquity, a careful analysis of the sources indicates that long-standing ordinances were not necessarily followed without interruption. Furthermore, education was not so general as is commonly supposed.

ELEMENTARY EDUCATION AND THE TALMUD TORAH SOCIETIES

Considering the importance attached to the study of the Torah in Jewish society through the ages, it is surprising to find that, in general, the community in the Crown of Aragon did not cater for the education of children. The community did not create a public educational system open to all boys; as for girls, no formal education was provided for them practically anywhere in the Jewish world. The rich and members of the middle class provided private tuition for their children by engaging teachers who came to their house to teach the boys of the family. These teachers were usually hired for a limited period, between several months and a year.[1] Lubona, from Santa Coloma, engaged Jucef Benveniste for 2 sb per week to teach her grandson *litteras hebraicas* between Pesah and Sukkot.[2] A contract was usually signed by the teacher and the parents or guardians of the children. Unless it was terminated by mutual consent, any breach of the contract could lead to a lawsuit.[3] Some contracts between parents and teachers, and the latters' conditions of employment, are extant.[4]

It was obvious that only the rich could afford to hire private teachers for their children. Not every Jew could afford such tuition.[5] To alleviate the financial

---

[1] Adret, i. 645.   [2] Segura, 'Documentos', p. 334.   [3] Adret, i. 873.
[4] For a few examples from Santa Coloma de Queralt, see Assis, *The Jews of Santa Coloma*, pp. 61–3; Segura, 'Aplech de documents', p. 248.
[5] Adret, v. 229.

burden, some parents joined together to hire a teacher for their children.⁶ In some instances, instruction was paid for in services. One person promised to teach his friend's son *halakhah* in return for attendance and service by the pupil throughout the period of instruction. In another case, the parent offered a book instead of a monetary fee.⁷ As the interest of teachers and parents might sometimes encourage an increase in the numbers of pupils studying together in one session, some parents or guardians took the precautionary measure of including a clause in the contract limiting the number or forbidding shared tuition altogether. The contract drawn up for the above-mentioned Lubona had a clause prohibiting the teacher to teach more than three pupils at a time.⁸

Where did the poor children who could not afford to pay for private tuition study? We have no information whatsoever on any special arrangements that the community initiated to cater for the elementary education of the poor. The first initiatives were taken by individual Jews who bequeathed funds for the education of the poor. Jewish philanthropists who left property and money in their wills to be used specifically for the education of poor children laid the foundations of a school system. In fact, the system was imposed on the community by the donors' explicit testamentary instructions: halakhically the community could not use such funds for any other purpose. Communities that inquired about such a possibility were categorically denied permission to do so by halakhic authorities.⁹

In view of all this, it is not surprising that the only officer of the community who was involved in setting up an establishment for elementary education was the treasurer of the *heqdesh*, who had to use the money left for this very purpose.¹⁰ In several communities, we can easily trace the beginnings of the school system to private initiatives to teach poor children. In Lérida a Jew left a fund to engage a teacher for the pupils. A salary was to be paid annually on Pesah to the teacher who was in charge of the education of the poor.¹¹ Yucef Cohen, from Tortosa, left in his will funds for the establishment of a *studium* or *midrash* for the poor. He also left for this purpose his house in the *call*, and numerous books and 1,000 sb. His nephew claimed that, after the death of the other two, the sole remaining trustee was misusing the fund of the *heqdesh* and causing damage to the *midrash*. In 1328 Alfonso IV ordered the Christian court to investigate the allegation. This lawsuit indicates clearly that the community leaders were behind the move of the trustee, leaving the nephew no other option but to complain to the king.¹²

The failure of the communities to organize elementary education led to the creation by philanthropists of *midrashim* for poor boys. These institutions operated under the terms set by the donor and, generally, under the supervision of the *heqdesh* officers. The funds left by the donors helped to pay teachers, help

[6] Adret, i. 643.
[7] Adret, iii. 319, vii. 515.
[8] Segura, 'Documentos', p. 334.
[9] Adret, v. 249.
[10] Adret, i. 1157.
[11] ACA, Reg. 392, fos. 245ᵛ–246ᵛ [Baer, *Spanien*, doc. 185].
[12] Rubió, *Documents*, p. 88.

pupils, and provide the various needs of the school, including oil for lighting. The money was often invested to add to the income for the benefit of the school, the expenses of which were rather high. Stipends were offered to poor pupils.[13] Some teachers taught in their houses, allocating rooms for this purpose.[14] Many community members found this arrangement to be unsatisfactory. The establishment of educational societies in the fourteenth century was the outcome of widespread dissatisfaction with the community's inability or unwillingness to assume responsibility for elementary education. As the children of the wealthy and many of the middle class received private tuition, the problem remained that of the poorer classes. The leadership of the community, composed of members of the wealthy families, showed little sensitivity and concern for what became essentially a problem of the poor. The Talmud Torah societies did not operate as agencies of the communal administration, but acted as voluntary societies with funds of their own. In some respects they were part of a protest movement within Jewish society that aimed at solving, outside the framework of the establishment, a variety of problems in the Jewish community.

In Barcelona, a society known as Confrare del Maldar or Tamutera (*talmud torah*) existed in the fourteenth century. A number of buildings in the *call* belonged to it, serving as premises for a *beth midrash* and a source of income.[15] The aim of these societies in the Crown of Aragon is stated in several sources. The society in Murviedro aimed at providing poor children with free education.[16] The Talmud Torah society in Perpignan was one of the four, later five, confraternities in the community. They were all on the list of institutions to which donations were offered during the weekly reading of the Torah.[17] The society in Gerona had serious financial difficulties in the first half of the fifteenth century following the demographic and economic decline of the community. It was then that the society merged within the *aljama*'s establishment.[18] In Tortosa a Confradia de Thamutora existed in the fourteenth century.[19]

The Talmud Torah confraternity in Saragossa was one of the oldest in the Iberian peninsula. It was established with the consent of the authorities and operated as an autonomous body within the *qehilah*. It had its own premises in the *judería*. Its income came from membership fees and rentals of its property. In the fourteenth century the finances of the society were sufficiently strong to enable it to advance loans to the community.[20]

---

[13] Adret, i. 669, v. 249, vii. 194, viii. 268.
[14] Adret, viii. 220.
[15] Baer, *Spanien*, doc. 399, p. 641; ACA, CR, Pedro IV, C 4, no. 475.
[16] ACA, Reg. 2338, fo. 152^v; Chabret, *Sagunto*, ii, pp. 343–4.
[17] Gerondi 75; ACA, Reg. 1687, fo. 198^v.
[18] Girbal, 'Beneficencia judaica', pp. 3–4 [= Romano (ed.), *Per a una història*, pp. 545–6].
[19] AHPT, Protocolos de Tortosa, lib. 1145, fos. 252^v–253^v [= Cubells, *The Jews of Tortosa*, nos. 135–6].
[20] Serrano, *Orígenes*, i, pp. ix, xliii; Blasco, 'Instituciones sociorreligiosas', docs. 4–5, and p. 26, n. 208, 210.

Some of the Talmud Torah societies catered for both children and adults, while some were formed in the first place to offer programmes of adult education. Thus we find in one community Jews who formed a confraternity and hired a scholar for a year to preach and teach every Sabbath.[21] In another community young students hired a teacher for a year.[22] Some projects did not succeed because of differences in ability and interests among the members. The withdrawal of one member naturally affected the whole project, which depended on the contributions of all members. In one particular case, ten students hired a rabbi to teach them the Talmud. More members joined the group but one of the original founding members decided to leave the group, claiming that the rabbi refused to teach them the commentary of Rashi.[23]

YESHIVOT AND TALMUDIC STUDIES

Talmudic scholarship was promoted in *yeshivot* which were established by eminent scholars. The *yeshivah* depended entirely on the expertise and personality of an individual Talmudic scholar in a particular locality. In the thirteenth and fourteenth centuries there were three prominent centres of Torah study in the Crown of Aragon: Barcelona, Gerona, and Perpignan. Talmudic studies in Barcelona followed the lead of Nahmanides, who combined the *tossafists*' method with the Spanish tradition. R. Jonah Gerondi taught for a while in Barcelona between his return from France and his departure for Toledo. His disciple R. Shelomo ben Adret headed the famous *yeshivah* in Barcelona, where students from various lands studied under his guidance and that of R. Aharon Ha-Levi de Na Clara. The two had some common students. The heads of the Barcelona *yeshivah* in the fourteenth century were R. Nissim Gerondi and R. Isaac ben Sheshet Perfet.

In Gerona a centre of kabbalistic studies developed in the thirteenth century. The first mystics of the Geronese school included R. Ezra and R. Azriel, among others.[24] A different kabbalistic trend was followed by Nahmanides, who opposed the popularization of the kabbalah. The centre in Gerona declined from the middle of the thirteenth century.[25] Apparently Nahmanides headed a *yeshivah* in Barcelona where he taught a restricted number of students *halakhah* and kabbalah. The most important of his disciples, who followed his kabbalistic teachings, was R. Shelomo ben Adret. In Perpignan there was also a *yeshivah* headed by R. Menahem ha-Meiri in the first half of the fourteenth century.

The number of the students in the *yeshivah* was usually around twenty-five.[26]

---

[21] Adret, ii. 260.   [22] Adret, i. 1042.   [23] Adret, viii. 1.
[24] Scholem, *Origins of the Kabbalah*, pp. 365–93.
[25] Idel, 'La història de la Cábala', pp. 59–74; id., 'Jewish Thought', pp. 272–5; id., 'R. Moshe ben Nahman'.
[26] See e.g. Adret, i. 460.

Students came from various communities and from both neighbouring and distant lands.[27] The duration of studies varied from one student to another: some studied for a limited period of one year or so,[28] while others studied for longer periods. Studies were often held in the house of the head of the *yeshivah* or in a building that belonged to the *heqdesh*. Some philanthropists let their houses be used as the house of study. The *yeshivah* was usually maintained through the generosity of such philanthropists, and funds bequeathed for charity were at times used to support it.[29] Donations were offered to the *beth midrash*.[30] Books were expensive and some works were rare or unavailable. The *yeshivah* of R. Shelomo ben Adret had very important manuscripts of the Talmud which were written or corrected in the Babylonian academies.[31]

CURRICULUM AND METHODS OF STUDY

By the middle of the thirteenth century the Babylonian Talmud was almost the only text studied in the *yeshivot*. The Jerusalem Talmud was hardly studied at all; its neglect goes back to the beginnings of Talmudic studies in Muslim Spain. By the thirteenth century the *tossafist* method of Talmudic study had supplanted the Sephardi system, which consisted of examining the Talmudic text in order to reach the halakhic decision. The novellae of great halakhists like Adret no longer aimed to reach the *halakhah* but rather to interpret the Talmudic theme under discussion.[32] This was precisely the criticism expressed by R. Yehudah ibn Abbas, who was opposed to the introduction of the *tossafists*' method into the Sephardi *yeshivot*.[33] This did not mean that in the *yeshivot* they actually studied the Talmud with the glosses of the *tossafot*; it was usually considered enough to study Rashi's commentary and the novellae of Nahmanides, Adret, Asibili, and others.[34] Special intonation was used for the study of Bible and Talmud.[35]

Great emphasis was put on pedagogy in the *yeshivah* of Barcelona. The individual student's intellectual capacity and the relationship between master and disciple were considered of special import.[36] In particular, it was understood that a great scholar was not necessarily a great teacher, and that the art of teaching was not something that could be acquired through extensive and scholarly study alone.[37]

The rationalists opposed the exclusive study of the Talmud and presented an alternative curriculum which greatly emphasized the importance of the Bible. Shem Tov ibn Falaquera, who lived in thirteenth-century Tudela, expressed the

[27] For students from Germany in Barcelona, see Adret, i. 395.
[28] Adret, vii. 537.   [29] Adret, i. 386, iii. 276.
[30] For such a donation to the *beth midrash* of Huesca by a Jewess, see Adret, iv. 243.
[31] Adret, ii. 11, vi. 57.   [32] Adret, ii. 374.
[33] See Assaf, *Sources*, ii, p. 30; Grossman, 'Relations between Spanish and Ashkenazi Jewry', p. 229; Gross, 'Centers of Study', p. 405.   [34] See e.g. Zacut, *Sefer Yuhasin*, ch. V, p. 221.
[35] Adret, v. 9.   [36] Adret, i. 1042, viii. 1.   [37] Adret, v. 229.

Sephardi view well. He attached great importance to Biblical exegesis. He suggested that pupils learn the written Law first, before starting Talmudic studies, and that scriptural commentaries be studied methodically. The oral Law is, after all, the interpretation of the written Law. Furthermore, he maintained, it is sufficient to study Alfasi's *Halakhot* and Maimonides' *Mishne Torah* in order to know the *halakhah*. He recommends then Maimonides' commentary on the *Mishnah*. Only then should the student start to study the Talmud, which is excellent as an intellectual exercise designed to sharpen the mind. He objected, however, to the view that students should devote themselves exclusively to Talmudic studies. Falaquera also proposed secular studies that should include all the sciences and subjects that do not contain heretical ideas, among them mathematics, geometry, optics, astronomy, and music. It was also important to study the Hebrew language, an essential instrument in any study programme, this to be followed by poetry.[38] A good style and a beautiful calligraphy were recommended in curricula proposed by rationalist scholars.[39] The rationalists argued that since the danger of idol worship had vanished and everyone believed in God and in providence, the study of philosophy could cause the student no harm.[40]

[38] Falaquera, *Sefer ha-Mevagesh*, pp. 72-3, 52-3.
[39] See e.g., Qalonimus ben Qalonimus, 'Igeret Musar', p. 107 [= Dinur, ii. 6, p. 69, no. 19].
[40] Adret, i. 418.

CONCLUSION

THE GOLDEN AGE OF ARAGONESE JEWRY was a remarkable period in medieval Jewish history. It was a period when the Jews achieved a great degree of integration in the political and economic life of a Christian country, while reaching a high level of religious and cultural productivity that made the Crown of Aragon one of the major centres of Jewish scholarship. It is enough to review the impressive list of the eminent rabbis of the period to appreciate the quality of Jewish scholarship that was achieved during one century: R. Jonah Gerondi, R. Moshe ben Nahman, R. Shelomo ben Adret, R. Aharon Ha-Levi de Na Clara, R. Yom Tov Asibili, R. Bahye ben Asher, and R. Nissim Gerondi.

This Golden Age was one of the most exciting eras of medieval Jewish history. The political, social, and economic achievements of the Jews created tension and gaps in Jewish society. During a period of deep social dissent, we witness a bitter struggle conducted by the poor who sought ways to take part in the management of their community or, failing that, to create the appropriate institutions to resolve their problems.

The religious conflicts and polemics of these years were the outcome of intellectual and spritual maturity. The sad results of the antagonism between the religious trends cannot obscure the significance of the crisis. This religious ferment was evidence of a Jewish society that was rich, creative, exciting, and imaginative in its intellectual and spiritual scope. It exerted great influence on near and distant communities, but was equally receptive to influences from other centres. Catalan Jewry became versatile in the Judeo-Arabic tradition of Sepharad while also absorbing much of the heritage of Franco-German or Ashkenazi Jewry. It was in the Crown of Aragon, where bitter religious conflicts tore apart the Jews in the Maimonidean controversies and the crisis over the study of secular sciences, that the Jewish cultures of Sepharad and Ashkenaz clashed. It was primarily an inner conflict, between those who adopted many of the religious concepts of Ashkenaz, like Gerondi, Nahmanides, and Adret, and those who wanted to retain the religious and philosophical perceptions of Sepharad. Only in a community that produced intellectual giants could such significant conflicts occur. Peace and quiet are the destiny of communities whose religious and intellectual aridity condemns them to stagnation.

Physical destruction was, alas, to precede cultural extinction. Following the reigns of Alfonso IV (1327–36) and Pedro IV (1336–87), during which the Jews managed to maintain a certain level of culture and enjoy a fairly secure existence, despite the occasional crisis (the Black Death, for instance), there came the period of Juan I (1387–95). In 1391 the massacres that began in Andalusia and spread throughout the peninsula struck the communities of the Crown of Aragon. After the attacks in Valencia, Majorca, and Catalonia in the summer of 1391 there remained very little of the glory of the previous century and a half. A large number of the surviving Jews were baptized while many fugitives went abroad, particularly to North Africa. The dead were many, and the survivors were busy attempting to rebuild their ruined lives, while fanatical churchmen were already planning the next attacks to reduce even further the small community that was the remnant of a glorious past. The Tortosa Disputation was the most serious but by no means the only calamity that befell the descendants of the survivors.

When the day of expulsion came, there were few left of the Jews in the Crown of Aragon. Of these, some left, others remained as *conversos*. The refugees from Aragon, Valencia, and Catalonia joined their brethren from Castile. They were too few in number to leave much impact on the emerging Sephardi diaspora. Besides names, such as Catalan, Saragoussi, Tarragano, Gerondi, Benardout, Benveniste, Valencia, and some customs and liturgical pieces and names of congregations in Rome or the Ottoman Empire, such as *Qahal Aragon* and *Qahal Catalan*, little was left in the mainly Castilian–Portuguese Sephardi diaspora that emerged in the east and the west, except a religious and cultural legacy. This legacy, bequeathed by the eminent scholars of the Golden Age in the thirteenth and fourteenth centuries, was absorbed by World Jewry in general, and by the Sephardi Jews in particular. Their literary production remains, to the present day, one of the richest contributions to Jewish culture and civilization.

APPENDIX I

The Monetary System in the Medieval Crown of Aragon

DURING the thirteenth century and the beginning of the fourteenth century the currency in the territories of the Crown of Aragon was based on silver bullion. Money units followed the Carolingian system and consisted of three denominations:

	£	s	d
Latin	*libra*	*solidus*	*denarius*
Catalan	*lliura*	*sou*	*diner*
Aragonese/Castilian	*libra*	*sueldo*	*dinero*

£1 = 20s; 1s = 12d.

The *libra* and the *solidus* did not exist and were only used for computation. The *denarius* was the actual coin in use.

Each of the constituent territories of the Crown had its own currency. Aragon had the *dineros jaqueses* or *de Jaca* or *sanchetes*. The name *Jaca* was derived from the mint which operated in the Aragonese town of that name, while the name *sanchetes* owed its origin to the founder of the mint, Sancho Ramírez. The coin was made of silver and copper.

In Catalonia, the coins used were the *diners de Barcelona*.

In Valencia, Jaime I issued in 1247, following the conquest of the territory and the establishment of the kingdom, the *real de Valencia* which was divided into three *diners*. In the second half of the thirteenth century, one *dinero de Jaca* was worth ⅘ of the *real de Valencia*. Later, the rate of exchange was 1.5 *real de Valencia* = 1 *dinero de Jaca*.

The *real de Valencia* was also in use in Majorca. In 1300 Jaime II issued the *real de Mallorca* or the *real menut*. One *real de Mallorca* was worth ¾ of the *diner de Barcelona*.

Under Jaime I all four currencies of his four territories were valid in his treasury. In 1254 he introduced the *diner barcelones de tern* which was designed to achieve uniformity in the Crown of Aragon. This new *diner* was worth three old *diners*. Half a *diner de tern* was called an *obolo* or a *mailla*. In 1266 Jaime I adopted the Franco-English model: *sou = gros tornes* (containing 4.05 grammes of silver) The *gros* was worth £4 of English currency.

Pedro III issued the *denarius argenti* which was worth 12 *vellon*, a mixture of silver and copper, or *solidi*. The coin was also called *croat* (*cruzado*), after the cross that appeared on one side.

In 1296, following the conquest of Alicante, Jaime II introduced the *grossos* in the south. In 1299 the *puguese* appeared in Lérida. Its value was ½ *obolo* = ¼ d. In 1310 the *croat gross* or *dihuite* of silver was in use in Valencia: 1 *croat gros* was worth 18 d of Valencia or 6 *reales*.

During most of the period, the *sou* of Barcelona was worth less than the *sou* of Valencia and the *sueldo de Jaca* but more than the *sou* of Majorca.

The relations that the Crown of Aragon maintained with European countries and Muslim Granada had their influence on the currencies used within its boundaries. The Muslim coins *almoravides*, *amorabetis*, or *maravedis* were used in the Crown of Aragon, particularly after the conquest of Valencia. The coins which were in use in Muslim Valencia, the *masmudinas* or the *semidirhemes*, and the *besantes* of the Muslims in Majorca, remained legal currencies for a long time. The *besant* was worth half a *morabeti*. The *denari melgorienses* or the *melgoresos* of Montpellier, which was under Catalan rule, were also in use in the Crown of Aragon. The *diners torneses* of France, too, constituted a legal currency in the Crown.

The final accounts in the royal treasury were made in *sous de Barcelona*.

APPENDIX 2

The Sovereigns of the House of Aragon in the Crown of Aragon, Majorca–Roussillon, and Sicily 1213–1336

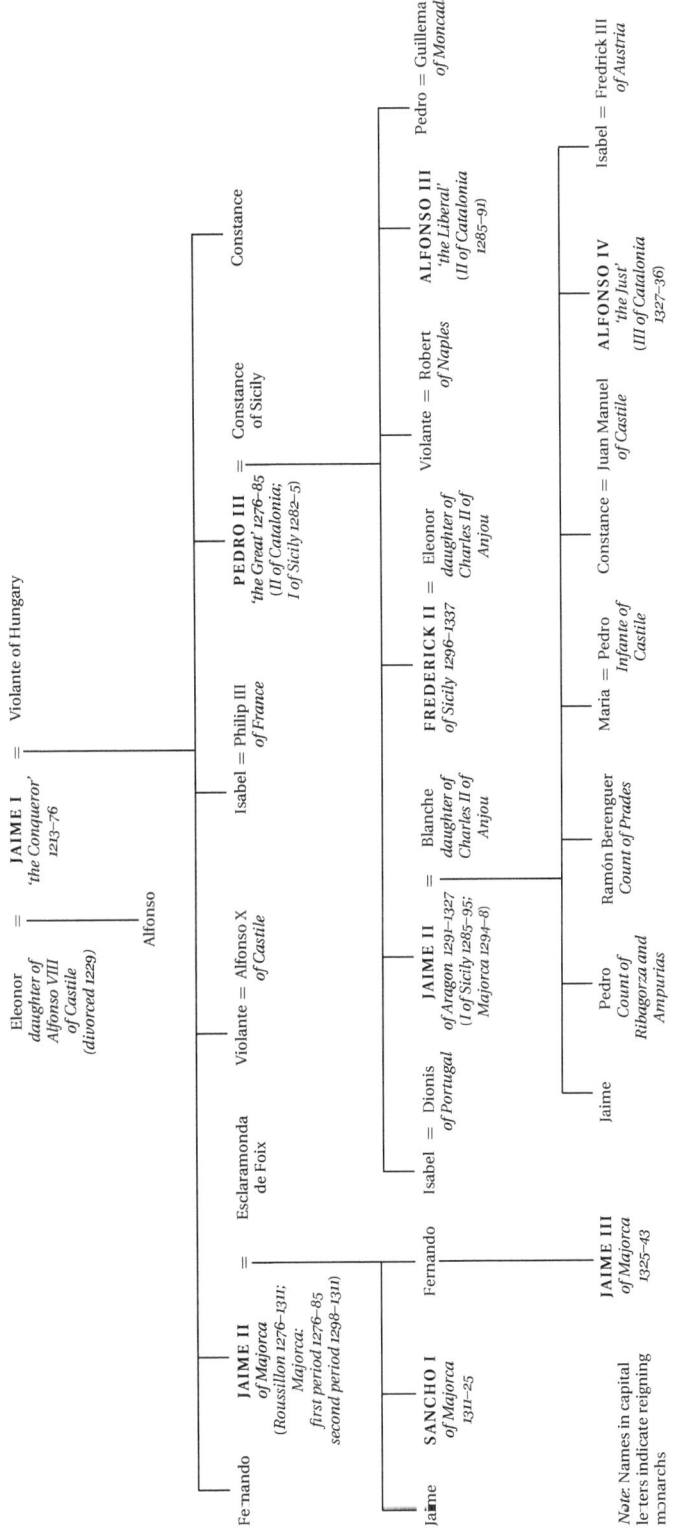

Glossary

açoch, azoch (Arabic)   The market.

adelantado (Castilian)   Member of the executive body in Jewish communities in Aragon, Valencia, and the other Hispanic kingdoms, Castile and Navarre. *Muqadem* in the Hebrew sources.

agadah (Hebrew)   The non-legal parts of the Talmud.

alatma (Arabic)   Ban imposed by the community. *Herem* or *nidduy* in Hebrew.

albedin, bedin, bedi (Hebrew)   Jewish or Christian officer with police jurisdiction.

aljama (Arabic)   Name of the legally constituted Jewish or Muslim community in all the Hispanic kingdoms.

almagran (Catalan and Arabic)   Fine paid by Muslims, and in Valencia by Jews as well.

almidraz (Hebrew or Arabic)   House of study or rabbinic academy with premises for prayers.

almosna, almoyna, almoina, elmosine (Catalan; Castilian *limosna*; Latin *eleemosyna*)   Charity fund or charity tax.

almoyner (Catalan; Latin)   Officer in charge of collecting and distributing charity in the community.

'atarot (Hebrew)   Crowns placed on the scroll of the Torah.

ayuda, ajuda (Castilian; Catalan)   Contribution or subsidy paid to king to meet his private needs. Subsequently tax imposed on meat and wine.

'azarah (Hebrew)   Ladies' gallery or prayer hall in the synagogue.

baile (Castilian; Aragonese)   King's representative in charge of administration and finance.

baror (pl. berurim) (Hebrew)   Member(s) of the executive body in the Jewish communities in the Iberian peninsula.

berure 'averot (Hebrew)   Officers in the communal government appointed to oversee religious and moral behaviour.

berure midot (Hebrew)   Officers in the communal government in charge of weights and measures.

berure tevi'ot (Hebrew)   Officers in the communal government in charge of criminal and civil charges.

beth midrash (Hebrew)   House of study with prayer premises.

bimah (Hebrew)   Central platform in synagogue where the services are conducted.

call (Latin or Hebrew)   The Jewish quarter in Catalonia.

capa (Catalan)   Mantle worn by Jews.

capella, capellano (Latin and Romance)   Person in charge of conducting the services in the synagogue.

carcelatge, carcelage, carcellagium (Romance; Latin)   Payment made by prisoners to the prison authorities.

cena (Latin)   Tax paid in the Crown of Aragon in money or in kind to provide for the needs of the king and his retinue while staying in the locality.

cisa (Latin)   Indirect tax on foodstuffs.

clavario (Castilian or Aragonese)   Treasurer or tax-collector.

cohen (Hebrew)   A descendant of the priestly family of Aaron, Moses' brother. Since the destruction of the Temple in Jerusalem the title has been largely honorific. Its bearer enjoys priority in some ceremonies but is subject to extra restrictions in marital laws.

collecta (Latin)   Inter-communal organization in Catalonia headed by a major community, originally created for tax collection, later catering for other communal needs as well.

concell, concejo, concilium (Catalan; Aragonese; Latin)   Municipal and communal council.

Cortes, Corts (Aragonese or Castilian; Catalan)   Assembly of the three estates in each of the constituent territories of the Crown of Aragon.

çunna, çuna, açuna, azuna (Arabic)   Muslim law and by extension Jewish law, the Torah, in many archival sources.

cuyraça, cyracia, curacia, coiraza   Name of Jewish quarter in Lérida.

darshan (Hebrew)   Preacher in synagogue.

dayan (Hebrew)   Judge in Jewish court.

ebreismo (Aragonese)   Rare name of Jewish quarter in Aragon.

'eza (Hebrew)   Name of community council.

fanega, faneca (Aragonese; Catalan; orig. Arabic)   Measure of volume equivalent to between 33 and 55 litres depending on the locality. Also name of the measuring instrument.

franco (Aragonese)   Jews exempt from payment of tax with the community, mainly in Saragossa.

fueros, furs (Aragonese; Catalan)   Collection of ordinances, laws, and privileges of a locality or city confirmed by the king.

gabay (Hebrew)   Community leader or officer.

get (Hebrew)   Bill of divorce according to Jewish law.

gizbar (Hebrew)   Treasurer.

halakhah (Hebrew)   Jewish law.

haskamah (Hebrew)   Communal ordinance.

havurah, haburah, hevrah (Hebrew)   Jewish confraternity whose members belong to the same profession or are dedicated to a common cause.

hazan (Hebrew)   Officiating minister in Jewish prayers and in synagogue.

hekhal (Hebrew)   Ark facing Jerusalem where scrolls of the Torah are kept in synagogue.

heqdesh (Hebrew)   Property donated to community.

herem (Hebrew)   Ban imposed on transgressor by the community.

hospital (Latin and Romance)   Hospice for sick, poor people and visitors.

hostalatge, ostalatge, hostagius (Catalan; Latin)   Accommodation or payment towards it given to king or to the royal family or household.

infante, infanta (Castilian; Aragonese)   King's son[-e] or daughter[-a].

irusin (Hebrew)   Betrothal according to Jewish law.

judería (Castilian; Aragonese)   Jewish quarter in all Spain, except Catalonia.

justicia (Castilian; Aragonese)   Magistrate in charge of administering justice in Castile, Aragon, and Valencia.

kafiç, kahiç, cafiç (Catalan; Castilian; orig. Arabic)   Unit of capacity, equivalent to 180 litres in Aragon, 140 litres in Valencia.

ketubah (Hebrew)   Marriage contract according to Jewish law.

lezda, lleuda (Aragonese; Catalan)   Toll on merchandise.

libra (Latin)   Monetary unit, equivalent to 20 *sous* or *solidi*. Also unit of weight.

mà, mano, manus (Catalan; Aragonese; Latin)   Social class, estate.

ma'amad (Hebrew)   Assembly of community members. In post-expulsion period, executive board of community.

maestre racional (Romance)   Royal official in charge of finance or treasury in each constituent state of the Crown of Aragon.

malcuç, malqut (Hebrew)   Flagellation.

malshin, malsin (Hebrew)   Informer.

malshinut (Hebrew)   Act of informing.

mapah (Hebrew)   Strap of cloth to wrap a Torah scroll.

maravedí (Arabic)   Monetary unit from Almohadic Spain, also used in Christian Spain.

matzah (Hebrew)   Unleavened bread eaten by Jews on Passover.

merino (Castilian, Aragonese)   Royal official with judicial power acting in a city.

meshumad (Hebrew)   Apostate.

mezuzah (Hebrew)   A piece of parchment containing two Pentateuchal passages rolled and placed on the doorpost of a Jewish house.

minyan (Hebrew)   Quorum of ten adult men necessary to hold prayers in public and recite certain parts of the prayers.

miqve (Hebrew)   Ritual bath of Jews built according to certain specifications and using rain or river water.

missatger (Catalan)   Envoy, representative.

mohel (Hebrew)   Expert who circumcises Jewish male babies.

mozarabs (Arabic)   Arabic-speaking Christians in Muslim Spain whose theology, liturgy, and music differed substantially from those of the Roman Church.

mudéjar (Castilian; Aragonese)   A Muslim living in Christian Spain. Used also of art, architecture, style, and taste in Christian Spain reflecting Muslim influence.

muqadem, muqademin (Hebrew; orig. from Arabic)   Community leader, member of the executive board. In Romance sources *adelantado*.

mustaçaf (Arabic)   Municipal official in charge of the market.

nedunia (Aramaic; Hebrew)   Dowry.

ne'eman (Hebrew)   Community leader, member of the executive board.

niduy, nitduy (Hebrew)   Ban, of a less severe nature than a *herem*.

nisu'in (Hebrew)   Marriage.

ostages, hostatge (obscure etymology; prob. from Latin)   Methods of election by electors who remain secluded until their choice is made.

parnas (Hebrew)   Community leader.

peatge, peaje (Catalan; Castilian)   Road tax.

procurator, procurador (Latin; Castilian)   Representative of one party in a trial.

prohomens, probi homines (Latin)   Municipal leaders.

qahal (Hebrew)   The entire Jewish population in a community. Leaders of the community.

qehilah (Hebrew)   Organized Jewish community.

qinyan (Hebrew)   Act, contract, or ceremony by which something is acquired. Right over such an acquisition. Name of ceremony whereby the bride is promised to the groom.

reconquista (Castilian)   Series of wars conducted by the Christians in Spain for the conquest of the Iberian peninsula from the hands of the Muslims.

renegat (Catalan)   Derogatory term for apostate.

repartiment, repartimiento (Catalan; Castilian)   Distribution of conquered territories and property by Christian kings. List of recipients of such property.

responsum, responsa (Latin)   Legal decisions given in form of answers to questions sent by communities, courts, and individuals to halakhic experts.

rimonim (Hebrew)   Ornamental pieces, usually made of silver, placed on the scroll of the Torah.

scrivano (Aragonese)   Scribe or notary.

secretarius (Latin)   Leader of the community, member of the executive board. *Ne'eman*, *adelantado*, or *baror*.

shaliah (pl. shelihim) (Hebrew)   Representative(s) of the community in Jewish conventions and in negotiations with Jewish communities, municipal and ecclesiastical authorities, and the royal court.

shamash (Hebrew)   Beadle and caretaker of synagogue.

shamay (pl. shamain) (Hebrew)   Tax-assessor(s).

shehitah (Hebrew)   Ritual slaughter according to Jewish law.

shekhunat Yisrael, shekhunat ha-Yehudim (Hebrew)   Jewish quarter.

shofar (Hebrew)   Ram's horn used as a wind instrument on festivals and other solemn occasions.

shohet (pl. shohatim) (Hebrew) Slaughterer of animals and fowl in accordance with Jewish ritual.

sinagoga, sinoga (Romance) Synagogue.

sindich (Catalan) Member of executive board in Jewish community.

sofer (Hebrew) Scribe in charge of drawing up legal documents, such as marriage contracts, divorce bills, etc., and expert in writing on parchment Torah scrolls, phylacteries and *mezuzot* (q.v.).

solidus, solido (Latin; Castilian) Monetary unit, twenty of which made one *libram* (see Appendix 1).

sou (Catalan) Monetary unit, twenty of which made one *libram* (see Appendix 1).

talit (Hebrew) Rectangular piece of cloth with fringes on four corners, worn by Jewish men during morning prayers.

taqanah (Hebrew) Ordinance or by-law of the community.

tatxador (Catalan) Tax-assessor or collector.

tevah (Hebrew) Platform in synagogue, usually in the centre, on which the officiating minister stands.

tiq (Hebrew) Wooden case or cloth mantle in which the scrolls of the Torah are put.

tossafists (from Hebrew) Twelfth- and thirteenth-century Talmudic scholars in Franco-Germany whose glosses and comments on Rashi's commentary are found in the standard editions of the Talmud.

veguer (Castilian; from Latin *vicarius*) Magistrate in Aragon, Catalonia, and Majorca; representative of the king, in charge of civil and criminal justice in a certain district.

vicinalium (Latin) Communal tax.

yeshivah (Hebrew) Academy for Talmudic and Jewish studies.

yo'ez (pl. yo'azim) (Hebrew) Councillor member of communal council, called the *'eza*.

zalmedina (Castilian; Aragonese; from Arabic *Sahib al-Madina*) Supreme judge of Muslims and, in Aragon, inspector of the city.

Bibliography

※

D'ABADAL I VINYALS, R., and VALLS I TABERNER, F. (eds.), *Usatges de Barcelona* (Barcelona, 1913).

ABBA MARI, R., *Minhat Qenaot* (An Offering of Zeal) (Pressburg, 1838).

ABULAFIA, D., 'Catalan Merchants and the Western Mediterranean, 1236–1300: Studies in the Notarial Acts of Barcelona and Sicily', *Viator, Medieval and Renaissance Studies*, xvi (1985), 209–42.

—— 'The Problem of the Kingdom of Majorca (1229/76–1343). 1. Political Identity', *Mediterranean Historical Review*, v, 2 (1990), 150–68; and '2. Economic Identity', *Mediterranean Historical Review*, vi, 1 (1991), 35–61.

—— 'From Privilege to Persecution: Crown, Church and Synagogue in the City of Majorca, 1229–1343', in D. Abulafia, M. Franklin, and M. Rubin (eds.), *Church and City, 1000–1500: Essays in Honour of Christopher Brooke* (Cambridge, 1992), 111–26.

—— *A Mediterranean Emporium: The Catalan Kingdom of Majorca* (Cambridge, 1994).

ABULAFIA, R. MEIR BEN TODROS HA-LEVI, *Sheelot u-Teshuvot, Or Zaddiqim* (Responsa) (Salonica, 1899).

ADLER, E. N., 'Provençal and Catalonian Responsa', *JQR*, xii (1900), 143–9.

ADRET, R. SHELOMO BEN, *Sheelot u-Teshuvot* (Responsa), vols. i (Bologna, 1539); ii, iii (Leghorn, 1657, 1778); iv (Vilna, 1881); v (Leghorn, 1825); vi, vii (Warsaw, 1868); viii (Adret's Responsa attributed to Nahmanides) (Warsaw, 1883).

ALANYA, L., *Aureum Opus Regalium Privilegiorum Civitatis et Regni Valentie* (Valencia, 1515; republ. Valencia, 1972).

ALARCÓN, M. A., and GARCIA LUNARES, R., *Los documentos arabes diplomáticos del Archivo de la Corona de Aragón* (Madrid, 1940).

ALART, B., *Documents sur la langue catalane* (Paris, 1881).

—— *Privilèges et titres du Roussillon* (Perpignan, 1874).

ALDEA VAQUERO, Q., MARÍN MARTÍNEZ, J., and VIVES GATELL, J., *Diccionario de historia eclesiastica de España*, 4 vols. and supplement (Madrid, 1972–87).

ALTISENT, A., 'El monasterio de Poblet y unos judíos prestamistas de la Segarra (s. XIV–XV)', *Sefarad*, xxvii (1967), 282–9.

AMADOR DE LOS RÍOS, J., *Historia social, política y religiosa de los judíos de España y Portugal*, 3 vols. (Madrid, 1875–6).

ARABAL I DE VINYALS, R. D', *Moments crucials de la història de Catalunya* (Barcelona, 1962).

ARAMA, R. YIZHAQ, *Agedat Yizhaq* (The Sacrifice of Isaac), (Pressburg, 1849).

ARCO, R. DEL, 'Ordenanzas inéditas, dictadas por el concejo de Huesca (1284 a 1456)', *RABM*, xxix (1913), 427–52.

Arco, R. del, 'La judería de Huesca: Noticias y documentos inéditos', *BAH*, lxvi (1915), 321–54.
—— 'La aljama judaica de Huesca', *Sefarad*, vii (1947), 271–301.
—— 'Nuevas noticias de la aljama judaica de Huesca', *Sefarad*, ix (1949), 350–92.
—— 'Las juderías de Jaca y Zaragoza', *Sefarad*, xiv (1954), 79–87.
Arribas i Palau, A., *La conquista de Cerdeña por Jaime II de Aragón* (Barcelona, 1952).
—— *La conquesta de Sardenya: Episodis de la història*, no. 17 (Barcelona, 1961).
Asher ben Yehiel, R., *Sheelot u-Teshuvot* (Responsa) (Venice, 1607).
Ashtor, E., *The Jews of Moslem Spain*, 3 vols. (Philadelphia, 1973–8).
Asibili, R. Yom Tov, *Responsa, The Works of the Ritba (Kitve HaRitba)*, ed. M. Y. Ha-Cohen Blau (New York, 1957).
—— *Sheelot u-Teshuvot* (Responsa), ed. Y. Kapah (Jerusalem, 1959).
Assaf, S., *Courts of Law and their Methods in Post-Talmudic Times* (Jerusalem, 1924) (Hebrew).
—— *Punishments in Post-Talmudic Times* (Jerusalem, 1924) (Hebrew).
—— *Sources for the History of Education in Israel*, 4 vols. (Jerusalem, 1925–42) (Hebrew).
—— 'Slavery and the Slave-trade among the Jews during the Middle Ages', *Zion*, iv (1939), 106ff. (Hebrew).
—— *Texts and Studies in Jewish History* (Jerusalem, 1946) (Hebrew).
Assis, Y., 'The "Ordinance of Rabbenu Gershom" and Polygamous Marriages in Spain', *Zion*, xlvi (1981), 251–77 (Hebrew).
—— 'Crisis in the Community of Saragossa in the Years 1263–1264 according to Hebrew and Latin Sources', *Proceedings of the Seventh World Congress of Jewish Studies*, vol. iv (Jerusalem, 1981), 37–42 (Hebrew).
—— 'The Jews of Aragon under James II', unpubl. doctoral diss. (Jerusalem, 1981) (Hebrew).
—— 'Juifs de France réfugiés en Aragon (XIIIe–XIVe siècles)', *REJ*, cxlii (1983), 209–27.
—— 'Crime and Violence in Jewish Society in Spain (XIII–XIVth Centuries)', *Zion, Jubilee Volume*, l (1985), 221–40 (Hebrew).
—— 'Jewish Diplomats from Aragon in Muslim Lands (1213–1327)', *Sefunot*, iii [18] (1985), 11–34 (Hebrew).
—— 'The Papal Inquisition and Aragonese Jewry in the Early Fourteenth Century', *Mediaeval Studies*, xlix (1987), 391–410.
—— 'La participación de los judíos en la vida económica de Barcelona, s. XIII–XIV', *Jornades dels jueus a Catalunya: Actes, Girona, abril 1987*, Girona (1990), 77–92.
—— 'The Jews of Barcelona in Maritime Trade with the East', in A. Mirsky, A. Grossman, and Y. Kaplan (eds.), *Exile and Diaspora* (Jerusalem, 1988), 257–83 (Hebrew).
—— *The Jews of Santa Coloma de Queralt: An Economic and Demographic Case Study of a Community at the End of the Thirteenth Century* (Jerusalem, 1988).
—— 'Sexual Behaviour in Medieval Hispano-Jewish Society', in A. Rapoport-Albert and

S. J. Zipperstein (eds.), *Jewish History: Essays in Honour of Chimen Abramsky* (London, 1988), 25–59.

—— 'Social Unrest and Class Struggle in Jewish Communities in Spain before the Expulsion', in Y. Dan (ed.), *Tarbut ve-Historia* (Culture and History) (Jerusalem, 1988), 121–45 (Hebrew).

—— 'The Jews of Spain in Gentile Courts (XIIIth–XIVth Centuries)', in M. Ben-Sasson, R. Bonfil, and J. Hacker (eds.), *Tarbut ve-Hevrah be-Toledot Yisrael Biyeme ha-Benayim* (Culture and Society in Medieval Jewish History) (Jerusalem, 1989), 399–430 (Hebrew).

—— Les Juifs de Montpellier sous la domination aragonaise', *REJ*, cxlviii (1989), 5–16.

—— 'Jewish Capital and the Conquest of Sardinia by the Catalans', *Italia*, ix (1990), 7–18.

—— 'Los judíos de Cataluña: Fuentes y posibilidades de estudio', *Actes del Ier Col·loqui de Història dels Juheus de la Corona d'Aragó* (Lleida, 1991), 139–155.

—— 'Poor and Rich in Jewish Society in Mediterranean Spain', *Pe'amim*, xlvi–xlvii (1991), 115–38.

—— 'Les Institutions économiques d'avant la modernité', in S. Trigano (ed.), *La Société juive à travers l'histoire* (Paris, 1992), 259–92; notes 563–70.

—— 'Les Institutions sociales médiévales: Les Logiques de la charité collective et de l'association', in S. Trigano (ed.), *La Société juive à travers l'histoire* (Paris, 1992), 181–217; notes 552–60.

—— 'Jewish Attitudes to Christian Power in Medieval Spain', *Sefarad (Homenaje al Prof. David Romano Ventura)*, lii (1992), 291–304.

—— 'The Jews in the Crown of Aragon and its Dominions', in H. Beinart (ed.), *The Sephardi Legacy*, vol. i (Jerusalem, 1992), 44–102.

—— 'Synagogues in Medieval Spain', *Jewish Art*, xviii (1992), 7–29.

—— 'Welfare and Mutual Aid in the Spanish Jewish Communities', in H. Beinart (ed.), *The Sephardi Legacy*, vol. i (Jerusalem, 1992), 318–45.

—— 'Responsa Rabínicos y Cartas Reales: Fuentes para el estudio de la historia de los judíos en la Corona de Aragón', *Espacio, Tiempo y Forma, Revista de la Facultad de Geografía e Historia (UNED)*, 3rd ser., vi (1993), 363–76.

—— 'El concepto del judaismo de Nahmanides', in *Mossé ben Nahman i el seu temps* (Girona, 1994), 79–90.

—— 'Jewish Physicians and Medicine in Medieval Spain', in S. Kottek (ed.), *Medical Ethics in Medieval Spain (13th–14th Centuries)* (Jerusalem, 1996), 33–49.

—— 'The Judeo-Arabic Tradition in Christian Spain', in D. Frank (ed.), *The Jews of Medieval Islam: Community, Society, and Identity* (Leiden, New York, and Cologne, 1995), 111–24.

—— *Jewish Economy in the Medieval Crown of Aragon, 1213–1327: Money and Power* (Leiden, forthcoming).

—— (ed.), *The Jews in the Crown of Aragon. Regesta of the Cartas Reales in the Archivo de la Corona de Aragón, Part II: 1328–1493* (Jerusalem, 1995).

—— and MAGDALENA, R., *The Jews of Navarre* (Jerusalem, 1990) (Hebrew).

Assis, Y., Magdalena Nom de Déu, J. R., and Lleal, C., *Aljamía romance en los documentos hebraiconavarros (siglo XIV)* (Barcelona, 1992).

Baer, F. *Die Juden im christlichen Spanien, Urkunden und Regesten*, vol. i: *Aragonien und Navarra* (Berlin, 1929); vol. ii: *Kastilien und Inquisitionsakten* (Berlin, 1936).

Baer, I., 'Todros ben Judah Halevi and his Time', *Zion*, ii (1937), 19–55 (Hebrew).

Baer, Y., *Studien zur Geschichte der Juden im Königreich Aragonien während des 13. und 14. Jahrhunderts* (Berlin, 1913).

—— 'The Foundations and Beginnings of a Jewish Community Structure in the Middle Ages', *Zion*, xv (1950), 1–41 (Hebrew).

—— *A History of the Jews in Christian Spain*, 2 vols. (Philadelphia, 1966).

Bahye ben Asher, R., *Kad ha-Qemah* (A Jar of Flour), in *Kitve R. Bahye bar Asher* (The Works of R. Bahye ben Asher), ed. C. B. Chavel (Jerusalem, 1970) (Hebrew).

—— *Commentary on the Pentateuch*, ed. C. B. Chavel, 3 vols. (Jerusalem, 1977) (Hebrew).

Ballesteros y Beretta, A., *Historia de Españā* (Barcelona, 1948).

Barnai, J., 'Jewish Guilds in Turkey in the 16th–19th Centuries', in N. Gross (ed.), *Jews in Economy* (Jerusalem, 1985), 133–48 (Hebrew).

Baron, S. W., *The Jewish Community*, 3 vols. (Philadelphia, 1942).

Batlle Gallart, C., 'Notícies sobre els jueus de la Seu d'Urgell: els Bedoz (1336–1348)', *Urgellia*, x (1990–1), 375–406.

—— 'Solución al problema de las dos sinagogas de Gerona', *Sefarad*, xix (1959), 301–20.

Beinart, H., 'A 15th Century Hebrew Formulary from Spain', *Sefunot*, v (1961), 75–134.

—— 'The Image of Jewish Courtiers in Christian Spain', in *Elites and Leading Groups* (Jerusalem, 1966), 55–71 (Hebrew).

—— 'Hispano-Jewish Society', *Cahiers d'Histoire Mondiale*, x (1968), 220–38; republ. in *Jewish Society through the Ages*, ed. H. H. Ben-Sasson and S. Ettinger (London, 1971), 220–38.

Ben-Sasson, M., 'Sources for the History of the Jewish Communities in Spain in the Fourteenth Century', in A. Mirsky, A. Grossman, and Y. Kaplan (eds.), *Exile and Diaspora* (Jerusalem, 1988), 284–336 (Hebrew).

Bergua Camón, J., 'Fueros de Aragón de 1265 a 1381', *Anuario de Derecho Aragonés*, v (1949–50), 455–79.

Bertan Roige, P., 'La fiscalidad extraordinaria de las aljamas de judíos de la Corona de Aragón (1309–1317)', *Sefarad*, lii (1992), 305–22.

Blasco Martínez, A., '"Ebreismo" sinónimo de judería', *Sefarad*, xli (1981), 111–13.

—— 'Los judíos de Zaragoza en el siglo XIV—su evolución social', *Minorités et marginaux en Espagne et dans le Midi de la France (VIIe–XVIIIe siècles): Actes du Colloque de Pau, 27–29 mai 1984* (Paris, 1986), 177–202.

—— *La judería de Zaragoza* (Saragossa, 1988).

—— 'Instituciones sociorreligiosas judías de Zaragoza (siglos XIV–XV)—Sinagogas, cofradías, hospitales', *Sefarad*, xlix (1989), 227–36; l (1990), 3–46.

—— 'Los judíos del reino de Aragón: Balance de los estudios realizados y perspectivas', *Actes; I" Col·loqui de Història dels Juheus a la Corona d'Aragó* (Lleida, 1991), 13–97.

BLIDSTEIN, G. J., 'A Note on the Function of "the Law of the Kingdom is Law" in the Medieval Jewish Community', *Jewish Journal of Sociology*, xv (1973), 213–19.

BOFARULL Y DE SARTORIO, M. DE, 'Gremios y cofradías de la antigua Corona de Aragón', *CDIA*, xl (1876).

BOFARULL Y SANS, F. DE, 'Judíos en Montblanch', *Memorias RABLB*, vi (1898), 560–73.

—— 'Jaime el Conquistador y la comunidad judía de Montpellier', *BABLB*, v (1910), 484–92.

—— *Los judíos en el territorio de Barcelona (siglos X al XIII), Reinado de Jaime I, 1213–1276* (Barcelona, 1910).

—— 'Ordinaciones de los concelleres de Barcelona sobre los judíos en el siglo XIV', *BABLB*, vi (1911), 97–102.

—— 'Los judíos malsines', *BABLB*, viii (1919), 207–16.

BONFIL, R., 'The Image of Judaism in Raymundus Martini's Book "Pugio Fidei" ', *Tarbiz*, xl (1971), 360–75 (Hebrew).

BOSCH VILÁ, J., 'Escrituras oscences en aljamía hebraico-arabe', *Homenaje a Millás Vallicrosa*, vol. i (Barcelona, 1954), 183–214.

—— 'Referencias a moneda en los documentos árabes y hebreos', *EEMCA*, vi (1956), 229–46.

BOSWELL, J., *Christianity, Social Tolerance and Homosexuality: Gay People in Western Europe from the Beginning of the Christian Era to the Fourteenth Century* (Chicago and London, 1980).

BRAMONS D., *Contra moros i jueus* (Valencia, 1981).

BURNS, R. I., *The Crusader Kingdom of Valencia: Reconstruction of a Thirteenth-Century Frontier*, 2 vols. (Cambridge, Mass., 1967).

—— *Islam under the Crusaders: Colonial Survival in the Thirteenth Century Kingdom of Valencia* (Princeton, 1973).

—— *Medieval Colonialism: Postcrusade Exploitation of Islamic Valencia* (Princeton, 1975).

—— *Jaume I i els Valencians del s. XIII* (Valencia, 1981).

—— *Moros, cristians i jueus en el regne croat de Valencia* (Valencia, 1987).

CABARTE, P., *Fueros y observaciones del reyno de Aragón* (Saragossa, 1624).

CABEZUDO ASTRAIN, J., 'Testamentos de judíos aragoneses', *Sefarad*, xvi (1956), 136–47.

—— 'La judería de Epila', *Sefarad*, xvii (1957), 103–18.

—— 'Nuevos documentos sobre judíos zaragozanos', *Sefarad*, xx (1960), 407–17.

CAGIGAS, I. DE LA, *Minorías etnico-religiosas de la Edad Media Española*, vol. i, *Loz Mozárabes* (Madrid, 1947).

CANTERA BURGOS, F., 'La Cofradía de "malvisar" de Zaragoza y un censal de Oliete', *Sefarad*, vii (1947), 147–51.

—— *Sinagogas españolas* (Madrid, 1955).

—— and MILLÁS VALLICROSA, J. M., *Las inscripciones hebraicas de España* (Madrid, 1956).

CAPMANY Y MONTPALAU, A. DE, *Memorias históricas sobre la marina, comercio y artes de la antigua ciudad de Barcelona* (Madrid, 1779–92; republ. Barcelona, 1962).

CARBONEL, P. M. 'Opuscules inèdits', *CDIA*, xxvii (Barcelona, 1865).

CARDONER PLANAS, A., 'Nuevos datos acerca de Jafuda Bonsenyor', *Sefarad*, iv (1944), 287–93.

—— 'Muestra de protección real a físicos judíos españoles conversos', *Sefarad*, xii (1952), 378–80.

—— 'El hospital para judíos pobres de Barcelona', *Sefarad*, xxii (1962), 373–5.

CARINI, I., *Gli archivi e le biblioteche di Spagna* (Palermo, 1884).

CARRASCO PÉREZ, J., 'Acerca del préstamo judío en Tudela a fines del siglo XIV', *Príncipe de Viana*, clxvi–clxvii (1982), 909–48.

—— 'Los judíos de Viana y La Guardia (1350–1408): aspectos sociales y económicos', in *Vitoria en la Edad Media* (Vitoria-Gasteiz, 1982).

—— *Sinagoga y mercado, Estudios y textos sobre los judíos del reino de Navarra* (Pamplona, 1993).

CARRERAS I CANDI, F., *Lo Montjuich de Barcelona, Memorias RABLB*, viii (Barcelona, 1903).

—— 'Evolució històrica dels juheus y juheissans barcelonins', *EUC*, iii (1909), 404–28, 498–522; iv (1910), 45–65, 359–73.

—— 'Ordinacions urbanes a Catalunya, Ordinacions de Barcelona (Any 1301)', *BABLB*, xi (1924), 292–334.

—— 'Ordinacions de bon govern a Catalunya: Ordinacions de Valls (1299–1325)', *BABLB*, xii (1925–6), 368–72.

—— 'L'aljama de juheus de Tortosa', *Memorias RABLB*, ix (1928).

CASAS I NADAL, M., 'El "Liber Iudeorum" de Cardona (1330–1334), edició i estudi', Els 'Libri Iudeorum' de Vic i de Cardona, *Miscel·lànea de Textos Medievals*, iii (Barcelona, 1985). 121–314.

CDIA, 'Procesos de las antiguas Cortes', vi.

—— 'Rentas de Rosellón. Rentas reales, 1315', xii.

—— 'Rentas de la antigua corona de Aragón', xxxix (Barcelona, 1871).

—— P. de Bofarull y Mascaró, 'Repartimiento de Mallorca, Vallencia', xi (Barcelona, 1856).

CHABRET, A., *Sagunto, su història y sus monumentos*, 2 vols. (Barcelona, 1888).

CHAZAN, R., 'The Barcelona "Disputation" of 1263: Christian Missionizing and Jewish Response', *Speculum*, lii (1977), 824–42.

—— *Barcelona and Beyond: The Disputation of 1263 and its Aftermath* (Berkeley, Los Angeles, and Oxford, 1992).

CHAVEL, C. B. (ed.), *Nahmanides' Commentary on the Pentateuch* (Jerusalem, 1959) (Hebrew).

—— *The Works of Nahmanides (Kitve ha-Ramban)*, 2 vols. (Jerusalem, 1964) (Hebrew).

—— *The Works of R. Bahya bar Asher* (Jerusalem, 1970) (Hebrew).

—— (ed. and trans.), *Ramban (Nachmanides) Commentary on the Torah*, 5 vols. (New York, 1971).

CINTA MAÑE, M. (comp.) and ASSIS, Y. (ed.), *The Jews in the Crown of Aragon: Regesta of the Cartas Reales in the Archivo de la Corona de Aragón, Part I: 1066–1327* (Jerusalem, 1993).

COHEN, J., 'The Christian Adversary of Solomon ibn Adret', *JQR*, lxxi (1980), 48–55.

—— *The Friars and the Jews* (Ithaca and London, 1982).

COHEN, M. A., 'Reflections on the Text and Context of the Disputation of Barcelona', *Hebrew Union College Annual*, xxxv (1964), 157–92.

COLL, J. M., 'Escuelas de lenguas orientales en los siglos xiii y xiv', *Analecta Sacra Tarraconensia*, xix (1946), 217–40.

Constitucions y altres drets de Cathalunya (Barcelona, 1704; republ. 1909).

Corbella, M. R., *La aljama de juheus de Vich* (Vich, 1909).

CORCOS, D., 'The Jews of Morocco under the Marinides', *JQR*, lv (1964), 271–87; lv (1965), 53–81, 137–50.

—— 'The Attitude of the Almohadic Leaders towards the Jews', *Zion*, xxxii (1977), 137–60 (Hebrew).

COROLEU, J., *Documents historichs catalans del sigle XI* (Barcelona, 1889).

Cortes de los antiguos reinos de Aragón y Valencia y principado de Cataluña, 7 vols. (Madrid, 1896–1903).

CORTES MUÑOZ, FERMIN, 'Aportaciones al estudio de las instituciones mercantiles de la Valencia foral', *Boletín de la Sociedad Castellonense de Cultura*, xxiv (1948), 218–35.

COWDREY, H. E. J., *The Cluniacs and the Gregorian Reform* (Oxford, 1970).

CUBELLS I LLORENS, J., *The Jews of Tortosa 1373–1492, Regesta of Documents from the Archivo Histórico de Protocolos de Tarragona*, ed. Y. Assis (Jerusalem, 1991).

CUBELLS, M. (ed.), 'Documentos diplomáticos aragoneses (1259–1284)', *Revue Hispanique*, xxxvii (1916), 105–250.

DANVILA Y COLLADO, F., 'El robo de la judería de Valencia en 1391', *BAH*, viii (1886), 358–96.

—— 'Clausura y delimitación de la judería de Valencia en 1390 a 91', *BAH*, xviii (1891), 142–58.

DARWIN SWIFT, F., *The Life and Times of James the First* (Oxford, 1894).

DECLOR, M., 'Les Juifs de Puigcerdà au XIIIe siècle', *Sefarad*, xxvi (1966), 17–46.

DENIFLE, H., 'Quellen zur Disputation Pablos Christiani mit Moses Nachmani zu Barcelona, 1263', *Historisches Jahrbuch der Gorres-Gessellschaft*, viii (1887), 225–44.

DINUR, B. Z., *A Documentary History of the Jewish People*, 2nd ser.: *Israel in the Diaspora*, 2nd ed., 2 parts, 10 vols. (Jerusalem, 1961–72) (Hebrew).

DRORI, R., 'The Hidden Context: On Literary Products of Tri-cultural Contacts in the Middle Ages', *Pe'amim*, xlvi–xlvii (1991), 9–28 (Hebrew).

DUFOURCQ, CH., *L'Espagne catalane et le Maghrib* (Paris, 1966).

DURAN Y SANPERE, A., *Referencies documentals del call de juheus de Cervera* (Barcelona, 1924).

—— and MILLÁS VALLICROSA, J. Mª, 'Una necropolis judaica en el Montjuich de Barcelona', *Sefarad*, vii (1947), 232–59.

ELFENBEIN, I., 'Jewish Communal Government in Spain', *Students' Annual, Jewish Theological Seminary*, ii (1915), 102–21.

EMERY, R. W., *The Jews of Perpignan in the Thirteenth Century: An Economic Study based on Notarial Records* (New York, 1959).

—— 'Jewish Physicians in Medieval Perpignan', *Michael*, xii (1991), 113–34.

EPSTEIN, I., *Responsa of Rabbi Solomon ben Adreth of Barcelona (1235–1310) as a Source of the History of Spain* (London, 1925; 2nd edn. *Studies in the Communal Life of the Jews of Spain*, New York, 1968).

ESCRIBÀ I BONASTRE, G., and FRAGO I PÉREZ, M. P., *Documents dels jueus de Girona, 1124–1595* (Gerona, 1992).

FALAQUERA, R. SHEM TOV, *Sefer ha-Mevaqesh*, ed. Mordekhay ben Yishaq Tamah (The Hague, 1778).

FELIU I MABRES, E., and RIERA I SANS, J. (eds.), *Poemes hebraics de jueus catalans: Segles XI–XV* (Barcelona, 1976).

—— 'Els acords de Barcelona de 1354', *Calls*, ii (1987), 145–64.

FELLER, A., '"Purim of Saragossa" and its Implications on the Sephardi Method of Dressing the Torah Scroll', *Jewish Art*, l (1992), 79–85.

FERNANDEZ Y GONZÁLEZ, F., *Estado social y político de los mudéjares de Castilla* (Madrid, 1866).

FINKE, H., *Acta Aragonensia. Quellen zur deutschen, italienischen, französischen, spanischen, zur kirchen und Kulturgeschichteaus der diplomatischen Korrespondenz Jaymes II (1291–1327)*, 3 vols. (Berlin and Leipzig, 1908–22).

FINKELSTEIN, L., *Jewish Self-government in the Middle Ages* (New York, 1924).

FITA Y COLOMÉ, F., 'El cementerio hebreo de Barcelona en 1111', *BAH*, xvii (1890), 190–9.

—— 'El Montjui de la ciudad de Gerona y la sinagoga y concejo hebreo de Castellón de Ampurias', *BAH*, xlviii (1906), 169–74.

—— 'La judería de la ciudad de Vich', *BAH*, lx (1912), 291–302.

—— and LLABRÉS Y QUINTANA, G., 'Privilegios de los hebreos mallorquines en el códice Pueyo', *BAH*, xxxvi (1900), 15–35, 122–48, 185–209, 273–306, 369–402, 458–94 [= *España hebrea*, ii (1898)].

FITER E INGLÉS, J., 'Bandos dados por el concejo municipal de Barcelona', *Revista Historica*, iii (1876), 340–1.

FLORIANO CUMBRENO, A. C., *La aljama de judíos de Teruel y el hallazgo de su necropolis* (Teruel, 1926).

FONT I RIUS, J. M., 'Orígenes del regimen municipal de Cataluña', *Anuario de Historia del Derecho Español*, xvi (1945), 389–529; xvii (1946), 229–589.

FORT I COGUL, E., *Catalunya i la inquisició* (Barcelona, 1973).

FREIMANN, A., *Ha-Rosh Rabbeinu Asher bar Yehiel and his Descendants* (Jerusalem, 1986) (Hebrew).

GARCÍA I SANZ, A., 'Los intereses de los préstamos de los judíos de Vich durante la primera mitad del siglo XIV', *Ausa*, iv (1962), 247-55.

GERONDI, R. JONAH, *Sha'are Teshuvah* (Gates of Repentance) (Vilna, 1886; Hebrew and English edn. Jerusalem, 1967).

GERONDI, R. NISSIM BEN REUVEN, *Sheelot u-Teshuvot* (Responsa), ed. L. A. Feldman (Jerusalem, 1984).

GIMÉNEZ SOLER, A., 'La Corona de Aragón y Granada', *BABLB*, iii (1905-6), 101-34, 186-224, 295-324, 333-65, 450-76, 486-96; iv (1907), 49-91, 146-80, 200-25, 271-98, 342-75 [= *La Corona de Aragón y Granada* (Barcelona, 1908)].

—— *El sitio de Almería en 1309*, (Barcelona, 1909).

—— *D. Juan Manuel: biografía y estudio crítico* (Saragossa, 1932).

GIRBAL, C., *Los judíos en Gerona* (Gerona, 1870) [= D. Romano (ed.), *Per a una història de la Girona jueva*, vol. i (Gerona, 1988)].

—— 'Beneficencia judaica en Gerona', *Revista de Gerona*, xviii (1884), 1-5 [= D. Romano (ed.), *Per a una història de la Girona jueva*, vol. ii (Gerona, 1988)].

GOITEIN, S. D., 'Slaves and Slavegirls in the Cairo Geniza Records', *Arabica*, ix (1962), 1-20.

GONZÁLEZ ANTÓN, L., *Las Uniones Aragoneses y las Cortes del reino*, 2 vols. (Saragossa, 1975).

GONZÁLEZ HURTEBISE, E., *Libros de tesorería de la casa real de Aragón*, vol. i (Barcelona, 1911).

—— *Guía histórico-descriptiva del Archivo de la Corona de Aragón en Barcelona* (Madrid, 1920).

GONZÁLEZ PALENCIA, C. A., *Los mozárabes de Toledo en los siglos XII y XIII* (Madrid, 1926).

GONZÁLO RUBIÓ, C., 'Zaragoza en la historia del judaismo español', *Miscelánea de Estudios Arabes y Hebraicos*, xvi-xvii (1967-8), fas. 2, 97-105.

GOROSCH, M., *El Fuero de Teruel* (Stockholm, 1950).

GRAU MONTSERRAT, M., 'La judería de Morella (siglos XIII-XIV)', *Sefarad*, xxii (1962), 69-81; xxiv (1964), 288-321.

—— 'Medicina a Besalú (segle XIV), Metges, apotecaris i manescals', in *Patronat d'Estudis Historics d'Olot i Comarca, Annals 1982-83* (Olot, 1984), 99-133.

GRAYZEL, S., *The Church and the Jews in the Thirteenth Century* (Philadelphia, 1933; repr. New York, 1966).

—— 'Popes, Jews and Inquisition', in A. I. Katsch and L. Nemoy (eds.), *Essays on the Occasion of the Seventieth Anniversary of the Dropsie University (1909-1979)* (Philadelphia, 1979), 151-88.

GROSS, A., 'Centers of Study and Yeshivot in Spain', in H. Beinart (ed.), *The Sephardi Legacy*, vol. i (Jerusalem, 1992), 399-410.

GROSS, H., *Gallia Judaica* (Paris, 1897).

GROSSMAN, A., 'The Origins and Essence of the Custom of "Stopping-the-Service"', *Milet*, i (1983), 199–219

—— 'Between Spain and France—Relations between the Jewish Communities of Muslim Spain and France', in A. Mirsky, A. Grossman, and Y. Kaplan (eds.), *Exile and Diaspora* (Jerusalem, 1988), 75–101.

—— 'Biblical Exegesis in Spain during the 13th–15th Centuries', in H. Beinart (ed.), *The Sephardi Legacy*, vol. i (Jerusalem, 1992), 137–46

—— 'Relations between Spanish and Ashkenazi Jewry in the Middle Ages', in H. Beinart (ed.), *The Sephardi Legacy*, vol. i (Jerusalem, 1992), 220–39.

GUILLERÉ, C., 'Juifs et Chrétiens à Gérone au XIVème siècle', in *Jornades d'història dels jueus a Catalunya* (Girona, 1990), 45–65.

GUTWIRTH, E., 'Jewish Hospices in Spain', *Pe'amim*, xxxvii (1989), 140–50 (Hebrew).

HACKER, J., 'The Sephardim in the Ottoman Empire in the Sixteenth Century', in H. Beinart (ed.), *The Sephardi Legacy*, vol. ii (Jerusalem, 1992), 109–33.

HALKIN, A., 'History of the Almohadic Persecutions', *Joshua Starr Memorial Volume* (New York, 1953), 101–10 (Hebrew).

HALPER, B., *Post-biblical Hebrew Literature*, 2 parts (Philadelphia, 1921).

HAVLIN, S., 'The Taqquanot of Rabbenu Gershon Me'or ha-Golah on Family Law in Spain and Provence (in the Light of Manuscripts of Responsa of RaSHBA and R. Isaac de Molina)', *Shenaton ha-Mishpat ha'Ivri*, ii (1975), 200–57 (Hebrew).

HEFELE, C. J., *Histoire des conciles* (Paris, 1913).

HEYD, W. VON, *Histoire du commerce du Levant au Moyen Age* (Leipzig, 1885).

HILLGARTH, J. N., 'The Problem of a Catalan Mediterranean Empire 1229–1327', *English Historical Review*, supplement, viii (1975).

—— *The Spanish Kingdoms 1250–1516*, 2 vols. (Oxford, 1976).

—— and NARKISS, B., 'A List of Books (1300) and a Contract to Illuminate Manuscripts (1335) from Majorca', *REJ*, cxx (1960), 297–320.

HINOJOSA MONTALVO, J., 'Los judíos valencianos durante la época de las Vísperas Sicilianas (1276–1336)', *XI Congreso de Historia de la Corona de Aragón*, vol. iii (Palermo, 1984), 195–219.

—— 'El préstamo judío en la ciudad de Valencia en la secunda mitad del siglo XIV', *Sefarad*, xlv (1985), 315–39.

—— 'Bosquejo histórico de los judíos en tierras alicantinas durante la baja edad media', *Actes; Ier Col·loqui de Història dels juheus a la Corona d'Aragó* (Lleida, 1991), 207–20.

—— 'La sociedad y la economía de los judíos en Castilla y la Corona de Aragón durante la baja edad media', *II^a Semana de Estudios Medievales* (Nájera, 1992), 79–109.

HIRSCHMAN, A., *Rabbi Isaac ben Sheshet Perfet and his Times* (New York, 1943).

HUICI, A., *Colección diplomática de Jaime I, el Conquistador* (Valencia, 1916).

HUNT, N., *Cluny under S. Hugh* (London, 1967).

IDEL, M., 'We Have No Kabbalistic Tradition on This', in I. Twersky (ed.), *Rabbi Moses Nahmanides (Ramban): Explorations in his Religious and Literary Virtuosity*, (Cambridge, Mass., 1983), 51–73.

—— 'La història de la Cábala a Barcelona', in *La Cábala* (Barcelona, 1989), 59–74.
—— 'Jewish Thought in Medieval Spain', in H. Beinart (ed.), *The Sephardi Legacy*, vol. i (Jerusalem, 1992), 261–81.
—— 'R. Moshe ben Nahman: Kabbalah, Halakhah and Spiritual Leadership', *Tarbiz*, lxiv (1995), 535–80.
ISAACS, A. L., *The Jews of Majorca* (London, 1936).
JACOBS, J., *An Inquiry into the Sources of the History of the Jews in Spain* (London, 1894).
KAHN, S., 'Documents inédits sur les Juifs de Montpellier', *REJ*, xix (1889), 259–81; xxii (1891), 265–79.
KAPLAN, Y., 'The Sephardim in North-western Europe and the New World', in H. Beinart (ed.), *The Sephardi Legacy*, vol. ii (Jerusalem, 1992), 240–87.
KAUFMAN, D., 'Jewish Informers in the Middle Ages', *JQR*, viii (1896), 217–38.
KAYSERLING, M., 'Un contrat de mariage en langue catalane', *REJ*, xxiv (1892), 291.
—— 'Raymond Lulle, convertisseur des Juifs', *REJ*, xxvii (1893), 148–9.
—— 'Les Juifs à Barcelone', *REJ*, xxviii (1894), 109–10.
—— 'Les Juifs à Saragosse', *REJ*, xxviii (1894), 115–17.
—— 'Critical Notes: The Jews of Spain', *JQR*, viii (1896), 486–99.
—— 'Jehuda Bonsenyor and his Collection of Aphorisms', *JQR*, viii (1896), 632–42.
KLÜPFEL, L., 'El règim de la confederació catalano-aragonesa a finals del segle XIII', *Revista Juridica de Catalunya*, xxxv (1929), 34–40, 195–226, 289–327; xxxvi (1930), 18–37, 97–135, 298–331.
KRIEGEL, M., *Les Juifs à la fin du Moyen Age dans l'Europe méditerranéenne* (Paris, 1979).
LACAVE, J. L., 'La carnicería de la aljama Zaragozano a fines del siglo XV', *Sefarad*, xxxv (1975), 1–33.
—— 'Las juderías aragonesas al terminar el reinado de Fernando I', *Sefarad*, xxxix (1979), 209–24.
—— *Juderías y sinagogas españolas* (Madrid, 1992).
LACRUZ BERDEJO, L., 'Fueros de Aragón hasta 1265', *Anuario de Derecho Aragonés*, ii (1945), 223–361.
LAZAR, M., 'Catalan–Provençal Wedding Songs (14th–15th Centuries)', *Hayim (Jefim) Schirman Jubilee Volume* (Jerusalem, 1970), 159–77 (Hebrew).
LECOY DE LA MARCHE, R. A., *Les Relations politiques de la France avec le Royaume de Majorque*, 2 vols. (Paris, 1892).
LEROY, B., *The Jews of Navarre in the Late Middle Ages* (Jerusalem, 1985).
LIEBERMAN, S., 'Raymund Martini and his Alleged Forgeries', *Historia Judaica*, v (1943), 87–102.
LINEHAN, P., *History and Historians of Medieval Spain* (Oxford, 1993).
LLABRÉS Y QUINTANA, G., *Jahuda Bonsenyor, Llibre de paraules e dits de savis e filosofs* (Palma de Mallorca, 1889).
—— 'Permiso concedido a Ramón Lull para predicar en sinagogas y mezquitas (1299)', *Boletin de la Sociedad Arqueológica Luliana*, iii (1889), 104.

LLORENTE, J. A., *Historia crítica de la Inquisición en España*, 2 vols. (Barcelona, 1880).
LOEB, I., 'Actes de vente hébreux originaires d'Espagne', *REJ*, x (1885), 108–122.
—— 'Les Administrations juives', *REJ*, xiv (1887), 262–4.
LONGPRÉ, E., 'Le. B. Raymond Lulle et Raymond Marti', *Butletí de la Societat Arqueològica Luliana*, xliv (1933), 269–71.
MACKAY, A., *Spain in the Middle Ages: From Frontier to Empire, 1000–1500* (London, 1977).
MAGDALENA NOM DE DÉU, J. R., 'Delitos y "calonies" de los judíos valencianos en la segunda mitad del siglo XIV (1351–1384)', *Anuario de Filología*, ii (1976), 181–225.
—— 'Delitos de los judíos de Aragón a inicios del siglo 14 (1310 a 1312): Aportación documental', *Anuario de Filología*, v (1979), 219–27.
—— 'Un zoco judaico en la Valencia medieval (1351–1389)', *Sefarad*, xxxix (1979), 309–31.
—— 'Etimología no semítica de "call"', *Calls*, ii (1987), 7–16.
—— 'Sinagogas, madrazas y oratorios de la aljama de Calatayud', *Anuario de Filología*, xiv (1991), 117–23.
—— *Three Jewish Communities in the Medieval Kingdom of Valencia: Burriana, Castellón de la Plana, Villareal* (Jerusalem, 1991).
MARQUÉS CASANOVAS, J., 'Alfonso II el Casto y el Seo de Gerona', in *Crónica, Ponencias y Comunicaciones* (Barcelona, 1962).
MARTINEZ FERRANDO, J. E., *Catálogo de la documentación relativa al antiguo Reino de Valencia*, 2 vols. (Madrid, 1943).
—— *Jaime II, su vida familiar*, 2 vols. (Barcelona, 1948).
—— *Indice cronológico de la colección de documentos inéditos del Archivo de la Corona de Aragón*, vol. i (Barcelona, 1958).
—— 'Estado actual de los estudios sobre la repoblación en los territorios de la Corona de Aragón (siglos XII–XIV)', *VII Congreso de Historia de la Corona de Aragón*, i (1962), 143–84.
—— *Jaume II o el seny Català* (Barcelona, 1963).
MAS Y CASAS, J. M. DE, *Ensayos históricos sobre Manresa* (Manresa, 1882).
MAS LATRIE, M. L. DE, *Relations et commerce de l'Afrique septentrionale au Maghreb avec les nations chrétiennes au moyen âge* (Paris, 1886).
MASIA DE ROS, A., *La Corona de Aragón y los estados del norte de Africa* (Barcelona, 1951).
—— 'Aportación al estudio de los "Pastorellos" en la Corona de Aragón', *Homenaje a Millás Vallicrosa*, vol. ii (Barcelona, 1956), 9–30.
MIERES, T., *Apparatus super constitutionibus curiarum generalium Cathaloniae*, 2 vols. (Barcelona, 1621).
MILLÁS VALLICROSA, J. M., 'Un manuscrit hebraic-valencià', *Butlletí de la Biblioteca de Catalunya*, vi (1920–2), 341–57.
—— 'Documents hebraics de jueus catalans', *Memories, Instituts de Estudis Catalans*, (Barcelona, 1927), vol. i, fas. 3.

—— 'Descubrimiento de una miqwah en la población de Besalú', *Sefarad*, xxv (1965), 67–9.

—— and BATLLE, L., 'Inventaris de llibres de jueus gironins', *Butlletí de la Biblioteca de Catalunya*, viii (1928–32), 5–45.

MIQUEL ROSELL, F. J., *Regesta de letras pontificas del ACA, sección Cancillería Real (Pergaminos)* (Madrid, 1948).

MIRET Y SANS, J., 'Le Massacre des Juifs de Montclús en 1320', *REJ*, liii (1907), 255–66.

—— 'El procès de les hosties contra els jueus d'Osca en 1377', *Anuari, Institut de Estudis Catalans*, iv (1911–12), 59–80.

—— and SCHWAB, M., 'Documents sur les Juifs catalans aux XIe, XIIe et XIIIe siècles', *REJ*, lxviii (1914), 49–83, 174–97 [= *Documents sur les Juifs catalans* (Paris, 1915)].

MOLHO, M., *El fuero de Jaca* (Saragossa, 1964).

MONFAR I SORS, D., 'Historia de los condes de Urgel', *CDIA*, x (Barcelona, 1853).

MOREL-FATIO, A. P. V., 'Notes et documents pour servir à l'histoire des Juifs des Baléares sous la domination aragonaise du XIIIe au XVe siècle', *REJ*, iv (1882), 31–56.

MORRIS, C., *The Papal Monarchy: The Western Church from 1050 to 1250* (Oxford, 1989).

MOSHE OF COUCY, R., *Sefer Mitzvot Gadol* (Venice, 1547).

MOSHE BEN MAIMON, R. [Maimonides], *Mishne Torah* (Amsterdam, 1702).

MOSHE BEN NAHMAN, R. [Nahmanides], 'Sheelot u-Teshuvot' (Responsa), in S. Assaf (ed.), *Sifran shel Rishonim* (Jerusalem, 1935), 51–119.

MOTIS DOLADER, M. A., 'Los judíos oscenses en la Plena y Baja Edad Media', in *Los judíos de la Corona de Aragón en los siglos XIV–XV* (Valencia, 1989), 96–113.

—— 'Los judíos turolenses en la Edad Media (siglos XIII–XV)', in *Los judíos de la Corona de Aragón en los siglos XIV–XV* (Valencia, 1989), 61–76.

—— *Los judíos en Aragon en la edad media (siglos XIII–XV)* (Saragossa, 1990).

—— and AINAGA ANDRES, M. T., 'Patrimonio urbanístico aljamial de la judería de Tarazona (Zaragoza): Las sinagogas, la necrópolis y las carnicerías', *Cuadernos de Historia Jerónimo Zurita*, lvi (1987), 83–130.

MÚNERA BASSOLS, C., 'Una miqwah judía a Besalú', *Noticiario arqueológico hispánico*, viii–ix (1964–5), 259–62.

—— 'Sobre la sinagoga de Besalú', *Sefarad*, xxviii (1968), 69–79.

NARKISS, B., 'The Heikhal, Bimah, and Teivah in Sephardi Synagogues', *Jewish Art*, (1992), 31–47.

NEUBAUER, A., 'Jewish Controversy and the "Pugio Fidei"', *The Expositor*, vii (1888), 81–105, 179–97.

NEUMAN, A. A., *The Jews in Spain: Their Social, Political and Cultural Life during the Middle Ages*, 2 vols. (Philadelphia, 1942).

NICOLAU DE OLWER, L., *Catalunya en la Mediterránea oriental* (Barcelona, 1960).

O'CALLAGHAN, J. F., *A History of Medieval Spain* (London, 1975).

OLIVA PRAT, M., 'Importante descubrimento arqueológico en Besalú', *Revista de Gerona*, xxix (1964), 57–60.

OLIVA PRAT, M., 'Un importante monumento hebraico descubierto en Besalú (Gerona)', *Pirineos*, lxxxiii–lxxxvi (1967), 9–16.

OLIVER Y ESTELLA, B., *Libre de les costums generals escritas de la ciudad de Tortosa* (Madrid, 1881).

OLLICH I CASTANYER, I., 'Una familia jueva de Vic (1266–1278)', *Ausa*, vii (1972–4), 160–3.

—— 'Aspectes economicos de l'activitat dels jueus de Vic, segons els "Libri Iudeorum" (1266–1278)', Els 'Libri Iudeorum' de Vic i de Cardona, *Miscel·lànea de Textos Medievals*, iii (Barcelona, 1985), 3–118.

ORFALI, M., 'R. Selomo ibn Aderet y la controversia judeo-cristiana', *Sefarad*, xxxix (1979), 111–20.

PARKES, J., *The Jew in the Medieval Community* (London, 1938).

PERFET, R. YISHAQ BEN SHESHET, *Sheelot u-Teshuvot* (Responsa) (Riva di Trenta, 1559).

PERLES, J., *R. Salamo b. Abraham b. Adreth sein Leben und seine Schriften* (Breslau, 1863).

PILES ROS, L., 'La judería de Sagunto, sus restos actuales', *Sefarad*, xvii (1957), 352–73.

—— 'La judería de Alcira', *Sefarad*, xx (1960), 363–76.

PONS, A., *Los judíos del reino de Mallorca durante los siglos XIII y XIV*, 2 vols. (Palma de Mallorca, 1984).

PROCTER, E. C., 'The Development of the Catalan "Corts" in the Thirteenth Century', *EUC*, xxii (1936), 525–46.

QALONIMOS BEN QALONIMOS, 'Igeret Musar' (Epistle of Morality), ed. I. Sonne, *Qovez 'al Yad*, n.s., xi (1936), 101–10.

QIMHI, R. YOSEF, *Sefer ha-Berit* (Book of the Covenant), trans. F. E. Talmage (Toronto, 1972); in Hebrew, ed. F. E. Talmage (Jerusalem, 1974).

RAKOVER, N., 'Coercive Marital Relations between a Man and his Wife', *Shenaton ha-Mishpat ha-'Ivri*, vi–vii (1979–80), 295–317 (Hebrew).

RÉGNÉ, J., *History of the Jews in Aragon, Regesta and Documents 1213–1327*, ed. Y. Assis (Jerusalem, 1978; first publ. in *REJ* (1910–1925) under the titles 'Catalogue des actes de Jaime Ier, Pedro III et Alfonso III rois d'Aragon, concernant les Juifs (1213–1291)' and 'Catalogue d'actes pour servir à l'histoire des Juifs de la Couronne d'Aragon sous le règne de Jaime II (1291–1327)').

REPARAZ, G. DE, *Catalunya a les mars* (Barcelona, 1930).

RIERA I SANS, J., 'La Catalunya jueva del segle XIV', *L'Avenç*, xxv (1980), 52–5.

—— 'La conflictividad de l'alimentació dels jueus medievals (segles XII–XIV)', in *Alimentació i societat a la Catalunya medieval* (Barcelona, 1988), 295–312.

—— and FELIU, E., *Disputa de Barcelona de 1263 entre mestre Mosse de Girona i fra Pau Cristia*, introd. J. Riera i Sans, trans. and ann. Eduard Feliu (Barcelona, 1985).

—— and UDINA I MARTORELL, F., 'Els documents en hebreu conservants a l'Arxiu de la Corona d'Aragó', *Miscellanea Barchinonensia*, xlix (1978), 21–36.

RIGLA I CAMPISTOL, J., 'El comercio entre Francia y la Corona de Aragón en los siglos XIII y XIV y sus relaciones con el desenvolvimiento de la industria textil catalana', *Actas del I Congreso Internacional de Pirenaicos*, vol. vi (San Sebasti, 1950).

RIU I CABANAS, R., 'Aljama hebrea de Solsona', *BAH*, xxi (1982), 20–4.

ROBERT, U., 'Etude historique et archéologique sur la roue des Juifs depuis le XIIIᵉ siècle', *REJ*, vi (1882), 81–95; vii (1883), 94–102.

—— *Les signes d'infamie au moyen-âge* (Paris, 1891).

ROCA TRAVER, F. A., 'Un siglo de vida mudéjar en la Valencia medieval (1238–1338)', *EEMCA*, v (1952), 115–208.

—— *El justicia de Valencia (1238–1321)* (Valencia, 1970).

ROMANO, D., 'Estudio histórico de la familia Ravaya, bailes de los reyes de Aragón en el siglo XIII', unpubl. doctoral diss. (Barcelona, 1952).

—— 'Análisis de los repertorios documentales de Jacobs y Régné', *Sefarad*, xiv (1954), 73–86.

—— 'Los hermanos Abenmenassé al servicio de Pedro el Grande de Aragón', *Homenaje a Millás Vallicrosa*, vol. ii (Barcelona, 1956), 243–92.

—— 'Restos judíos en Lérida', *Sefarad*, xx (1960), 50–65.

—— 'Responsa y reportorios documentales (Nuevos detalles sobre el caso de Vidalón de Porta)', *Sefarad*, xxvi (1966), 47–52.

—— 'Los funcionarios judíos de Pedro el Grande de Aragón', *BABLB*, xix (1969–70), 5–40.

—— 'Conversión de judíos al islam (Corona de Aragón 1280 y 1284)', *Sefarad*, xxxvi (1976), 333–7.

—— 'La Transmission des sciences arabes par les Juifs en Languedoc', in *Juifs et judaisme de Languedoc* (Toulouse, 1977), 363–86.

—— 'Judios escribanos y trujamanes de arabe en la Corona de Aragón (Reinados de Jaime I a Jaime II)', *Sefarad*, xxxviii (1978), 83–7.

—— 'Aljama frente a judería, call y sus sinónimos', *Sefarad*, xxxix (1979), 347–54.

—— *Judíos al servicio de Pedro el Grande de Aragón (1276–1285)* (Barcelona, 1983).

—— '"Courtisans" juifs dans la Couronne d'Aragon', in *Les Juifs dans la méditerranée médiévale et moderne* (Nice, 1986), 79–95.

—— 'Cortesanos judíos en la Corona de Aragón', in *Destierros Aragoneses*, vol. i (1988), 25–37.

—— 'El papel judío en la transmisión de la cultura', *Hispania Sacra*, xl (1988), 955–78.

—— (ed.), *Per a una història de la Girona jueva*, 2 vols. (Gerona, 1988).

—— 'Los judíos y el campo en los estados hispánicos', *Proceedings of the Tenth World Congress of Jewish Studies*, div. B, vol. ii (Jerusalem, 1990), 135–42.

—— 'The Jews' Contribution to Medicine, Science and General Learning', in H. Beinart (ed.), *The Sephardi Legacy*, vol. i (Jerusalem, 1992), 240–60.

ROTH, C., 'The Disputation of Barcelona (1263)', *Harvard Theological Review*, xliii (1950), 117–44.

ROTH, N., '"Deal Gently with the Young Man": Love of Boys in Medieval Hebrew Poetry in Spain', *Speculum*, lvii (1982), 20–51.

ROVIRA I ERMENGOL, J. (ed.), *Usatges de Barcelona* (Barcelona, 1933).

ROVIRA I VIRGILI, A., *Història nacional de Catalunya*, 7 vols. (Barcelona, 1922–31).

RUBIÓ Y LLUCH, A., 'Notes sobre la ciencia oriental a Catalunya en XIV sigle', *EUC*, iii (1909), 389–98, 489–97.

—— *Documents per l'història de la cultura catalana mig-eval*, 2 vols. (Barcelona, 1908–21).

SAIGE, G., '*Les Juifs du Languedoc antérieurement au XIVe siècle* (Paris, 1881).

SALARRULLANA DE DIOS, J., 'Estudios históricos acerca de la ciudad de Fraga: La aljama de judíos de Fraga', *RABM*, xl (1919), 69–90, 183–206, 431–46.

SANCHEZ HERRERO, J., 'Cofradías, hospitales y beneficencia en algunas diocesis del Valle del Duero, siglos XIV y XV', *Hispania*, xxxiv (1974), 5–51.

SÁNCHEZ MARTÍNEZ, M., 'La fiscalidad catalanoaragonesa y la aljama de judíos en la epoca de Alfonso IV (1327–1331): Los subsidios extraordinarios', *Acta Historica et Archaeologica Medievalia*, iii (1982), 93–141.

SÁNCHEZ REAL, J., 'Los judíos en Tarragona', *Boletín Arqueológico de Tarragona*, xlix (1949), 15–45.

—— 'La judería de Tarragona', *Sefarad*, xi (1951), 339–48.

SANPERE Y MIQUEL, S., *Las costumbres catalanas en tiempo de Juan I* (Gerona, 1878).

SARACHEK, J., *Faith and Reason—the Conflict over the Rationalism of Maimonides* (Williamsport, Pa., 1935).

SARRET Y ARBOS, J., *Jueus a Manresa* (Manresa, 1917).

SCHIRMAN, H., *Shirim Hadashim min ha-Genizah* (New Poems from the Geniza) (Jerusalem, 1966) (Hebrew).

SCHOLEM, G., *Major Trends in Jewish Mysticism*, (New York, 1941).

—— 'Le Centre kabbalistique de Gérone', in *Les Origines de la Kabbale*, trans. J. Loewenson (Paris, 1966), 387–500.

—— *Origins of the Kabbalah* (Princeton and Philadelphia, 1987).

SCHREINER, M., 'Die apologetische Schrift des Salomo b. Adreth gegen einen Muhammedaner', *Zeitschrift der Deutschen Morgenlandischen Gesellschaft*, xlviii (1894), 39–42.

SECALL I GÜELL, G., *Els jueus de Valls i la seva època* (Valls, 1980).

—— *La comunitat hebrea de Santa Coloma de Queralt* (Tarragona, 1986).

SEGURA I VALLS, J., 'Aplech de documents curiosos e inèdits fahents per la història de les costums de Catalunya', in *Jochs Florals de Barcelona* (Barcelona, 1885–7).

—— 'Documentos para las costumbres de Cataluña durante la edad media', *Revista de Ciencias Historicas*, v (1887), 216ff., 326ff., 329ff., 534.

SEPTIMUS, B., 'Piety and Power in Thirteenth Century Catalonia', in *Studies in Medieval Jewish History and Literature* (Cambridge, Mass., 1979), 197–230.

—— *Hispano-Jewish Culture in Transition* (Cambridge, Mass., and London, 1982).

SERRA VILARÓ, J., *Baronies de Pinos i Montaplana, investigació als seus arxius*, Biblioteca Histórica de la Biblioteca Balmes, 2nd ser. vol. xix (1947).

SERRANO Y SANZ, M., 'Notas acerca de los judíos aragoneses en los siglos XIV y XV', *RABM*, xxxvii (1917), 324–46.

—— *Orígenes de la dominación española en America: Estudios históricos* (Madrid, 1918).

SHATZMILLER, J., 'Rabbi Isaac Ha-Cohen of Manosque and his Son Rabbi Perez: The Rabbinate in its Professionalization in the Fourteenth Century', in A. Rapoport-Albert and S. J. Zipperstein (eds.), *Jewish History: Essays in Honour of Chimen Abramsky*, (London, 1988), 61–83.

—— 'Paulus Christiani: Un aspect de son activité anti-juive', in G. Nahon and Ch. Touati (eds.), *Hommage à George Vajda: Etudes d'histoire et de pensée juives* (Louvain, 1980), 203–17.

SHILO, S., 'Two Communal Ordinances from Spain', *Sinai* (1967), 291–7 (Hebrew).

SHNEIDMAN, J. L., 'Jews as Royal Bailiffs in XIIIth Century Aragon', *Historia Judaica*, xix (1957), 55–66.

—— 'The Jews in the Royal Administration of XIIIth Century Aragon', *Historia Judaica*, xxi (1959), 37–52.

—— 'Protection of Aragonese Jewry in the Thirteenth Century', *REJ*, cxxi (1962), 49–58.

—— *The Rise of the Aragonese–Catalan Empire 1200–1350*, 2 vols. (New York, 1970).

SILVER, D. J., *Maimonidean Criticism and the Maimonidean Controversy, 1180–1240* (Leiden, 1956).

SIMONET, F. X., *Historia de los mozárabes de España*, vol. xiii of *Memorias of the Real Academia de Historia* (Madrid, 1903).

SOBERANAS I LLEÓ, A. J., 'La biblioteca de Salamó Atzarell, jueu de Santa Coloma de Queralt (1373)', *Boletín de la Real Sociedad Arqueológica Tarraconense*, lxvii–lxviii (1967–8), 191–204.

SOLDEVILA, F., *Història de Catalunya*, 3 vols. (Barcelona, 1962).

—— (ed.), *Les Quatre grans cróniques* (Barcelona, 1971).

STITSKIN, D., *Judaism as a Philosophy: The Philosophy of Abraham bar Hiyya* (New York, 1960).

STOBER, S., 'On Two Questions Posed to R. Abraham b. Maimonides (Concerning Servant-Concubines)', *Shenaton ha-Mishpat ha-'Ivri*, vi–vii (1979–80), 339–403.

SUÁREZ FERNANDEZ, L., *Historia de España, Edad media* (Madrid, 1970).

—— *Los judíos españoles en la Edad Media* (Madrid, 1980).

TA SHEMA, I. M., 'Rabbeinu Dan from Ashkenazi', in J. Dan and J. Hacker (eds.), *Studies in Kabbalah, Philosophy and Ethical Literature Presented to Isaiah Tishby on his Seventy-Fifth Birthday* (Jerusalem, 1986), 385–94.

—— 'Ashkenazi Hasidism in Spain: R. Jonah Gerondi—the Man and His Work', in A. Mirsky, A. Grossman, and Y. Kaplan (eds.), *Exile and Diaspora* (Jerusalem, 1988), 165–94.

TAZRAT, R. ABRAHAM BEN R. SHELOMO IBN, *Huqat ha-Dayanim* (Rules for Judges), in N. N. Coronel (ed.), *Five Treatises* (Vienna, 1864).

TILANDER, G., *Los fueros de Aragon* (Lund, 1937).

—— *Documento desconocido de la aljama de Zaragoza del año 1331*, *Leges Hispaniae Medici Aevi*, vii (Stockholm, 1958).

TOLEDANO, Y. M., 'Conditional Marriage and the Abrogation of Marriage', *Ozar ha-Hayim*, vi, ed. H. Y. Ehrenreich (1930), 211–14 (Hebrew).

TORRES BALBÁS, L., 'La judería de Zaragoza', *Al-Andalus*, xxi (1956), 172–90.

TORROELLA, J. BTA, *La jueria de Banyoles* (Gerona, 1928).

TOUATI, CH., 'La Controverse de 1303–1306 autour des études philosophiques et scientifiques', *REJ*, cxxvii (1968), 21–37.

—— 'Les Deux conflits autour de Maimonide et des études philosophiques', in *Juifs et judaisme de Languedoc* (Toulouse, 1977), 173–84.

TREPPO, M. DEL, *Els mercaders catalans i l'expansió de la Corona catalano-aragonesa al segle XV*, trans. J. Riera i Sans (Barcelona, 1976).

TWERSKY, I., *Rabad of Posquieres, a Twelfth Century Talmudist* (Cambridge, Mass., 1962).

—— 'Aspects of the Social and Cultural History of Provençal Jewry', *Cahiers d'Histoire Mondiale*, ix (1968), 85–207 [= *Jewish Society throughout the Ages*, ed. H. H. Ben-Sasson and S. Ettinger (London, 1971), 85–207].

URBACH, E. E., 'Sheelot u-Teshuvot HaRaShBa' (Responsa of the RaShBA), *Shenaton ha-Mishpat ha-'Ivri*, ii (1975), 141–3 (Hebrew).

VENDRELL GALLOSTRA, F., 'Al margen de la organización de la aljama judía zaragozana', *Sefarad*, xxiv (1964), 81–106.

—— *Rentas reales de Aragón de la época de Fernando I (1412–1416)* (Madrid and Barcelona, 1977).

VERNET, J., 'Un embajador judío de Jaime II, Selomo b. Menassé', *Sefarad*, xii (1952), 125–54.

VICAIRE, M. H., *S. Dominic and his Times* (London, 1964).

VICENS VIVES, J., *Historia social y económica de España y America*, 4 vols. (Barcelona, 1957–9).

—— *Historia de España y America* (Barcelona, 1961).

VIDAL, P., *Les Juifs de Roussillon et de Cerdagne* (Paris, 1888). First publ. in *REJ*, xv (1887), 19–55, xvi (1888) 1–23, 170–203; also publ. in Catalan, trans. E. Feliu, 'Els jueus dels antics comtats de Rosselló i Cerdanya', *Calls*, ii (1987), 27–112.

VILADES CASTILLO, J. M., 'Materiales procedentes de la sinagoga de Monzón (Huesca) en el Museo Provincial de Zaragoza', *Boletín de la Asociación Española de Orientalistas*, xx (1984), 307–15.

VILLANUEVA, J., *Viage literario a las iglesias de España*, 22 vols. (Madrid, 1803–52).

VINCKE, J., *Documenta Selecta* (Barcelona, 1936).

VIVES Y CEBRIÀ, P. N., *Usatges de Catalunya: Traducción al castellano de los usages y demás derechos de Cataluña . . . ilustrada con notas*, 5 vols. (Madrid, 1864–7).

WEINRYB, B. D., 'Responsa as a Source for History, Methodological Problems', in *Tif'eret Israel: Essays Presented to Chief Rabbi Israel Brodie* (London, 1967), 399–417.

WISCHNITZER, M., *A History of Jewish Crafts and Guilds* (New York, 1965).

YAHUDA, A. S., 'Hallazgo de pergaminos en Solsona: Un capítulo sobre la poesia hebraica religiosa de España', *BAH*, lxvii (1915), 513–49.

YEHUDAH BEN ASHER, R., *Zikhron Yehudah* (Berlin, 1846).

ZACUT, R. A., *Sefer Yuhasin*, ed. Z. H. Filipowski (Frankfurt, 1925).

ZIMMELS, H. J., 'The Contribution of the Sephardim to the Responsa Literature till the Beginning of the 16th Century', in R. Barnett (ed.), *The Sephardi Heritage*, vol. i (London, 1971), 367–401.

ZLOTNIK, Z., 'Two Passages for the Completion of *Sefer ha-'Ittim'*, Sinai, xvi (1945), 116–38 (Hebrew).

ZURITA Y CASTRO, J., *Anales de la Corona de Aragón*, 6 vols. (Saragossa, 1610–70).

Index

Individuals are listed under their first name: Abraham de Portella, not Portella, Abraham de.

A
Abamari Adret 269
abattoirs, *see* slaughterhouses
Abba Mari 306
Abraffim Abnayub 108
Abraham Abendavid 228
Abraham Abingavet, *see* Abrahim Abingavet
Abraham Abnayub, *see* Abraffim Abnayub
Abraham Alfaquim, *see* Abram Alfaquim
Abraham son of Çadia Abenaçaya 320
Abraham Camis 293
Abraham Fierro 211
Abraham ibn Gallel 15
Abraham bar Hiyya 5
  Hibbur ha-Meshikhah ve-ha-Tishboret 5
  Megillat ha-Megalleh 5
Abraham ibn Menasse 16
Abraham ben Natan ha-Yarhi 301, 305
  Sefer ha-Manhig 301
Abraham son of Omar Tahuyl 108
Abraham de Portella 15
Abraham son of Salamo Adret 271
Abraham Sento 269
Abraham ben Shelomo ibn Tazrat or Tazarte
  132, 137, 142, 310
  Huqat ha-Dayanim 137, 310
Abraham de Tolosa 269, 313
Abraham de Torre 266, 296
Abrahim Abingavet 57
Abram Alfaquim, '*alfaquin*' 222–3
Açach Abenbruch 151
Açach Avenecara 271
Açach Çalema 60
Açach el Calvo 291
Açach Çibili 114
Açach Manuel 136
academies, *see yeshivot*
açuna, *see halakhah*
adelantados 84, 86, 125–6, 130, 133
  authority of 113–16, 120, 155, 205
  of burial societies 250
  in charge of finance 120–2
  in charge of taxes 117–20
  contacts with authorities 287, 293, 316
  duties of 112–13, 115, 150
  election of 77–8, 81, 88–92, 94–8
  as electors of communal functionaries 103,
    105–6, 135–6
  as judges 124–5
  as legislators 148
  supervision in religious matters 122–4
  the term and its synonyms 86, 110–11
Agramunt 44, 170, 187–8, 312
agriculture, Jewish involvement in 4
Aharon Ha-Levi de Na Clara
  Bedeq ha-Bayit 310
  dayan 146, 147, 152, 277, 311, 312, 313
  rabbi and scholar 139, 269, 303, 310, 330,
    333
Aharon ibn Jahia (Abinafia) 15, 214–15
Alaçar grandson of Vives de Limoux 287
Alagón 123, 127, 166, 168, 175, 287, 317
alatma, *see* bans
Alazar Alfaquim 229
Alazar son of Isaac Allatemi 294
Alazar grandson of Vives de Limoux, *see* Alaçar
  grandson of Vives de Limoux
Albalate de Cinca 187–8, 193
albedins 42, 105–6, 135–6, 160
Alcañiz 194
Alcañizo 189, 192
alcaydes 25
Alcira 177, 196, 272, 288
Alcolea de Cinca 224, 230, 232
Alcoletge 187–8
Alconstantini family 151, 291
Alcover 185
Alfonso I 4
Alfonso II 2, 39
Alfonso III, the Liberal 4, 11, 99, 124, 141,
  164, 175, 180, 184, 186, 187, 261, 283
  attitude to judiciary 146, 154, 261–2, 269,
    274, 291, 311–13
  employment of Jews by 14–16, 102

Alfonso III (cont.):
  gives permission to build synagogue 211
  Inquisition under 59
  interference in Jewish life 74, 81, 90, 94, 103, 108, 275, 276, 317, 321
  policy on the Jewish quarter 201–4, 211
  privileges granted by 37–9, 113, 172, 178
  taxes paid to 117, 119, 174
Alfonso (future Alfonso IV) 44, 89, 106, 120, 142, 188, 207, 224, 232, 287, 294, 328, 333
Alforja 185
Alicante 45, 176, 195–6
Aljohar, wife of Ya'aqov ben Yosef 272
  slave 265
almidraz, see *beth midrash*
Almohads 299, 304
Almoravids 304
almoyners 107, 127, 243
Ampurias 2
  Count of 11, 45
Andalusia, Andalus 13, 299–301, 303, 305, 334
apostates, see converts
Arabic 135, 176, 304
  Jewish experts in 15
  Jewish secretaries and interpreters for 16, 229
  Judeo-Arabic 300
  literature 134
  notary for 133
  study of 49
  terms in 145, 157
  use of by Christians 303
  use of by Jews 68, 177
Aragon, Kingdom of 2, 3, 9, 19, 31, 79, 97, 115, 124, 125, 172, 173, 174, 188, 199, 214, 252, 284, 288, 293, 295, 303
  currency of 180
  extent of 2
  Inquisition in 62
  Jewish communities of 76, 83, 99, 102, 104–5, 112, 116, 119, 127, 130, 135, 151, 164, 170, 173–6, 178, 187, 192, 194, 238, 239, 240, 244, 305, 312, 317
  Jewish refugees from 334
  Jews of 5, 19, 34–5, 102, 141, 163, 175, 289, 300, 310
  noblemen of 13
  Qahal 334
Aragonese 110
  Judeo-Aragonese 326
Aramaic 259
arbitration, arbitrators 154, 170, 260, 274, 311–13

Arbós 185
aristocracy, Jewish 96, 114, 120, 125, 252
Aristotelianism 304
Arnaldo de Bastida 321
arrab, see rabbis
Asher ben Yehiel 302–3
Ashkenazim 299, 302, 305, 333
  customs and traditions 158, 302–3
  influence 263, 305, 309
Assach Abnelfalir 261
Assach Alcutavi 293
Astruc Caravida 271, 293
Astruc de Porta 51
Astruc Saltell 89, 120
Astruc Xaprut 294
Astrug Avincendut 270
Astrug Bonsenyor 107, 133
Astrug Jacob Xixó 223
Astrug Lunel 290
Astrug Obrador 137
autonomy, Jewish
  its character 71, 122, 172, 267, 315
  the Crown attitude to 73–5
  in the medieval period 101
  religious 224, 324
Avenfalaud family 105
Avenrodrich family 294
Aytona 168–9, 188
Azach Abinhalim 158
Azariam or Azariah Abenjacob 107, 133–4, 137
Azmel Sahadia 294
Azmell Abengalell 119
Azriel (Gerona) 330

B

badge, to distinguish Jews 30, 46, 284
Bahye Alconstantini 141
Bahye Alconstantini (Calatayud) 214
Bahye ben Asher
  Kad ha-Qemah 140, 310
  rabbi and scholar 139, 239, 303, 310, 333
bakeries, see food, Jewish
Balaguer 188
Balearic islands 2
Bañolas 186
bans (*herem, niduy*) 113
  by Maimonideans and anti-Maimonideans 305–6, 315
  by Monzón Jews on wine imports 166, 171
  proclamation of 86, 139, 219–20
  public 86, 113, 157, 219–20, 285, 316
  as punishment for Jews 22, 140, 144, 156–8, 168, 214, 320, 323

of Rabbenu Gershon against bigamy 261–3
against secular studies and allegorization
    (1305) 125, 129, 149
as a weapon against another community 171
baptism, *see* converts
Barbastro 83, 89, 92, 96, 98–9, 104, 107, 130,
    133, 155, 165, 171, 175, 194, 204, 211,
    225, 293–4
Barcelona 32, 60, 146, 164, 181, 207, 218, 224,
    263, 269–71, 274, 286, 288, 300, 305,
    313–14, 321, 330
  aljama 39, 44, 89, 95, 97, 99, 101, 102, 125,
    128, 129, 134, 149, 167, 170, 173, 179,
    184, 243, 312
  bailes of 4, 120, 230, 269, 274, 313
  ban against study of sciences in 149
  barrio gótico 233
  brothel in 287
  Castell Nou 223, 287
  charitable institutions in 243, 248
  collecta of 22, 26, 28, 30, 33, 37, 46, 90, 95,
    105, 112, 119, 168, 179–84, 186–7, 189,
    194, 203, 316
  communal functionaries of 137, 144
  communal leaders of 22, 90, 100, 115,
    118–20, 127, 129, 165
  communal ordinances of 111
  Condes de Barcelona street 234
  counts of 222
  County of 2, 174, 306
  Jafiel street 248
  Jewish cemetery of 24, 233–4
  Jewish council of 128, 243
  Jewish education in 309–10, 329
  Jewish judges of 153, 269, 311
  Jewish quarter of 43, 201–2, 206, 209, 287,
    329
  Jews of 28, 30, 33, 34, 46, 90–1, 119, 173,
    187, 208, 283–4
  Marlet street 248
  Moncada street 234
  moratorium on debts to Jews in 182
  municipal council of 226, 284
  Palau de Vicrey 233
  privileges of the Jews in 21, 34, 48, 234
  public baths in 223
  religious life in 230
  synagogues of 50, 210, 213–14, 216
Barcelona Haggadah 216–17
Baron Almelich 109
baror, see berurim
baths, public, *see miqve*
beadles, *see shamash*
bedins, see albedins
Belshom son of Bonanasch 262, 275
Belshom Levi 290
Belshom Momet 271
Benardout 334
Benavides 196
Benedict Jona or Benedictus Biona, *see* Jonah
    Gerondi, the younger
Benito de Limos 313
Benvenist Barzilay 57
Benvenist de Porta 51, 275
Benveniste 334
Berga 184
Bernardo de Podio 60–1
Bertrand de Jorba 56, 228
berurim 81, 92–3, 160
  authority and jurisdiction of 78, 84, 113–15,
    120, 128, 148, 154, 315
  berure 'averot (berurim daveros) 87, 104, 111,
    315
  berure midot 87
  berure tar'omot 111
  berurim dayanim 92, 111, 124–5
  berurim de tavioz (berure tevi'ot) 87, 94
  of confraternities 250–1
  election and appointment of 82–3, 93
  functions and duties of 87, 105, 107, 115–16,
    118–23, 205, 219, 272, 315–16
  proceedings against 108, 126
  terminology 86, 110–12
Besalú 2, 21–2, 33, 111, 186, 207, 211, 222,
    231, 246, 262, 267, 271, 290
beth din
  appeal from 312
  attitude of king to 147–8, 152, 154, 261, 291
  authority and jurisdiction of 153–5, 160,
    166, 262, 277, 289–90, 292, 315
  its composition and establishment 102, 124,
    151, 269, 274, 305, 310–11
  lawsuits 217, 258–60, 266, 270, 272, 277,
    281, 285–6
  its scribe 135
  status of 101, 146, 150
beth midrash
  Beth HaMidrash of Farhi (Calatayud) 214
  of Biqur Holim (Huesca) 245, 247
  of the Burial Society (Huesca) 250
  confiscation of by Inquisition 62
  donations for 331
  fine for repairs of 212
  the Great Beth HaMidrash (Calatayud) 214
  studium or *midrash* of the poor (Tortosa) 328,
    331

beth midrash (cont.):
  the Weavers' Midrash (Calatayud) 214
Bible
  ban on allegorization of 129
  confiscation of 62
  study of 299, 304, 331
Biel 60
bigamy, *see* marriage
Black Death 232-3, 334
Blanca, Queen 109, 228
Blanca, wife of Abraham Sento (daughter of Abamari Adret) 269
blasphemy
  by Christians 288
  in Jewish books 58
Bonadona, wife of Jahuda de Limos 275-6
Bonafilia, daughter of Druda 293
Bonafilia, wife of Abraham de Tolosa 269
Bonafos Adit 323
Bonanat 56
Bonanat Salamo 210, 214
Bonasruch Alfaquim 223
Bonastrug de Porta, *see* Nahmanides
Bondavid Bonsenyor 15-16
Bonjuda 290
Bonjudas Salomo 273, 312
Borja 175, 194, 217
Burgos, Council of 304
Burriana 165, 177, 196, 211, 232, 249, 291

C
Çadia Abenaçaya 106, 320
Calatayud 175, 261
  attacks against the Jews of 208
  collecta of 192-3
  Inquisition against Jews of 58, 61-2
  Jewish cemetery of 233
  Jewish oath in 42
  Jewish poor of 241
  Jewish quarter of 200, 204, 205
  Jewish self-government in 77, 83, 105, 124, 150, 155
  the king and Jewish autonomy in 136, 146, 158, 174
  privileges of the Jews of 21, 22, 38, 39, 124, 155, 227, 270
  synagogues in 208, 213, 214, 215
  violence among the Jews of 292-4
Caldas de Montbuy 183, 223
Çalema Çuri 109
Çalema Sahadia 294
call, *see* quarter, Jewish
Camprodón 186

Canet 196
capella, *see* synagogues: *hazan*
carcelatge 46, 48, 159
Cardona 184
Carolingians 4
Castellón de Ampurias 45, 186, 262
Castellón de Farfaña 188
Castellón de la Plana 177, 196, 232
Castile 2, 4, 11, 77, 80, 140, 155-6, 195, 199, 211, 265-6, 292, 300, 315, 334
Catalan
  as family name 334
  letters in 173-4
  synagogue 217
  terms for Jewish leaders 110
  Valencian dialect of 177
  works in 134
Catalonia 2-5, 9, 19, 31, 58, 79, 97, 104, 115, 172, 174, 176, 180-1, 187, 199, 215, 238, 248, 255, 261, 266, 269, 283, 288, 300, 302-3, 308, 334
  Jewish communities of 76, 99, 102, 112, 116, 119, 125, 127-8, 151, 154, 157, 164, 167, 174, 178, 240, 305, 312
  Jews of 11, 33, 35, 37, 40, 145, 163, 168, 172-4, 179-81, 186, 189-91, 194, 212, 263, 283, 291, 333
  noblemen of 14
Cathars 58
Cazola, Treaty of 2
cemeteries, *see* death and burial, Jewish
cena 25
censorship, of Jewish books 58
Cerdagne 2-3, 191
Cervera 46, 105, 130, 165, 183-4, 224, 232, 249
Ceti, *rabisse* 106, 143
charity 242-4
  charitable societies 245-6
  see also confraternities, Jewish
charters, *see* privileges
class system 76, 99
  agreements between classes 117
  characteristics of 238-9, 291, 326
  inter-class struggle 79, 82-4, 114, 125, 128, 141, 239-41, 244-5, 254, 295
  representation of classes 86, 93-5, 97-8, 103-4, 105, 129, 130
  representative electors of classes 104
Clement IV 58
clergy or clerics 3, 21, 209, 211, 216, 231, 288
clerks 239
clothes, Jewish 30, 46, 178, 283-5
  aldifara (mantle) 283

capa (mantle) 283
capero 284
gonela (mantle) 283
jewellery 284
patinas (shoes) 284
Cluny 303–4
collectas 21, 46, 115, 117, 180, 182, 189
   Catalan 128, 173–4, 179–80, 183–5, 192, 196
   sub-*collectas* 181, 184–5, 188
   see also under individual place-names
collidores, *see* taxes
colonization 12–13, 45, 177
commerce, *see* trade
concejo, see *'eza*
concell, see *'eza*
concilium, see *'eza*
confiscation of property, *see* property, Christian; property, Jewish
Conflent 190–1
confraternities, Jewish 214–15, 243–5, 247–9, 251–4, 325–6, 329–30
   Biqur Holim 215, 246–7, 253
   'Ose Hesed 245
   'Ose Zedaqot 245–6
   Rodfe Zedeq 245, 248
   Shomre Holim (Guardians of the Sick) 247
Constanza 12
constitutions, of communities 88–9, 95–9, 101, 105, 112, 125, 129, 172
controversies, religious 304, 305, 333
converts
   to Christianity 49, 51, 53–7, 61, 73, 209, 212, 228, 276, 289, 321
   to Judaism 57, 60
   return to Judaism 57–8, 61, 63, 248
   see also missionary activities
Corda de Gardeny (Lérida) 233
Cordova 304
Cortes 55, 57
Corts
   of Barcelona 11
   Catalan 173
   of Lérida 284
   of Tarragona 54
council, see *'eza*
Council of One Hundred 128
Council of Thirty 95, 105, 115, 128–31, 243, 306
councillors, see *yo'azim*
courtiers, Jewish 14–16, 74, 124, 126, 151, 207, 228, 237–8, 287, 290–1, 295–6, 311
courts of law
   ecclesiastical 191

Gentile 147–8, 151, 154, 191, 259–62, 268–70, 277, 287, 293
   Jewish, see *beth din*
craftsmen, *see* merchants and craftsmen, Jewish
Cresques Zarch 290
crime 288
   kidnapping 274
   murder 150, 170, 240, 291, 293–6, 312–13
   robbery 279, 288–9, 296
   transgressors 71, 315
   see also punishment; violence
Çulema Abinçulana 271
çuna, see *halakhah*

D

Dan Ashkenazi 302
Daroca 38, 106, 136, 140, 175, 193–4, 218, 289, 293, 317, 323
darshanim 106, 139–40, 303, 310
Davi, rabbi of Daroca 140, 144
David Abnarrabi 109
David Mascaran, or Almascaran 152, 170, 295, 311
David Qimhi 62
   Sefer ha-Shorashim 62
dayanim
   albedins acting as 135
   appointment or election of 36, 85, 87, 91, 92, 95, 101–3, 129, 149, 151
   berurim serving as 92, 111, 124–5
   communal rabbis as 140
   contact of authorities with 146, 152, 269, 311
   famous rabbis serving as 146, 152, 310, 311, 312
   in matrimonial lawsuits 258, 269, 312
   non-judicial duties of 115, 129
death and burial, Jewish
   burial societies (*hevrat ha-qabarim*, *kat ha-qabarim*) 215, 249–51
   cemeteries 24, 29, 165, 209, 232–4, 249
   funerals 137
   privileges regarding Jewish burial 233
   see also inheritance
Denia 195–6
diet, Jewish, *see* food, Jewish
diplomats, Jewish 15, 18, 237
disputations
   of Barcelona 28, 30, 50–2, 58, 208, 210, 212, 308–9, 314
   of Paris 58
   of Tortosa 334
divorce 146, 152, 260, 268, 273–4, 290, 296, 312

divorce (*cont.*):
    alimony 268–9
    get (bill of divorce) 133, 146
    see also marriage
Domingo de la Figera 227
Dominicans 28, 49, 50–2, 54, 58–60, 183, 209, 211–12, 275
dowries, see marriage
Dulcia, wife of Mosse Cabrit 248

E
ebreismo, see quarter, Jewish
Ebro, river 203, 222
education
    of adults 141, 250, 330
    of children 142, 243, 327–8
    higher 330–1
    see also teachers, Jewish; *yeshivot*
Egea 103, 124–5, 166, 175, 194, 200, 206
Elche 45, 176, 195–6, 225
elections 77, 81–2, 84, 86, 88–105, 107–9
Ella 196
emigration, Jewish 10, 12, 166, 168–9, 192, 206, 302, 304
Enrique II 155
Epila 246, 248
Escapat Açach 270
Estadilla 187–8, 193
Evreux 301
exegesis 301, 310, 332
expulsion 60, 62
'*eza* (council) 79, 82, 84, 87, 95, 97–9, 101, 112, 128
Ezra (Gerona) 330

F
Fariza 193, 293
festivals 23, 41, 46, 139, 283, 316, 320
    Easter 231
    Passover 230, 283, 316, 321–2, 327–8
    Purim 320–1
    Rosh Hashanah 100
    Succoth (Sukkot) 123, 316, 327
Figueras 186, 266, 291, 296
Fluvia, river 222
food, Jewish
    bakery 38, 205, 230–1, 282, 322
    butchery 224–8
    control over 123, 143, 228, 317, 321
    Jewish prisoners provided with 41, 159
    matzah 230, 322
    monopoly of Christians on *kasher* meat 225, 227–8, 321

offences related to 289
price of 149
privileges relating to 144, 224, 227, 230, 324
right to provide 23, 24, 207, 224, 227, 323
sale to Christians of 41, 225–6
sale monopoly of 56, 228, 321
shohatim 106, 123, 132, 140, 143–4, 225, 317, 323–4
trefa 227
wine 166, 171, 282–3, 318, 321, 322
Fraga 167, 187–8, 193
France 2–3, 45, 58–9, 63, 190, 206, 214, 263, 301–2, 304–5, 308–9, 330
Franciscans 28, 49, 62–3
Franco-Germany 255
    immigrant rabbis from 140
    influence of 146, 261–3, 333
    Jewish communities in 158–9
    scholarship in 300–4
francos 5, 126, 240, 252
fueros 14, 165, 178, 293
funerals, see death and burial, Jewish
furs, see *fueros*

G
gabay 86, 126
    gabae zedaqah 126–7
    gabay ha-heqdesh 127
Galceran Andreu 43
gambling 285–6, 288
Gandia 177, 195–6
Garcia Garces 229
gate-keepers (*porteros*) 136–7
Gatova 196
Gavarell, butcher from Huesca 123
Gemila 293
Genton, butcher from Jaca 123
Genton Assibili, see Yom Tov Asibili
Germany 61, 301, 303, 308–9
Gerona
    bishop of 50
    cemetery of 233
    as centre of kabbalah 302, 303, 330
    collecta of 129, 173, 179–81, 184, 186–7, 189
    community or *aljama* of 21, 22, 30, 81, 94, 111, 126, 168, 179, 207, 267, 311, 314
    county of 2
    Jewish institutions in 129, 329
    Jewish moneylenders of 33
    Jewish property in 45
    Jewish quarter of 204, 206, 209
    Jews of 39, 103, 152, 268, 270, 271, 291, 312

Gerona-Besalú, *collecta* of 21–2, 37–9, 59, 91, 186
Gerondi 334
Gershon, Rabbenu 261–3
get, see divorce
gizbar heqdesh 142
Gorrea 192
Gradella 187
Granada 15, 179
Granollers 167, 184
Gregory VII 304
Guillem Dufort 223
Guillem II of Montcada 188

H

Hacen son of Salamon 140
halakhah
 application of 102, 156, 272, 273, 278, 285
 as the basis of Jewish life 69, 70, 123, 145–6, 183, 252, 255, 262–4, 270, 315, 316
 deviation from 155, 160, 256, 257, 323
 documents according to 133, 134, 147, 183
 experts in 36, 85, 92, 103, 119, 124, 125, 134, 147, 151–6, 160, 170–1, 216, 258, 268, 274, 277, 287, 290, 308, 311, 313
 judicial system according to 150, 154, 269
 royal recognition of 36, 147–8, 259, 268, 269, 274–5, 291, 312
 rules of slaughter according to 24, 41
 study of 310, 328, 331–2
 transgression of 104, 122, 293
halizah, see marriage
Hasdai Cresques (Crescas) 264
Hasdai ibn Shaprut 299
hasidim, see pietists
haskamot, see ordinances
havurah, havurot, see confraternities, Jewish
hazan, see synagogues
Hebrew
 books in 62, 299
 documents and signatures in 77, 107, 114, 138, 146, 147, 148–9, 269, 274–5, 309
 sources in 53, 57, 86, 100, 103, 155, 156, 158, 165, 179, 199, 249, 250, 255, 256, 257, 262, 272, 292, 293
 study and knowledge of 5, 49, 125, 247
 terms and titles in 110–12, 126, 131, 135, 157, 199, 242, 248–9
heqdesh (funds or property donated to the community) 127, 152, 206, 243–5, 247, 249, 311, 328, 331
Hevrat Heqdesh synagogue 214
herem, see bans

heresy 58–9, 299
hospices, *see* hospitals
hospitals (hospices) 206, 243, 245, 247–9, 253
housing, Jewish, *see* quarter, Jewish
Huesca 60, 175, 266
 charitable societies and institutions 245, 248, 250, 253
 collecta of 193–4
 communal administration in 92, 96, 98, 130
 communal functionaries of 134, 138, 142, 323
 elections in 89, 99
 Jewish judiciary in 22, 124, 150, 266
 Jewish shops in 207
 Jews and Christians in 318
 king's interference in affairs of 109, 123
 murder in 293
 ordinances of 226
 poor Jews of 83, 142, 245
 rabbis of 170, 312
 status of the *aljama* of 25, 42, 174
 synagogues in 213, 218

I

Içach Abnayub 108
Içach Çaporta 137
incest, *see* sexual relations
informers within the Jewish community 113, 123, 126, 136, 152, 155–6, 240, 311
inheritance, legal aspects of 147, 274–5, 276–8, 286
Innocent IV 288
Inquisition 56–63
interpreters, Jewish 18, 228, 237
Isaac Abenbruch, *see* Açach Abenbruch
Isaac Abingalell, *see* Isach Abingalell
Isaac Abinhalim, *see* Azach Abinhalim
Isaac Abnayub, *see* Içach Abnayub
Isaac Abnelfalir, *see* Assach Abnelfalir
Isaac Alcutavi, *see* Assach Alcutavi
Isaac Alfasi, *see* Yishaq Alfasi
Isaac Allatemi 294
Isaac ibn Asfura, *see* Yishaq ibn Asfura
Isaac Avenecara, *see* Açach Avenecara
Isaac Çalema, *see* Açach Çalema
Isaac el Calvo, *see* Açach el Calvo
Isaac Çaporta, *see* Içach Çaporta
Isaac Çibili, *see* Açach Çibili
Isaac Cohen, *see* Yishaq Cohen
Isaac Daray, *see* Izach Daray
Isaac Manuel, *see* Açach Manuel
Isaac Nisim, *see* Issach Nisim

Isaac ben Reuven Al-Bargeloni, *see* Yishaq ben Reuven Al-Bargeloni
Isaac ben Sheshet Perfet, *see* Yishaq ben Sheshet Perfet
Isaac Vitalis 248
Isaac Vives, *see* Isach Vives
Isach Vives 263
Ismael Abengalell, *see* Azmell Abengalell
Ismael Avinabez de Ablitas 140
Ismael ibn Crisp 292
Ismael de Portella 15, 141
Ismael Sahadia, *see* Azmel Sahadia
Ismael Thercullut 108
Israel Israeli 300
Issach Nisim 61
Izach Daray 286

J

Jaca 46, 79, 93–4, 123, 175, 194, 208, 213, 271, 315–16, 318
Jacob Abinhalim 158
Jacob ben Khalina, *see* Ya'aqov ben Khalina
Jacob ben Yosef, *see* Ya'aqov ben Yosef
Jaffuda (Jahuda) Acdarra 107, 133
Jaffudan Abnayo 108
Jahia Morcat 294
Jahuda Aladef 287
Jahuda Alazar 296
Jahuda son of Astrug Bonsenyor 107, 133
Jahuda Aveaçfora 261
Jahuda Avinceit 158
Jahuda de la Cavallería 101–2, 114, 151, 229, 275
Jahuda Golluf 109
Jahuda de Limos 275–6
Jaime I, the Conqueror 54, 63, 180, 186, 190, 222, 223
  administration of 3, 176
  attitude to Jews 19–22, 24, 27, 28, 30–1, 50–1, 59, 176, 206, 283–4
  his charters relating to Jews 35, 37, 39, 48, 135, 144, 173, 187, 200–1, 204, 226, 230–1
  conquests by 2, 3, 76
  his involvement in Jewish affairs 74, 117, 166, 319–20
  his involvement in Jewish autonomy 77, 88, 90, 91, 101, 102, 119, 134, 150, 158–9, 163, 275
  Jewish moneylending under 33, 182
  Jewish settlers under 10, 12, 13, 19
  Jews in the service of 228
  protection of Jews by 25, 26, 28–9, 182, 191, 204, 208–9, 213, 287
  religious life under 24, 207, 210–12, 224, 226, 232, 234, 262, 319–20
  his taxation of Jews 174, 239, 314
Jaime II 76, 150, 174–5, 189, 196
  appointment of Jews by 133, 135, 144
  attitude to Jews 10–11, 16, 38, 102, 141, 168, 207, 284, 294
  his charters relating to Jews 39–43, 45–8, 145, 155, 187, 203, 233
  Christian–Jewish relations under 56–60, 62–3
  employment of Jews by 14, 16
  foreign policy of 4
  his involvement in Jewish affairs 74, 123, 136, 166, 167, 193, 205, 206, 240, 264, 265, 312–13
  his involvement in Jewish autonomy 75, 81, 82–3, 89–90, 96–7, 103–7, 109, 120, 135, 138, 144, 158, 172–3, 268–9, 320, 323
  Jewish settlers under 45–6
  his policy on Jewish converts 55–6
  protection of Jews by 43, 44–5, 54–5, 203, 204, 208, 233
  religious life under 211, 216, 225–7, 230, 322, 323
  status of Jews under 17, 41, 63
  taxes and subsidies of Jews to 118, 127, 164, 170, 184, 186, 188
Jaime II (of Majorca) 283
Jaime Perez 212
Játiva 21, 29, 43, 177, 195–6, 201, 209, 212, 216, 227, 234, 270, 285
Jehuda ibn Menasse 16
Jehudah ibn Abbas, *see* Yehudah ibn Abbas
Jehudah Abnayo, *see* Jaffudan Abnayo
Jehudah Acdarra, *see* Jaffuda (Jahuda) Acdarra
Jehudah Aladef, *see* Jahuda Aladef
Jehudah Alazar, *see* Jahuda Alazar
Jehudah Alharizi, *see* Yehudah Alharizi
Jehudah son of Astrug Bonsenyor, *see* Jahuda son of Astrug Bonsenyor
Jehudah Aveaçfora, *see* Jahuda Aveaçfora
Jehudah Avinceit, *see* Jahuda Avinceit
Jehudah ben Barzilay al-Bargeloni, *see* Yehudah ben Barzilay al-Bargeloni
Jehudah de la Cavallería, *see* Jahuda de la Cavallería
Jehudah Golluf, *see* Jahuda Golluf
Jehudah de Limos, *see* Jahuda de Limos
Jehudah ibn Menasse, *see* Jehuda ibn Menasse
Jehudah ben Yaqar, *see* Yehudah ben Yaqar
Jento Caracallo 136
Jenton Assibili, *see* Yom Tov Asibili

Jerba 3, 13
Joce Avenjacob 133, 135
Jonah Avinceit, *see* Junis Avinceit
Jonah Gerondi, the elder 139, 265–6, 270, 301, 303, 305, 309, 311, 330, 333
Jonah Gerondi, the younger (cousin of Jonah Gerondi the elder) 152, 156, 311, 314
Jonas Çibili 114
Josef de Orta 15
Joseph Picho 155
Jossuas Abnarrabi 109
Juan I 334
Juan Ferrand 56–7
Juan de Llotger 60
Juce Bienbiniest 214
Jucef, royal treasurer 4
Jucef, gate-keeper of Barcelona 137
Jucef Abenalahut 291
Jucef Abenvives 287
Jucef Abinhalim 158
Jucef Alatronay 312
Jucef Alorqui, *see* Juceff Alorqui
Jucef Alphavel, *see* Juceph Alphavel
Jucef Avenaçfora, *see* Juceff Avenaçfora
Jucef Avenhalahu 271
Jucef Avenjacob, *see* Joce Avenjacob
Jucef Avinceit 158
Jucef Avinxaprut 223
Jucef Azday 103
Jucef Baro, *see* Yucef Baro
Jucef Benveniste 327
Jucef Bienbiniest, *see* Juce Bienbiniest
Jucef Coffe, *see* Juceff Coffe
Jucef Cohen, *see* Yucef Cohen
Jucef Contatxich 292
Jucef Daray 286
Jucef Faquim 302
Jucef de Faro 294
Jucef de Grasse 262
Jucef Hasdai 268
Jucef son of Jaffudan Abnayo, *see* Juceff son of Jaffudan Abnayo
Jucef Maçana 60
Jucef Morcat 294
Jucef Moreno 289
Jucef de Orta, *see* Josef de Orta
Jucef Picho, *see* Joseph Picho
Jucef Qimhi, *see* Yosef Qimhi
Jucef Ravaya 166
Jucef Sachs (or Jaches), *see* Juceff Sachs
Jucef Xaprut 293
Jucef ibn Yahya (or Abinafia), *see* Yosef ibn Yahya

Juceff Alorqui 114
Juceff Avenaçfora 261
Juceff Coffe 205
Juceff son of Jaffudan Abnayo 108
Juceff Sachs (or Jaches) 44
Juceph Alphavel 312
judaismo, *see* quarter, Jewish
Judeo-Arabic 299–302, 306, 308, 333
juderia, *see* quarter, Jewish
judges, *see dayanim*
judiciary 101, 104, 145, 155, 274, 311
  privileges of 145, 151, 172
Junis Avinceit 158

K
kabbalah, kabbalists 302–3, 307–8, 310, 330
kasher food, *see* food, Jewish
kat ha-havurah 117, 239, 244, 254
Kerkennah 13
ketubah, *see* marriage

L
La Bisbal 186
Languedoc 2, 20, 58, 303
Lascara, Infanta 118
Lateran Council, Fourth 284
Latin
  literature 134
  milieu 300
  sources 76, 78, 100, 110, 111, 126, 156, 160, 247, 250, 292
  terms 110, 199
  validation of Hebrew documents 267, 274
law
  biblical 71
  Catholic or ecclesiastical 75, 212
  civil 147
  criminal 153, 155
  Jewish, *see halakhah*
  matrimonial 146–7, 267–8
  Talmudic 71
lawsuits, *see* trials
Leon 300
Lérida
  attitude to apostates in 57
  children's education in 140, 328
  collecta of 21, 38, 46, 173, 179–82, 187–9, 193
  community of 21, 37, 78, 79, 81, 83–4, 89, 92–4, 98–101, 103, 105–6, 126, 130, 134, 322
  disputes with other communities 170
  family life in 266, 269, 275, 312

Lérida (cont.):
  interference in autonomy of 158, 320
  Jewish cemetery of 24, 232–3
  Jewish creditors in 33
  Jewish judiciary in 145, 151, 312, 313
  Jewish quarter (cuyraça, curacia, coiraza) 199, 201, 203, 204, 207, 208
  Jews in the courts of 40, 47, 61, 152
  Jews in the vicinity of 167–8, 187
  protection of Jews of 23, 32, 166, 208
  religious life in 230, 316, 322
  taxes and subsidies paid by 179
  violence by Jews in 291
lezda, *see* taxes
Liria 196
liturgy, *see* synagogues
Lope Ferrench de Luna 168, 192
Lubona 327–8
Luna 106, 136, 175

M

Maalux Alcoqui 228
ma'amad 86–7
Mahir, scribe of Huesca 134
Maimonidean Controversy 58, 302, 305–6, 309, 315
Maimonides 69, 299, 301, 305, 308–9, 312, 332
  Guide of the Perplexed 305, 309
  Mishne Torah 50–1, 69, 305, 332
Majorca, kingdom or island of
  conquest of 2
  island 13, 91, 98, 103, 172, 334
  Kingdom 3, 40, 91, 130, 190, 306
Majorca, city or community of
  charters of the Jews in 47, 150, 224, 233
  city 288
  community 23, 31, 32, 38, 76, 99, 103, 129
  emigration to 302
  Jewish quarter in 199, 201–2, 204–5, 225
  Jews of 33, 37–8, 54, 211, 230
  missionaries in 208
malshinim, *see* informers within the Jewish community
Malta 3, 13
Manresa 43, 184
Manuel son of Açach Manuel 136
mapah, *see* Torah
María, daughter of Jaime II 62
Marines 196
marriage 256–7, 273, 277–8
  adultery 272–3, 287, 296, 312
  betrothal 220, 256–7
  bigamy 146, 257, 261–5, 277, 320
  concubines 54, 265–7
  courtship 255–7
  documents, Jewish, concerning 267–9
  financial aspects of 267–8, 284–5
  halizah 256
  illegal 264–5, 288
  ketubah 133, 138, 145, 158, 183, 259–3, 266–8, 273, 277, 290, 313
  and lawsuits 258–9
  legal aspects of 145–7
  marital offences 156
  nedunya 146, 260, 268–9, 273
  qinyan ceremony 220, 256
  trousseaux 284
  weddings 144, 214, 221, 240, 259, 273–4, 279, 288, 290–2, 294–6
  see also divorce
Martin Pere 57
Martorell 185
massacres 209, 243–4, 310, 334
Maymo de Forn 207, 226
Meir ha-Levi Abulafia 301, 305
Meir of Trinquetaille 301
Menahem Ha-Meiri 190, 330
merchants and craftsmen, Jewish 129, 139, 166, 206, 238–9, 279
  cloth merchants 202, 206–7
  jewellers 109
  shoemakers 253
  silk manufacturers 109
  silversmiths 109, 214
  tailors 248, 253
  tanners 253
  tradesmen's guilds 251–2
  weavers 214
Mérida 304
Midrash, literature and sources 308
minyanim, *see* synagogues
Miquel de Cariñena 227
miqve (ritual bath) 206, 222–3, 258, 281, 293
Mishnah 332
Mishne Torah, *see* Maimonides
missionary activities, Christian
  among Jews 52–4, 208, 212
  missionaries 50, 53, 55, 208
  among Muslims 303
  sermons 28, 50, 52–6, 212–13
moneylenders, moneylending 32–3, 139, 191, 310, 314
  Jewish financiers 18
  see also under individual place-names
monopolies
  of Jewish scribes 107, 133, 135

of Jews in commerce 56
of Jews on communal enterprises 18
of royal bakery 231
of wealthy Jews 78, 240
Montblanch
  baile of 268
  cemetery of 232
  city of 179
  community of 105, 183
  Jewish help to converts 57, 61
  Jewish quarter of 203
  Jews of 103, 185
  kasher meat in 56, 224, 225, 227–8
  privileges of Jews in 46
  synagogue of 212
Montcada, house or lords of 168, 184, 188
Montclús 166–7, 175, 209, 232, 290
Montjuich 233
Montpellier 2, 20–1, 27, 30, 32, 90, 158, 212, 224, 234, 262, 305–6, 309
Monzón 56, 107, 166, 171, 173, 175, 181, 187–8, 193–4, 211, 221, 293
Morella 21, 177, 196
Morocco 15, 218
Moses ibn Ezra 300
Moshe of Courcy 301, 303
mosques, *see* Muslims
Mosse Abendavid 228–9
Mosse Aieig 103
Mosse Alconstantini 102
Mosse Alcotanti 261
Mosse Alfaquim 126
Mosse Bonavia 294
Mosse Cabrit 248
Mosse of Courcy, *see* Moshe of Courcy
Mosse ibn Ezra, *see* Moses ibn Ezra
Mosse Jumiz 106, 320
Mosse ben Nahman, *see* Nahmanides
Mosse de Portella, *see* Muça de Portella
Mosse Ravaya 15
Mozarabs 303–4
Muça de Portella 15, 124, 286
muqademin, see *adelantados*
Murcia, city and kingdom 4, 13, 176, 195
Murviedro 34, 83, 89, 97, 105, 119, 177, 196, 223, 232, 247, 329
Muslims
  baile of 56
  Christian mission among 303
  clothes 283
  concubines 266–9
  conversion to Judaism 53–4
  emigration of 2, 12
  influence in Spain of 67, 176–7, 265, 299
  Jewish converts to Islam 53
  Jewish offences against 288–9, 295
  Jews attacked by 44, 213
  Jews' relations with 201, 203, 225
  mosques 55
  numbers of 2–3
  property of, given to Jews (*repartiment*) 201
  prostitutes 286
  sexual relations with Jews 270
  status of 20, 47
  wars between Christians and 49, 155, 303

N

Naçan Lobell 294
Naci Azday 101
Nahmanides
  attitude to concubinage 265–6
  his concept of magic 302
  customs of 282
  in Disputation of Barcelona 50–1
  Dominicans against 58
  as a scholar 139, 302, 303, 308, 330, 331, 333
  his status 309, 314
Narbonne 44
Navarre 2, 144, 199, 300
Neci Azday 151
nedunya, see marriage
ne'emanim
  authority of 78, 84, 105, 106, 205, 306
  in charge of tax collection 104
  duties of 113, 115, 117, 126, 129, 135
  election or appointment of 89–90, 95, 96–7, 101, 108, 130
  eligibility for office 92, 99
  as judges 125
  number of 97–8
  responsibilities of 118–20
  status of 76, 128, 310
  term of office 86, 110–12
Neoplatonism 304
niduy, see bans
Nissim Gerondi 139–40, 215, 243, 266, 302, 310, 330, 333
nobility 3, 12–13, 21, 80, 167, 168, 294
North Africa 2, 12, 15, 310, 334
notarial acts 133–4, 261, 268
notaries, *see* scribes and notaries

O

oath-taking 31–2, 42, 91, 114, 123, 126, 136, 178, 219, 239, 293
oligarchy 76, 78, 83, 92, 99

Olot 186
Omar Tahuyl 108
Onda 177, 196
ordinances (*taqanot*)
  announcement of 139, 219
  on clothes 284–5
  communal and administrative 99, 107, 111, 128, 151
  of confraternities 250
  financial and economic 81, 122, 126
  infringement of 148–9
  Jews' right to enact 71, 113, 148
  moral and religious 123, 315, 316, 318, 322
  on taxes 170, 240
  validity of 108
  against violence 289
  on weddings 259
  writing of 133–4
Oriola 45, 176, 195–6, 225, 319
ostages 93, 100, 130
Osuna 2
Oto de Montcada 167
Ottoman Empire 218, 254, 334

P
Pallars 2
Pantelleria 13
papacy 3–4
pardon, royal 44
Paris 304
parnas 86
Passover, *see* festivals
Pastoureaux ('Shepherds' Crusade') 232
Paulus Cristiani 50–2, 58, 212, 308
Pedro I 4
Pedro II 2, 223, 228
Pedro III, the Great
  administration 3, 13
  arbitration between communities 166
  attitude to Jews 10, 12, 13, 34, 39, 54, 91, 119, 146, 163, 165, 172, 201, 225, 227, 269, 273
  charters relating to Jews 34–6, 37, 40, 112, 113, 145, 154, 173, 230, 234
  Christian missionaries 212–13
  conquests 3–4
  interference in Jewish affairs 74, 94, 102, 103, 105, 108, 117, 126, 175, 228–9, 269, 273, 274, 275, 286, 311, 312, 313
  Jews' attitude towards 276
  Jews under the reign of 69, 79, 84, 85, 124, 150, 177, 180, 184, 186, 187, 192

  Jews in his service 13, 14, 15–16, 80, 102, 141, 228
  protection of Jews 53, 178, 209, 211, 234
  support of Jewish autonomy 146, 154, 157, 163, 267, 268, 291, 293
  taxation of Jews 174, 181, 189
Pedro IV 89, 104, 129–30, 232, 250, 253, 333
Pedro, Infante (son of Jaime II) 120
Pedrola 168, 192
Pere de Puig 44
Perelada 186
Perez Ha-Cohen 140, 302
Perpignan
  charters of 21, 23, 25, 26
  clothing of Jews of 30, 283
  collecta of 190–1
  confraternities in 243, 246, 247, 249, 250, 253, 325
  council of community 129
  gambling in 260, 285
  Jewish education in 329, 330
  Jewish quarter of 25, 202, 208
  Jewish scholarship in 190, 330
  protection of Jews in 208
  violence in 288
Pesach, *see* festivals: Passover
physicians, Jewish 15, 18, 48, 109, 129, 132, 134, 137, 139–40, 204, 237–8, 246, 292, 309, 314
pietists 301–2, 311
Pina 192, 213
polemics
  Jewish–Christian 51
  Jewish–Muslim 53
  see also disputations
polygamy, *see* marriage: bigamy
Pomar 187–8, 193
Pons 170, 188, 312
Portugal 2, 248, 300
prayers, *see* synagogues
preachers, Jewish, *see* *darshanim*
privileges
  of autonomy 88, 124, 163, 174, 270, 291
  of communal functionaries 77, 138
  confirmation of 187
  conflicts over 168
  financial 172, 191
  of individuals 5, 73, 114, 228–9, 292
  as models 193
  protection of Jews 182–3, 219, 316
probis homines, prohomines 78, 110, 112, 128
procuradores, procuratorii 110
promissory notes, *see* notarial acts

property 4–5, 39, 42–3, 45, 46, 118, 134, 147, 158, 167, 201, 238, 286, 316
property, Christian, confiscation of, permitted to Jews 33
property, Jewish, confiscation of
  books 50–1, 62, 183
  by Jewish community 160
  Jewish protests over 45
  by king 201, 218, 234
  by papal Inquisition 60
  royal promise of immunity from 20, 25–6, 46, 316
proselytes, see converts
protection, royal 44
Provence 2, 140, 263, 299, 303–5, 308–9
  Provençal influence 305
  Provençal Jews 261, 306
  Provençal mystics 302
Puigcerdá 190
punishment
  according to Jewish law 154
  arrests 20, 26, 39, 41, 45, 46
  capital 77, 124, 153, 155–6, 271, 287
  corporal 155–6
  expulsion from Jewish quarter 123
  fines 106, 107, 126, 135–6, 154, 185, 289–91
  imprisonment 124, 153, 159
  by *lex talionis* 27
  prisoners, Jewish 41, 46, 208, 294–5
  privileges 155, 156, 157
  sanctions on crafts and trades 123
  torture 42
  see also crime
Purim, see festivals
Pyrenees 2, 63, 67, 159, 190, 263, 300, 303, 306, 309

Q
qinyan 154, 220, 256
quarrels, between Jews 289–90
quarter, Jewish
  Christians in 43, 200, 201, 203, 206, 227
  closure of its gates 32, 46, 75, 136, 202, 203, 204
  communal work in 132, 136–7
  electors acting outside 93–4
  establishment of 201–2, 204–5, 225, 230
  expulsion from 156
  Jewish homes in 204, 206, 279–81, 328
  Jews outside 50, 52, 54, 165, 200, 207, 208, 219, 223, 226
  jurisdiction in 73, 112, 115, 159, 165, 205
  king's stay in 25, 203, 207, 208
  life and institutions of 40, 122–3, 124, 209, 213–14, 243, 248, 249, 254, 279, 286–7, 294, 323, 328, 329
  location of 200–2
  maintenance of 116, 203, 281
  municipal influence in 128, 200
  name of 199
  protection of 29, 42, 200, 201, 204, 207, 209
  security in 25, 182, 200, 209
  structure and extent of 202–3, 204, 205–6, 232, 280–1
  terms for 199
  walled 38, 136

R
rabbis
  acting as judges and arbitrators 151, 170, 311–12
  acting as preachers 140
  acting as scribes 135
  appointment of 101, 106, 320
  Ashkenazi 140, 302
  attitude to transgressors 255, 256, 257, 258, 266–7, 318
  Catalan 262, 272, 274, 311, 314, 311
  as communal functionaries 139
  communal and local 140, 141, 222, 261
  of confraternities 250
  Crown-appointed 102, 141, 289
  practising medicine 109
  professionalization of 140
  Provençal 262
  role in administration 77, 117, 124, 150
  royal consultation with 269, 311–312
  as spiritual leaders 139, 303
  violence against 292
  see also responsa
Ramón Berenguer I 4
Ramón Berenguer IV 9, 222
Ramón Berenguer, Infante 169
Ramón Lull 55, 212
Ramon de Miedas 62
Rashi 301, 330–1
rationalists 304, 306, 332
Raymundus de Peñaforte 51
Reconquista 2, 13, 19, 23, 45, 49, 145, 176, 210, 237, 299, 303–4
Reina, wife of Samuel de Forn 273–4
repartiment, see Muslims
responsa 112, 122, 258, 272, 308–10, 317
Ribagorza 2
Ricla 193
Ripoll 186

Romance 100, 112, 126, 148–9, 160, 250, 267, 300
Judeo-Romance 149
Rosh Hashanah, *see* festivals
Roussillon
  collectas of 184, 190, 191
  communities of 22
  county of 2, 199
  Jews of 20, 26, 29, 190, 212, 285
  part of Crown of Aragon 20, 172
  part of Kingdom of Majorca 3
Roven son of Vidal 270
Rueda 175
Ruesta 167, 175, 192, 200

S
Sa'adiah Abenaçaya, *see* Çadia Abenaçaya
Sabadell 185
Sabbath
  arrest on 41, 46, 316
  clothes for 283, 284
  desecration of 316
  family life on 257
  observance of 250, 282, 316, 320
  right to observe 23
  sermons on 139, 330
sacristan, see *shamash*
Salamo d'en Adret 275
Salamo Avenjacob 109
Salamon, physician from Egea 140
Salamon Abençaprut 296
Salamon Abendavid 228–9
Salamon Abinçulama, *see* Çulema Abinçulana
Salamon ben Adret, *see* Shelomo ben Adret
Salamon d'en Adret, *see* Salamo d'en Adret
Salamon Alfaquim, or Alconstantini 11, 101, 102, 141, 151, 229
Salamon Alfayat 296
Salamon Avenbruch, or Ibn Baruch 102, 150, 295, 313
Salamon Avenjacob, *see* Salamo Avenjacob
Salamon Avenlatemi 312
Salamon Constantin, *see* Salamon Alfaquim
Salamon Çuri, *see* Çalema Çuri
Salamon Gratiani, or Graciani, *see* Shelomo Gratiani
Salamon of Montpellier, *see* Shelomo of Montpellier
Salamon de Portella 15
Salamon Sahadia, *see* Çalema Sahadia
Salamon Scapa 294
Salamon Zarfati, *see* Shelomo Zarfati
Saltel Astruch 152, 311

Saltell, baile of Barcelona 4
Saltell Gracia 89
Samuel Alfaquim 15
Samuel Almeridi 151
Samuel de Forn 273–4, 312
Samuel ibn Menasse 15–16
Samuel Nageri 211
Samuel de Orta 15
Samuel Pariente 248
Samuel Peniel 272
Samuel ha-Sardi, *see* Shemuel ha-Sardi
San Lorenzo de Lamuga 186
San Mateo 196
San Pedro de Galligans, monastery 233
Sancho, the Great 2
Santa Coloma de Queralt 245–8, 253, 325, 327
Santa María de Albarracín 193
Santa María de la Serra, monastery 212
Saragossa
  appointments in 106
  baile of 151
  bishop of 211
  charitable institutions in 243–4, 245, 246, 248, 251, 254
  class struggle in 77, 79, 89, 104, 114, 117, 130, 150, 238–40
  crime and violence in 289, 291, 296
  crisis in 94, 120
  debts of the *aljama* of 316
  elections in 77, 104, 108, 149
  emigration from 168
  exemption of physicians from office in 109
  francos of 126
  Jewish abattoir of 228, 229
  Jewish baile of 124, 126
  Jewish baths in 222
  Jewish cemetery of 233
  Jewish cloth-merchants in 206–7
  Jewish judges in 101, 102, 111, 125, 150, 151, 310, 313
  Jewish oath in 42
  Jewish prostitutes in 124, 286
  Jewish quarter of 202, 204, 206–7
  Judeo-Arabic culture in 300
  judiciary in 145, 154
  lawsuits between Jews and community 152, 311
  meeting-place of Jewish delegates of the *aljamas* 127, 163, 174, 175
  missionary sermons in 55
  murder in 102, 150, 293
  preachers in 140, 310
  privileges of Jews in 20, 23, 38, 48, 103

protection of Jews of 208
rabisse of synagogue in 143
relations between communities in 166, 167, 312
religious fraternities in 325, 326, 329
scribe of 107, 137
status of the *aljama* in 174, 175
synagogues of 213, 214-15
taxes in 118
trade guilds in 252-3
Saragoussi 334
Sarajevo Haggadah 216-17
Sardinia 4, 294
Sarrión 193
scribes and notaries 182, 185, 267
 Jewish 107, 132-5, 137, 140
 royal 106
secretarii, see *ne'emanim*
Segorbe 177, 196
Segre, river 233
Sepharad 299, 301-2, 305, 333
 Sephardi culture 300, 332
 Sephardi refugees in Italy 218
sexual relations 266-7, 270-2, 295
 homosexuality 287
 incest 265, 296
 between Jews and Muslims 270
 prostitutes: Jewish 123-4, 279, 286-7; Muslim 286
 sexual offences 156, 259, 279, 287, 292-3, 296
shamash 106, 142-3, 218
shekhunah, see quarter, Jewish
Shelomo ben Adret
 as arbitrator between communities 168, 170-1, 312
 attacks against 150, 290-1
 '*Avodat ha-Qodesh* 309
 his ban on secular sciences 129, 149, 306
 on communal government 81, 84, 88, 95, 179, 182, 183
 as a communal leader and representative 119, 125, 228, 310
 on the community's jurisdiction 80, 108, 179
 on community's source of power 19
 his criticism of rabbis 140, 141, 289
 on elections 94
 on the establishment of the *qehilah* 70-1
 as a jurist 104, 146, 147, 152, 153, 160, 166, 252, 269, 273, 277, 311-13
 on the leadership of the community 76, 78, 91-2
 on marriage and marital relations 255, 256, 257, 262, 263, 267
 as a master and teacher 132, 331
 as a moneylender 312
 on prayers 221
 as a scholar 139, 263, 303, 306, 309, 330-1, 333
 Torat ha-Bayit 309, 310
 on validity of documents 134
Shelomo Gratiani, or Graciani 147, 277
Shelomo of Montpellier 305
Shelomo Zarfati 302
Shem Tov ibn Falaquera 332
Shemuel ha-Sardi 158, 248
Shepherds' Crusade, see *Pastoureaux*
shohatim, see food, Jewish
Sicily 2-3, 13, 16, 127, 164, 189
Sigena, monastery 62
sindichs 110
slaughterhouses 113, 143, 165, 207, 224-9, 317
 see also food, Jewish
slave trade 34
Sobarbe 2
sofer, see scribes and notaries
Sol 276
Solsona 184
Soria 200
Sos 204, 293
subsidies, paid by Jews to king 118, 163-4, 167, 169, 171, 173, 175, 177-9, 181, 184, 188-9, 195
Succoth (Sukkot), *see* festivals
synagogues
 arrest and detention in 26, 182
 as community centres 48, 100, 139, 148, 149, 185, 219-20, 256, 259
 construction and architecture of 24, 204, 206, 210, 211, 212, 214, 215-18, 221, 243, 319
 correct behaviour in 221, 290, 296
 establishment of 36, 38, 213-14
 hazan 100, 106, 132, 137-40, 143, 157, 217, 219-20, 221, 256, 259, 320
 hekhal 216-18
 liturgy: Mozarabic 304; *piyutim* 301; Roman 304
 maintenance of 325-6
 minyan 137-8, 214, 247
 missionary sermons in 28, 50, 52, 53, 55, 56, 208, 212-13
 ner tamid 218
 as political centres 86, 97, 103, 117, 219
 prayers, interruption of 157-9, 220
 rabbis 106

synagogues (*cont.*):
  ritual objects in 218–19, 289
  seating in 295, 320
  sermons in 140
  shamash of 142–3
  site of 201
  supervision of 113, 123
  suspension of prayers in 157–9
  types of 213–15, 245, 247, 248, 253
  women in 143, 216
  worship in 219–21

T
tailors, *see* merchants and craftsmen, Jewish
Talmud 299–300, 302–3, 308, 330–2
taqanot, *see* ordinances
Tarazona 175, 194, 284, 321
Tarragano 334
Tarragona 10, 46, 57, 60–1, 105, 183, 185, 203, 224, 284, 312
Tárrega 46, 106, 138, 143, 187–8, 211, 215–16, 233, 291
Tauste 140, 166, 175, 194, 211
taxes
  charters on 46
  cisa 104
  collidores (tax-collectors) 18, 90, 91, 104–5, 109, 126–7, 144
  communal 242
  conflicts over 166, 171, 192
  distribution of 79, 105, 128, 167, 170, 175, 183–6
  exemptions from 18, 75, 120, 188
  leaders' responsibility for 119, 121
  lezda 227
  offences 48
  ordinances concerning 149
  privileges regarding 239
  property tax 158, 166
  punishment for non-payment of 41, 45, 157, 160, 320
  reductions in 34, 75, 120, 196
  royal intervention over 74
  royal taxes 34, 40, 117, 118, 163, 168, 169, 173, 174, 182, 219, 312
  tax-assessors 91, 97, 104–5, 126–7, 158, 239
  tax collection 82, 104, 116–17, 119, 182, 178–86, 190, 193–5
  tax-payers 78, 91, 92, 95, 96, 105, 116–17, 134, 160, 166, 175, 213, 238–40
  tax roll 78, 194
teachers, Jewish
  appointed by community 132, 140
  of children 142, 327–9
  private 327, 328
  in *yeshivot* 139, 330
Telmecen 15
Templars 59, 166, 187, 193
Teruel 56, 83, 105, 175, 211, 233, 247, 291, 293, 296
  collecta of 193–4
Toledo 300–5, 330
Torah
  application of its laws 19, 156, 160
  book of, for oath-taking 126
  commentaries on 310
  fraternities of 326
  fulfilment of its commandments 36, 40, 315
  learning 134, 140, 250, 327
  mapah 218
  rimonim 218
  scroll of (*sefer*) 218–19, 221, 247, 325
  silver ornaments of 289
  terms for 145
  tiq 218
  see also *halakhah*
Torroella de Montgrí 186
Tortosa 38, 48, 127, 158, 163–4, 173, 179, 188–9, 203, 225, 231, 265, 288, 328–9
  collecta of 173, 179, 181–2, 188–9
tossafists 301–3, 308–10, 330–1
trade 47, 190
  local 118, 207
  maritime 222–3
  see also merchants and craftsmen, Jewish
translators 237
trials 126, 152, 167, 177–8, 258, 260, 269, 274–6, 291–2, 311, 313, 321, 327–8
  Jewish and Christian witnesses in mixed trials 39, 41, 165, 177–8, 291
  oaths of witness 293
  right to give testimony in *call* 182
Tudela 140, 300, 332

U
Uncastillo 175, 200, 293
Urgell 2, 179, 184, 186, 188–9, 194
Usatges of Barcelona 5

V
Valencia, city and community 176
  appointment of *dayanim* in 103
  baths owned by Jews in 223
  cemetery of the Jews in 232
  communal appointments by Christians 106, 107, 144

conflicts with other communities 152
constitution of *aljama* in 96, 97
Council of Thirty in 130
elections and appointments in 89, 92, 93, 104
exemption from office-holding 108
hazan of 137
Jewish market of 207
Jewish quarter in 201, 206, 209, 289
Jews and Jewish life in 177, 178, 271, 290, 291, 292, 294, 312, 313
leaders of 98, 100, 114–15, 119, 150, 165, 312
oaths taken by Jews in 219
privileges of Jews in 20–1, 30, 38, 122, 224
royal support of communal authority 157
shamash of 143
social classes in 82, 83, 238
status of *aljama* 196
synagogues in 213, 219
Valencia, Kingdom 43, 196, 199, 272, 288, 290
  baile general of 201
  citizens of 14
  communities of 26, 76, 96, 97, 99, 112, 116, 119, 125, 127, 151, 164, 176–8, 195, 240
  fur of 178
  Inquisition in 58
  Jewish communal government in 99
  Jewish judge in 102
  Jewish oath in 32
  Jews of 20–3, 34–5, 37, 45, 163, 165, 178, 283, 295, 334
  Mishne Torah in 69
  Muslims of 20
  noblemen of 13
  as part of the Crown of Aragon 2, 3, 172, 195
  rights of Jewish women in 146, 178, 268
Vallmoll 185
Valls 60–1, 185, 227
veguer 43, 45, 48, 152, 283
Vicente Stefan 56
Vich 168, 184, 211, 216, 233
Vidal, scribe of Barbastro 133
Vidal Abulbaca (Abulbach) 48, 205
Vidal Çibili 114
Vidal de España 274
Vidal Malet 270
Vidal de Porta (Vidalon) 15, 152, 155, 275, 311, 313
Vidal Salamon 4
Vidal Thercullut 108
Villafranca de Conflent 190

Villafranca del Panades
  accusations against Jews of 271, 320–1
  attacks against the Jews of 43
  charters of the Jews in 38
  clothes of Jews of 46, 284
  Jewish cemetery in 24, 232, 233, 234
  Jewish life in 51, 275
  Jewish quarter of 203
  part of a *collecta* 183, 184
  taxation of Jews in 105
  violence by Jews in 150, 290, 313
Villagrassa 187–8
Villareal 196
violence
  among Christians 288
  by Christians against Jews 213
  by husbands against wives 273
  among Jews 144, 221, 240, 259, 279, 290–1, 294–6
  in synagogues 221, 290
  of women against men 292
  see also crime
Vives son of Jahuda de Limos (Limoux) 275
Vives son of Jucef Abenvives 287

W
wills, *see* inheritance

X
Xúcar, river 176, 178, 195

Y
Ya'aqov ben Khalina 214
Ya'aqov ben Yosef 272
Yehudah ibn Abbas 301
Yehudah Alharizi 300
Yehudah ben Barzilay al-Bargeloni 5
  Sefer ha-'Ittim 5
  Sefer ha-Shetarot 5
Yehudah ben Yaqar 301
yeshivot 95, 243, 263, 300–1, 309, 330–1
  see also teachers, Jewish
Yishaq Alfasi 80, 308, 310, 332
  Sefer Halakhot 310, 332
Yishaq ibn Asfura 296
Yishaq Cohen 272
Yishaq ben Reuven Al-Bargeloni 5
Yishaq ben Sheshet Perfet 139, 266, 310, 330
yo'azim 79, 81, 84, 86–7, 92, 96–101, 103, 105, 110, 115, 127–30, 151
Yolanda, Queen 202
Yom Tov, butcher from Jaca, *see* Genton

Yom Tov Asibili 72, 78, 139, 154, 156, 303, 310–11, 313, 331, 333
Yom Tov Caracallo, *see* Jento Caracallo
Yom Tov Farhi 214
Yosef Qimhi 288
Yosef ibn Yahya (or Abinafia) 214
Yucef Baro 44

Yucef Cohen 328

Z
Zaidin 188
zalmedina 42
Zarch Malet 152, 311
Zuera 192

www.ingramcontent.com/pod-product-compliance
Ingram Content Group UK Ltd.
Pitfield, Milton Keynes, MK11 3LW, UK
UKHW021316180426
11947UKWH00015B/1262